SLAVERY
IN THE
UNITED STATES

SLAVERY

IN THE

UNITED STATES

A SOCIAL, POLITICAL,

AND HISTORICAL ENCYCLOPEDIA

VOLUME ONE

Junius P. Rodriguez, Editor

A B C ⬛ C L I O

Santa Barbara, California   Denver, Colorado   Oxford, England

Library of Congress Cataloging-in-Publication Data
Slavery in the United States : a social, political, and historical
    encyclopedia / Junius P. Rodriguez, editor.
        p. cm.
    Includes bibliographical references and index.
    ISBN-13: 978-1-85109-544-5 (hardcover : alk. paper)
    ISBN-13: 978-1-85109-549-0 (e-book)
    ISBN-10: 1-85109-544-6 (hardcover : alk. paper)
    ISBN-10: 1-85109-549-7 (e-book)
    1. Slavery—United States—History—Encyclopedias. 2.
Slavery—Political aspects—United States—History—Encyclopedias. 3.
Slavery—Social aspect—United States—History—Encyclopedias. 4.
United States—Biography—Encyclopedias. I. Rodriguez, Junius P.

E441.S635 2007
306.3'6209703—dc22
                                                                    2006101351
    11   10   09   08   07   /   1   2   3   4   5   6   7   8   9   10

Production Editor: Anna A. Moore
Editorial Assistant: Sara Springer
Production Manager: Don Schmidt
Media Editor: Jason Kniser
Media Resources Coordinator: Ellen Brenna Dougherty
Media Resources Manager: Caroline Price
File Manager: Paula Gerard

ABC-CLIO, Inc.
130 Cremona Drive, P.O. Box 1911
Santa Barbara, California 93116-1911

This book is also available on the World Wide Web as an ebook.
Visit http://www.abc-clio.com for details.

This book is printed on acid-free paper. ∞
Manufactured in the United States of America

TO

GERALD T. PELTIER

(1932–1999)

Teacher, mentor, and friend

O Mother Race! to thee I bring

This pledge of faith unwavering,

This tribute to thy glory.

I know the pangs which thou didst feel,

When Slavery crushed thee with its heel,

With thy dear blood all gory.

— PAUL LAURENCE DUNBAR,
"Ode to Ethiopia"

Contents

Volume One

Contextual Essays

Entries

A

B

E

F

G

H

I

J

K

L

M

Volume Two

N

O

P

Q

R

S

T

U

V

W

Y

Primary Source Documents

Acknowledgments

When I started working with ABC-CLIO in 1995 to develop *The Historical Encyclopedia of World Slavery* (2 vols., 1997) I could never have imagined the influence that the relationship would have on my career and the long-lasting partnership that would emerge. After receiving positive reviews for that initial project, I was later able to produce *Chronology of World Slavery* (1999) and *The Louisiana Purchase: A Historical and Geographical Encyclopedia* (2002) for ABC-CLIO, two other reference works that were also well received.

From the moment that I began envisioning *Slavery in the United States: A Social, Political, and Historical Encyclopedia* it was clear that this was going to be a massive undertaking but the necessity of the work made it a worthy challenge. Three years in development, the task certainly had its highs and lows as looming deadlines created euphoria when met, but more long nights and weekends when targets were missed. In the process, the project taught me much about dedication, focused determination, and humility—lessons that I hope have made me a better editor and a better person.

I appreciate the assistance of the professional staff of ABC-CLIO for their patience and counsel during the development of this project. It has been a pleasure to work with Alicia Merritt and Steve Danver, senior acquisitions editors, who have provided a wealth of guidance from the moment this work began to its final publication. In addition, Submissions Editors Peter Westwik and Alex Mikaberidze have helped to polish this work in countless ways.

The work of seventy-five scholars who have examined the history of slavery appears in this work in the form of 305 encyclopedia-style entries. Having worked with many of these authors over the years, I have developed an admiration for their work and am pleased that they contributed their scholarship to this publishing effort. I value the friendships that have formed in the development of these volumes as many of these colleagues have also extended their encouragement and support to me.

Several of my students at Eureka College have worked over the years as research assistants and have helped me with developing portions of this manuscript. I am appreciative of their assistance and wish to express my sincere gratitude to them for their tremendous efforts. Special thanks are extended to Sarah Wilson, Jon Hackler, Lance Hrdlicka, Mitch Pinkston, and Abbre McClain for their tireless dedication to this work. In addition, I must thank all my students, past and present, whose stimulating questions about slavery have been a valuable resource in my own intellectual growth as I have had to fashion and hone interpretations. Their invariable quest to learn has challenged me and sustained me through the years.

The Eureka College Faculty Development Committee generously supported start-up costs for this project and assisted in supporting research trips that were necessary to collect materials for this work. In addition, I must thank Joy Kinder, who has always offered expert secretarial assistance as well as a kind word when I was working intently to get mailings out on time. Eldrick Smith always solved my computer problems, both great and small, which kept me on task and generally sane. In addition, the support of Ginny McCoy, Tony Glass, Kelly Fisher, Brent Etzel, Lynne Rudasill, and Ann Shoemaker was especially helpful in tracking down the bits and pieces that can make an editor's life challenging.

I take responsibility for the failings and inevitable shortcomings of this work. Any attempt to examine an issue as large and as perplexing as slavery in the United States in an encyclopedia format will undoubtedly require editorial choices that will not be pleasing to everyone. The necessity of blending social history with political history in a historical context is a challenging task, but these volumes represent a genuine effort to strive for the mean and fashion a viable synthesis. It is hoped that students, scholars, and general readers alike who use this work will find it to be informative and insightful.

— Junius P. Rodriguez
June 20, 2006

Contributors

Valerie Abrahamsen
Tunde Adeleke
Thanet Aphornsuvan
Andrea M. Atkin
Jim Baugess
Jackie R. Booker
Stefan Brink
Christopher L. Brown
Ron D. Bryant
Beverly Bunch-Lyons
Keith Byerman
Sydney J. Caddel-Liles
Charles W. Carey
Mark Cave
Constance J. S. Chen
William L. Chew III
Boyd Childress
David M. Cobin
Philip R.P. Coelho
Dallas Cothrum
Charles D'Aniello
Enrico Dal Lago
Brian Dirck
Elizabeth Dubrulle
Jonathan Earle
Raingard Eßer
Patience Essah
Peter S. Field
Roy E. Finkenbine
James C. Foley
Daniel L. Fountain
Dan R. Frost
DoVeanna S. Fulton
Gwilym Games
Larry Gara
Henry H. Goldman
Marquetta L. Goodwine

John Grenier
Sally E. Hadden
Judith E. Harper
Sharon A. Roger Hepburn
Timothy S. Huebner
Anthony A. Iaccarino
Eric R. Jackson
Claude F. Jacobs
Mark L. Kamrath
Frances Richardson Keller
Stephen C. Kenny
Yitzchak Kerem
Jeffrey R. Kerr-Ritchie
Hyong-In Kim
Stewart King
Sharon Landers
Tom Lansford
Lori Lee
Kurt E. Leichtle
David J. Libby
Richard D. Loosbrock
David B. Malone
Chandra M. Manning
Jennifer Margulis
Charles H. McArver, Jr.
Dwight A. McBride
Robert A. McGuire
Scott A. Merriman
Debra Meyers
Mary Jo Miles
Dennis J. Mitchell
Andrew P. Morriss
Bruce L. Mouser
Caryn E. Neumann
Elsa A. Nystrom
Onaiwu W. Ogbomo
Craig S. Pascoe

Julieanne Phillips
Michael Phillips
Jan Pilditch
Michael Polley
James M. Prichard
John W. Pulis
Maria Elena Raymond
Douglas S. Reed
Richard A. Reiman
Junius P. Rodriguez
Barbara Ryan
Arnold Schmidt
Jason H. Silverman
Malik Simba
Frederick J. Simonelli
Manisha Sinha
James L. Sledge, III

Dale Edwyna Smith
Gene A. Smith
John David Smith
Richard D. Starnes
John Stauffer
Torrance T. Stephens
Harold D. Tallant
Anthony Todman
Eric Tscheschlok
Peter Wallenstein
Nagueyalti Warren
Michael Washington
Mary Ellen Wilson
Yolandea Wood
John J. Zaborney
Robert J. Zalimas, Jr.

Maps

—m—

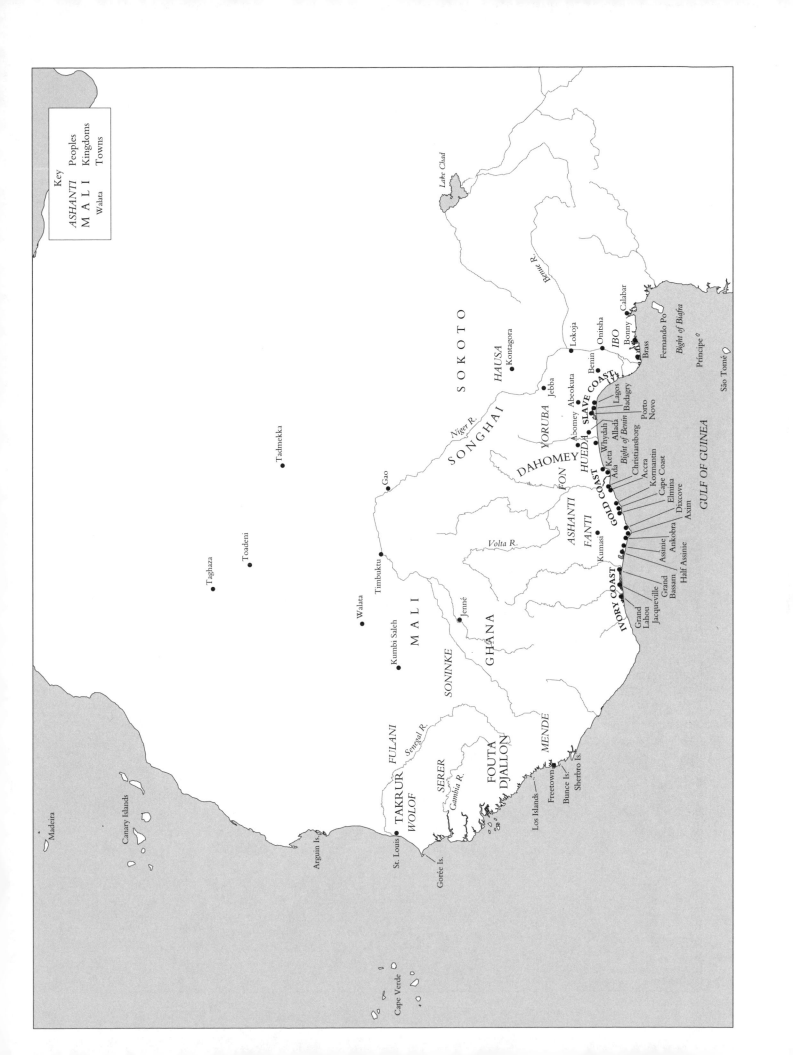

Key

ASHANTI	Peoples
M A L I	Kingdoms
Walata	Towns

Madeira

Canary Islands

Cape Verde

Arguin Is.

St. Louis

Gorée Is.

TAKRUR

FULANI

WOLOF

SERER

Senegal R.

Gambia R.

FOUTA
DJALLON

MENDE

Los Islands

Freetown

Bunce Is.

Sherbro Is.

Taghaza

Toadeni

Tadmekka

Gao

Niger R.

Timbuktu

Walata

Kumbi Saleh

MALI

SONINKE

Jenné

GHANA

Volta R.

ASHANTI

FANTI

Kumasi

IVORY COAST

GOLD COAST

Grand
Lahou

Jacqueville

Grand
Bassam

Assinie

Half Assinie

Ankobra

Axim

Dixcove

Elmina

Cape Coast

Kormantin

Accra

Christiansborg

Ada

Keta

Whydah

HUEDA

Allada

Bight of Benin

FON

DAHOMEY

YORUBA

Abomey

Porto
Novo

Badagry

Lagos

SLAVE COAST

Benin

Abeokuta

Jebba

Kontagora

HAUSA

SOKOTO

Benue R.

Lake Chad

Lokoja

Onitsha

IBO

Benin

Calabar

Bonny

Brass

Fernando Po

Bight of Biafra

Príncipe

São Tomé

GULF OF GUINEA

SONGHAI

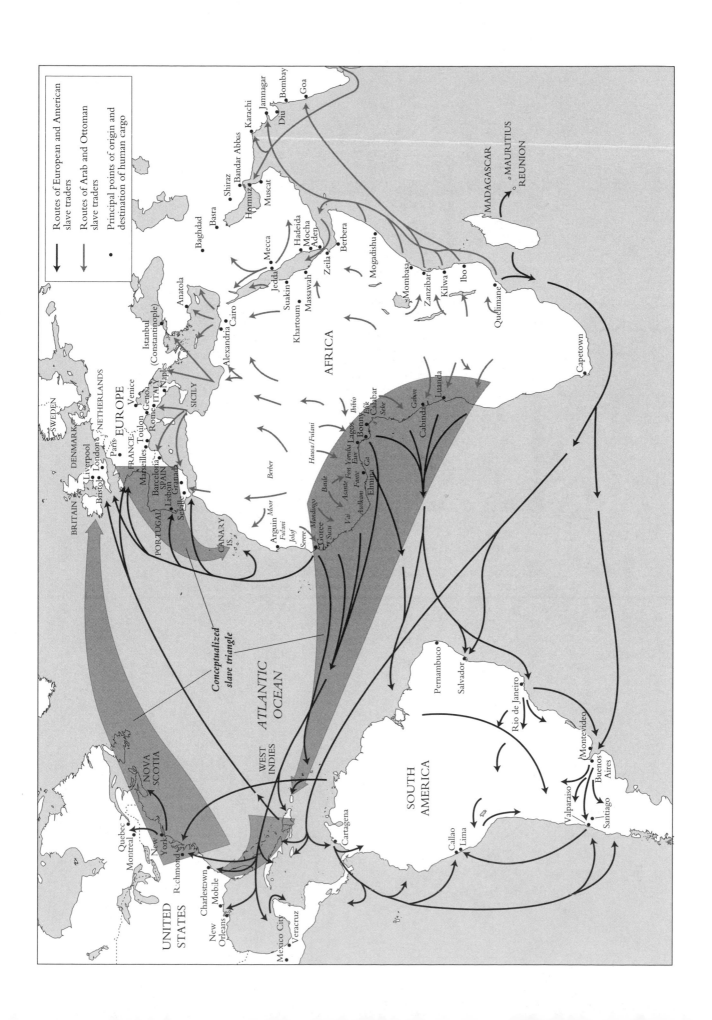

SWEDEN

DENMARK

BRITAIN

Liverpool
London
Bristol

NETHERLANDS

EUROPE

Paris

FRANCE

Marseilles
Toulon

PORTUGAL

SPAIN

Barcelona
Lisbon
Seville

Granada

Venice
Genoa
Rome
Naples

ITALY

SICILY

Anatola

Istanbul
(Constantinople)

Alexandria
Cairo

Baghdad
Basra

Shiraz
Hormuz
Bandar Abbas
Muscat

Karachi
Jamnagar
Diu
Bombay
Goa

Mecca
Jedda

Hadeida
Mocha
Aden

Suakin
Massawah
Khartoum

Zeila
Berbera

Mogadishu

Mombasa
Zanzibar
Kilwa
Ibo

Quelimane

MADAGASCAR

MAURITIUS
REUNION

AFRICA

Capetown

CANARY
IS.

Arguin

Jolof

Serere

Ciotee
Sisin

Fulani

Moor

Berber

Hausa/Fulani

Mandingo

Baule

Val

Asante
Fanti

Ga
Elmina

Ewe

Fon

Aukkam

Yoruba

Lagos
Bonny
Efik
Calabar

Ibibio

Seke

Cabinda
Luanda

Gabon

WEST
INDIES

ATLANTIC
OCEAN

Conceptualized
slave triangle

NOVA
SCOTIA

Quebec
Montreal

New York

Richmond

UNITED
STATES

Charlestown
Mobile

New
Orleans

Mexico City
Veracruz

Cartagena

SOUTH
AMERICA

Pernambuco
Salvador

Callao
Lima

Rio de Janeiro

Montevideo
Buenos
Aires

Valparaiso
Santiago

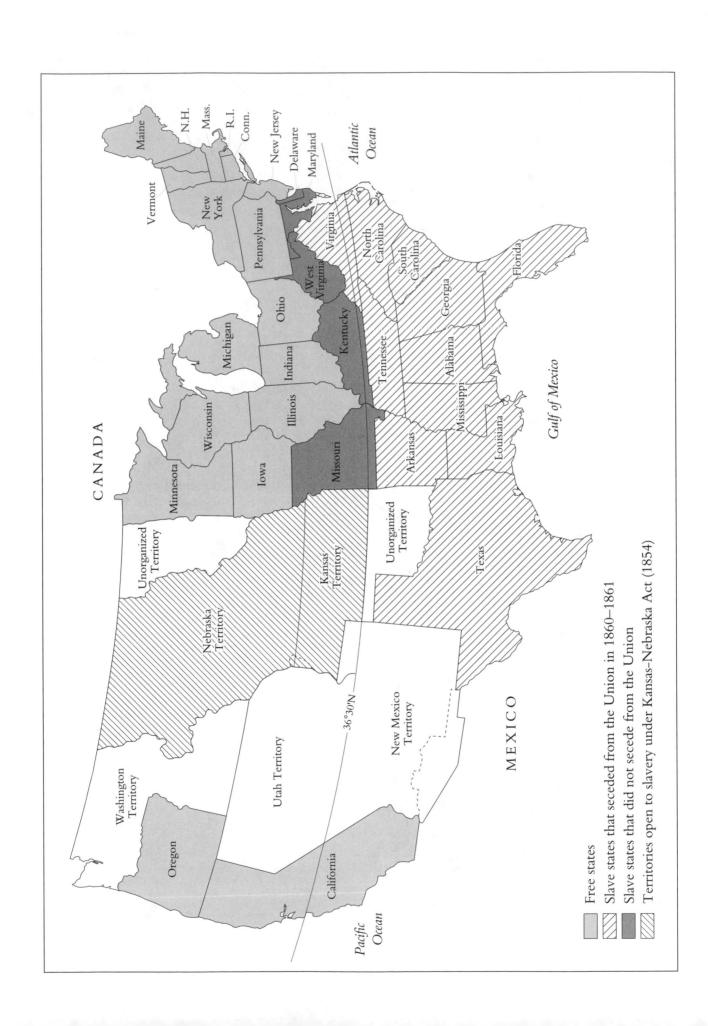

CANADA

MEXICO

Pacific
Ocean

Atlantic
Ocean

Gulf of Mexico

Maine
N.H.
Mass.
R.I.
Conn.
New Jersey
Delaware
Maryland
Vermont
New York
Pennsylvania
Virginia
North Carolina
South Carolina
Georgia
Florida
West Virginia
Kentucky
Ohio
Michigan
Indiana
Tennessee
Alabama
Mississippi
Wisconsin
Illinois
Minnesota
Iowa
Missouri
Arkansas
Louisiana
Unorganized Territory
Nebraska Territory
Kansas Territory
Unorganized Territory
Texas
Washington Territory
Utah Territory
New Mexico Territory
Oregon
California

36°30′N

Free states
Slave states that seceded from the Union in 1860–1861
Slave states that did not secede from the Union
Territories open to slavery under Kansas–Nebraska Act (1854)

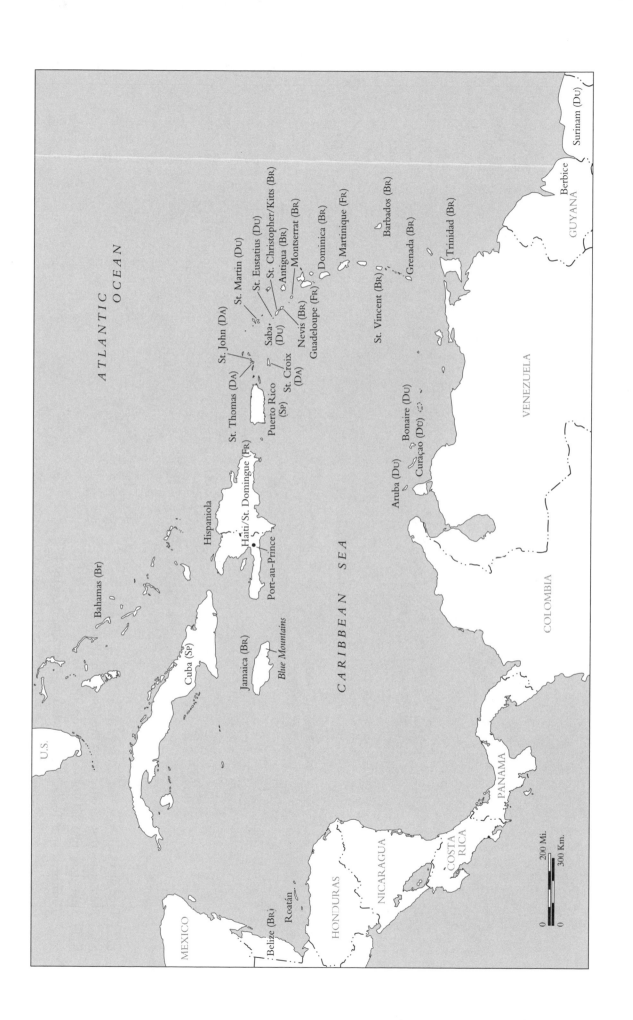

SLAVERY

IN THE

UNITED STATES

Chronology of Slavery in the United States

—⁂—

1528

Estevanico, also known as Esteban or Black Stephan, was likely the first person of African descent to set foot upon North America during the expedition led by the Spanish explorer Álvar Núñez Cabeza de Vaca.

1563

A French Huguenot refuge was established at Fort Caroline, near modern-day Jacksonville, Florida. Slaves were used as laborers in the Fort Caroline settlement.

1565–1568

The Spanish founded St. Augustine in Florida, the oldest town in what eventually became the United States. During the first three years of the settlement's existence, five hundred slaves were introduced to the area.

1619

On August 20, African American history began when a Dutch ship delivered "twenty and odd" Africans to the English settlement at Jamestown, Virginia, where they were sold by bid as indentured servants. Although they did not become slaves immediately, these twenty individuals represented the first permanent involuntary African immigrants to come to the region that eventually became the United States. According to the contemporary records of John Rolfe, "About the last of August came in a dutch man of warre that sold us twenty Negars." Most indentured servants were released after serving a term, generally four to seven years, and then were allowed to become property owners and participate in civic affairs. Within the first generation of their arrival in Virginia, most of the initial African servants had their period of indenture extended to the point where they became servants for life.

1620

A public school that taught both blacks and Indians was established in the Virginia colony. As time went by, most of the colonies would enact restrictions that prohibited most nonwhite inhabitants from receiving an education.

1621

The Dutch West India Company, a corporation that would be very involved in establishing colonial outposts and in conducting the transatlantic slave trade, was created. Willem Usselinx and other Dutch merchants chartered this corporation to organize trade and to encourage further colonization efforts by the Netherlands in the New World. The Dutch West India Company received a trading monopoly in its charter and soon established the colony of New Netherlands (New York) as the headquarters for its colonial enterprises.

1622

The Virginia House of Burgesses enacted a law that "imposed fines for fornication with a Negro" in an effort to prevent interracial liaisons within the colony.

Virginia would not adopt an antimiscegenation law until 1691. The primary justification for laws of this type was that colonial assemblies were particularly concerned about the problems that arose in determining the legal status of children who were born from interracial encounters.

Virginia colonial court records from Old Accomack (Northampton) County indicate that the first free blacks in the colony were Anthony and Mary Johnson. Anthony Johnson eventually became an owner of African slaves.

1624

John Phillip, one of the Africans who arrived at Jamestown, testified in court against a white man. This was the first time in England's North American colonies that a black man testified against a white man in a court of law.

Church records indicate that William Tucker was baptized at Jamestown, Virginia. He was the first black child to be born in England's North American colonies. Although this child's parents were likely to have been indentured servants, it is probable that this young man grew up to be a slave in the Virginia colony. Throughout the colonial and early national periods, churches would continue to record significant genealogical information about the lives of those slaves who were Christians.

1626

The Dutch introduced eleven Africans as indentured servants into their newly established colony of New Netherlands. Dutch colonial records identify Paul d'Angola, Simon Congo, Anthony Portuguese, and John Francisco as four of these early servants. These Africans were imported to serve as laborers on Hudson Valley farms. As was the case in Virginia, many of the African servants saw their period of indenture extended to the point where they became servants for life. According to Dutch law as applied within the colony, the children who were born to slaves who had been manumitted (freed) were still bound to slavery in New Netherlands.

1629

Africans were imported as slaves into the region that became the colony of Connecticut.

1630

In the Massachusetts Bay Colony, a fugitive law that protected slaves who fled owners because of ill treatment was enacted. According to the language of this statute, those fugitive slaves who sought self-protection because of abuse were protected "till due order be taken for their relief."

In Virginia, the white colonist Hugh Davis was publicly whipped as punishment for his being guilty of "defiling his body by lying with a Negro."

1634

Africans were imported as slaves into the Massachusetts Bay Colony.

Slavery was first introduced into the colony of Maryland.

1634

In the French colony of Louisiana, Catholic settlers urged colonial authorities to provide educational opportunities for blacks, including those blacks that were slaves in the colony.

1636

Slavery was first introduced into the colony of Delaware.

1638

On December 12, Governor John Winthrop of the Massachusetts Bay Colony reported that Boston received its first shipment of black slaves from Barbados with the arrival of the slave ship *Desire*. The slaves were transported as cargo along with other commodities including cotton and tobacco. Captain William Pierce of Salem, Massachusetts, who commanded the *Desire*, regularly traded indigenous Pequot Indians as slaves in the West Indies in exchange for Africans whom he transported (as slaves) to Boston.

1639

Virginia's House of Burgesses enacted a statute that prohibited blacks from carrying firearms within the colony.

1640

In Virginia in July, the black indentured servant John Punch was sentenced to lifetime service for having run away. Two other white indentured servants who ran away with John Punch were sentenced to lesser punishment. In this episode it becomes clear that black indentured servants were quickly becoming enslaved in the colony of Virginia.

A slave trader named Captain Smith carried a group of Africans to Massachusetts after he had illegally attacked their village in West Africa. Massachusetts authorities refused to accept the cargo of Africans and ordered that they be returned to Africa at the colony's expense. Captain Smith was arrested for the offense of capturing Africans who were not taken as a result of a "just war" situation in which enslavement would have been morally acceptable.

Events in Virginia demonstrated the extent to which racial distinctiveness had already affected crime and punishment within the colony. A Virginia court charged that a white man and a black woman had been "associated" in an inappropriate manner and meted out the punishment deemed necessary. The man was ordered to do penance while the woman was publicly whipped.

1641

In December, Massachusetts became the first colony to legalize slavery by giving statutory recognition to the practice in Section Ninety-one of the *Body of Liberties,* but added a caveat that forbade capture by "unjust violence." This provision was later incorporated into the Articles of the New England Confederation, and all of the other New England colonies eventually added this provision to their statutes regarding the institution of slavery. The Massachusetts law recognized the slave trade as a legal enterprise and allowed for the enslavement of blacks and Indians.

1642

The Virginia House of Burgesses passed a law imposing fines upon anyone who harbored runaways. The penalty assessed for harboring a runaway was 20 pieces of tobacco per night of refuge granted. The same measure authorized the branding of slaves who attempted a second escape. This measure is viewed as the precursor of other fugitive slave acts that would be imposed in future years.

1643

An intercolonial agreement drafted for the New England Confederation stated that mere certification by a local magistrate could serve as enough evidence to convict a runaway slave. This decision formed the basis for many of the fugitive slave acts that would be enacted in the eighteenth and nineteenth centuries.

The Virginia House of Burgesses took action to standardize the period of service for indentured servants to a span of four to seven years (previously a range from two to eight years had been common). Colonial records do indicate that the period of indenture assigned to African servants tended to be longer than that assigned to white servants. By 1661, Virginia authorities would consider black servants to be servants for life.

1644

The first recorded marriage of blacks in the region that eventually became the United States occurred at the Boulweire Chapel on Manhattan Island in the Dutch Colony of New Netherlands. In this ceremony Antony van Angola and Lucie d'Angola were married.

Dutch authorities in New Netherlands presented land grants to the first eleven blacks introduced into the colony in 1626. The land grants were located in the areas that today comprise Brooklyn and Greenwich Village.

1645

The *Rainbowe,* which was the first slave ship ever constructed in England's North American colonies, sailed for Africa and began to operate in the transatlantic slave trade.

Slavery was introduced into the colony of New Hampshire.

1648

Governor William Berkeley of Virginia began to plant rice on his plantation. Some of Berkeley's slaves had suggested the crop because they noted the similarity between Virginia and their former homeland in West Africa.

1649

A colonial census states that there were only three hundred indentured servants of African descent in Virginia.

The British Parliament incorporated the Society for Propagating the Gospel in New England. This missionary effort, which was established by John Eliot, had enjoyed a great deal of success in converting Native Americans, and Eliot would expand the society's efforts into areas of educating blacks and converting them to Christianity.

1650

The colony of Connecticut legally recognized the institution of slavery by passing statutes to regulate the practice.

1651

In North Hampton, Virginia, Anthony Johnson, a free black man, imported five servants, which entitled him to receive a 200-acre land grant along the Puwgoteague River. Johnson and a group of other free blacks attempted to establish an independent black community; at one point the community contained twelve homesteads.

With passage of the British Navigation Act of 1651 Parliament attempted to limit the commercial influence of the Dutch West India Company in the British North American colonies. The act limited the colonial slave trade to English merchants only. The British would fight against the Netherlands in two colonial wars in the hope of winning greater concessions in the African slave trade. By the end of the War of the Spanish Succession (Queen Anne's War), 1701–1714, the British would wrest control of the slave trade away from the Dutch.

1652

On May 18, the colonial assembly of Rhode Island enacted the first legislative measure in America to declare slavery illegal, but later legislation enacted in 1700 would reverse this decision.

Also on May 18, Quakers meeting in Warwick, Pennsylvania, approved of a resolution that black slaves should be afforded the same status as white indentured servants within the colony of Pennsylvania. The language of the resolution stipulated that no one could be enslaved for a term of more than ten years.

The government of the Netherlands granted the Dutch West India Company specific permission to import African slaves into the Dutch colony of New Netherlands. Colonial laws prohibited the mistreatment of slaves, and whippings were not allowed without the specific permission of colonial authorities.

1654

In Northampton County, Virginia, Anthony Johnson, himself a free black, filed suit in court to make his black indentured servant John Casor a servant for life. This is the first recorded case in a Virginia civil court where an indentured servant was effectively transformed into a slave.

1657

Quaker founder George Fox encouraged his American brethren to "the duty of converting the slaves" and demonstrated his personal commitment to this ideal by ministering to the slaves in the West Indies.

1658

A group of black and Indian slaves revolted in the area of Hartford, Connecticut.

1660

The English political philosopher John Locke drafted a constitution for the Carolinas that gave every free man in the colony complete power and authority over his slaves. Locke's constitution was never enacted, but subsequent colonial and state charters would grant slaveowners much power over their slaves.

1660

On March 13, the Virginia House of Burgesses enacted a measure that limited the amount of tax that could be charged upon the sale of a slave.

The colonial assembly in Connecticut enacted a statute that prohibited blacks from serving in the militia.

1661

By this point, slavery had come into practice in the British colony of Virginia. A law that was passed in 1661 recognized the condition in which some blacks were assumed to serve their masters for life. Although white indentured servants who committed an offense might be punished by an extended period of indenture, the law described blacks as "persons incapable of making satisfaction by addition of time." This measure suggests that a gradual transformation occurred between 1619 and 1661 as the condition of indentured labor for black servants became transformed into a condition of enslavement.

Administrators of the Dutch colony of New Netherlands received a petition for freedom presented by a slave.

1662

The colonial assembly in Virginia passed a law declaring that the status of all children—whether bound or free—shall be determined by the condition of the mother only. With the passage of this measure, slavery became hereditary in the colony of Virginia.

1663

Laws within the British colony of Maryland reveal that all imported black servants within the colony were servants for life (slaves). The law further declared that free white women who married slaves became slaves themselves during the lifetime of their spouse. Children born of such a union were also slaves. This measure was later repealed in order to prevent the forced marriages of white servant women to slaves.

Governor Charles Calvert of Maryland wrote to Lord Baltimore in England and suggested that the colony had a great need for African slaves. Calvert was looking for other means of acquiring slaves: he had become concerned that the Company of Royal Adventurers might not be interested in providing slaves to Maryland, which was too poor to purchase large numbers of Africans.

On July 27, the British Parliament approved the second Navigation Act, which developed a stronger mercantile arrangement between the mother country and its colonies. According to this legislation, all imports were to be carried to the colonies on British vessels, but an exception was made for certain imports, including servants. At this time, the British were not yet actively involved in the African slave trade, but this situation would eventually change.

On September 13, a house servant named Berkenhead in Gloucester County, Virginia, betrayed a planned uprising that involved a conspiracy between black slaves and white indentured servants. This episode is believed to be the first serious slave conspiracy in the British North American colonies. Throughout the colonial and early national periods, local authorities would maintain a careful vigilance to suppress all episodes of organized resistance by slaves.

As settlement of the Carolina colony began, settlers were promised 20 acres of land for each male slave that they brought into the colony and 10 acres for every female slave.

1664

Maryland law stated that Christian baptism did not affect the slave status imposed on black servants within the colony—effectively, blacks were considered servants for life. This measure was necessary because certain precedents in English common law allowed for the emancipation of slaves who became converts to Christianity and then established a legal domicile within the colony. Eventually, colonial assemblies in New York, New Jersey, North Carolina, South Carolina, and Virginia (but not Georgia, Pennsylvania, and Delaware) would enact similar laws.

The colonies of New York and New Jersey legally recognized the institution of slavery, by passing respective statutes to regulate the practice. Slavery had existed in both of these colonial regions prior to 1664, when the area was still under Dutch control, but the statutes passed in these colonies in 1664 marked the first time that British authorities in these colonies officially recognized slavery's legal status.

On September 20, the colonial assembly in Maryland enacted an antimiscegenation statute to prevent "freeborn women from . . . shameful matches." The assembly was particularly concerned about the problems that arose in determining the legal status of children who were born from interracial encounters.

1665

The laws that the duke of York (the future King James II of Great Britain) developed for governing the colony of New York recognized the legality of slavery within the colony and did not prevent the enslavement of Native American peoples or Christian Africans.

1667

In England, Parliament passed the "Act to Regulate the

Negroes on the British Plantations." This measure described persons of African descent as possessing a "wild, barbarous and savage nature, to be controlled only with strict severity."

On September 23, Virginia repealed an earlier enacted statute that enfranchised blacks who converted to Christianity. The new law stated that Christian baptism did not affect the slave status imposed on black servants within the colony—effectively blacks were considered servants for life. In the Preamble to this statute, Virginia lawmakers urged the colony's slaveowners to be more diligent in converting slaves to Christianity.

Virginia authorities declared that it was not to be considered a felony if one's slave died while being "corrected"—that is, punished.

1668

The Virginia House of Burgesses enacted a measure declaring that free black women in the colony should not "be admitted to the full fruition of the exemptions and impunities of the English."

1669

In October, the Virginia House of Burgesses enacted a statute that acquitted slaveowners who killed their slaves. The law stated that "it cannot be presumed that premeditated malice (which alone makes murder a felony) should induce any man to destroy his own estate." The law was based on the assumption that the slave's value as an item of property superseded the slave's value as a person.

1670

On October 13, the Virginia House of Burgesses passed legislation asserting that all non-Christian servants who were imported by sea were thereafter to be considered as servants for life and that the condition of all issue must follow the status of the mother. Because of the moral concerns raised by the possible enslavement of Christians, the law further stipulated that blacks who were Christians before their arrival in Virginia could not be enslaved for life, but this provision was repealed in 1682. The law also stated that servants who entered the colony by land were to serve until they reached the age of thirty if they were

adult men and women when their period of servitude began.

Statutes within the Body of Liberties for the colony of Massachusetts were revised so that the enslavement of a slave woman's offspring was legalized. According to this policy, the status of the child was viewed as the same as the status of the mother in all circumstances. The previous language of this section had created a legal loophole in which the children of certain slaves had attempted to sue for their freedom.

The settlement of South Carolina began in earnest as two thousand emigrants from the island of Barbados in the British West Indies moved to the mainland colony and brought their slaves with them.

1671

Virginia governor William Berkeley believed that there were two thousand blacks in Virginia and six thousand white indentured servants out of a total population of forty thousand inhabitants. Slaves constituted about 5 percent of the colony's population.

The colonial assembly in Maryland enacted a measure declaring that the conversion of blacks to Christianity, either before or after their enslavement in the colony, did not affect their condition of service for life. This measure was necessitated by the apprehension of slave traders who believed that their economic welfare was dependent on such a declaration. With passage of this measure, slave importers were more likely to encourage the conversion of slaves to Christianity.

1672

The British Parliament passed enabling legislation that chartered the Royal African Company and granted it a monopoly in conducting the British slave trade between Africa and the Americas. The British were eager to acquire profits from the slave trade that previously had enriched other rival European powers. The Royal African Company held its exclusive monopoly status until 1698, when the Parliament opened the slave trade to all British subjects.

In Virginia, a new law placed a bounty on the head of "maroons"—black fugitives who formed independent communities in the mountains, swamps, and forests of the colony. These communities were viewed with disdain; occasionally the residents of maroon communities would raid towns and plantations in order to obtain needed provisions.

1674

After having had success with Native American peoples, John Eliot and the Society for Propagating the Gospel in New England began to support the education of persons of African descent.

1676

Dutch slave traders carrying Africans to the Americas were engaged in a lucrative business. Africans purchased in Angola cost the Dutch traders 30 florins each, and they sell slaves in the Americas for prices ranging between 300 and 500 florins. The Dutch traders transport approximately fifteen thousand Africans per year for sale as slaves in the Americas.

English Quaker William Edmondson addressed a general letter to the slaveholders of Great Britain's North American colonies. In the letter Edmundson argued that Christianity was incompatible with slaveholding, and he urged his colonial brethren to separate themselves from the vile institution of slavery.

Colonial legislators in New Jersey prohibited the practice of slavery from the western portion of that colony.

1680

A Virginia law prohibited blacks from gathering in large groups or carrying weapons of any type.

On October 31, the General Court of Massachusetts imposed fines and prohibited any ship from sailing from a Massachusetts port with "any servant or Negro" aboard without having obtained specific permission from the governor.

1681

A colonial census estimated that three thousand blacks resided in Virginia.

A slave girl named Maria was burned alive in the colony of Massachusetts after she was convicted of setting fire to her master's home. This case of arson was especially disturbing because it had caused the death of a child in the home.

A Maryland colonial law freed black children who were born either of European mothers or of free black mothers. With the passage of this measure, the status of slaves in the colony of Maryland effectively followed the status of the father. Legislators enacted this measure because many colonial planters had been encouraging white indentured women to marry slaves so that their offspring would become slaves.

1682

The British colony of South Carolina legally sanctioned the practice of slavery within its borders, thus giving statutory recognition to the "peculiar institution."

The Virginia House of Burgesses passed a law that reduced all non-Christian bondservants to permanent status as slaves regardless of any future religious conversion experiences. The new law also allowed slaves who were Christians at the time of their arrival in Virginia to be enslaved for life. This measure reversed existing policies that had been established in 1670. The previous legislation had caused economic distress by limiting the number of slave imports into the Virginia colony.

The Pennsylvania colonial assembly chartered the Free Society of Traders in Pennsylvania that recognized the legality of slavery in the colony but sought to introduce a new commercial scheme. The society established a system of slave apprenticeship in which slaves would be freed after fourteen years, provided that they continued to cultivate plots allotted to them and submitted two-thirds of their agricultural produce annually to the society.

1685

The French government enacted the *Code Noir* in all of its colonial settlements. In North America, this involved the French colony of Louisiana, but settlers often ignored the provisions of this decree. The code required religious instruction for slaves, permitted intermarriage, and outlawed the working of slaves on Sundays and on holidays. The code also forbade the liberation of mulatto children who reached the age of twenty-one if their mothers were still enslaved.

The Virginia House of Burgesses passed a statute that prohibited slaves within the colony from participating in any of the Quaker meetings that were held for educational purposes.

1687

In Westmoreland County, Virginia, rumors of a planned slave insurrection abounded. Public gatherings of slaves in the region were banned by local authorities, and slaves were not allowed to hold public funerals for other slaves.

In New England, fugitive slaves were often captured and returned to slavery by various indigenous peoples who served as slave catchers and were paid a small bounty by colonial slaveowners to perform this service.

1688

On February 18 in Germantown, Pennsylvania, the famous "Germantown Protest" occurred as a group of Pennsylvania Mennonite Quakers declared openly at their monthly meeting that slavery was contrary to Christian principles and signed an antislavery resolution to that effect. The document was prepared by Franz Daniel Pastorius and his brethren. This antislavery tract is viewed as the first public condemnation of the institution and practice of slavery in the Western Hemisphere, and it is also viewed as one of the first examples of nonviolent protest in American history.

1690

The colonial assembly in Connecticut enacted a pass law, which made it unlawful for black and Indian servants to travel freely in the colony without specific written permission from their masters or some other person of authority. Those guilty of violating this policy were deemed fugitives and could be disciplined accordingly.

1691

Virginia's House of Burgesses enacted an antimiscegenation law designed to prevent intermarriage between races. Virginia officials also sought to restrict the practice of manumission within the colony and ordered any blacks who were freed to leave the colony within a six-month period. If a slaveowner did free a slave under this new policy, it was the responsibility of the owner to pay all costs necessary for transporting the freed slave beyond the borders of Virginia. Officials in Virginia did not desire to have a large free black population within the colony because they feared that such a group might endanger regional security "by their either entertaining . . . slaves or receiving stolen goods or being grown old and bringing a change upon the country."

1692

The colonial assembly in Maryland imposed a penalty of seven years of indenture on any white man who either married or fathered a child with a black woman. The law also imposed penalties on both the white women who were "associated" with blacks and the black men themselves.

Virginia colonial law stated that a fugitive slave might be legally killed and that the owners who experienced such a loss would be compensated by the colony with 4,000 pounds of tobacco.

Pennsylvania statutes imposed strict penalties on any slave who was loitering in an unauthorized area without a pass from his owner. Such a slave could be imprisoned without food or drink and could receive thirty-nine lashes "well laid on, on their bare backs" as part of a public whipping.

In Salem, Massachusetts, the frenzy of a witch craze swept the community, and twenty citizens of Salem were executed after having been accused and convicted of being witches. Much of the initial fear had grown from stories of black magic that a slave woman named Tituba had shared with a group of adolescent girls in the home of Reverend Samuel Parris. Tituba was not executed for her role in Salem's witchcraft hysteria, but she remained a slave in Massachusetts.

1693

Quaker George Keith published *An Exhortation and Caution to Friends Concerning Buying or Keeping of Negroes.* Keith's hoped that Quakers who owned slaves would free them as soon as possible. This tract was presented as a paper at the Quaker annual meeting in Philadelphia.

In Boston, Puritan minister Cotton Mather prepared the "Rules for the Society of Negroes." This group represented the first black religious association known to have formed in early America.

1695

In Goose Creek Parish, South Carolina, Reverend Samuel Thomas established a school that taught black children.

1696

During their annual meeting, American Quakers (Society of Friends) admonished their membership for participating in the importation of slaves. The Quakers threatened those who continued to import slaves with possible expulsion from the Society of Friends.

1698

Blacks comprised 12 percent of the population in the colony of New York.

Pennsylvania Quaker William Southeby petitioned Quakers in Barbados to stop shipping blacks to Pennsylvania as slaves. As a result of his sustained efforts against slavery, Southeby was eventually expelled from the Society of Friends.

The Royal African Company lost its monopoly status for conducting the British slave trade between Africa and the Americas. As a result, participation in the slave trade was opened to all British subjects, and many New Englanders became involved in extensive slave trading as they realized the lucrative profits that this enterprise afforded. Parliament considered the slave trade to be "highly beneficial and advantageous to this kingdom and to the Plantations and Colonies." Private traders could enter into the enterprise once they paid a 10 percent duty to the Royal African Company for the maintenance of the West African forts and factories. From this date onward, the so-called triangular trade developed as slaves, sugar/molasses, and rum would become the dominant goods exchanged between Africa, the West Indies, and the colonies of British North America.

Officials in Massachusetts changed the colonial tax codes so that "all Indian, mulatto, and Negro servants be estimated as other personal estate." Prior to 1698, Massachusetts listed slaves as persons on tax lists, but this action changed their legal status to property.

1699

Virginia's House of Burgesses imposed an import duty of 20 shillings on each slave that was imported into the colony.

1700

The British colonies of Pennsylvania and Rhode Island passed legislation that sanctioned the practice of slavery within their borders.

Slave population in the British North American colonies was estimated at 27,817, with 22,611 of these living in the southern colonies and 5,206 living in the northern colonies. As a group, slaves constituted 10 percent of the total population in the British colonies.

On June 24, Judge Samuel Sewall published *The Selling of Joseph* in Boston, Massachusetts. This antislavery tract based its arguments against the institution and practice of slavery on biblical sources and questioned those who used biblical interpretation to condone the practice of slavery.

In the same year, Judge Sewall organized an antislavery organization known as the Boston Committee of 1700 that lobbied for implementation of a high duty on slave imports. The group believed that excessive taxation might be one means of destroying the slave trade in Massachusetts, but the group's efforts were unsuccessful.

1700

Quakers began to make an effort throughout the colonies to provide religious instruction to slaves. In Pennsylvania, William Penn organized a monthly meeting for blacks.

1701

The Anglican Society for Promoting Christian Knowledge, better known as the Society for the Propagation of the Gospel in Foreign Parts, was founded in England by Thomas Bray. One of the group's primary concerns of the society was the religious conversion of Native American peoples and persons of African descent in the British colonies.

1702

New Jersey colonial legislators enacted statutes that gave legal recognition to the practice of slavery within the colony.

1703

Colonial legislators in South Carolina imposed a duty on all slave imports into the colony.

A work entitled *John Saffin's Tryall* was published in Boston. This work initiated the literary genre of the slave narrative that would be popular throughout the colonial and early national periods. Many of the slave narratives would be published and used by antislavery supporters as powerful propaganda tools to agitate for an end to the slave trade, and eventually, an end to slavery itself.

Rhode Island colonial legislators enacted statutes that gave legal recognition to slavery within the colony.

1704

The first school established to educate black children in what eventually became the United States was founded when Elias Neau, a French Huguenot immigrant, opened the Catechism School for Negroes at Trinity Church in New York City. The school was suspected of being somehow involved in a antislavery plot when rumors of revolt surfaced in the city in 1712.

In Connecticut, a mulatto slave named Abda sued his owner, Thomas Richards of Hartford. Abda maintained that he should be free because of his white blood; a Connecticut court agreed and set him free. Later, the Connecticut General Assembly reversed the colonial court's decision and returned Abda to slavery.

1705

On October 23, Virginia's black code placed severe restrictions on slave mobility and also authorized heavy penalties to discourage the practice of miscegenation within the colony. The measure also recognized slaves as being real estate rather than persons, thus serving to dehumanize the slaves, conferring on them the status of nothing more than chattel property that could be bought, sold, and traded at whim.

Following the lead taken by other colonies, legislators in Massachusetts imposed a duty of £4 on all slaves imported into the colony. This customs imposition was not severe enough to tax the slave trade out of business as Samuel Sewall and the Boston Committee of 1700 had desired.

Also on October 23, the Virginia Assembly declared that "no Negro, mulatto, or Indian shall presume to take upon him, act in or exercise any office, ecclesiastic, civil, or military." Blacks were also forbidden from serving as witnesses in court cases. They were condemned to lifelong servitude, unless they had previously been Christians in their native land or free men in a Christian country. In addition, slavery was defined as a legal condition that was limited to blacks only with the exception of "Turks and Moors in amity with her majesty."

The colonial legislature in Massachusetts enacted an antimiscegenation law designed to prevent intermarriage between races. The goal of "An Act for the Better Preventing of a Spurious and Mist Issues" was to insure that problems arising from determining the legal status of such offspring would be reduced in colonial Massachusetts. This prohibition remained in effect until its repeal in 1843.

The colonial legislature in New York developed a measure to reduce the incidence of slaves running away from their owners by enacting stiff punishments for fugitives. The legislation called for the death penalty to be imposed against any fugitive slave who was captured in the region beyond a line forty miles north of Albany, New York, as capture within that area was sufficient evidence of the fugitive slave's desire to reach Canada.

1706

A statute enacted by colonial legislators in New York prohibited the testimony of a slave against a freeman in both civil and criminal cases.

1707

Colonial legislators in Massachusetts imposed a fine of 5 shillings on any free black who helped to harbor a fugitive slave. A significant number of slaves were imported into Massachusetts at this time, and the problem of slave runaways was becoming acute in the colony.

In Philadelphia, Pennsylvania, a group of mechanics and artisans banded together into a guild to protest the economic competition that their crafts faced because of the amount of work performed by slaves who were hired out within the city. The mechanics and artisans believed that they faced unfair competition from the labor performed by slaves.

In Massachusetts, selected free blacks were allowed to join the colonial militia.

1708

Virginia officials estimated that twelve thousand blacks resided within the colony.

A census in the Carolina colony showed that the combined total of black and Indian slaves in the region surpassed the population of whites.

In October, a slave uprising in the community of

Newton, on Long Island, New York, killed seven whites. The event was suppressed and four blacks were executed. The legislature responded to this event by enacting a new law aimed at preventing slave conspiracies.

Pennsylvania authorities responded to the protest of white mechanics and artisans and moved to restrict the further importation of slaves into the colony, but the British Crown invalidated these restrictive policies.

1709

Colonial authorities in Virginia discovered and suppressed a conspiracy in which black and Indian slaves had planned to revolt.

1710

Slave population in the British North American colonies was estimated at 44,866. Approximately 36,563 of slaves were in the southern colonies, and 8,303 were in the northern colonies.

Virginia's House of Burgesses agreed to manumit a slave named Will because he had informed colonial authorities of a planned slave conspiracy. The practice of rewarding slave informants with freedom was a common practice during the colonial and early national periods as local authorities sought to maintain peace and security in the plantation districts by discouraging conspiracies.

Colonial Governor Alexander Spotswood tried to discourage the further importation of slaves into Virginia as white residents became alarmed at the growing number of blacks within the colony.

1711

At the insistence of Quakers and Mennonites, the Pennsylvania colonial assembly outlawed slavery, but the action was immediately overruled by the British Crown.

The South Sea Company was organized in England, and this trading company received the right to transport Africans to the Americas where they could be sold as slaves.

In South Carolina, Governor Robert Gibbes and other colonial authorities struggled to combat a sustained campaign of slave resistance that was inspired by a large community of maroons led by a fugitive slave named Sebastian. The people of the colony were fearful of the maroon attacks until Sebastian was killed by an Indian hunter.

On September 22, the Tuscarora Indians became alarmed when British colonists in the Carolinas moved into their lands in the region of the Roanoke and Chowan rivers. A series of skirmishes between the Tuscarora and the colonists followed, and a number of slaves were able to use the chaos as an opportunity to escape from their owners.

1712

From April 7 to 8, nine white residents were killed and seven were wounded in a slave revolt that erupted in New York City. Once the tumult subsided, twenty-one slaves were convicted and sentenced to death for their roles in the uprising. Six other blacks committed suicide.

On June 7, the colonial assembly in Pennsylvania banned the further importation of slaves into the colony. In taking this action, Pennsylvania became the first of the British colonies to prohibit the slave trade. The Pennsylvania action followed efforts by William Southeby to have the assembly abolish slavery within the colony.

The colonial assembly in South Carolina enacted "An Act for the Better Ordering and Governing of Negroes and Slaves." This comprehensive measure became the model that was used by many other slave codes developed in the South during the colonial and national periods.

In response to the slave revolt that occurred in New York City, the colonial assemblies in New York and Massachusetts both enacted measures designed to prevent, suppress, and punish slave conspiracies and insurrections within their colonies.

1713

On March 26, during the negotiation of the Treaty of Utrecht, which ended the War of the Spanish Succession (Queen Anne's War, 1701–1713), the British South Sea Company received the *asiento*, the contract to supply slaves to the Spanish colonies in the Americas. This contract permitted the South Sea Company to carry 4,800 slaves per year to the Spanish colonies in the Americas for a period of 30 years (144,000 total). In addition, the British were allowed to send one merchant ship per year to the Spanish colonies for trading purposes. British slave traders would hold the *asiento* throughout most of the eighteenth century.

1714

Rhode Island colonial legislators enacted a measure to limit the mobility of slaves within the colony. Slaves were not permitted to travel on a ferry without the specific written permission of their owners.

Colonial legislators in New Hampshire enacted statutes that recognized the legality of slavery within the colony.

1715

A census taken in the New England colonies revealed that two thousand blacks lived in the region.

Approximately twenty-five hundred slaves were imported into the British North American colonies annually. In 1715 the population of the British colonies was estimated to be 434,600, and the total population of slaves was 58,850. According to these estimates, slaves constituted 13.5 percent of the colonial population at this time.

The colony of North Carolina enacted legislation that legalized the practice of slavery within its borders. The legislature also enacted an antimiscegenation law designed to prevent intermarriage between races. Slaves within the colony were also denied the right to have their own religious meetinghouses.

Quaker John Hepburn published the tract entitled *The American Defence of the Christian Golden Rule.* Hepburn presented many arguments against slavery, but stressed that most importantly, slavery was a practice that robbed individuals of the freedom of choice.

Quaker Elihu Coleman published the tract, *A Testimony Against that Anti-Christian Practice of Making Slaves of Men.*

Virginia officials estimated that 24 percent of the colony's population consisted of slaves.

Encouraged by agitators from Spanish Florida, on April 15 the Yamassee Indians attacked colonial settlements in South Carolina and killed hundreds of white settlers. During this conflict the Yamassee freed many slaves who had been held in South Carolina.

1716

On June 6, in the French colony of Louisiana, the first slaves were introduced by two slave ships of John Law's Company of the West.

An antislavery tract appeared in the Massachusetts colony. It argued that the presence of slavery in the British colonies had a debilitating effect on encouraging the immigration of additional white settlers. The author contended that slavery reduced the number of occupations that remained open to white settlers and that this type of economic competition did not encourage whites to immigrate to the British colonies.

1717

In Boston, Massachusetts, Cotton Mather established an evening school to educate Indian and slave youth.

The colonial legislature in South Carolina enacted an antimiscegenation law designed to prevent intermarriage between races. Many colonies adopted similar measures because of the problems that were associated with determining the legal status of children born of interracial unions.

The colonial legislature of Maryland enacted a measure designed to discourage interracial marriage within the colony. According to the provisions of this statute, if a free black married a white colonist, the black spouse became the slave of the white spouse.

1719

In the summer, the first large shipment of slaves arrived at New Orleans in the French colony of Louisiana. The ships *Grand Duc du Maine* and *Aurora* delivered approximately five hundred Africans to the colony. John Law, who was then the proprietor of the colony through his Company of the Indies, built a slave-trading station along the Mississippi River directly across from New Orleans. At this so-called Plantation of the Company, Africans were sold and distributed to the Louisiana colonists.

1720

It was estimated that two thousand slaves resided in the colony of Pennsylvania.

The population of the British North American colonies was estimated to be 474,000 and the total population of slaves was 68,839. According to these estimates, slaves constituted 14.5 percent of the colonial population at this time.

In May, a slave insurrection that was described as "a very wicked and barbarous plott" occurred in Charleston, South Carolina, and was put down by local authorities. Twenty-three slaves were arrested in conjunction with the incident, and three were eventually executed for their role in the revolt.

1721

The colonial legislature in Delaware enacted an antimiscegenation law designed to prevent intermarriage between races. According to this statute, the child who was born to a white mother and a slave father was legally bound to the county court until the mixed-race child reached the age of thirty-one.

On May 21 in Boston, Zabdiel Boylston administered the first smallpox inoculations in America; he gave them to his son and two African slaves. Reverend Cotton Mather had recommended the experiment after one of his slaves, Onesimus, had informed him that various African tribes had successfully used inoculations. This use of an African medical technology in a Western setting helped to save the lives of many Boston residents during the smallpox epidemic of 1721.

1722

In Virginia, authorities detected a conspiracy among slaves in several counties. The leaders of the plot were imprisoned, and several others associated with the plan were sold and transported out of Virginia.

The colonial assembly in Pennsylvania denounced the "wicked and scandalous practice" of blacks cohabitating with white colonists.

Pennsylvania officials again responded to the protest of white mechanics and artisans by declaring that the practice of hiring slaves into the trades was "dangerous and injurious to the republic and not to be sanctioned." Pennsylvania's action applied to both slaves and free blacks, and several other colonies followed the lead of Pennsylvania and enacted similar prohibitions designed to protect white mechanics and artisans against "unfair" competition from blacks.

1723

The Virginia legislature disenfranchised free blacks and Native Americans within the colony and also discriminated heavily against them in the imposition of colonial taxes. With its reliance on race as a controlling factor, this law represented a departure from policies that had been in effect since 1670, policies that had only restricted the suffrage on the basis of property qualifications. In addition, free blacks were also denied the right to carry weapons of any sort within the colony.

On April 13, after an extensive arson campaign affected the colony, acting governor of the Massachusetts colony, William Dummer, issued a proclamation announcing "fires which have been designedly and industriously kindled by some villainous and desperate negroes or other dissolute people as appears by the confession of some of them." Apprehension was high for many weeks as the white citizens of Boston feared that blacks planned to destroy the city.

In May, seven slaves from Middlesex and Gloucester counties were sold and transported out of Virginia because of their involvement in a planned slave uprising.

1724

In March, the *Code Noir* (or Black Code) went into effect in the French colony of Louisiana when it was instituted by Governor Bienville. The Code contained fifty-five provisions that regulated the life of slaves within the colony of Louisiana. Although this code primarily affected the slaves of the colony, certain provisions also directed the liberties afforded to free blacks. In addition, the code ordered that all Jews leave the colony and prohibited "the exercise of any other religion than the Catholic."

A religious tract published in Virginia encouraged slaveowners to baptize and educate their slaves. The author of this document suggested that owners should be exempt from paying taxes on baptized slaves who were under the age of eighteen.

1725

After many years of pressure by white settlers, the colonial assembly in Pennsylvania enacted an antimiscegenation law designed to prevent intermarriage between races. The assembly was particularly concerned about the problems that arose in determining the legal status of children who were born from interracial encounters.

An estimate placed the population of slaves in the British North American colonies at seventy-five thousand.

The Virginia House of Burgesses granted permission for free blacks in Williamsburg to establish the first Church of Colored Baptists.

The South Carolina colonial assembly imposed a £200 fine on those slaveowners who brought slaves to the western frontier of the colony. It was believed that such close proximity to the wilderness beyond the frontier would prompt slaves to escape. The law also sought to diminish the likelihood that slaves might conspire with Native Americans to harm the frontier settlements.

1726

Colonial Governor William Burnet of New York requested that the chiefs of the Six Nations of the Iroquois Confederacy surrender all fugitive slaves who had sought asylum among the Iroquois. Although the chiefs agreed to comply with Burnet's request, no fugitives were ever returned to colonial authorities.

Peter Vantrump, a free black, was kidnapped under false circumstances and sold into slavery in North Carolina by a Captain Mackie who had promised to take Vantrump to Europe. When Vantrump sued for his freedom, the General Court of North Carolina denied his petition, and he remained a slave.

1727

In Pennsylvania, Benjamin Franklin, a noted opponent of slavery, established a benevolent association called the Junto. Upon joining the organization, members pledged that they would work toward the abolition of slavery and other forms of inhumanity to man.

In the French colony of Louisiana, the Roman Catholic Ursuline Nuns began to educate black children in New Orleans.

1729

In Rhode Island, the colonial assembly required slaveowners to post a one-hundred-pound bond to insure that their slaves would not become a public charge "through sickness, lameness" or for other reasons.

Quaker Ralph Sandyford [Sandiford] published an antislavery tract entitled A Brief Examination of the Practice of the Times, By the Foregoing and the Present Dispensation. The work was published in Philadelphia by Benjamin Franklin, who supported efforts to abolish the institution of slavery.

The Society for the Propagation of the Gospel was reorganized, and the group changed its name to Dr. Bray's Associates. Reverend Thomas Bray had worked since 1701 to support the religious education of blacks in the British colonies.

1730

In Virginia, white residents were placed on heightened alert as slave conspiracies were detected in Norfolk and Princess Anne counties. Governor William Gooch authorized white males in the affected region to carry weapons with them when attending church services. Other conspiratorial plots were detected and suppressed in 1730 in South Carolina and in the French colony of Louisiana.

Slaves constituted 13.9 percent of the total inhabitants of the British North American colonies. Of the 91,021 slaves who lived in the colonies, 17,323 lived in the northern colonies and 73,698 lived in the southern colonies.

At Williamsburg, Virginia, slaves planned a rebellion as a rumor spread that the former colonial governor, Alexander Spotswood, had returned to the colony from London with the authority to free all persons who were baptized as Christians. Authorities in the colony crushed the conspiracy and executed four of the slaves who were believed to be the leaders of the planned rebellion.

On August 15, authorities in South Carolina discovered a plot that involved as many as two hundred slaves who were planning to revolt. Part of the plan allegedly included an attack on a church at the mouth of Virginia's Rappahannock River.

1731

British monarch George II provided royal instructions to all colonial governors that specifically prohibited the imposition of any customs duties on slave importations. This action was consistent with British mercantile policy and reflected the Crown's concern with the well-being of the slave-trading enterprise, which was quite lucrative for British merchants.

1732

The Virginia House of Burgesses imposed a 5 percent import duty on all slaves brought into the colony, and this provision remained in effect for many years. In 1759, colonial authorities attempted to raise the duty to 20 percent, but the British Crown rejected this duty as excessive.

1733

Georgia was founded as the last of the thirteen British North American colonies. It was viewed as an experimental colony in that slavery was not permitted when the colony was founded, but eventually authorities within the colony relaxed this prohibition. Philanthropist and colony founder James Oglethorpe was a slaveholder himself in the Carolinas, and he also served as the deputy governor of the Royal African Company, which was actively involved in the slave trade.

Because of persistent attacks by maroons upon plantations and farms in South Carolina, Governor Robert Johnson announced a reward of £20 for anyone who assisted in apprehending fugitives who operated as maroons within the colony.

Slaveowners in several southern colonies feared that slaves might conspire and organize an exodus to Spanish Florida. Spanish officials in Florida had promised to liberate any slave who escaped from a Protestant colony and sought refuge in Catholic Florida. This call was in large part responsible for much of the unrest that rocked South Carolina in 1739.

1735

In New York, the Dutch burgher John Van Zandt whipped to death a slave who had been picked up outside of his quarters beyond a curfew. A coroner's jury heard Van Zandt's case and declared that the slave was killed "by the visitation of God" rather than the actual beating. Van Zandt was found innocent of any criminal wrongdoing.

1736

Virginia planter William Byrd II commented on the hypocrisy of New England Puritans who criticized slavery but nonetheless participated actively in the African slave trade. Byrd commented that "the Saints of New England" were responsible for importing so many Africans into Virginia that "the Colony will some time or other be Confirmed by the name of New Guinea."

1737

The Quaker author Benjamin Lay published a radical antislavery work entitled *All Slave-Keepers that Keep the Innocent in Bondage; Apostates.* The controversial tract, which blended biting satire and advocacy of nonviolent resistance, was printed by Benjamin Franklin, who was himself an opponent of slavery.

1738

In Nantucket, Massachusetts, authorities discovered a well-planned conspiracy among Native American peoples to attack the community in the night and kill all the white settlers while sparing the blacks.

The Moravian Church established a mission in Bethlehem, Pennsylvania, that was created specifically to minister to blacks in the region.

1739

On September 9, in the British colony of South Carolina, a slave named Cato led a serious slave revolt along the Stono River in a region in which blacks constituted a very large majority of the population. The group of slaves involved reportedly sought to leave the South Carolina colony and travel to St. Augustine, Florida, where Spanish missionaries had reputedly promised liberation. Anyone who tried to prevent the migration was targeted as a victim. Thirty white residents and forty-four blacks died during the insurrection and its eventual suppression. This revolt was the most intense of three outbreaks that plagued South Carolina during the year. The two other events took place at Stone Creek and in St. John's Parish in Berkeley County, South Carolina.

The trustees of the Georgia colony received petitions from two groups, one supporting the introduction of slavery into the colony and the other opposing such action. For the time being, the trustees decided that it was best to keep slavery out of the colony.

Fugitive slaves who escaped to Spanish Florida and thus liberated themselves built a fort at St. Augustine, Florida. The purpose of this installation was to protect their own self-earned freedom and to prevent the British from sending expeditions into Spanish Florida to try to recapture fugitives.

1740

Of the 150,024 slaves who lived in the British North American colonies, 23,598 lived in the northern colonies, and 126,066 lived in the southern colonies.

In January, in response to concerns raised by the Stono Rebellion, fifty blacks were put to death by hanging when rumors of another slave conspiracy were uncovered in Charleston, South Carolina.

The colonial legislature in South Carolina imposed a harsh slave code that prohibited slaves from raising livestock, provided that any animals previously owned by slaves be forfeited, and set very high penalties for slaves who made "false appeals" to the governor on the grounds that they had been enslaved illegally.

Colonial governor James Oglethorpe mounted a limited incursion into Spanish Florida and captured Forts Picolata and San Francisco de Pupo, but his small force was eventually pushed out of Florida. The Spanish forces were assisted by Seminole Indians and nearly two hundred fugitive slaves who had escaped to Florida and found refuge there.

An insurrectionary panic swept New York City when it was believed that slaves in the city had poisoned the water supply in an effort to kill their masters and win their freedom.

1741

Between February and April, a series of arsonist acts in New York City helped spread wild rumors about a unified conspiracy in which slaves and poor whites planned to burn or to seize control of the city. Although evidence for such a plot was slight, a general hysteria developed and eighteen blacks were hanged, eleven were burned alive at the stake, and seventy were banished from the colony. The white backlash against slaves stemmed from their presence in the city rather than from any hard evidence of their connection with a criminal conspiracy.

1742

On April 15, the General Court of Massachusetts granted a divorce to a slave named Boston. Boston had charged that his wife Hagar had an adulterous affair with a white man and had given birth to a mulatto child.

Spanish officials in Florida mounted an invasion of the Georgia colony in retaliation for Oglethorpe's raid in 1740. The Spanish troops that fought in Georgia included a regiment of black troops that was commanded by black officers.

1743

In the New Jersey colony, John Woolman, an itinerant Quaker clergyman, initiated a series of sermons that called for an end to slavery and urged greater consideration of racial equality. Woolman eventually published his ideas in *Some Considerations on the Keeping of Negroes* (1754). Woolman would carry his antislavery message to Quaker meetings in several colonies.

In Charleston, South Carolina, Mr. Garden's School was established. This institution was created to teach black youth in the city, and the school was supported by both the free black and the white residents of Charleston.

A school specifically designed to train black missionaries was established in Charleston, South Carolina by the Society for the Propagation of the Gospel in Foreign Parts.

1744

The Virginia Assembly revised its 1705 law regarding the rights of blacks to serve as witnesses in court proceedings. The amended statute entitled "any free Negro, mulatto, or Indian being a Christian," the right to serve as a witness in criminal or civil suits involving another Negro, Mulatto, or Indian.

Anglican missionary Samuel Thomas established a school for free blacks in South Carolina.

1745

Thomas Ashley published *A New General Collection of Voyages and Travels*. In this work, Ashley responded to those proslavery supporters who said that slavery was beneficial to the African. Ashley challenged that if slavery was indeed beneficial, it would follow that the Africans should be allowed to choose for themselves whether or not they wanted to be enslaved.

1746

Lucy Terry, a slave poet, wrote "Bars Fight," a commemorative poem that is considered to be one of the best accounts of the Indian massacre of Deerfield, Massachusetts. Terry is generally considered to be the first black poet in America. She later unsuccessfully tried to convince the Board of Trustees at Williams College to admit her son to the school.

In New Jersey, the colonial assembly met at Perth Amboy and authorized John Hamilton, the commander of the colonial militia, to raise a regiment of five hundred free blacks and Native Americans to be used as soldiers against the French in Canada.

1747

The South Carolina Assembly thanked black slaves for demonstrating "great faithfulness and courage in repelling attacks of His Majesty's enemies." The Assembly also made cautious provisions for using black troops in times of dire emergency, but warned that black recruits should never constitute more than one-third of the colony's troop strength.

1748

The Virginia Militia Act became law within the colony of Virginia. According to this measure, free blacks and Native Americans were prohibited from carrying weapons. During the years of the American Revolution, this provision was revised so that free blacks could serve as soldiers in the Continental Army.

1749

On October 26, the trustees of the Georgia colony repealed their initial prohibition against the importation of slaves into the colony. This measure was later approved by the British Parliament, which indicated Parliament's effectual endorsement of slavery within the British North American colonies. This same measure also attempted to protect slaves from being hired out and from cruel treatment that might be imposed on them. Legislation within the Georgia colony established a ratio stipulating that four slaves could be kept in the colony for every white servant.

1750

On September 30 in Framingham, Massachusetts, Crispus Attucks escaped from his master. Attucks would later become a heroic figure for his role in the Boston Massacre (1770).

An estimated seventy-five hundred slaves were imported into British North America each year.

In Philadelphia, Pennsylvania, Anthony Benezet and a group of his Quaker brethren established an evening school for free blacks in the city. The school was taught by Moses Patterson.

The slave population was estimated to be 236,420, with 206,198 living in the southern colonies and 30,222 in the northern colonies. Although slaves comprised roughly 20 percent of the entire population of all colonies combined, they formed more than 40 percent of the population of the Virginia colony alone.

The French had established five colonial villages in the western territory that eventually became the state of Illinois. The population in this region was indeed sparse, but the 1,100 white settlers in those communities owned 300 black slaves and 60 Native Americans were also held in slavery. Although the Northwest Ordinance of 1787 would later prohibit slavery in this region and Illinois would eventually join the Union as a free state in 1818, a strong proslavery element remained active in some of the region's older French communities.

The British Parliament enacted a modification to its slave trade policies that had far-reaching implications on the enterprise. When Parliament ended the Royal African Company's monopoly on the trade in 1698, lawmakers opened the enterprise to other English corporations (syndicates) that were willing to pay a set duty in order to participate in the trade. The 1750 modification allowed private individuals to engage in the slave trade provided that they paid the duty to the Royal African Company for maintaining the West African forts and factories. The net result of this change was that more people became involved in the African slave trade and the business became more notorious at the same time that increased calls to end the trade were coming from many British colonists.

1751

Benjamin Franklin wrote a pamphlet entitled "Observations Concerning the Increase of Mankind and the Peopling of Countries." In this tract, Franklin argued that slave labor represented one of the most inefficient forms of production that was used in the world.

The Jesuits introduced the cultivation of sugarcane into the French colony of Louisiana. The large-scale cultivation of sugarcane in Louisiana that ensued necessitated the more massive importation of slaves into the region just as the "sugar revolution" of the previous century had brought enormous numbers of slaves to Brazil and to the islands of the West Indies.

1752

In July, there were eighteen slaves at the estate of Mount Vernon in Virginia when George Washington inherited the property upon the death of his half-brother. During his ownership, the number of slaves at Mount Vernon grew to 200. Washington was concerned with the physical well-being of his slaves, but he was never certain about his willingness to grant them freedom or to do without their services to the estate. After Washington's death in 1799, however, his final testament did manumit his slaves.

Maryland became the first of the British colonies to enact a manumission statute.

1753

Phillis Wheatley, the future child-prodigy poet, was born in West Africa.

1754

In Philadelphia, John Woolman published *Some Considerations on the Keeping of Negroes: Recommended to the Professors of Christianity of Every Denomination,* a tract designed to challenge his fellow Quakers to manumit their slaves on moral grounds. Woolman was one of the most influential Quaker abolitionists of the eighteenth century.

In Baltimore, Maryland, a twenty-two-year-old free black named Benjamin Banneker became the first person in the British North American colonies to build a clock. Although Banneker had never before seen a clock, the device that he created worked accurately for twenty years.

In Charleston, South Carolina, two female slaves belonging to an owner named Croft were burned alive because they had burned some of the buildings on the owner's estate.

1755

Having previously made a denominational stand against the practice of slavery, American Quakers (Society of Friends) excluded from their denomination all members who continued to import slaves.

Two slaves belonging to John Codman of Charlestown, Massachusetts, were executed after they conspired and poisoned their owner. The slaves Mark and Phillis had learned that they were to be freed upon the death of Codman, and they decided to expedite the date of their liberation. Authorities tried to set an example to other slaves with swift and certain punishment. Mark was hanged and disemboweled, while Phillis was burned to death.

The colonial assembly in Georgia enacted statutes making slavery legal within the colony.

1756

The population of the Virginia colony was estimated

to have reached two hundred fifty thousand; slaves constituted 40 percent of the population.

1757

The English writer Edmund Burke wrote *An Account of the European Settlements in America.* In this work Burke encouraged methods of increasing colonial productivity, and he warned of the danger of possible slave insurrections if steps were not taken to improve the conditions of slaves in the colonies.

1758

In Mecklenberg, Virginia, William Byrd established the Bluestone African Baptist Church on his plantation located near the Bluestone River.

Antislavery supporter Anthony Benezet and other Pennsylvania Quakers began meeting yearly to discuss and plan strategies for the abolition crusade. This group became the basis of the Society for the Relief of Free Negroes Unlawfully Held in Bondage that was later organized in Philadelphia, Pennsylvania, in April 1775.

1760

The slave trade was banned completely in South Carolina upon action to that effect taken by the colonial assembly, but the British Crown disallowed this measure because of its conflict with British mercantile interests.

On February 14, Richard Allen, who would eventually become a religious leader and founder of the African Methodist Episcopal Church, was born a slave in Philadelphia.

In Boston, Briton Hammon published a pamphlet entitled *A Narrative of the Uncommon Sufferings and Surprising Deliverance of Briton Hammon, a Negro Man.* This work is considered to be the first prose work to be published by a black author in America.

On December 25, in New York City, the black poet Jupiter Hammon published *Salvation by Christ with Penitential Cries.*

1761

The colony of Virginia tried to impose an importation duty of 20 percent upon slaves who were brought into the colony, but the British Crown did not allow this action to stand. The British government viewed such a measure as an excessive tax that was contrary to the economic interests of the British mercantile system.

The Society of Friends (Quakers) voted to exclude slave traders from church membership, but many of the Quakers continued to be slaveowners.

An eight-year-old African child named Phillis Wheatley arrived in Boston, Massachusetts, as a slave. She would become known as a poet of the late-colonial period.

1762

James Derham, who became recognized as the first black physician in America, was born a slave in Philadelphia.

Anthony Benezet, a Pennsylvania Quaker who was an opponent of slavery, published *A Short Account of that Part of Africa Inhabited by the Negroes.* Although the work was ostensibly a study of African life and culture, Benezet also included a clear antislavery message in his study.

1763

In Massachusetts, free blacks formed a significant social group constituting 2.2 percent of the colony's inhabitants. Out of a total population of 235,810 residents, there were 5,214 free blacks in Massachusetts.

1764

With Parliament's passage of the Sugar Act, New England merchants and slave-ship captains protested the increase in the price of sugar and molasses, declaring these items to be indispensable to the slave trade, which they described as "vital commerce" for the region. A group of merchants published a pamphlet entitled *A Statement of the Massachusetts Trade and Fisheries,* in which they protested that the increased duties on such essential commodities might bring economic disaster to the region.

James Otis wrote *The Rights of the British Colonies Asserted and Proved* to protest the British Parliament's action in imposing the Sugar Act on the colonists. Otis maintained that the British action represented "taxation without representation," and he further claimed that slaves had a right to be free. Sensing an inconsistency between coercive action and liberalism, Otis viewed a connection between the infringement upon colonists' liberties by the British and the institution of slavery. Otis criticized slavery as an evil that "threatens

one day to reduce both Europe and America to the ignorance and barbarity of the darkest ages."

1765

The population of the British North American colonies was estimated to be 1,750,000, and slaves constituted approximately 20 percent of this total.

1766

"Negro Tom," one of George Washington's slaves at Mount Vernon, was punished for running away. As punishment, Washington ordered that the unruly slave be sold to the West Indies for a hogshead of rum and other goods including molasses, rum, limes, tamarinds, sweet meats, and spirits. Washington ordered the ship captain who carried Tom away to keep the slave chained until he was at sea.

On November 6, a group of Massachusetts slaves tried to initiate court action against their owners by citing a violation of trespass laws, but the colonial courts did not support the claim.

1767

"A Poem by Phillis, A Negro Girl, On the Death of Reverend Whitefield" is written by Phillis Wheatley, a fourteen-year-old slave girl in Boston. The poem was eventually published in 1770, and Wheatley was soon thereafter recognized internationally as a prodigy.

Denmark Vesey was born. In 1822 Vesey would be put to death for allegedly organizing a vast conspiracy of slaves and free blacks who had planned an insurrection at Charleston, South Carolina.

1769

At the age of twenty-six, Thomas Jefferson was elected to the Virginia House of Burgesses. His first action as an elected official was to lead an unsuccessful attempt to pass a bill that would emancipate slaves within the colony of Virginia.

1770

The population of the British North American colonies was estimated at 2,312,000, which included

462,000 slaves. Slaves constituted approximately 20 percent of the colonial population.

On March 5, Crispus Attucks, a runaway slave from Framingham, Massachusetts, was the first to fall in the Boston Massacre. In November 1750 Attucks had escaped from his owner, Deacon William Browne.

On June 28, in Philadelphia, Pennsylvania, Anthony Benezet led a successful campaign among the Quakers to establish a school for blacks in the city. When Benezet died in 1784, he left his personal fortune to endow the school, known as the Binoxide House, which had been established in 1770.

In Virginia, George Washington was one of several planters who signed a petition circulated by the Association for the Counteraction of Various Acts of Oppression on the Part of Great Britain. Washington and the others who signed promised not to purchase slaves who had not been in North America for at least one year. This measure was designed to create economic distress for the British government by not supporting the African slave trade.

The colonial assembly in Rhode Island enacted a statute that prohibited the further introduction of slaves into the colony.

The colonial assembly in Massachusetts debated a proposed bill that would have prohibited the further introduction of slaves into the colony, but legislators defeated the measure.

1771

The Massachusetts colonial assembly approved of a resolution calling for an end to the importation of Africans as slaves in the colony, but Colonial Governor Thomas Hutchinson refused to support the measure.

For the first time in many years, the average annual number of Africans imported as slaves into the American colonies declined. This statistical change reflected the growing opposition of many people within the British colonies to the slave trade.

The colonial assembly in Connecticut enacted a statute that prohibited the African slave trade within the colony.

1772

In May, in a landmark judicial ruling, Chief Justice Lord Mansfield's (William Murray, first earl of Mansfield) decision in the case of *Somersett v. Knowles* abolished slavery within England. In this decision Mansfield declared that "the air of England has long been too pure for a slave, and every man is free who breathes it. Every man who comes to England is entitled to the protection of English law, whatever oppression he may heretofore have suffered, and whatever may be the color of his skin."

In Virginia, the House of Burgesses enacted a substantial tariff on slave imports in an effort to curtail the practice within the colony. Officials in Virginia requested that the British government support this action against "a Trade of great Inhumanity," but the Crown did not allow this action to stand. The British government viewed this measure as contrary to the economic interests of the British mercantile system. The House of Burgesses enacted thirty-three different measures that called for an end to the slave trade, but this action was taken primarily in defiance of Parliament's passage of the Townshend Acts rather than in sincere support of the end of the slave trade upon moral grounds.

In Boston, Massachusetts, John Allen published the tract "Oration upon the Beauties of Liberty." Allen used a philosophical natural rights argument in this pamphlet to support the slaves' right to rebellion, and he called for the immediate end of slavery in the British colonies.

1773

On January 6 in Massachusetts, a group of slaves petitioned the colonial legislature for their freedom. During the years of the American Revolution, eight petitions of this type were presented to the legislature of Massachusetts. Much of the action of slaves seeking liberation from their enslavement in the colonies was inspired by the success of the *Somersett* case, which had effectively ended slavery in England.

A slave child named Sally Hemings is born in Virginia. In subsequent years she would become the slave mistress of Thomas Jefferson.

The idea of colonizing West Africa with free blacks was first discussed and promoted publicly by Ezra Stiles, the president of Yale College, and Samuel Hopkins, a Congregational minister. The idea of colonization would continue to be popular, and in the early nineteenth century the American Colonization Society would support such a program, but some white abolitionists and many free blacks were opposed to this strategy. Stiles and Hopkins also sent a circular to many New England churches urging their opposition to the slave trade.

The slave Phillis Wheatley published her first book of poetry, *Poems on Various Subjects, Religious and*

Moral, when she was about twenty. It was the second book to be published by an American woman. Wheatley was manumitted shortly after the publication of the book of verse.

1773

In Savannah, Georgia, David George, George Lisle, and Andrew Bryan established the first Negro Baptist church in the colony. Another church was established in Silver Bluff, South Carolina.

In Philadelphia, Pennsylvania, Dr. Benjamin Rush published the antislavery tract *An Address to the Inhabitants of the British Settlements, on the Slavery of the Negroes in America.* This document is perhaps the most significant expression of the American antislavery position to be published in the eighteenth century.

Residents of Leicester, Massachusetts, urged their elected representatives to enact legislation against slavery and the slave trade.

1774

On December 1, George Washington chaired a meeting at which delegates from several Virginia counties approved of the Fairfax Resolves, authored by George Mason, which condemned the slave trade. Resolution Number 17 stated, "it is the opinion of this meeting that during our present difficulties and distress, no slaves ought to be imported into any of the British colonies on this continent; and we take this opportunity of declaring our most earnest wishes to see an entire stop forever put to such a wicked, cruel and unnatural trade." As a result of this action, the Virginia Association suspended further importation of slaves into the colony and threatened a boycott of all British exports.

During the First Continental Congress, Thomas Jefferson and Benjamin Franklin convinced delegates to approve a measure that called for an end to the slave trade effective December 1, 1775, and sought to impose economic sanctions on those countries that continued to participate thereafter in the slave trade. These pledges were included in the Articles of Association that were adopted by the Continental Congress.

After a slave conspiracy was discovered in Boston, Abigail Adams wrote to her husband, John Adams, who was attending the Continental Congress and discussed the matter. She wrote, "I wish most sincerely there was not a slave in the province. It always appeared a most iniquitous scheme to me—fight ourselves for what we are daily robbing and plundering from those who have as good a right to freedom as we have."

In Philadelphia, the Society of Friends (Quakers) adopted rules at the society's annual meeting that prohibited Quakers from buying or selling any additional slaves. Those Quakers who owned slaves were advised that they should prepare their slaves for emancipation.

The Rhode Island legislature enacted a measure that freed any future slaves that were introduced into the colony, but the measure did not change the status of those persons who were slaves within the colony at the time the measure was enacted.

Thomas Jefferson wrote his first published work, *A Summary View of the Rights of British America.* In this pamphlet, Jefferson argued that the British colonists supported the abolition of slavery. Jefferson wrote that "the abolition of slavery is the great object of desire in those colonies where it was unhappily introduced," but also cautioned that it would first be necessary "to exclude all further importations from Africa."

In Rhode Island and Connecticut, the colonial legislatures in each colony forbade the continuation of slave imports into each colony. The Rhode Island legislation declared that any new slave who was brought into the colony would be made free, but the legislation did not emancipate the slaves who were already laboring within the colony.

Delegates met at a convention in New Berne, North Carolina, for the purpose of organizing a provincial congress. The delegates who gathered there believed that the colonies should immediately end the importation of African slaves.

In St. Andrews Parish, Georgia, a slave revolt resulted in the death of four white colonists and the injury of three others. The two slaves who led the revolt were burned to death as punishment.

1775

On April 14, in Philadelphia, Pennsylvania, a group of Quakers organized the Society for the Relief of Free Negroes Unlawfully Held in Bondage, the first secular antislavery society in the American colonies. Benjamin Franklin and Benjamin Rush were among the founding members of this group. The society would suspend its operations during the years of the American Revolution, but it was reorganized again in 1787.

On April 19, the American Revolution began as shots were fired at Lexington and Concord. Free blacks were among the minutemen who took part in these opening battles for American freedom.

On the Natural Variety of Mankind (Humani Varietate Nativa) was published in Germany by Johan Friedrich Blumenback. This work was the first of its kind to challenge the prevailing racist assumptions that viewed blacks as racially inferior and thus prone to be enslaved by superior peoples. Blumenback's work challenged the ideas of "enlightened" thinkers such as Voltaire, Hume, and Linne, who had argued that blacks were somehow related to apes. Blumenback proved that the skulls of blacks and Europeans and the brain size of each were similar.

On May 10, the black soldier-patriots Lemuel Haynes, Primas Black, and Epheram Blackman fought with Ethan Allen and the Green Mountain Boys during the capture of Fort Ticonderoga, generally considered to be the first aggressive action taken by American forces during the American Revolution.

On June 17, during the battle of Bunker Hill, several black soldier-patriots, including Peter Salem and Salem Poor, fought and distinguished themselves.

On July 10, General Horatio Gates, in his capacity as adjutant general of the Continental Army, issued a general order that banned free blacks from serving in the Continental Army.

On October 8, in a decision made by the Council of General Officers of the Continental Army, it was determined that neither slaves nor free blacks would be allowed to fight in the Continental Army.

On October 23, the Second Continental Congress specifically prohibited blacks from joining the American Continental Army.

On November 7, in an effort to raise a local Loyalist army, Lord Dunmore, the British governor of the Virginia colony, promised to free any male slave who deserted their plantations and farms and joined British forces in an effort to suppress the rebellion that had been begun by the American patriot forces. Approximately eight hundred Virginia slaves accepted Dunmore's invitation and joined the king's forces. Dunmore lost the support of many Loyalist planters by initiating this policy.

On November 12, General George Washington, commander of the Continental Army, issued a general order prohibiting all recruiting officers from enlisting blacks, both slave and free, into the service of the Continental Army.

On December 31, apparently alarmed by Lord Dunmore's action, George Washington, who originally opposed the use of black troops, modified his initial position on the matter and ordered his recruiting officers to enlist any free blacks who offered their services to the Continental cause, but Washington continued to resist the use of slaves as soldiers.

Sally Hemings, then a two-year-old child, arrived as a slave at Monticello, Thomas Jefferson's home in Virginia.

The colonial assembly in Delaware approved of a measure that would have prohibited the introduction of any additional slaves into the colony, but Governor John McKinly vetoed the bill.

Thomas Paine published his first antislavery essay entitled "African Slavery in America" in *The Pennsylvania Journal.* Paine signed the article "Humanus" and argued that slavery should be abolished and that land and other economic opportunities should be offered to freed slaves.

1776

On January 16, the Second Continental Congress gave its approval to George Washington's policy of accepting enlistments from free blacks who wished to join the Continental Army.

On April 9, by resolution, the Second Continental Congress called for an eventual end to the importation of slaves from Africa. During the course of the American Revolution, it is estimated that five thousand slaves supported the Continental forces in their efforts against the British.

On July 4, Thomas Jefferson penned the Declaration of Independence while serving as a delegate to the Second Continental Congress. Jefferson was swayed by the protest of southern delegates from South Carolina and Georgia and finally deleted lines critical of the slave trade and denouncing slavery from the final draft of the Declaration. The deleted passage had stated that King George encouraged "cruel war against human nature itself, violating its most sacred rights of life and liberty in the persons of a distant people who never offended him, captivating and carrying them into slavery in another hemisphere."

Later that year, Jefferson drafted a plan proposing a colonization plan to return former slaves to Africa.

The marquis de Lafayette praised the efforts of black troops for their role in covering Washington's retreat to Long Island.

In December, two black soldiers, Prince Whipple and Oliver Cromwell, took part in Washington's crossing of the Delaware River in order to attack British forces and their Hessian mercenaries at Trenton, New Jersey.

Reverend Samuel Hopkins, a Congregational minister in Newport, Rhode Island, published an antislavery tract entitled "A Dialogue Concerning the Slavery of the Africans." Hopkins forwarded a copy of his work to the Second Continental Congress in hopes that his argument might help to sway the officials there to abolish slavery within the colonies.

In Delaware a new constitution was drafted. It included a provision that prohibited the further importation of slaves into the region.

In Philadelphia, the Society of Friends (Quakers) approved of a measure at their annual meeting that urged other Quakers to shun fellow Quakers who refused to manumit their slaves.

In Williamsburg, Virginia, a group of free blacks organized the African Baptist Church.

1777

In North Carolina, the assembly readopted an older colonial statute that had prohibited the manumission of slaves by private citizens except for cases of meritorious service that were documented and verified by a local magistrate. It was the intention of North Carolina officials to make "the evil and pernicious practice of freeing slaves" more difficult.

On July 2, Vermont's state constitution abolished slavery within its borders. At this time Vermont had declared itself to be an independent state on January 16, 1777, but it was not yet an official part of the United States. Therefore, Pennsylvania's action against slavery in 1780 is generally considered to be the first time that a state abolished the institution of slavery in the United States.

Schools within the colony/state of New Jersey began to segregate black and white students.

1778

In Maryland, Quakers decided that the continuing ownership of slaves by fellow Quakers after the Society of Friends had declared manumission a moral offense that warranted disownment.

In February, in an unprecedented act made necessary by wartime exigencies, a black battalion of three hundred slaves was formed in Rhode Island after they were promised freedom upon the successful conclusion of the war. This group eventually engaged in battle and was responsible for killing one thousand Hessians. The same group eventually took part in the battle at Ponts Bridge in New York.

Upon the motion of Thomas Jefferson, the House of Burgesses enacted a statute that prohibited the importation of additional slaves into Virginia.

1779

On November 12, the New Hampshire colonial assembly received a petition from twenty slaves urging that body to abolish slavery. The petition requesting emancipation argued that "the God of nature gave them life and freedom upon the terms of most perfect equality with other men; that freedom is an inherent right of the human species, not to be surrendered but by consent."

In the Continental Congress, South Carolina representative Henry Laurens proposed that 3,000 slaves be used as soldiers in the southern colonies. Many of the southern representatives contested the proposal, but Alexander Hamilton of New York supported the idea. Hamilton stated: "I have not the least doubt that the Negroes will make very excellent soldiers . . . for their natural faculties are as good as ours." Although the Continental Congress approved of the recommendation, the South Carolina legislature rejected the proposal.

1780

On February 10, in Dartmouth, Massachusetts, Paul Cuffee led a group of seven free blacks that petitioned against the Continental Congress for imposing taxation without representation because they were denied the benefits of citizenship.

On March 1, Pennsylvania's legislature passed a measure aimed at the gradual abolition of slavery within the state's borders. According to this legislation, no child born after its enactment would be a slave in the state of Pennsylvania. According to the terms of this legislation, children who were born to slaves after 1780 would be considered to be bond servants until they reached the age of twenty-one. With this action, Pennsylvania effectively became the first state to abolish slavery. (Vermont had not yet become a state when action was taken there in 1777.)

In April, in Botecourt County, Virginia, a slave named Jack was hanged because he had threatened to lead a group of slaves to the British army of Lord Cornwallis in an effort to escape.

It was estimated that there were 575,420 slaves in the United States in 1780, with 56,796 in the northern states and 518,624 in the southern states.

There were rumors of a slave conspiracy in and around the city of Albany, New York, and a combined force of slaves and a few white associates did plot and burn the Half-Moon Settlement near Albany.

In Newport, Rhode Island, Newport Gardner and

his associates formed the African Union Society, a mutual-benefit organization designed to assist free blacks in the region. In 1803 the society merged with the African Benevolent Society.

1781

On July 20, shortly after the defeat of British General Cornwallis at Yorktown, there were reports of maroon attacks on plantations in the region, and a report of a planned slave uprising near Williamsburg surfaced when slaves burned several buildings including the capitol. One white colonist was killed in this incident.

1782

Thomas Jefferson wrote his *Notes on Virginia* in which he presented a mixed view of slavery and of the role of blacks in society. Jefferson wrote that "the whole commerce between master and slave is a perpetual exercise of the most boisterous passions," but he later penned the strange assessment that blacks' "griefs are transient."

Virginia's slave population was estimated to be 260,000.

As a result of Thomas Jefferson's insistence, the Virginia legislature enacted a measure legalizing the emancipation of slaves by private citizens through manumission in the state. According to this measure, it was permissible for one "by last will and testament or other instrument in writing sealed and witnessed, to emancipate and set free his slaves." It is particularly ironic that when Jefferson died in 1826, he freed some, but not all, of the slaves that he had held in bondage.

The state legislature of Rhode Island freed the slave Quaco Honeyman because of the services he rendered as a spy during the American Revolution.

British ships carried off an estimated five thousand slaves when they departed from Savannah, Georgia. Many of these "black Loyalists" would eventually settle in the Canadian provinces of New Brunswick and Nova Scotia. The following year the British ships left the New York City area carrying off three thousand slaves, and other ships that left Charleston, South Carolina, transported sixty five hundred slaves out of the region.

In the state of Massachusetts, the legislature received a "Petition of an African" from a seventy-year-old slave woman named Belinda. She was requesting freedom and protection for herself and her daughter from their owner. This petition seeking freedom from slavery is believed to be the first to be filed by a slave in the United States of America.

1783

Legislative action in Maryland prohibited involvement in the African slave trade, but not the institution of slavery, within the state.

The slave James C. Derham purchased his freedom from his owner, Doctor Robert Dove. Derham remained in New Orleans as a free black and established his own practice there as a doctor.

A Massachusetts court heard a case that was brought by Paul Cuffee and his brother John. The judges ruled that free blacks who paid taxes to the state of Massachusetts were entitled to suffrage rights within the state.

Diplomats in Paris signed the Treaty of Paris, which officially ended the American Revolution. Article VII of the treaty included a provision in which the British government agreed to return all slaves that were taken from their American owners. The British government did not comply with this provision.

By the end of the American Revolution, at least ten thousand blacks had served in the continental armies. Nearly half of these served as regular soldiers.

The county court in Great Barrington, Massachusetts, heard a case brought by a fugitive slave woman named Elizabeth [Mumbet] Freeman who had escaped her abusive master in 1742. Freeman was fighting efforts against reenslavement, which had been threatened, and she appealed to Thomas Sedgwick, an attorney, to defend her. Freeman won her case, and her former master was ordered to pay damages in the amount of 30 shillings.

On July 8, in a landmark judicial decision, slavery was abolished in Massachusetts by the action of the Massachusetts Supreme Court in the case of *Commonwealth v. Jennison,* which involved efforts of the slave Quock Walker to obtain his freedom. The decision in this case was based on an interpretation of the Massachusetts Declaration of Rights, which was included in the Massachusetts state constitution of 1780 and which stated that all men were "born free and equal." Chief Justice William Cushing and other Massachusetts jurists interpreted this phrase to be a repudiation of slavery. Many opponents of slavery believed that the Massachusetts ruling signified the removal of any judicial sanction for the institution and practice of slavery.

On October 7, the Virginia House of Burgesses passed a measure that granted freedom to those Virginia slaves who served in the Continental Army during the American Revolution.

On December 31, by the end of 1783, all states north of Maryland had taken effective legislative action to ban the further importation of Africans for use as slave laborers.

Shortly before his death in 1784, Anthony Benezet published *A Serious Address to the Rulers of America*. In this antislavery pamphlet, Benezet chided the American people for having shrouded the rhetoric of the American Revolution as a struggle against British tyranny and slavery while keeping thousands of people in bondage as slaves themselves in a land that claimed to love liberty.

1784

The Pennsylvania Abolition Society was organized in Philadelphia.

The Congress under the Articles of Confederation government considered a "Report of Government for the Western Territory," which Thomas Jefferson had drafted. Before enacting the measure, Congress deleted certain controversial provisions. By a vote of seven to six, the Congress defeated Jefferson's proposal that would have prohibited slavery and involuntary servitude from all western territories after 1800.

Members of the Methodist Episcopal Church met at a conference in Baltimore, Maryland, to adopt proposals that required Methodists who owned slaves to begin manumitting them or face the possibility of excommunication from the church.

The states of Connecticut and Rhode Island enacted legislative bills aimed at providing for the abolition of slavery within their respective states.

On December 5, the black American poet Phillis Wheatley died in Boston.

In Virginia, the Society of Friends (Quakers) required all Quakers in the state who owned slaves to manumit them.

1785

The New York state legislature took action making slavery illegal within the state. An effort to enact a program of gradual emancipation failed to win legislative approval because the measure would have denied civil and political rights to free blacks living within the state.

On September 28, the future abolitionist David Walker was born as a free child in Wilmington, North Carolina. In 1829, he would publish his *Appeal to the Coloured Citizens of the World*.

The New York Society for Promoting Manumission was chartered, with John Jay selected to serve as the first president of the group.

The General Committee of Virginia Baptists took action within their denomination to condemn the institution of slavery as being "contrary to the word of God."

John Marrant published *A Narrative of the Lord's Wonderful Dealings with J. Marrant, a Black . . . Taken Down from His Own Relation*. This work was the first autobiography of a person of African descent to be written in the English language.

The Methodist Conference, meeting at Baltimore, voted to suspend the 1784 ruling that required Methodists to manumit their slaves.

1786

The New Jersey state legislature declared slavery illegal within the state and adopted a program of gradual emancipation.

The state legislature of Virginia freed the slave James, who had been owned by William Armstead, because of the services that James rendered as a spy during the American Revolution.

George Washington wrote a letter to the marquis de Lafayette, the young Frenchman who had assisted him during the American Revolution. In the letter, Washington shared some of his views on the question of slavery. Washington wrote, "To set the slaves afloat at once would, I believe, be productive of much inconvenience and mischief; but, by degrees it certainly might, and assuredly ought to be, effected, and that too, by legislative authority." On the basis of this statement, it would seem that Washington endorsed a plan of gradual emancipation to bring an end to slavery.

1787

John Cabot and Joshua Fisher established the first cotton factory in the United States at Beverly, Massachusetts. As the factory system spread throughout New England, textiles became a major item of manufacture and northern-based production of cotton cloth became increasingly dependent on southern-based cotton production.

On April 12, Richard Allen and Absalom Jones formed the Free African Society in Philadelphia, which they described as "the first wavering step of a people toward a more organized social life."

On April 23, Benjamin Franklin and Benjamin Rush were among the members of the recently revived Pennsylvania Society for Promoting the Abolition of Slavery, the Relief of Free Negroes Unlawfully held in

Bondage, and Improving the Condition of the African Race. Franklin served as the honorary president of the organization.

On July 13, slavery was prohibited from all territories north of the Ohio River (the Old Northwest Territory) when the Congress under the Articles of Confederation approved passage of the Northwest Ordinance.

On September 12, Prince Hall, who had participated in military service during the American Revolution, established African Lodge No. 459, the first black Masonic Lodge in America. The charter for this new group was granted by the Grand Lodge of England.

On September 17, the United States Constitution was created. This document included a "three-fifths clause," which counted only three of every five slaves for purposes of representation and taxation. The document also stipulated that Congress could not act to prohibit the African slave trade until 1808.

On September 24, the black poet Jupiter Hammon published *An Address to Negroes in the State of New York.* In this essay Hammon urged slaves to be obedient and faithful to their masters. Hammon wrote, "Now whether it is right, and lawful, in the sight of God, for them to make slaves of us or not, I am certain that while we are slaves, it is our duty to obey our masters, in all their lawful commands, and mind them unless we are bid to do that which we know to be sin, or forbidden in God's word."

A group of blacks in Philadelphia led by Richard Allen and Absalom Jones established their own religious congregation when they were forced to leave a white church.

In a detailed proposal quite comparable to the Underground Railroad that would arise in the nineteenth century, Quaker Isaac T. Hopper, of Philadelphia, promoted a plan in which northerners could aid slaves who tried to escape from the southern states.

In response to numerous Quaker petitions, the legislature of Rhode Island enacted a law specifically prohibiting Rhode Island citizens from participating in the slave trade.

On October 17, under the leadership of Prince Hall, Boston blacks petitioned the Massachusetts legislature to establish equal educational facilities for black students within the state.

On November 1, in New York City, the New York Manumission Society established an African Free School.

The South Carolina legislature approved of a temporary halt to slave importations into the state.

1788

From February 27 to March 26, a group of free blacks led by Prince Hall petitioned the Massachusetts state legislature after a shocking incident occurred in Boston. A group of free blacks were seized on the streets of Boston, kidnapped, and transported as slaves to the French colony of Martinique in the West Indies. Governor John Hancock used his influence to win the release of the blacks who had been captured illegally. Legislators in Massachusetts then enacted a measure declaring the slave trade illegal and providing a fund to pay for compensatory damages to victims of such kidnapping incidents.

In Newport, Rhode Island, the Negro Union Society advocated a campaign of repatriating free blacks to Africa through an emigration program, but the Free African Society of Philadelphia opposed this strategy.

In November and December, "An Essay on Negro Slavery" was published in the journal *American Museum.* The anonymous author of this essay used the pen name Othello of Maryland.

Legislative action taken by Connecticut, Massachusetts, New York, and Pennsylvania prohibited citizens of those states from participating in the African slave trade.

1789

On March 4, a sufficient number of states ratified the Constitution of the United States, and the first session of the United States Congress was called into session. At this time the nation consisted of thirteen states, seven of which had become free states and six of which remained slave states.

The Delaware state legislature approved a resolution that prohibited citizens of Delaware from participating in the African slave trade.

The Providence Society for Abolishing the Slave Trade was established in Rhode Island.

A slave named Josiah Henson was born in Charles County, Maryland. He would later become the inspiration for the character of "Uncle Tom" in Harriet Beecher Stowe's novel *Uncle Tom's Cabin* (1852).

1790

The First Census of the United States revealed that 757,181 blacks resided in the United States—59,557 were identified as free blacks and 697,624 were slaves. Blacks constituted 19.3 percent of the total population of the United States in 1790. In this census only Massachusetts and Maine reported having no slaves.

The United States government entered into its first treaty with the Creek nation. The treaty included a provision requiring the Creek to return any fugitive slaves who sought protection in Creek territory.

Between February 3 and February 11, Congress received its first formal petition calling for the emancipation of slaves. The petition was presented by the American Quaker (Society of Friends) denomination and the Pennsylvania Abolition Society. Benjamin Franklin had signed the memorial and urged the Congress to remove "this inconsistency form the character of the American people."

On March 23, Benjamin Franklin, writing as "Historicus," wrote "An Essay on the African Slave Trade" in the *Federal Gazette*. In this essay Franklin used biting satire to parody the prevailing proslavery view in the Congress. His essay presented the Muslim argument that could be used for justifying the enslavement of Christians.

The Virginia Abolition Society was organized at a meeting in Richmond.

On November 1, in Charleston, South Carolina, a group of free blacks organized the Brown Fellowship Society. The organization was limited to emancipated blacks of good character who paid annual dues. The group served as a benevolent organization, supported schools, and operated a clubhouse and a private cemetery for society members.

1791

On January 5, free blacks in Charleston, North Carolina, presented a petition to the state legislature protesting recent legislation that prohibited black-initiated lawsuits in the courts and disallowed the testimony of blacks to be heard in the courts. The state legislature rejected the petition, and the condition of inequality before the law remained in effect.

At the request of Thomas Jefferson, Benjamin Banneker was appointed to the surveying commission that would establish plans for a new national capital at Washington, D.C.

The United States Congress enacted a measure that prevented blacks and Indians from serving in the peacetime militia.

Pierre Charles L'Enfant, the architect who designed the original plans for the District of Columbia, hired slaves from owners in Maryland and Virginia to begin construction of the new federal buildings in the national capital.

After some of President George Washington's slaves were brought to Pennsylvania, officials there claimed that they could not be returned to Virginia as slaves. Washington asked Tobias Lear to offer his assistance so that the slaves might be returned in a fashion that would "deceive both the slaves and the public."

1792

George Mason, a noted Virginia statesman, spoke out in opposition to slavery. Mason said that the institution of slavery was a disgrace to mankind, and he compared it to a slow poison that, in time, would corrupt future politicians.

On June 1, Kentucky entered the Union as a slave state. The region had previously been a part of Virginia's western territory. At this point the United States consisted of fifteen states, eight of which were free states and seven of which were slave states.

In Portsmouth, Virginia, Joshua Bishop, a free black preacher, was appointed to be the new pastor of the First Baptist Church, which served a white congregation.

In April, Presbyterian clergyman David Rice attempted unsuccessfully to have the Kentucky constitutional convention exclude slavery from that state. A later attempt to achieve the same objective failed in 1799.

Virginia Quaker Warner Mifflin sent an antislavery memorial to the United States Congress. The petition created a contentious debate in the Congress. One South Carolina congressman questioned whether the First Amendment's right to petition expressly included the "mere rant and rhapsody of a meddling fanatic."

1793

The New Jersey Abolition Society was organized.

On February 12, the United States Congress enacted a federal Fugitive Slave Law, which made it a criminal offense for anyone to harbor a slave or to prevent the arrest of a fugitive. The law based its legality upon Article IV, Section 2, of the United States Constitution, which established the legal mechanism for the recovery of fugitive slaves. This measure would remain in effect until Congress passed a stronger Fugitive Slave Law in 1850.

The General Committee of Virginia Baptists reached the conclusion that since emancipation was a political question, it should be addressed by legislative action and not through pronouncements agreed upon by church convocations.

On October 28, Eli Whitney invented the cotton gin in Mulberry Grove, Georgia. This invention revolutionized southern agriculture by making short-staple (upland) cotton easier to process. As planting of upland cotton increased in the Old Southwest, the region of slaveholding also increased. Whitney received the patent for his invention on March 14, 1794.

On November 25 in Albany, New York, a slave revolt took place as a group of insurrectionists rebelled and burned several buildings in the city. The property damages caused by the arsonists were estimated to be $250,000, and three slaves were eventually executed for these crimes.

Free blacks in South Carolina petitioned the state legislature to express their opposition to the state's poll tax.

The Virginia legislature passed a law making it illegal for any free blacks to enter the state.

The Georgia legislature enacted a measure prohibiting the importation of any slaves from the West Indies or Spanish Florida, but the importation of slaves directly from Africa was still allowed.

1794

On March 22, Congress prohibited the slave trade to all foreign ports and also prohibited the outfitting of any foreign vessels for the purposes of slave trading in any American port.

On July 29, Richard Allen and his followers established the Bethel AME Church ("Mother Bethel") in Philadelphia. This was the first African Methodist Episcopal church established in the United States. The church is the oldest piece of property in the United States that has continuously been owned by blacks.

The Connecticut legislature considered a bill that would have provided for immediate emancipation, but the measure failed to win final approval. This measure would also have required masters to care for old and infirmed blacks and provide for the education of black children.

In Philadelphia, the first meeting of the Convention of Delegates from the Abolition Societies was held. Delegates representing nine antislavery societies from several states discussed long-range strategies that should be employed to advance the cause of abolition.

George Washington wrote a letter to Alexander Spotswood in which he shared some of his views on slavery. Washington wrote, "Were it not then, that I am principled against selling *African Americans,* as you

would cattle at a market, I would not in twelve months from this date, be possessed of one as a slave. I shall be happily mistaken if they are not found to be a very troublesome species of property ere many years pass over our heads."

1795

In Louisiana in April, Spanish colonial officials put down a slave revolt in Pointe Coupée Parish and hanged twenty-three slaves who were implicated in the conspiracy. Local authorities also deported three white sympathizers from the colony. Officials in Louisiana believed that this rebellion was related to the insurrection that had rocked the French colony of St. Domingue in 1791.

George Washington published an advertisement notice calling for the return of one of his slaves who had escaped from Mount Vernon. Washington stipulated that the notice not be run in any state north of Virginia.

The average price of a slave laborer who worked as an agricultural field hand was $300.

1796

On June 1, Tennessee was admitted to the Union as a slave state, but the state's constitution did not deny the suffrage to free blacks. At this point, the United States consisted of sixteen states that were evenly divided, with eight being free states and eight slave states.

In New York City the free black community organized the Zion Methodist Church.

Forty-four free blacks were the charter members who organized the Boston African Society.

St. George Tucker, a professor of law and police at the College of William and Mary in Williamsburg, Virginia, published a work entitled *A Dissertation on Slavery: With a Proposal for the Gradual Abolition of It, in the State of Virginia,* which put forward the view that slavery was inconsistent with the high moral purpose of the Bill of Rights. Tucker called for Virginia to adopt a program of gradual abolition of slavery that would end the practice within a century.

1797

On January 30, a group of free blacks petitioned Congress protesting against a North Carolina law that required that slaves, though freed by their

Quaker masters, must be returned to the state and to their former condition, but the petition was rejected by the Congress.

Sojourner Truth (born Isabella Baumfree) was born a slave on an estate near Hurley, New York.

Polish General Tadeusz Kosciuszko received a land grant in the Ohio Valley as compensation for his service to the American cause during the American Revolution. Kosciuszko requested that his land grant be sold and that the revenues raised be used to establish a school for black children.

In Kentucky, a young lawyer named Henry Clay urged the state legislature to enact a program of gradual abolition of slavery. Clay often defended slaves who sued for their freedom.

1798

During the undeclared naval war with France, Secretary of the Navy Benjamin Stoddert refused to allow the deployment of blacks on American naval vessels, thus overturning the nonracial policy that the Navy had used previously. Despite this ban, blacks like William Brown and George Diggs did manage to serve on board American naval vessels.

A school for black children was established in the home of Primus Hall, a free black in Boston, Massachusetts.

The Georgia legislature enacted a measure that prohibited the further importation of slaves into the state.

The United States Congress debated a resolution that would have prohibited slavery from the Mississippi Territory, but the measure was defeated.

A collection of stories was published under the title *A Narrative of the Life and Adventures of Venture*. The stories were based on the life of Venture Smith, a Connecticut slave, who had been the son of a West African prince.

1799

In his last will and testament, George Washington declared, "It is my will and desire that all the slaves which I hold in my right, shall receive their freedom."

On March 29, a bill that provided for the gradual abolition of slavery was enacted by the legislature of New York.

In Boston the first minstrel performance occurred when Gottlieb Graupner performed a repertoire of songs that he had learned from blacks in Charleston, South Carolina. The young German immigrant would later form the Boston Philharmonic Society.

1800

The Second Census of the United States records that blacks, both slave and free, constituted 1,002,037 persons, or 18.9 percent of the national population.

On January 2, the United States House of Representatives rejected a petition advanced by a group of free blacks from Philadelphia who sought to end slavery in the United States through a system of gradual emancipation.

The petition also protested against the slave trade and the enforcement of the Fugitive Slave Law of 1793. The measure was defeated by an 85 to 1 margin.

On May 9, John Brown, the future white abolitionist who participated in antislavery activities during "Bleeding Kansas" and attempted to seize the Harpers Ferry arsenal in 1859, was born in Torrington, Connecticut.

The Virginia Assembly enacted legislation that supported development of a colonization plan to return former slaves to Africa.

The assembly would enact similar nonbinding resolutions on colonization in 1802, 1805, and 1816.

On August 30, Virginia authorities discovered and suppressed the plot of Gabriel Prosser and Jack Bowler to capture Richmond and surrounding regions in a large-scale slave insurrection involving thousands of slaves.

Prosser and fifteen of his associates were hanged on October 7 for their role in the conspiracy after the betrayal of the plot by two slaves. Governor James Monroe requested that federal troops be sent into the region to quell any further efforts at insurrectionary violence.

On September 2, on a plantation in Southampton County, Virginia, a slave child named Nat Turner was born. He would eventually become a slave preacher and would organize and lead a slave insurrection in the region in 1831.

1801

In the aftermath of Gabriel Prosser's conspiracy in Virginia, the American Convention of Abolition Societies issued a public statement affirming that "an amelioration of the present situation of the slaves, and the adoption of a system of gradual emancipation . . . would . . . be an effectual security against revolt."

1802

Residents of the Indiana Territory met in a convention at Vincennes that was called by Territorial Governor

William Henry Harrison. The convention forwarded a memorial to the Congress asking that the Northwest Ordinance of 1787 be suspended so that slaves might be introduced into Indiana. The Congress did not support Governor Harrison's recommendation, but a measure was later enacted that did allow indentured servants to be brought into the Indiana Territory. Since the Northwest Ordinance had prohibited both slavery and involuntary servitude, the admission of indentured servants into Indiana permitted a de facto form of slavery to exist in territory that was deemed to be free. (For more on the Northwest Ordinance of 1787, see Document 32.)

The United States Congress considered a proposed bill that would have strengthened the Fugitive Slave Law of 1793, but the measure was defeated.

In May, authorities in North Carolina were on alert throughout the year as several rumors of revolt surfaced in Charlotte, Elizabeth, Hertford, Wake, Warren, and Washington counties. In May, a disturbance near Elizabeth City was organized by Tom Cooper, a fugitive slave who lived in the swamps as a maroon. Local authorities restored order in the county, and fifteen slaves were executed for their role in the plot.

In the Mississippi Territory, the legislature considered a bill that would have prohibited the importation of male slaves into the region, but the measure was defeated.

1803

On February 19, Ohio became the seventeenth state to be admitted to the Union. At this point in the nation's history, there were nine free states and eight slave states. Since the area was carved from the Old Northwest Territory, Ohio was the first state to join the Union in which slavery was prohibited by law from the beginning of statehood.

On February 28, the United States Congress enacted "An Act to Prevent the Importation of Certain Persons into Certain States, Where, by the Laws Thereof, Their Admission Is Prohibited." This measure was enacted because many feared that slaves who had been "tainted" by the insurrection in St. Domingue would carry seeds of discontent into the American South if they were permitted into the region.

South Carolina's legislature, which previously had tried to limit slave imports, authorized the importation of slaves from South America and from the West Indies. This move was especially controversial as many feared that slaves who had been "tainted" by the insurrection in St. Domingue would carry seeds of discontent into the American South. With the expansion in cultivation of upland cotton that followed Eli Whitney's invention of the cotton gin, states like South Carolina soon realized the economic pressure for greater numbers of slaves to work the new lands that were brought under cotton cultivation.

In February, free blacks and slaves in York, Pennsylvania, rioted and attempted to burn the town to protest the conviction of Margaret Bradley on the charges that she attempted to poison two white citizens. Governor Thomas McKean ordered the state militia into the city to restore order, and the legislature funded a $300 reward for information that would aid in the capture of the revolt's leaders.

Lunsford Lane was born a slave on a plantation in North Carolina. By 1839, Lane would become a well-known lecturer for the American Anti-Slavery Society, and in 1842, he would publish a narrative of his life.

1804

On January 5, Ohio, a state that was carved from the Old Northwest Territory, enacted Black Laws that restricted the rights and movements of free blacks within the state. Illinois, Indiana, and later Oregon would later adopt similar policies or insert anti-immigration provisions into their respective state constitutions.

Between February and March, the United States Congress debated legislation that organized the Louisiana Territory. In keeping within the guidelines of the Louisiana Purchase Treaty, the federal government agreed to recognize and protect the property of Louisiana slaveowners who had been protected by Spanish and French laws. In addition, the Congress voted to restrict the slaves that could be brought into the territory to those slaves who were actual property of settlers moving into the region. The Congress defeated a proposal that would have limited the period of servitude of slaves in the territory to one year.

On February 15, the legislature of New Jersey enacted a bill to provide for the abolition of slavery within the state. After the passage of this measure, all states north of the Mason-Dixon Line took steps to prohibit slavery within their borders or provide for its gradual demise.

On May 14, the Lewis and Clark Expedition left St. Louis on a two-year-long-journey to explore the upper portion of the Louisiana Purchase Territory. A slave named York accompanied the expedition and served as William Clark's valet.

Thomas Branagan, who had been a slave trader himself, published *A Preliminary Essay on the Oppres-*

sion of the Exiled Sons of Africa. This work was a brutally frank denunciation of the African slave trade from the vantage point of someone who had experienced the enterprise directly.

1805

The Virginia state legislature approved of a resolution that was forwarded to the United States Congress calling for establishment of a new territory in the upper portion of the Louisiana Purchase where free blacks could be settled.

On October 9, Benjamin Banneker died. The noted mathematician and astronomer had helped to survey the District of Columbia when a new national capital was established.

A Kentucky court decided the case of *Thompson v. Wilmot.* Thompson, who was a free black man in Maryland, was taken to Kentucky to serve a specified number of years as an indentured servant. When his period of indenture expired, Wilmot attempted to enslave Thompson. The courts ruled that Thompson had been illegally enslaved and ordered him freed. The verdict was sustained upon appeal in 1809.

On December 10, William Lloyd Garrison was born in Newburyport, Massachusetts. In his lifetime, Garrison would become the most famous abolitionist in the United States. From 1831 to 1865 he would publish and edit *The Liberator,* an abolitionist weekly.

1806

The Virginia Assembly enacted legislation requiring anyone who was manumitted after May 1 of that year to leave the state within one year.

On December 2, President Thomas Jefferson sent a message to Congress urging the passage of legislation ending all slave importation to the United States effective January 1, 1808. Jefferson's desire was that the government should act upon this question as soon as it was permissible. When the Constitution of the United States was written in 1787, a twenty-year moratorium on any legislative action regarding the suppression of the African slave trade (Article I, Section 9) had been included as part of the document.

1807

On March 2, the United States Congress passed landmark legislation that prohibited the importation of African slaves into any region within the jurisdiction of the United States effective January 1, 1808, and President Thomas Jefferson signed the measure into law. Despite the United States government's efforts to enforce this measure, violations of this law would occur until the time of the American Civil War.

In Charleston, South Carolina, two boatloads of Africans who had been brought to the Americas as slaves starved themselves to death rather than submit to slavery.

Although slavery was prohibited in the region by the Northwest Ordinance of 1787, legislators in the Indiana Territory enacted a measure that established a strict indenture system in the region. This virtual form of slavery remained in effect for three years until the law was repealed in 1810. (For more on the Northwest Ordinance of 1787, see Document 32.)

New Jersey amended its 1776 state constitution to limit the right of suffrage so that only free white males could vote.

In Kentucky several antislavery supporters established a new abolitionist society called Friends of Humanity. Even though it was considered a slave state, there were active abolitionists in Kentucky right up to the time of the American Civil War.

1808

On January 1, the ban on the importation of Africans as slaves took effect. It is estimated that there were 1 million slaves in the United States at this time. Many believed that the elimination of external imports would set the stage for the gradual elimination of slavery within the country, but by 1860 there would be nearly 4 million slaves in the southern states.

Judges in the District of Columbia heard the case of *United States v. Mullany.* The judges declared that free blacks were competent to testify as witnesses in court proceedings.

The General Conference of the Methodist Episcopal Church decided to remove the church's rules on slavery from copies of its *Discipline* that would be sent to the southern states.

1809

On February 12, Abraham Lincoln was born in Hardin County, Kentucky. In 1860 Lincoln would be elected the nation's sixteenth president. With his decision to issue the Emancipation Proclamation, Lincoln became known as the "Great Emancipator" to future generations.

The population of New Orleans increased dramatically as six thousand new immigrants arrived in the Louisiana colony. These immigrants were originally from the French colony of St. Domingue, but they had left that island when a slave insurrection took place in 1791. They had initially moved to Cuba but were expelled from that island in 1809 after Napoleon's forces invaded Spain and relations between France and Spain grew cold. Many in the Louisiana colony feared that the introduction of these immigrants and their slaves might bring the taint of insurrection to the colony.

A Louisiana court heard the case of *Girod v. Lewis.* Judges decided in this case that the marriages of slaves had no binding civil effect, while the individuals involved remained slaves; upon manumission, however, such a marriage held the same legal standing as white marriages.

1810

The Third Census of the United States documented that blacks, both slave and free, constituted 19 percent of the national population, or 1,377,808 persons.

Louisiana courts heard the case of *Adelle v. Beauregard* and declared that a black was considered free unless it was otherwise proven that the person in question was a slave. Louisiana courts would issue a similar ruling in the case of *State v. Cecil* in 1812.

On February 1, the black abolitionist Charles Lenox Remond was born in Salem, Massachusetts. In 1838 he would become the first black to be hired as a lecturer by the Massachusetts Antislavery Society.

Lewis Dupre published an antislavery tract entitled *An Admonitory Picture and a Solemn Warning Principally Addressed to Professing Christians in the Southern States.* Published in Charleston, South Carolina, this pamphlet urged southern slaveowners to adopt an enlightened view and work to bring about an end to slavery.

1811

Between January 8 and 10, a massive slave revolt erupted along the River Road plantations 35 miles west of New Orleans (a region commonly called the German Coast) in the parishes of St. Charles and St. John the Baptist. Nearly five hundred were estimated to be involved in the uprising that was organized and led by Charles Deslondes. A combined force of planter militia and United States Army troops quelled the rebellion and restored order but apparently with great bloodshed. It is estimated that one hundred slaves were either killed in the suppression of the revolt or executed as a result of trials that followed the episode.

On June 14, Harriet Beecher [Stowe], the future author of *Uncle Tom's Cabin,* was born in Litchfield, Connecticut.

Paul Cuffee (1759–1818) sailed with thirty-eight blacks to the colony of Sierra Leone in West Africa. Cuffee spent $4,000 of his own funds to finance this expedition. Cuffee favored a program of colonization in which free blacks could be repatriated to Africa, and he used this voyage to promote that position. In subsequent decades many other individuals and organizations would take up the cause of colonization.

The Delaware state legislature enacted a law that prohibited free blacks from moving into the state. Any free black who arrived in Delaware was given a ten-day grace period to leave the state. After that time expired, free blacks were fined $10 per week until they removed themselves from the state.

North Carolina militia attacked a maroon community in Cabarrus County that contained several fugitive slaves. As a result of the attack, two slaves were killed and one was wounded, but most of the maroons were captured and returned to slavery.

A Maryland court heard the case of *Commonwealth v. Dolly Chapple.* The judges decided that blacks were permitted to testify against whites in those cases where a white defendant stood accused of having committed an act of mayhem upon a black person.

1812

On April 30, Louisiana entered the Union as a slave state. According to the state constitution, freedmen were allowed to serve in the state militia. At this point the United States consisted of eighteen states that were evenly divided—nine states free and nine states slave.

Paul Cuffee wrote *A Brief Account of the Settlement and Present Situation of the Colony of Sierra Leone.*

The General Conference of the Methodist Church met in New York City. The group decided that slaveowners were no longer eligible to be elders in the Methodist Church.

On May 6, the black abolitionist Martin Robinson Delany was born in Charles Town, Virginia (now in West Virginia).

1813

Judges in the United States Circuit Court for the District of Columbia heard the case of *United States v.*

Douglass. The judges declared that free blacks were competent to testify as witnesses in court proceedings against whites.

Letters from a Man of Color on a Late Bill was published anonymously in Philadelphia, Pennsylvania, but it was believed that James Forten was the author. In this tract the author criticized a bill that the Pennsylvania state legislature was considering that would have prohibited the introduction of additional free blacks from the state. The legislature did not enact the measure.

1814

In September, authorities in Louisiana tried to end the slave-trading and other business ventures of Jean Lafitte and his pirates in the Barataria Bay region south of New Orleans. Naval commander Daniel Patterson and Army Colonel George T. Ross conducted an amphibious assault on the pirate's compound and disrupted Lafitte's the activities. Eventually, the pirates relocated these illegal activities to the area of Galveston Island, Texas.

On September 21, in an emergency proclamation issued from Mobile, Alabama, General Andrew Jackson called upon free blacks "to rally around the standard of the eagle" and help to defend the American cause during the War of 1812.

On December 18, General Andrew Jackson issued his proclamation to the free black troops at New Orleans. Jackson stated, "TO THE MEN OF COLOR.—Soldiers! From the shores of Mobile I collected you to arms; I invited you to share in the perils and to divide the glory of your white countrymen. I expected much from you, for I was not uninformed of those qualities which must render you so formidable to an invading foe. I knew that you could endure hunger and thirst and all the hardships of war. I knew that you loved the land of your nativity, and that like ourselves, you had to defend all that is most dear to you. But you surpass my hopes. I have found in you, united to these qualities, that noble enthusiasm which impels to great deeds."

On December 24, in the Treaty of Ghent, which ended the War of 1812 between the United States and Great Britain, both nations agreed to cooperate in naval efforts to suppress the African slave trade. Both nations had enacted legislation in 1807 that outlawed the African slave trade in their respective regions.

A Louisiana court heard the case of *Davenport v. the Commonwealth.* In their decision, the judges fined and imprisoned a white man who had kidnapped and sold a free black woman as a slave.

Charles Osborne and other antislavery associates established the Manumission Society of Tennessee.

The territorial legislature in Illinois passed enabling legislation that allowed settlers to hire slaves from outside the territory and to bring them into Illinois as laborers.

1815

On January 8, at the Battle of New Orleans, two battalions of free blacks (about six hundred soldiers) served along with Andrew Jackson's forces to defend the city from the attack of British forces.

Quaker abolitionist Benjamin Lundy organized the Union Humane Society in St. Clairsville, Ohio. This organization was one of the first abolitionist societies to form in the Midwest.

On December 23, Henry Highland Garnet, who later became a minister, an abolitionist, and a diplomat, was born a slave on a plantation in Kent County, Maryland.

In October, George Boxley, a white man, failed in his attempt to foment a slave rebellion in Spotsylvania and Orange County, Virginia. Boxley and his fellow conspirators had planned to attack the community of Fredericksburg during the harvest season. A slave woman reported the conspiracy to authorities, and the leaders of the planned attack were arrested before they could commence their plans. Boxley was never captured, but six slaves were executed for their role in the affair.

1816

The Virginia state legislature asked the federal government to establish a colony in the Pacific Northwest where free blacks from Virginia might be resettled as part of a colonization scheme.

Louisiana law prohibited slaves from testifying in court against whites or free blacks unless the case in question involved a slave insurrection.

North Carolina Quakers who supported the abolition of slavery established the Manumission Society within the state.

The Bethel Charity School for Negroes was founded in Baltimore by Daniel Coker.

Between April 9 and 11, in Philadelphia, the African Methodist Episcopal Church (AME) was organized at a convention. It was the first black church in the United States to be totally free and independent of the white churches. Richard Allen was ordained as its first bishop. The AME Church established a policy of denying membership to anyone who was a slaveowner.

In June, South Carolina authorities discovered a slave conspiracy that involved a planned attack upon Camden on July 4. A slave who learned of the plot alerted his master before the violence began, and local authorities were able to arrest the leaders of the plot. The state legislature eventually emancipated the slave who betrayed the plot and provided him with a lifetime pension for his services to the state.

On July 27, as part of the United States Army's efforts to stem the anarchy and lawlessness in Florida, United States Army forces attacked and destroyed Fort Blount on Apalachicola Bay. The fort had been renamed "Negro Fort," after it was manned by nearly three hundred escaped slaves and twenty Creek Indian allies who had sought asylum in the Spanish colony of East Florida. During the attack on the fort, the fugitive slaves who defended the site suffered tremendous casualties. Only forty defenders were still alive when the fort was surrendered to the American forces. United States troops also conducted an expedition against a large fugitive settlement in South Carolina.

On December 28, the American Colonization Society (ACS) was founded in Washington, D.C., in the hall of the House of Representatives. The purpose of this organization was to assist former slaves to return to Africa. The ACS would be instrumental in establishing the colonial outpost of Liberia on the West African coast as a homeland for repatriated Africans.

Virginia congressman John Randolph of Roanoke proposed a resolution requesting that Congress halt the "infamous traffic" of slaves in the nation's capital. Since Washington, D.C. was a southern city that was located in a federal district carved out of Maryland and Virginia, two slave states, the presence of the slave trade in the nation's capital was disturbing to many who opposed slavery. Congress would receive many memorials urging the end of the slave trade in the District of Columbia until the practice was finally abolished as a part of Henry Clay's Compromise of 1850 legislation.

George Bourne published his work, *The Book and Slavery Irreconcilable,* which is considered to be one of the most radical antislavery tracts to be published in America.

1817

In January, James Forten led a protest meeting of three thousand free blacks in Philadelphia who opposed the work of the American Colonization Society. The group met at the Bethel AME Church. They protested against the efforts of the American Colonization Society, believing that the organization sought "to exile us from the land of our nativity."

On February 14, Frederick Douglass was born a slave on a plantation near Tuckahoe, in Talbot County, Maryland. He would eventually escape from slavery and become the best-known black abolitionist in the United States.

On April 7, a revolt involving as many as two hundred slaves occurred in St. Mary's County, Maryland.

On August 29, In Mount Pleasant, Ohio, the white abolitionist Charles Osborn began publishing an antislavery newspaper entitled *The Philanthropist.*

On October 17, Samuel Ringgold Ward, who became a noted abolitionist, minister, and author, was born a slave on Maryland's Eastern Shore. In 1855 he would publish *The Autobiography of a Fugitive Negro.*

On December 10, Mississippi entered the Union as a slave state. At this point the United States consisted of twenty states that were evenly divided with ten being free states and ten slave states.

The New York state legislature enacted a second gradual abolition bill. According to this measure, all blacks who would not yet have been emancipated by the first gradual emancipation act of 1799 would become free effective upon July 4, 1827.

A Maryland court heard the case of *Burrows Admiralty v. Negro Anna.* In this case, the court decided that a master provided freedom to a slave by implication if he granted the slave a gift of property. This decision was based on the understanding that a slave could not own property; therefore if property was given, it was apparent that the owner desired that the slave be emancipated.

Most abolitionists did not support the colonization plans that had started returning freed blacks to Africa. At the yearly meeting of the American Conventions of Abolition Societies, delegates approved a resolution stating that "the gradual and total emancipation of all persons of colour, and their literary and moral education, should precede their colonization."

1818

On April 18, in the Battle of Suwanee, General Andrew Jackson defeated a combined force of Indians and blacks, thus ending the First Seminole War. Jackson had termed the conflict "this savage and negro war" in his communications during the war.

A Mississippi court heard the case of *Harvy and Oth-*

ers v. Decker. In a case closely related to the 1857 *Dred Scott* decision, judges determined that slaves who were transported from Virginia into Indiana and then later brought into Mississippi were legally free. The Mississippi judges ruled that the Northwest Ordinance of 1787 had made the slaves free when they were brought into the free territory of Indiana. (For more on the Northwest Ordinance of 1787, see primary source 32, "Constitution of the Manumission Society of North Carolina")

Action by the state legislature disenfranchised blacks in the state of Connecticut.

A South Carolina court decided the case of *Arthur v. Wells.* The judges declared that the killing of a fugitive slave was lawful only if the fugitive resisted recapture and thus threatened the safety of the slave catcher.

In Philadelphia a group of free blacks established the Pennsylvania Augustine Society "for the education of people of colour."

Judges in the United States Circuit Court for the District of Columbia heard the case of *Sarah v. Taylor.* The judges declared that children who were born between the date of promised manumission and the date of actual manumission were entitled to be freed at the same time that their mother was freed.

New York Congressman James Tallmadge, Jr., tried to stall the admission of Illinois into the Union because he was concerned that the proposed state constitution did not contain a clear and strong prohibition of slavery.

A Delaware court heard the case of *Meunier v. Duperrow.* Judges convicted two free black women upon the charge that they had been kidnapping other free blacks and selling them into slavery.

1819

On January 26, Congress considered a measure to create the Arkansas Territory out of Arkansas County in the Missouri Territory. This action was approved, but not before the Congress had to defeat an amendment, proposed by New York Representative John W. Taylor, that would have prohibited slavery from the Arkansas Territory.

On February 13, when the Missouri Territory sought admission to the Union as a slave state, the action was challenged by New York Representative James Tallmadge, Jr. Tallmadge proposed that two antislavery amendments be attached to the bill proposing Missouri statehood. The first would have prevented the further importation of slaves into Missouri, and the second would have emancipated all children born to slaves in Missouri, after its admission as a state, to be free at the age of twenty-five. Even though the House of Representatives approved both of these amendments, the Senate defeated both measures. Nonetheless, the admission of Missouri into the Union was mired in controversy.

Former President James Madison promoted a plan that slavery should end through gradual abolition, with freed slaves being allotted western homesteads because he foresaw that the difficulties of "incorporation of the people are insuperable." Although Madison wanted slavery to end, he believed that racial separation would be necessary in America in order to maintain civil order.

On March 3, even though the Congress legally ended the African slave trade, a lucrative illegal trade continued as slave ships tried to smuggle shiploads of Africans into American coastal waters. In order to end these smuggling efforts, the Congress enacted a measure creating a reward of $50 per slave to any informer who provided reports that helped to stem the illegal importation of slaves to the United States. The measure also gave the president the power to return any Africans who were captured in this fashion back to Africa.

In the spring, a slave named Coot was captured and executed for having organized a conspiracy among slaves who planned to burn the city of Augusta, Georgia.

On December 14, Alabama entered the Union as a slave state, but the state constitution did provide the legislature with the ability to abolish slavery and compensate slaveowners should it see fit to take such action. At this point the United States consisted of twenty-two states that were evenly divided—eleven free states and eleven slave states.

The United States Congress granted authority to President James Monroe to dispatch armed vessels to the coast of West Africa. These American warships became a part of the African Squadron, which was a joint British and American venture launched to try to suppress the illegal African slave trade.

Attorney Roger B. Taney defended Reverend Jacob Gruber who was accused of inciting slaves to riot. In his defense of Gruber, Taney cited slavery as a great evil that had to be destroyed. Years later, Taney would be the chief justice of the United States Supreme Court who sat in judgment over the case of *Dred Scott v. Sandford* in 1857.

The white abolitionist Charles Osborn began publishing an antislavery newspaper entitled *The Manumission Intelligencer* in Tennessee.

1820

According to the Fourth Census of the United States, the black population of the country, both slave and free, was 1,771,656, or 18.4 percent of the nation's population.

Free blacks organized the New York African Society as a benevolent association to assist the needs of the free black population. The success of this organization would spawn the creation of other such groups including the Union Society, the Clarkson Association, the Wilberforce Benevolent Society, and the Woolman Society of Brooklyn.

In February, President James Monroe signed a Presidential Order that allowed the United States Army to enact a policy denying blacks or mulattoes the right to serve in the United States military.

On February 6, the *Mayflower of Liberia* (previously the brig *Elizabeth*) sailed from New York City to Sierra Leone on the western coast of Africa with eighty-six blacks who had agreed to return to Africa as part of a colonization scheme. The ship arrived in Sierra Leone on March 9. The British had established Sierra Leone as a colony where former slaves could be repatriated to Africa. The colony had been accepting freed blacks and fugitive slaves for the past three decades.

On February 17, the United States Senate passed the measure known as the Missouri Compromise. In this measure it was understood that Missouri would enter the Union as a slave state and Maine as a free state, thus maintaining the delicate balance of votes that existed in the Senate chamber. Senator Jesse B. Thomas of Illinois introduced an amendment to this measure calling for the prohibition of slavery in those areas within the Louisiana Territory north of the line 36°30' north latitude. The measure passed as amended in the Senate.

On February 28, the House of Representatives defeated the Senate version of the Missouri Compromise legislation. Members of the House attempted to pass a modified version of the bill that included the controversial Taylor Amendment that would have barred slavery from the western territories. Taylor had earlier tried to introduce this measure on January 26, 1819, but the proposal had been defeated at that time.

On March 3, Congress agreed to the Missouri Compromise, which allowed Missouri to enter the Union as a slave state provided that Maine entered the Union as a free state. The measure also prohibited slavery from being allowed in any territories north of the 36°30' parallel line. (In developing the Compromise, the Thomas Amendment had been incorporated and the Taylor Amendment had been rejected.)

From April to October, Quaker Elihu Embree began publishing *The Emancipator,* an antislavery newspaper, in Jonesboro, Tennessee. One year earlier, Embree had published the short-lived *Manumission Intelligencer,* which was probably the first antislavery newspaper published in the United States.

On May 15, in an effort to stop the illegal importation of African slaves to America, the Congress of the United States declared that thereafter the involvement in the African slave trade would be considered as an act of piracy. Punishments for those found guilty of such action would be the forfeiture of all vessels and cargo, and execution of any American citizens found to be participating in this illegal activity.

On July 19, the Missouri Territory drafted a constitution for the proposed state of Missouri, but this constitution included a discriminatory prohibition keeping mulattoes and free blacks from entering the future state. This controversial provision would present problems when the Congress reviewed this constitution on November 14, 1820.

The American Colonization Society established Liberia on the coast of West Africa. This site would be used as an outpost for colonization efforts aimed at returning free blacks to Africa. Many antislavery advocates like Margaret Mercer would work tirelessly to support the society's colonization efforts. In 1847, Liberia would declare its independence as an independent republic.

The premise that slaves received their freedom when they were transported from a slave state to a free state or territory was confirmed in two legal decisions of 1820. Kentucky courts upheld this principle in the case of *Rankin v. Lydia,* and Virginia courts reached the same decision in the case of *Griffith v. Fanny.*

1821

In January, Benjamin Lundy, a Quaker, began publication of the *Genius of Universal Emancipation* in Mount Pleasant, Ohio. This publication was one of the earliest abolitionist newspapers in the United States. Although Lundy relocated his publication to Baltimore (1824), Washington, D.C. (1830), and Illinois (1838), the newspaper remained in print rather regularly from 1821 to 1839.

In New York the State Constitutional Convention altered provisions made in the state's 1777 constitution by increasing property and residence requirements for blacks. This action effectively limited the suffrage to fewer free blacks.

On March 2, Speaker of the House Henry Clay negotiated a last-minute Compromise as the Congress balked at discriminatory provisions in the proposed constitution of Missouri that would have barred free blacks and mulattoes from the state. The Congress voted to approve statehood for Missouri provided that state officials did not attempt to limit the rights of citizens, especially free black citizens, as guaranteed by the United States Constitution. On June 26, 1821, the Missouri legislature approved of this stipulation.

On June 21, in New York City, James Varick was installed as the first bishop of the newly established African Methodist Episcopal Zion (AMEZ) Church.

On August 10, Missouri entered the Union as a slave state. At this point the United States consisted of twenty-four states that were evenly divided—twelve free states and twelve slave states.

In December, the Maryland State Supreme Court ruled in the case of *Hall v. Mullin* that a master provided freedom to a slave by implication if he left a bequest of property to that slave in a will or final testament. This decision was based on the understanding that a slave could not own property; therefore if property was willed, it is apparent that the former owner desired that the slave be emancipated.

United States Attorney General William Wirt advised port officials in Norfolk, Virginia, that blacks could not legally command naval vessels. Wirt claimed that maritime law required that all naval commanders be citizens of their country and that this provision prevented free blacks from such service because they were not considered to be citizens of the United States.

Harriet Tubman was born a slave on a plantation in Dorchester County, Maryland. She would escape from slavery in 1849, and thereafter, she became one of the most celebrated "conductors" along the Underground Railroad as she assisted hundreds of other slaves as they escaped from slavery in the southern states.

1822

The American Colonization Society settled its first group of repatriated Africans in a settlement at Monrovia, Liberia, in West Africa. Eventually about fifteen thousand persons settled in the colony. Much of the success of the Liberian colony was due to the efforts of Jehudi Ashmun who was sent to Liberia by the American Colonization Society to direct efforts there.

On May 30, authorities in Charleston, South Carolina, learned of a slave insurrection that was planned by the free black Denmark Vesey when a house servant alerted them to the wide-ranging conspiracy. Vesey, who was a sailor and carpenter, organized one of the most elaborate slave conspiracies in the history of the United States. He was eventually hanged along with thirty-six of his conspirators, while 130 blacks and four whites were arrested during the intensive investigation that followed the discovery of the plot. South Carolina and several other southern states took immediate action to restrict the mobility and education that was afforded blacks in light of this plot.

On July 2, Denmark Vesey and five of his principal accomplices were hanged at Blake's Landing in Charleston, South Carolina.

Free blacks were disenfranchised in Rhode Island.

Judges in the United States Circuit Court for the District of Columbia heard the case of *Matilda v. Mason*. The judges declared that it was not necessary to remove all antislavery supporters from a potential jury pool if a case involved questions regarding slaveowners and their property. Evidently, this discriminatory practice was common in many of the southern states.

A struggle began in Illinois as proslavery supporters tried to create a state constitution that would legalize slavery in Illinois. The debates would rage in the state until the proposal was effectively defeated in 1824 when Governor Edward Coles refused to call a constitutional convention that, most likely, would have drafted a proslavery document.

The premise that slaves received their freedom when they were transported from a slave state to a free state or territory was again confirmed in a state court. A Pennsylvania court heard the case of *Commission v. Robinson* and held that transporting a slave from a slave state to a free state did in fact make a slave free.

The Tennessee Manumission Society addressed a memorial to the United States Congress calling for an end to slavery in Washington, D.C.

A New York court heard the case of *Overseers of Marbletown v. Overseers of Kingston*. In this case it was decided that a marriage between a free black and a slave did not change the status of either party involved. The judge further ruled that the children of such a union would be born free only if the mother was free.

The abolitionist John Finely Crowe began publishing *The Abolition Intelligencer* in Shelby, Kentucky.

1823

A decision in a United States Circuit Court in the case of *Elkison v. Deliesseline* asserted that the removal of a slave from a slave state to a free state effectively bestowed freedom.

The Mississippi state legislature enacted a measure that made it illegal to teach a slave to read or write. In addition, any gathering that consisted of more than five slaves or free blacks was also deemed illegal by legislative action.

Judges in the United States Circuit Court for the District of Columbia heard the case of *United States v. Brockett*. In rendering their decision, the judges declared that "to cruelly, inhumanely, and maliciously cut, slash, beat and ill treat one's own slave is an indictable offence at common law."

1824

State laws in Illinois, Iowa, Indiana, and Michigan required that blacks must post bond to guarantee good behavior in order to be qualified for suffrage rights.

In December, the Indiana state legislature enacted a measure that made enforcement of the Fugitive Slave Law of 1793 more difficult. The new Indiana law allowed justices of the peace to settle cases in fugitive slave cases, but both the fugitive and the claimant had the right to demand a trial by jury. This action made the work of reclaiming a fugitive more time-consuming and in effect, more expensive. The Indiana law would eventually be invalidated with the passage of the new Fugitive Slave Law in 1850.

The Louisiana state legislature enacted a new slave code that updated some of the provisions of the older *Code Noir*, which had been in operation for the previous century.

The Missouri Supreme Court decided the case of *Winny v. Whitesides*. In their decision, the justices declared that a slave did indeed become free by residing for a time in Illinois or any other free jurisdiction.

1825

The legislatures in eight of the twelve northern free states approved of resolutions calling upon the federal government to enact a program of compensated emancipation to end the practice of slavery in the United States. Southern politicians in the Congress blocked efforts to consider these proposals.

The slave Josiah Henson, who was later used as the prototype for the character "Uncle Tom" in Harriet Beecher Stowe's *Uncle Tom's Cabin* (1852), led a group of slaves from Maryland to freedom in Kentucky. He would later cross the border into Ontario (Upper Canada), where he led a community of former slaves.

1826

Frances Wright established Nashoba plantation, a utopian community near Memphis, Tennessee, that was designed to train blacks for their eventual settlement outside of the United States. Wright also published the tract *A Plan for the Gradual Abolition of Slavery in the United States without Danger of Loss to the Citizens of the South*.

In June, President John Quincy Adams requested Senate confirmation of two delegates whom he wished to send to the Panama Conference of Latin American States that Simón Bolívar had organized. Even though some senators opposed participation because international involvement ran counter to American diplomatic tradition, Vice President John C. Calhoun, who presided over the Senate, opposed the appointment because nations that were governed by blacks would participate in the conference. The Senate eventually approved of the appointments, but because of the delay that the partisan debate had caused, neither of the diplomats who was appointed ever made it to Panama in time for the conference.

Upon his death in Virginia, Thomas Jefferson freed only five of his slaves, but bequeathed the rest to his heirs.

An antislavery newspaper called *The African Observer* began publication in Philadelphia, Pennsylvania.

Reverend Samuel E. Cornish, a free black from New York, published an antislavery tract entitled *A Remonstrance Against the Abuse of the Blacks*.

In an effort to weaken enforcement of the Fugitive Slave Law of 1793, the Pennsylvania legislature passed a law making the crime of kidnapping a felony and required slave catchers to obtain a special "certificate of removal" before fugitive slaves could be removed from the state. The United States would eventually strike down this law in the case of *Prigg v. Pennsylvania* (1842).

1827

On March 16, the first black newspaper to be published in the United States, *Freedom's Journal,* began publication in New York City. The paper was cofounded and coedited by John B. Russwurm and the Reverend Samuel Cornish, who stated, "We wish to plead our own cause. Too long have others spoken for us." In the newspaper's prospectus, Russwurm and Cornish stated, "In the spirit of candor and humility we intend to lay our case before the public with a view to arrest the progress of prejudice, and to shield ourselves against its consequent evils."

Abolitionist editor Benjamin Lundy was attacked in Baltimore by Austin Woolfolk, a slave dealer. Woolfolk was angered by remarks that Lundy had published in *The Genius of Universal Emancipation.*

A North Carolina court heard the case of *Trustees of the Quaker Society of Contentnea v. Dickenson.* The judge in this case ruled that ownership of slaves by Quakers was illegal in North Carolina because it was tantamount to emancipation. Since the state of North Carolina permitted manumission only in specialized cases, the courts held that the ownership of slaves by Quakers, who were obligated by their faith to manumit their slaves, would be contrary to North Carolina law.

On July 4, slavery was officially abolished in the state of New York as 10,000 slaves were set free with the passage of the New York State Emancipation Act.

The abolitionist William Goodell began publication of *The Investigator,* an antislavery newspaper, in Providence, Rhode Island. In 1829 the paper merged with *The National Philanthropist.*

1828

In Bennington, Vermont, an abolitionist writer named William Lloyd Garrison began to publish a series of articles that attacked slavery in the *National Philanthropist.*

An antislavery newspaper called *The Liberalist* began publication in New Orleans, Louisiana. Milo Mower, the publisher of the paper, would later be imprisoned in 1830 for circulating advertisements of his abolitionist newspaper in New Orleans.

Thomas Dartmouth Rice, "the father of American minstrelsy," popularized the practice of using blackface during minstrel shows when he danced and sang to a tune called "Jim Crow." Over the course of the nineteenth century, the term "Jim Crow" would become synonymous with blacks in the United States as later segregation laws became known as Jim Crow laws.

An antislavery newspaper called *The Free Press* began publication in Bennington, Vermont.

On December 19, United States Vice President John C. Calhoun wrote the document *South Carolina Exposition and Protest* anonymously to decry what he believed to be unjust and oppressive action by the federal government upon the state of South Carolina. Calhoun would use the states' rights argument to defend his position, and he would endorse the right of individual states to nullify federal law. Calhoun did

not speak for all South Carolinians as James Louis Petigru, South Carolina's attorney general, and others did not agree with Calhoun's doctrine.

1829

On August 10, a serious race riot erupted in Cincinnati, Ohio, in which whites attacked black residents and burned and looted their homes. As a result of this attack, 1,200 black residents fled the area and started a new life in Canada.

On September 15, the government of Mexico abolished slavery.

On September 28, David Walker, a free black who lived in Boston, published *An Appeal to the Colored People of the World.* It was a militant antislavery publication that advocated the resistance by blacks to the institution of slavery. The pamphlet was distributed throughout the United States and greatly disturbed southern slaveowners who believed that its message would incite unrest among the slave populace.

In New York City, free black Robert Alexander Young wrote and published *The Ethiopian Manifesto, Issued in Defense of the Black Man's Rights in the Scale of Universal Freedom.* Young used passages from the Bible to condemn the institution of slavery, and he predicted the coming of a black Messiah who would smite slaveholders and bring emancipation to the black masses.

On December 2, after encountering the protest of slaveowning American settlers who had emigrated to Texas, Mexican President Vincent Guerrero exempted Texas from the Mexican antislavery proclamation of September 15, 1829.

After John B. Russwurm emigrated to Liberia, Reverend Samuel E. Cornish continued to publish the antislavery newspaper *Freedom's Journal* under the new masthead *The Rights of All.*

A book of poetry entitled *The Hope of Liberty* was published by George Moses Horton, a North Carolina slave. Horton's work was the first book of poetry by a black author to be published since the time of Phillis Wheatley. The collection included Horton's poem "The Slave's Complaint." Horton published this book of verse in an effort to raise funds so that he might be able to purchase his own freedom, but sales of the book were poor.

1830

In North Carolina slaveowners manumitted more than

four hundred slaves and turned them over to Quakers living within the state. The Quakers retained legal ownership, but allowed the "slaves" to live in virtual freedom until they could afford to transport them to a true life of freedom in the northern states.

According to the Fifth Census, 3,777 black heads of families were listed as slaveowners. Most of these black slaveowners were found in Louisiana, Maryland, Virginia, North Carolina, and South Carolina. Blacks, both slave and free, constituted 18.1 percent of the national population, or 2,328,642 persons.

The state legislature of Louisiana petitioned the Congress with a complaint that slaves from the state were escaping to Mexico.

Massachusetts abolitionist Edward Beecher became the president of Illinois College in Jacksonville, Illinois. In the Midwest Beecher became a friend and supporter of the antislavery work of editor Elijah Lovejoy. Shortly after the murder of Lovejoy, Beecher returned to Massachusetts to accept the position of pastor at the Salem Street Church in Boston.

The Louisiana state legislature enacted a measure that made it a criminal offense to teach a slave to read or write.

On January 21, municipal authorities in Portsmouth, Ohio, forcibly deported all black residents from the community.

On April 6, Mexican authorities prohibited the further colonization of Texas by United States citizens. This action also prohibited those American settlers who were already in Texas from importing additional slaves into the region.

On April 30, much of the debate between the North and the South over slavery was based on the states' rights views of the political leaders who represented the interests of their regions. Occasionally these views were articulated in less-than-subtle fashion. At the Jefferson Day dinner in 1830, President Andrew Jackson presented the toast "Our Federal Union—it must be preserved!" Jackson's vice president, John C. Calhoun of South Carolina, responded to Jackson's remarks with his own toast, "The Union—next to our liberty, the most dear!"

Between September 20 and 24, Richard Allen chaired the first National Negro Convention, which met in Philadelphia at the Bethel AME Church. The purpose of this gathering was to launch a church-affiliated program to uplift and improve the status of American blacks.

In December, the *Comet,* an American schooner that was transporting slaves between Alexandria, Virginia, and New Orleans, Louisiana, as a part of the domestic slave trade, was wrecked off of the Bahamas. British officials in the Bahamas set the slaves on board the vessel free, much to the chagrin of the Americans who owned the slaves. The manner in which the *Comet* episode was handled would be a matter of diplomatic contention between the United States and Great Britain for more than a decade.

1831

On January 1, William Lloyd Garrison, one of America's more radical abolitionists, began publication of *The Liberator* in Boston. It would continue publication weekly through December 1865 making it the longest-running, most successful, and best known of all antislavery newspapers. In establishing this organ for the abolitionist cause, Garrison declared, "I am in earnest—I will not equivocate—I will not excuse—I will not retreat a single inch—AND I WILL BE HEARD!" Garrison promised that he would continue to publish his newspaper until slavery had been abolished in the United States.

The term "Underground Railroad" was used for the first time to describe the system that existed in the northern states in which whites and free blacks sympathetic to the abolitionist cause aided fugitive slaves to make their way to freedom.

Residents of Mississippi formed the Mississippi Colonization Society to establish a colony for the purpose of repatriating former slaves from that state to Africa.

The Georgia state legislature announced a reward of $5,000 to anyone who would capture William Lloyd Garrison and turn him over to Georgia authorities. It was the belief of the Georgia legislators that the abolitionist editor of *The Liberator* should face criminal prosecution and conviction in a Georgia courtroom.

From August 21 to 22, in Southampton County, Virginia, a large-scale slave insurrection was led by Nat Turner, a literate slave preacher, who claimed that voices inspired him to lead the revolt. Turner's owner, Joseph Travis, and his family were among the fifty-seven whites who were killed by Turner and his seventy associates during the rampage, and the entire South experienced panic because of the shocking violence. In the end, Turner was captured in the swamps on October 30 after an exhaustive search, and he was eventually convicted and sentenced to death by hanging in Jerusalem, Virginia, on November 11.

On December 12, in the United States House of Representatives, Congressman John Quincy Adams of

Massachusetts began a pro-abolition campaign against slavery that he would maintain until his death in 1848. Adams introduced fifteen petitions that Pennsylvania residents had organized calling for the abolition of slavery in the District of Columbia. Although the Congress abolished the slave trade in the nation's capital as part of the Compromise of 1850, it would not be until 1862 that slavery itself was abolished in the District of Columbia.

In Philadelphia the first annual meeting of the Convention of the People of Color was held at the Wesleyan Church. Delegates discussed the possibility of creating Canadian settlement communities but voiced strong opposition to the African emigration policies of the American Colonization Society.

John E. Stewart, a black abolitionist, published the antislavery newspaper entitled *The African Sentinel and Journal of Liberty* in Albany, New York.

Alexis de Tocqueville, the French bureaucrat who eventually wrote the seminal study *Democracy in America,* toured the United States for several months as he tried to learn about American culture. At a dinner party in Boston, de Tocqueville sat next to former President John Quincy Adams and had an opportunity to question Adams about his views on slavery. When asked "Do you look on slavery as a great plague for the United States?," Adams responded to de Tocqueville saying, "Yes, certainly that is the root of almost all the troubles of the present and the fears for the future."

Maria W. Stewart published *Religion and the Pure Principles of Morality—The Sure Foundation on Which We Must Build.* Stewart was a free black who opposed slavery and is considered to be the first African American political writer in the United States.

Virginia state legislator and college professor Thomas Roderick Dew described his state as a "Negro-raising state" for the remainder of the South. During the following three decades nearly 300,000 slaves would be exported from Virginia to the other states as part of the internal slave trade.

Between 1831 and 1832, in Virginia a state convention used the winter session to debate the issue of slavery within the state. Various plans of gradual emancipation and colonization were considered, but in the end all of the measures involving changes in the state's involvement with slavery were defeated by the proslavery element that attended the convention. On January 21, 1832, Thomas Jefferson Randolph, the grandson of former President Thomas Jefferson, presented the assembly with a proposal for gradual emancipation that his grandfather had promoted nearly forty years earlier.

The plan did not sway the convention, and the proposal was defeated.

1832

In Canterbury, Connecticut, Prudence Crandall, a white teacher, admitted a black student named Sarah Harris to the school that she ran and suffered public admonishment for this action. Crandall would eventually be arrested on June 27, 1833, for teaching black children. The school was targeted by vandals, and it was eventually demolished.

A serious academic debate between students and faculty was held at Lane Theological Seminary in Cincinnati, Ohio, on the topics of abolition and colonization. When the trustees of the seminary ordered an end to this discussion in May 1833, many of the students left the Seminary and eventually moved to a more open educational setting at Oberlin College.

On January 6, a group of twelve white abolitionists met at the African Baptist Church on Boston's Beacon Hill to organize the New England Anti-Slavery Society. William Lloyd Garrison played an important role in the founding of this organization, and the group supported the concept of "immediatism" as it believed that gradual abolition was an inadequate response to the sin of slavery.

Thomas Roderick Dew, a professor of political economy at William and Mary College, published his "Review of the Debate in the Virginia Legislature of 1831 and 1832." Dew was a southern apologist for slavery, and his presentation represented a one-sided view that emphasized the proslavery perspective. Dew also published an essay in 1832 entitled "The Proslavery Argument" in which he provided an intellectual foundation for the racist assumptions that southern slaveholders used to justify the institution and practice of slavery.

From November 19 to 24, using the defense of a states' rights argument, the legislature of South Carolina nullified the federal Tariff Acts of 1828 and 1832. This action would precipitate a showdown between the state of South Carolina and the executive authority of President Andrew Jackson. The question of states' rights and the doctrine of nullification would be divisive issues in the decades leading up to the American Civil War.

1833

Oberlin College was founded in Ohio, and from the start it became an institution that was integrated and that took a leading role in the growing abolitionist movement. By the time of the American Civil War, one-third of Oberlin's students were black. Many black abolitionists like John Mifflin Brown were strong advocates of the institution because of its antislavery heritage.

Eliza Lee Cabot Follen and other female abolitionists organized the Boston Female Anti-Slavery Society. The group would remain active until 1840.

John Rankin, a Presbyterian minister and Tennessee abolitionist, published *Letters on American Slavery.* Rankin was forced to leave the South because of his antislavery views, but his book became a handbook for abolitionist speakers around the country.

Quaker abolitionist Elijah P. Lovejoy began to publish the *Observer,* an antislavery newspaper in St. Louis, Missouri.

On August 28, the British Parliament enacted a measure that provided for the compensated, gradual abolition of slavery in all British colonial possessions. This action would energize the abolitionist movement in the United States as America was increasingly viewed as a pariah nation for maintaining the practice of slavery. In future decades, a true transatlantic abolitionist movement formed as British and American abolitionists worked together to try to bring an effective end to slavery in the United States.

Also on August 28, the British Parliament appropriated £20,000,000 to be used as a package of compensated emancipation for slaveholders in the British West Indies who would suffer economic losses as a result of Britain's policy of abolishing slavery within the Empire. A total of 700,000 slaves were emancipated in the British colonies.

Abolitionist editor Joshua Leavitt and others organized the New York City Anti-Slavery Society.

Justice and Expediency, a popular antislavery tract, was published by the American poet John Greenleaf Whittier.

On December 4, William Lloyd Garrison, Theodore Dwight Weld, Arthur Tappan, Lewis Tappan, and several other black and white abolitionists met in Philadelphia to establish the American Anti-Slavery Society. This organization was the first national abolitionist society to form in the United States.

Also in December, Quaker Lucretia Mott became the first president of the Female Anti-Slavery Society, which she helped to organize in Philadelphia, Pennsylvania.

The white abolitionist David Lee Child published *The Despotism of Freedom—Or The Tyranny and Cruelty of American Republican Slavemasters.*

1834

The South Carolina legislature enacted a measure making it a crime to teach black children, slave or free, to read.

In New Orleans, Louisiana, a riot developed when authorities discovered a torture chamber where slaves were horribly abused in the home of Madame Lalaurie's. City residents rose in righteous indignation over the alleged cruelty that had occurred in the home, but Madame Lalaurie was able to escape the mob's wrath and flee to France.

From July 4 to 12, rioting rocked the city of New York for eight days after a proslavery mob attacked an antislavery society meeting that was held at New York's Chatham Street Chapel on Independence Day. The proslavery group was angered because black and white abolitionists were sitting together in the audience. In the rioting, several churches and homes were destroyed by fire.

In October, the homes of nearly forty free blacks in Philadelphia, Pennsylvania, were destroyed when a proslavery mob went on a riotous rampage through the city.

1835

William Lloyd Garrison, the abolitionist editor and publisher of *The Liberator,* was attacked and beaten by a white mob in Boston.

Theodore Dwight Weld began to train abolitionist agents for the American Anti-Slavery Society who would spread the antislavery message as disciples throughout rural communities of the northern states and the border states. Members of this group, known as "The Seventy," were physically attacked by proslavery supporters in many communities.

From June 1 to 5, one recommendation to come out of a National Negro Convention meeting in Philadelphia was that blacks should remove the word "African" from all of their organizations and institutions.

On July 6, in Charleston, South Carolina, Alfred Huger, the local postmaster, requested of Postmaster General Amos Kendall that antislavery tracts be prohibited from the United States mail. Huger's request was denied by Kendall, who maintained that he did not have the authority to make such a decision, but he did suggest that Huger might act on his own initiative. Kendall stated that "We owe an obligation to the laws, but a higher one to the communities in which we live."

On July 29, antislavery pamphlets and other abolitionist literature were removed from the public mail in Charleston, South Carolina, and publicly burned in the streets.

North Carolina became the last southern state to deny the suffrage to free blacks by making changes to its state constitution. In addition, the state legislature made it illegal for whites to teach free blacks.

On August 10, mob violence forced the closure of Noyes Academy in Canaan, New Hampshire. The school was burned to the ground because it had operated on an integrated basis with fourteen black students and had thus irritated community sensibilities.

The Georgia state legislature enacted a measure that provided for the death penalty in the case of anyone convicted of publishing abolitionist tracts that might foment insurrection among the slaves within the state.

On September 13, in a letter to abolitionist Gerrit Smith, James G. Birney wrote, "The antagonist principles of liberty and slavery have been roused into action and one or the other must be victorious. There will be no cessation of strife until slavery shall be exterminated or liberty destroyed."

The state of South Carolina, like most of the southern states, made an effort to keep abolitionist literature out of the hands of slaves and free blacks. In a report to the state legislature, South Carolina Governor George McDuffie commented that "the laws of every community should punish this species of interference by death without benefit of clergy."

On October 21, a scheduled address by British abolitionist George Thompson to the Female Anti-Slavery Society in Boston was disrupted by a proslavery mob.

On the same day, efforts to organize an antislavery society in Utica, New York, were disrupted by a proslavery mob.

Also on October 21, William Lloyd Garrison, the radical abolitionist editor of *The Liberator,* was attacked by a mob that was estimated to include two thousand people. Garrison was delivering a speech on the theme that "all men are created equal," when the enraged mob turned against the antislavery orator. Garrison was rescued and lodged in Boston's Leverett Street Jail for his personal safety.

In December, just before the Second Seminole War began in Florida, John Caesar organized an attack of hundreds of slaves on plantations in the region of St. Johns River. Many fugitive slaves took part in the fighting of the Second Seminole War.

On December 7, bowing to pressure from states' rights advocates, President Andrew Jackson considered measures that would allow southern postmasters the right to restrict the mailing and distribution of abolitionist tracts in the southern states. Jackson asked the Congress to consider enacting a law that would prohibit the circulation of antislavery literature through the mail.

On December 15, Mexican president Antonio López de Santa Anna announced his intention to establish a unified constitution for Mexico. This decision would mean that the exemption granted to Texas in 1829, which allowed for the continuation of slavery in the region, would now be invalidated. American settlers in Texas who are slaveholders vowed that they would fight a war of secession from Mexico rather than surrender their right to hold slaves in Texas.

Unitarian minister William Ellery Channing, the pastor of Boston's Federal Street Church, published *Slavery,* an antislavery tract in which he openly promoted abolitionist sentiments.

The poet and abolitionist John Greenleaf Whittier published the poem "My Countrymen in Chains."

1836

In January in Philadelphia, James G. Birney began publishing a new antislavery newspaper called the *Philanthropist.*

On January 11, Congress received several petitions from abolitionists calling for the abolition of slavery in the District of Columbia. Senator John C. Calhoun of South Carolina described these petitions as a "foul slander" upon the South.

On March 11, in the United States Senate, the practice began of hearing antislavery petitions that were presented to the body and then rejecting them.

On March 17, Texas, which declared itself an independent republic, drafted a constitution that legalized slavery in the Republic of Texas. Texan settlers would fight the Texas Revolution against Mexico in order to win their independence. Shortly after achieving their independence, Texans would seek annexation as a state to the United States.

On May 26, the United States Congress began using the so-called gag rule, which prevented the reading and circulation of all antislavery petitions that were received by the Congress. As a parliamentary maneuver, the House of Representatives must renew the "gag rule" at the start of every year's congressional session. The rule would remain in effect until 1844.

On June 15, Arkansas entered the Union as a slave state. At this point the United States consisted of twenty-five states, of which twelve were free states and thirteen were slave states. This was the first time in the nation's history that the number of slave states surpassed the number of free states.

On July 12, after he relocated his abolitionist press to Cincinnati, Ohio, James G. Birney encountered a proslavery mob that was upset with him for publishing the *Philanthropist,* an antislavery newspaper. The mob attacked Birney's press and destroyed the type that he used to publish the newspaper.

In a tract entitled *An Appeal to the Christian Women of the South,* the South Carolina-born abolitionist Angelina E. Grimké urged the abolition of slavery and advocated social equality for free blacks. Copies of her pamphlet were burned when they were found in the mail at several South Carolina post offices.

The Missouri Supreme Court decided the case of *Rachael v. Walker.* In their decision the justices declared that a slave did indeed become free by residing at northern military bases and in territories where slavery had been prohibited.

The white abolitionist Lydia Maria Child published *An Appeal in Favor of that Class of Americans Called Africans.*

The Massachusetts Supreme Court ruled that any slave who was brought within the state's borders by a master became legally free.

Richard Hildrith, a white historian, published the novel *The Slave: Or, Memoirs of Archy Moore.* Hildrith attempted to write this novel in the style of a slave autobiography.

Softening its previous antislavery tone, the Methodist Church stated its intention to avoid interfering in the civil and political relationships that existed between master and slave.

In Granville, Ohio, a meeting of the Ohio Anti-Slavery Society was disrupted by ruffians who had been hired for the task by community leaders.

Elizabeth Buffum Chace and other antislavery supporters organized the Ladies Anti-Slavery Society of Fall River, Massachusetts.

In a tract entitled *An Epistle to the Clergy of the Southern States,* the South Carolina-born abolitionist Sarah Moore Grimké called for the overthrow of the institution of slavery. Copies of her pamphlet were burned when they were found in the mail at several South Carolina post offices.

By the end of 1836 it was estimated that five hundred different abolitionist societies were active in the northern states.

1837

William Whipper, a free black from Philadelphia, Pennsylvania, published "An Address on Non-Resistance to Offensive Aggression." This article was published twelve years before Henry David Thoreau's essay on nonviolence, and it may be the first literary reference in United States history to the concept of nonviolent protest.

In Boston the Reverend Hosea Eaton published *A Treatise on the Intellectual Character and Political Condition of the Colored People of the United States.*

Quaker Richard Humphreys established the Institute for Colored Youth in Philadelphia, Pennsylvania. In 1902 the school would move to Cheney, Pennsylvania, where it became known as Cheney University.

John Greenleaf Whittier published *A Narrative of Events Since the First of August, 1834,* which he believed to be the true narrative of a slave named James Williams. Impressed by the powerful message of this narrative, the American Anti-Slavery Society distributed a copy of the work to every member of the United States Congress. It was later discovered that the story that Williams told, however powerful, was untrue.

The Panic of 1837, a serious economic recession, affected the institution of slavery. Prior to the economic downturn, a prime fieldhand in Virginia might have sold at auction for $1,300, but these prices declined significantly during the recession.

In Canada, blacks received the suffrage.

On February 6, a resolution was approved in the United States House of Representatives asserting that slaves did not possess the right of petition that was guaranteed to citizens in the United States Constitution.

On May 10, the *Weekly Advocate* was first published in New York City. It was the first black newspaper to be published in the United States.

In August, in Rapides Parish, Louisiana, a planned slave conspiracy was detected when the slave Lewis Cheney alerted authorities to the plot. Cheney earned his freedom for this action even though he was the person who had initiated the planned uprising. In the aftermath of this episode, United States troops were sent into Alexandria, Louisiana, to put an end to the vigilante-based hangings of suspected black conspirators.

On November 7, in Alton, Illinois, the antislavery newspaper publisher Elijah Lovejoy was murdered by an antiabolition mob as he refused to stop publishing antislavery material and defended his press from mob attack. Lovejoy's press had been attacked on two previous occasions and had been smashed and then thrown into a river, but his press had been replaced by the Ohio Anti-Slavery Society.

On December 4, during a brief moment when the "gag rule" was not in effect, Vermont congressman William Slade presented a series of antislavery petitions to the Congress. The angry debate that followed prompted the Congress to enact an even stronger "gag rule" on December 19. The measure had to be renewed each year at the start of the congressional term, and it remained in effect until 1844.

On December 8, motivated by the brutal lynching of the Quaker abolitionist Elijah Lovejoy, Wendell Phillips delivered his first abolitionist address at Faneuil Hall in Boston, Massachusetts. In his oration, Phillips declared "my *curse* be on the Constitution of the United States" because the document protected slavery as a legal and permissible institution.

On December 25, during the Second Seminole War, American forces defeated a Seminole party under the command of the black chief, John Horse, in the battle of Okeechobee. Chief John Horse shared his command responsibilities with Alligator Sam Jones and Wild Cat.

1838

Throughout the South, slaveowners became increasingly suspicious of how religious services might sway the passions of the slaves. Black preachers found it more and more difficult to conduct services, and slaves were required to worship in those settings where they could be under the direct supervision of the slaveowners.

From January 3 to 12, South Carolina Senator John C. Calhoun, alarmed by efforts of northern abolitionists to have slavery outlawed in the District of Columbia and to prohibit the domestic slave trade, presented a series of proposals to the Senate that were designed to bolster the legal protection of slavery. The Senate did approve of Calhoun's measure, which affirmed that the national government should "resist all attempts by one portion of the Union to use it as an instrument to attack the domestic institutions of another."

On February 15, Massachusetts congressman John Quincy Adams introduced 350 antislavery petitions in defiance of the "gag rule" that the House of Representatives had instituted. The petitions opposed slavery and the annexation of Texas.

On March 14, Robert Purvis led free blacks in Philadelphia, Pennsylvania, as they held a mass meeting to protest the disenfranchisement of blacks in the state.

Robert Purvis published *Appeal of Forty Thousand Citizens Threatened with Disenfranchisement to the People of Pennsylvania.*

On May 17, Philadelphia's Pennsylvania Hall was burned to the ground by a proslavery mob. The group was angered that the building had been used to host recent antislavery meetings.

In August in New York City, black abolitionist David Ruggles began publication of *Mirror of Liberty,* the first black magazine to be published in the United States.

On September 3, Frederick Douglass escaped from slavery in Baltimore, Maryland, and made his way to New York City.

The Massachusetts Antislavery Society hired Charles Lenox Remond to serve as a lecturer for the organization. Remond became the first black abolitionist to be employed in this capacity.

On December 3, Representative Joshua Giddings took his seat in the United States House of Representatives. The Ohio Whig was the first abolitionist to be elected to the United States Congress. Among other issues, Congressman Giddings would work tirelessly to do away with the "gag rule," which prohibited the Congress from considering any antislavery petitions that were submitted.

On December 11, the United States House of Representatives voted to renew the "gag rule" that it had adopted in 1836 prohibiting the consideration of any antislavery petitions that were received by the Congress. The 1838 renewal became known as the Atherton Gag because the measure had been introduced by Congressman Charles G. Atherton, a New Hampshire Democrat.

1839

On February 7, Senator Henry Clay of Kentucky planned to run for the presidency in 1840 as a candidate of the Whig Party, but Clay believed that many Americans associated the Whigs with the abolitionist cause. In a Senate debate on slavery, Clay criticized the abolitionists and said that they had no legal right to interfere with slavery in those areas where it already existed. Clay hoped that he could gain support among northern and southern conservatives by speaking out against the abolitionists who were considered the extremists of their day. Despite his efforts, Clay was unable to secure the Whig Party's nomination in 1840; the Whig standard-bearer, General William Henry Harrison, was elected president in 1840.

On February 25, during the Second Seminole War, captured Seminoles along with their black allies were shipped from Tampa Bay, Florida, to their new home in the Indian Territory of Oklahoma.

On April 5, Robert Smalls, who later became a hero during the American Civil War and eventually served as a Reconstruction-era congressman from South Carolina, was born into slavery in Beaufort, South Carolina.

American Slavery As It Is: Testimony of a Thousand Witnesses was published by Theodore Dwight Weld. This work was an attempt to present a documentary history—based on southern newspaper accounts and eyewitness testimony—that would identify the true condition of slaves in the American South. Weld was assisted in this project by South Carolina abolitionist Angelina Grimké, and the two abolitionists were married later in the year.

On November 13, the Liberty Party, the first antislavery political party in the United States, was established by James G. Birney at a convention in Warsaw, New York. Some of the leading supporters of this new political party included the black abolitionists Samuel Ringgold Ward and Henry Highland Garnet. Prominent white supporters included Gerrit Smith and Salmon P. Chase. The convention nominated Birney for the presidency, and Francis J. Lemoyne was nominated for vice president. As part of the party's political activism, members urged boycotts of southern-made products and crops.

In July, the Spanish slave ship *L'Amistad* was seized off the coast of Cuba when the fifty-four Africans on board, led by Cinqué, revolted and killed the captain. The Africans on board demanded that the remaining crewmen return the vessel to Africa. Later in the summer the vessel was captured off the coast of Montauk, Long Island, and a series of trials began. Eventually, the *Amistad* captives won their freedom when former president John Quincy Adams defended them before the United States Supreme Court.

The United States State Department declared that blacks were not considered citizens and therefore denied a black applicant's request for a passport.

In a papal letter, Pope Gregory XVI declared the official opposition of the Roman Catholic Church to the slave trade and to slavery. In the United States, Catholic slaveholders generally ignored the papal pronouncement and continued to participate in the peculiar institution of slavery.

Antislavery advocate Elizur Wright became the editor of the abolitionist newspaper *Massachusetts Abolitionist,* and he used his paper as a forum to advocate political action to bring an end to slavery. Wright was later active in efforts to establish the Liberty Party.

The American Anti-Slavery Society hired Presbyterian minister Samuel Ringgold Ward to serve as an abolitionist lecturer.

1840

Unitarian minister William Ellery Channing, the pastor of Boston's Federal Street Church, published *Emancipation,* an antislavery tract that urged the United States government to follow the same path as the British Parliament and abolish slavery. Channing believed that the success demonstrated in the British government's experience at ending slavery throughout its vast empire proved that the abolition of slavery was indeed a real possibility in the United States.

Theodore Dwight Weld, a non-Garrisonian abolitionist, broke with the Garrisonians concerning the tactics that should be used in the abolitionist movement. Weld eventually established the American and Foreign Anti-Slavery Society.

On April 1, the Liberty Party held its first national convention in Albany, New York. The convention confirmed the candidacy of James G. Birney for the presidency. Birney became the first antislavery candidate to seek the presidency.

On May 14, in an effort to prevent the kidnapping of free blacks that resulted in their being sold into slavery in the South, the legislature of New York enacted "An act more effectually to protect the free citizens of this State from being kidnapped, or reduced to Slavery."

In June, the American Anti-Slavery Society began publishing *The National Anti-Slavery Standard* as its official organ to support immediate emancipation. The publication would remain in operation under various titles until April 1870.

From August 18 to August 20, the New York State Convention of Negroes was held in Albany, New York.

Both New York and Vermont instituted a new judicial policy of holding a jury trial in all cases involving fugitive slaves who had been captured within their respective states. In the case of Vermont, the law creating this new procedure was rescinded in 1843, but the policy was reestablished in 1850 upon passage of the new Fugitive Slave Act.

Reverend Samuel E. Cornish and Theodore S. Wright published *The Colonization Scheme Considered in Its Rejection by the Colored People.* This work outlined the reasons why free blacks in the United States should oppose all efforts to recolonize them in West African locations like Liberia and Sierra Leone.

A group of abolitionists from the United States traveled to London to attend the World Anti-Slavery Convention, but were dismayed by the convention's policy denying seats to the female abolitionists who had planned to participate in the event. American abolitionists Elizabeth Cady Stanton and Lucretia Mott walked out of the convention in protest when they were denied seats as delegates, and William Lloyd Garrison showed his solidarity with the female abolitionists by leaving the meeting as well. In some respects, the poor treatment that was afforded the female abolitionists helped to encourage the eventual development of an American women's rights movement.

hamas where all of the slaves on board the vessel, except those accused of murder, were granted asylum and eventually set free by British officials. This event sparked an international diplomatic incident between the United States and Great Britain. Secretary of State Daniel Webster put forth the argument that slaves on board an American vessel were bound by American law, but the British maintained that the seizure took place in international waters and that American law did not apply in this instance.

Thornton Stringfellow, a proslavery apologist from Virginia, published *A Brief Examination of Scripture Testimony on the Institution of Slavery.* Stringfellow believed that the Bible's many references supporting slavery were sufficient proof of the practice's moral legitimacy.

In New York the state legislature gave public schools the authority to segregate students by race in all educational facilities.

1841

In March in Washington, D.C., the free black Solomon Northup was kidnapped and sold into slavery in the South. Northup would spend the next twelve years of his life as a slave on several Louisiana cotton plantations. Abolitionists in the North would work to win his eventual release.

On March 1, Blanche K. Bruce was born a slave on a plantation in Prince Edward County, Virginia. During the Reconstruction Era, Bruce would represent the state of Mississippi in the United States Senate. He would be the only black to serve a full term in the Senate during the era of Reconstruction.

On March 9, the U.S. Supreme Court upheld a lower court's decision and found the Africans from the ship *l'Amistad* to have been illegally kidnapped and ordered them set free to be returned to Africa as soon as possible. Former president John Quincy Adams had defended the Africans in legal arguments before the Supreme Court.

In August, Frederick Douglass began to speak on the abolitionist lecture circuit in behalf of the Massachusetts Anti-Slavery Society.

Between August 23 and August 25, the Pennsylvania State Convention of Negroes was held in Pittsburgh, Pennsylvania.

On November 7, while they were being transported from Hampton Roads, Virginia, to New Orleans, Louisiana, slaves on board the *Creole* revolted and took control of the vessel. They sailed to Nassau in the Ba-

1842

On January 24, Congressman John Quincy Adams of Massachusetts introduced a petition to Congress drafted by the citizens of Haverhill, Massachusetts, which called for the peaceful dissolution of the Union.

On March 1, the United States Supreme Court ruled in the case of *Prigg v. Pennsylvania* that a Pennsylvania statute that interfered with the enforcement of the Fugitive Slave Law of 1793 was unconstitutional. A state court had previously convicted Edward Prigg of kidnapping when Prigg, a slave catcher, tried to remove the fugitive slave Margaret Morgan from Pennsylvania back to slavery in Maryland. The Supreme Court upheld the validity of the Fugitive Slave Act of 1793 and the primacy of federal law over state efforts to block enforcement, but most of the northern states found means to avoid assisting the efforts of southerners to have fugitive slaves recaptured and returned to the South. The decision stated, however, that it was a federal responsibility to enforce the Fugitive Slave Law since the states could not be obliged to enforce federal laws through state officers, and many northern states used this interpretation as a judicial loophole. Most northern states soon thereafter enacted Personal Liberty Laws that helped state officials circumvent enforcement of the federal Fugitive Slave Law.

Between March 21 and March 22, Congressman Joshua Giddings, an Ohio Whig, introduced a series of measures collectively called the Giddings Resolutions in which he attacked the federal sanction of slavery and the coastal slave trade. Giddings's actions were largely a response to the controversy that had been caused by the *Creole* incident. His measures went so far as to encourage resistance like the one that had taken place on board the *Creole* the previous year when slaves mutinied and took control of the vessel. Giddings was censured by his colleagues on March 23 and resigned, but was reelected by his district and returned to Congress the following month.

In October, in Boston, George Latimer, an escaped slave, was captured. The case surrounding his efforts to avoid being returned to southern slavery sparked an intense North-South struggle over the effective enforcement of existing fugitive slave laws and northern attempts to circumvent these measures by passing personal liberty laws. In the case of Latimer, a Boston abolitionist eventually forced Boston authorities to allow him to purchase Latimer from his southern owner on November 17, thereby allowing the fugitive to become free. The debates regarding this case did prompt Frederick Douglass to publish his first printed articles in behalf of the abolitionist movement.

William G. Allen, a free black abolitionist, began publication of *The National Watchman,* an antislavery newspaper, in Troy, New York.

The Rhode Island legislature granted the suffrage to free blacks living within the state.

1843

Diplomats of the United States and Great Britain met at Washington, D.C., to negotiate the Webster-Ashburton Treaty. As a result of one of the articles of this treaty, the African Squadron was formed as naval officials of the United States and Great Britain agreed to cooperate and patrol the waters off the coast of West Africa in an effort to intercept ships that might engage in the slave trade. When ships were captured by the squadron, Africans on board were repatriated either to Liberia or to Sierra Leone. Treaty negotiations did not reach a final agreement as to how the slave trade within the Western Hemisphere might be best restricted.

In March, in an action that ran counter to the prevailing national trend, the Massachusetts legislature decriminalized miscegenation by repealing a 1786 law that had prohibited interracial marriage. As a result, intermarriage between whites, blacks, mulattoes, or Indians was legalized by Massachusetts state law.

On June 1, Sojourner Truth (born Isabella Baumfree), who had been born a slave in New York, became the first black woman to join the abolitionist lecture circuit and speak openly from a public platform in behalf of antislavery and women's causes.

On August 22, at the annual meeting of the National Convention of Colored Men in Buffalo, New York, Henry Highland Garnet called for slaves in the South to rise up and revolt and urged free blacks to participate in a general strike to improve the conditions for blacks in the country. Other delegates, including Frederick Douglass, disapproved of the message that Garnet delivered.

Between August 30 and 31, the Liberty Party held a national convention in Buffalo, New York, and Samuel Ringgold Ward, Henry Highland Garnet, and Charles B. Ray participated, thereby becoming the first blacks to take an active role in a national political gathering. Ward led the convention in prayer, Garnet served on the nominating committee, and Ray was one of the convention secretaries. The convention nominated James G. Birney for president and Thomas Morris for vice president. The party platform opposed the extension of slavery into any western territories, but it did not take a stand on the question of Texas annexation.

From October 23 to October 27, free blacks in Michigan held their first statewide convention in Detroit, Michigan.

On December 27, black abolitionist David Jenkins founded the antislavery newspaper *Palladium of Liberty* in Columbus, Ohio.

In light of the recent Supreme Court decision in the case of *Prigg v. Pennsylvania* (1842), the state legislatures in Massachusetts and Vermont specifically forbade any state officials from aiding and abetting anyone, including federal authorities, in efforts to remove fugitive slaves from their respective states and return them to the condition of enslavement in the South.

1844

The slavery question began to cause a schism in many American religious communities. The Methodist Episcopal Church of the United States divided over the question of whether or not bishops within the church could hold slaves. This schism grew out of the decision by Georgia Bishop James O. Andrews to continue holding his slaves after church authorities had told him to manumit them or else to give up his bishopric. As a result of this division, white southerners formed the Methodist Episcopal Church, South.

Proslavery forces in South Carolina were energized by a speech supporting disunion that "fire-eater" Robert Barnwell Rhett delivered in Bluffton, South

Carolina. The "Bluffton Movement" was a short-lived effort to stir the political passions of South Carolina residents over the issues of states' rights and nullification.

The Baptist Church suffered a schism in regard to the slavery question that was reflective of society at large. The church divided into northern and southern conventions over the question of whether or not slave-owning missionaries should be sent into the territories of the expanding Southwest.

On June 8, the United States Senate rejected a treaty that would have provided for the annexation of the Republic of Texas and its admission to the Union as a slave state. Antislavery forces within the Senate were able to convince a majority that the sectional division that would be caused by admitting another slave state to the Union outweighed any possible benefits that might come from such action.

On June 24, free blacks in Massachusetts held a series of protest meetings in opposition to the state's segregated school policy.

On December 3, after eight years of difficult enforcement, the House of Representatives lifted the "gag rule," which had prohibited the discussion of any antislavery petitions that were received by the Congress. Much of the agitation against the "gag rule" had been led by Congressman John Quincy Adams of Massachusetts and Congressman Joshua Giddings of Ohio. The resolution calling for repeal of the "gag rule" passed by a vote of 108–80.

1845

Frederick Douglass published the *Narrative of the Life of Frederick Douglass: An American Slave.* The autobiographical slave narrative included a preface written by William Lloyd Garrison and a supporting letter by Wendell Phillips.

Les Cenelles, the first anthology of African American verse, was published. Several of the poems included were written by Camille Thierry, a New Orleans Creole.

In the state of New York, the Democratic Party found itself divided over the question of slavery, and two factions formed to run slates of candidates for statewide office. The "Barnburners" were considered the more radical antislavery wing of the party, and the "Hunkers" were the more traditional Cotton Democrats who did not share antislavery sentiments. The "Barnburners" would eventually leave the Democratic Party and join the Free Soil Party because of their views on slavery.

On March 3, Florida was admitted to the Union as a slave state. At this point the United States consisted of twenty-seven states, of which thirteen were free and fourteen were slave. This was the second time in the nation's history that the number of slave states surpassed the number of free states.

After years of contention, and especially the efforts of Congressman John Quincy Adams of Massachusetts, the Congress rescinded the so-called gag rule that had prohibited the discussion of antislavery petitions in the Congress.

On December 29, Texas was admitted to the Union as a slave state. At this point the United States consisted of twenty-eight states, of which thirteen were free and fifteen were slave. The imbalance between the number of slave and free states caused many antislavery supporters to ponder the fate of the nation as new territories prepared for statehood.

Free blacks in the New England region organized the Freedom Association. The purpose of this group was to assist fugitive slaves in their efforts to escape from the southern states and find freedom in the North.

1846

On January 16, in Lynn, Massachusetts, a convention of New England workingmen adopted an antislavery resolution and urged their elected representatives to continue the fight against slavery until abolition had been achieved.

Many workers in the North felt a particular kinship with the slaves of the antebellum South. On January 23, the labor newspaper *Voice of Industry* published a poem entitled "What it is to be a Slave."

On August 8, Democratic Congressman David Wilmot of Pennsylvania introduced the Wilmot Proviso, which proposed that slavery should be excluded from any territory that might be acquired from the war with Mexico. Wilmot borrowed part of the language in his Proviso from the Northwest Ordinance of 1787, which stated that "neither slavery nor involuntary servitude shall ever exist in any part of" the territory that the United States might acquire from the war with Mexico. Since the Mexican government had abolished slavery in 1829, many feared the message that the United States would send with the possible reintroduction of slavery into free territory. The Senate defeated the Proviso, but the measure would reappear before the Congress many times over before the beginning of the Civil War. Votes on this measure did not follow a party line, but rather were based on a clear geographical delineation between northern and southern representatives. (For more on the Northwest Ordinance of 1787, see Document 32.)

Antislavery supporters in Great Britain pay £150 ($711) to purchase the freedom of Frederick Douglass. After Douglass had gained celebrity as an abolitionist lecturer, his former owner had sought to have him returned under the terms of the Fugitive Slave Act of 1793. With the purchase of his freedom, Douglass was legally free when he returned to the United States after conducting a successful lecture tour in England and Scotland.

Reverend Moses Dickson and eleven other free black leaders met in St. Louis, Missouri, and organized the Knights of Liberty. The purpose of the secret militant group was to gain a national following that would make the violent overthrow of slavery a real possibility. A decade later the organization claimed to have 47,240 members.

In Louisiana, the multiple-effect vacuum evaporation process for processing sugar was patented by Norbert Rillieux, a mulatto. This process would revolutionize the sugar industry by creating a more efficient means of processing refined sugar from cane juice.

1847

William Wells Brown published the *Narrative of William W. Brown, a Fugitive Slave, Written by Himself.* It was one of the few slave narratives that was written by the subject and not dictated to white abolitionists. The book quickly became a best-seller.

Antislavery advocate Gamaliel Bailey became the editor of the *National Era,* the weekly newspaper published by the American and Foreign Anti-Slavery Society. It was Bailey's *National Era* that would begin publication of Harriet Beecher Stowe's *Uncle Tom's Cabin* in serial form in 1851.

Free blacks constituted a sizable and somewhat affluent segment of Philadelphia's population. The collective taxable income of all free blacks in that city was estimated at four hundred thousand dollars.

New York abolitionist Gerrit Smith attempted to form a community of free black farmers by dividing his sizable landholdings in New York and making the lands available to prospective black farmers. Unfortunately, the poor quality of the land and the inability of black farmers to afford such a purchase reduced the effectiveness of this experimental community.

New York voters defeated an amendment to the state constitution that would have granted the suffrage to free blacks within the state of New York.

On January 16, the United States House of Repre-

sentatives passed the Oregon Bill, which excluded slavery from the Oregon Territory on the basis of the Northwest Ordinance of 1787. On March 3, 1847, the Senate would table the measure. (For more on the Northwest Ordinance of 1787, see Document 32).

On February 19, the United States Senate approved passage of the army appropriations bill after defeating the Wilmot Proviso, which had been attached as an amendment. During the debates on this matter, South Carolina senator John C. Calhoun made an impassioned argument that it was the duty of the Congress to protect slavery. Calhoun used the property rights argument to suggest that Congress had no right to limit the expansion of slavery into any state or territory. Essentially, Calhoun's arguments questioned the legality of measures like the Missouri Compromise of 1820. Even though the Senate did not endorse Calhoun's position, one decade later the Supreme Court would decide the case of *Dred Scott v. Sandford* (1857) and state the same basic positions that Calhoun supported in 1847.

On June 30, in St. Louis, Missouri, the slave Dred Scott filed the initial lawsuit seeking his freedom in the Circuit Court of St. Louis. This case would travel through several judicial venues through the following decade. Eventually, in 1857, the United States Supreme Court would decide the case of *Dred Scott v. Sandford.*

On July 26, Liberian president Joseph Jenkins Roberts, who had been born a free black in Petersburg, Virginia, declared the West African nation of Liberia to be an independent republic.

In November, the Liberty Party held a convention in New York City and nominated John P. Hale of New Hampshire as the party's candidate for president and Leicester King of Ohio was nominated for the office of vice president. Hale would later decline the nomination of the party in deference to former President Martin Van Buren when the Liberty Party merged with the Free Soil Party in 1848.

On December 3, Frederick Douglass and Martin Delany started publishing the *North Star,* an antislavery newspaper, in Rochester, New York. This abolitionist newspaper opposed the methods and strategies that William Lloyd Garrison and Wendell Phillips advocated.

On December 14, the concept of popular sovereignty as a possible solution to the question of slavery's expansion into the western territories first entered the national political vocabulary. New York Senator Daniel S. Dickinson, a Democrat, introduced a resolution that would have allowed territorial legislatures to determine whether or not slavery would be permitted in each respective territory.

On December 29, Michigan Senator Lewis Cass, a Democrat who intended to seek his party's nomination for president in 1848, lent his support to the idea of popular sovereignty that New York Senator Daniel S. Dickinson had proposed two weeks earlier. In a letter written to Alfred O. P. Nicholson, a Tennessee politician, Cass argued that the question of reaching a decision regarding slavery in the territories should be left up to the territorial legislatures. The idea received serious consideration in national political discourse, and it would be employed later as part of the Kansas-Nebraska Bill (1854). Many politicians were attracted to the idea of popular sovereignty because it allowed them to avoid the moral and legal implications of any decision regarding slavery since they turned the issue over to the will of the majority.

1848

Abolitionists Frederick Douglass and John Brown met for the first time in Springfield, Massachusetts.

Captains Daniel Drayton and Edward Sayres who operated the *Pearl,* a small coastal vessel, attempted to transport seventy-six slaves, valued at $100,000, from Washington, D.C., to freedom in the northern states. The vessel was seized in Chesapeake Bay, and Drayton and Sayres were arrested and charged with attempted slave stealing. The two men were convicted and were sentenced to prison time in Maryland.

June 2, in Rochester, New York, an abolitionist organization called the Liberty League held a national convention and nominated a slate of antislavery candidates for national office. The group nominated Gerrit Smith of New York for president and Charles E. Foot of Michigan for vice president.

On July 27, the United States Senate approved the Clayton Compromise, named after Senator John M. Clayton, a national Republican from Delaware. The measure proposed that slavery be excluded from Oregon, that any legislation regarding slavery by the territories of California and New Mexico be prohibited, and that the Supreme Court hear the appeal of all territorial slave cases. The measure was tabled by the House of Representatives the day after it was approved by the Senate.

On August 9 and 10, a coalition that included various abolitionists and Conscience Whigs gathered in Buffalo, New York, to organize the Free Soil Party. Several black abolitionists took part in this gathering. The antislavery party nominated Martin Van Buren for president and Charles Frances Adams for vice president. The phrase "free soil, free speech, free labor, and free men" was adopted as the campaign slogan of the Free Soil Party.

On August 14, President James K. Polk signed the bill that established the Oregon Territory without slavery. Southern political leaders did not challenge this point as they were willing to have a free Oregon with the implied understanding that other western territories would be open to the possible expansion of slavery.

The legislature of the state of Vermont supported a resolution calling for the prohibition of slavery in the western territories and its outright abolition in the District of Columbia. The measure was nonbinding and largely symbolic, but it reflected the growing spirit of the free soil position in American national life.

Virginia enacted a law requiring postmasters to inform the local police whenever any proabolition literature arrived at a post office within the state. The law further stipulated that this literature must be surrendered to state authorities who would burn the materials.

The legislature of the state of Alabama supported a resolution calling upon the Congress to do its duty and protect the rights of all people and their property in the western territories.

On December 22 in Washington, D.C., a group of southern congressmen held a caucus to discuss the slavery question and to determine a strategy that could be used to protect slaveholders' rights.

On December 26, in one of the most dramatic slave escapes of the antebellum era, William and Ellen Craft made their way from slavery in Georgia to freedom in Philadelphia. Ellen impersonated a white slaveowner who was traveling north to seek medical treatment, and William acted as his "master's" trusty servant. The Crafts lived in England for a number of years before returning to the United States in 1868. While in England, they published their story in the book *Running a Thousand Miles for Freedom; or The Escape of William and Ellen Craft from Slavery* (1860).

Black abolitionist Henry Highland Garnet published *The Past and Present Condition and the Destiny of the Colored Race.*

Southern "fire-eater" William Lowndes Yancey of Alabama drafted the Alabama Platform, a proslavery missive that was created to counter the arguments supporting the Wilmot Proviso. Yancey believed that it was the duty of the national government to protect the life and property, including slaves, of all citizens who lived in the western territories. Several other southern states adopted the stand enunciated by Yancey's Alabama Platform.

From January 10 to January 13, the Connecticut State Convention of Negroes was held in New Haven,

Connecticut. During this time, the Ohio State Convention of Negroes was also held in Columbus, Ohio.

On March 10, the state legislature in Missouri approved of a resolution that declared that "the right to prohibit slavery in any territory belongs exclusively to the people thereof." The language of this measure indicated support for the concept of popular sovereignty.

Between March 29 and March 30, the Virginia slave Henry "Box" Brown found an ingenious way to obtain his emancipation. He hid himself in a box that was mailed to abolitionists in Philadelphia. Two years later, Brown told his story in his *Narrative of the Life of Henry Box Brown*.

During the summer of 1849, Harriet Tubman escaped from slavery in Maryland. After her escape she became active in the so-called Underground Railroad that helped fugitive slaves make their way to freedom in the northern states, and eventually to Canada. Tubman was reported to have made nineteen trips back into the states of the Upper South in which she helped more than three hundred slaves escape to freedom. For this heroic action she became known as the "Moses" of her people.

Between September 1 and October 13 in Monterey, California, a statehood convention was called by Territorial Governor Bennett Riley. Without waiting for congressional sanction to begin the statehood process, the gathering created a state constitution that prohibited slavery, and the measure was approved by California voters on November 13.

In November, Massachusetts attorney Charles Sumner broke new ground by introducing the legal concept of equal protection under the law in a racial controversy in the case *Sarah C. Roberts v. the City of Boston*. This foundational legal principle would later be introduced into the United States Constitution with passage of the Fourteenth Amendment after the Civil War. In this case, Benjamin Roberts had filed the first school integration lawsuit on behalf of his daughter Sarah who had been denied admission to a white school. The Massachusetts Supreme Court rejected the lawsuit and established the controversial "separate but equal" precedent that would later reappear in the case of *Plessy v. Ferguson* (1896).

On December 4, President Zachary Taylor recommended that the Congress accept California's request to join the Union as a free state. There was considerable opposition to this action by southern politicians who did not desire to create another free state, which would upset the delicate political balance between northern and southern states. The level of political bickering caused by this debate is reflected in the difficulty the Congress encountered in choosing a new speaker. After sixty-three ballots and three weeks of debate, Georgia congressman Howell Cobb was selected as speaker of the House of Representatives.

James William Charles Pennington, an American fugitive slave who became a noted black abolitionist, published *The Fugitive Blacksmith* in London. Pennington hoped that his autobiographical narrative would help to expose the true horrors of slavery as it existed in the United States.

The Wisconsin state legislature enacted a statute that disenfranchised free blacks within the state.

1850

On January 29, dismayed by the rhetoric of extremists on both sides of the slavery issue, Senator Henry Clay began work on obtaining passage of a series of resolutions that would become known collectively as the Compromise of 1850. It was Clay's wish that the Union be preserved, and he believed that the give-and-take of good-faith compromise was the only way to achieve this end.

From February 5 to February 6, in his last great speech before the United States Senate, Henry Clay argued that the Senate should enact the compromise measures that he had proposed as a means of preserving the Union, which was so threatened by sectional discord. Extremists from both sides of the issue questioned Clay's actions and motives. New York senator William Seward declared that "there is a higher law than the Constitution which regulates our authority," and South Carolina Senator John C. Calhoun, near the end of his life, said that abolitionists in the North must "cease the agitation of the slavery question."

On March 7, sensing the extreme levels of discontent in the preceding debate, Senator Daniel Webster offered his support of Senator Henry Clay's efforts to enact the series of compromise resolutions that eventually became law as the Compromise of 1850. In a speech to the Senate, Webster supported the provisions of the Fugitive Slave Bill, which to many northern lawmakers was the most odious part of Clay's package. The poet John Greenleaf Whittier would later immortalize Webster's "fall" in the poem "Ichabod." Whittier wrote:

> *"All else is gone from those great eyes*
> *The soul has fled;*
> *When faith is lost when honor dies*
> *The man is dead."*

During the contentious debates associated with passage of the Compromise of 1850, Senator Henry Clay remarked, "I would rather be right than be president."

On May 8, a Senate committee composed of seven Whigs and six Democrats worked with the series of resolutions that Henry Clay had introduced to the Senate in January. The committee refined the measures into two bills: the first, an Omnibus Bill that affected slavery in the western territories, and the second, a bill that would outlaw the slave trade in the District of Columbia.

In June, debate over Henry Clay's compromise resolutions dominated the affairs of the Congress. In an impassioned speech in the House of Representatives, Georgia congressman Robert A. Toombs used a classical allusion and likened himself to Hamilcar, the father of the Carthaginian general Hannibal, a mortal enemy of Rome. Toombs warned his northern colleagues, "I will . . . bring my children and my constituents to the altar of liberty, and like Hamilcar I would swear them to eternal hostility to your foul domination."

From June 3 to June 12, the Nashville Convention was held as delegates from nine southern states met in Nashville, Tennessee, to discuss the issues of slavery and states' rights. Some of the most radical delegates, the so-called fire-eaters favored immediate secession as the only means of preserving southern traditions and rights, but the moderates prevailed at this meeting. Delegates approved of several resolutions including one that would have extended the Missouri Compromise line of 36°30' north latitude all the way across the western territories to the Pacific Ocean.

On August 2, the Underground Railroad had been operational for nearly two decades as antislavery supporters in the northern states assisted fugitives who made their escape from slavery in the South. Unfortunately, there are no accurate numbers of how many fugitives were assisted by this method. The black abolitionist William Still, who was an active "conductor" on the Underground Railroad, began keeping statistical records of how many fugitives escaped from this date onward. The passenger records that remain are some of the best source materials available for determining the effectiveness of the Underground Railroad. Many white abolitionists, like John and Hannah Pierce Cox of Pennsylvania, were actively involved in the Underground Railroad.

Between September 9 and September 12, the Compromise of 1850 admitted California to the Union as a free state; adjusted the borders of Texas; established the territories of Utah and New Mexico with the understanding that popular sovereignty would decide the fate of slavery in those regions; prohibited the slave trade, but not slavery, in the District of Columbia; and

provided for the passage of a newer and stronger Fugitive Slave Law. As a result of the New Fugitive Slave Law, thousands of fugitive slaves in the northern states would cross the international boundary and enter Canada.

In New York City, a group of black and white abolitionists rushed into a courtroom to rescue James Hamlet, a fugitive slave.

The Seventh Census of the United States revealed that 37 percent of the free black population was identified as mulatto. Also, the entire black population, slave and free, was 3,638,808 persons, or 15.7 percent of the national population.

Samuel R. Ward became the first president of the American League of Colored Laborers. This organization was a union of skilled black workers who sought to encourage free black artisans to develop black-owned businesses.

Vermont became the first state to enact a Personal Liberty Law, which was designed to circumvent enforcement of the federal Fugitive Slave Law that had been recently enacted.

On October 21, the City Council in Chicago, Illinois, passed a resolution criticizing recent congressional approval of the Fugitive Slave Law as part of the Compromise of 1850.

On October 25, the Southern Rights Association was established to provide united opposition to all antislavery efforts mounted by abolitionist groups.

From November 11 to November 15, southern delegates held a second Nashville Convention and again considered the possibility of seceding from the Union.

From December 13 to December 14, in Georgia a state convention declared the intention of the state of Georgia to remain in the Union, but warned that this action was contingent on the northern state's willingness to enforce all of the measures recently enacted in the Compromise of 1850, especially the new federal Fugitive Slave Law.

1851

On February 15, a group of black abolitionists rushed into a Boston, Massachusetts, courtroom in order to rescue the fugitive slave Shadrach.

From May 7 to May 9, Frederick Douglass and William Lloyd Garrison split over disagreements concerning the tactics and strategies to be employed in the antislavery movement during the eighteenth annual meeting of the American Anti-Slavery Society. It was the issue of moral force versus political force that caused this rift.

On May 28, black abolitionist, and former slave, Sojourner Truth (born Isabella Baumfree) attended a Women's Rights Convention in Akron, Ohio. Her presence at the gathering helped to demonstrate the illogical underpinnings of sex discrimination as she compared these views to the racism that justified slavery. In her own eloquent style, Truth's declaration that "ar'n't I a woman" became a powerful testimony to the twin evils of racism and sexism in American society.

On June 5, *The National Era,* a Washington-based abolitionist newspaper, began publishing a story called "Uncle Tom's Cabin" by Harriet Beecher Stowe in serial form.

On September 11, in the so-called Christiana Riot, a group of free blacks and antislavery whites dispersed a party of slave catchers at Christiana, Pennsylvania. In the melee, one white man was killed and another was wounded. This episode represents the heightened levels of passion that were caused by passage of the new Fugitive Slave Law. The Christiana Riot was the most violent instance of civil disobedience and outright resistance to this unpopular legislation.

On October 1, in Syracuse, New York, a group of black and white abolitionists rushed into a courtroom to rescue Jerry M'Henry, a fugitive slave.

On December 1, the results of the recent congressional elections indicated that southerners approved of the Compromise of 1850. In several of the southern states, Unionists were elected to office over more radical "fire-eaters" who supported secession. In the northern states, the opposite effect seemed to have been working. The state of Massachusetts elected the abolitionist Charles Sumner to the United States Senate.

A group of black abolitionists rushed into a Baltimore, Maryland, courtroom in order to rescue the fugitive slave Rachel Parker.

The United States Supreme Court decided the case of *Strader v. Graham.* In their decision the justices declared that three slaves who had returned to Kentucky after visiting Indiana and Ohio were to be governed by the laws of Kentucky. In what was viewed as a proslavery ruling, the court maintained that it was the states themselves that determined the status of all persons living within their respective jurisdictions.

Services of Colored Americans in the Wars of 1776 and 1812 was published by the abolitionist William C. Nell. This work is considered to be the first extended study on the history of African Americans.

In Boston, Massachusetts, Thomas Sims, a fugitive slave who had been captured, was returned to his owner in Georgia. Abolitionists had considered an attempt to rescue Simms by force, but were unable to carry out such a plan.

The Colored Man's Journal, an antislavery newspaper operated by free blacks, began publication in New York City.

The Virginia legislature enacted a measure requiring free blacks who had been recently manumitted to leave the state within one year of their emancipation or else face the possibility of renewed enslavement in Virginia.

1852

On January 28, during a speech that he delivered before the Massachusetts Anti-Slavery Society, abolitionist Wendell Phillips first spoke the oft-quoted phrase, "Eternal vigilance is the price of liberty."

On March 20, the first edition of *Uncle Tom's Cabin, or Life Among the Lowly* was published by Harriet Beecher Stowe. This work offered a moving account of the brutality of the institution of slavery in its many forms. The work was considered to be a literary classic in the nineteenth century, and it was one of the seminal works that influenced American attitudes about the institution and practice of slavery in national life. The story had first been published in serial form in 1851 by the *National Era,* but in its first year of publication as a novel more than 1 million copies had been sold.

On July 4 in Rochester, New York, city officials invited Frederick Douglass, the city's most famous resident, to deliver an oration to commemorate the nation's independence. Douglas delivered his "What to the Slave is the Fourth of July?" speech. In this address, Douglas noted "To him your celebration a sham; your boasted liberty an unholy license, your national greatness, swelling vanity; your sounds of rejoicing are empty and heartless; your denunciation of tyrants, brass-fronted impudence; your shouts of liberty and equality, hollow mockery; your prayers and hymns, your sermons and thanksgivings, with all your religious parade and solemnity, are to him mere bombast, fraud, deception, impiety, and hypocrisy—a thin veil to cover up crimes which would disgrace a nation of savages."

On August 11, the Free Soil Party held its first national convention in Pittsburgh, Pennsylvania, and nominated John P. Hale of New Hampshire for president with George W. Julian of Indiana as the vice presidential candidate. The party platform condemned slavery and decried the recent enactment of the Compromise of 1850 by stating that "Slavery is a sin against God and a crime against man."

On September 27, in Troy, New York, a dramatic version of *Uncle Tom's Cabin* was performed for the first time by George L. Aiken, an actor and playwright. The performance was judged to be a huge success, and the play ran for 100 nights.

On October 26, abolitionist Senator Charles Sumner of Massachusetts delivered a four-hour speech in the Senate chamber during which he chastised the Congress for passing the Fugitive Slave Law as part of the Compromise of 1850.

"The Pro-Slavery Argument" was published by a group of southern apologists including William Harper, Thomas R. Dew, and James Henry Hammond. This work contained a collection of essays, including many th0at had been previously published, that used a wide range of theoretical justification based on biblical and classical sources to defend the institution of slavery as it existed in the American South.

The Missouri Supreme Court decided the case of *Scott v. Emerson*. In their decision the justices declared that Dred Scott was a slave. This decision reversed Missouri precedents that had been in place since the *Winny v. Whitesides* (1824) decision.

In response to the passage of the Fugitive Slave Law, the black abolitionist Martin Delany published *The Condition, Elevation, Emigration, and Destiny of the Colored People of the United States Politically Considered*.

Sojourner Truth (Isabella Baumfree) spoke before a gathering of the National Women's Suffrage Convention that met in Akron, Ohio.

A total of thirty-five hundred free blacks were living in Cincinnati, Ohio. Among this group, 200 were identified as prosperous property owners who had an aggregate wealth of $500,000. Despite this, free blacks were often the targets of violent episodes in Cincinnati that were racially motivated.

tioned the state legislature for permission to join the state militia.

Clotel; or, The President's Daughter: a Narrative of Slave Life in the United States, the first novel to be written by an African American author, was published in London by William Wells Brown. The story was based loosely on the rumored affair between Thomas Jefferson and his slave, Sally Hemings.

Frederick Douglass published the short story "The Heroic Slave." The story was based on the exploits of Madison Washington who had participated in the seizure of the slave ship *Creole* in 1841 when it was traveling from Virginia to Louisiana. The slaves on board the vessel sailed the *Creole* to the Bahamas where they gained their freedom.

James Dyson, an Englishman who ran a school in New Orleans, was arrested and charged with conspiracy for trying to organize a slave insurrection.

Growing nationwide support became visible for a large-scale campaign to deport free blacks to colonial settlements on the coast of West Africa. In Virginia, a poll tax was imposed on free blacks in order to generate funds to support such a project. The *New York Herald* supported the idea of emigration and stated that "racial inferiority" makes such a program desirable.

In December, by the end of 1853, Harriet Beecher Stowe had sold more than 1.2 million copies of *Uncle Tom's Cabin*. The book was criticized by many who claimed that Stowe had exaggerated the true condition of slaves in the South in order to create a sympathetic antislavery propaganda tract. Stowe responded to her critics by publishing the *Key to Uncle Tom's Cabin* in which she defended her work and outlined the factual basis upon which the novel was written.

1853

In January, Solomon Northup, a free black who had been illegally kidnapped and held as a slave for twelve years, was freed from his enslavement in Louisiana after an extended campaign on his behalf was conducted by northern abolitionists. In March, Northup would publish his story in the book, *Twelve Years a Slave*.

From July 6 to July 8, the National Council of Colored People was founded in Rochester, New York. This organization was established by delegates from several states who wished to encourage the mechanical training of blacks. The group grew out of the Negro Convention Movement, which had been active in several states for more than a decade.

On August 1, free blacks in Massachusetts peti-

1854

On January 1, the Ashmum Institute was founded at Oxford in Chester County, Pennsylvania. Known today as Lincoln University, it was the first black college to be established in the United States.

On January 16, as the Congress debated the merits of the Kansas-Nebraska Act, Senator Archibald Dixon, a Kentucky Whig, introduced a resolution that would have repealed the Missouri Compromise of 1820, which had established the line of 36°30' north latitude as the boundary between potential slave and free territory in the Louisiana Purchase lands. The following day, Massachusetts senator Charles Sumner introduced a resolution that reaffirmed the Missouri Compromise.

On January 24, six prominent abolitionists from the

northern states signed their names to a document entitled "The Appeal of the Independent Democrats in Congress, to the People of the United States." The document was allegedly written by Salmon P. Chase of Ohio, and it was signed by Charles Sumner of Massachusetts, Joshua Giddings of Ohio, Gerrit Smith of New York, Edward Wade of Ohio, and Alexander De Witt of Massachusetts. The manifesto voiced strong opposition to the Kansas-Nebraska Act, which it described as a plot by slaveholders. It is credited as having galvanized public sentiment in favor of creating the Republican Party.

On February 28, in response to the political discord caused by debates over the proposed Kansas-Nebraska Bill, a group of fifty disillusioned Whigs, Free Soilers, and northern Democrats held a preliminary meeting in Ripon, Wisconsin, to discuss the possibility of creating a new political party that was opposed to the expansion of slavery into the western territories. This meeting represents the earliest beginnings of the Republican Party.

On April 26, in Worcester, Massachusetts, abolitionist Eli Thayer established the Massachusetts Emigrant Aid Society. The purpose of this organization was to send at least 2,000 free blacks and antislavery supporters to Kansas in order to prevent the territory from becoming an area open to slavery. In 1855, the organization changed its name to the New England Emigrant Aid Company. Under its auspices, many free soil communities were established in Kansas.

On May 24 in Boston, a United States deputy marshal arrested the fugitive slave Anthony Burns and began the process of returning him to his owner in the South as stipulated by the Fugitive Slave Act (1850). Black and white abolitionists, including Wendell Phillips, rallied to the cause of supporting Burns, but were unable to prevent his extradition. Burns's owner in Virginia had rejected an offer by northern abolitionists to purchase Burns for $1,200 in order to set him free.

On May 30, with the support of Illinois senator Stephen A. Douglas, Congress passed the Kansas-Nebraska Act. This measure repealed the clause in the Missouri Compromise (1820) that prohibited slavery in the territories north of 36°30' and instead allowed popular sovereignty to determine the status of slavery in those regions. The measure was responsible in large part for the founding of the Republican Party, which opposed the expansion of slavery into any of the western territories.

On June 3, the United States government spent $100,000 to return one fugitive slave to the South. In Boston, hundreds of state militia and two thousand federal troops were required to maintain order as the fugitive slave Anthony Burns was escorted from his jail cell through the streets of Boston to Long Wharf to be returned to his owner in Virginia. It was estimated that fifty thousand Bostonians lined the streets in protest as this event occurred. During the dramatic march to the dock, Boston church bells tolled and buildings along the route were draped in black. One year later, Boston abolitionists were able to purchase Burns from his owner, thereby granting Burns the freedom that had eluded him in the Massachusetts courts. The citizens of Massachusetts were so aroused by this unpleasant episode that the state of Massachusetts never again returned another fugitive slave to the South.

Sociology for the South; or, The Failure of Free Society was published by George Fitzhugh, a southern apologist.

William Grayson published "The Hireling and the Slave" in an effort to counter Harriet Beecher Stowe's dark portrayal of southern life in *Uncle Tom's Cabin.* Grayson's long, didactic poem tried to contrast the benefits of the slave's ideal life in the South with the wretched conditions experienced by "wage slaves" in the industrial North.

On July 6, in response to the political discord caused by passage of the Kansas-Nebraska Act, a group of disillusioned Whigs, Free Soilers, and northern Democrats met in Jackson, Michigan, and formed the Republican Party.

On July 19, the Wisconsin State Supreme Court decided the case of *In re Booth and Rycraft* as the Wisconsin jurists declared the Fugitive Slave Law of 1850 to be unconstitutional. Sherman Booth and John Rycraft, who had rescued the fugitive Joshua Glover from extradition back to slavery in the South, were ordered freed by the court. The case was appealed to the United States Supreme Court, and in the *Ableman v. Booth* (1859) decision, the federal court ruled that state courts did not have the authority to declare federal laws unconstitutional.

From August 24 to August 26, the Negro Emancipation Convention was held in Cleveland, Ohio. The gathering was attended by delegates from eleven states.

In October, Abraham Lincoln made his first public statement on slavery in a speech given in Peoria, Illinois. Lincoln stated that he opposed the extension of slavery into the western territories.

On October 18, American diplomats Pierre Soulé (minister to Spain), John Y. Mason (minister to France), and James Buchanan (minister to Great Britain) met in Ostend, Belgium, to discuss a strategy that the United States might follow in order to purchase Cuba from Spain or to seize it by force if necessary. The Ostend Manifesto was the confidential diplomatic dispatch, written primarily by Soulé, which proposed that the United States offer the Spanish government no more than $120 million for Cuba, and that, should Spain reject that offer, the United States should take the island by force. The document was made public by enemies of President Franklin Pierce who wanted to discredit the proslavery Pierce administration. Expansionists, who tended to be proslavery supporters, hoped that Cuba might be used to form two additional slave states.

On November 19, after an estimated sixteen hundred "Border Ruffians" crossed from Missouri into Kansas to influence an election by voting for a proslavery candidate, J.W. Whitfield was elected to be the Kansas Territory's representative to the Congress. This event established the pattern for subsequent elections in the Kansas Territory that would be fraught with intimidation and fraud. It was in this setting that Kansas would use the system of popular sovereignty to settle the slavery question.

Sociology for the South was published by George Fitzhugh, a southern proslavery polemicist. The work contained a series of proslavery newspaper articles that Fitzhugh had previously published in the *Richmond Examiner.*

Connecticut and Rhode Island each enacted personal liberty laws, which were designed to circumvent enforcement of the federal Fugitive Slave Law of 1850.

1855

My Bondage and My Freedom was published by Frederick Douglass. In this autobiographical account, Douglass described himself as a self-proclaimed graduate of the institution of slavery.

Frederick Douglass was nominated by the antislavery-based Liberty Party as a candidate for secretary of state in New York. Douglass became the first black to be nominated for a statewide office in the United States.

William Wells Brown published *The American Fugitive in Europe: Sketches of Places and People Abroad.* The work was an account of Brown's travels as a publicist for the antislavery cause.

The legislatures of Maine, Massachusetts, and Michigan all enacted personal liberty laws, which prohibited state officials from assisting in the capture or return of fugitive slaves who might be found within their borders. These measures polarized northern-southern attitudes as they were designed specifically to have state officials circumvent the mission and purpose of the Fugitive Slave Law of 1850 by failing to assist federal marshals in enforcing a federal law.

John Mercer Langston, who had been born a slave on a Virginia plantation, became the first African American to win elective office in the United States. He was elected clerk of Brownhelm Township in Lorain County, Ohio. Langston later served in the Freedmen's Bureau, as the first dean of the Howard University Law School, and as United States minister to Haiti.

On January 9, the United States and Great Britain finally agreed to a monetary settlement in regard to the *Creole* incident of 1841. The British had freed a shipload of slaves who mutinied at sea and found refuge in the Bahamas. For years the British action had caused a diplomatic rift between the two nations. Joshua Bates, an American-born British banker, negotiated a settlement between representatives of the two nations in which the British government agreed to compensate $119,330 in damages to the owners of the slaves who were emancipated by Bahamian authorities in 1841.

On February 6, Eureka College was chartered after a group of Kentucky abolitionists moved to central Illinois and established an educational institution in the hope of continuing the antislavery struggle.

On March 30, the first territorial elections were held in the Kansas Territory. A group estimated at five thousand "Border Ruffians" entered Kansas from Missouri and forced the election of a proslavery legislature in an election that was wracked by fraud. There were many more votes cast than there were eligible voters in the territory. Despite these irregularities, Territorial governor Andrew H. Reeder allowed the election results to stand because he feared that an escalation of violence would occur if he failed to do so.

On April 28, the Massachusetts legislature abolished racial segregation in all Massachusetts public schools, and integration proceeded without incident.

On July 2 in Pawnee, Kansas, the new proslavery territorial legislature met and enacted a series of measures that protected slavery in Kansas. The proslavery majority within the legislature went so far as to expel the antislavery faction ("jayhawkers") that had been elected in the spring.

On July 31, President Franklin Pierce ordered the removal of Andrew H. Reeder as territorial governor in the Kansas Territory. Pierce cited a conflict of interest as his reason for making the change because Reeder was speculating in Kansas lands, but in reality, Reeder's greatest offense to President Pierce was that he did not support the proslavery legislature that had been elected in March 1855. Pierce replaced Reeder with Wilson Shannon, a proslavery supporter from Ohio.

On August 4, in Lawrence, Kansas, a free soil community that had been founded by the New England Emigrant Aid Company, a group of antislavery supporters ("jayhawkers") gathered together to call for their own constitutional convention since the sitting proslavery legislature had come to power through election fraud.

On September 5, a convention was held at Big Springs, Kansas, in which antislavery supporters ("jayhawkers") repudiated the results of the fraudulent elections that had been held on March 30. The jayhawkers formed the free state forces and soon started to receive shipments of arms from the northern states. John Brown eventually arrived in Kansas and became a leader of the free state forces.

On October 1, J.W. Whitfield was again elected as the Kansas Territory's representative to Congress as proslavery men in Kansas and "Border Ruffians" from Missouri manipulated the balloting. In response to this fraud, the jayhawkers of Kansas held their own balloting on October 9 and elected former territorial governor Andrew H. Reeder as the territory's representative to the Congress. In Washington, D.C., faced with representatives elected from each side in the Kansas dispute, the Congress refused to seat either Whitfield or Reeder.

From October 23 and November 12 in the Kansas Territory, free state forces drafted the Topeka Constitution, which outlawed slavery and elected a governor and legislature supportive of this position. The Topeka Constitution also included a curious provision that barred all blacks from Kansas. For nearly two years the Kansas Territory would operate with two governments: a proslavery government seated at Lecompton and an antislavery government seated at Topeka. The political repercussions of "Bleeding Kansas" would also force battle lines to form in the Congress as the rhetoric over this situation intensified.

From November 20 to November 22, the first California Negro Convention was held in Sacramento, California.

Between November 26 and December 7, in the Kansas Territory, the Wakarusa War erupted as a group of 1,500 "Border Ruffians" from Missouri entered Kansas and fought a series of skirmishes with antislavery groups in the Wakarusa River region. The "Border Ruffians" had intended to attack the community of Lawrence, but refrained from doing so when they learned that the town was well-defended. The fighting diminished when Territorial Governor Wilson Shannon intervened and sent the territorial militia into the affected region.

On December 15, free soil supporters in the Kansas Territory held a referendum and approved the Topeka Constitution, which outlawed slavery in Kansas and also prohibited blacks from the region as well.

In Ohio, abolitionist senator Salmon P. Chase was elected governor of Ohio. Many within the Republican Party believed that Chase would make an excellent presidential candidate.

Peter H. Clark, a black abolitionist, began publishing *The Herald of Freedom,* an antislavery newspaper, in Ohio.

1856

David Christy published *Cotton Is King, or the Economical Relations of Slavery.* It was from this work that the popular expression "cotton is king" came into the national discourse.

On January 15, in the Kansas Territory free soil supporters elected Charles Robinson as their territorial governor, and they also elected an antislavery legislature. The free soil Kansans took this action in behalf of the Topeka Constitution, which they had ratified in a December 1855 referendum. In Washington, D.C., President Franklin Pierce looked upon the actions taken by the free soil Kansans as an act of rebellion against federal authority because the national government had already recognized the proslavery legislature that was elected in March 1855.

On January 24, Georgia senator Robert A. Toombs delivered a proslavery address at the Tremont Temple in Boston, Massachusetts.

On February 2, the polarization that the country faced regarding the issue of slavery was greatly exacerbated by the Kansas-Nebraska Act, and nowhere was this more apparent than in the United States Congress. It took the House of Representatives more than two months to decide on a speaker for that body. Eventually, Congressman Nathaniel P. Banks of Massachusetts was elected speaker of the House of Representatives.

On February 11, President Franklin Pierce, a northern doughface who supported the proslavery element in Kansas, issued a special proclamation to the residents of the Kansas Territory. Pierce called upon both the "Border Ruffians" and the free soil supporters to cease all hostilities in the territory.

On February 22, delegates from the Republican Party held their first national meeting in Pittsburgh, Pennsylvania.

On March 4, the free soil government in the Kansas Territory with its legislature seated at Topeka petitioned the United States Congress to admit Kansas to the Union as a free state. Even though the proposal was popular among many Republicans in the Congress, Illinois senator Stephen A. Douglas proposed a bill that would make Kansas statehood contingent on the promulgation of a new state constitution.

On April 5, Booker Taliafero Washington was born into slavery in Franklin County, Virginia.

On May 19, after delivering his "Crime Against Kansas" speech, Senator Charles Sumner of Massachusetts was savagely beaten with a cane by Congressman Preston Brooks of South Carolina. The attack took place in the Senate chamber of the United States Capitol, and Sumner would require three years of recuperation before he could return to his position in the Senate. The state of Massachusetts kept the position vacant for this period so that Sumner's empty chair in the Senate chamber remained a symbolic reminder of the attack. In his speech, Sumner had insulted the aged Senator Andrew Butler of South Carolina, the uncle of Congressman Brooks. Preston Brooks believed that his action in attacking Sumner was justified as he defended both the honor of his family and the interests of his state and region.

On May 21, a group of proslavery forces attacked and sacked the town of Lawrence, Kansas, which had acquired the reputation of being an abolitionist, free soil stronghold and was reputedly a station on the Underground Railroad. One antislavery supporter was killed in the attack. The radical abolitionist John Brown led a group of antislavery men ("jayhawkers") in a nighttime attack that killed five proslavery settlers at Pottawotamie Creek as retaliation for the attack on Lawrence. These episodes began the two-year long struggle that was known as "Bleeding Kansas." During the violent struggle over the issues of slavery and popular sovereignty, more than 200 Kansas settlers would die.

On June 2, an antislavery faction within the American Party (Know-Nothing Party) held its own nominating convention in New York City. At this meeting, John C. Frémont of California was nominated for the presidency, and W. F. Johnston of Pennsylvania was nominated for the vice presidency.

From June 17 to June 19, the Republican Party held its first national nominating convention. John C. Frémont was nominated as the first Republican candidate for the presidency, and William L. Dayton was nominated for vice president. Frémont ran on a platform that did not support the expansion of slavery into the western territories. The slogan "Free Soil, Free Speech, Free Men, Frémont" was used throughout the campaign. In November, Frémont would lose the election to the Democrat James Buchanan.

On July 3, although the House of Representatives voted to accept Kansas as a state with its Topeka Constitution, which prohibited slavery, the Senate rejected the measure. The question of Kansas statehood, and the nature of whether Kansas would become slave or free, remained undecided at the conclusion of the Thirty-fourth Congress.

On July 4, with the support of the administration of President Franklin Pierce, federal troops from Fort Leavenworth in the Kansas Territory were dispatched to Topeka to break up the free state legislature that was convened there. Since the national government had gone on record as recognizing the proslavery government in the Kansas Territory, President Pierce believed that the legislature that convened in Topeka represented a challenge to federal authority in the region.

In August, the Kansas Territory experienced the horror of civil war as the specter of "Bleeding Kansas" resulted in nearly 200 deaths and more than $2 million worth of property damage. During the struggle between proslavery and antislavery ("jayhawkers") forces, two different governments were seated simultaneously in the Kansas Territory, and the Congress refused to seat representatives from either government. The matter would not be completely resolved until October 1857.

On August 18, in the Kansas Territory Governor Wilson Shannon resigned his position and was replaced by John W. Geary.

On August 30, the Methodist Episcopal Church founded Wilberforce University in Ohio. The African Methodist Episcopal Church later purchased the university.

On September 15, in the Kansas Territory, Governor John W. Geary used federal troops to prevent an army of twenty-five hundred "Border Ruffians" from Missouri from marching into Kansas.

Free blacks in Ohio were granted the right to control their own schools.

The Knights of Liberty, a secret society of free blacks, claimed to have a membership of 47,240 throughout the country. The purpose of this secret militant group was to bring about the end of slavery through violent action.

Governor James H. Adams of South Carolina called for the reopening of the African slave trade, which had been illegal since 1808. Adams believed that South Carolina planters were having a difficult time obtaining sufficient numbers of slaves through the domestic slave trade, and he feared the economic implications that a shortage of slave laborers might mean to his state. Adams's apprehension seems to have been somewhat dubious, for according to census figures, slaves constituted 57.6 percent of South Carolina's population in 1850, and by 1860, slaves made up 57.2 percent of the state's population.

1857

Between January 12 and February 15, the Kansas Territory's proslavery legislature held a session in Lecompton, Kansas, and issued a call for a territorial census and a constitutional convention. Governor John W. Geary vetoed the measures, but the legislature overrode the governor's actions.

On January 15, delegates who favored the peaceful separation of the North and South met in Worcester, Massachusetts, at the State Disunion Convention. Abolitionist William Lloyd Garrison addressed the crowd that had gathered for the meeting, and, in an impassioned speech, he declared "No union with slaveholders!" This phrase became the slogan of the organization.

On March 6, the United States Supreme Court by a vote of seven to two decided the case of *Dred Scott v. Sandford* and declared that blacks were not citizens of the United States, but were property that had no right to sue for freedom in a court of law. In the words of Chief Justice Roger B. Taney, slaves had "no rights a white man need respect." The court also asserted that the Congress had no power to exclude slavery from any of the territories, thus in effect declaring the Missouri Compromise to be unconstitutional.

On May 1, the state of Massachusetts adopted a literacy test as a requirement for voting.

On May 26, Robert J. Walker of Mississippi was appointed governor of the Kansas Territory. The new governor pledged that he would make sure that any proposed state constitution that was offered to the voters would be presented in a fair election.

In June, by a very narrow margin the California state legislature defeated a proposal that would have prohibited the further immigration of free blacks into the state.

On October 5, in the Kansas Territory Governor Robert J. Walker supervised the elections to ensure that fraudulent votes were not cast. Frederick P. Stanton of Tennessee, who served as territorial secretary, saw to it that several thousand fraudulent proslavery ballots were rejected by election officials. When the votes were finally counted, the Free State Party had won a majority in both houses of the territorial legislature. The lingering struggle that "Bleeding Kansas" had endured demonstrated the difficulties that would arise if popular sovereignty became the means employed to settle the issue of slavery's expansion into the western territories.

From October 19 to November 8, proslavery forces in Kansas held a constitutional convention in Lecompton and drafted a document that legalized slavery in Kansas. Upon realizing that passage of this document was unlikely, delegates to the convention drafted a separate article on slavery that would be put before the voters in a referendum. Regardless of how the vote turned out on the slavery article, the constitution would still protect the institution in Kansas. Although Kansas territorial governor Robert J. Walker opposed the efforts of the delegates at Lecompton, President James Buchanan, who hoped to maintain a strained sense of unity within the Democratic Party, endorsed the work of the Lecompton Convention.

Legislators in Maine and New Hampshire granted freedom and citizenship to all persons of African descent who resided within their respective borders. This action represented further evidence of efforts by the northern states to negate the effects of the Fugitive Slave Law of 1850.

On December 21, when antislavery supporters ("jayhawkers") in the Kansas Territory refused to take part in the referendum on the proslavery Lecompton Constitution, the proslavery document was approved for the territory.

Hinton Rowan Helper of North Carolina, an abolitionist who despised blacks, published *The Impending Crisis of the South: How to Meet It*. Helper based his arguments on statistical information that he garnered from the Seventh Census of the United States taken in 1850. Helper asserted that slavery had caused great economic distress to the nonslaveholders and the poor whites of the South. He urged the South's poor whites to rise up and overthrow slavery, but he also advocated the deportation of freed blacks to Africa. Sixty-eight members of the House of Representatives endorsed Helper's book, most without having read it, and the Republican Party distributed 100,000 copies of it in the northern states. Once the book was published, it was banned in the southern states. Helper was considered a pariah in the region, and he was forced to flee to New York for his personal safety.

George Fitzhugh of Virginia, a noted proslavery polemicist, published *Cannibals All!: or, Slaves Without Masters*. In this work Fitzhugh presented the argument that northern "wage slaves" were essentially worse off than slave laborers in the South. Fitzhugh believed that the exploitative nature of industrial capitalism did not provide a system of economic security to northern workingmen that was similar to the benevolence found in the paternalistic institution of slavery that was found in the South. Fitzhugh lived until 1881, and in the years following the American Civil War he supported efforts to attract northern industry to the New South.

1858

On January 4 in the Kansas Territory, the Lecompton Constitution appeared on the ballot for a second time in a popular referendum. In a reversal of the initial vote, proslavery voters boycotted the election and the free soil supporters were able to defeat the measure.

On February 2, President James Buchanan urged the Congress to admit Kansas to the Union with the Lecompton Constitution that allowed slavery, even though Kansas voters rejected the document in January. Buchanan was criticized strongly by Illinois Senator Stephen A. Douglas who believed that the Lecompton Constitution did not represent the true wishes of Kansas voters as expressed through the system of popular sovereignty.

In February, the radical abolitionist John Brown, who was wanted by federal authorities for murder charges in the Kansas Territory, spent a month living in the home of Frederick Douglass in Rochester, New York. During this time, Brown began to develop the plan for his raid on the Harpers Ferry arsenal in Virginia.

On March 23, Illinois senator Stephen A. Douglas was unable to find the votes to block President James Buchanan's wishes, and the United States Senate voted to allow Kansas to enter the Union under the Lecompton Constitution, which permitted slavery, even though the free soil voters of Kansas had previously rejected this constitution. In the House of Representatives it was decided that the people of Kansas should be able to vote on this constitution once more through a third popular referendum. On April 1, the House of Representatives passed a resolution that required voters in the Kansas Territory to vote again on the Lecompton Constitution.

William Wells Brown published *The Escape; or, A Leap for Freedom*. It was the first play to be written by an African American. Brown had previously written an unpublished antislavery drama that he titled "Experience, or How to Give a Northern Man a Backbone."

On April 14, in California's most celebrated fugitive slave case, the Mississippi-born fugitive Archy Lee won the right to his freedom and then moved to Victoria, British Columbia. Several other fugitive slaves living in California also moved to British Columbia to avoid the possibility that California courts might be used to

try to return them to a condition of slavery in the southern states.

On May 4, in an effort to find a compromise that could settle the impasse on Kansas statehood, Indiana congressman William H. English proposed that the Congress provide statehood to Kansas in the event that voters there approved of the Lecompton Constitution. The Congress agreed to the compromise offered in the English Act.

On May 8, the American abolitionist John Brown held an antislavery convention in Chatham, Canada. Twelve whites and thirty-four blacks attended the gathering.

On June 16, Abraham Lincoln delivered the "House Divided" speech as he accepted the Republican Party's nomination for senator from Illinois. In the speech Lincoln declared, "A house divided against itself cannot stand. I believe this government cannot endure permanently half *slave* and half *free*. I do not expect the Union to be *dissolved*. I do not expect the house to *fall*, but I do expect it will cease to be divided."

On August 2, voters in Kansas rejected the Lecompton Constitution, and the territory became a free (nonslaveholding) territory. In rejecting this constitution and the stipulations attached in the English Act of May 4, Kansans turned away from the notion of immediate statehood, opting instead for an opportunity to keep the region free of slavery. Kansas did not enter the Union as a state until 1861, but it joined the Union as a free state.

Kansas and Wisconsin each enacted personal liberty laws, which were designed to circumvent enforcement of the federal Fugitive Slave Law of 1850.

From August 21 to October 15, Abraham Lincoln and Stephen A. Douglas conducted a series of seven debates in conjunction with the race for the United States Senate seat for Illinois. These debates were held in the communities of Ottawa (August 21), Freeport (August 27), Jonesboro (September 15), Charleston (September 18), Galesburg (October 7), Quincy (October 13), and Alton (October 15). During the debates Douglas made statements that alienated many of his southern supporters, thus making his chances of a successful presidential bid less likely. Lincoln used the debates to state his opposition to slavery, but he also declared his belief that it would be impossible to achieve racial equality in the United States.

In September in Wellington, Ohio, a group of several hundred Oberlin College students, led by one of their professors, local abolitionists, and free blacks rescued a fugitive slave named [Little] John Price and helped him to escape to Canada. This action was taken in direct violation of the Fugitive Slave Law of 1850.

The federal government brought charges against thirty-seven of the alleged rescuers in the Oberlin-Wellington cases.

On September 25, New York senator William H. Seward had hoped to be the Republican Party's nominee for the presidency in 1860. Seward spoke at a public rally in Rochester, New York, during the midterm elections, when he stated, "It is an irrepressible conflict between opposing and enduring forces, and it means that the United States must and will, sooner or later, become either entirely a slaveholding nation or entirely a free-labor nation." Although the Republicans did gain additional congressional seats in 1858, Seward's "irrepressible conflict" statement had painted him to be a radical within the party, and his chances of securing the Republican Party's presidential nomination in 1860 diminished.

The decision was made that slaves could not patent an invention because they were not considered citizens of the United States. In addition, Jefferson Davis was unable to obtain a patent on a type of boat propeller that his slave, Benjamin Montgomery, had invented. It was ruled that slaves could not assign any of their inventions to their owners.

1859

In February in Arkansas, the state legislature presented free blacks with the choice of either exile or enslavement.

On March 7, the United States Supreme Court decided the case of *Ableman v. Booth*. This case first began in 1854 when the Wisconsin Supreme Court freed Sherman M. Booth, an abolitionist editor, after he had been convicted in a federal court of violating the federal Fugitive Slave Law. The United States Supreme Court maintained that the states did not have the right to interfere in federal cases, and the justices upheld the constitutionality of the Fugitive Slave Law of 1850. In light of the ruling, the Wisconsin state legislature declared that "this assumption of jurisdiction by the federal judiciary . . . is an act of undelegated power, void, and of no force." In an unusual twist of fate, it was a northern antislavery state that used the argument of states' rights here to defend its actions.

On May 12, in Vicksburg, Mississippi, southern delegates gathered to participate in the annual Southern Commercial Convention. The convention delegates approved a resolution stating, "In the opinion of this Convention, all laws, State or Federal, prohibiting the African Slave Trade, ought to be repealed." This measure was approved despite the opposition of several delegates from Tennessee and Florida.

On July 5 in the Kansas Territory, delegates gathered at Wyandotte (later Kansas City), Kansas, in order to hold a constitutional convention. The primary issue that was debated concerned whether or not Kansas should allow slavery. On October 4, 1859, Kansas voters would ratify a constitution that contained antislavery provisions. The measure would be approved by a nearly two to one margin.

From August 1 to August 2, the New England Colored Citizens Convention was held in Boston, Massachusetts.

On August 20, John Brown held a secret meeting with Frederick Douglass at a stone quarry near Chambersburg, Pennsylvania. Brown told Douglass of his planned raid at Harpers Ferry and hoped to gain Douglass's support of the project. Douglass cautioned Brown that the plan was ill-advised, and Douglass refused to offer his support to the project.

On September 5, Harriet E. Wilson, a free black woman, published the novel *Our Nig; or Sketches from the Life of a Free Black*. The work, which was published in Boston, was the first novel to be written by an African American woman and the first novel to be published by an African American author in the United States. It was also the first work that explored the exploitation and race-based abuse that free blacks faced in the antebellum North.

A group of Maryland slaveholders held a convention in Baltimore. During the event businessmen complained that many of the jobs in the service industries were monopolized by free blacks. Despite these reservations, the convention did not support a resolution to deport free blacks from the state of Maryland.

From October 16 to 17, John Brown and his associates (thirteen whites and five blacks) raided the United States Army arsenal at Harpers Ferry, Virginia, hoping to seize weapons that would help foment a massive slave uprising. During the attack, two blacks were killed, two were captured, and one escaped. Brown was captured by forces led by Colonel Robert E. Lee, and transported to Charleston, Virginia, where he was tried for treason, convicted, and executed by hanging. Upon his death on December 2, Brown became to many a martyr for the abolitionist cause. Four black co-conspirators, Shields Green, Dangerfield Newby, Sherrard Lewis Leary, and John A. Copeland were also hanged with Brown.

On December 2, abolitionist editor William Lloyd Garrison delivered a speech at Tremont Temple in Boston, Massachusetts, upon the death of John Brown.

On December 5, the House of Representatives again took two months to settle the question of who would serve as speaker. Ohio congressman John Sherman had hoped to win the post, but his earlier endorsement of Hinton Rowan Helper's book *The Impending Crisis* made him an unacceptable candidate to southern congressmen. In the end, the House elected New Jersey congressman William Pennington as the speaker of the House of Representatives for the Thirty-sixth Congress.

On December 14, the Georgia state legislature enacted a measure that made it illegal for a slaveowner to manumit slaves through a final will or testament.

On December 16, two black accomplices of John Brown, John Copeland and Shields Green, were hanged at Charleston, Virginia for their role in the failed plot.

On December 17, the Georgia state legislature enacted a measure that permitted any free black within the state of Georgia who was indicted for vagrancy to be sold as a slave.

On December 19, President James Buchanan used the occasion of his annual message to Congress to state his opposition to any effort to reestablish the African slave trade. Although Buchanan pledged to use the government's resources to stop the illegal slave trading that had persisted, he also criticized the detention and search of American merchant vessels by British patrols off the coast of West Africa.

American sculptor John Rogers created a work of group sculpture that he called "The Slave Auction." The work was featured at an art showing in New York City from 1859 to 1860.

1860

The results of the Eighth Census revealed that of the more than 8 million white residents of the South, only 383,637 were identified as slaveowners. Black population, both slave and free, was recorded at 4,441,830, or 14.1 percent of the nation's population. Of this total, 448,070 were identified as free blacks and 3,953,760 were slaves.

Free blacks in New York petitioned the state legislature to grant them equal suffrage rights with white citizens.

Although involvement in the African slave trade had been illegal since January 1, 1808, *The Clothilde,* the last recorded slave ship to carry slaves to the United States, landed a shipment of Africans at Mobile, Alabama.

The approximate price of a slave fieldhand averaged between $1,200 and $1,800.

Skilled slave artisans could earn $500 to $600 per year by hiring their services out in the community.

The legislature of the state of Virginia enacted a measure that made it possible for free blacks to be sold into slavery as punishment for committing acts that would otherwise be considered as imprisonable.

On February 2 in the United States Senate, Senator Jefferson Davis of Mississippi introduced a series of resolutions that maintained that the federal government did not have the authority to prevent the expansion of slavery into the western territories and that the government must actually protect slaveholders and their property in these regions. Although Davis was aware that the Senate would not support these measures, his effort was more of a calculated political move that was aimed at swaying the Senate's Democrats to this position. Davis hoped to derail the presidential aspirations of Illinois senator Stephen A. Douglas who was an advocate of the popular sovereignty position.

On February 27, Abraham Lincoln delivered an address to the Young Men's Central Republican Union at the Cooper Institute in New York City. In this speech Lincoln outlined the principles of the Republican Party and stated his no-compromise position on the issue of slavery. The publicity attained from this address helped to make Lincoln a front-runner for the Republican Party's presidential nomination.

Legislators in Maryland outlawed the practice of manumission within the state.

From April 23 to May 3, the Democratic Party held its national nominating convention in Charleston, South Carolina. The party rejected a proslavery plank in its platform, a decision that caused the delegates from eight southern states to walk out of the convention. This convention would adjourn without selecting a presidential nominee for the Democratic Party.

On May 9, the Constitutional Union Party was formed at a convention in Baltimore, Maryland, as southern Unionists, former members of the Whig Party, and former members of the American (Know-Nothing) Party came together in an effort to preserve national unity through effective compromise. These like-minded delegates believed that secession was a greater evil than slavery. The platform of the Constitutional Union Party did not mention slavery, but the party pledged loyalty to the Union, support for the Constitution, and the willingness to enforce all national laws. The party nominated John Bell of Tennessee for the presidency, and Edward Everett of Massachusetts was the party's vice presidential nominee.

Abraham Lincoln, in a speech prior to his nomination as a presidential candidate, identified slavery "as an evil not to be extended, but to be tolerated and protected only because of and so far as its actual presence among us makes that toleration and protection necessary."

Between May 16 and 18, the Republican Party held its nominating convention in Chicago, Illinois, and nominated Abraham Lincoln of Illinois as its presidential candidate and Hannibal Hamlin of Maine as vice president. The Republican platform stated the party's opposition to the expansion of slavery into the western territories, but pledged that the party would not interfere with slavery in the states where it already existed.

Between June 18 and 23, as a result of their failed convention in Charleston, South Carolina, the Democratic Party held a second nominating convention in Baltimore, Maryland. Southern delegates again stormed out of the convention in protest of the party's unwillingness to include a strong proslavery plank in its platform. After the southern delegates left the convention, the remaining delegates selected Illinois senator Stephen A. Douglas to be the party's presidential nominee.

On June 28, the southern delegates who had walked out of previous Democratic Party conventions in Charleston and Baltimore held their own rump convention in Baltimore. The southern Democrats drafted a party platform that demanded federal protection of the right to own slaves. The delegates nominated then Vice President John C. Breckinridge of Kentucky as their presidential nominee and Senator Joseph Lane of Oregon for the vice presidency.

On November 6, Abraham Lincoln was elected to the presidency of the United States on a platform that opposed the extension of slavery into the western territories. Lincoln garnered only 40 percent of the popular vote in a race that featured four prominent candidates, but he won a resounding victory over his opponents in the Electoral College.

In December, President James Buchanan urged the Congress to pass constitutional amendments that upheld the fugitive slave acts.

On December 18, Senator John J. Crittenden of Kentucky chaired a special Senate committee that sought to find an eleventh-hour compromise that might prevent the secession of the southern states and the possibility of civil war. Among other things, Crittenden's compromise measures would include the call for a constitutional amendment that would have taken the 36°30' north latitude boundary, first used in the Missouri Compromise of 1820, and applied it across all of the western territories. The efforts of Crittenden's committee were ineffective. President-elect Abraham Lincoln had been elected on a platform that called for prohibiting the expansion of slavery into the western territories, and Lincoln could not support a measure that would have granted the possibility of slavery expanding into these lands.

On December 20, South Carolina became the first southern state to secede from the Union by declaring itself to be an "independent commonwealth." By February 1, 1861, six other southern states had followed South Carolina out of the Union. These included: Mississippi (January 9), Florida (January 10), Alabama (January 11), Georgia (January 19), Louisiana (January 26), and Texas (February 1).

1861

Between February 4 and 9, delegates from the seven southern states that had seceded from the Union met at Montgomery, Alabama, and adopted the provisional constitution of the Confederate States of America. On February 9, the body elected Senator Jefferson Davis of Mississippi as the provisional president of the Confederacy.

On February 18, Confederate president Jefferson Davis described slavery as a practice "as necessary to self-preservation" in his inaugural address.

Harriet Jacobs published *Incidents in the Life of a Slave Girl*. The work is considered one of the most important slave narratives and presents a vivid portrayal of the multifaceted exploitation faced by women who were slaves.

On March 2, the United States Congress adopted a proposed constitutional amendment, which it sent to the states for final ratification. This proposed amendment stated that the federal government would have no right to subsequent action that would "abolish or interfere . . . with the domestic institutions" of the states. With the outbreak of the American Civil War in April 1861, the proposal would fail to be ratified by the states.

On March 4, Abraham Lincoln was inaugurated as the nation's sixteenth president in Washington, D.C. In his inaugural address, Lincoln stated unequivocally, "I have no purpose . . . to interfere with the institution of slavery." Nonetheless, Lincoln cautioned the southern states, "In *your* hands, my dissatisfied fellow countrymen, and not in *mine,* is the momentous issue of civil war. The government will not assail *you*. You can have no conflict, without being yourselves the aggressors. *You* have no oath registered in Heaven to destroy the government, while *I* shall have the most solemn one to 'preserve, protect and defend' it."

Also in March, Alexander Stephens, the vice president of the Confederate States of America, stated that his government "rested upon the great truth that the Negro is not equal to the white man, that slavery, subordination to the superior race, is a natural and normal condition . . . our new Government, is the first in the history of the world, based upon this great physical, philosophical, and moral truth."

On April 12, Confederate forces began the bombardment of the federal garrison at Fort Sumter in Charleston Harbor, South Carolina. This incident marks the beginning of the American Civil War.

On April 15, President Lincoln issued a national call for 75,000 troops for three months. Rather than describing the situation as one of war, he used the term *rebellion*. Free black troops sought to volunteer to Lincoln's call but were rejected.

On May 20, North Carolina became the eleventh and final southern state to secede from the Union. Other states of the Upper South had waited until after the incident at Fort Sumter before deciding upon secession. Once it became clear that Abraham Lincoln would use force against the South, four additional states seceded, joining the seven that had left the Union earlier. Besides North Carolina, the other three states were Virginia (April 17), Arkansas (May 6), and Tennessee (May 6).

On May 24, Union general Benjamin F. Butler put a group of fugitive slaves to work at Fortress Monroe, Virginia. Butler described the fugitive slaves as "contraband of war."

In the summer, slaves on several plantations located along Second Creek in Adams County, Mississippi, planned an uprising that was to coincide with the arrival of Union troops in the region. Local planters discovered the plot, executed nearly forty slaves who were suspected of involvement, and then kept silent about the extent of the plot in the hope that other slaves might not be inspired to similar acts by this episode.

On July 22, the United States Senate declared that "this war is not waged . . . for any purpose . . . of overthrowing or interfering with the rights or established institutions of . . . southern States." The resolution further stated that the specific aim of the war was "to preserve the Union" and not the abolition of slavery in the southern states.

On August 6, with the passage of the First Confiscation Act, Congress authorized the freeing of those slaves who were in regions under Union army control and who had previously been employed to aid the Confederate cause.

On August 30, acting upon his own initiative and without the backing of officials in Washington, Major General John C. Frémont invoked martial law and issued a proclamation that freed the slaves of all disloyal owners in Missouri. Lincoln later effectively nullified the order by asking Frémont to revise his proclamation so that it would not overstep congressional laws regarding emancipation. Lincoln later reassigned Frémont to a different department.

Black volunteers had already fought in behalf of the Confederacy both on land and at sea, but in September the Union army had officially rejected the application of free black volunteers who had offered their services to fight in the war.

On September 11, General John C. Frémont refused to comply with President Lincoln's request that he revise his proclamation freeing the slaves of disloyal owners in Missouri. Using his power as commander-in-chief of the nation's armed forces, Lincoln ordered General Frémont to comply.

On September 17, Mary Peake, a black teacher, established a school at Fortress Monroe, Virginia. This school marked the beginning of what eventually became the Hampton Institute.

On September 25, the secretary of the navy authorized the enlistment of black slaves.

On December 1, at President Lincoln's request, Secretary of War Simon Cameron deleted several controversial clauses from his annual report to the Congress. The passages in question had advocated the use of emancipation as a wartime necessity and related to the use of former slaves as military laborers and soldiers. Lincoln would soon remove Secretary Cameron from the War Department by naming him the minister to Russia and appointing Edwin M. Stanton as his replacement.

1862

On March 6, Abraham Lincoln sent a message to the Congress in which he proposed that a plan of gradual, compensated emancipation be enacted.

In Memphis, Tennessee, the Lincoln School for Negroes was established as an elementary school for black children. The institution eventually grew and developed into LeMoyne-Owen College.

In a letter to newspaper editor Horace Greeley, Abraham Lincoln stated that saving the Union was his primary concern and that "not either to save or destroy slavery" was an issue that motivated his directing of the war efforts.

On March 13, with the adoption of a new article of war, the Congress prohibited northern military commanders from capturing any fugitive slaves or helping to return any fugitives to their owners.

In March, the National Freedmen's Relief Association was established in New York City. The purpose of this organization was to help former slaves to make the transition from slavery to freedom. Similar Freedmen's Societies were eventually established in Boston, Philadelphia, Cincinnati, and Chicago. These groups later were consolidated into the American Freedmen's Aid Commission under the leadership of James Miller McKim.

On April 3, Union general David "Black David" Hunter requested permission from the War Department to recruit and arm blacks in the South Carolina Sea Islands for military service. When officials in Washington failed to respond to his request, Hunter initiated the plan on his own accord.

On April 10, the United States Congress agreed to cooperate with any state that sought to establish a plan of gradual abolition of slavery with compensated emancipation.

On April 16, Congress ended slavery in the nation's capital when a program of compensated emancipation for slaves held in the District of Columbia was enacted into law. The Congress appropriated $1 million to compensate the owners of slaves who were freed by this measure. Congress also appropriated $100,000 in funds for the resettlement of freed blacks in Liberia, Haiti, or other locations that were deemed appropriate.

On May 9, without prior approval of Union military authorities, General David "Black David" Hunter organized the First South Carolina Volunteers, the first all-black regiment to be formed during the Civil War. (Later, when the War Department failed to pay or equip the regiment, Hunter was forced to disband it.) Hunter also issued a proclamation that freed the slaves owned by all rebels in Georgia, Florida, and South Carolina.

On May 19, President Lincoln revoked the proclamation issued by General Hunter on May 9. Lincoln feared that an emancipation edict instituted in any setting might be sufficient cause to encourage the border states to leave the Union. Lincoln urged the border states (Missouri, Kentucky, Maryland, and Delaware) to adopt a program of gradual, compensated emancipation.

On May 13, the slave Robert Smalls commandeered a Confederate steamer, *The Planter,* and surrendered it to the Union navy as war booty in Charleston Harbor, South Carolina. Smalls would later serve as a congressman during the Reconstruction Era.

The First Regiment Louisiana Heavy Artillery and the Massachusetts Fifty-fourth and Fifty-fifth Infantry Regiments were formed. These units were the first authorized black combat units to be used in the Civil War.

On June 19, the United States Congress approved of a resolution that prohibited slavery from all federal territories, but not the states.

On July 12, President Lincoln lobbied the senators and congressmen from the four border states to support a plan of gradual, compensated emancipation, which would be followed by the systematic colonization of freed slaves to points outside the United States. Lincoln cautioned that if the political leaders failed to act, slavery "will be extinguished by mere friction and abrasion—by the mere incidents of the war." On July 14, the political leaders from the border states voted to reject President Lincoln's proposal.

On July 17, Congress enacted the Second Confiscation Act, which granted freedom to slaves of masters who supported the Confederacy, but this did not provide universal emancipation. With the passage of this measure, the president was also authorized to employ "persons of African descent" in any fashion deemed necessary, including their use as armed troops in the military service.

On July 17, Congress enacted the Militia Act, which permitted the employment of blacks in "any military or naval service for which they may be found competent." The measure also bestowed freedom on any slave who was employed in this capacity.

On July 22, Abraham Lincoln submitted a working draft of the Emancipation Proclamation to his cabinet for the first time. The cabinet decided that the president should wait until a major Union victory was achieved on the battlefield before making the Proclamation public. Lincoln postponed announcement of the proclamation until after the Union victory in the battle of Antietam on September 17, and he then announced the Emancipation Proclamation on September 22.

In August, General Jim Lane began to organize the First Kansas Colored Volunteers.

On August 14, Abraham Lincoln held a meeting with prominent black leaders in which he urged them to support a colonization plan either to Central America or to Africa. Although this was the first time that an American president conferred with black leaders on a matter of public policy, many free blacks in the North were highly critical of President Lincoln's suggestions.

On August 22, shortly after the capture of New Orleans, General Benjamin F. Butler, acting on his own initiative, issued a call to the free blacks of New Orleans to organize a military unit in support of the Union cause.

Also on August 22, President Lincoln responded to Horace Greeley's editorial "A Prayer of Twenty Millions," which appeared in the August 20 edition of the *New York Tribune.* Greeley's editorial was, in effect, an open letter to the president calling for action on the issue of emancipation. Despite his having previously drafted the Emancipation Proclamation, Lincoln responded to Greeley's challenge by stating, "My paramount object in this struggle *is* to save the Union, and it is *not* either to save or to destroy slavery. If I could save the Union without freeing *any* slave I would do it, and if I could save it by freeing *all* the slaves I would do it; and if I could save it by freeing some and leaving others alone I would also do that."

On August 25, Secretary of War Edwin M. Stanton authorized General Rufus Saxton, the commander of the Southern Department, to arm up to 5,000 slaves and to train them as guards for plantations and settlements in the South Carolina Sea Islands.

On September 22, Abraham Lincoln issued the preliminary draft of his Emancipation Proclamation shortly after the Union victory in the battle of Antietam. In this statement President Lincoln warned the southern states that he intended to free the slaves in all regions that remained in rebellion against the national government effective upon January 1, 1863. Lincoln also used this occasion to pledge financial support to any border state that adopted a program of gradual, compensated emancipation. He also stated his support for the colonization of freed slaves to points outside of the United States such as Liberia or Haiti.

On September 23, only one day after publicly announcing the Emancipation Proclamation and stating his intention to end slavery, Abraham Lincoln met with his cabinet to discuss the acquisition of new territory that might be used for the deportation of free blacks upon the abolition of slavery.

On September 27, the First Louisiana Native Guards, the first black regiment that received officially sanctioned recognition by the United States government, was mustered into service to assist the Union army. Free blacks from New Orleans comprised most of the membership of this regiment.

On October 11, fearing the potential for unrest on plantations that might arise because of the absence of proper supervision, the Confederate Congress enacted a measure that exempted from military service those slaveowners who held more than twenty slaves. Many cynics observed that this action was another example of how the American Civil War was a rich man's war but a poor man's fight.

On October 28, black troops took part in battle for the first time during the American Civil War. The First Kansas Colored Volunteers, which had been organized by General Jim Lane, engaged and repulsed a large rebel force at Island Mound, Missouri.

On December 1, still supporting a plan of compensated emancipation, Abraham Lincoln sent a message to the Congress urging that federal bonds be used to fund a compensation scheme for those states that agreed to abolish slavery before 1900.

On December 23, Confederate president Jefferson Davis signed an order immediately mandating that any black Union troops and the white officers who commanded them when captured in battle were not to be treated as prisoners of war. Rather, they were to be turned over to state authorities where they would be prosecuted as criminals.

1863

On January 1, the Emancipation Proclamation became effective and declared free all slaves except those in states, or parts of states, that were no longer in rebellion. The Proclamation did not apply in the border states, nor did it apply in those areas that were already under control of the Union army. These areas included thirteen parishes in southern Louisiana (including the city of New Orleans), the forty-eight counties that made up West Virginia, seven counties in eastern Virginia (including the city of Norfolk), and the state of Tennessee. President Lincoln also announced the Union's intention of recruiting blacks as sailors and soldiers.

On January 26, Secretary of War Edwin M. Stanton authorized the governor of Massachusetts, John A. Andrew, to organize a company of black troops. The Fifty-fourth Massachusetts Volunteers, under the command of Colonel Robert Gould Shaw, was the first black regiment to be raised in the North.

In February, Pennsylvania Congressman Thaddeus Stevens pushed a bill through the Congress that called for the enlistment of 150,000 United States Colored Troops.

On March 10, the city of Jacksonville, Florida, was captured and occupied by the First and Second South Carolina—two black regiments. The fear of white communities being occupied by black troops caused great distress in many parts of the South.

On March 16, Secretary of War Edwin M. Stanton established the American Freedmen's Inquiry Commission within the War Department. This commission was charged with investigating the conditions faced by freed slaves and making recommendations that would aid their future welfare and potential for employment.

A colonization attempt was made with the support of President Abraham Lincoln. An American vessel carried 500 black settlers to Cow Island, off the coast of Haiti, but the colonization attempt failed.

On May 1, the Confederate Congress, responding to the worst fears of white southerners, declared that all black troops, and the white officers who commanded them, would thereafter be considered criminals in the South. For blacks, this action meant that black troops captured in battle would either be executed or forced into slavery. If the white officers who commanded blacks were captured, they would be executed.

On May 22, the United States War Department issued General Order No. 143, which placed control of black troops under the United States Colored Troops. An aggressive recruiting campaign began to attract black troops who were willing to fight for the cause of freedom.

In July, thirty regiments of United States Colored Troops were armed and equipped.

Between July 13 and 17 in New York City Draft Riots occurred, and white mobs displayed a vast amount of antiblack sentiment in perhaps the bloodiest race riot in American history. Twelve hundred deaths, mostly black, were reported. The combined effects of fearing the economic competition of free blacks, the new cause of freedom for which the war was being waged, and hostility to the draft all contributed to the rage among poor white immigrant mobs in New York City.

On July 18, the Fifty-fourth Massachusetts Volunteers, an all-black regiment, made its famous assault on Fort Wagner at Charleston Harbor, South Carolina.

On July 30, Abraham Lincoln announced that the United States government would "give the same protection to all its soldiers, and if the enemy shall sell or enslave anyone because of his color, the offense shall be punished by retaliation upon the enemy's prisoners in our possession." The immediate result of this "eye-for-an-eye" policy was that the Confederate government backed away from its May 1 position, but individual commanders continued to execute captured black troops.

On October 3, the War Department began recruiting blacks for military service in the border states of Maryland and Missouri as well as in the state of Tennessee, which was effectively under Union control. The Congress appropriated funding to compensate owners of these slaves, provided that they had remained loyal Unionists throughout the rebellion.

On December 8, President Abraham Lincoln issued his Proclamation of Amnesty and Reconstruction, which outlined the basis of his "Ten Percent Plan." Should southerners take an oath of allegiance to the Union and promise to accept emancipation, Lincoln was willing to offer a federal pardon and restore all property, except slaves, that had been taken during the rebellion. Lincoln's proposal also outlined the procedure by which the southern states could begin the process of gaining readmission to the Union.

1864

A new federal law enabled northern states to recruit black soldiers in the South.

Sergeant William Walker of the Third South Carolina Regiment was shot by order of a court martial after he protested against the inequality in pay received by black troops during the Civil War.

On March 16, pro-Union voters in occupied Arkansas ratified a new state constitution that abolished slavery in the state.

On April 8, the United States Senate approved by a vote of thirty-eight to six a proposed constitutional amendment that would abolish slavery in the United States.

On April 12, during the battle at Fort Pillow, near Memphis, Tennessee, nearly three hundred blacks were massacred by Confederate troops under the command of Nathan Bedford Forrest. Confederate troops had been told that black troops used in battle would not be taken as prisoners of war.

On June 7, the United States War Department began the enlistment of blacks into the Union military in the border state of Kentucky whether or not slaves had the permission of their owners to do so. As was the case in other regions, loyal owners who had maintained Unionist sympathies during the rebellion were compensated for the slaves who were taken for military service.

On June 15, the United States House of Representative failed to approve the proposed constitutional amendment abolishing slavery in the United States, which the Senate had approved on April 8. There were ninety-five votes for the measure and sixty-six against, but the proposed amendment failed because it was thirteen votes shy of the two-thirds majority that was needed for approval before the measure could be sent to the states for final ratification.

Also on June 15, Congress equalized the bounties that were paid for enlistment of white and black soldiers with the passage of the Army Appropriations Bill. The same measure equalized pay, arms, equipment, and medical services that were provided to black troops. The adjustment in pay, from $10 per month to

$13 per month was made retroactive to January 1, 1864, for slaves who served in the military, and it was made retroactive to the time of enlistment for all free blacks who served.

On June 20, the United States Congress enacted a pay increase for all Union soldiers, black and white alike. Privates would now earn $16/month.

In July, Congress authorized that families of black troops who were killed in the war were entitled to receive government pensions.

On July 5, Horace Greeley, editor of the *New York Tribune,* received a letter from Canada suggesting that Confederate diplomats in that country were prepared to negotiate a peaceful settlement to the Civil War. Greeley informed President Lincoln of this correspondence, and on July 9 Lincoln informed Greeley that anyone who wanted to negotiate should contact the proper authorities in Washington. Nonetheless, Lincoln did allow Greeley to travel to Niagara Falls, Canada, on July 18 to meet with the Confederate diplomats. The negotiations proved to be unsuccessful as the southern negotiators would accept nothing short of southern independence.

On July 23 in occupied Louisiana, pro-Unionist delegates drafted a new reunion constitution at a state constitutional convention that was called by Governor Michael Hahn. This new constitution abolished slavery, but it did not grant the suffrage to blacks immediately. The new constitution did allow the legislature to extend the franchise to blacks at a later date.

On September 5 in occupied Louisiana, a new state constitution was approved by pro-Unionist voters who had taken an oath of allegiance to the federal government. This constitution eliminated slavery, but it did not immediately give blacks the right to vote. Instead, suffrage was postponed.

On October 4 in New Orleans, the *New Orleans Tribune (La Tribune de la Nouvelle Orleans)* began publication. It was the first black daily newspaper, and it was published in both French and English. Louis Charles Roudanez and his brothers operated the newspaper, and it remained for many years one of the most influential black newspapers in the United States.

On October 10, President Abraham Lincoln wrote to Henry W. Hoffman, a Maryland political leader, urging ratification of the proposed state constitution that would abolish slavery in the state. Maryland voters were scheduled to vote on the measure in an October 13 referendum, and many believed that the passage of the constitution was doubtful. Lincoln wrote, "I wish all men to be free. I wish the material prosperity of the already free which I feel sure the extinction of slavery would bring. I wish to see, in process of disappearing, that only thing which ever could bring this nation to civil war."

On November 1, in the border state of Maryland, a new state constitution that abolished slavery went into effect. The measure had been approved by state voters in an extremely close vote on October 13.

On November 8, President Abraham Lincoln was reelected to a second term in office as he defeated his Democratic rival, General George B. McClellan. In many respects, the election was a referendum on Lincoln's conduct of the war effort and his decision to issue the Emancipation Proclamation. The Republican Party also increased its majority in the House of Representatives and the Senate.

1865

The American Missionary Association established Atlanta University in Georgia as an institution of higher education for African Americans. The institution later merged with Clark College and changed its name to Clark-Atlanta University.

The Baltimore Association for the Moral and Educational Improvement of Colored People established the Baltimore Normal School in order to educate free black children. The institution eventually grew and developed into Bowie State University.

On January 9, pro-Unionist delegates attending a constitutional convention in occupied Tennessee adopted an amendment to the state constitution that abolished slavery in Tennessee. Pro-Unionist voters would ratify the proposed amendment in a referendum on February 22.

On January 11, General Robert E. Lee recommended that the Confederacy begin arming slaves as a means of filling the ranks of the Confederate army.

Also on January 11 in St. Louis, delegates attending a constitutional convention in the border state of Missouri ratified a new constitution that abolished slavery within the state.

On January 12, Secretary of War Edwin M. Stanton traveled to Savannah, Georgia, to confer with General William T. Sherman and twenty black leaders to discuss the welfare of freed slaves in the aftermath of the rebellion.

Also on January 12, in a speech before the House of Representatives, Congressman Thaddeus Stevens of Pennsylvania described slavery as "the worst institution upon earth, one which is a disgrace to man and would be an annoyance to the infernal spirits." During the Reconstruction Era, which followed the American

Civil War, Congressman Stevens would become one of the most influential Radical Republican leaders to direct Reconstruction policy.

On January 16, General William T. Sherman issued Special Field Order 15. This measure set aside 40-acre plots in the coastal islands of Georgia, South Carolina, and Florida that were to be distributed to freed slaves who would receive "possessory title" to the lands. The property in question had constituted large plantation estates in the years prior to the Civil War, but the lands had been seized when Union forces entered the region.

On January 17, realizing the difficult conditions that he faced, General Robert E. Lee said that it was "not only expedient but necessary" that slaves be used as soldiers by the Confederate government to fill the ranks of the Confederate Army.

On January 31, the House of Representatives finally approved a proposed constitutional amendment that would abolish slavery in the United States by a vote of 119 to 56. The election of more Republicans to the Congress in the November 1864 elections had made it easier for the measure to obtain the two-thirds majority that was necessary for approval. The Senate had originally approved the measure on April 8, 1864, but the initial vote in the House of Representatives had failed on June 15, 1864. Upon ratification by the states, this measure would become the Thirteenth Amendment to the Constitution of the United States.

On February 3, President Abraham Lincoln met with Confederate vice president Alexander Stephens at an abortive peace conference at sea off the coast of Hampton Roads, Virginia. Continuing Confederate demands that the South be granted autonomy as a sovereign independent republic resulted in the failure of the negotiations.

On February 12, Henry Highland Garnet became the first black minister to preach in the United States Capitol building. Garnet delivered a memorial sermon on the abolition of slavery.

On March 3, in anticipation of the work that would have to take place upon the conclusion of the Civil War, Congress authorized creation of the Bureau of Refugees, Freedmen, and Abandoned Lands, a government agency that became the first public welfare program in the history of the United States. The Freedmen's Bureau was designed to assist freedmen and refugees as they made the difficult social and economic transition from slavery to freedom after the war.

Also on March 3, a joint resolution of Congress emancipated the wives and children of all blacks who served in the Union military during the Civil War.

On March 13, the government of the Confederate States of America authorized the filling of military quotas by using slaves, with the permission of their owners. The government did stipulate however that the number of slaves was not to exceed 25 percent of the able-bodied male slave population between the ages of eighteen and forty-five. This last-ditch effort was enacted too late to assist the Confederate war effort.

On April 9, Confederate General Robert E. Lee surrendered to Union General Ulysses S. Grant at Appomattox Court House, Virginia. This event marked the end of the American Civil War.

On April 11, Abraham Lincoln recommended that the Congress consider granting the suffrage to black veterans and to other blacks who were considered to be intelligent.

Lincoln had been assassinated on the evening of April 14 by John Wilkes Booth, a southern sympathizer. Upon Lincoln's death, Vice President Andrew Johnson of Tennessee became the nation's seventeenth president.

On May 11, blacks in Norfolk, Virginia, held mass meetings to demand the suffrage and equal rights with whites.

On May 29, President Andrew Johnson publicly announced his plans for the reconstruction of the southern states. Johnson believed that the states of the defeated Confederacy had to ratify the Thirteenth Amendment to the Constitution, which repudiated slavery, but he did not believe that the suffrage should be extended to freedmen.

On June 6, blacks in Petersburg, Virginia, held mass meetings to demand the suffrage and equal rights with whites.

On June 19, blacks in Vicksburg, Mississippi, held mass meetings to demand the suffrage and equal rights with whites.

Also on June 19, news about the Emancipation Proclamation finally reached slaves in Texas when Union general Gordon Granger arrived at Galveston Bay, Texas, and liberated nearly two hundred thousand slaves. The celebration of "Juneteenth" as a commemoration of Emancipation Day became popular among African Americans within the state of Texas. Today the celebration is recognized in communities all across the United States.

From August 7 to the 11, blacks in Nashville, Tennessee, held mass meetings to demand the suffrage and equal rights with whites.

On September 16, Pennsylvania congressman Thaddeus Stevens urged the confiscation of all estates belonging to former Confederate leaders. Stevens believed that these lands should be redistributed to adult freedmen. This was the basis of the "forty acres and a mule" idea of providing freedmen with the economic means to survive in a world after slavery.

On September 18, blacks in Richmond, Virginia, held mass meetings to demand the suffrage and equal rights with whites.

Between September 29 and October 3, blacks in Raleigh, North Carolina, held mass meetings to demand the suffrage and equal rights with whites.

On October 7, blacks in Jackson, Mississippi, held mass meetings to demand the suffrage and equal rights with whites.

From November 20 to November 25, blacks in Charleston, South Carolina, held mass meetings to demand the suffrage and equal rights with whites.

In the fall and winter, legislatures in states that constituted the former Confederate States of America enacted black codes that were designed to restrict the civil rights and liberty of movement of the newly emancipated freedmen.

On December 18, the Thirteenth Amendment, which abolished slavery, became part of the United States Constitution.

1866

On January 9, Fisk University was founded in Nashville, Tennessee. It was one of the first historically black colleges and universities to be established in the United States.

On February 19, Congress attempted to expand the power and authority of the Bureau of Refugees, Freedmen, and Abandoned Lands that had been established in March 1865. The action was caused by the creation of black codes in states throughout the South that were designed to deny civil rights to former slaves. President Andrew Johnson vetoed the measure.

On February 22, supporters of President Andrew Johnson marched to the White House in the evening to celebrate the president's veto of the Freedmen's Bureau Act.

On March 16, Congress passed a Civil Rights Act that was designed to extend citizenship rights to African Americans. Calling the measure an infringement on the rights of the states, President Andrew Johnson vetoed the measure.

On April 2, President Andrew Johnson declared that the state of insurrection had ended in all of the former Confederate states with the exception of Texas.

On April 9, Congress passed the Civil Rights Act of 1866 by overriding the veto that President Andrew Johnson had issued on March 16.

Between May 1 and May 3, a serious racial disturbance took place in Memphis, Tennessee, that resulted in the death of forty-eight individuals. Many of the people targeted were black veterans of the Civil War.

On June 16, Congress sent the Fourteenth Amendment to the U.S. Constitution to the states for ratification. If approved, the measure would extend citizenship rights to African Americans and provide for equal protection of the law to all Americans.

In July, Congress reduced the number of justices on the U.S. Supreme Court from nine to seven in order to prevent President Andrew Johnson from making any appointments to the court.

On July 16, Congress passed a new Freedmen's Bureau Act by overriding the veto that President Andrew Johnson had issued on February 19.

On July 24, upon its ratification of the Fourteenth Amendment to the U.S. Constitution, the state of Tennessee was restored to the Union by action of the U.S. Congress.

On July 30, a race riot occurred in New Orleans, Louisiana, that left 37 dead and 119 wounded.

On August 2, President Andrew Johnson declared that the state of insurrection had ended in Texas and that civil authority had been restored in all parts of the former Confederate states.

On August 14, a group of moderates from the North and the South held a National Union Convention in Philadelphia, Pennsylvania, to try to rally support for President Andrew Johnson and his policies, but the gathering has no real effect upon national Reconstruction policy.

Between August 28 and September 15, President Andrew Johnson spent time campaigning for congressional candidates who supported his Reconstruction policies. Johnson hoped to affect the outcome of the midterm elections of 1866 that would produce a new Congress. Although Johnson hoped to diminish the political power of the Radical Republican faction, that group gained sufficient seats in the new Congress to make it "veto-proof."

On November 6, midterm elections produced sweeping victories for the Radical Republicans in Congress who gained enough new seats to command a two-thirds majority in both the House of Representative and the Senate. At this point, the Radical republicans had enough power to override any presidential veto that might be issued.

1867

On January 8, Congress enacted a law that extended

the suffrage to African American men living in the District of Columbia.

On January 22, Congress authorized a special session of the new Congress to begin on March 4, thus allowing the Radical Republican-dominated Congress to begin its work nine months earlier than normal. This measure was designed to take Reconstruction policy effectively out of the hands of the president.

On February 7, Frederick Douglass led a delegation of black leaders who met with President Andrew Johnson to urge that suffrage rights be extended to all blacks who met the qualifications for voting.

On February 18, Morehouse College was founded in Augusta, Georgia (and later moved to Atlanta, Georgia). This educational institution quickly became one of the premier historically black colleges and universities to be established in the United States.

On February 27, James D. B. DeBow died. As the editor and publisher of *DeBow's Review of the South and Southwest,* DeBow had been one of the strongest proponents of industrialization in the South prior to the Civil War.

On March 2, Congress voted to charter Howard University in Washington, D.C. The school was named after General Oliver Otis Howard who was the director of the Freedmen's Bureau.

Also on March 2, Congress enacted the Command of the Army Act, a measure stipulating that all military orders from the president of the United States must emanate from the general of the army in Washington, D.C. Congress further stated that this officer could not be removed from his post without the consent of the Senate.

In the Tenure of Office Act of March 2, Congress prohibited the president of the United States from removing any cabinet-level civil officials from their posts without the consent of the Senate. The measure was passed over President Johnson's veto. Subsequently, this legislation would be used to bring impeachment charges against the president when he sought to remove Secretary of War Edwin M. Stanton from office.

On the same day, the First Reconstruction Act was passed by Congress over the veto of the president. This measure divided the South into five military districts and imposed martial law in the region. States desiring to enter the Union under the terms of this act would need to establish new state constitutions that granted suffrage rights to African American men and ratified the Fourteenth Amendment to the U.S. Constitution.

On March 11, Republican representative Thaddeus Stevens of Pennsylvania introduced a slave reparations bill in the House of Representatives. The bill was defeated by a vote of 126 to 37.

On March 23, Congress passed the Second Reconstruction Act. The measure called for the registration of all qualified African American males as voters.

On April 1, the Ku Klux Klan held its first national convention in Nashville, Tennessee.

On May 1, Howard University was founded in Washington, D.C. This educational institution quickly became the premier historically black university to be established in the United States.

On July 19, Congress passed the Third Reconstruction Act. In addition to complying with previous measures, states in the South were required to ratify the Fifteenth Amendment to the U.S. Constitution before they could be readmitted to the Union.

On August 12, President Andrew Johnson removed Secretary of War Edwin M. Stanton from office and appointed General Ulysses S. Grant as an interim appointee to replace Stanton. Congress viewed this action as a violation of the Tenure of Office Act and began to consider charges of impeachment against the president.

1868

As a former White House seamstress and confidante of Mary Todd Lincoln, the former slave Elizabeth Keckley created a stir when she published *Behind the Scenes: Thirty Years a Slave and Four Years in the White House.*

William Wells Brown published *The Negro in the American Rebellion,* the first work to examine the role of African Americans during the Civil War.

On January 13, Congress refused to accept the removal of Secretary of War Edwin M. Stanton. Interim appointee General Ulysses S. Grant turned the position back over to Stanton.

On February 21, President Johnson formally dismissed Secretary of War Edwin M. Stanton from the cabinet and had him forcibly removed from his office.

On February 23, W. E. B. (William Edward Burghardt) DuBois, one of the leading intellectuals and social activists of the African American community, was born. As a historian, DuBois wrote extensively on the topic of slavery and its legacy for the United States.

Between February 24 and May 16, Congress considered the matter of the impeachment of President Andrew Johnson.

The impeachment trial of President Andrew Johnson took place from March 5 to May 16. At the end of the trial, the U.S. Senate voted to convict by a vote of 35 to 19, but this fell one vote shy of the two-thirds needed for conviction. President Andrew Johnson would remain in office, but he was tremendously weakened and largely ineffective for the remainder of his term.

On March 11, Congress passed the Fourth Reconstruction Act. The measure stated that a majority of votes cast (rather than a majority of registered voters) would determine the adoption of state constitutions in the South. This measure was adopted to counter the intimidation of black voters in the South by groups like the Ku Klux Klan.

On March 17, Congress denied the U.S. Supreme Court the power to hear appeals of any habeas corpus cases that might reach the court. The effort was a preemptive one designed to prevent the Court from possibly declaring the First Reconstruction Act unconstitutional.

In April, Samuel Chapman Armstrong established the Hampton Institute in Hampton Roads, Virginia. Designed to provide a practical education for former slaves, one of its graduates, Booker T. Washington, would go on to become one of the leading African American educators of the era.

On April 30, Decoration Day (later named Memorial Day) was recognized for the first time as an opportunity to commemorate the service of those who had lost their lives during the Civil War. The idea was developed by John A. Logan, who was then serving as national commander of the Grand Army of the Republic (GAR), an association of Union army veterans.

On June 13, the African American officeholder Oscar J. Dunn, a former slave, became the lieutenant governor of Louisiana.

On June 22, upon its ratification of the Fourteenth Amendment to the U.S. Constitution, the state of Arkansas was restored to the Union by Congress.

On June 25, upon their ratification of the Fourteenth Amendment to the U.S. Constitution, the states of South Carolina, North Carolina, Alabama, Florida, and Louisiana were restored to the Union by action of the U.S. Congress.

On July 28, Congress declared that the Fourteenth Amendment to the U.S. Constitution had been ratified by a sufficient number of the states to make it a part of the Constitution.

On August 11, Pennsylvania congressman Thaddeus Stevens, one of the key architects of the Radical Republican plan of Reconstruction, died.

On November 3, Republican candidate General Ulysses S. Grant was elected president of the United States by defeating his Democratic rival, Governor Horatio Seymour of New York.

On December 25, a presidential proclamation of unqualified amnesty was granted by President Andrew Johnson to all who had participated in the "insurrection or rebellion" of the Civil War.

On February 27, Congress sent the Fifteenth Amendment to the U.S. Constitution to the states for ratification. If approved, the measure would extend voting rights to African American men.

On September 22, a serious race riot took place in New Orleans, Louisiana.

On September 28, a serious race riot took place in Opelousas, Louisiana.

On October 26, a serious race riot took place in St. Bernard Parish, Louisiana.

1870

On February 2 in South Carolina, the African American officeholder Jonathan Jasper Wright began serving as an associate justice on the state supreme court. Wright held the post for seven years, during which he was the highest ranked African American judicial officer in the United States.

On February 25, the U.S. Senate seat from Mississippi that was once held by Jefferson Davis became occupied by Hiram R. Revels, the first African American to serve in the U.S. Senate.

In March, the Forty-first Congress gathered in Washington, D.C. It included two African American members of the House of Representatives Joseph H. Rainey and Robert Brown Elliot both from South Carolina.

On March 30, Congress declared that the Fifteenth Amendment to the U.S. Constitution had been ratified by a sufficient number of the states to make it a part of the Constitution.

On April 9, the American Anti-Slavery Society held its final meeting and decided to disband since it had accomplished its task of ending slavery in the United States.

On May 31, Congress enacted the first of the Force Acts, commonly called the Ku Klux Klan Acts, to outlaw the activities that vigilante organizations like the Klan were carrying out against freedmen in the South.

On October 12, General Robert E. Lee died. During the Civil War, General Lee had commanded the Army of Northern Virginia and eventually became commander-in-chief of all Confederate Armies.

On October 20, the black abolitionist James W. Pennington died. In 1841, Pennington had authored *A Textbook of the Origin and History of the Colored People*, the first African American history textbook to be published in the United States.

On December 12, Joseph H. Rainey, a congressman from South Carolina, became the first African American to serve in the U.S. House of Representatives. In addition to completing the term to which he had been appointed, Rainey was subsequently elected to the next four Congresses.

1871

On January 25, Quaker abolitionist Thomas Garrett died. Hearing of Garrett's passing, William Lloyd Garrison commented: "His rightful place is conspicuously among the benefactors, saviors, martyrs of the human race."

In March, the Forty-second Congress gathered in Washington, D.C. It included five African American members of the House of Representatives: Benjamin S. Turner of Alabama; Josiah T. Walls of Florida; and Robert Carlos DeLarge, Robert Brown Elliot, and Joseph H. Rainey of South Carolina.

On April 20, Congress enacted the second of the Force Acts, commonly called the Ku Klux Klan Acts, to outlaw the activities that vigilante organizations like the Klan were carrying out against freedmen in the South.

On December 11, Congress passed a law making it illegal for U.S. citizens to participate in the slave trade or to own slaves in any other country. This effectively meant that the Thirteenth Amendment to the U.S. Constitution would have a bearing on all U.S. citizens regardless of where they might live or work.

1872

Slavery in the United States began to be treated in a scholarly fashion as historians Henry Wilson and Samuel Hunt published *History of the Rise and Fall of the Slave Power in America*.

William Still, a black abolitionist and conductor on the Underground Railroad published *The Underground Railroad*, a history of the antislavery network that had helped thousands of fugitives to escape from slavery. Still's work was one of the first to highlight the important role that the fugitives themselves had played in achieving their own freedom by "stealing themselves away from slavery."

On May 22, Congress passed the Amnesty Act and restored civil rights to most former Confederates who had been barred from voting or holding public office. Within a few years, many of these individuals would rise to positions of power in the South.

On November 5, President Ulysses S. Grant was re-elected to a second term.

On December 11 in Louisiana, the speaker of the state legislature P. B. S. Pinchback, an African American officeholder, was elevated to the post of acting-governor, a position he held for forty-three days. He is considered to be the first African American to serve as a governor in the history of the United States.

1873

In March, the Forty-third Congress gathered in Washington, D.C. It included six African American members of the House of Representatives: Benjamin S. Turner of Alabama; Josiah T. Walls of Florida; and Robert Carlos DeLarge, Robert Brown Elliot, Joseph H. Rainey, and Robert Smalls of South Carolina.

1874

On March 11, the death of Massachusetts Senator Charles Sumner marked the passing of one of the last great supporters of congressional reconstruction policy as crafted by the Radical Republicans.

In November, in the midterm congressional elections, the Democratic Party regained control of the House of Representatives as the Republicans lost eighty-five seats.

1875

The sculpture *Emancipation* was unveiled in Lincoln Park in Washington, D.C. Created by Thomas Ball, the sculpture showed President Abraham Lincoln with his hand lifted over a kneeling slave.

The Supreme Court ruled in the case of *U.S. v. Cruikshank* and weakened the effect of the Fifteenth Amendment. The Court stated that "the right of suffrage was not a necessary attribute of national citizenship." The Court also determined that "the right to vote in the States comes from the States" and not from the national government.

In March, the Forty-fourth Congress gathered in Washington, D.C. It included six African American members of the House of Representatives: Benjamin S. Turner of Alabama; Josiah T. Walls of Florida; and Robert Carlos DeLarge, Robert Brown Elliot, Joseph H. Rainey, and Robert Smalls of South Carolina.

On March 1, Congress enacted the Civil Rights Act of 1875, which gave all citizens equal rights in all public places and prohibited the exclusion of African Americans from jury duty. Several years later in the *Civil Rights Cases* (1883), the U.S. Supreme Court would rule the measure to be unconstitutional.

On March 15, Blanche K. Bruce, the second African American to serve in the U.S. Senate, took his seat as a senator from Mississippi. He was the only African American senator to serve a complete six-year term during the nineteenth century.

On July 31, former president Andrew Johnson died.

On December 19, Carter G. Woodson was born. The future historian would be one of the founders of the Association for the Study of Negro Life and History. He established the *Journal of Negro History* and was the founder of Negro History Week.

1876

On March 8, the U.S. Senate refused to seat P. B. S. Pinchback as a senator from the state of Louisiana. As an African American political figure who had previously served as acting-governor of Louisiana, members of the Senate claimed that Pinchback did not have the proper qualifications to serve in the Senate.

On July 8, racial disturbances began in South Carolina that persisted until October 26. Federal troops were sent into the area to restore order after five blacks were killed in racial violence in Hamburg, South Carolina.

On November 7, Republican Rutherford B. Hayes and Democrat Samuel Tilden were candidates for president of the United States, but the election did not produce a winner. Although Tilden had a slight lead in the popular vote, neither candidate had an electoral vote majority. Disputed votes from four states had to be reconciled before a winner could be declared.

On December 6, electoral votes were counted in Washington, D.C., but did not yield a winner to the disputed presidential contest. Twenty-three electoral votes from Florida, South Carolina, Louisiana, and Oregon remained in dispute.

1877

On January 29, an Electoral Commission was appointed by Congress to determine how the electoral votes that remained in dispute from the presidential election of 1876 should be distributed. The commission eventually decided to award all twenty-three disputed electoral votes to Republican candidate Rutherford B. Hayes.

On February 26, representatives of Rutherford B. Hayes met with southern political leaders at the Wormly Hotel, a black-operated hotel in Washington, D.C., to work out the final details of a compromise that would allow Hayes to become president if he agreed to end Reconstruction and remove federal troops from the South.

On March 2, after intense negotiations, representatives from the Republican and Democratic parties agreed to the terms of the so-called Compromise of 1877 that settled the disputed election of 1876. By the terms of the agreement, Republican Rutherford B. Hayes became president, but in exchange the Republicans promised to remove federal troops from the South, appoint southerners to the cabinet and the Supreme Court, and provide money for generous internal improvements to aid the South.

On March 4, Rutherford B. Hayes became the nineteenth president of the United States.

On March 18, in the face of opposition from the South as well as within the Republican Party, President Rutherford B. Hayes appointed the prominent African American leader Frederick Douglass to the post of federal marshal for the District of Columbia.

From April 10 to April 14, President Rutherford B. Hayes removed the last federal troops from the states of Louisiana, South Carolina, and Florida, thereby marking an end to the Reconstruction Era.

On April 24, the last federal troops withdrew from Louisiana and South Carolina ending what southerners termed "carpetbag rule" that had prevailed during Reconstruction.

On June 15, Henry O. Flipper became the first African American to graduate from the U.S. Military Academy at West Point, New York.

On September 16, Levi Coffin died. During the antebellum era, Coffin had been known as the self-proclaimed "President of the Underground Railroad."

On October 29, Nathan Bedford Forrest died. He had been a Confederate cavalry officer and founder of the Ku Klux Klan.

On November 4, Ulrich Bonnell Phillips was born in LaGrange, Georgia. The future historian would write *American Negro Slavery* (1918), which became the dominant historiographic interpretation of the institution during the first half of the twentieth century. Phillips believed that slavery was a benevolent institution that resulted from planter paternalism, and he viewed the plantation as an educational institution that trained the slaves.

Contextual Essays

～m～

EARLY CONQUEST, COLONIALISM, AND THE ORIGINS OF AFRICAN SLAVERY

The origins of slavery as a social institution can be traced back to the very beginnings of civilization. The settlement of villages, made possible by the invention of farming and the domestication of animals, meant that humankind was no longer reliant on a nomadic, hunter-gatherer existence. As such, a more stable type of life based on sedentary farming became common in many civilizations.

We measure our ability to live together in community by the degree to which we can coexist within settled societies. Curiously, our terms "city" and "civilization" share the same Latin root ("civis") in celebration of the human achievement that was attained when nomadic existence gave way to what was perceived as a better way. Civilization—life in community—represented the highest of achievements in many respects,

but it also contained the seeds of discontent that have plagued much of human history. Civilization gave way to disparities in wealth as legions of "have" and "have not" societies emerged and the progeny of this social and economic reality—war and slavery—emerged.

Social scientists have long recognized an immediate connection between war and slavery. The ancient practice of fighting to the death was a difficult and bloody business that evolved into something that was viewed as more humane and more pragmatic. War captives became understood as having an economic value if they were enslaved rather than killed on the battlefield; thus the earliest consideration of a human being as a commodity occurred when this concept was first realized. War captives, in essence, became prizes that provided great advantage to societies that were victorious in battle. In an almost never-ending cycle, the economic value of the prizes of war (particularly slaves) gave rise to more conflict as societies sought a distinct economic advantage over their rivals and sought to subjugate and enslave the "socially dead" captured on the field of battle.

In ancient societies of Mesopotamia, Egypt, China, India, Greece, and Rome, this practice persisted in varying degrees from the beginnings of civilization. Slavery was a social status that was bestowed upon the vanquished. It had no particular racial, ethnic, or religious connotation, but simply meant that slaves or their ancestors had experienced the misfortune of defeat at some point in the past. This was the type of slavery that existed for centuries in the ancient and classical civilizations that gave rise to the modern world.

The Origins of a New Slave Trade

The ancient form of slavery was quite distinct from the new practice that emerged in the mid-fifteenth century as Europeans began to conduct a trade in West African slaves. The new form of slavery recognized the slave as an object: as chattel that could be bought, sold, and traded. This concept also defined the slave as African. For the first time, a distinct group of people was recognized as potential slaves not because of a loss on the battlefield but simply because of the circumstances of their birth. Within a few generations the term "African" became synonymous with slavery.

Europeans first became interested in the exploration and conquest of Africa in the early fifteenth century. A military expedition in 1415 commanded by Portugal's Prince Henry ("the Navigator") resulted in the conquest of Ceuta, a fortified African city (located in modern-day Morocco) that became the first portion of the African continent to fall under European colonial occupation. The conquest of Ceuta was primarily an economic venture of the Portuguese, but rooted within this new adventure were ulterior motives: gold, glory, and God that would inspire subsequent exploration of Africa and eventually the Americas. Once the Portuguese possessed Ceuta they desired to know more of Africa and the potential riches that it might contain.

The exploration of coastal Africa was made difficult by the limitations of sailing technology and the virtual absence of cartographic knowledge in the early fifteenth century. Prince Henry sought to stimulate further exploration in 1421 by outfitting a school for sailors at Sagres, on Portugal's most southwestern point, to look outward to the seas and perfect new navigational tools and methods that might render sailing craft better able to overcome challenges that coastal Africa might present. New types of ship design, such as the caravel, which combined square-rigged and lateen sails, were developed and tested along with modifications to primitive navigational instruments like the magnetic compass and the astrolabe. The sailors and technicians at Sagres labored to develop sailing vessels that could explore the unknown parts of the world beyond.

The physical geography of coastal Africa also contributed to the difficulty experienced by early Portuguese navigators who sought to explore and chart the coastline of the African continent. The vast expanse of the African continent made the business of exploring difficult and time-consuming. Expeditions generally remained within sight of the coastline as they explored so that they would not become lost in an unknown sea, and the shape and size of the continent caused peculiar problems that the sailors had to overcome. Changes in latitude brought about differences in the prevailing winds, and shifting directions of coastline might mean sailing with the wind at times or sailing against the wind at others. Facing these obstacles and limitations, Portuguese exploration of the African coast persisted throughout the fifteenth century, albeit at a slow pace.

Forces greater than the acquisition of knowledge for its own sake motivated the venture that the Portuguese sailors began after their initial success at Ceuta. The economic desire to acquire great wealth was one of the primary factors that inspired technological innovation and persistence among those who plied the waters of the African coastline. Europeans understood that Africa was the landmass of indeterminate size that stood between Europe and the markets of Asia. For centuries exotic Asian products—silks and spices—had reached European markets via an overland-caravan route, but the uncertainties of wars and of banditry had made the overland-trade route dangerous and expensive. Many believed that an all-water route to Asia could produce a savings in costs that would enhance the profits garnered by Asian goods. The Portuguese wanted to round the African continent in order to realize the great profits that Asian markets could garner in European markets.

Faith and fear were other motivating factors that prompted the European expeditions along coastal Africa. Many Europeans had come to believe that Western European Christendom was under attack by the numerically superior forces of Islam. The combination of the Reconquista (711–1492), the seven-hundred-year experience with Muslims in the Iberian

Peninsula, with Muslim excursions into the area of southeastern Europe made many Christians fear that they were under attack and surrounded by enemies to the east and to the west. Many began to imagine that there might be other Christian kingdoms, perhaps in Africa, that could join forces with European Christians to counter the threat posed by Islam. There arose a belief that Africa contained a large Christian kingdom ruled by a semilegendary figure named Prester John, and many Europeans hoped to find this Christian ruler and form an alliance with him. The mythical kingdom of Prester John may have emerged from stories that Europeans had heard of the Coptic Christian population that lived in Ethiopia.

Europeans also felt threatened by the economic hegemony that Muslims were achieving in the eastern Mediterranean world. In 1453 the Ottoman Turks had seized control of the trading center of Constantinople, one of the principal entrepôts for Asian caravan trade routes. The Europeans did not want to deal with Muslim middlemen and the higher prices that might be involved in trade, and increasingly they wanted to find their own all-water route to Asia, which prompted further exploration of coastal Africa.

Portuguese sailors hoped to make the seas their domain as they explored the waters of coastal Africa. In 1425 they captured the Canary Islands, which had been occupied by the Spanish (Castilians) since 1405. In 1431 Portuguese sailors Diogo de Seville and Gonçalo Cabral claimed the uninhabited Azores for Portugal. With these two archipelagoes in their possession, the Portuguese sailors began to explore and map the western coast of Africa. Shortly thereafter, in 1433, they reached Cape Bojador (in modern-day Morocco) and continued sending expeditions farther southward.

The expeditions continued until Portuguese sailors had made their way south of the Sahara. It was here that the Europeans first came into contact with black Africa in the early 1440s. In 1441 the Portuguese sailor Antam Gonçalvez returned to Lisbon with ten captured Africans, who were sold as slaves in the public market. This was the first recorded episode of Europeans transporting and marketing Africans as slaves.

Expeditions continued as Nino Tristram reached the mouth of the Senegal River in 1444 and Dinís Dias reached Cape Verde (in modern-day Senegal) the following year. A Portuguese chronicler in 1445 noted that a large slave auction, which he described as "a terrible scene of misery and disorder," was conducted in the city of Lagos, Portugal. There were more than nine hundred African slaves in Portugal by 1447. The formalized trading of Africans became more institutionalized when, in 1448, Portugal's Prince Henry authorized

construction of the first European slave-trading center and fort on the African coast at Arguin Bay. Exploration had given way to commerce, and the institutional structure of the slave trade began to emerge.

Regular trade in African captives to Portugal continued into the 1450s as an estimated eight hundred Africans were transported to Europe each year and were sold as slaves. The market for these captives expanded beyond Portugal as slave traders found ready buyers in Spain and other sugar islands in the Mediterranean. The hand-in-hand exploration and commercial exploitation of Africa continued as navigators continued southward while further establishing the mechanics of the slave trade. By 1462 the Portuguese had created a huge slave-trading center at Cacheu (in modern-day Guinea-Bissau) that was capable of holding thousands of captives at one time.

By 1471 the Portuguese sailors had reached the Gold Coast (modern-day Ghana) where they established a trading center at Elmina. This location would eventually become the site of one of the largest and most notorious slave-trading castles (São Jorge da Mina) on the west coast of Africa. Other sailors reached the Bight of Benin by 1472, São Tomé by 1475, and the mouth of the Congo River by 1482. Reports from all of the locations indicated that numerous Africans were present who could be easily subdued and enslaved. The Portuguese had found an almost endless supply of potential slaves, but there was not yet a tremendous demand for the slaves that could be provided.

The nature of the slave trade changed in 1486 when the Portuguese conducted a trade agreement with the rulers of Benin. In exchange for captured Africans, the Portuguese agreed to trade European-made firearms. This decision, and others that followed, changed the nature of warfare and conquest in much of West Africa and destabilized states and kingdoms. The escalation of warfare in Africa that was prompted by the introduction of new weapons and the slave-raiding expeditions that were conducted to acquire captives began to produce more and more captives. War begat the taking of prisoners, and prisoners found themselves as captives who would be sold as slaves.

By the time the Portuguese sailor Bartolomeu Dias reached southern Africa at the Cape of Good Hope in 1488, the mechanics of the slave trade were well established, and a series of forts, castles, and trading centers had been set up along much of the West African coastline. Even though finding a route to Asia remained the primary goal and finding Prester John's kingdom was perhaps a distant second, the Portuguese had come to realize that trade in Africans as slaves was a potentially lucrative business that, for the time being, was Portugal's private monopoly. The same year that Dias stood at the Cape of Good Hope, the king of Portugal presented Pope Innocent VII with a gift of one hundred African slaves.

Another Route to the Indies

Christopher Columbus's 1492 assertion that Asia could be reached by sailing west from Europe did not find many ready believers. It was not the concept of a round earth that troubled learned Europeans; instead, it was Columbus's belief that earth was small enough that sailing vessels of the day could safely make a transoceanic voyage. After several European courts rejected his ideas, Columbus found support in the court of Ferdinand and Isabella, rulers of Castille, who agreed to support his proposed expedition in the hope that they might arrive in Asia before their Portuguese rivals. Since the Spanish had been preoccupied by their efforts to remove the Muslims from the Iberian Peninsula, a task they completed at Grenada in 1492, any expedition that might overcome the Portuguese in the race to Asia was worth the risk.

The discovery of land on October 12, 1492, changed the course of modern history in ways that Columbus could never have fathomed. Despite the four voyages that he made, Columbus resisted the claim that a "New World" had been found; he preferred to believe that he had found the outer reaches of Asia. Yet even before his death in 1506, Columbus had witnessed the introduction of African slaves as laborers; slaves were first delivered to Hispaniola in April of 1502. Even before the introduction of the first Africans, the practice of enslaving the Indians—the indigenous Arawak and Carib (later called Taino) who inhabited the islands of the Caribbean—had begun.

The decimation of the indigenous populations that followed the discovery and conquest of the Americas was not effected as part of Spain's design. The destruction of millions, a genocide of immense proportions, was largely the result of epidemics and disease against which the indigenous peoples of the Americas had no natural immunity and were highly susceptible. In the so-called Columbian exchange whereby germs were transmitted, nearly 80 percent of some indigenous populations were killed within the first half-century of Spain's arrival in the New World; among some groups there were no survivors.

Besides disease, the enslavement of the indigenous people and the mistreatment that they received at the hands of the Spanish caused the tremendous decline in their numbers. As early as 1511, some Spaniards began to take note of the destruction that was taking place, and a few began to speak out on the unpopular topic.

On the island of Hispaniola Father Antonio Montesinos delivered a pointed sermon on the first Sunday of Advent in December 1511 in which he took the Spanish to task for the poor treatment of the Indians that was taking place on the island. Other clergymen would soon lend their voices to the crusade for social justice.

The Dominican friar Bartolomé de Las Casas began to speak out on behalf of the Indians after serving as a missionary on the island of Cuba. He appealed directly to the Spanish Crown to intervene so that the indigenous peoples of the Americas would not be destroyed by the abuses of the Spanish. Known as the "Apostle to the Indies," Las Casas wanted the Spanish Crown to protect the Indians so that they could be converted to Christianity. Recognizing that the need for a ready labor supply was an ever-present demand of the New World colonies, Las Casas recommended that Africans be introduced into the Spanish colonies to serve as laborers. In his efforts to protect the rights of the indigenous peoples of the Americas, the advice of Las Casas made possible the importation of millions of Africans to the Americas. Although he imagined that the Africans would be wage laborers who could also be converted to Christianity, the Africans who were brought to the Americas were transported across the Atlantic and sold as slaves.

Initially, the Spanish Crown questioned what types of Africans should be sent to the New World. In the early sixteenth century the Spanish considered *ladinos,* Africans who had been brought to Spain and made Christians, to be of a different quality than *bozales,* who were described as wild Africans. The first Africans who were transported to the Americas as slaves were *ladinos,* and at first they were sent exclusively to Hispaniola to assist with gold-mining efforts.

The Spanish also established the contractual mechanism through which they conducted the slave trade when they established the *asiento* in 1518. Under this system, the *asiento* (contract) would be assigned to slave traders to deliver up to four thousand Africans per year to the Spanish colonies in the Americas. The Portuguese were the first to hold the *asiento* and deliver slaves to the Spanish colonies, but in subsequent years the contract would be held by the Dutch, the French, and the British. The number of slaves that could be imported rose with time, especially after the labor demands substantially increased during the sugar revolution of the eighteenth century. The *asiento* was a very lucrative business arrangement, and the nations that held it tended to profit immensely from the trade.

Even though the Spanish Crown had only authorized the importation of *ladino* slaves (considered to be superior because of their time in Spain and their religious conversion), the Spanish soon realized that their expectations differed from social realities. In 1521, slaves belonging to Diego Colón, the son of Christopher Columbus, revolted on Christmas Day on the island of Hispaniola. This was the first slave insurrection to take place in the Americas. The revolt lasted for about a week and was eventually suppressed by Spanish authorities, who used great cruelty in restoring order to the colony.

Incorporating Slave Labor in the Americas

The initial colonization of the Americas by Spain was followed by similar exploration and conquest by other European powers. During the sixteenth century, the Portuguese began to develop the colony of Brazil, and various island possessions or territorial claims on the Guinea coast were made by England, France, Holland, and Denmark. In all of these possessions, the initial colonization pattern followed that of the Spanish model as Europeans sought out riches in gold or silver. If precious metals were not found, Europeans generally tried to cultivate a cash crop that could benefit the mother country through an economic order based on mercantilism. In such a system, colonies supplied the raw materials that could be used in the production of manufactured goods, and they also provided markets where finished goods might eventually be sold. It was an exploitative economic structure designed to generate profits in specie (gold or silver) that would grow the national treasury and determine the nation's relative wealth and power.

The other European colonial powers followed the pattern that Spain had begun by incorporating African slave labor as a central element of colonial economic life. The business of the slave trade became increasingly regularized as colonial powers depended on a steady supply of Africans to labor on the plantations and farms and in the mines of the Americas. In most of the colonies there was a clear preference for male slaves as laborers; as a result, a gender imbalance developed in practically all of the colonies in the Americas. It therefore became difficult for slave families to form, and consequently the slave population grew not through natural increase, but rather through continual importation of new Africans to the New World colonies.

The practice of enslaving Indians alongside Africans persisted in some New World colonies for the first few generations after the conquest of the Americas. Despite efforts to curb the practice of enslaving Indians, the custom did not end immediately. In 1537, Pope Paul III issued the bull "Veritas Ipsa," in which he de-

creed that the indigenous peoples of the Americas should not be enslaved. However, this proclamation did not carry the weight of law. Spain's New Laws of the Indies, promulgated in 1542, echoed these sentiments, but many of the Spanish settlers in the Americas circumvented the law and continued to enslave Indians. In time, however, the decimation of the Indian populations made further reliance on Indian slaves impractical, and so Europeans turned to the exclusive use of imported Africans as slave laborers.

Many of the Caribbean colonies operated what became known as "breaking plantations," in which new Africans were conditioned to their new role as slaves. Slaveowners were always uncertain about whether a new slave would be able to tolerate the combined effects of the heat, oppressive humidity, diseases, and the labor regimen imposed in the Americas. Those slaves who survived for at least one year on the breaking plantations became known as "seasoned slaves" because they had proven their ability to survive and labor effectively under the conditions of the New World. Planters hoping to resell slaves knew that seasoned slaves would be worth much more at an auction than newly arrived Africans, who had not yet proven their mettle.

Another, equally important task performed on the breaking plantation was to discourage the slave from retaining African cultural values. Slaves had to be indoctrinated into the culture of slavery, and in doing so they had to lose all aspects of their African identity. African names were taken away, and new slave names, usually nonsensical or humorous in origin, were assigned in their place. It was common, for example, to hear of slaves named Cato, Cicero, or Caesar after figures from classical Roman history, or perhaps mythological figures like Jupiter or Apollo. Slaves were also deprived of their African religious identity. Whether a slave was a Muslim or had practiced an indigenous African animist faith, planters in the Americas believed that they had to be stripped of that cultural identity. If a slave was to have religious beliefs, they were limited to Christian beliefs, and planters were careful about who could preach to slaves. African languages and other traditions were also stripped.

Academics have continued to argue about the degree to which traditional African identities were maintained in what are called "Africanisms"—cultural carryovers that survived the attempt to break the slaves of a remembered past. Some have argued that the physical and emotional anguish of the transatlantic Middle Passage to the Americas and the breaking plantations was strong enough to destroy all cultural ties with an earlier African life. According to this view, slave culture was a formulation of new, learned cultural practices that formed through accretion in the New World setting. Other scholars believe that some Africanisms did survive, and that modern phenomena such as the role of a matriarchal family structure is evidence that some African cultural forms persisted through slavery.

European powers also developed slave codes that they promulgated in their colonies and enforced strictly. These codes severely limited the liberties that were granted to slaves and made them learn to live in fear of patrollers and other enforcers who operated within the plantation districts and made sure that the codes were being enforced. The French *Code Noir*, first issued in 1685, contained harsh provisions but tempered them with certain religious concerns. Under the *Code Noir*, religious instruction was required for all slaves, slave marriages were permitted, and slaves were prohibited from working on Sundays and holidays. Other slave codes, however, were less liberal in the privileges they permitted.

Since the slaves' liberties were strictly regulated by the codes and enforced within the colonies, slaves had few means of resisting. Still, opposition did exist. One of the greatest means of agency available to the slave was running away, or "stealing oneself away from slavery," and causing a financial loss to the slaveowner. Slaves frequently ran away and sometimes lived on the fringes of settled areas as "outlyers" who would periodically raid plantations and farms for needed food and provisions. Other groups of slave fugitives lived together in settlements called "maroon communities" (from the Spanish cimmaron, or "wild horse") that were established in dense forests, swamps, or rugged mountains. Maroon communities were known as *palenques* among the Spanish and as *quilombos* among the Portuguese, and the French term *marronage* was used to describe the general practice of living in the wilderness as a fugitive. Several maroon communities existed for many years in places such as Jamaica's Blue Mountains, the interior of Suriname, and perhaps the most famous, the *quilombo* of Palmares in Brazil.

The slaves who lived in maroon communities generally reverted to the African tribal customs and traditions with which they were familiar. Housing architecture and village styles resembled those of West African communities. Indigenous religious practices, including the application of conjure/vodou, was common in many of these settlements. Elements of the Americas were also present, as many of the customs and traditions represented syncretic forms as Christian tradition blended with elements of Islam or animist religious practices. The maroon communities were usually well defended, and on occasion the colonial militias that attempted to subdue the settlements were repulsed by maroon fighters. The Palmares *quilombo* survived for nearly eighty years, and some maroons were able to negotiate peace settlements with colonial authorities that won a degree of autonomy for the maroon settlements. As early as 1542, Spanish authorities reported that three thousand of the thirty thousand slaves who were estimated to be in Hispaniola were maroons.

One of the curious aspects of slavery in the New World colonies is that, while a concerted abolitionist movement emerged to protect the natural rights of the Indians, no similar movement emerged to protect slaves' rights. Bartolomé de Albornoz, a law professor at the University of Mexico, wrote a 1573 essay that attacked the legal foundation on which Spain's enslavement and sale of Africans was based, but no popular antislavery movement resulted. Although there were clerics who cared deeply and sincerely about saving the souls of African slaves, few rose to be their patrons and criticize the institution that held them in bondage. Although the Jesuit priest Peter Claver baptized an estimated three hundred thousand slaves during his forty years of ministry in the area that became Colombia, he did not become an advocate in the model of Las Casas but chose instead to remain silent on the injustice of slavery.

Slavery generated tremendous profits in the New World colonies, and few Europeans were willing to criticize the system. This became especially clear during the eighteenth century, when the expansion of sugar cultivation across Brazil and throughout much of the Caribbean basin transformed the plantation-based economy of the colonies in the New World. As sugar cultivation exploded in the Americas, the demand for African slaves also increased. This rapid transformation skewed the demographic profile of most of the European colonies. Blacks held a significant numerical advantage over white settlers in the sugar islands, and only the presence of vigilant militia mitigated the dangers emanating from the potential for mutiny. When resistance did occur, repression was always swift and brutal.

The Complexity of Race and Status

Colonial society in the Americas began with a tripartite division in which Europeans and colonial whites (*creoles*) were free and Indians and Africans were capable of being enslaved. Over time, as laws and decrees changed Indians' status, they too became free. With the abolition of Indian slavery, only Africans remained enslaved, but over time some Africans became free.

This complexity of race and status created a unique social dimension in the New World colonies.

Africans could become free in a variety of ways. Sometimes a master might legally free a slave in a will, and legislative assemblies also had the power to manumit, or free, a slave who had performed some type of valuable or meritorious service. Slaves could also become free through purchasing their own freedom, a privilege that was sometimes only available to skilled slaves who had knowledge of a special craft or trade. Other slaves became free at birth because they were the offspring of a master who desired his mixed-race child to be born free. Since the laws in most colonial settings declared that the status of a child was determined by the condition of the mother, slave mothers would have given birth to slave children unless a white father intervened and freed the child at birth.

In addition to the original tripartite division of society among whites, Indians, and Africans, other racial combinations soon emerged. Among the Spanish, the practice of identifying *castas* (or racial identities) was maintained until it was mathematically impossible to distinguish identities. Terms like *mulatto* (white and African), *mestizo* (white and Indian), and *zambo* (African and Indian) were used to distinguish mixed-race offspring born in New World colonies. Notions of racial or ethnic solidarity were made more tenuous by the many admixtures that were found in the Americas.

One of the most challenging aspects of the cultural milieu that emerged in the Americas was the relationship that existed between free blacks and slaves. In many respects, the presence of a free black population within any colony seemed to negate any theoretical assumptions upon which a race-based system of slavery was structured, and therefore white colonists generally viewed free blacks as a troublesome. Still, free blacks could own property and were sometimes persons of considerable wealth—some were even slaveowners themselves. Free blacks were not provided with all of the political and civil liberties that were given to whites; thus the free blacks were, in effect, slaves without masters.

Free blacks were torn over the question of identity. Some, particularly those who had been slaves themselves, resented the institution of slavery but viewed themselves as incapable of doing anything to challenge a system that was so well entrenched and so pervasive. Other free blacks felt very little racial solidarity with enslaved Africans and sought instead to fashion their culture on the basis of a European model that was deemed more cultured and proper. Since free blacks were often so divided in their sympathies and loyalties, African slaves in the early colonial era often lacked the support of those who might have been capable of being their advocates and mitigating the harsher demons of enslavement.

A Well-Oiled Machine

The system of the transatlantic slave trade that first emerged in the early sixteenth century was perfected as trade to the Americas grew. In the process of this growth, the slave trade emerged as a business that was both sordid and quite lucrative. There were tremendous profits to be earned in the slave trade, but it was a dangerous enterprise. Slave ship captains operated their vessels under conditions designed to maximize profits, but these conditions often did very little for the Africans who were being transported. Ships were periodically overloaded by captains, who used a system called "tight packing" to transport as many Africans as possible on the transoceanic leg of the voyage known as the Middle Passage. Cramped quarters, lack of food and fresh water, the persistence of disease, and the stench of human misery and filth made the Middle Passage a horrid experience for the African slaves aboard the slave ships. Not all of the Africans survived the voyage, and the dead and near-dead were often tossed into the sea during the crossing. The certainty of profitability was guaranteed by insurance companies that issued policies protecting ship owners from human losses.

Mortality rates were high among the Africans aboard slave ships, but the rates were even higher for crewmembers. The coastal areas of Africa were known as the "white man's grave" because many tropical diseases killed European sailors who had no immunity to malaria and other such maladies. The danger posed by insurrection at sea also made crewmembers's work quite precarious. Slave vessels were usually well armed and sometimes even included small cannon, but if weapons fell into the hands of the Africans, the lives of crewmembers could be at risk. In addition, slave ships also had to be concerned with pirates who robbed slave ships of their cargoes on the high seas and killed crewmembers.

After the British acquired the *asiento* in the War of the Spanish Succession (1702–1714), English ports like Liverpool and Bristol became some of the primary home ports of slaving vessels. Fine city houses symbolized the wealth accrued through the triangular trade as ships plied their way from Britain to the West African coast, from West Africa to the Caribbean, and from the Caribbean back to Britain. During this exchange, the commodities of rum, slaves, and sugar, filled the holds of the ships that operated their routes like clockwork and generated profits from each leg of their venture. The slave trade may not have been the most respectable trade, but it was a lucrative business. By 1744, 50 percent of the ships that operated out of Liverpool were involved in the slave trade.

Requiem

In 1441 the Portuguese carried ten Africans to Lisbon, where they were auctioned at a market. By the time the colonial era drew to a close, an estimated 10 million Africans had been transported across the Atlantic Ocean to labor on plantations, farms, and mines in the Americas. What had begun as a trickle quickly turned into a mighty stream. The slave trade that emerged was partly the result of the simultaneous growth of Europeans' familiarity with Africa and exploration of the New World. The magnitude of the trade was amplified by the establishment of cash crops such as sugar, and later cotton, that became staples in spite of the means of production associated with their cultivation and harvest.

Although slavery had monumental consequences for the Americas—the effects of which are still being felt—the impact of slavery on Africa itself was also consequential and tragic. The depopulation of the African continent during the Diaspora paved the way for subsequent generations of European colonialism. In spite of decolonization and twentieth-century independence movements, much of Africa is still reeling from the ill effects of the slave trade and European colonialism.

The historical reality of the transatlantic slave trade changed the history of the world and certainly impacted the development of the New World colonies in consequential ways. The system of slavery that originated in the Caribbean islands and eventually spread into Mexico, Central America, and South America would also take root in isolated colonies established by the British on the Atlantic seaboard of North America. With 178 years of experience already accomplished and the infrastructure of the slave trade in place, slavery would take root in the North American colonies and soon flourish. The words of the Senegalese poet Leopold Sedar Senghor seem appropriate: "Listen to the voices of our Forebears . . . in the smoky cabin, souls that wish us well are murmuring."

EARLY AMERICAN SLAVERY IN THE COLONIES AND THE HARDENING OF RACIAL DISTINCTIONS

England established its first permanent colony on the Atlantic seaboard of North America at Jamestown in 1607. The settlement was formed on an island in the James River in a region the settlers named Virginia. The colony's location on an island, particularly one that was 30 miles inland from the coast, was believed to provide a degree of protection from the ravages of Atlantic storms and the dangers posed by possible Indian attack. The decision was seen as a wise one, since previous efforts to establish a settlement on Roanoke Island two decades earlier had failed for these suspected reasons. Still, Jamestown was not the most ideal location for planting a colony.

From its start, Jamestown was a tenuous settlement. The elevation of the island was low, and the region was prone to occasional flooding. Swamps abounded in the area, but the settlement's location north of the tropical latitudes meant that many of the diseases and maladies that plagued warmer climates were not present at Jamestown. The settlement fell within the coastal region of Virginia known as the Tidewater, a region that was affected by the daily ebb and flow of tidal changes. Thus the potential contamination of groundwater and of the James River—the sources of the colony's fresh water supply—was always a concern as habitation of the region by English colonists affected the local ecology.

Tremendous numbers of colonists died within the first year of their arrival in Virginia, and the pattern continued for the first three years of the colony's existence. The difficulties of this "starving time" as it came to be known caused some of the initial settlers to leave the colony and live among the Indians where food was more abundant, while other reports suggested that cannibalism may have occurred in the island settlement as well. Famine reduced the settlement's population from a height of 500 residents down to only 60. Conditions were so bad in Jamestown and the mortality rates were so high that by 1610 the colonists had decided to abandon the venture and return to England. They were only halted in their evacuation by the arrival of a royal governor, Thomas Lord De La Warr, who brought much-needed provisions and additional settlers to the incipient colony.

Virginia was settled by English colonists sent to North America by the London Company of Adventurers, a joint-stock venture of English merchant-capitalists who hoped to profit from the colony's economic success. Judging primarily from the Spanish experience in the Americas, many English investors believed that precious metals like gold and silver would be as abundant in North America as they had been in Mexico and Peru. If this were true and if an indigenous labor force could be utilized to exploit such resources, the economic potential of a colony in Virginia was boundless. Much of this belief, however, was premised on speculation that had very little real bearing on the conditions in Tidewater Virginia.

The business of carving a colony in the wilderness of a New World environment was a difficult one that few of the colony's initial settlers had fully contemplated before their arrival. The labor-intensive efforts were made even less appealing when it became clear that precious metals did not abound in the region. Many of the colonists' and their capitalist financiers' initial hopes were dashed as it became clear that easy wealth was not to be had in colonial Virginia. The success of the venture and the profitability that its investors deemed essential would have to be obtained through alternative means.

In other parts of the Americas, the Spanish and Portuguese colonizers had begun to cultivate cash crops in areas in which precious metals had not been located. As early as 1580, the Portuguese settlers in Brazil had begun to cultivate sugar on a large scale, and Spanish colonists had begun to grow coffee and tobacco on some of their Caribbean possessions. In those colonies developing single-crop, agricultural-based economies, two unique, supply-oriented issues had arisen. One was the delivery of sufficient foodstuffs and other necessary provisions to the colonies was essential, and the other was the introduction of a labor force that could handle the intensive agricultural demands of large-scale production. The British would learn from the experiences of other European colonizers in the Americas

and would seek to transform Virginia into a profitable venture based on export-oriented agricultural production.

Tobacco became Virginia's main cash crop. Indians had cultivated a strain of tobacco, and their knowledge convinced some of the early English settlers that large-scale production of the crop in the colony might be possible. By 1612, an Englishman named John Rolfe had introduced a variety of tobacco that had been successfully cultivated in the West Indies, and the crop acclimated well to the soil and conditions in Virginia. Europeans had become familiar with tobacco, a product of the Americas that had first been introduced to Europe only after the Spanish conquest, and both the novelty and the addictive nature of the new product had made it fashionable in social circles of European society. Interestingly, as early as 1604, King James I of Great Britain had written "A Counterblaste to Tobacco," an essay that criticized the noxious leaf, and by 1620, a Dutch physician named Tobias Venner had issued the first medical warning of the harmful effects associated with tobacco.

Early success in growing tobacco in Virginia convinced both investors in London and officials in the colony that further cultivation and expansion of the colony were warranted. During the 1610s, additional colonists were transported to Virginia not to seek and find precious metals, but rather to become farmers. It was a time of extraordinary transformation in the colony, as the infrastructure for a plantation-based society and an export-oriented economy converged to produce and distribute tobacco. The growth of colonial Virginia did not follow a prescribed path; instead, the colony's growth and expansion were determined by the exigencies of a burgeoning market. In many respects, the society and culture that emerged in Virginia, and subsequently in other British colonies in North America, were a product of market forces that drove colonial policy.

Land Rich and Labor Poor

It did not take the English colonists long to realize that North America was a vast region that possessed ample lands for agricultural development, but this awareness was tempered by the understanding that legions of settlers would be needed to tap the land's productive potential. The early colonists were a hardy lot who were willing to undertake a treacherous ocean voyage and plant themselves in an unknown and alien environment in the hope that they might encounter success.

Stories about the "starving time" in early Virginia, reports of high mortality, and the difficulties of enduring in the harsh conditions of frontier life were not particularly appealing to those who might otherwise have considered life as a Virginia colonist. It soon became clear to both the colony's financial patrons and its officials that Virginia was in need of an influx of settlers who would become the center of a tobacco-based export economy.

England contained a substantial population of landless, dispossessed peasants who were potential North American colonists. The enclosure movement, which arose when traditional rights to share common pasture lands in villages throughout the English countryside were eliminated to foster development of an early woolens industry, created a growing population of the poor that presented a deep social and economic dilemma. English jails became filled with individuals who were imprisoned because of their debts, and the fear of peasant rebellion in the countryside was an ever-present concern. Authorities believed that the many dangers posed by a disaffected peasant population could be remedied through colonization.

With land as the most available resource in North America, colonial officials in Virginia and subsequent English colonies devised the headright system, in which settlers who relocated to the North American colonies were guaranteed 50 acres of land as an incentive. Such a promise would certainly have been appealing to the landless in England, but many did not have the means of making the transoceanic voyage to North America to claim the headright that had been promised. The system was also fraught with abuses. Unscrupulous ship captains sometimes transported colonists to the North American colonies with the intention of claiming the headrights of their passengers as payment for the cost of the voyage. As such, there were many individuals who became owners of huge tracts in Virginia and other colonies by claiming property that was not rightfully theirs.

The headright system seemed to make sense for an area that was land rich but labor poor. Yet the circumstances by which impoverished English peasants who might otherwise have become colonists faced limited options reduced the overall effectiveness of the system, and the policy was eventually suspended. Still, the need for colonists remained great, and the profitability of the entire colonial enterprise hinged on delivering a steady labor supply to North America to render productive the agricultural capabilities of the land.

The solution that evolved in the British colonies was the introduction of contract laborers known as indentured servants. Although the terms of their individual contracts varied, the typical indentured servant would agree to sell his or her labor for a period of three to seven years as payment for the cost of their transoceanic transport to North America. In exchange, those who issued the contracts generally promised to equip the servants with so-called freedom dues—the tools and a parcel of land provided upon completion of their indenture so that these individuals could become independent farmers in the tradition of the English yeoman. The contracts generally circumscribed the rights and privileges of the indentured servants, making them beholden to the prerogatives of the masters who had financed their voyages. The contracts were written in such a way that any servant who violated the terms of the contract might be punished by having additional years of service, without pay, added to their period of indenture.

The indentured servant system clearly exploited laborers, but nonetheless thousands of impoverished English peasants, along with Europeans of other nationalities, accepted the offer and sold themselves into a period of limited servitude in North America. Ships packed with European indentured servants plied the waters of the Atlantic in a fashion similar to that of slaves in the Middle Passage, but the indentured servants traveled with the assurance that they would one day be freed. Estimates are that by the time that the colonial period ended, nearly half of the residents of Great Britain's North American colonies could trace their ancestry through individuals who had first arrived in the colonies as indentured servants.

After their service was complete, white indentured servants emerged as independent landowners who could blend into the social and political life of the colony. Since there was no particular onus placed upon the freed indentured servant and no racial or ethnic distinctiveness made them stand out, the transition from indentured servitude to freedom was relatively seamless, and former indentured servants experienced the blessings of freedom and citizenship upon completion of their labor tenure. In this fashion, for some the society that emerged in the British colonies had the appearance of being egalitarian.

The work of the indentured servants varied tremendously. Many found themselves employed in agricultural labor since the profitability of the colonial venture depended on the success of the tobacco crop. Other indentured servants, particularly women, found employment as household and domestic servants. Others still were engaged in the difficult task of creating a colony out of wilderness. The clearing of timber, brush, and stumps to create and till fields was a time-consuming and laborious task, but it needed to be done as the colony grew and agricultural lands under cultivation expanded. Other aspects of the colonial infrastructure also needed to be created, and indentured servants found themselves employed in these capacities. Indentured servants also cleared roads, constructed bridges over streams, and erected fortifications to secure the colonial outposts from potential enemies.

Even with the promise of freedom at the end of their contracted service, indentured servants in the British colonies experienced tremendous hardships. Mortality rates remained high among the indentured population, so there was not always the guarantee that one would survive to see freedom and become an independent farmer. In addition, the contracts for indentured servants could be bought and traded, so the indentured servant labored at the whim of the master who issued the contract. Many indentured servants found the labor expected of them in the British colonies to be much more severe than that experienced by apprentices in England, and many indentured servants were physically and sexually exploited.

Indentured servants frequently ran away from their masters in an effort to void the terms of their contracted labor. Those who were captured generally had additional years of service added into their contracts. For the particularly recalcitrant, indentured servitude could become a virtual lifetime of forced labor. Sometimes indentured servants were beaten as a means of punishment, some were branded, and egregious offenders often filled the colonial jails. Occasionally, indentured servants who escaped lived among Indian communities, and after the introduction of African slavery into the British colonies, they sometimes lived in isolated maroon communities or helped organize potential slave revolts.

Indentured servitude remained in use even after the introduction of Africans into the British colonies and the growth of slave labor. The custom of indentured servitude that largely involved white laborers was a striking contrast to slavery that relied exclusively on black laborers. The white versus black dichotomy of race would eventually fashion the freedom-versus-slavery pattern that persisted throughout subsequent generations.

1619 and Beyond

African American history and the approximate start of slavery in the British North American colonies began on August 20, 1619, when a Dutch ship delivered "twenty and odd" Africans to the English settlement at Jamestown, Virginia, where they were sold at auction as indentured servants. Although they did not become slaves immediately, these twenty individuals represented the first permanent involuntary African immigrants in the region that eventually became the United States. According to the contemporary records of John Rolfe, "About the last of August came in a dutch man of warre that sold us twenty Negars." Most indentured servants were released after serving a term, generally three to seven years, and then were allowed to become property owners and participate in civic affairs. Within the first generation of their arrival in Virginia, most of the first African servants had witnessed their period of indenture extended to the point where they became servants for life.

It is difficult to say exactly when slavery began in the English colonies. Africans were first introduced in Virginia in 1619, but the first laws specifically recognizing the status of slaves as a class of persons do not appear until December of 1641, when section 91 of the Massachusetts *Body of Liberties* recognized the existence of a class of slaves within the colony. It is clear that the legal status of Africans began to emerge within the first two decades of their introduction into the English colonies, but the details of that transformation and the complexities contained therein are difficult to fathom. In Virginia, for example, a free black named Anthony Johnson imported five servants into the colony.

The use of Africans as slave laborers in the British colonies presented clear advantages over the continued use of white indentured servants. Slaves were much cheaper and easier to obtain than were indentured servants. Since no "freedom dues" were involved, the mere provision of food, shelter, and clothing was all that was necessary to sustain a slave laborer and the quality and extent of these sustenance benefits could vary tremendously through the colonies. In addition, the procurement necessary to obtain a ready supply of indentured servants was not a problem with the use of African slave labor. The transatlantic slave trade had emerged by the early seventeenth century as a global enterprise that regularly transported thousands of Africans to various destinations in the Americas where they were sold as slaves. The adoption of slavery within the British colonies simply tapped into the existing slave trade network that had perfected the efficient delivery of large numbers of Africans to the Americas.

In addition, the badge of racial distinctiveness set the Africans apart from European indentured servants. Although an indentured servant might escape from one location and try to blend into another community as just another English settler, this opportunity was not a viable option for Africans. Racial distinctiveness made the African stand out and indirectly made all colonial observers part of the elaborate maintenance network that was necessary to establish and sustain a slave-based economic order. Although the Africans did find occasional allies among disaffected indentured servants and Indians, they found themselves placed in a setting in which white residents were de facto slave catchers upon whom the peace, stability, and economic success of the colonies relied.

Africans also were alien to the English political and civil tradition. Although indentured servants could always appeal to their traditional rights and prerogatives as Englishmen, such was not the privilege of African slaves. Although white indentured servants could expect the benefits that English tradition and precedent accorded them, Africans were effectively a class of persons outside of the law who were not naturally entitled to the hereditary rights of Englishmen. For example, Englishmen could enter into contracts with other Englishmen by which both parties would be honor bound to comply with terms and stipulations, but such was not the case with Africans. In 1661, Virginia authorities declared that thereafter all black indentured servants would be servants for life.

The Frontier of Slave Territory

Virginia was the first of the thirteen British colonies planted on the Atlantic seaboard of North America. It would remain the only colony in the region until religious dissenters from England settled at Plymouth, Massachusetts, in 1620, and were followed to the region by a large contingent of English Puritans by the end of the decade. Even with two colonies—Virginia and Massachusetts—there existed vast expanses of frontier that remained unsettled on the Atlantic seaboard. Those fugitives who sought to escape from their conditions in either colony had ample space in which to navigate should they decide to run away.

In 1624 the Dutch planted a colony at New Netherlands (which included parts of present-day Delaware, New Jersey, New York, and Connecticut), located between the English colonies of Virginia and Massachusetts. Building on their active involvement in the transatlantic slave trade, the Dutch introduced Africans into their colony in substantial numbers. It was common for Dutch slaving vessels to sell as many Africans as they could in the Caribbean islands and then to bring those Africans who could not be sold to New Netherlands. Such Africans, often the elderly,

the lame, or the otherwise infirm, were frequently enslaved as household servants among the early Dutch families that settled New Amsterdam (New York City after 1665) and some of the patroon estates in the Hudson Valley region. Throughout the colonial period, New Netherlands would contain a substantial slave population.

During the seventeenth and eighteenth centuries, much of the North American continent would become contested terrain as the French in Canada and the Spanish from Mexico and the Gulf borderlands worked to extend their colonial hegemony into the interior of North America. At times the amorphous boundaries that separated colonial spheres became ideal ground for slave fugitives who sought escape and prospects of freedom. In the case of Spanish Florida, invitations were extended in the early-eighteenth century to slaves in the colonies of Georgia and the Carolinas; these invitations said that freedom would be granted to any slave from British territory who escaped and ventured into Florida.

The British established a number of new colonies after the restoration of the Stuart monarchy in 1660 following the English Civil War and the rule under Oliver Cromwell. These colonies, known as the Restoration Colonies, included the Carolinas, New Jersey, Pennsylvania, and New York. (New York was wrested from the Dutch in 1664.) Slavery took root in these and all the British colonies that formed on the Atlantic seaboard.

Slavery Becomes Institutionalized

The British did not establish colonies in North America with the purposeful intent of establishing a slave-based economy. Nonetheless, circumstance and opportunity had created just such an environment in the developing colonies. As a result, there was no institutional design of how a slave system would develop in North America, and the independent formulation and regulation of slavery in thirteen separate colonies created an imperfect system. Still, by the time of the American Revolution (1775–1783), a rather unified code had emerged through custom and tradition as each colony defined the nature of slavery and the laws that would regulate the practice.

As early as 1630, the Massachusetts Bay colony enacted a measure that dealt with the subject of fugitive slaves. Freedom, it seems, was not just an aspiration of English colonists but was seemingly a desire of Massachusetts slaves as well. Over subsequent years, all of the colonies would pass measures that protected the rights of slaveowners and called for the return of fugitive slaves who sought escape.

Early statutes regarding slavery were designed to focus on the notion of racial purity, an issue that was of theoretical concern to white Europeans but not one they followed in practice. Antimiscegenation laws tried to prevent marriage or intercourse between individuals of different races by judging such behavior to be a criminal offense. Although all of the colonies developed laws to regulate this matter, enforcement was uneven. In Virginia a white man named Hugh Davis was publicly whipped in 1630 for "defiling his body by lying with a Negro," but such cases were rarely brought before the courts. A double standard existed that criminalized in the harshest means possible such action committed by a male slave upon a white woman, but white men were seldom censured for committing similar acts with slave women.

Colonial assemblies enacted general slave codes that regulated the rights and the liberties of the slaves. These regulations were seldom designed for the protection or benefit of the slave, but rather were legal controls that were employed to maintain the peace and security of white residents, particularly those living in areas that contained a substantial black majority. Laws were passed that prohibited slaves from carrying firearms within a colony, prohibited blacks from serving in the militia, and made slave insurrection a capital offense. Yet despite the bevy of laws instituted, the slaves had no real standing before the courts.

Slaveowners were encouraged to provide Christian religious instruction to their slaves in the hope that such training would help to bestow the blessings of civilization on their bonded laborers, but the acceptance of Christianity did not change their status as slaves. Once again, numerous laws such as Maryland's 1664 measure were passed, stating that Christian baptism did not change one's status as a slave. Similar measures were eventually enacted in New York, New Jersey, North Carolina, South Carolina, and Virginia, but not in Pennsylvania and Delaware.

The British Parliament even offered its advice on how policies toward the colonial slaves should be instituted. In its 1667 measure, "An Act to Regulate the Negroes on the British Plantations," Parliament described persons of African descent as possessing a "wild, barbarous and savage nature, to be controlled only with strict severity." The colonial assemblies responded with measures that exacted severe punishments for violators.

Resistance

Colonial assemblies sought to protect their citizens from the greatest possible danger that slave-based societies could face: the specter of slave insurrection. In efforts to restrict the liberties of slaves to maintain a strict discipline on colonial plantations and farms, public officials and the owners of slaves often instituted repressive policies that relied on harsh treatment of slaves, but these measures sometimes fanned the flames of insurrection instead. Most slaves had a rudimentary idea of what justice was, and when owners and overseers crossed the line and committed egregious offenses, slaves often lashed out in retribution.

In addition to actual outbreaks of slave revolt, the mere existence of rumors of revolt was usually enough to strike fear in many communities and hasten the use of extralegal justice to punish the alleged conspirators. Fears of rebellion would often stir paranoia and hysteria in the colonies, and such episodes often resulted in the executions of those presumed guilty. Suspicious action like the burning of a barn or the theft of weapons stirred rumors that assumed a life of their own. Sometimes isolated incidents that had no real bearing on fact resulted in the colonial militia being called out and white residents maintaining increased vigilance.

Despite the persistence of a few isolated slave plots or rumored conspiracies in the seventeenth century, most of the significant rebellions in the British colonies occurred during the early eighteenth century. South Carolina's Stono Rebellion of 1739 was the largest and most serious uprising of the colonial era. Fomented by the hope that freedom awaited them in Florida, a number of South Carolina slaves began to make their way southward to reach the Spanish settlement at St. Augustine. South Carolina militia caught up with the slave exodus and did battle with the fugitives. Peace was restored in the colony and a harsher slave code was enacted, but the threat of persistent revolt continued for many years.

The threat of slave revolt was not limited to the southern colonies. Nine white residents were killed and seven wounded in a slave revolt that occurred in New York City in April 1712. Once the tumult had subsided, twenty-one were convicted and sentenced to death for their role in the uprising, and six others committed suicide. In response to the revolt, the colonial assemblies of New York and Massachusetts enacted measures designed to prevent, suppress, and punish slave conspiracies and insurrections within their colonies.

New York City faced another plot in 1741 when a series of arson attacks set off wild rumors of a unified conspiracy between slaves and the city's poor white residents either to burn or seize control of the city. Although the evidence of such a plot was slight, a general hysteria developed, and eighteen blacks were hanged, eleven were burned alive at the stake, and seventy were banished from the colony. The white backlash against the slaves stemmed from their mere presence in the city rather than from any real evidence of their connection with a criminal conspiracy.

Slave Country

Slavery existed in all of the thirteen British colonies in North America, but slavery's relative significance varied significantly by region and the demographic distribution of slaves was equally varied. In general, slavery was much more essential to the six plantation colonies—Georgia, South Carolina, North Carolina, Virginia, Maryland, and Delaware, which were all located south of Pennsylvania. The rocky soils and small farms of the northern colonies were not well suited for large-scale plantation agriculture, but slaves did labor in those colonies often as domestic workers.

The largest concentrations of slaves in the British colonies were found in two locations. The Chesapeake Bay region, encompassing portions of Virginia, Maryland, and Delaware, had the greatest per capita density of slaves of all of the regions along the Atlantic seaboard. Much of the Chesapeake region consisted of lands where tobacco cultivation was the principal crop. In addition to the Chesapeake, the region of Charleston, South Carolina, and its surrounding coastal lowlands and Sea Islands also had a high population density of slaves. Much of this region was devoted to the cultivation of rice and indigo, with limited production of cotton on the Sea Islands.

Slave populations tended to be located in the eastern portions of the colonies where plantations lined rivers that provided access to the sea and world markets that lay beyond. Counties in the Piedmont had substantially fewer slaves as conditions in the region, much like those of the northern colonies, were not conducive to large-scale slave-based agricultural enterprises. These skewed demographics were made even more challenging by the distribution of political power in several colonies. In Virginia, for example, populous counties in the Piedmont found their relative political influence limited by Tidewater counties that contained fewer white residents. The political structure of colonial Virginia was set up in such a way that the plantation owners of the Tidewater maintained political control in the region even though growing numbers of poor, Scots-Irish, and other immigrants were settling the mountainous backcountry. If laws were needed to maintain and support slavery, it was necessary for the planters to control the colonial government.

The settlement patterns found within the thirteen British colonies left many communities isolated from one another. No real transportation infrastructure existed in colonial America, and north-south roads were practically nonexistent. In addition to the absence of a transportation infrastructure, there was no real communications network in place in the British colonies, which helps to explain why rumors were often accepted as fact. Even though newspapers eventually existed in larger cities like Philadelphia, there was no single paper that had anything more than a local readership in colonial America. In order to protect a colonial population that was so scattered and so isolated that standing armies and militias would have little effect, each community had to be prepared and capable to defend itself against any possible contingency that might befall the region. It was from this understanding that the notion of extralegal justice came to be an accepted concept in determining how order and stability would be maintained in slave country.

Other Cash Crops

Although tobacco was clearly the cash crop that saved the Virginia colony in its early years, it was not the only crop that was cultivated by slave labor in North America. In portions of South Carolina and Georgia, conditions were suitable for the cultivation of other crops, and indigo and rice were introduced to the region. Since these were considered to be specialized crops, slaveowners often sought out African slaves who had some experience with the cultivation of these crops in the West Indies or in Africa.

Blacks from the Gold Coast in Africa were believed to be familiar with indigo production, and Africans from Angola had technical experience with the intricacies of rice cultivation. The planters who cultivated these crops wanted to purchase slaves who were familiar with their production. As a result, planters developed a keen understanding of the different attributes and qualities of Africans from different regions. Although a particular understanding of African tribal, linguistic, or ethnic variations was typically not a concern of most slaveowners, such subtle clues were important to rice and indigo cultivators in determining what slaves they would purchase.

Colonial Slave Culture

A tremendously rich slave culture existed in colonial America. Because many of the slaves who were introduced into the Chesapeake region were imported directly from Africa, elements of African custom and tradition had not completely vanished from their memory as they fashioned a new culture in captivity in the Americas. Similarly, many "seasoned slaves" were still introduced to the North American colonies after having labored in the West Indies for a period of time. As a result, these slaves often transmitted elements of Spanish, French, Creole, or West Indian cultural influence when they were sold and traded. Still, many slaves were individuals who were born in North America, perhaps living for several generations within some families by the end of the colonial era, and their cultural perception was therefore totally different from that of African-born or West Indian-resident slaves.

Within the rich cultural milieu that existed, slaves formulated the limited cultural space that was allowed to them. Within the slave community on the plantations and farms, they created their own cultural identity from the African, West Indian, and American elements that were known to them. In this cultural fusion a synthesis of practices occurred, and a new type of cultural identity took shape. This identity was expressed in story, song, and dance, through religious practices, in cooking, and in the limited family experience that slaves were permitted to have.

Slaves incorporated elements of Christianity into the cultural identity they formed. Quaker and Methodist missionaries made an effort to visit the plantation districts of the British colonies to convert slaves and to spread the gospel. Although some plantation owners were leery of allowing slaves to worship on their own, they generally did not resist the introduction of Christianity, believing that the faith might help to make slaves more docile. Some owners believed that the otherworldly focus of the Christian message might make slaves more willing to accept an onerous yoke in this life, knowing that something better awaited them in eternity. Christian slaves who were perceptive found a common bond with biblical stories of the captive Hebrews and longed for the day when their Moses might appear and lead them into the promised land of freedom.

By 1770, near the end of the colonial era, the population of British North America was estimated at 2,312,000, which included 462,000 slaves, or approximately 20 percent of the colonial population. In the era of the American Revolution, many of the colonial Patriots felt themselves to be Americans, products of seven generations of free people born on the North American continent—a new breed of men. Similarly, descendants of Africans looked curiously at the Patriots and wondered how the slaves might be identified. Born into captivity, perhaps several generations raised in North America, they, too, had formed a new breed of men, but they only knew freedom from a distance.

During the American Revolution, the Patriots would compare their relationship with Great Britain as a condition of slavery and servitude without sensing the irony in the claim. Perhaps the Americans were a new breed and there was some validity to a claim of American exceptionalism, but part of what made the experience unique was the presence of slavery. Generations removed from a tenuous outpost on the James River, more than 2 million British colonists had fashioned a land and were prepared to carve a country, but the sons and daughters of Africa had helped to shape the land.

The transformation of the British colonies from 1607 to 1776 was remarkable. In the view of many, civilization had extended its blessings to a once heathen land and the prosperity that emerged was a sure sign that nature and the heavens were pleased with what had transpired. Although many would have sung such high hosannas, not all would have agreed. Slaves played an essential part in the planting, building, and developing of the British colonies, but they were rendered an almost invisible presence in the story of the national founding that followed. They were there and they mattered, they were there and they toiled, they were there and they struggled because they were there.

REVOLUTIONARY IDEOLOGY,
CITIZENSHIP, AND SLAVERY

The last generation of the eighteenth century and the first of the nineteenth century witnessed an age of revolutions that transformed much of the Western world. Starting with the political and social change wrought by the American Revolution (1775–1783) and the French Revolution (1789–1792), the revolutionary ideology of the era further inspired independence movements in Haiti (1791–1804) and throughout the colonies of Latin America. As colonized people clamored to be free and couched their rhetoric in the natural rights philosophy that was prevalent at the time, freedom prevailed for some, but in most settings the status of slavery remained largely unchanged.

The ideological origins of the age of revolution emerged during the era of the Enlightenment, a period of intellectual liberation in which rationalism broke free of all restraining tendencies that heretofore had limited human thought. Although intellectual revolutions do not of their own accord naturally inspire a popular response, many of the writers of the Enlightenment era, known as the *philosophes,* believed that their duty was to become promoters and popularizers of the new ideas so that a true societal transformation could be achieved. In the wake of the intellectual changes that were occurring, a new appreciation of ideas like justice, liberty, and freedom began to emerge in the hearts and minds of those who realized that their capacity for even greater opportunity was restricted by archaic traditions and beliefs that were maintained in spite of their illogical nature. Inspired by Voltaire's rallying cry of "Ecrasez l'infame" (Crush infamy!), the authors of the Enlightenment hoped to dispel the illogical myths and traditions of the past to create a better and more rational world.

For many Enlightenment thinkers, the movement was motivated by a desire to restrict what they considered the stifling power of organized religion to limit human thought and understanding. Some of the authors took an antagonistic position against the theological perspectives that they charged had enshrined misconception and pretense in the place of truth. Such a worldview, they argued, unduly limited the capacity of human logic to counter the horrid abuses that had been perpetuated throughout history as unquestioned matters of tradition and faith. For some of the early abolitionists, who were inspired by the notions of Enlightenment thought, the failure of organized religion to speak to the evils of slavery was an example of how such perversity, if left unchecked, could limit human potential.

Much of revolutionary ideology centered on the multiple meanings of freedom in human affairs. All of the transformations that occurred during the age of revolution were motivated by people who desired a greater degree of freedom in their lives, but did not necessarily believe that the blessings of freedom should extend to all in equal measure. Despite the hypocrisy that one might observe in reading behavior through a modern lens, those who sought greater freedom did so within the confines of a socially-stratified, class-based patriarchal system that did not consider all persons to be equal in all things. Even when such revolutionaries spoke of freedom in glowing universal terms, their specific point of reference was much more limited and circumscribed than their rhetoric.

Slavery and Revolutionary Rhetoric

Enlightenment thought alone does not explain the rise of antislavery sentiment in the Western world. The roots of abolitionist thought have complex origins: not all of the Enlightenment thinkers objected to the institution of slavery while some individuals found the means to criticize the practice from within the confines of organized religious movements. Abolitionism was for many an intellectual commitment that was borne by their inability to find a rational foundation for the practice, but for others the antislavery impulse was an emotionally charged belief that aroused great passion among those who recognized sin as the motivating factor in man's inhumanity to man. Abolitionism was essentially a movement of both the heart and the mind that emerged in the Western world during the eighteenth century and found expression through the revolutionary ideology that was swirling at the time.

Emotionalism also experienced a resurgence at the same time that rationalism was emerging. In North America, the thirteen British colonies witnessed a profound spiritual rebirth during the Great Awakening that began during the 1730s. This movement of religious revivalism was inspired by an evangelical fervor that reawakened the spiritual lives of many colonial residents. Inspired by the preaching of Puritan divines like George Whitefield and Jonathan Edwards, thousands of individuals found themselves reconnected to their faith and inspired to lead lives that would show an outward expression of their inner light. The motivation for individuals to lead righteous lives that would make manifest their godliness was an important spiritual legacy of the Great Awakening, but it was a difficult task to accomplish in a society where slavery prevailed.

Much of the popular appeal of the evangelism associated with the Great Awakening took place in the 1730s and 1740s throughout colonial America. The genuine religiosity that was experienced by many during this era was tempered by the social reality of slavery becoming manifest in colonial America at the same time. In 1730 it was estimated that there were 91,000 slaves in British North America, but by 1750 that number had more than tripled to 236,000 slaves. During the same period, the colonial population of white residents had not quite doubled, rising from an estimated 538,000 in 1730 to 935,000 in 1750. It was impossible to fail to notice the transformation that was occurring in colonial life as more and more slaves were imported to North America, but it was also increasingly difficult to avoid recognizing the incongruity between supposed lives of godliness and a world where slavery prevailed.

Abolitionism was essentially a radical doctrine that challenged the prevailing orthodoxy of the time. In order to be an abolitionist, one had to believe that organized religions were wrong since there were no biblical injunctions against slavery and the practice seemed to be sanctioned by scripture. In addition, those who avowed an antislavery perspective had to denounce as wrong the thousands of years of human history, custom, and tradition that suggested slavery to be a normal practice of peoples worldwide. Even the Greek and the Roman societies of classical antiquity on which much of the Western heritage was founded had been slave-based societies. Abolitionists had to assert that the laws were wrong. One of the key principles of maintaining civil society was the respect for and the maintenance of the law; yet radical abolitionists spoke of injustices that were inherent within the laws that protected and defended slavery. In addition, besides criticizing orthodoxy the abolitionists had to maintain that they were right—that their views were superior to all of the collective wisdom that had come before. In the context of eighteenth-century values in which personal modesty was deemed a virtue, the notion of voicing antislavery sentiment called attention to oneself in a fashion that was considered outrageous by standards then prevailing.

Voices in the Wilderness

The first public criticism of slavery in the North American colonies appeared in Pennsylvania on February 18, 1688, when a group of Mennonite Quakers (from the Society of Friends) openly declared at their monthly meeting that slavery was contrary to Christian principles and signed an antislavery resolution to that effect. Known as the Germantown Protest, the document prepared by Francis Daniel Pastorius and his fellow brethren is viewed as the first public condemnation of the institution and practice of slavery in the Western Hemisphere. It is also seen as one of the first examples of nonviolent protest in the history of the United States.

Although the Germantown Protest called upon Pennsylvania residents to disavow all connections with the slave trade and with slavery itself, such changes did not immediately follow. Slavery had become so entrenched in colonial America and had proven to be so profitable that many colonial economies were dependent on its continuation for their survival. Even in Pennsylvania, a number of Quakers were engaged in aspects of the slave trade that represented a lucrative enterprise. Efforts to reconcile matters of profit with matters of faith did not always produce a quick or easy remedy.

The Quaker brethren continued their efforts to instill an antislavery consciousness among the faithful. In 1693 the Quaker author George Keith published *An Exhortation and Caution to Friends Concerning Buying or Keeping of Negroes,* which had been presented as a paper at the Quaker annual meeting in Philadelphia. It was Keith's desire that those Quakers who owned slaves should free them as soon as possible. By the time of the 1696 annual meeting, Quakers admonished members for participating in the importation of slaves and threatened those who continued to import slaves with possible expulsion from the Society of Friends.

Having not yet adopted an exclusively antislavery perspective, members of the Quaker community struggled with the moral dilemma of slavery. In 1698 the Pennsylvania Quaker William Southeby petitioned fellow Quakers in Barbados to stop shipping blacks to Pennsylvania as slaves. Because of his sustained efforts to combat slavery, Southeby was eventually expelled from the Society of Friends, which had not yet adopted abolitionism in principle.

The early voices against slavery were not limited to Pennsylvania. Judge Samuel Sewall of Massachusetts published the antislavery tract, *The Selling of Joseph,* in 1700, in which he argued that slavery was not condoned by biblical sources and urged his fellow citizens to work for the abolition of slavery. That same year,

Sewall organized an antislavery organization known as the Boston Committee of 1700, which lobbied the colonial assembly to impose a higher duty on slave imports. Members of the group believed that excessive taxation might be one effective means of destroying the slave trade in Massachusetts, but their efforts were unsuccessful. Early efforts at encouraging antislavery sentiment in Massachusetts continued in 1703 with the publication of *John Saffin's Tryall,* a narrative that examined the life and sufferings of a slave. In subsequent years, the literary genre of the slave narrative would emerge as one of the abolitionists' most effective tools to convey their message and attract supporters to the antislavery cause.

The sustained efforts of William Southeby and other early Quaker abolitionists appeared to gain ground in Pennsylvania in 1711 when the colonial assembly enacted a measure that outlawed slavery in the colony, but the measure was immediately overruled by the British Crown. Despite this setback, the assembly voted on June 7, 1712, to ban the further importation of slaves into the colony, thus making Pennsylvania the first of the British colonies to ban the slave trade.

Early abolitionists began to employ a variety of strategies to encourage support to the antislavery cause. The Quaker author John Hepburn published the tract, *The American Defence of the Christian Golden Rule* (1715), in which he presented many arguments against slavery but stressed that most importantly, slavery was a practice that robbed individuals of the freedom of choice. Using a different strategy, abolitionists in colonial Massachusetts began to advance the argument that the presence of slaves in the colony had a debilitating effect on encouraging the immigration of additional white settlers to the colony.

Benjamin Franklin joined the abolitionist movement in 1727 when he established a benevolent association in Philadelphia, Pennsylvania, that was called the Junto. Members who joined the organization pledged that they would work toward the abolition of slavery and other forms of inhumanity to man. Within a few years, Franklin's printing press in Philadelphia was used regularly to publish antislavery tracts by abolitionists like Ralph Sandyford and Benjamin Lay that could further the cause of abolition.

All of the early efforts by abolitionists in Pennsylvania and Massachusetts met with limited success; few individuals became convinced of the necessity of ending slavery. The economic life of the North American colonies seemed secure, and many believed that the prosperity resulted from the success of the slave trade and slave-based agricultural productivity. Few were willing to challenge the prevailing orthodoxy and the economic well-being of the colonial settlements to defend the purported natural rights of the slave. To many in the North American colonies, the economic success of the colonial experiment was evidence of God's approval of the enterprise. Challenging slavery would be to venture into disrupting the divine order that prevailed at the time.

Britain's Rule in North America

The Stirrings of Discontent

The economic hegemony that the British maintained within their North American colonies was made possible through the effective use of mercantile policies that emerged through the course of the colonial period and often found expression in the various Navigation Acts. Although these measures were ultimately designed to enrich the mother country by maintaining a favorable balance of trade that strengthened the national treasury, the colonies themselves did benefit through the trade and commerce that ensued. The slave trade and the production of cash crops for export produced by slave labor were essential elements of the colonial economic system that had emerged since the early seventeenth century.

British success in North America was threatened, however, by the continuous growth and expansion of other colonial enterprises on the continent maintained by their European rivals, the Spanish and the French. Since mercantilism was premised on the notion that national wealth was determined by the amount of gold and silver in a nation's treasury, the competition for scarce resources and markets created a zero-sum game in which economic rivalry was merely an expression of economic warfare. With respect to the competing interests for North American colonies and the potential resources and markets that they represented, economic warfare turned into actual warfare during much of the eighteenth century as the European powers struggled for mastery of the North American continent.

Despite a pledge that the British and French kings made in the Peace of Whitehall (1687), whereby both monarchs pledged that their nations would never fight over colonial interests, the promise was broken almost as soon as it had been made. During the course of the eighteenth century, a series of wars that pitted Great Britain and France as constant rivals emerged, and some of these conflicts brought about territorial changes in North American colonial possessions. A progression of conflicts including the War of the Grand Alliance (War of the League of Augsburg, or King William's War, 1688–1697), the War of the Spanish Succession (Queen Anne's War, 1702–1714), the War of the Austrian Succession (King George's War, 1740–1748), and the French and Indian War (Seven Years War, 1755–1763) had the effect of a continuous campaign designed to wrest control of colonial possessions in North America. In this bitter struggle, the British would ultimately emerge victorious and drive the French from the North American mainland.

The British fought these wars ostensibly to guarantee their economic hegemony and to ensure further development of their national coffers, but protection of the colonies was tantamount to achieving this desired end. As a result, it became difficult for the British to distinguish between measures taken to secure its colonies and measures taken to secure its own economic interests since both of these were associated roles. The difference was made more real, however, when the British tried to determine who should pay for the cost of defending the North American colonies. The efforts taken to answer this question and the colonial responses they engendered would set in motion conflict between Britain and its North American possessions.

The Rights of Englishmen

Colonists in North America would come to discover the limitations of their freedom as British taxation policies became more stringent during the 1760s, and increasingly they began to express their dismay at being treated as slaves by the British Crown. On the eve of the American Revolution, the Virginia Patriot leader Patrick Henry would ponder the rhetorical question, "Is life so dear or peace so sweet to be purchased by the price of chains and slavery?" before exhorting his compatriots to choose between liberty or death. Virginians certainly knew what slavery was, but they seemed quite uncertain at parsing the various gradations that existed between those who were completely free and those whose hereditary rights faced infringement of one degree or another.

The North American colonists initially appealed to their rights as Englishmen in an effort to protect themselves from burdensome taxation that was imposed to cover the costs of their own protection and help pay the debt incurred by the French and Indian War. The colonists appealed to the Parliament with the understanding that their rights as colonists were no different than the rights of those who lived in England, so they expressed their concerns in terms of justice, equity, and fairness. Tradition, however, indicated otherwise as the tax burden placed on those living in England was more severe than the share that was apportioned to the North American colonists. Even Sir William

Blackstone's *Commentaries on English Law*, considered the penultimate source of the English legal tradition, suggested the weakness of the colonial claim that the traditional rights of Englishmen extended to countrymen in the North American colonies. Facing such a difficult argument, the North American colonists found support in an alternative approach that would help them define, and eventually win, their freedom.

The English political philosopher John Locke first articulated the "natural rights" theory in his *Second Treatise on Civil Government* (1690), a work considered one of the founding documents of liberal political theory. Written largely as a defense of England's Glorious Revolution (1688) when Parliament deposed the Stuart king James II and invited William and Mary to become the coregents of the realm, Locke's political theory had to determine a legal foundation for the right of revolution in order to confer legitimacy on Parliament's extraordinary actions. He was able to formulate such a theory by hearkening back to the considerations that he assumed had motivated the invention of civil government when it emerged from what Locke termed a "state of nature."

In Locke's view, government existed by virtue of a contract that had been formed from the beginning of civil society. According to the nature of this contract theory of government, the purpose of forming a government had been to protect the natural rights that were inherently due to all. In Locke's formulation of the theory, he identified three rights—life, liberty, and property—as the natural or God-given rights that were due to all and could not be alienated. Since, in Locke's view, government existed only to protect these natural rights, any government that became abusive of these ends or failed to protect the natural rights of the people was in violation of the terms of the contract that had brought about its creation. Under such circumstances, Locke argued, the people had a right to abolish such government and institute new government in its place. Locke's theory had fashioned a defense of revolution in civil society, and this would become the new line of reasoning used by the North American colonists to strive for their natural rights that presumably had been violated.

"No Taxation without Representation"

After the Parliament's passage of the Sugar Act (1764), New England merchants and the captains of slave ships protested the increase in the prices of sugar and molasses, declaring these items to be indispensable to the slave trade, which they described as "vital commerce" for the region. A group of merchants published a pamphlet entitled *A Statement of the Massachusetts Trade and Fisheries* in which they protested that the increased duties on such essential commodities might bring economic disaster to New England. That same year, James Otis published *The Rights of the British Colonies Asserted and Proved* to protest Parliament's imposing the Sugar Act. Otis maintained that the British action represented "taxation without representation," and he further claimed that slaves had a right to be free. Sensing an inconsistency between coercive action and liberalism, Otis saw a connection between the infringement on colonists' liberties by the British and the institution of slavery, and he criticized slavery as an evil that "threatens one day to reduce both Europe and America to the ignorance and barbarity of the darkest ages."

Although many colonists shared Otis's sentiments regarding "taxation without representation," few supported his antislavery views. Most colonists in North America were able to distinguish between the economic bondage that Britain tried to impose on the colonies and the chattel bondage of black slaves that they considered an economic necessity for the strength and security of the colonies. They were able to despise one form of slavery and laud the merits of another.

By the time Parliament passed the Stamp Act in 1765, slaves made up an estimated 20 percent of the North American colonial population. The ever-expanding commerce of the slave trade and the slave-produced colonial exports constituted a tremendous source of revenue for the British Crown that far exceeded what new tax measures might garner. The number of slaves imported into the North American colonies continued to increase annually until 1771, when for the first time, importation of Africans into the colonies began to decline as antislavery sentiment began to emerge in Great Britain.

First Blood

Tensions between the North American colonies and Great Britain escalated throughout the 1760s as a series of new tax initiatives enacted by Parliament were met with an increasing air of resistance by the colonists. Measures of civil disobedience against "taxation without representation" carried out in a nonviolent fashion gave way to more brazen acts of assault as British revenue officials were assaulted and occasionally tarred and feathered by aggrieved colonists. As early as the summer of 1765, private militia groups had begun to form and drill in some communities as the Sons of Liberty began to organize and carry out attacks in the interest of the North American colonists.

Sensing the increased hostility by colonial residents, the British government had maintained a troop presence in the colonies, particularly in the New England region where resistance seemed the strongest. In addition to protecting royal interests in the colony, the troops also sought to protect the lives and property of revenue officials who ably performed the tasks that would benefit Great Britain's treasury. Over time, the association of British taxation and royal troops would become indelibly linked in the mind of many colonial Patriots who viewed the presence of standing troops as another aspect of the enslavement that Britain was forcing on its rightfully free colonists.

On the evening of March 5, 1770, the association of unlawful taxation and military oppression would become inextricably linked in the hearts and minds of many Bostonians when violence erupted near the colonial State House. The event that became known as the Boston Massacre marked the spilling of the first blood in a conflict that eventually led to the independence of the North American colonies. The first of five Patriots to die in the encounter was Crispus Attucks, a mulatto and former slave who perished when British forces opened fire into an increasingly unruly mob. In a North American colonial setting where 20 percent of the residents were slaves, that the first of five to die was a former slave seems almost a prophetic omen, but such an awareness appears to have escaped notice at the time of the event.

Colonial discontent reached a fevered pitch after the Boston Massacre as committees of correspondence were organized throughout the North American colonies to keep residents of distant communities informed of the reputed atrocities conducted by the British in defense of the onerous taxes. Violent encounters between the Patriots and the British revenue officials grew more frequent and more pointed as when the Sons of Liberty torched the revenue cutter *Gaspée* after it became grounded in Narragansett Bay off the Rhode Island coast in 1772. Parliament passed the Tea Act in March 1773 in an effort to prop up the failing East India Company by creating a monopoly for their product in the North American colonies, but the Patriots responded in December by staging the Boston Tea Party and dumping 342 chests of tea into the icy waters of Boston Harbor.

When Parliament sought to punish the citizens of Boston with the Coercive Acts of 1774, sentiments throughout the North American colonies were unified in the view that these punitive measures were unlawful. Thomas Jefferson of Virginia authored *A Summary View of the Rights of British America* in July 1774, a pamphlet that argued Parliament had overstepped its authority with the Coercive Acts and that the residents of the North American colonies were only beholden to obey King George III. At this point, Jefferson and other Patriot leaders still believed that well-intentioned appeals to reason could inspire the king to action that would lead to a redress of grievances.

An Appeal to Arms

The North American colonists held to their beliefs that petitions to the king could remedy the problems that were at hand in the early 1770s. When delegates met at a Continental Congress in 1774, they hoped that by issuing a petition and launching a boycott of British goods they could persuade the king to move Parliament to rescind its taxes and other coercive legislation that had caused the breach between the mother country and its colonies. Despite these well-intentioned efforts, and the naive assumptions on which they were based, neither the king nor Parliament was moved to action by the request of the North American colonists. Both sides in the dispute were quickly approaching a point of no return.

Delegates at the Continental Congress agreed to meet again the following spring if redress of the grievances outlined in the petition to the king were not met. Few understood at the time the momentous events that would transpire between the time of the two meetings. In some New England towns, volunteer militias began to drill openly in preparation for defending their natural rights by force of arms if necessary. In many communities residents began to hoard arms, ammunition, and powder for what they believed would be the coming assault on their traditional liberties. The free citizens of the North American colonies were no longer willing to be enslaved by British taxes and mercantile policies.

Just weeks before a second Continental Congress was set to meet in Philadelphia, open warfare between colonial and British forces erupted near Boston on April 19, 1775. In what the poet Ralph Waldo Emerson would later call "the shot heard round the world," the North American colonists stood their ground at Lexington and inflicted casualties on the British at Concord in the first encounters of what became the American Revolution. Even as delegates gathered in Philadelphia in May, military operations continued to be conducted in and around Boston. By mid-June 1775 colonial forces engaged British troops in battle at Bunker Hill where they inflicted more than 1,000 casualties on the British before they were forced to retreat from the hill.

Although the second Continental Congress took measures to prepare for war, including the creation of the Continental Army and the appointment of George Washington as its commander, the delegates at Philadelphia also sought to negotiate a peaceful resolution of their differences with Great Britain, though that prospect seemed increasingly fleeting. The colonists extended an Olive Branch Petition to the king, still hoping to settle outstanding concerns short of war, but George III rejected any attempt to negotiate with rebels who had assaulted royal forces and committed treason against the Crown.

We Hold These Truths to Be Self Evident

In June 1776 the second Continental Congress approved of a resolution introduced by Richard Henry Lee of Virginia. The measure called for independence from Great Britain. Upon passage of the resolution, the Congress formed a committee of five to draft a declaration of independence that would outline the reasons for why such a break with the mother country was necessary. The committee included Thomas Jefferson of Virginia, Benjamin Franklin of Pennsylvania, John Adams of Massachusetts, Roger Sherman of Connecticut, and Robert Livingston of New York. Jefferson would become the primary author of the final document.

By basing his argument for independence on the natural rights philosophy of John Locke, Jefferson argued that Britain's repeated offenses against the North American colonies represented a violation of the original contract upon which government is premised and justified the colonists' act of rebellion to create new government. In addition to explaining succinctly the key elements of Locke's theory, the declaration also included an enumeration of twenty-seven grievous offenses that either the king or Parliament had inflicted on the North American colonists. These measures were included to convince the faint of heart who might otherwise have believed that rebellion against the British Crown was unwarranted.

The Declaration of Independence, as penned by Thomas Jefferson, was adopted by the second Continental Congress on July 4, 1776. In the final deliberations, Jefferson was swayed by the arguments of delegates from South Carolina and Georgia who had objected to his inclusion of lines that were critical of the slave trade and denounced slavery. He agreed to delete a passage that had criticized George III for encouraging "cruel war against human nature itself, violating its most sacred rights of life and liberty in the persons of a distant people who never offended him, captivating and carrying them into slavery in another hemisphere." Although Jefferson deleted these references from the final draft of the Declaration of Independence, the second Continental Congress had previously passed a resolution on April 9, 1776, calling for an eventual end of the transatlantic slave trade.

Jefferson's hesitancy to include language critical of the slave trade and slavery in the Declaration of Independence reflects the colonial mentality on the issue. Recognizing what all might recognize as self-evident truths was easier to accomplish if the slave trade and slavery were not made part of the argument. Although it is admirable that Jefferson and the other Founders applied Locke's natural rights philosophy to their call for independence, it is particularly telling that they understood rights to be natural for some and not so for others. The document that gave birth to freedom was one that still enshrined slavery.

Workers in the Vineyard of Freedom

When it became clear that the North American colonists intended to make war on the British Crown, the British seized on an opportunity to raise a Loyalist army in the colonies by promising freedom to slaves who would flock to the royal cause and take up arms in defense of Great Britain. On November 14, 1775, John Murray, fourth earl of Dunmore, who was the royal governor of Virginia, issued a decree in which he promised to free any male slaves who deserted their plantations and farms and joined British forces in an effort to suppress the rebellion that had been initiated by the colonial forces. An estimated eight hundred Virginia slaves accepted Dunmore's invitation and joined the royal forces, but Dunmore lost the support of many Loyalist planters by initiating this policy.

Although the second Continental Congress initially decided against arming either slaves or free blacks to support the American cause, it tempered its policy by 1779 and more than five thousand black troops saw service during the American Revolution. Most of the slaves who fought were promised that they would be emancipated upon the conclusion of the war.

Black troops fought nobly as workers in the vineyard of freedom during the American Revolution. On May 10, 1775, Lemuel Haynes, Primas Black, and Epheram Blackman fought with Ethan Allen and the Green Mountain Boys during the capture of Fort Ticonderoga in New York. This event was considered to be the first aggressive action taken by colonial forces during the American Revolution. Several weeks later, the black soldiers Peter Salem and Salem Poor distinguished themselves through service at the battle of Bunker Hill. Two black soldiers, Prince Whipple and Oliver Cromwell, took part in George Washington's famed crossing of the Delaware River in December 1776 to attack British forces and their Hessian mercenaries at Trenton, New Jersey.

The courageous actions by more than five thousand black troops during the American Revolution convinced many of the North American colonists to recognize their bravery and appreciate their humanity. In many respects, the participation of black troops as soldiers during the war helped lead to the first emancipation in the northern states following the American Revolution.

Varieties of Emancipation

War with Great Britain produced an independent United States of America where free citizens could enjoy the blessings of liberty free from the bondage that had been associated with colonial rule, but this was not true for all residents of the new republic. Slavery would end in some parts of the new nation, but in the southern states where it was most prevalent, its status was not altered.

Some slaves found freedom by supporting the Loyalist cause and aiding the British during the war. In 1782 British ships carried off an estimated five thousand slaves when they sailed from Savannah, Georgia. Many of these black Loyalists would eventually settle in the Canadian provinces of New Brunswick and Nova Scotia. In 1783, British ships would similarly evacuate black Loyalists from New York City, where three thousand were evacuated, and from Charleston, South Carolina, where another sixty-five hundred slaves were removed and resettled as free citizens in other British possessions.

By the end of 1783, all of the states located north of Maryland had enacted measures to ban the further importation of Africans for use as slave laborers. Many of the northern states began to consider legislation that would emancipate slaves within their jurisdiction.

In Massachusetts the courts intervened before the state assembly could take positive action to end slavery. The case of *Commonwealth v. Jennison* concluded that the Massachusetts Declaration of Rights, which was included in the state constitution of 1780, stated that all men were "born free and equal." According to their interpretation of this measure, the jurists declared that slavery was thus repudiated within the Commonwealth of Massachusetts.

Subsequent action by state assemblies emancipated slaves in Connecticut and Rhode Island in 1784, New York in 1785, and New Jersey in 1786. The legislation through which slavery was ended employed different methods and timetables, thus producing varieties of emancipation within the northern states. In some cases slaves were emancipated immediately, as in the case of Massachusetts, while many states, including Pennsylvania, New York, and New Jersey, adopted gradual emancipation measures.

In some states the status of slavery persisted even though the burden of slave labor was no longer expected. In the case of the well-known black abolitionist Sojourner Truth (born Isabella Baumfree), though she was born circa 1797 in New York State, she did not escape from her owner until 1826. She became free in 1827 according to the terms of New York's gradual emancipation law that had been enacted in 1785.

In the case of New Jersey, slaveowners were given advanced warning of the date when slavery would end in the state, and some owners were able to sell their slaves to other owners in the southern states where slavery remained legal. By employing these means, some New Jersey owners did not realize a financial loss from emancipation in their state, but the slaves they sold did not gain the emancipation that had been promised them by the state's legislative action.

When the American Revolution began in 1775, slavery existed in all thirteen of Britain's North American colonies, but by the end of the conflict it only remained legal in six southern states. Although the initial flurry of activity by northern legislatures held promise that freedom was on the ascendancy, it soon became increasingly clear that slavery was well entrenched in the southern states and would not be ending anytime soon. However, the ideology of the Enlightenment and the fervor of evangelical Christianity had indeed made inroads in challenging the power of slavery; yet a long and bitter campaign lay ahead to realize the true meaning of liberty and justice for all.

THE END OF THE SLAVE TRADE AND THE RISE OF ABOLITIONISM

The same intellectual and evangelical religious attitudes that fomented the American Revolution and the many other political revolutions that transformed the Western world in the late eighteenth and early nineteenth centuries also played an important role in beginning to challenge the underpinnings of slavery. The age of revolution was closely paralleled by the rise of a powerful transatlantic abolitionist movement that started to challenge the foundations on which slavery had been supported and maintained for centuries. The opponents of slavery would develop tactics that viewed the abolition of the African slave trade as a first and necessary step toward the eventual abolition of slavery itself. Despite their marginalized status as fanatics who sought to undo the social fabric on which much of economic power and public order had been maintained, the abolitionists maintained the intensity of their struggle with a buoyant optimism that their cause was not only right but also essential.

Although much of the support for early abolitionism grew out of the religious community, it was not the mainline denominations that took the lead in advancing the cause, but rather some of the groups that were considered to be either beyond the mainstream of traditional Christianity or at odds with some of the more traditional groups. In both Great Britain and the United States, much of the early antislavery agitation stemmed from the Quakers (Society of Friends) and after the 1740s from the Methodists. In this era each of these religious congregations was perceived as a radical faith community. Among the Quakers, the lack of characteristic religious hierarchy, the nondescript nature of services, and the individualistic reliance on one's "inner light" to motivate and inspire spirituality were perceived as being at odds with the more staid traditional Christian congregations. Similarly, the Methodists were initially viewed as a communion of believers who were revolting against the trappings of Anglican (or Episcopalian) ceremony and practice. Yet unlike the Puritan revolutionaries of an earlier era, reliance on a rational "method" of spiritual practice made the Methodists seem to be too modern or too closely affiliated with notions of the Enlightenment and its presumed antireligious sentiments. Only after Quaker and Methodist abolitionists initiated the antislavery movement did supporters from other religious communities join the social and moral crusade to end slavery.

Early abolitionists also faced another criticism as they rooted their antislavery beliefs in their faith and sought to impart their moral beliefs to society at large. The notion of the social gospel, or the view that one's faith must be made manifest by reforming real-world conditions that are in need of moral improvement, was not yet fully accepted as part of the responsibility that Christians were expected to bear. The belief that one's faith must direct one's works or that spirituality must transform itself into action in the world of the present was at odds with the view of those who saw religion as directed to an otherworldly existence exclusively. Concerns about being "too much of this world" caused many to resist the abolitionist impulse since the tradition of reading social justice into the calling of the gospels had not yet become an accepted practice within many religious communities.

Still others resisted the abolitionist movement in its early stages because they perceived the antislavery movement as being contrary to the social and political order that was necessary to maintain a civil society based on laws, customs, and traditions. The long history of slavery and the legal framework that had been created to support it were considered to be de facto evidence that the practice was a necessary and proper element of the social order of things. Those who questioned the justification of slavery were seen as challenging the most basic foundations of order in the eyes of traditionalists who did not view civil disobedience as evidence of good citizenship. In addition, any suggestion that the slave was the equal of those who were born free was perceived as a dangerous form of social leveling in societies that viewed stratified, class-based distinctions as both necessary and proper for the maintenance of public order and security.

In addition to all of these tendencies, the individual dispositions of many of the early abolitionists also prevented some from supporting the antislavery movement. Most abolitionists were viewed as unequivocating advocates of their cause who were totally convinced of the moral certainty of their position, and this practice of calling attention to oneself was not characteristic of late eighteenth-century sensibilities. Thus the composite perception of the abolitionist as the dissenter, the radical, the social leveler, and the unreserved individualist all contributed to the resistance that antislavery advocates faced as they challenged the status quo and sought to remake society.

A Transatlantic Movement

Much of what transpired in Great Britain influenced the rise of the abolitionist movement in the United States. During the eighteenth century, an estimated 5 million Africans were transported to the Americas by slave-trading vessels. A large portion of this trade was conducted by British merchants and traders who prof-

ited immensely from the insatiable demand for slaves that resulted from the ever-increasing production of sugar in the Americas. The profits that Britain would accrue from its involvement in the transatlantic slave trade would set in motion the forces that started an abolitionist movement by the late eighteenth century.

When the Treaty of Utrecht ended the War of the Spanish Succession, or Queen Anne's War (1702–1714), British merchants and traders won a major concession from the Spanish as they acquired the *asiento,* the contract that authorized British vessels to deliver African slaves to Spain's New World colonies. This lucrative trade was a prize of war that coincided with what would become the most massive century of the transatlantic slave trade. Vessels packed with captive Africans ventured across the Atlantic throughout the eighteenth century as suppliers tried to keep up with the incessant demands for more and more slaves in the Americas. The profitability of the enterprise was enormous.

In many respects, the transatlantic slave trade was an invisible form of commerce to most Britons. Seaports like Bristol and Liverpool witnessed an increased activity as the construction and outfitting of new ships kept many laborers employed throughout the century; these vessels regularly sailed in and out of the port cities to other ports of call and destinations unknown to most. The trade that some Britons saw did not contain the human cargo of slaves, but only the raw material of sugar or the manufactured product of rum—essentially the *cause* and *effect* of the need for a slave trade. The sailors who manned the ships of the slave trade witnessed aspects of the business that were beyond the sight and the imagination of most Britons, but few of these seasoned sailors shared their tales of the trade. The profitable commerce remained intact largely through an understood conspiracy of silence among many of its members and most immediate observers.

The necessity of the transatlantic slave trade was argued by the sugar planters of the West Indies, who demanded a steady supply of slave laborers to plant, cultivate, harvest, and refine the sugarcane that had made the colonies such a lucrative setting. Since disruptions in slave supply could translate into poor harvests and decreased profitability, the planters had agents who worked on their behalf in Great Britain to make sure that slave ships regularly supplied the demands of the sugar colonies. Over the course of time, the agents and supporters of the colonial plantation interests formed a West India lobby in order to guarantee that Parliament would enact no measures that were detrimental to the slave trade and the financial well-being of the sugar producers.

Out of Sight, Out of Mind?

As long as the business of the slave trade remained a distant enterprise that was isolated from the thought and awareness of most Britons, it was unlikely that the issue would cause much concern or motivate any social agitation. Profits from the trade in sugar and slaves streamed into Britain during the eighteenth century, but few if any devoted much consideration to the basis of this wealth. Aside from limited populations in Bristol and Liverpool, the slave trade was largely out of sight and out of mind.

The feigned ignorance of the slave trade began to change in the 1760s as more information about the conditions of the slave trade emerged and some began to experience moral qualms about the inhumanity of the slave trade. Coincidentally, the birth of William Wilberforce (1759–1833) and Thomas Clarkson (1760–1846), two British abolitionists and members of Parliament who would lead the struggle against the slave trade and slavery itself, occurred at the dawn of an era when the issue of slavery became a prominent social concern in British society. It is not surprising that men like Wilberforce and Clarkson would be influenced by the changing temper of their times to view the slave trade and slavery as social ills that needed to be addressed through legislative remedy.

Granville Sharp became one of the first British abolitionists who publicly questioned the conditions associated with the slave trade. After being contacted by Africans in Britain who sought his assistance as a solicitor to help them obtain their freedom, Sharp became an advocate for the cause of the Africans and devoted much of his time and energy into researching the slave trade and making his findings available to the general public. Sharp was responsible for bringing forward the case *Knowles v. Somersett* (1772), which resulted in the abolition of slavery in England. In 1783 Sharp would investigate the case of the *Zong*, a British slaving vessel that had been associated with the criminal act of tossing 133 Africans who were near death into the waters of the Atlantic.

Knowledge about slavery also increased as Britons began to read about the practice through firsthand accounts that were written and published by former slaves. In 1787 the former slave Quobna Ottobah Cugoano published *Thoughts and Sentiments on the Evil and Wicked Traffic of the Slavery and Commerce of the Human Species, Humbly Submitted to the Inhabitants of Great Britain, by Ottobah Cugoano, a Native of Africa.* Similarly, a young African named Olaudah Equiano was captured sometime around 1756 and sold into slavery. He would later publish *The Interesting Narra-* *tive of the Life of Olaudah Equiano, or Gustavaus Vassa, the African, Written by Himself* (1789).

Appeals for a Parliamentary Inquiry

Encouraged by the early successes, Granville Sharp and other British abolitionists pressed their case in the 1770s for an investigation by Parliament into the operations and conduct of the transatlantic slave trade. Their efforts were met with stiff resistance by the West India Lobby, which had the support of many members of Parliament who were not favorably disposed to such an inquiry because of the potential dangers it might pose to the colonial sugar interests. Thus, even when Parliament appeared to take an interest in the matter of the transatlantic slave trade, its actions were halfhearted, and its findings were always a foregone conclusion.

In 1776 the British Parliament briefly debated a measure that called for an end to the African slave trade. This event was especially noteworthy, for it was the first time that Parliament had ever considered the question. In the same year, the House of Commons defeated a resolution that condemned slavery as being contrary to the laws of God. Despite these setbacks, Sharp and the other British abolitionists continued to press their case.

The House of Commons agreed to establish a parliamentary committee in 1778 that would investigate the transatlantic slave trade. That same year, Joseph Knight, a slave who had been taken from Jamaica to Scotland, sued for his freedom in the Edinburgh Court of Session. The Scottish court declared Knight to be free, basing its ruling on the judicial precedent established in *Knowles v. Somersett* (1772).

Granville Sharp appealed to Anglicans in 1779 to voice their opposition to the African slave trade, but they chose not to become involved in the political fray. Despite this failure, Sharp did attract some support when the British political leader Edmund Burke, an opponent of slavery and a member of Parliament, wrote the essay "Sketch of a Negro Code" as a means of preparing slaves for a future life of "civilization and gradual manumission."

New and more strident voices joined the British abolitionist movement in the 1780s as antislavery advocates continued to press their case against the transatlantic slave trade. In 1788 the British abolitionist Thomas Clarkson published *An Essay on the Impolicy of the African Slave Trade,* and fellow abolitionist James Ramsey published *Objections to the Abolition of the Slave Trade with Answers.* British abolitionists organized a petition drive throughout the nation to have Parliament outlaw the transatlantic slave trade, and leading abolitionists such as William Pitt, William

Wyndham Grenville, and William Wilberforce addressed Parliament in support of the proposal. For its part, Parliament enacted the Dolben Act, a statute regulating the conditions permitted in conducting the African slave trade, but the measure fell far short of abolition, which the antislavery supporters had demanded.

Limiting Slavery's Expansion in the United States

In the immediate aftermath of the American Revolution, seven of the original thirteen states enacted measures that provided emancipation in various forms to the slaves within their jurisdiction. Slavery remained legal in the six southern states where large-scale agricultural production on plantations remained the principal form of commercial activity. All legislative action to abolish slavery or to preserve and maintain it was conducted at the state level, and the national government made no effort to address the question or the status of slavery.

The government of the United States that was organized during the early years of the republic was fashioned by the Articles of Confederation, an early constitution that formed a weak national government with limited powers while sustaining autonomous state governments that continued to maintain their traditional powers. This arrangement of a weak national government paired with strong autonomous state governments characterized political life in the 1780s as the young nation sought to implement a form of federalism that rendered state powers supreme. In such a system, the national government had no ability to speak to the status of slavery within the individual states since that was a matter of local control.

In 1784 the Congress under the Articles of Confederation government considered a "Report of Government for the Western Territory" that had been drafted by Thomas Jefferson. Before adopting the measure, Congress deleted certain controversial provisions, including by a vote of seven to six, a proposal that would have prohibited slavery and involuntary servitude from all western territories after 1800.

Congress did adopt the Northwest Ordinance in 1787 to provide a framework for settlement of and future statehood by the western territories located north of the Ohio River. In enacting this measure on July 13, 1787, the Congress ruled that slavery was prohibited from all territories north of the Ohio River (the "Old Northwest" that later included Ohio, Indiana, Illinois,

Michigan, and Wisconsin). Speaking as the legislative body of the national government, Congress made clear that the prerogative of determining the status of slavery in the territories fell within the purview of the national government.

A More Perfect Union

Throughout the summer of 1787, delegates from the various states met in Philadelphia to draft a new constitution for the United States that would replace the largely ineffective Articles of Confederation. The document that would be produced was revolutionary in nature as it formulated a powerful national government at the expense of weakened powers left to the autonomous states. Although the new document never specifically mentioned the word "slave," the implied protection of the slave trade and slavery itself were enshrined and protected in the new document.

On September 17, 1787, delegates signed the U.S. Constitution and submitted the document to the states for ratification. The new document included a "three-fifths clause," which meant that only three of every five slaves would be counted for purposes of representation and taxation. The U.S. Constitution also stipulated that the Congress could not act to prohibit the transatlantic slave trade for twenty years.

It had been the decision at the Constitutional Convention to establish a bicameral Congress and to apportion seats in the House of Representatives on the basis of population that precipitated much of the debate over slavery. A division of states allied on the basis of small states versus large states, which was notoriously similar to free states versus slave states, debated the key question of whether or not slaves would be counted as population when apportioning seats in the House of Representatives. The "three-fifths clause" was inserted into the U.S. Constitution to settle this matter.

The twenty-year moratorium on consideration of ending the transatlantic slave trade was inserted into the U.S. Constitution as part of a commerce-related compromise between northern and southern states. Although the southern states hoped to maintain the right to import Africans as slaves without the threat of government suspension of the trade, northern states were fearful that a strong national government might tax the region's exports, thus making manufacturing interests fearful. The solution was to satisfy both sides by including both protections in the U.S. Constitution. The national government prohibited the taxation of exports, and the issue of ending the African slave trade could not be considered until 1807 at the earliest.

In addition to these two key provisions, other portions of the U.S. Constitution also provided inherent protections to slavery. The states were made to extend "full faith and credit" to the laws of fellow states, thereby preserving the status of slave for any fugitive who might escape to seek liberty in a free state. The states also were made to honor preexisting contracts through which it became understood that northern states were duty-bound to return fugitive slaves to their owners. This matter would be further explicated upon passage of the Fugitive Slave Act of 1793, which made clear the responsibility of northern states to remand into custody any fugitive slaves who were captured within their jurisdictions. In addition, the weight of the U.S. military was available to "insure domestic tranquility" should the threat of a slave insurrection affect the peace and security of any slaveholding region.

In subsequent years, some abolitionists would charge that the U.S. Constitution was a document that had been designed specifically to protect and preserve the interests of slaveholders in the United States. Some even argued that a "slave power conspiracy" existed within the nation as a result of the undue influence the U.S. Constitution gave to the southern slaveholding states.

Early Government

Having been ratified by a sufficient number of states, the U.S. Constitution became effective on March 4, 1789, when the first meeting of the U.S. Congress was called into session. By late April George Washington took the oath of office in New York City and became the first president of the United States, a young nation of thirteen states divided almost evenly on the question of slavery.

In 1790 the first census of the United States revealed that 757,181 blacks, representing 19.3 percent of the national population, resided in the thirteen states with 59,557 identified as free blacks and 697,624 as slaves. Only Massachusetts (and Maine, which was a part of Massachusetts) reported having no slaves.

The issue of slavery quickly emerged as an issue of concern in the new nation. In early February 1790, the U.S. Congress received its first formal petition calling for the emancipation of the slaves. The petition was presented by the American Quakers (Society of Friends) and the Pennsylvania Abolition Society. Benjamin Franklin had signed the petition and urged Congress to remove "this inconsistency from the character of the American people." After having failed to persuade Congress to his position, Franklin published "An Essay on the African Slave Trade" in the March 23 issue of the *Federal Gazette*. Using the biting satire for which he had become well known, Franklin parodied the prevailing proslavery attitude in the Congress by presenting a Muslim argument that could be used for justifying the enslavement of Christians.

In 1790 the U.S. government also entered into its first treaty with the Creek Indian nation. The treaty included a provision that required the Creek to return any fugitive slaves who sought protection by escaping to Creek territory. To many abolitionists it became clear that the agency of the government of the United States under the Constitution supported the legal rights of slaveholders to maintain the institution of slavery. Many antislavery advocates began to question whether abolitionist legislation could ever be obtained by working within the strictures of the government.

Warner Mifflin, a Virginia Quaker, sent an antislavery petition to the U.S. Congress in 1792, and the matter caused a contentious debate. One South Carolina congressman questioned whether the First Amendment's right to petition expressly included the "mere rant and rhapsody of a meddling fanatic."

On February 12, 1793, the U.S. Congress enacted a federal Fugitive Slave Act that made it a criminal offense for anyone to harbor a slave or to prevent the arrest of a fugitive. The law based its legality on Article 4, Section 2 of the U.S. Constitution, which established the legal mechanism for the recovery of fugitive slaves. The measure would remain in effect until Congress passed a stronger Fugitive Slave Act in 1850.

Seeds of Discontent

Eli Whitney invented the cotton gin in Mulberry Grove, Georgia, on October 28, 1793. This invention revolutionized southern agriculture as it made short-staple (upland) cotton easier to process, and as the planting of upland cotton increased in the Old Southwest (territories south of the Ohio River), the region of slaveholding also increased. Whitney received the patent for his invention on March 14, 1794.

A particularly telling sentiment of the times appeared in a letter from President George Washington to fellow Virginian Alexander Spotswood in which Washington shared some of his views on slavery. Washington wrote:

> Were it not then, that I am principled against selling African Americans, as you would cattle at a market, I would not in twelve months from this date, be possessed of one as a slave. I shall be happily mistaken if they are not found to be a

very troublesome species of property ere many years to pass over our heads."

Ending the Transatlantic Slave Trade

Efforts to abolish the African slave trade proceeded in both the British Parliament and the U.S Congress. In both settings, many believed that the abolition of the slave trade was the necessary first step toward ending slavery. Viewing the matter as a question of supply and demand, many believed that eliminating the supply of Africans as slaves would cause the institution of slavery to flounder.

On March 22, 1794, the U.S. Congress voted to prohibit the slave trade to all foreign ports and also prohibited the outfitting of any foreign vessels in any American port for the purpose of slave trading. Although this legislation was a welcomed sign to abolitionists, it was not the comprehensive ban on the slave trade that antislavery advocates desired, so they continued in their efforts to petition until the matter would be concluded to their liking.

The U.S. House of Representatives rejected a petition advanced by a group of free blacks from Philadelphia on January 2, 1800. The petitioners sought to end slavery in the United States through a system of gradual emancipation. The petition also protested against the transatlantic slave trade and the enforcement of the Fugitive Slave Act of 1793. The measure was defeated by a margin of 85 to 1.

On December 2, 1806, President Thomas Jefferson sent a message to Congress urging passage of legislation ending all slave importation to the United States effective January 1, 1808. This proposal was designed to address the twenty-year moratorium on addressing the slave trade that had been written into Article 1, Section 9, of the U.S. Constitution. The U.S. Congress enacted the recommended legislation on March 2, 1807, and Jefferson signed it into law. Despite the U.S. government's efforts to enforce the measure, violations did occur all the way to the time of the Civil War.

Having twice defeated similar measures in 1804 and 1805, the British Parliament took up a measure to outlaw the African slave trade on March 25, 1807. With the backing of Lord Grenville's government, the Parliament enacted the measure that would outlaw the transatlantic slave trade effective on March 1, 1808. The Parliament also enacted measures that permitted the Royal Navy to enforce the terms of the legislation to ensure that slaving vessels would no longer ply the waters of the Atlantic.

Emboldened by their victories against the slave trade in both the United States and Great Britain, abolitionists on both sides of the Atlantic set their sights on achieving their next main objective—the abolition of slavery itself. That campaign would be effected through different means and on different occasions in each respective nation.

Retrenchment and New Objectives

When the ban on further importation of Africans as slaves took effect on January 1, 1808, it is estimated that there were 1 million slaves in the United States. To optimists, elimination of the supply of additional African slaves was going to initiate the inevitable decline of slavery, but such would not be the case. By 1860 there would be nearly 4 million slaves in the United States. The failure of abolition to be achieved through the laws of supply and demand meant that new measures, and a sustained antislavery effort, would be required to effect emancipation in the United States.

Results of the Third Census of the United States, completed in 1810, revealed that 1,377,808 blacks, slave and free, constituted 19 percent of the nation's population. When the Fourth Census of the United States was taken a decade later, the incomprehensible seemed to be happening. The black population of the United States had increased to 1,771,656, or 18.4 percent of the nation's population. The laws of supply and demand were not moving the nation toward abolition as the natural increase of the slave population was sustaining and enlarging the labor supply of slaves. In response to this reality, new types of antislavery organizations and new methods of agitation began to be employed in the United States to hasten the coming of emancipation.

Although the slave population of the United States was expanding in the 1810s, it was the growing population of free blacks in both the northern and southern states that first attracted the attention and concern of many. A curious blend of reformers, some of whom were motivated by the best interests of free blacks and some of whom were driven by ulterior motives, coalesced around the concept of emigration—the idea that free blacks should be allowed, if they chose to do so, to return to Africa. The idea of emigration had support in Great Britain as well as in the United States.

Supporters of emigration to Africa gathered in Washington, D.C., on December 28, 1816, to form the American Colonization Society (ACS), an organization that endeavored to return free blacks who sought its services to Africa. Meeting in the chamber of the House of Representatives in the U.S. Capitol building, the ACS members vowed to support the emigration of free blacks to Africa. By 1820 the ACS had established the colonial outpost of Liberia on the western coast of Africa to receive those free blacks who chose to emigrate.

Most abolitionists in the United States did not support the colonization plans of the ACS. Delegates attending the 1817 meeting of the American Convention of Abolition Societies approved of a resolution stating "the gradual and total emancipation of all persons of colour, and their literary and moral education, should precede their colonization." A group of 3,000 free blacks in Philadelphia, led by the free black community leader James Forten, met to protest the plans of the ACS to encourage the removal of free blacks to Africa.

In 1820 the *Mayflower of Liberia* (formerly the brig *Elizabeth*) sailed from New York City with eighty-six free blacks who had agreed to return to Africa as part of the colonization plans of the ACS. The group was brought to Sierra Leone, a colonial outpost that the British had established for former slaves who wished to be repatriated to Africa. Between the time of its founding and the Civil War, the ACS would repatriate nearly fifteen thousand free blacks to Liberia.

Agitation

New independent organizations that employed distinct strategies aimed at effecting the abolition of slavery began to form in the United States during the 1810s and 1820s, and by 1833 when the American Anti-Slavery Society was organized, the movement assumed a national following even though its strongest support was limited to New England. The preponderance of new antislavery organizations and the strategies that they employed suggest that there were *varieties* of abolitionism under consideration rather than a single unified approach. The divisions that were apparent within the antislavery movement tended to keep it weak and likely delayed the eventual achievement of emancipation in the United States.

Lewis Dupre published the antislavery tract *An Admonitionary Picture and a Solemn Warning Principally Addressed to Professing Christians in the Southern States.* Published in Charleston, South Carolina, in 1810, the pamphlet urged southern slaveowners to adopt an enlightened view and work to bring about an end to slavery through principles of Christian justice. Such appeals on the basis of faith were designed to bring about abolitionism without the necessity of resorting to a legislative solution that would have been difficult to attain. Despite such goals, working toward emancipation through religious denomina-

tions became increasingly difficult. The General Conference of the Methodist Church determined in 1812 that slaveholders were no longer eligible to be elders within the congregation.

The presence of limited antislavery sentiment existed in the southern states during this era. In 1814, Charles Osborne and other antislavery advocates established the Manumission Society of Tennessee and by 1819 had founded the antislavery newspaper the *Manumission Intelligencer.* The goal of the group was to encourage slaveholders to emancipate their slaves so that abolition could be achieved through voluntary means. A society with similar motives was established by North Carolina Quakers in 1816.

In St. Clairsville, Ohio, the Quaker abolitionist Benjamin Lundy organized the Union Humane Society in 1815. In addition to later publishing and editing antislavery newspapers, Lundy was also one of the promoters of the "free produce" movement that encouraged individuals to purchase only those commodities that were produced by free laborers who earned wages rather than supporting slavery by purchasing slave-produced goods. Lundy and other abolitionists would operate free stores where no slave-produced items were sold.

Another path followed by antislavery advocates was the more radical approach. In 1816 the abolitionist George Bourne published *The Book and Slavery Irreconcilable,* often considered to be one of the most radical antislavery tracts ever published in the United States. In Bourne's view, one could not be a Christian and a slaveholder since the two concepts were incompatible.

Although moral suasion, voluntary manumission, economic boycotts, and radicalism were all approaches that individually might advance the antislavery cause, the different strategies did not coalesce into a unified course of action that all abolitionists should pursue. The number of slaves in the United States continued to increase, and the relative political influence of the slaveowners also grew during an era when abolitionists were struggling to focus attention on the antislavery cause.

Gradualism vs. Immediatism

Abolitionists in both the United States and Great Britain were also divided on a key strategy in the antislavery debate—the question of the timetable and the process whereby emancipation might be achieved. Some abolitionists on both sides of the Atlantic believed that a system of gradual emancipation was the most efficient and least disruptive method that could be used to bring about the end of slavery. Others claimed that since slavery was evil, only immediate emancipation could rid the nation of its sin and begin the process of redemption. Those who supported gradualism generally adopted a more conservative stance, believing that the abolition of slavery would take an extended period of time to achieve, while the more radical immediatists believed that swift action could free slaves all at one time.

Most of the early abolitionists in the United States fell into the gradualist camp. When slavery had been abolished by seven northern states after the American Revolution most of the states had used a form of gradualism to bring about emancipation. Although the system was somewhat cumbersome to employ and held the possibility of long-delayed freedom for many, it had produced emancipation in the northern states without causing the social disruption that many had feared. Support for gradualism remained strong in the United States until the late 1820s when more strident voices began to call for immediate emancipation.

Intellectual support for gradualism declined after the publication of an 1824 antislavery work by the British abolitionist Elizabeth [Coltman] Heyrick. In her work *Immediate, Not Gradual Abolition, or, An Inquiry into the Shortest, Safest, and Most Effectual Means of Getting Rid of West Indian Slavery*, Heyrick supported immediate emancipation because she believed that slavery was a moral question rather than an economic or political concern.

The transition from support for gradual emancipation to immediate emancipation was associated with a dramatic change in the tone of antislavery rhetoric. Antislavery advocacy couched in genteel appeals to reason gave way to more vitriolic prose that attacked not merely the institution of slavery itself, but also those who supported and sustained it. The war of words intensified as immediatism became the primary strategy, and rhetoric on both sides of the question—proslavery and antislavery—became sharper by the 1830s. The intensification of the debate caused a retrenchment in both camps as proslavery defenders and antislavery agitators became true believers in the certainty of their cause.

On the Precipice

The abolitionist editor William Lloyd Garrison launched his antislavery newspaper the *Liberator* on January 1, 1831. Vowing "No Union with Slaveholders" and disavowing political action as a means to effect emancipation, Garrison's strategy was to confront slavery as the evil that he believed it to be and to labor to rid the nation of the odious stain of slavery. In his inaugural issue of the *Liberator*, Garrison declared, "I am in earnest—I will not equivocate—I will not excuse—I will not retreat a single inch—AND I WILL BE HEARD!"

When many in the South saw a cause-and-effect relationship between the launch of Garrison's newspaper and the outbreak of the Nat Turner insurrection in Virginia in August 1831, the fear of Garrison and his fiery rhetoric grew even stronger than it had been before. The belief, however mistaken, that antislavery rhetoric in New England could foment slave rebellion in Virginia increased Garrison's stature within the abolitionist movement and made him a pariah in the eyes of southern slaveowners. Garrison relished the criticism and used it to attract new recruits to the antislavery cause.

On December 4, 1833, Garrison, along with other black and white abolitionist leaders including Theodore Dwight Weld, Arthur Tappan, and Lewis Tappan, met in Philadelphia where they established the American Anti-Slavery Society. This organization, with Garrison as its titular leader, became the leading antislavery organization in the United States until a rift in the 1840s caused factions to form within the Society. Garrison's ideology of immediatism and his fiery rhetoric animated the cause as abolitionists in the United States finally coalesced, at least momentarily, into a unified reform movement with clearly defined objectives. Garrison published the *Liberator* continuously until December 1865 once the Civil War had concluded, and the American Anti-Slavery Society remained in operation until 1870 when it ceased to exist after passage of the Fifteenth Amendment granted the right to vote to African American males. William Lloyd Garrison had been heard.

THE RISE OF "KING COTTON"
AND THE ECONOMICS OF SLAVERY

Just as the colonies that Britain had developed on the North American continent needed to be economically viable communities in order to survive, the thirteen independent states that formed the United States faced similar challenges. The new nation faced tremendous obstacles as it emerged onto the world stage since its economic potential was not yet realized and it carried mounting debt that had accrued throughout the revolutionary era. Structurally, the United States was an agricultural economy with only limited manufacturing taking place in selected portions of New England, and the immediate prospects for development in 1789 as the new U.S. Constitution took effect did not augur that any dramatic transformations were imminent. Without the solid foundation that a sound national economy would provide, the young nation might have found itself perpetually relegated to the ranks of lesser states for whom the status of dependency on the great powers became the mode of financial life.

The Constitution of the United States was formed to provide a stronger national government to the United States, a task that clearly had not been achieved under the Articles of Confederation. Although the principal doctrines of a stronger government were largely perceived as being political matters, there were certainly other means through which national strength could accrue through better and more effective government. For many, the success or failure of the U.S. Constitution would hinge largely on the new government's ability to provide the framework on which a sound economy might be fashioned so that the new country could emerge strong and prosperous within the family of nations.

During George Washington's first presidential administration, the responsibility for formulating an adequate strategy to achieve the nation's short-term and long-term financial objectives fell squarely on Secretary of the Treasury Alexander Hamilton. Realizing that national power stemmed from fiscal strength, Hamilton envisioned a vibrant economic life that could animate the young republic through the creation of wealth. In both his *Report on the Public Credit* (1790) and *Report on Manufactures* (1791) that he prepared for the Congress, Hamilton outlined a financial plan for the United States that would include debt management, limited taxation, and fiscal responsibility, but all of this was rooted in the promise of free market capitalism, which, if left unfettered, could stimulate economic growth and promote the creation of wealth. Hamilton's plans largely created an engine for economic prosperity but did not specifically identify the fuel that would power the transformation.

The economic impact of the early Industrial Revolution had begun to be realized in Great Britain in the eighteenth century as textile factories emerged and began to transform the social landscape. The rise of urban population centers as an ancillary component of the nascent factory system was not yet fully understood in the early stages of industrialization, as elements of the British model began to emerge in the United States as well. Unlike most Americans of the time, Hamilton, realized the potential social and economic change that manufacturing could bring to the United States, and he relished the prospect of growth that lay in the nation's future. Others, who saw the nation's destiny tied to the maintenance of an agricultural-based economy, feared the potential expansion of a manufacturing sector and viewed such changes not in terms of increased national prosperity but in terms of lost national virtue.

Whether one was a protoindustrialist or an advocate of the citizen farmers in 1789, their fortunes were inextricably tied together. The United States was an agricultural society and would remain so for quite some time, but the emergence of a manufacturing sector would grow out of and in response to the exigencies of the nation's farm- and plantation-based productivity. In many respects, the rise of manufacturing interests in the United States was largely driven by the expansion of the nation's agricultural sector.

Changing the Old Ways

The creation of a vibrant national economy would require the establishment of a commercial infrastructure that was sorely lacking in the early United States. During the colonial era, the nature of the colonies acting as autonomous economic entities had not fostered the development of any unified system that linked the activities of one region with another. Coordination, for example, between Massachusetts and South Carolina was nonexistent as each colony had viewed its fiscal ties directly with Britain rather than with other colonies that were generally seen as economic rivals.

The development of roads, bridges, and port facilities emerged to service local economic needs, but the macroeconomic concerns of a region or a nation did not drive commercial life.

In the southern colonies where a plantation-based agricultural economy had emerged, many large estates operated autonomously even within their specific colonial setting. Located along navigable rivers, many plantations had created their own dock and wharf facilities where products of the land could be loaded onto vessels that were destined for British ports, thus bypassing the need for regional ports and harbors. In general, colonial economic transactions more regularly occurred on an east-west axis than on a north-south one as transatlantic trade largely surpassed intercolonial financial activity.

Even under the days of the Articles of Confederation, the notions of sovereignty that had been retained by the thirteen independent states perpetuated the perceptions of economic rivalry and political suspicion that had emerged during the colonial era. The primary task of a nation that wanted to live up to its motto of *E pluribus unum* ("Out of many, one") rested in the ability of its people to see the interconnectedness that was essential to national life. Putting aside differences and quelling regional passions would be difficult tasks, but they were essential elements to formulating a new nation whose political solidarity and economic stability were premised on the belief that unity was attainable.

Convincing citizens that the interests of the tobacco planter in Tidewater Virginia were comparable with those of the farmer who grew corn in western Pennsylvania or that the Connecticut dockworker had similar economic passions as the South Carolina artisan were challenges of the highest order. In many respects, the success or failure of the American experiment with democracy rested not on the theoretical foundations on which the national government was based but more on winning the hearts and minds of a disparate citizenry to recognize their common interest as stakeholders in the new nation. More challenging perhaps would be the tacit understanding that slave states and free states existed because of the mutual dependence of one on the other in the complexities of national economic life.

The Emergence of Cotton

On the eve of the American Revolution in 1770, the commodities that were produced by slave labor in the North American colonies had constituted much of the bulk of goods traded with Great Britain. Tobacco (27.1

percent), rice (10.1 percent), and indigo (3.9 percent) together formed 41 percent of all colonial exports at the time, and no manufactured goods seemed poised to threaten the economic supremacy that the plantation interests maintained. By the time the U.S. Constitution took effect in 1789, exports stemming from fisheries and iron ore rose slightly, but the dominance of exports based on slave-produced commodities had changed little.

Cotton cultivation and trade, which came to dominate southern plantation agriculture and stimulate American manufacturing, was an infinitesimally small specialized crop localized to the Sea Islands of South Carolina and Georgia at the time of the nation's founding. Few would have imagined at the time that cotton would transform all sectors of the national economy during the early nineteenth century.

A variety of cotton that was acclimated to the Sea Islands had been under cultivation for many years but did not rival the profits from indigo and rice. The fibers of Sea Island, or long-staple, cotton were considered to be of high quality and had a smooth or silky texture, but cultivation of the crop was geographically limited to those areas that provided an ideal growing season without the danger of early-season frosts that could ruin the harvest. The moderating influence of warm Gulf Stream currents made the Sea Islands well suited for the cultivation of long-staple cotton, but few other locations in the United States were appropriate for large-scale cultivation of the crop on a plantation model.

Slave labor was used in the locations where Sea Island was cultivated to plant, tend, and harvest the crop as well as to remove the seeds from the cotton once it was picked. This was a labor-intensive task that was often relegated to women and children, but it was made somewhat easier because the black seeds of long-staple cotton generally separated rather easily from the cotton fibers. The removal of the seeds was done by hand by slave laborers.

Other varieties of cotton existed and were grown in parts of the South. One type, known as upland or short-staple cotton, grew practically like a weed in almost any soil type or climate zone of the South. Short-staple cotton could be cultivated in the red clay soils of the upland South in areas that were otherwise thought unfit for large-scale agricultural development. Although its growth in various settings was ubiquitous, the cultivation of short-staple cotton had not emerged as a plantation crop because the time-consuming efforts of seed removal and the perceived lesser quality of the cotton fiber made it a less attractive product than Sea Island cotton.

Technological innovation would transform the nature of southern agriculture, and subsequently of American manufacturing, when short-staple cotton became a viable crop for large-scale production on a plantation model using slave labor. This change was wrought when Eli Whitney invented the cotton gin in Mulberry Grove, Georgia, on October 28, 1793, since this invention revolutionized southern agriculture as it made short-staple (upland) cotton easier to process. As the planting of upland cotton increased after 1793 and both new and marginal lands came under cultivation, the profits that were realized fostered the expansion of cotton production into new lands that were farther inland. The settlement of the Old Southwest and the concomitant expansion of slaveholding in the region would accompany the rise of cotton cultivation and trade.

A Need for Slave Laborers

As cotton cultivation expanded during the years of the early republic, it became increasingly clear that a large supply of slave laborers would be needed to develop the new acreage coming under cultivation as new plantations and farms were established in portions of the upland South. At the time when the U.S. Constitution was being written in 1787, the Founders had included in the document a twenty-year moratorium on any consideration of ending the transatlantic slave trade. Thus the Congress could not consider such a legislative item until 1807 at the earliest. Accordingly, the importation of Africans as slaves into the United States continued unheeded during the late eighteenth and early nineteenth centuries, and many of these new slaves were introduced to plantations and farms in the Lower South where cotton cultivation was expanding.

In addition to the importation of Africans until the transatlantic slave trade was outlawed, there emerged a large-scale domestic slave trade business in the United States that provided the sale and transit of slaves from the Upper South to the Lower South throughout the antebellum era. In many respects, some slaveowners in the Upper South were beginning to realize the marginal utility of slave labor on their plantations and farms and began to sell their slaves to the Lower South to recoup their investment and often garner handsome profits. Although the prices of slaves varied considerably from one period to another, the nearly constant demand for slave laborers on southern cotton plantations made it likely that one could profit considerably from selling slaves through the domestic trade.

The dependency on the African slave trade and the domestic slave trade to provide plantation laborers in the late eighteenth and early nineteenth centuries is in-

congruous with the pattern that had emerged at the end of the American Revolution as northern states manumitted slaves and outlawed the practice of slavery. The trend that emerged in the United States in the 1780s was that slavery was being diminished both in theory and in practice in the new nation. Not only had northern states abolished slavery, but the Northwest Ordinance of 1787 had also prohibited slavery from being introduced into the territory north of the Ohio River. The first decade of American independence had seemingly indicated that freedom in the United States was a growing tendency that might one day be appreciated by all, but the circumstances of the 1790s indicated that slavery was not dead yet.

Cotton Land

The widespread cultivation of cotton meant that not only would additional slave laborers be needed to establish new plantations and farms, but new territory would also be needed to meet the insatiable demand for cotton exports that were being demanded by world markets. The expansion of cotton cultivation was motivated by the incessant demands of textile manufacturers in Europe and in the northern states of the United States who spun cotton into manufactured products that had mass appeal. Drawn almost inextricably into a classic economic model of supply and demand, southern producers responded intuitively to the urgent calls for more cotton and the profits it would accrue, and the twin requirements of additional slaves and additional land became endemic necessities.

Although the acquisition of additional slaves was an economic activity that individual planters had to effect through their own initiative and means, the acquisition of new territory in which plantation agriculture might be expanded was a task that sometimes involved geopolitical gamesmanship and in which the United States government became a willing participant. Certain parts of the Old Southwest, such as the Natchez District, were well suited for cotton cultivation. Those areas were being farmed commercially in the early years of the republic, but other areas would require different government efforts before they could come under possession of the United States and eventual agricultural development.

Diplomatic initiatives of the United States government during the early nineteenth century would help to form the eventual "Cotton Kingdom" that emerged by the late-antebellum period. The Louisiana Purchase (1803), the annexation of West Florida (1810), the purchase of East Florida (1819), and the annexation of Texas (1845) were all part of the territorial expansion of the United States, but all of these acquisitions permitted the extension of cotton cultivation and the expansion of slavery.

In addition to the territorial acquisition that stemmed from international treaties and disputes, the United States also maintained a consistent policy of territorial aggrandizement in its relation with the various domestic nations, or Indian tribes, that initially inhabited the lands of the Old Southwest. Starting with the Treaty of Fort Jackson at the conclusion of the Creek Indian War and continuing through the Indian Removal of the 1830s and the Seminole Wars, the efforts of the United States to remove the five "Civilized Tribes" from the southeast to reservation lands in Oklahoma was designed to acquire more territory that could come under cultivation by southern planters and their slaves. Even though the United States government couched the language of Indian Removal in rhetoric that was seemingly beneficial to the Indian and motivated through acts of benevolence, the clearing of the land for a higher economic purpose was central to the Indian Removal efforts.

Consciously or unconsciously, whether contrived or unintentional, the systematic expansion of the United States during the early nineteenth century and the removal of Indian tribes from the region served the economic interests of southern cotton planters and helped facilitate the expansion of slavery into the region. Although such a self-serving policy to advance the cause of southern interests may seem likely, it provides only a partial explanation for government actions. The economic expansion of the United States was rooted in the interconnectedness that existed between raw cotton produced in the South by slave laborers and the textile mills of the North that spun southern cotton into manufactured products. Some abolitionists criticized a "slave power conspiracy" for controlling the apparatus of government and determining policy only in support of slaveholding interests, but the complexity of the truth is more damning of all parties. Cotton had become so essential a commodity to the United States that its economic power held sway over many decisions made at the national level. Both as an export commodity and as a natural resource that powered a growing manufacturing sector in the young nation, cotton had tremendous economic implications. It seemed as though slavery was safe in the United States as long as the benefits of a cotton economy accrued to all parts of the nation both North and South.

A Better Way

In an amoral sense, profit is profit and no nation should be expected to question the foundations on which its prosperity is based. Even the residents of those portions of the United States that had abolished slavery after the American Revolution found themselves benefiting from the perpetuation of slavery in the southern states and from the market commodities that slave labor produced. America's national prosperity in the antebellum era did not produce widespread pangs of guilt, but it did have its detractors who argued that there must exist a better way to create wealth without stealing the labor of others. To such critics, slavery could not be excused as merely a necessary first step toward economic maturation in a young nation because slavery was a moral abomination, a practice that was inexcusable in any civil society.

Some of the early Quaker abolitionists believed that the purchase of slave-made goods was a sin of commission through which individuals perpetuated the institution of slavery by creating a ready market for such products. Believing that every dollar spent in the marketplace was, in effect, an endorsement, such abolitionists argued that only by purchasing exclusively those products that were made by free laborers who earned wages could one effectively fight against the practice of enslaving fellow human beings. Abolitionists like Benjamin Lundy and others established free stores in Quaker communities that only handled products that were produced or manufactured by free laborers who earned wages. They argued that only through the deliberate and conscious act of avoiding any endorsement of slavery through purchase could one honestly consider himself to be an abolitionist. Although the movement was small and had limited effectiveness, it presented an alternative to the free market capitalistic model in that individuals were willing to pay higher prices for goods if they knew that their conscience would be clear that they were not supporting the perpetuation of slavery.

The free store concept was not the only economic alternative that abolitionists presented in their efforts to promote antislavery ideals. In 1826 the British abolitionist Frances Wright established Nashoba plantation near Memphis, Tennessee, as a utopian community experiment that was designed to train blacks for eventual settlement outside of the United States. Wright hoped to demonstrate that cotton produced on a plantation where laborers received wages could be just as competitive in the marketplace as slave-produced cotton. Although Wright's experiment ended when her plantation faced bankruptcy in 1830, the argument about the relative merits of free produce as compared to slave produce continued until the time of the Civil War.

The "Cotton Kingdom" Emerges

Settlement of the Old Southwest was marked by the creation of new slave states that joined the Union in rapid succession in the early nineteenth century. Louisiana (1812), Mississippi (1817), and Alabama (1818) quickly emerged as areas where expansive agriculture on a plantation-based model existed, and portions of western Georgia that were cleared for white settlement after Indian Removal in the 1830s followed a similar pattern. By the early 1840s, the demographic profile of the Old Southwest began to reflect the emergence of the "Cotton Kingdom" in which large plantations with many slaves fashioned the social and economic base of the region's identity. The area's so-called Black Belt began to take shape as plantation lands fanned out in crescent shape across the Old Southwest from northeast Georgia across Alabama to northeastern Mississippi in what became some of the prime cotton lands of the region.

The cotton monoculture that dominated the lands of the Old Southwest was an essential element of the regional identity that formed, but it was augmented by a proslavery ethos that emerged in the 1830s and became embedded in the cultural identity of the Cotton Kingdom. Among southern slaveholders and non-slaveholders alike, it became common to hear stirring defenses of the positive aspects of slavery as the economic practice became enshrined as an essential component of the southern way of life. In this fashion, slavery became a part of the moral order of society, and its perpetuation was argued not in terms of profitability but instead in terms of social necessity. Those like the abolitionists who would dare to question the moral legitimacy of slavery were challenging what southerners perceived to be a basic institution on which civil society itself was structured. Accordingly, the ideologies of such economic radicals and social levelers needed to be confronted in every possible fashion.

The antebellum Cotton Kingdom also emerged in the aftermath of the Nat Turner Revolt that shook Southampton County, Virginia, in August 1831. This event, convergent with the rise of "radical" abolitionism as evidenced by William Lloyd Garrison's *Liberator* that began publication in 1831, heightened tensions in the South and convinced most southerners that only a united and sustained effort to combat the enemies of slavery would prevent the forces of insurrection from threatening the peace and security of the South and its inhabitants. Southern defenders of slavery became increasingly fanatical in their rhetoric as they decried northern efforts to interfere with slavery in any fashion.

Southern politicians, too, became vocal advocates of the economic and social necessity of protecting and perpetuating the institution of slavery. Congressional defenders of slavery were able to institute a "gag rule" in the House of Representatives that remained in effect from 1836 to 1844. The rule was curiously coincidental with the emergence of the cotton South, as southern legislators sought to prohibit consideration of any antislavery petitions or memorials that might be presented to the Congress. When Arkansas became the twenty-fifth state in June 1836, the slaveowning states constituted, for the first time in the nation's history, a majority of states in the Union. In many respects, the ascendant power of slavery seemed quite real in the 1830s as the expansion of cotton cultivation in the United States changed the nature of the debate over slavery.

The Global Economy

The cultivation of cotton in the United States impacted not only the economic power of the United States, but also much of international trade during the antebellum era. A casual review of the expansion of cotton as a commodity on the world market reflects the power of the cotton interests to influence the nation's economic policy. In 1820 cotton exports totaled $22 million, by 1830 they totaled $30 million, by 1840 $64 million, by 1850 $72 million, and by 1860 cotton exports had jumped to $192 million in U.S. exports. Although these figures represent dollars alone and not the volume of cotton traded, the 1840 and 1860 figures are especially revealing. During the 1830s the value of cotton exports doubled, and the 1850s witnessed cotton exports increasing by 267 percent more than in the previous decade. In 1850 U.S. cotton production was estimated to be 2.5 million bales (400 pounds each), and this level of production had more than doubled by 1860. These astronomical growth rates suggest the power inherent within the cotton economy of the South to influence national policy.

Most of the cotton exports during the antebellum era fed the textile mills of northern England as free wage-based laborers transformed the slave-produced cotton into manufactured goods that were then sold on the world market. To borrow the notion from the Quaker abolitionists that all were sullied who trucked with slave-produced goods, the transoceanic shippers, the British manufacturers, and all who purchased cotton products that were manufactured shared complicity, if not compunction, with the system of slavery that existed in the South. Far from being an economic matter of limited concern, the slave-produced commodities of the southern states influenced the global economy of the nineteenth century and thus had far-reaching consequences.

In the United States, too, the textile mills worked with cotton cultivated by slaves. In the heart of abolitionist New England, the mill towns of Waltham, Lowell, Chicopee, and Lawrence, Massachusetts, all spun cotton that was cultivated on the plantations and farms of the southern states. In 1820 these mills had 220,000 spindles working with cotton, and by 1840 the number of spindles was just under three million. The jobs held by many workers in the northern textile industry were grounded in the perpetuation of slave-based cotton production in the southern states, and few abolitionists rose from the ranks of the mill workers.

Abolitionists in both Great Britain and the United States recognized that convincing their respective governments to wean themselves away from slave-produced goods was an almost hopeless challenge. Using the empty power of moral suasion to overcome the incalculable profits that tens of millions in exports and manufacturing could generate was an obstacle to effective advocacy of the antislavery position.

Perils of the Trade

Cotton was a commodity on the world market, subject to all the vagaries and uncertainties of market conditions. Thus cotton prices varied considerably. Adverse weather patterns and dangers of crop infestation could produce temporary fluctuations in cotton prices, while more sustained economic panics could inflict severe drops in commodity prices. Since the world demand for cotton grew tremendously during the early nineteenth century, these economic downturns created a buyer's market in which relatively cheap cotton could be purchased and warehoused for later manufacture. Planters generally saw decreased profits during the downturns, and since most plantation costs of production were fixed, little could be done to offset such losses. Despite these occurrences, there were good years when cotton prices were high, and these gains more than offset the losses created in the panic years. But as a general trend, cotton prices declined during much of the antebellum era.

Since slave laborers were also bought, sold, and traded as chattel property, the relative cost of buying and selling slaves also varied with changes in the market. The cost of purchasing a prime cotton fieldhand might have varied from a high of $1,200 on the eve of the Civil War to a low of perhaps $800 in the immediate aftermath of the Panic of 1837. The prices of slaves were always dependent on the age, health, and general appearance of the slave, so even within a particular era the prices paid for individual slaves might have varied tremendously.

The price of public lands remained fairly consistent during the expansion of the Cotton Kingdom in the Old Southwest. Planters and farmers wishing to acquire additional acreage could purchase public land for as little as $1.25 per acre, though better quality land would draw a higher price. In many cases, planters wishing to expand their lands under cultivation would often clear marginal lands and place these under cultivation rather than purchase additional acreage. This effort kept costs down and provided tasks that slaves could perform in the off-season when planting and harvesting were not taking place.

Historians have long speculated as to whether or not slavery was profitable. Some nineteenth-century abolitionists speculated that the demise of slavery would come about in response to its economic viability. Such observers believed that the moment slavery ceased to be profitable it would be abandoned and wage labor would take its place. Apologists for slavery, both during the nineteenth century and since, claimed that slavery was maintained as a social institution out of a sense of benevolent paternalism and that its maintenance was not associated with any supposed link to its profitability. Most studies that have examined the economic history of slavery in the United States have concluded that slave labor was indeed profitable for southern cotton planters who were garnering profits ranging from 6 to 12 percent on the eve of the Civil War.

Texas

One factor that expanded cotton production in the United States and enlarged the Cotton Kingdom was the annexation of Texas in 1845. The rich lands of eastern Texas were considered to be prime cotton lands on a par with the Black Belt of the Old Southwest and the Delta region of the Mississippi Valley. The productivity of Texas cotton lands helped to satisfy market demands of the 1850s, even though cotton prices diminished somewhat because of fears of overproduction and the impact of the Panic of 1857.

The impact of market forces on Texas cotton production is reflected in the state's demographic transformation during the decade prior to the Civil War. In 1850 Texas had a slave population of 58,161, but by 1860 that figure had increased to 212,592. Texas had the fastest growing population of any slave state in the Union on the eve of the war. During the decade of this expansion in slave population, Texas increased its cotton production by 600 percent over 1850 levels.

When cotton prices dropped in the late 1850s, many British manufacturers, fearing the escalating tension in the United States, bought up large quantities of Texas cotton at reduced prices and warehoused these bales. As a result of acquiring such a supply, British manufacturers were not adversely affected by the disruption of supply caused by the Civil War. This supply of warehoused cotton prevented the British government from being forced into recognizing the Confederate States of America in order to maintain a ready cotton supply. The Confederacy's strategy, known as "King Cotton Diplomacy," failed to effect the diplomatic recognition so desperately sought during the war years.

Other Crops

Although much attention is paid to the power and impact of the Cotton Kingdom in influencing antebellum economic life, the southern states produced other crops and farm commodities that had an impact on both the regional and national economy. Cotton was certainly the dominant cash crop of most of the southern states, but other crops under cultivation by slave laborers were equally profitable.

Most of the parishes of southeastern Louisiana were under cultivation in sugarcane, and the annual productivity from the region had been steadily increasing throughout the antebellum era. New technologies in sugar making, such as the multiple-effect vacuum evaporation process, had been implemented to extract the greatest possible quantity and the highest possible quality of product from the cane cultivated in Louisiana.

Tobacco cultivation remained the principal crop cultivated by slave laborers in Virginia, North Carolina, Tennessee, and Kentucky during the antebellum era. Even though the acreage under tobacco cultivation had declined somewhat owing to soil depletion and to planters making the transition to corn and other foodstuffs, the volume of tobacco produced in the region remained consistently high.

Other regions used slave labor to produce different cash crops. Sections of coastal South Carolina and Georgia still cultivated much of the rice that was grown in the United States. In areas like Virginia's Shenandoah Valley, slave labor was used to cultivate foodstuffs such as corn and wheat, which were under intensive cultivation. The Shenandoah Valley would become the breadbasket of the Confederacy during the Civil War. In addition, slave labor supported the cultivation of livestock in many parts of the South. In particular, cattle and pigs augmented the profits attained through crop cultivation.

The Balance Sheet

The results of the eighth census of the United States, completed in 1860, revealed that of the more than 8 million white residents of the South, only 383,637 were identified as slaveowners. The black population, both slave and free, was recorded at 4,401,830, constituting 14.1 percent of the nation's population. Of this total, 448,070 were identified as free blacks and 3,953,760 were slaves.

As the slave population in the United States had experienced a fourfold increase from 1808 when the transatlantic slave trade had been outlawed, the economy of the South had also witnessed a dramatic transformation. The cultivation of short-staple (upland) cotton had generated economic growth in the agricultural South, and it had fueled manufacturing in the free states of the North. Cotton had also provided an export commodity that made the United States the key trading partner with Great Britain in the early nineteenth century.

In many respects, the Founding Fathers' economic dreams had been realized. Alexander Hamilton had envisioned an America where factory workers and shopkeepers would dominate an urban-industrial society. Thomas Jefferson had pictured an America in which the produce of the land would constitute the nation's riches. To an extent they were both right as elements of each vision had been achieved by the cultivation of cotton and the manufacture of textiles.

A significant portion of America's prosperity in the antebellum era stemmed from the economic viability of slave-based agricultural productivity and its linkage to the trade networks of a transnational economy. The magical powers of free market economics directed the forces of supply and demand in such a way that the "invisible hand" of which Adam Smith spoke in *The Wealth of Nations* (1776) fashioned a way for cotton produced in the Black Belt of Alabama to reach the boutiques of London and Paris. The creation of wealth that emerged from such a process was phenomenal.

Some southern planters showcased their wealth in ostentatious displays, lavishing enormous sums on grand homes to mark their economic prowess. Others used their newfound wealth to purchase more slaves.

A Voice in the Wilderness

Hinton Rowan Helper, a North Carolina abolitionist who despised blacks, ignited a firestorm of protest when he published *The Impending Crisis of the South: How to Meet It* (1857). Helper based his arguments on statistical information he had gleaned from the seventh census of the United States taken in 1850 and asserted that slavery had caused great economic distress to nonslaveholders and poor whites of the South. He urged the South's poor whites to rise up and overthrow slavery, but he also advocated the deportation of freed blacks to Africa. Sixty-eight members of the U.S. House of Representatives endorsed Helper's book, most without having read it, and the Republican Party distributed 100,000 copies of it in the northern states. Once the book was published it was banned in the southern states. Helper was considered such a pariah in the region that he was forced to flee to New York for his personal safety.

The Impending Crisis presented an alternative, albeit controversial, interpretation of the economic impact of slavery on southern society. Rather than focusing on the dualism of the master-slave arrangement, Helper gave his attention to marginalized groups like nonslaveholders and poor whites and questioned the presumed benefits of a slave-based cotton economy. He also highlighted the limited extent to which any real economic transformation had occurred in the region. By attacking the economic premise that had sustained slavery as a system, Helper attracted critics who were eager to quell any voice of discontent challenging the status quo.

By the eve of the Civil War, the voices of critics like Helper were drowned out by the stirring rhetoric of proslavery apologists who touted the economic benefits of the institution of slavery and praised the important social role that slavery provided in an ordered, class-based society. Their argument was smug, but they were the true believers. The world they knew and the economic system they envisioned was a world apart from that of the slave or even that of the poor white or nonslaveholder in the South. Preaching to the solidarity and common aspirations of their own social group, the proslavery apologists affirmed what they hoped was plausibly true as a bulwark against their unspoken fears.

SLAVERY, PATERNALISM,
AND ANTEBELLUM SOUTHERN CULTURE

All efforts to examine slavery through the lens of modernity make it difficult to comprehend how individuals supported and sustained an institution for centuries that degraded and dehumanized others for the exploitation of profit. Slavery was a multidimensional practice that influenced economic thought in its time but also affected the social, cultural, and moral ethos of both its defenders and its detractors. The slaveholder and the nonslaveholder alike were sullied by maintaining a slave-based society, and all individuals, whether they lived in the South or North, found their life and times circumscribed by the necessities inherent in preserving slavery and preserving civil society simultaneously. The response to this challenge led to the formation of a defensive posture that acknowledged the place of slavery in the natural order of things and viewed abolitionist challenges to the "peculiar institution" as errant beliefs that would only produce social discord.

It is difficult to understand how a society might fashion an attitude that legitimates the buying, selling, trading, and owning of others as an acceptable form of commerce. Even more disconcerting is the level of blind hypocrisy that is readily apparent when defenders of slavery in the United States who mouthed the revolutionary rhetoric of liberty and freedom as natural conditions of humankind found common cause to support the enslavement of their fellow human beings. That people of faith with a clear conscience recognized the need to perpetuate slavery seems terribly at odds with modern sensibilities of morality and social justice, but the intellectual foundation of the times created a bulwark against all contrary notions. As such, slavery was seen as part of the moral order on which society rested, and slaveowners were viewed by many as benevolent individuals who maintained an essential social task.

Defenders of slavery found ideological support for the practice in their society's cultural heritage as they rooted their beliefs in commonly held assumptions and historic precedent and practice. The language of the Bible was used to espouse the enslavement of Africans and to justify its moral necessity. They also mined intellectual tradition dating back to classical antiquity to find the rhetoric that would support a class-based society where slaves were meant to benefit and serve others. The discipline of science, and the use of pseudoscience, fashioned explanations that defended the "natural" inclination of Africans to be enslaved by their social betters. Moreover, the proslavery apologists employed a careful reading of history to explain the notion of human progress through the perpetuation of class-based societies that relied on slave labor. To challenge the legitimacy of slavery would therefore require a denunciation of all the intellectual antecedents that justified, rationalized, and buttressed the practice.

God's Will

At the same time that abolitionists were acknowledging that slavery was contrary to Christian practice and were urging coreligionists to end the practice, defenders of slavery were finding an alternative message in scripture that justified the moral necessity of the institution. The apologists believed that Christians had a moral imperative to be slaveowners because the system conferred beneficial effects on the enslaved. Other people of faith interpreted the same sacred text in a widely different way. Nonetheless, both sides in the debate were certain of the moral urgency of their calling, and both were animated with the evangelical fervor of true believers.

Thornton Stringfellow, a Baptist minister and proslavery apologist from Virginia, published *A Brief Examination of Scripture Testimony on the Institution of Slavery* (1841) to refute the abolitionist argument that slavery was contrary to Christian practices. Stringfellow believed that the number of references in the Bible supporting slavery was sufficient proof of the moral legitimacy of the practice. His work challenged the notion that "the gain of freedom to the slave, is the only proof of godliness in the master" because he held that owning and maintaining order among slaves provided a form of moral education that would uplift and enlighten the slave. Stringfellow confronted what he perceived was the antislavery advocate's misreading of scripture. He found it inconceivable that "God has ordained slavery, and yet slavery is the greatest of sins?" as the abolitionists had argued.

Others found a defense for slavery, particularly for the enslavement of Africans, in the story of Noah in Genesis, which became known as the "Curse of Ham." According to this tradition, Noah placed a curse on his son Ham that implied his son's descendants would be "servant of servants" for all eternity. An interpretation of this passage by the twelfth-century religious scholar Benjamin of Tudeal implied a racial association of blackness, which he ascribed to Ham, thus equating the notion of servant with the badge of racial exclusiveness. Religious leaders in the antebellum South regularly used the "Curse of Ham" to defend the enslavement of Africans as something that was divinely inspired and biblically sanctioned. They questioned the motives of anyone who would challenge the class-based doctrines on which southern society was structured.

The fact that mainline Christian denominations were not quick to condemn slavery was perceived as a tacit endorsement of the practice by many. Pope Gregory XVI did not declare the Roman Catholic Church's opposition to the slave trade and slavery until he issued the 1839 papal letter *In supremo*. But Roman Catholics in the United States generally ignored the papal pronouncement and continued to hold slaves. Among the Protestant religious communities in the United States, slavery did not emerge as a key moral concern until the 1850s when schisms divided many denominations over the question of slavery.

The religious argument in support of slavery was a primary defense presented in "The Pro-Slavery Argument" (1852), published by a group of southern apologists including William Harper, Thomas R. Dew, and James Henry Hammond. This work contained a collection of essays, many of which had been previously published, that based their theoretical justification for the institution of slavery on biblical and classical sources.

The incongruity of slavery with religious belief does not seem to have registered with those who considered themselves righteous before God. The sincerity of these beliefs is apparent as slaveowning southerners endeavored to introduce their slaves to Christianity as a means of moral uplift for the slave and evangelical urgency to the owners. Sensing themselves as virtual trustees of a benighted people, slaveholders considered bringing faith to the faithless to be one of their highest callings. They accepted this duty without hesitation, never allowing their Christian zeal to grasp the enormous inconsistencies between belief and practice.

Classical Antecedents

The classical origins of Western culture were made

manifest through the ancient Greeks who articulated the individual's place in the universe through an understanding of a well-ordered society. In the vast marketplace of ideas, the Greeks posited questions of relationship as they strove to understand the interconnectedness of all things around them. Central to this discussion was the place of human beings and the relative abilities of each to contribute to the ultimate good of society. Humans' ability to actualize their potential, however great or small, was deemed essential to the well-being of society.

Classical antiquity suggests that slaves existed from the beginning of civilized society. Homer makes reference to the presence of slaves in both the *Iliad* and the *Odyssey,* thus implying that the origins of slavery were organic to social development as captives of war became servants to the victors. These mores and values were accepted without question. In his *Works and Days,* the Greek author Hesiod acknowledged the existence of slaves but did not distinguish them greatly from free workers who also toiled laboriously. By not describing the slave as a commodity that could be traded, he implicitly viewed slaves as a protected class of laborers who were not subject to many of the burdensome anxieties and responsibilities that befell free citizens.

Slavery was also defended in the earliest formulations of philosophy. Plato and Aristotle not only affirmed the condition of slavery, but also owned slaves themselves, attesting to the ancients' justification of the institution. When Plato tried to create a model of the ideal state in *The Republic,* he included slavery as part of the social order of this perfect state. In his view, there was nothing wrong with the enslavement of foreigners, and he believed that slavery should be confined to barbarians exclusively. Furthermore, he did not believe that freed slaves should be allowed to become citizens of the ideal state. Aristotle, in his *Politics,* wrote, "From the hour of their birth some are marked out for subjection, others for rule." When he died in 322 BCE, Aristotle left an estate that included fourteen domestic slaves.

Similarly to their Greek counterparts, the Romans defended the institution and practice of slavery in their society. The security of an ordered society was always given precedence over the rights and liberties of the individual; thus maintaining slavery was viewed as being more beneficial socially than the particular liberties denied the individual slave. The Roman scholar Marcus Terentius Varro in his treatise *De re rustica* ("On Farming") advised that slaves "should be neither cowed nor high-spirited," and he warned owners to "avoid having too many slaves of the same nation, for this is a fertile source of domestic quarrels."

Later Christian writers such as Augustine and Thomas Aquinas did not challenge the sense of order that slavery created in society. In *The City of God,* Augustine observed that slavery was a status that "has been imposed by the just sentence of God upon the sinner." Later Aquinas developed Augustine's views into the notion of "just war," which could be pursued for divinely sanctioned purposes. Over time, European slave traders would come to understand the operations of the slave trade to be a manifestation of just war.

With such rich intellectual antecedents, it is not surprising that proslavery apologists in the United States South found evidence to support their claims that slavery was both necessary to maintain an ordered society and beneficial to the slave. A flurry of proslavery literature appeared during the antebellum era as abolitionist rhetoric was matched by the intellectual defense of slavery.

In 1832 Thomas Roderick Dew, a professor of political economy at William and Mary College in Virginia and a southern apologist for slavery, published his "Review of the Debate in the Virginia Legislature of 1831 and 1832." Dew emphasized the proslavery perspective of the debates that had followed the Nat Turner insurrection of 1831. In 1832 Dew also published an essay entitled "The Pro-slavery Argument," in which he provided an intellectual foundation for the racist assumptions that slaveholders used to justify the institution and practice of slaveholding.

George Fitzhugh of Virginia, a noted proslavery polemicist, published *Cannibals All! Or, Slaves without Masters* (1857), in which he presented the argument that northern "wage slaves" were essentially worse off than slave laborers in the South. Fitzhugh believed that the exploitative nature of industrial capitalism did not provide a system of economic security to northern workingmen similar to that found in the South's paternalistic institution of slavery.

Southern rhetoric in defense of slavery grew more vociferous after 1831. With the beginning of the radical abolitionist movement, as shaped by William Lloyd Garrison's publication of the *Liberator,* and the outbreak of the Nat Turner Revolt in Virginia, many slaveholders became more vocal in their belief that slavery was divinely sanctioned and intellectually sound. They believed that only through the sustained defense of the "peculiar institution" could they protect it—and essentially themselves—from the dangerous doctrines advocated by abolitionist fanatics.

Scientific Error

Although both religious and intellectual arguments were offered in defense of slavery, some of the strongest support by proslavery apologists came from men of science. The idea that rational arguments rooted in science could defend slavery was a new argument first expressed in the United States during the antebellum era. With findings supposedly rooted in scientific inquiry, proslavery apologists believed that such support would be able to counter the emotionally laden charges that abolitionists had leveled against the institution. The assumption was that the facts would not lie.

Many of the prevalent notions about race in the nineteenth century were fashioned by the Mobile, Alabama, physician Josiah Clark Nott who wrote *Connection between the Biblical and Physical History of Man* (1849), *Types of Mankind* (1854), and *Indigenous Races of the Earth* (1857). An avowed apologist for slavery who tried to couch his defense of the institution in the rationalism of science, Nott studied the physiological traits of the African and deemed that the Africans' physical endurance and limited mental capacity made them a "race" specially suited for slavery. Arguing that there were "fixed races" of humankind, Nott hypothesized that a racial hierarchy existed that identified those who must rule and those who must by nature be ruled.

Using Nott's work as a foundation, southern proslavery apologists found it fashionable to use the language and appearance of science to defend slavery. The New Orleans, Louisiana, physician Samuel A. Cartwright, for example, published articles in the *New Orleans Medical and Surgical Journal* in the 1850s that focused on new findings about the ethnology of the slave population in the South. Cartwright tried to use science to mask and defend his own racist assumptions, and he began to use pseudoscience to make claims about the relative attributes of slaves. He argued, among other things, that the propensity of slaves to run away was not a natural desire for human freedom but rather a malady that he called *drapetomania*. In similar fashion, *dysaesthesia aethiopica* was distinguished as the illness that caused "rascality" to appear in some slaves but not in others.

Both Nott and Cartwright misused the scientific method to suit their own interests. Rather than letting scientific research take them to an undetermined goal, which is the key objective of empiricism, both men began with a predetermined goal and sought out only what they considered to be appropriate evidence supporting that goal. Their writings are more characteristic of propaganda or boosterism than of true science.

Slavery in History

Slave-based societies have existed throughout the history of the world, but none of these civilizations ever gave rise to an abolitionist movement. Defenders of slavery used this sense of historical awareness to argue that the antislavery activism that emerged in the late eighteenth and early nineteenth centuries in Great Britain and the United States was an anomaly that had no antecedents and thus should be dismissed. Proslavery forces believed that the absence of comparable abolitionist movements in the history of past societies was sufficient evidence that slavery was part of the accepted nature of things and that it was a normal condition in society.

In past societies where slavery had emerged or receded, it had done so in response to market forces and not in reaction to popular agitation rooted in antislavery morality. Since slavery was viewed primarily in economic terms as a labor force that was necessary to maintain a certain level of market production, proslavery apologists deemed as unworthy any criticism of the practice on any basis other than market-based principles. As such, agitation rooted in emotionalism and sentimentality had no place in determining market decisions that would influence the economic well-being of society.

History also demonstrated that some of the world's most powerful and longest-lasting empires had been those societies that used slave-based labor on a large scale. This was certainly the case with the Greeks and especially with the Romans, and the Roman model had inspired British imperial designs. Since the United States emerged from the thirteen British North American colonies, many believed that the cultural antecedents of greatness, which included slavery, were rooted within the young nation almost as a birthright. To proslavery apologists, any criticism of slavery was interpreted as a criticism of the American experiment with liberty and was designed to reduce the economic capacity of the new nation. To its defenders, any criticism of slavery was perceived as disloyalty to the dreams and aspirations of the American Founders. Freedom could not exist without slavery.

At Home on the Plantation

Many slaveowning southerners believed that their ownership of slaves was a necessary form of social control that was rooted in paternalism. According to this view, the slaves were almost childlike creatures who were ill-prepared to be left to their own devices. It was necessary, nay essential, for white southerners to "look after" their slaves and tend to them much as a parent might govern and discipline a child who was not yet prepared to accept responsibility and act independently without supervision. The slaveowner was the mentor and teacher, and some would later argue that the plantation or farm was essentially a school where tutelage occurred.

A parent–child relationship is marked by genuine bonds of affection and is usually characterized by a sense of mutuality or reciprocity in which both parties to the arrangement comprehend at least some aspect of the benefits that occur. This aspect was not, of course, always present in the form of paternalism that existed on plantations and farms in the South. Even though many of the slaveowning whites may well have had genuine feelings of goodwill, mutuality did not exist, for the tacit appreciation of the relationship was not universally acclaimed. This is not to say that genuine bonds of affection did not exist in some cases.

Tremendous variations in the master–slave relationship existed throughout the antebellum South. The relationship between the owner and the slaves was much different on small farms where an owner might have a small number of slaves than what it was on a large plantation with a large number of slaves. On the large estates owners had very little direct contact with slaves inasmuch as a hierarchy of managers consisting of overseers and slave drivers had more day-to-day contact with slaves during the operation of the plantation. On a small landholding, an owner would likely work side by side with slaves—an arrangement that would not have occurred on a large plantation.

In addition, the level of paternalism would have also been affected by the slave's degree of autonomy. Skilled slaves who were hired out as day laborers had a different type of relationship with their owners than did slaves who remained constantly on the plantation or farm. In addition, different levels of paternalism, or perhaps favoritism, might have developed in the case of house slaves as compared to common field laborers. Since familiarity often breeds affection over time, those slaves with whom the owners were most acquainted would likely have experienced treatment that was different than that accorded to the more isolated field laborers.

Southern planters often viewed their estates in patriarchal terms as the "plantation household"—an extended kinship network that included all immediate family members, employees, and slaves who operated the plantation. But this household was more fictive than real. Slaves found themselves living within two worlds, one the fictive plantation household that was dominated by their owner and defined by the values of an almost alien culture and another that took place within the slave quarters of the plantation in which the slave community maintained its own mores and values. The persistence of these two worlds always meant that paternalism, if it did exist, had limited influence within the slave community.

Divide and Conquer

Throughout the South during the antebellum era, white slaveholders constituted a minority of the population, but in all of the southern states they controlled the mechanism of state and local government. The dominant population group in the South consisted of nonslaveholders, who might be broadly defined in two groups: affluent nonslaveholders and poor whites. The affluent nonslaveholders were individuals who owned some form of real property, typically in land, but also in the form of livestock. Poor whites were generally landless and worked as tenant farmers on the land of others. Most slaveowners tended to be quite wealthy by relative comparison to the affluent nonslaveholders and the poor whites.

Racial exclusivity was used during the antebellum era (as it would later be used in the post–Civil War era) to maintain a wall of separation between the interests of economically disaffected whites and the slave population. Rather than permitting individuals to recognize their common association through the economic forces that united them, the divisive issue of race was used to separate the loyalties of individuals on a basis that had a purely constructed meaning. It is true that on occasion poor whites sometimes aided slaves who were conspiring to revolt, but generally poor whites and other nonslaveholders in the South viewed their loyalties to the white slaveowners as being more immediate than any connection with slaves.

Planters dominated state legislatures in the South and controlled the southern governorships during the antebellum era. The legislation they enacted and enforced was generally beneficial to the planter class. Although they used their bond of common racial interests to create white solidarity in the South, they only paid lip service to the needs of economically disadvantaged white southerners, instead developing policies beneficial to the planters. For example, most states in the South provided very little funding of public education prior to the Civil War because slaveowners feared that increased literacy in the South might lead to the emergence of a dangerous slave population. Thus, in an effort to keep the mass of slaves illiterate, all white southerners, except for those wealthy enough to hire tutors or send their children outside the region for an education, suffered.

Patriarchy and Power

The dominance of the planter class on the regional political level was paralleled by their unchecked supremacy within the plantation household. Decisions about plantation management or any actions associated with the buying or selling of slaves were made by the master and perhaps his sons. In most cases, women were not permitted a role in plantation management, though this situation differed on smaller farms. In addition, in isolated instances women managed plantations effectively and were able to run a profitable enterprise. This later became evident during the war when many women were required to operate plantations and farms while their husbands and fathers were away.

Much of the myth of planter paternalism was shattered by the uncontested use of patriarchy and power on plantations and farms as white men abused women and girls whom they owned as slaves. The sexual exploitation of female slaves was prevalent from colonial times up to the Civil War, as evidenced by the growing population of mulatto offspring. Although some of these relationships were mutual and genuine, most were premised on power and authority and constituted rape. In the case of younger girls, the offense was even more onerous. Planters, the brothers, sons, and nephews of planters, and overseers often treated their plantation household as a private harem. Theirs were not typical family values.

White women in the South, trapped within the cycle of patriarchy and power, had only limited power to challenge the status quo. Wives and daughters of planters found themselves degraded by the sexual indiscretions of their husbands and fathers, but being economically beholden to the plantation, were hushed into a world of silent frustration. In some cases, white women in the South lashed out at slave women whom they suspected of "luring" their white men. In reality, however, all of the women concerned—both white and black—were being victimized by the same oppressors. In spite of their common suffering, the same myth of racial exclusivity that maintained the political hegemony of white planters also maintained their power within the household. Since divorce was rare in the antebellum South, white women endured fictive marriages, feeling bitter resentment toward both their husbands and slave mistresses.

Cavaliers versus Yankees

One of the myths associated with southern exceptionalism is that the region's values were uniquely inspired by its founding settlers, the Cavaliers of Old England. When the southern colonies were settled, in particular the Carolinas and Georgia, many of the English who emigrated to North America were former supporters of the royalist cause during the English Civil War, who were known as the Cavaliers. In appreciation of the Cavaliers' support of his deceased father, Charles I, the new Stuart monarch, Charles II, granted the restoration colonies established after 1660 to several of the Cavalier families. As the Old Southwest was settled in the early nineteenth century, many believed that it was the descendants of the early Cavaliers who moved into the newly opened territories and states.

During the English Civil War, the royalist forces of the Cavaliers fought against the parliamentary forces associated with the Puritan cause. Many in the Old South, viewing themselves as the descendants of the Cavaliers, believed that their nemesis in the northern states, the abolitionists and the manufacturers, were the descendants of the early Puritans who had populated the New England region during the colonial era. Ascribing the pejorative name "Yankees" to the descendants of the Puritans, the southern Cavaliers, as they styled themselves, recognized a sense of regional distinctiveness that was different from that of the Yankees and their monied interests.

Honor and violence were closely intertwined in the mythic South as those who sought to demonstrate their refinement dueled in the streets to settle old scores. Those who chose to perpetuate the mythic Cavalier image believed that the South was essentially a feudal aristocratic society in which planter lords controlled fiefs that were tended by slave vassals. Imagining the dutiful labor performed by slaves as evidence of *noblesse oblige,* the planter lords conveniently failed to remember that slave labor was the product of power and the lash, and not willingly given. While some imagined the South to be a genteel land of honor where gentlemen protected their ladies, the reality was much different.

If the South was indeed distinct from the North, it was the presence of its monoculture agriculture and slave labor that made for the differences. The culture fashioned in the South was more a response and coping mechanism to particular exigencies than it was a product of a feudal-aristocratic mentality magically transposed to the cotton lands of the Black Belt. Southern culture was more complex than moonlight and magnolias, and it was a contested culture.

Agricultural Economy

Partly in an effort to be unlike their northern "Yankee" brethren, southern planters established a regional economy based largely on agriculture. Although key cash crops varied by region, monoculture was the practice within specified areas: cotton, sugar, tobacco, and rice formed the bulk of southern production cultivated and harvested by slave laborers. As a result of its dependence on one-crop cultivation, the South lagged behind the North in developing a manufacturing capability, and the region's railroad infrastructure was sporadic at best.

Lacking industrial development, the South relied on imports from abroad or items purchased from northern manufacturers to supplement the paucity of goods produced in the region. In the case of imported products, southerners found themselves paying the bulk of the national tariff on imported goods; thus tariff policy was a long-standing political issue that raised the ire of southern residents and politicians alike.

Southerners believed that their lack of manufacturing was another factor that made their region distinctive. They celebrated this distinction by extolling the supposed virtues of agricultural productivity and decrying the poor conditions experienced by "wage laborers" in the northern states.

"A Troublesome Species of Property"

In 1794 President George Washington candidly addressed the topic of slaves in a correspondence with a friend and prophetically wrote, "I shall be happily mistaken if they are not found to be a very troublesome species of property ere many years pass over our heads." Washington's astute observation was made at a time when the total population of slaves and free blacks was less than 1 million, yet he could foresee difficulty if the United States sought to maintain a servile population over time.

By the eve of the Civil War, the black population of the United States, both slave and free, had grown to just over 4 million. In two states—South Carolina and Mississippi—blacks constituted a population majority, and in Louisiana the black population was slightly less than 50 percent of the state's total. Some counties in the Black Belt and in the Mississippi Delta had black population majorities of as much as 80 percent. Maintaining public safety in such areas was decidedly difficult as the "troublesome species of property" was perceived as a constant threat to regional security.

In some communities a "siege mentality" was an ever-present reality of life for white residents. Factors such as rural isolation, distance from militia gathering points, and general malaise often made it difficult to maintain concerted readiness against any possible contingency. Slave insurrection was perceived as the worst possible calamity that could befall a community, and individuals often lived in constant fear that such an episode would occur within their community. When actual outbreaks of violence did occur, the suppression by local authorities was swift and brutal.

Local authorities established patrol groups that enforced slave codes within their respective communities, and all able-bodied men were expected to participate in local militia efforts if outbreaks of slave violence threatened the region. Even when there were slave insurrection scares that did not culminate in actual revolt, momentary hysteria would give way to episodic outbreaks of extralegal justice. Many believed that only the most brutal means of suppression could strike sufficient fear into the slave populace to prevent future rebellion.

A Region unto Itself

As proslavery sentiment in the South hardened after 1830, the region increasingly began to distinguish itself from the northern states. Although there had been free and open discussion of antislavery views in previous decades, with antislavery newspapers even published in Tennessee in the 1820s, attitudes changed dramatically in the decades that followed as dissent was silenced.

Abolitionists who resided in upper southern states like Kentucky and Tennessee found it increasingly difficult to remain in the South and espouse antislavery sentiments. As attitudes grew more stringent, many of these abolitionists left the South and moved northward to locations in Ohio, Indiana, and Illinois. By the 1830s abolitionist newspapers were no longer being published in the southern states, and even those newspaper presses located in the North that were within reach of southern mobs found it difficult to operate. The antislavery editor Elijah P. Lovejoy was murdered in Alton, Illinois, in 1837, and antiabolition riots in Cincinnati threatened presses in that city during the 1830s.

The exodus of most abolitionists from the South and the closing down of the antislavery newspapers were indicative of the fact that freedom of thought in the South was increasingly coming under attack. The emerging belief was that all opinion with respect to slavery must be spoken in a unified voice that defended the institution at all costs and tried to silence all critics.

When northern abolitionists tried to flood the South with antislavery literature in the "Great Postal Campaign" of 1836, southern postmasters refused to deliver the materials. In the streets of Charleston, South Carolina, many abolitionist newspapers and pamphlets were burned in symbolic protests. Such action, though a violation of federal law, was condoned by Postmaster General Amos Kendall, who argued: "We owe an obligation to the laws, but a higher one to the communities in which we live."

When southerners became fearful that free blacks visiting port cities on merchant vessels might either try to entice slaves to escape or perhaps foment rebellion, they responded with proscriptive legislation that barred such free blacks from disembarking from their vessels while in southern ports. Through the Negro Seamen's Acts, the southern legislatures attempted to maintain freedom and security in their respective regions while denying freedom to others. Such an action was indicative of a region that had begun to view itself as not merely distinctive, but almost alien to the civil culture of the United States of which it remained a part.

No Middle Ground

In an 1858 speech, South Carolina Senator James Henry Hammond drew a distinction between the laborers of the South and the North by stating, "The difference between us is, that our slaves are hired for life and well compensated; there is no starvation, no begging, no want of employment among our people, and not too much employment either. Yours are hired by the day, not cared for, and scantily compensated, which may be proved in the most painful manner, at any hour in any street in any of your large towns." It was clear to Hammond that slave labor was not merely more efficient than wage labor, but more moral.

As the United States drew closer to civil war, it became apparent that the nation had divided into separate cultural worlds long before the first secession resolutions were ever introduced. Conditions had changed and attitudes had hardened in the generation that preceded the Civil War to the point that politicians of the North and the South could not find common cause on which they might reach compromise. Southern exceptionalism had come into being as the defense of slavery at all costs became the mantra of the region's political leaders. The Cavaliers were not willing to sound the retreat.

Southerners were so convinced of the righteousness of their cause that they would not retreat an inch on the defense of slavery. They considered their religious, intellectual, scientific, and historical justifications of slavery as superior to any abolitionist argument that could be posed to challenge the merits of slavery. Moreover, their genuine belief in their own benevolence, as evidenced in the spirit of paternalism that permeated the plantation South, represented a higher ethic than that of the money-grubbing interests of New England merchants and antislavery agitators. Finally, the purity of their culture and the virtue of their cause made southerners believe that God was on their side and they had nothing to fear.

AFRICAN AMERICAN CULTURE AND STRATEGIES FOR SURVIVAL

That a distinct culture was able to take shape during the generations of oppression that slaves endured in the United States is one of the most remarkable aspects of the "peculiar institution." Much of slavery was premised on the notion that Africans or blacks born in the Americas who were enslaved had to be separated from any knowledge of a cultural past and indoctrinated in the understanding that only servitude and bondage were fitting conditions for persons of their rank and status. Plantations and farms served to educate in only the most punitive terms, so that the enslaved accepted the conditions in which they found themselves and dared not fashion any sort of cultural defense against the stifling burden of labor and the demeaning sense of nothingness that slave status imposed on them. Bought, sold, owned, and traded, slaves were perceived as objects—things rather than persons—and the entire mechanism of the institution of slavery was predicated upon keeping them lowly and fit to be cowed by social betters who owned them. This worldview of the masters could only be replicated in the hearts and minds of slaves if they were prevented from having a culture of their own that resisted all of these efforts and fashioned a spirit of hope in an otherwise hopeless world.

Cultural formation is a complex process that involves

a culling of things past and things present into a viable worldview, a system that employs both continuity and change. Part coping mechanism and part defensive bulwark, the slave culture that developed on the plantations and farms of the South was a natural and essentially human response to an otherwise dehumanizing practice. It allowed the slaves to draw boundaries and say "no" to an institution that otherwise sought to maintain absolute control over their lives and activities.

Slaveowning southerners tried to control elements of the culture that slaves fashioned, but such a practice was difficult to control. Much of cultural creation is internalized and grows from what is accepted within the community rather than what is sanctioned from without. The power to accept or reject attributes of culture lies with those who must make use of it, and such decisions cannot be arbitrarily imposed by either the will or the whim of white southerners. In a society where slaves owned little that was theirs, the sense that they owned their own culture was a powerful force that helped to create an alternative reality for the slave community. Living essentially in two worlds—one that was fashioned by the slaveowners and imposed upon them and another that was formulated within their own hearts and minds—slaves found a way to endure the burden of slavery.

Am I Not a Man and a Brother?

The system of slavery that developed in the Americas was based on the assumptions that slavery was most ideally suited for Africans and that it represented a condition of servitude for life. All other elements aside, these two beliefs were the most basic defining characteristics of the system of chattel slavery that developed in the American colonies and became firmly established in the United States when it emerged as an independent republic. The necessity of maintaining such a system required that Africans be stripped of their essential humanity and relegated to the status of animals. It also required that the slaves passively accept such a status.

The mechanics of chattel slavery could only thrive through the systematic depersonification of the slave. If slaves could be commercially traded like livestock at auction, it meant that they needed to be perceived and treated in animalized form. The chaining, beating, and branding of slaves that transpired through the centuries was a symbolic effort to deny slaves the human qualities that they were due and to impose upon them the obtuse traits and behaviors of domesticated livestock. Physically shamed and culturally broken, such

slaves were assumed to become the docile creatures who would do the bidding of their social betters.

In order for this system to persevere, the twin conditions of slavery—low social standing and forced servitude for life—had to be maintained. Any deviation from this practice would present a challenge to the key assumptions on which chattel slavery was structured. Yet it was only natural that such challenges would emerge. The emancipation of some slaves through the process of legal manumission created the presence of a new social status—the free black. The existence of free blacks in slave-based societies was viewed as troublesome because it demonstrated that persons of color were not, after all, destined by nature to be slaves and that such servitude was not essentially a lifetime arrangement. Furthermore, the rise of literacy within the free black community demonstrated that the presumed animal nature of Africans was more mythic than real. The presence of free black communities and the success they experienced made it difficult either for white society to maintain or for slave society to accept the natural inferiority of Africans.

The essential humanity of Africans thus affirmed, whether tacitly or implicitly, made it difficult for slaveowners to maintain the ideological suppositions on which it was based. Nonetheless, they maintained the system because they argued that it benefited the slaves. The degradation of human beings that was key to slavery was understood as a form of tutelage necessary to instill the blessings of civilization and Western culture on otherwise benighted persons who had lived in ignorance. The slaves themselves had always recognized and understood their own humanity, and for them the condition of slavery was something that had to be endured for the sake of survival. However, African Americans clearly claimed ownership of their culture, and they carefully filtered and resisted any attempt to impose cultural change.

Most slaves were employed as agricultural laborers; much of their world was defined by the regimented system of forced labor. Operating within a cycle that was defined by the syncopation of the seasons, slaves found themselves planting, cultivating, and harvesting cash crops that varied by region in workdays that generally ran from sunup to sundown. On occasion the particular demands of the harvest might require additional hours of labor to guarantee that frost would not damage or destroy the crop. On most plantations and farms, the slaves employed in agricultural labor worked six days per week with Sundays off.

The type of labor performed by agricultural slaves could vary in several respects. Slaves who worked on smaller holdings might have experienced greater liberties than those who worked on larger plantation estates. In addition, plantation slaves would have experienced varieties within their labor regimen, depending on whether the task system or the gang system was used on the estate. A slave who was employed on the task arrangement might well have some spare time during the day after his work had been completed. This time could be devoted to tending private gardens, or provision grounds, where slaves grew foodstuffs to supplement their own diet or for sale in the plantation community. Slaves who worked on the gang system operated in groups that were directed by a slave driver, usually a trusted slave who represented a low-level manager in the plantation hierarchy. Depending on the slave driver's kindness and benevolence, other slaves could cover for those slaves who were weak, ill, or pregnant.

Men and women labored side by side in the fields of the plantation South in a gendered egalitarian setting. Only the young children and the elderly slaves were exempt from the more onerous tasks associated with southern agriculture. Elderly slaves were often granted oversight of groups of children who might walk the rows after the harvest to pick items that were missed. In the absence of formalized family structures, notions of "aunt" or "uncle" were often ascribed to fictive kin who assumed roles within the plantation community that needed to be filled. Older slaves, in particular, filling the role formerly held by tribal elders, would narrate stories and lessons that were passed from one generation to another within the slave community.

Behind the Big House

Much of slave culture was fashioned and formalized in the plantation quarters where slaves resided. Even though owners sought to maintain a degree of control over what happened within the slave quarters, this location served as a "world within" the plantation setting that maintained its own ethos and values. It was here that slaves cultivated and passed down social attributes that defined their sense of self-identity and navigated the tenuous boundaries that existed in the "world without" the slave quarters.

The slave family was one of the most essential cultural creations of the plantation community. In most parts of the antebellum South, slave marriages were not legally recognized, and thus families could be broken up when slaves were sold to different plantations. Marriage records were kept in portions of Roman Catholic Louisiana, but even there, slave marriages were often severed without question as resale separated

husbands, wives, and children from one another. Although examples of the nuclear family have been found on some plantations and farms as family units remained intact, this was not the most common experience throughout the plantation South. Customarily, family units were created out of circumstance and necessity as slave parents raised orphaned children along with their own. Kinship was determined more by a sense of mutual dependency than by a factor of blood relationship.

An enduring spirit of lovingness was found within the plantation community as slaves came to understand the importance of their relationship and bonds. Knowing that their self-interests could only be maintained and protected within the sense of the slave community, plantation slaves found the means to create group solidarity against the forces that held them in slavery. Sometimes these bonds were expressed through acts of active or passive resistance that were directed at obtaining greater liberties either for individuals or for the group. In many cases the group solidarity helped fashion a conspiracy of silence when slaves protected members from within the community who may have absconded or committed petty offenses on the plantation.

Natural Increase

One of the most dynamic attributes of the slave community in the United States was its ability to sustain itself through a natural population increase. Unlike the slave societies of Latin America and the Caribbean where the population of slave men far exceeded that of women, in the United States there was a relatively even gender distribution among slaves, and it was easier for slave families to form.

In addition to the equitable gender distribution, other demographic factors were at work contributing to the natural increase of the slave population. Among slave women in the United States, the fertility rate was nearly twice as high as that of their counterparts in Latin America and the Caribbean. On the eve of the Civil War, the average slave woman in the southern states had 9.2 pregnancies during her childbearing years. In addition to the high fertility rate, the mortality rate among slaves in the United States was considerably lower than comparable rates in other slave societies in the Americas. With the combined effect of a high fertility rate and a low mortality rate, the natural increase within the slave population was dramatic.

In 1808, when the United States outlawed the transatlantic slave trade, the estimated population of slaves was 1 million, but by 1860, the slave population had risen to 4 million. Many in 1808 had believed that slavery would die once the supply of African slaves was eliminated, but the dramatic rate of population growth through natural increase transformed and swelled the ranks of the slave community.

A Community of Believers

It was commonly assumed in the antebellum South that those slaves who had been exposed to Christianity tended to be better behaved and more passive than those who had not received religious training. Planters were encouraged to provide religious instruction to their slaves as a means of effective plantation management rather than for the presumed moral benefits that might accrue. Docility rather than dogma influenced policy in this regard.

Most slaveowning southerners were willing to provide religious instruction to slaves as long as they had some means of control over the religious messages that would be preached to the congregants. In many cases, only white ministers were allowed to conduct religious services with slaves, while slave preachers were sometimes permitted to conduct religious meetings under the supervision of white authorities. It was clear to white southerners that the gospel of liberation should not be a message that was extended to the slaves, but rather the message of long-suffering in this world to prepare for a better eternal life.

Among the slaves who accepted Christianity there was a common bond found in the Old Testament stories of the Hebrews being held in bondage. The story of Moses, though muted to conform to the wishes of southern planters, found special meaning among the long-suffering bondsmen who were longing for liberation. In many respects, the messianic language of redemption found in the Christian message offered hope to those who awaited a better day and also inspired the urgency of action to seek justice in the face of ever-present evil. Depending on the reading of the gospels, one might find their redemption awaiting in the hereafter, or a more immediate day of judgment might await them.

Matters of faith were not only relegated to church services, but were also embedded within the daily world of the slave's experiences. Spirituals that were rooted in biblical verse became associated with the toiling that slaves performed and served as both a pastime and a diversion during the workday while also reminding the faithful that a better day did await them. Slaves found a common bond with biblical figures like Job who endured and maintained faithfulness despite being tested beyond human limits.

The slave community found a way to incorporate its own cultural elements into the religious teachings that Christian ministers expressed to them. Elements of folk religious belief found their way into traditional Christian theology, and aesthetic elements of song and dance were incorporated into the more staid practices of white Christians. Open-air services that involved the participation of exhorters, rather than ministers, and utilized uniquely African expressive forms like the ring shout were conducted by slaves, who found a sense of liberation in their ability to make the religious practices their own through spiritual improvisation. In spite of their acceptance of Christian beliefs, slaves in some parts of the South continued to rely on elements of conjure and vodou in their comprehension of spirituality.

Connections to a Remembered Past

One of the strongest cultural elements within the slave community was the power of story to convey message and meaning while preserving the historical association with a remembered past. Among peoples who were largely illiterate, the use of story to convey knowledge and institutional history was quite powerful. Use of the oral tradition permitted the transgenerational migration of ideas and beliefs to occur, so that younger generations of slaves might have some connection with a dynamic, albeit distant, past.

Quite often, folk tales were used to convey life lessons in a form that might be easily remembered. In many of these stories, slaves, who were dehumanized in the embodiment of slavery, found themselves related to animals who used their powers of quick wit and common sense to outsmart other story characters who embodied the qualities of southern whites. The stories were entertaining and easy to remember and were premised on moral lessons and other virtues that provided encouragement to the slaves. As the rabbit could outwit the fox, so too could the slave survive the travail foisted on them by slaveowning whites.

Slaves also used their conversations within the slave quarters to learn of the world beyond their plantations and farms. Some skilled slaves were allowed to work off of their home plantations, and in the course of their travels they learned much from the surrounding community. This knowledge was not only limited to geographical knowledge about the surrounding region, but also included bits of conversations overheard in the community and reports of news that circulated in the region. On occasion, some slaves learned of the northern abolitionists and their efforts to bring an end to slavery. This knowledge existed within the plantation community and was discussed on occasion in the isolated security of the quarters.

Slaves planned their escape within the confines of

the slave quarters; some discussed their plans with other slaves, while others remained silent about their intentions. The knowledge and collective wisdom found within the plantation community could provide invaluable information to the prospective fugitive, and the heroic exploits of those who did escape successfully were often shared in stories many years after the deed was done. Although not everyone in the plantation community was willing to be a rebel, those who did find the means to escape were admired.

Literacy

As noted earlier, slaveowning southerners generally sought to prevent their slaves from learning how to read and write. Most southern states in fact had laws prohibiting the teaching of slaves, and these laws were enforced as much as possible. Still, some slaves did become literate.

It was feared that literacy among the slave population would lead to spreading the antislavery doctrine that abolitionists espoused, but such sentiments already existed in the hearts and minds of most slaves with or without the prompting of northern abolitionists. Perhaps the greatest fear was that the educated slave had a greater chance of becoming an articulate leader of a mass movement among the slaves. Literacy, it was believed, would produce leadership, which, in turn, would result in organization. White southerners were unwilling to risk such a danger.

The South also exhibited resentment of literate slaves since many southern whites, both nonslaveholders and poor whites, had not been provided with educational opportunities. For white southerners the notion of literate slaves was contrary to the social station deemed appropriate for slave laborers.

A Little Commonwealth

In many respects, the slave community on larger plantations functioned much as an African village. There was a clear sense of communal responsibility within the plantation's slave community as familial roles often were carried out on the basis of extended kinship. Group dynamics were at work as child-rearing responsibilities were often shared, as was the necessity of provision ground plots where produce was cultivated for consumption or sale. Even though they might be beyond their prime as field laborers, the advice and counsel of elderly slaves was valued, and they served almost as trusted tribal elders in the little commonwealth that existed within the plantation community.

Since slaves had so little that was their own, they sought to maintain a sense of control over what was theirs. Violations of their community, either by members of the slave community or by outsiders (white residents), were not condoned. Although a slave could steal from the plantation household, theft of possessions belonging to another slave was a violation of community standards and would earn the condemnation of others. Violations of the slave community by whites, usually in the form of sexual exploitation and indiscretion, were resented within the slave community, but only limited responses could be exacted for such transgressions.

Far from being a conspiratorial den where plots of insurrection were constantly hatched, the slave community often exerted a calming influence on irate slaves whose passions were quelled by the collective wisdom of fellow slaves. Rather than running headlong into insurmountable resistance for every point of contention that was raised, the slave community carefully chose its battles and forms of resistance. Weapons of the weak ranging from arson to tool breaking to foot dragging could be more effective to achieving specific objectives than overt resistance that was almost always doomed to fail.

Navigating Boundaries

One of the most important elements in the slave culture that formed in the antebellum South was its propensity for community survival. Slaves generally adopted a long-range strategy of endurance and survival rather than opting for a short-term solution that might involve suicidal resistance. By looking upon community survival as the most essential goal, the slaves sought to fashion the changes they could effect with the means at their disposal, but they also recognized that some desires were beyond their means and expectations.

Not all of the slaves in the South could cope with a strategy of strategic endurance, and many chose to run away to seek their own liberty. Many were successful in their pursuit of freedom, while others were recaptured and some died in the process of attempting to escape. No community has the absolute power to impose its values and standards on every member, and it is not surprising that individual acts of resistance far outweighed the number of incidents in which group resistance was readily apparent. Unable to communicate with other slaves throughout the South to coordinate their efforts, the mass of southern slaves, nearly 4 million individuals by 1860, operated on the basis of their common sense and their understanding of realistic expectations in the various communities in which they lived.

In some respects, the slave community mimicked

the methods and strategies of white southern society and demanded that traditional rights and responsibilities be honored through custom and practice. In recognizing that society was an association of structured classes, of which slaves constituted an integral part, each group in society found itself defined by hereditary rights or traditions that were associated with its status. Violations of community norms, such as making slaves work on Sunday, were considered to be unfair encroachments on traditional rights, and slaves might invoke passive forms of resistance to demand a return to traditional privileges. Such small battles, invoked in thousands of isolated settings throughout the South, were the means through which slaves helped to define the limits of what was tolerable and what was insufferable to the slave community.

White society, too, had to recognize that there were limits to what could be imposed on the slave community without exciting unrest. In parts of the plantation South where slaves greatly outnumbered white residents, slaves cherished the fluid boundaries of what was considered acceptable behavior, and white southerners had to avoid excesses that tested the limits of traditional social boundaries. Both communities—white and black—were motivated by their self-interest to maintain the social deference that was necessary in order to coexist peaceably without incident.

Coping Mechanisms

Some slaves learned quickly that feigned acquiescence to white authority and influence was the most effective survival strategy they could employ to cope with the realities of slavery. Since white perceptions of slaves were that they were almost childlike in their disposition and ill-equipped to cause any real disruption to southern society, many slaves found that behavior conforming to this stereotype was a form of personal security that would serve them well in the long run. Although one can speculate as to whether or not slaves were troubled by the charade, it is indisputable that the method served to protect many from the harsher abuses of slavery.

Historians like Stanley Elkins have argued that the Sambo image, the childlike simple slave, represented a deep-seated personality that had been formed by the psychological trauma wrought through slavery. It is possible, however, that this behavioral trait was purposeful in intent. If survival was the key goal of slaves when confronted by the harsh realities of slavery, resorting to a childlike persona that white society had imagined to exist could well be a brilliant strategy. One might appear on the outside to portray Sambo-like qualities while harboring seething resentment and hatred of those who perpetuated and maintained the

system of slavery. Far from a benign creature, the childlike slave could well have been a potential rebel.

Other coping mechanisms also helped slaves to survive the "peculiar institution." In many respects a keen maternal instinct motivated many slave women to survive and endure so that they could protect their children. It was physically difficult for many women to escape, and it was even more difficult for a fugitive to escape with small children. Many slave women found themselves practically trapped by repetitive pregnancies and the responsibilities of caring for young children and had to submit to the reality that they would likely spend their entire life in slavery. Such women often found an inner strength that permitted them to endure because the well-being of their children depended on their survival.

Faith was another mode of survival for many slaves. Resigning themselves to the understanding that they would be slaves for their entire lives, they found a means to bear the yoke of slavery by accepting the burden of their labors. Like the long-suffering characters of the Bible, such slaves viewed themselves as laborers in the vineyard who would face their tasks with Christ-like resolution, hoping that a better day lay ahead. They struggled diligently knowing that the salvation they sought to attain in this world would likely never arrive, but believing that a life beyond held great promise for the true Christian.

The Rebels

Not all slaves were willing to accept a life of quiet acquiescence with slavery. Resistance to slavery was a common part of the experience within the slave community, but it manifested itself in a variety of forms. Although there were occasional slave revolts or conspiracies that were discovered, much of the resistance was carried out in smaller, less spectacular events. Not every slave was a revolutionary at heart, but many grew tired of the burden imposed on them and dared to strike a blow at the institution that denied them their liberty and their dignity.

One of the most common forms of resistance to slavery was expressed by slaves who ran away from plantations and farms and sought to attain their own liberty as fugitives. In a process often described as "stealing oneself away from slavery," the fugitives not only desired to attain their liberty, but also to inflict an economic burden on their owners who stood to lose both the value of the escaped slave and the diminished labor capacity resulting from his departure. Even though not all slaves who sought to escape by running away were successful, there were many cases of slaves seeking to run away on multiple occasions. Despite the threat of punishment if caught or even the possibility of death, the desire to be free inspired countless slaves to rebel personally against the system that kept them in bondage.

Slave rebels had many other tools at their disposal. On occasion southern planters experienced severe financial losses from arson that resulted in the burning of plantation homes, barns, fields, cotton gins, and sugar refineries. Such attacks on the infrastructure of slavery were often timed strategically to coincide with the harvest, thereby causing severe financial losses to southern planters. The occurrences of arson were so common in the antebellum South that the crime was considered a capital offense in most states punishable by death.

Slave rebels also found other available means to resist slavery. They frequently broke tools and other equipment necessary to their labor. These actions were often masked as acts of ignorance or incompetence, but they were specifically targeted actions that reduced the burdensome labor to be performed and caused further economic loss. Broken tools needed to be replaced, and this was often a burden that required additional time and added cost during the time-sensitive seasons of planting or harvesting.

In thousands of actions both large and small, slave rebels successfully attacked the economic infrastructure of the system that kept them in bondage. Whether it was through theft of foodstuffs from the plantation household or through foot dragging that slowed down production, slaves found the means to effect some degree of control over their lives. Sabotage was a weapon of the weak that could empower, and slaves used every opportunity within their means to weaken the institution of slavery.

Women found the means to resist the institution of slavery in a variety of ways. In some instances they carried out acts of infanticide or chose to terminate a pregnancy by self-aborting as a means of denying their owner another child who would be raised to become a slave. Often these actions were carried out by women who had been assaulted and raped by owners or overseers and who viewed their actions as a deliberate effort to punish the men who had harmed them. On occasion other women within the slave community assisted in these actions but maintained a conspiracy of silence when confronted about the occurrence.

Nameless rebels confronted the institution of slavery and made the cultural statement that they were not powerless creatures, but resourceful individuals who desired liberty. The bolder among them left their names recorded to history in courageous deeds.

The Insurrectionists

Some slaves, not satisfied with employing minor acts of passive resistance to fight slavery, wanted to do more to end the practice outright. Plots and rebellions did take place throughout the history of slavery in the United States, but none achieved long-term success. Death and destruction could be visited upon localized areas and white hysteria could be evoked, but those who chose to conspire and those who were determined to revolt never attained their lofty goals.

The success of the Haitian Revolution (1791–1804) encouraged many potential rebels to believe that slave insurrection could be successful and could bring real results, but none of the incidents of revolt in the United States ever came close to achieving a similar outcome. Incidents like the German Coast Uprising in Louisiana in 1811 and the Nat Turner Rebellion in Southampton County, Virginia, in 1831 were large movements that inspired local panic but ended in immediate and brutal suppression. Even when conspiracies were detected before revolt was carried out, such as the Gabriel Prosser plot in Richmond, Virginia, in 1800 and the Denmark Vesey conspiracy in Charleston, South Carolina, in 1822, the execution of the principal leaders marked the savage repression of the incidents by local authorities. Officials in the southern states were determined that they would not permit the horrors of St. Domingue to occur in the United States.

Even though the slave revolts failed to effect real change during the antebellum era, plots were being hatched right up to the time of the Civil War. Potential slave insurrectionists were unwilling to dismiss the possibility that a well-timed revolt could foment a massive uprising similar to the race war that had led to the liberation of Haiti. Even the radical abolitionist John Brown believed that it was possible to incite large-scale revolt among the slaves in the southern states. His efforts to seize the U.S. arsenal at Harper's Ferry, Virginia, in 1859 were expressly designed to enable him to distribute guns throughout the states of the Upper South and to end the institution of slavery through force of arms.

Gone but Not Forgotten

The names of Gabriel Prosser, Denmark Vesey, and Nat Turner continued to be remembered in the stories that were shared in the slave community. Although white society called them insurrectionists, they were held in high regard by slaves. They, along with countless other nameless slaves who resisted and who perished, formed a litany of the silent, a cadre of brave souls who perished for a cause. Gone, but not forgotten, they were cultural heroes to many who still hoped and dreamed.

The United States was a country that was born of both liberty and the lash. In the case of slave rebels, the two symbols incongruously merged. The notion of freedom was a natural quality that endured in the hearts and minds of slaves, but seemed a distant aspiration. Strategies of survival fashioned to bear the burden of slavery had worked, but the cost had been tremendous. A unique culture, increasingly sorrowful and soulful, had survived through a pain-filled existence. People of faith had fought the good fight and found a way to thrive amidst unparalleled adversity.

The culture that took shape on southern plantations and farms was one that was tested by the most difficult methods, but it endured. In spite of the injustice of slavery and all the degradation that could be foisted upon a people, the slave population grew and its culture flourished. Born of adversity and hardship, the "world within" the plantation system had not been broken by the forces that sought to control and diminish it.

The Souls of Black Folk

A rich and vibrant culture came into existence on the plantations and farms of the southern states during the antebellum era. As noted earlier, by 1860, an estimated 4 million slaves inhabited the region and maintained an alternative culture that rivaled the one that white southerners had fashioned. Held in check by a power establishment that was armed to the teeth to suppress potential revolt, the slave community labored and endured as it had done for nearly eight generations in North America since 1619.

Although white southerners had feared that a Black Spartacus would emerge in the South, the region remained mysteriously quiet and serene during the antebellum era. Millions labored in fields of cotton, sugar, and tobacco from the Chesapeake to East Texas with freedom a distant dream. Living in a world of limits, white and black southerners had designed two worlds for themselves, existing side by side but terribly unequal. Slaves prayed to the same God as white southerners, but when each group sought redemption it likely had a different ambition in mind. Both groups prayed for a deliverance from evil, but each had a distinct image of the personification of evil and knew that it surrounded them.

Opulent mansions in the South reflected the treasure produced from the bounty of the land, and in the distance, beyond the big house, lay the cabins of the laborers. The lives of the lowly had been spent to procure great wealth, but at a terrible cost. Families formed and re-formed as fictive kin struggled to cope with the changing circumstances of market economics that knew no morality. "Aunts" and "uncles" told the stories of long ago and far-away places and reminded the young that they too must tell the stories in order to preserve tradition.

SLAVERY AND THE GROWTH
OF SECTIONAL CONFLICT

The seeds of political discord over slavery in the United States were first sown during the debates held at the Constitutional Convention of 1787. The Founding Fathers' decision to create a bicameral Congress with representation in the lower house based on a state's population led to a heated political debate as to what constitutes population. Central to this question, which no longer was an academic issue, was the place that slaves would hold in determining a state's population for purposes of representation in the Congress. As the southern slaveholding states pushed the issue to have all slaves counted and northern states that had abolished slavery balked at this proposal, it seemed that the deadlock might end all of the convention's deliberations without the proposal of a new document. When the Founders settled on the compromise solution of counting three of every five slaves for purposes of representation and taxation, they imagined that they had solved a vexing problem, but they had only initiated a growing crisis.

As a result of the so-called three-fifths compromise, the southern states received a virtual windfall of representatives for their slaves, who were persons holding no real political voice in American society. When the U.S. Constitution instituted an Electoral College to select the president and based the number of votes a state received on the total size of its congressional delegation, the southern states received what some imagined an inordinate amount of power and influence in choosing the nation's chief executive officer. Many would imagine in subsequent generations that the decisions enshrined in the Constitution of the United States helped to fashion a "slave power" conspiracy through which the southern slaveholding states determined much of the political direction of national life.

In the generations between the Founding and the Civil War, it appeared that southern political leaders held sway over national affairs. Presidents who hailed from southern states and owned slaves dominated the office in the years prior to the Civil War, and the occasional northern presidents who served were often sympathetic "doughfaces" who sided with pro-southern policy initiatives. Southern politicians dominated the position of speaker of the House of Representatives, and held control of most of the seats on the U.S. Supreme Court in the years prior to the Civil War. In addition, key cabinet-level posts such as attorney general and secretary of war were dominated by southern politicians. In many respects, much of the nation's political apparatus at the executive, legislative, and judicial levels was dominated by leaders who had southern roots or southern sympathies and seemingly used their posts to defend the institution of slavery.

Although there was no preconceived conspiracy to protect and defend slavery, the circumstances of American political life seemed to suggest that such was the case. The U.S. Constitution guaranteed that states would extend full faith and credit to the laws of other states, which meant that northern states that had abolished slavery would need to respect and honor the right of southern states to maintain the institution. Further still, once the Congress enacted the Fugitive Slave Act of 1793 it became incumbent on the northern states to return fugitive slaves to their previous condition of slavery when they were captured and remanded to the South. In addition, the federal government's pledge to "preserve domestic tranquility" warranted the use of the power and might of national forces to quell attempts at domestic insurrection that might upset the tranquility of the nation's plantations and farms.

The Firebell in the Night

Few could have imagined the central place that slavery would take in American political life during the antebellum era. For the first few decades of the early national era, the government seemed to operate smoothly without experiencing the rancorous discord that would characterize later years. Even though the Congress regularly received antislavery petitions from

its earliest years, the first being sent by Pennsylvania Quakers in February 1790, the issue of slavery did not have the divisive power that it would attain over time. There was a civility to political life and an optimism about making the American democratic experiment work that directed national affairs. Even though Federalists and Jeffersonian Republicans might vigorously debate political concerns of the day, the question of slavery had not yet reached the critical mass.

Even in 1807 when the Congress considered legislation to outlaw the transatlantic slave trade, southern legislators made no attempt to filibuster or otherwise block passage of the legislation. Although many believed that ending the slave trade was the first step toward hastening the end of slavery itself, the staunch defenders of slavery did not fight the measure as some might imagine. The legislation was encouraged by President Thomas Jefferson in his December 1806 message to the Congress, and it was enacted into law on March 2, 1807, and signed into law by Jefferson, a Virginia slaveowner.

Nearly a decade later, on December 28, 1816, many antislavery advocates and leading members of Congress gathered in the chamber of the House of Representatives in Washington, D.C., to found the American Colonization Society, an organization that would endeavor to return free blacks to Liberia in West Africa. Although the organization was not specifically abolitionist in its orientation, it did strive to remedy what it perceived to be a growing concern as more and more slaves were manumitted and the ranks of the nation's free black population swelled. Believing that freedom in Liberia was better than the arrested liberties that one might enjoy in the United States as a free black, political leaders like Henry Clay of Kentucky advocated the cause of the American Colonization Society.

The relative calm in American political life would be shattered in 1819 as the issue of slavery emerged in a heated congressional debate that belied what some had called the "era of good feelings." When the territory of Missouri applied for statehood, the question of whether or not slavery would be permitted in the new state became a key point of contention in congressional debate over the proposed constitution for Missouri. New York Representative James Tallmadge introduced an amendment that would have prohibited slavery from Missouri if it were allowed to enter the Union, and this effort to circumvent the wishes of the people of Missouri set off a firestorm of protest within the Congress and around the country. For the first time, the issue of slavery had become central to national political discourse, and the rhetoric of its proponents and its detractors was heated.

The debate over slavery in Missouri was so heated that Thomas Jefferson observed: "this momentous question, like a firebell in the night, awakened and filled me with terror." The aged Founder of the nation confided to a friend that he "considered it at once as the knell of the Union" and wondered if the civility of American political life could ever be restored. Noting that the debate was one that pitted justice against self-preservation, Jefferson surmised that "we have the wolf by the ears, and we can neither hold him, nor safely let him go." Indeed, it would be difficult to resolve the Missouri issue to everyone's satisfaction.

A Delicate Balance

The Missouri debate was so contentious in part because of the delicate balance of power that existed in the U.S. Senate when the territory sought statehood in 1819. At the time there were twenty-two states in the Union, and they were equally divided between eleven southern slave states and eleven northern states that had previously abolished slavery. The admission of Missouri to the Union either as a slave state or a free state was going to shift the balance of power in the Senate one way or another, and both sides were determined that they would not let their adversaries prevail in the political struggle.

Missouri's eventual admission to the Union as a slave state was made possible through a compromise engineered in 1820 by Kentucky Senator Henry Clay. According to the terms of the Missouri Compromise, the balance of power would be maintained in the Senate by admitting two states: Maine (until then a part of Massachusetts) entered the Union as a free state, with Missouri maintaining its status as a slave state. In addition, subsequent decisions on the status of slavery in the lands acquired through the Louisiana Purchase would be settled by drawing an arbitrary line at 36°30' north latitude, with only territory below that line permitted to have slavery. The Congress accepted the compromise, and the debate over slavery subsided for the time being.

Despite the compromise, it was difficult to return the proverbial genie to the bottle once it has been released, and the congressional debates over slavery that raged from 1819 to 1821 inspired greater public discourse on the topic of slavery. Supporters and detractors of slavery emerged and began to campaign to win the hearts and minds of the many Americans who were largely dispassionate about the slavery debate. The 1820s witnessed the rise of many antislavery societies in the northern states and even a few in the southern states, but by the end of the decade most southern abolitionists removed themselves from the region as passions about slavery hardened in the South. Two short-lived antislavery newspapers—the *Manumission Intelligencer* and the *Emancipator*—were published, respectively, in 1819 and 1820 in Tennessee, but open advocacy of abolitionist views in the South became increasingly rare as the 1820s progressed.

The delicate balance over slavery in the United States was part of a larger phenomenon that was occurring as the nation moved from an attitude that was predominantly nationalistic toward one that was motivated by parochial sectional interests. Although the Missouri debates were one of the forces that prompted the growth of sectionalism, other factors motivated the ideological shift. The economic distress that emerged during the Panic of 1819 had increased tensions between the regional interests of the South, the West, and the Northeast as the burden of blame was placed on regional action for hurting the national economy. In addition, the political discord that occurred during the disputed presidential election of 1824 also inspired regional animosities and heightened sectional discord. When the popular southerner (or westerner) Andrew Jackson lost the presidential race to John Quincy Adams, a New Englander and son of a former president, a struggle that pitted regional and class interests followed. In a sectionally divided nation it was impossible for the potent issue of slavery not to become a central political issue in American national life.

The Birth of the North

As the nationalism of the "Era of Good Feelings" gave way to the sectional rivalry that would characterize the antebellum period, three distinct regions emerged: the South, the West, and the Northeast. Although real political divisions and economic motivations characterized sectional interests, there was much that kept the nation unified as key national values and aspirations varied only slightly across the country. Despite the persistence of a national ethos that kept America unified, regional self-interests were furthered by the emergence of sectional mythologies that magnified differences and piqued the regional antagonism of rival areas. Operating like self-fulfilling prophecies, this process of regional self-definition fashioned sectional identities that remained quite potent. Each section produced its own political leaders whose strident voices perpetuated the mythic identities that had formed.

The period of sectional self-definition that emerged in the 1820s coincided with a tremendous surge in expansion of the nation's commercial infrastructure. A series of projects that involved canal construction, the building of early turnpikes, and river and harbor improvements were underway in much of the nation during the 1820s, and the subsequent decades would witness the development and expansion of an early rail network. Casual perusal of the network of internal improvements that were created during this era suggests an east-west axis that took shape as markets in the Northeast were linked with an agricultural hinterland in the West. Despite the presence of a North-South artery of commerce like the Mississippi River, it became more common for farmers in Illinois to see their economic fortunes tied to merchants and traders in New York than to longshoremen in New Orleans. The artificial arteries of commerce that emerged through linkages of canals, turnpikes, and rail made the West and the Northeast part and parcel of the same business network that increasingly alienated the South as an archaic region where slave-labor prevailed.

Although it was initially unspoken, the commercial ties that bound the economic interests of the Northeast and the West eventually came to be understood as social and political links that also joined the areas. The North, as the combined regions came to be known, was a region characterized by its work ethic, its capitalistic values, and its reliance on free laborers who earned wages. The commercial arteries that linked the two regions facilitated the expansion of a network of trade and commerce and the rise of a factory-based system of production. Increasingly separated from the agricultural South, the North became "modern" and industrial, while the South languished in a world reminiscent of the feudalism and manorialism that characterized an ancient age.

Antislavery societies, which initially emerged in New England and other parts of the Northeast, began to take root in the fertile ground of the West. Abolitionists appeared in places like Ohio, Indiana, and Illinois with values that were different from those of their southern brethren, but more in tune with the values of the New Englanders whom they emulated. Political ties with the Whig Party grew in the West as the pro-business agenda of supporting the tariff and the national bank, and advocating the further expansion of internal improvements, became as vital to the region's self-interest as it was to those of the Northeast. By comparison, southerners increasingly found themselves drawn to the Democratic Party and its defense of slavery and states' rights.

The Age of Jackson

The era of Jacksonian Democracy, which extended roughly from 1824 to 1845, was characterized by the political coming of age of the common man in Ameri-

can society. The adoption of universal manhood suffrage, which eliminated property ownership as a qualification for voting, empowered vast numbers of United States citizens with a political voice as they became stakeholders in the American democratic experiment. Equipped with the right to vote and animated by an almost passionate support for Andrew Jackson and the frontier values that he represented, the common man fashioned a bulwark against the unbridled expansion of the northern monied interests during the age of Jackson. Indirectly, these voters also aided the expansion of slavery into the states of the Deep South.

The Jacksonians disdained most of the platform that the Whigs supported and did everything within their power to limit its advancement. The Democrats were able to destroy the national bank, and they worked to reduce national tariff rates during the 1830s after the nullification crisis threatened to foment secession earlier in the decade. Under Jackson, federal dollars to fund internal improvements were restricted as states were directed to fund their own projects. The Jacksonians therefore damaged much of the program to aid the commercial expansion of the nation.

At the same time that the Whig platform was under attack by the Jacksonians, the nation was effecting the removal of the Five Civilized Tribes from the southern states and relocating them to reservation land in Oklahoma through a coordinated plan of Indian Removal. The lands in the South that were being cleared of Indian inhabitants were then opened for sale and subsequent agricultural expansion as planters and farmers entered the region to cultivate cotton. With the same intensity that they used in trying to limit the commercial development of the North, the Jacksonians were seeking to expand the agricultural, slave-based economy of the Cotton South.

Speak No Evil

The slavery debate grew increasingly intense during the 1830s as the number of antislavery societies grew and the methods of their political advocacy became more extreme. Although many of the early abolitionist groups were dominated by Quakers who opposed slavery but did not want to be "too much of this world," many of the new abolitionist leaders who emerged advocated various forms of direct action as a means of fighting slavery on multiple fronts. The abolitionists of the 1830s, perhaps best characterized by William Lloyd Garrison, refused to be silenced or cowed by the opposition and vowed to fight unceasingly until the stain of slavery had been removed from the fabric of the nation.

Although some viewed the U.S. Constitution as a document that enshrined and protected the institution of slavery, others recognized that the civil liberties guaranteed in the Bill of Rights protected the interests of those who would courageously dare to oppose slavery. Utilizing their First Amendment right to petition for a redress of grievances, hundreds of antislavery societies in the northern states sent petitions and memorials to the U.S. Congress calling for an end to slavery. Many believed that direct political action was necessary to combat slavery, and by the end of the 1830s efforts were underway to form the Liberty Party—a political party that stood on an exclusively antislavery platform. Not all antislavery advocates supported this course of action, however. Some saw the plan as nothing more than cooperation with a political system that existed to perpetuate and protect slavery. Such critics believed that moral suasion rather than political action was the most effective means to resist slavery in the United States.

The growing number of antislavery petitions that were sent to the Congress began to have an impact on the ability of federal legislators to deliberate effectively on all matters that came before the House of Representatives and the Senate. The petitions were unlikely to result in any congressional action against slavery. The legal status of slavery within the southern states was not viewed as a matter that fell under the purview of the U.S. Congress, but was instead seen as an internal matter that was left to the legislative devices of the respective states where it existed. Nevertheless, the arrival of each antislavery petition and efforts made to read it aloud in the Congress inspired countless battles as the divisive issue of slavery aroused the passions of political leaders on both sides of the question and reduced the capacity of the Congress to attend to the peoples' business. Unable thus to effect political action, but able to obstruct the legislative process, the antislavery petitions and memorials that poured into the nation's capital had a debilitating effect on the work of the Congress. Confronted by the conflicting interests of the right of petition and the necessity of conducting the business of government, the Congress had to act on the thorny question of slavery in the 1830s.

Starting on May 26, 1836, the U.S. House of Representatives began using the so-called gag resolution, a rule that prevented the reading and circulation of all antislavery petitions that were received by the Congress. As a parliamentary maneuver, the House had to renew the gag rule at the start of every year's congressional session until the rule was eventually repealed in 1844. With the adoption of this procedure, the effective means of restricting the peoples' freedom of petition was to limit the legislators' freedom of speech within the halls of the U.S. Congress.

Members of Congress who espoused antislavery sentiments and others who viewed the matter as a free speech question fought incessantly against the gag rule for the eight years that it was in effect in the House of Representatives. One of the most vocal opponents of the policy was Massachusetts congressman, and former president, John Quincy Adams. In spite of the procedural ban on reading antislavery petitions, Adams violated the policy unsparingly. He would be ruled out of order by the speaker of the House for carrying on his campaign of civil disobedience against a rule that he considered unjust and a violation of the Constitution.

Civil liberties were not only under attack in the halls of the Congress, but they were also being challenged in cities and towns across the southern states. Several northern antislavery groups initiated a direct-mail effort that became known as the Great Postal Campaign of 1835 when they began sending abolitionist literature in the form of newspapers and pamphlets to southern communities. The abolitionists hoped that the antislavery literature would fall into the hands of sympathetic readers who might share its contents with the slaves of the South. In the eyes of southern defenders of slavery, the action of the abolitionists was an effort to foment slave insurrection in the South and was viewed as a criminal undertaking that needed to be halted.

South Carolina, like most other southern states, made an effort to keep abolitionist literature out of the hands of slaves and free blacks in 1835. In a report to the state legislature, South Carolina Governor George McDuffie commented that "the laws of every community should punish this species of interference by death without benefit of clergy." In July of that year, Alfred Huger, the local postmaster in Charleston, requested that Postmaster General Amos Kendall prohibit antislavery tracts from the U.S. mail. Huger's request was denied by Kendall, who maintained that he did not have the authority to make such a decision, but he did suggest that Huger might act on his own initiative. Kendall stated, "We owe an obligation to the laws, but a higher one to the communities in which we live." By late-July 1835, antislavery pamphlets and other abolitionist literature was removed from the public mail in Charleston and burned in the city's streets.

Before the Storm

Among most abolitionists in the 1830s the notion of using moral suasion to effect an end to slavery held more promise than efforts to find a legislative solution. Conventional wisdom of the times held that the federal government could do little to impact the status of slavery within the sovereign states, and its action in the Missouri Compromise of 1820 had effectively addressed the question of slavery in the federal territories, where Congress did have the authority to legislate on the matter. Essentially, only the actions taken by slaveowning southerners themselves or their respective state legislatures could do anything to affect the status of slavery in the states where it continued to exist.

Others who took the long view and looked upon slavery as a historical phenomenon believed that the institution of slavery was a function of market economics. According to this view, slavery would only continue to exist in areas where it remained profitable, and when the economic burden of slavery became greater than its potential benefit, it was assumed that the institution would wither and die. Some even held out hope that the declining margin of profitability from slaveholding might bring an end to the practice within a generation.

Corollary to both of these views was the understanding that slavery would end of its own devices if it was contained to the states where it currently existed and not permitted to expand into any additional territory. This belief was premised on several factors, including declining profitability, the lessening productivity of depleted soils, and the theoretical notion that the southern states were close to reaching the maximum carrying capacity of their agricultural lands. If these assumptions were correct, the institution of slavery would begin to decline when it could no longer expand into additional lands that would offset these economic determinants. Slavery, thus limited to the states where it currently existed, seemed destined to experience an inevitable decline that would be precipitated by market forces.

A Frontier for Slavery

The intensity of political debate over slavery also escalated in the 1830s because of events in Texas. After the Texas Revolution (1836), the former Mexican province of Texas emerged as an independent nation and began to court the possibility of annexation to the United States. Although the actual annexation would not take place until 1845, the abolitionists became concerned that slavery might be expanded if Texas joined the United States. Since Mexico had abolished slavery in 1829, some antislavery advocates believed that if Texas was annexed and if the United States permitted slavery there, the nation would be reestablishing slavery in an area that had previously been declared free.

Texas did join the Union as a slave state on December 29, 1845, becoming the fifteenth slave state in the Union of twenty-eight states. Northern abolitionists were not only dismayed by the creation of another slave state, but they soon realized that additional lands in the Southwest might also come into the possession

of the United States as potential sites of new slave states. To many it appeared that the containment of slavery had failed and the institution was moving triumphantly into a western frontier that some believed was designed for the presence of slavery.

Actions taken by President James K. Polk in 1846 helped to precipitate a war with Mexico over the issue of a disputed southern boundary for Texas. Many northerners imagined that Polk, as slaveowner from Tennessee, was motivated by sectional interests rather than by policy that best served national objectives. To many, the Mexican War (1846–1848) was a blatant land-grab of territory from a weak neighbor that was conducted to suit the purposes of proslavery southerners.

On August 8, 1846, Democratic Congressman David Wilmot of Pennsylvania introduced the Wilmot Proviso, which proposed that slavery should be excluded from any territory that might be acquired from the war with Mexico. Wilmot borrowed part of the language for his proviso from the Northwest Ordinance of 1787, which stated that "neither slavery nor involuntary servitude shall ever exist in any part of" the territory that the United States might acquire from the Mexican War. Since the Mexican government had previously abolished slavery in the area, many people feared the message the United States would send if slavery were reintroduced into free territory. The U.S. Senate defeated the proviso, but the measure reappeared before the Congress many times over before the start of the Civil War. Votes on the Wilmot Proviso did not follow a party line but were instead based on a clear geographical delineation between northern and southern representatives.

By 1848 the United States defeated Mexican forces and concluded the Treaty of Guadalupe Hidalgo to end the war. According to the terms of the treaty, the United States received a clear title to Texas with the boundary line upon the Rio Grande that had been demanded. In addition, the United States received the Mexican Cession territory (roughly one-sixth of the continental United States), and the Mexican government received compensation of $15 million. Acquisition of this new territory immediately raised the question of whether or not slavery would be permitted to enter the lands formerly held by Mexico. This issue would dominate the political scene until the time of the Civil War.

Free Soil

A new political movement emerged in 1848 as it became clear that the territorial expansion of slavery was an issue that the United States would have to take on. Long-dormant antipathy toward slavery became evident in many as the debate essentially changed from one's opposition to slavery itself (a largely theoretical concern) to one's opposition to the expansion of slavery (a very practical concern). With the nation consisting of fifteen slave states and thirteen free states, and the looming prospect of vast new territorial acquisitions being exposed to the threat of slavery, it appeared that the history of the United States was going to be the story of slavery triumphant. In an age in which sister republics in the Western Hemisphere had enacted emancipation decrees and the transatlantic slave trade had been outlawed, the policy toward slavery in the United States was trending in the opposite direction as new lands were being opened to slavery's expansion. Some in the South were even questioning whether the African slave trade would need to be reestablished in order to fulfill the expected demand for slave labor in the Southwest.

Facing such threats, a coalition of diverse elements formed in 1848, united under their common belief in "free soil," and initiated a political party to espouse their shared values. The Free Soil Party consisted of abolitionists who opposed the expansion of slavery because of their genuine disaffection with slavery itself. Other elements within the new party were aroused not by abolitionism but by antiblack racist assumptions that the presence of slaves, or free blacks for that matter, would degrade the value of white wage laborers in the new western territories. Those who espoused these views wanted the new territories to be free of slaves and, what is more, to be an exclusive domain of white wage laborers. Defending the slogan "Free soil, free labor, free land, free men!" the new movement felt it imperative that the expansion of slavery be halted if the nation were not to be imperiled.

The potency of the free soil doctrine inspired various legislative solutions to the dilemma the nation faced after acquiring the lands of the Mexican Cession. Members of Congress bantered about political solutions ranging from permitting the expansion of slavery to prohibiting it, and some proposed that the Missouri Compromise line of 36°30' north latitude should simply be extended westward from the crest of the Rocky Mountains to the Pacific Coast, thus dividing the new territory on the basis of slavery. Other solutions, as yet untried, were also under consideration, including the notion of "popular sovereignty" that Democratic presidential candidate Lewis Cass had first introduced during the 1848 presidential campaign. According to this view, the question of slavery would be most equitably settled if the matter were left to the accords of popular democracy and permitted to be decided by the will of a territory's citizens as expressed in a referendum.

On the Precipice

By 1850 the rancorous debate over the disposition of the western territories with respect to slavery had become such a divisive political issue that the very survival of the Union seemed to be at stake. In the South the strident voices of "fire-eaters" like John Quitman, William Lowndes Yancey, and Edmund Ruffin urged disunion over compromise, and the specter of secession of the southern slaveholding states seemed real to a nation that was deeply divided over how to address the vexing problem of slavery's expansion into the western territories. Although some believed that the time for a political solution to the crisis had long passed, others turned to the Congress in the hope that a workable compromise could be crafted to avert the potential for disunion.

A series of controversial bills were pending before the Congress in 1850 and each of these measures pitted regional interests of the South against those of the North. Each of these legislative measures held the potential of shattering the fragile bonds that held the nation together, and it seemed, for the moment, that the nation was teetering dangerously on the precipice, with secession as an immediate threat. Leaders in the Congress hoped to avert a national crisis, while southern delegates met at the Nashville Convention in June 1850 to consider slaveholding's best course of action. Moderates at Nashville were able to prevail over the wishes of the "fire-eaters," and southerners decided to support congressional efforts to remedy the crisis through political compromise.

The aged Henry Clay, who had averted a national crisis thirty years earlier by effecting the Missouri Compromise, attempted to craft a legislative remedy in 1850 that could satisfy the disparate views of northerners and southerners over the potential expansion of slavery into the western territories. The Compromise of 1850 that emerged in the U.S. Congress was an imperfect solution that resulted from the give-and-take of political debate, but it was the best possible arrangement that the nation's political leaders could devise to address the growing crisis over slavery.

According to the terms of the compromise, California was allowed to enter the Union as a free state, but two new western territories were established with the understanding that popular sovereignty could decide the question of slavery's status if and when those territories applied for statehood. In addition to these measures, the northern and western boundaries of Texas were reduced and the slave trade (but not slavery) was prohibited in the District of Columbia. Certainly the most controversial aspect of the compromise was the creation of a new and stronger Fugitive Slave Act to replace the largely ineffective 1793 measure that had been diminished through legislative action in the northern states. Faced with the difficult choices of political gamesmanship, several northern politicians who opposed slavery found themselves voting in favor of the Fugitive Slave Act because they needed to win over southern support for the admission of California as a free state. Although the compromise implied that the Congress had come up with a legislative remedy to the divisive question of slavery, the truth was that the issue remained largely unsettled and passions on both sides of the question remained strong throughout the 1850s.

Bleeding Kansas

All doubt about the relative political stability that the Compromise of 1850 had produced was shattered in 1854 when Illinois Senator Stephen A. Douglas introduced the Kansas-Nebraska Act for consideration by the Congress. The measure, which was designed to create and settle new territories to the west of Missouri, shifted national attention from the newly acquired territories of the Southwest and focused instead on the yet-unsettled lands in the northern Louisiana Purchase territory. To most Americans, the disposition of the slavery question in this region was a matter of settled law that had been decided by the Missouri Compromise (1820), which prohibited slavery to the north of the line of 36°30' north latitude. Kansas and Nebraska were territories that were supposed to be free from slavery according to the terms of the Missouri Compromise, but Douglas wanted to insert the possibility that slavery might expand there by stipulating

that popular sovereignty would be used to determine the status of slavery in the new territories when they applied for statehood.

Those who imagined that a "slave power" conspiracy existed in the United States to further the influence of slaveowning interests saw in the Kansas-Nebraska Act all the evidence that they needed to confirm their worst fears. Like the phoenix rising from the flames, the question of slavery's expansion into the territories seemed to be an issue that could not be resolved. Some abolitionists, who heretofore had advocated passive nonresistance to fight against slavery, began to consider different tactics in their strategy to halt the expansion of slavery and destroy the "peculiar institution" itself.

Proslavery and antislavery advocates alike rushed into the Kansas Territory to establish homesteads so that they could participate in the referendum that would determine the status of slavery in the region. It did not take long for the popular sovereignty campaign to turn deadly as massacres occurred on both sides of the question, with advocates resorting to violence in order to further their ideology on slavery. The fevered violence even spilled over into the halls of Congress when Massachusetts Senator Charles Sumner was beaten by Congressman Preston Brooks in the Senate chamber after having given a speech that was critical of southern advocacy of slavery in Kansas.

It was becoming increasingly difficult for the United States to bridge the chasm that divided the nation on the slavery question. Although few things in history are essentially inevitable, it seemed that the nation had passed a point of no return after the episodic violence that marred the popular sovereignty campaign in Kansas. As noted earlier, to many it seemed that the time for compromise had passed and that other solutions would have to be found to settle the question of slavery and its place in American national life.

THE COMING OF THE WAR AND EMANCIPATION

Cracks in the American political landscape caused by slavery began to appear in 1846 when the Congress first considered the Wilmot Proviso and had to determine whether or not slavery would be permitted to expand into lands in the Southwest that the United States might acquire from Mexico. For the first time in American political life a key vote was based on a geographical political orientation rather than on an ideological perspective influenced by party. It was clear that northerners and southerners alike felt differently about the potential expansion of slavery and political leaders simply mirrored the interest of their respective region with their votes.

The passage of the Kansas-Nebraska Act in 1854 challenged the prevailing wisdom of the two-party system that had existed since the Jacksonian era, with Democrats battling Whigs to influence national policy. The pro-business Whigs, who had increasingly become associated with northern manufacturing interests, proved incapable of defending formerly protected free territory from the possible incursion of slavery. As the Kansas Territory convulsed with internecine warfare as proslavery partisans and antislavery advocates battled for control of the future state, the political sway of the Whigs was diminished and eventually extinguished. It was unclear what group would rise to fill the political vacuum created by the demise of the Whig Party.

A coalition of disaffected political elements began to converge in the summer of 1854 after the passage of the Kansas-Nebraska Act to form a new political organization. The central unifying tenet of this new political association was that the expansion of slavery into the western territories must be prevented. As abolitionists and the remnants of the Free Soil Party joined forces with "conscience" Whigs and disillusioned northern Democrats, a new organization that identified itself as the Republican Party came into existence. For the first time in the history of the United States a major political party adopted a stance that was antagonistic toward slavery.

Influential northern political leaders flocked to the banner of the new party. Men like William Seward and Salmon P. Chase, the governors of New York and Ohio, respectively, became prominent Republicans and began to speak critically of slavery. In Illinois, the former congressman and circuit lawyer Abraham Lincoln made his first public statement on slavery in a speech given in Peoria, Illinois, in October 1854. In the speech Lincoln stated his opposition to the expansion of slavery into the western territories. Within a few short years, Seward, Chase, and Lincoln would find themselves bound by a conflict that would challenge them to put their ideological beliefs into action as practical policy.

Equal Justice Under Law

The United States Constitution is structured on the existence of three separate branches of government that are theoretically equal and independent of one another except for the system of checks and balances that protect and maintain the integrity of the executive, legislative, and judicial branches. It seemed apparent to many in the 1850s that neither the executive nor the legislative branch of government was capable of dealing effectively with the thorny question of slavery. Some now began to wonder whether the judiciary was capable of rendering an impartial judgment that could speak to the legality of slavery within American society.

The courts were given an opportunity to address one part of the slavery question when a slave named Dred Scott brought a case forward in the federal courts to try to win his freedom through a judicial decree. The decision ultimately rendered in Scott's case would demonstrate that the courts, too, were incapable of adequately addressing the issue of slavery in American society. By the late 1850s, many in the United States believed that the constitutional system of government was broken and that the unbridled power of slaveholding interests reigned supreme in the United States.

The Missouri slave Dred Scott had seen much of the United States during his lifetime. As the slave of an army surgeon, Scott had lived for a time in Illinois and Minnesota, a free state and territory, respectively, and upon his original owner's death, Scott believed that his time spent in the North had made him free. Scott's case began in the district court in St. Louis in 1849, but after various appeals it finally reached the U.S. Supreme Court where a verdict was rendered in March 1857.

On March 6, 1857, the U.S. Supreme Court, by a vote of seven to two, decided the case of *Dred Scott v. Sandford* and declared that blacks were not citizens of the United States but property that had no right to sue for freedom in a court of law. In the words of Chief Justice Roger B. Taney, a former slaveholder from Maryland, slaves had "no rights a white man need respect." The court also asserted that the Congress had no power to exclude slavery from any of the territories—in effect, declaring the Missouri Compromise (1820) to be unconstitutional.

From the time of the American Revolution until 1857 the United States had existed with the understanding that there were "free states" and "slave states," but Taney's decision in the *Dred Scott* case said that property could be taken anywhere, and in effect, any state could be a slave state. By enshrining the property rights of individuals and holding that slaves were merely chattel property, Taney was asserting that one was free to own slaves anywhere in the nation. Although it is universally despised today as a poorly formulated judicial decision, it was Taney's hope that the *Dred Scott* decision would settle once and for all the vexing problem of slavery in American life. It was his hope that the courts would be able to speak where the executive and legislative branches had failed to act.

Debates on the Prairie

The impact of the *Dred Scott* decision was felt across the nation. For southerners the decision was a godsend that affirmed the legitimacy of slavery and seemingly settled any and all questions about the right of slavery to expand into other areas. For northerners, the decision was tremendously unsettling because it inferred that there were no legal means by which a community might prevent the institution of slavery from taking root. Few cases had ever excited such a level of popular interest and public debate.

Chief Justice Taney and the Court tried to interject the last word into the national dialogue on slavery, but the topic was one that was too intense to be settled by judicial fiat alone. The court could render its decision, but it had no minions at its disposal to refashion society at its behest, and neither the executive nor the legislative branch was prepared to issue a ringing endorsement of the Court's pronouncement. Many still believed that the Congress held the power to limit the expansion of slavery into the territories, but the Court's decision had certainly clouded the political landscape.

The nation was still deliberating the impact of the *Dred Scott* decision when the midterm elections were held in 1858 and campaigns held across the nation provided a venue for political discourse on the question of slavery. Nowhere was this discussion more pronounced than in the series of debates held in Illinois as incumbent senator Stephen A. Douglas and challenger Abraham Lincoln discussed the vital issues of the day in a series of seven debates held in the summer and fall of 1858.

As one of the leading proponents of the doctrine of popular sovereignty, Douglas had to use the debates to defend how this concept could continue to function in light of the *Dred Scott* ruling. For Lincoln, who was a relatively unknown political figure, the newspaper coverage of the Illinois debates made him a prominent spokesman for the cause of those who wanted to prohibit the expansion of slavery into the western territories. Even though Douglas would eventually win reelection to the Senate, it was Lincoln who received the greatest boost from the debates as his views became nationally known and his name more prominent. Only two years later, the failed Senate candidate from Illinois would be a candidate for the presidency.

As Lincoln and Douglas crossed the prairies of Illinois to debate the questions of the day, their journey reflected the temper of the nation—a land that was still willing to discuss civilly the political matters that affected national life. Neither Lincoln nor Douglas used anything except the power of ideas to sway the crowds that attended the series of debates. Americans had not yet abandoned their confidence that political discourse in the public square was the best assurance that a self-governing republic could remain free.

The Avenger

In November 1837 abolitionists across the northern states were shocked to learn of the murder of the abolitionist editor Elijah P. Lovejoy who died trying to defend his press from a proslavery mob in Alton, Illinois. Antislavery advocates gathered at memorial services across the North where Lovejoy was eulogized as a martyr to the cause of abolitionism. At one such service held in Ohio, a young man stood up and affirmed that he would not rest until the righteousness of Lovejoy's cause had been avenged and slavery was forever stricken from the land. The young abolitionist was named John Brown.

Nearly two decades later, John Brown emigrated to the Kansas Territory with several of his sons during the popular sovereignty referendum that was held to determine the status of slavery in the region. As ardent antislavery men, the Browns who had settled at Ossawatomie were determined that proslavery forces would not prevail during the election campaign, and they vowed that any excesses by proslavery interests would be met with a formidable response. On May 21, 1856, proslavery forces attacked the abolitionist stronghold of Lawrence and killed an antislavery supporter. Three days later, Brown and his sons carried out a nighttime attack on proslavery settlers at Pottawatomie

Creek and hacked five residents to death with broadswords. John Brown had baptized his cause in blood and had begun his campaign to avenge the national sin of slavery.

Wanted for murder in Kansas, John Brown went into hiding and was protected by abolitionists around the country who sympathized with his cause and were not critical of his methods. With the Supreme Court's decision in *Dred Scott v. Sandford* announced while Brown was in hiding, he came to believe that nothing short of armed insurrection could bring an end to slavery in the United States. Certain of the goodness of the abolitionist cause and believing that all means employed to fight evil were virtuous, Brown began to craft a plan that would foment the revolt he believed was necessary to bring an end to slavery in the United States. His role was simply to be God's avenging angel who would help the slaves attain salvation through freedom.

Portrayed by some as a raving lunatic, Brown worked with the methodical precision of one who believed in the certainty of his cause more than life itself. He discussed his plans with some of the leading abolitionists of the day in an effort to solicit financial backing for his conspiracy. Far from being perceived as a madman, he moved freely in antislavery social circles communicating with leading figures including the philanthropist Gerrit Smith, Thomas Wentworth Higginson, and Frederick Douglass. Although Douglass did not support the plan, others did, for by 1859 the thought of inciting a slave rebellion appeared to be a rational means of bringing an end to the "peculiar institution."

Brown's plan was to attack the U.S. army arsenal located at Harpers Ferry, Virginia, so that arms could be acquired for distribution among the slaves of the Upper South. Brown believed that once his small force had secured the arsenal, slaves would spontaneously join his cause and revolt in a massive uprising that would destroy slavery.

Brown and his small force of eighteen associates were able to capture the town of Harpers Ferry on the evening of October 16, 1859, but news of the raid was transmitted to public authorities by the conductor of a train that was permitted to travel through the captured town. On October 17 federal forces under the command of Colonel Robert E. Lee arrived at Harpers Ferry and assaulted the firehouse where Brown and his associates had taken refuge. After the brief battle that ensued, Brown was captured and taken to Charlestown where he would be tried for treason. He was convicted and subsequently executed on December 2, 1859.

An Irrepressible Conflict

When Abraham Lincoln accepted the nomination of the Republican Party in Illinois to challenge incumbent senator Stephen A. Douglas in June 1858, he spoke these words: "A house divided against itself cannot stand. I believe this government cannot endure permanently half slave and half free. I do not expect the Union to be dissolved. I do not expect the house to fall, but I do expect it will cease to be divided." The poetry of Lincoln's prose belies the truism reflected in this thought—the United States could not continue to exist as one nation if the slavery question was not resolved one way or another. His words did not suggest how the resolution might be produced or what the eventual outcome might be, but he was certain that change was inevitable.

Speaking in Rochester, New York, on September 25, 1858, New York Senator William H. Seward stated of slavery, "It is an irrepressible conflict between opposing and enduring forces, and it means that the United States must and will, sooner or later, become either entirely a slaveholding nation or entirely a free-labor nation." Although he was vehemently criticized for the radical tone of his rhetoric, Seward's words were prophetic and reflected a growing sensibility that many Americans shared at the time. Both Lincoln's careful rhetoric and Seward's more pointed observation reflect the growing awareness that America was nearing the point of reckoning over slavery and that a clear decision on the status of the "peculiar institution" would need to be reached if national unity was to survive.

After the Harpers Ferry raid, the likelihood of a civil discussion on the question of slavery seemed a quaint relic of a distant past. The intensity of passions among both proslavery and antislavery advocates was so inflamed that disunion became a viable alternative to many. If America could not resolve the divisive issue of slavery, it may well have been because indeed there were two nations, not one, that existed at the time. It was in this setting that the United States prepared to elect a new president in 1860.

Election of 1860 and Secession

Perhaps no other presidential contest in the nation's history has held more significance than that of November 1860. As the nation teetered on the possibility of disunion, four candidates vied for the presidency: Abraham Lincoln (Republican), Stephen A. Douglas (Northern Democrat), John C. Breckinridge (Southern Democrat), and John Bell (Constitutional-Union).

The contest was almost two elections in one as Lincoln and Douglas were the principal contenders in the northern states, while Breckinridge and Bell were the principal contenders in the South. Lincoln's name was not even listed on ballots in the southern states because he was perceived as being an abolitionist.

Abraham Lincoln was elected president of the United States by garnering only 40 percent of the popular vote but winning handily in the Electoral College. None of his electoral votes came from any of the slaveholding states. During his presidential campaign, Lincoln had remarked that slavery was "an evil not to be extended, but to be tolerated and protected only because of and so far as its actual presence among us makes that toleration and protection necessary." Such comments infuriated southerners who believed that instead of tolerating and protecting slavery, a Lincoln administration would promote an abolitionist agenda and attempt to destroy slavery. When it became clear that Lincoln had been elected president, the "fire-eaters" and other radicals within several of the southern states began to consider the appropriate response and secession from the Union seemed imminent.

On December 20, 1860, South Carolina became the first southern state to secede from the Union by declaring itself to be an "independent commonwealth." By February 1, 1861, six other southern states had followed South Carolina out of the Union–Mississippi (January 9), Florida (January 10), Alabama (January 11), Georgia (January 19), Louisiana (January 26), and Texas (February 1). Delegates from these seven states met in Montgomery, Alabama, during February 4–9, 1861, to adopt a provisional constitution for the Confederate States of America. Senator Jefferson Davis of Mississippi was elected president of the Confederacy with Alexander Stephens of Georgia as vice president.

The wave of secession that occurred during the winter of 1860–1861 came during the final months of James Buchanan's administration as president of the United States. Although Lincoln was the president-elect at the time and would not be inaugurated until March 4, 1861, there was nothing that he could do either to halt the wave of secession or to restore the Union. President Buchanan made no real effort to confront the crisis directly, choosing instead to leave the problem to his successor.

The Coming of the War

Abraham Lincoln was inaugurated as the nation's sixteenth president in Washington, D.C., on March 4, 1861. In his inaugural address, Lincoln stated unequivocally, "I have no purpose . . . to interfere with the institution of slavery." Nonetheless, he cautioned the southern states: "In your hands, my dissatisfied fellow countrymen, and not in mine, is the momentous issue of civil war. The government will not assail you. You can have no conflict, without being yourselves the aggressors. You have no oath registered in Heaven to destroy the government, while I shall have the most solemn one to 'preserve, protect and defend' it."

Despite Lincoln's rhetoric, the southern states that had seceded prepared for what they believed would be a short war. Confederate leaders believed that the North did not have the will to fight a war to restore the Union and imagined that swift action to seize federal properties in the South was a necessary step toward establishing hegemonic power in the region. Although federal authorities had warned that properties of the United States government would be defended if attacked, southerners continued to make plans for war.

On April 12, 1861, Confederate forces under the command of General P. G. T. Beauregard began the bombardment of the federal garrison at Fort Sumter in Charleston Harbor, South Carolina. This event marked the beginning of the Civil War. The following day Major Robert Anderson surrendered the garrison to Confederate forces.

President Lincoln responded to the attack on Fort Sumter by issuing a national call for 75,000 volunteers on April 15, 1861. These troops were expected to serve for a period of three months. In issuing his call for troops, Lincoln did not describe the situation as one of war, but used the word "rebellion" instead. Since Lincoln did not recognize the legitimacy of secession because he believed that the Union was inviolable, he believed that the action at Fort Sumter was part of a rebellion among states that were "out of their proper, practical relationship with the Union." Still considering himself the president of the entire country, Lincoln believed that he had the power to crush the rebellion with force.

Lincoln's call for troops in response to the attack upon Fort Sumter led to the secession of four additional states from the Upper South—Virginia (April 17), Arkansas (May 6), Tennessee (May 6), and North Carolina (May 20). Four remaining slaveholding states—Missouri, Kentucky, Maryland, and Delaware—did not leave the Union, but remained as border states and provided support to both sides during the Civil War. Much of Lincoln's strategy during the early months of the war was designed to keep the border states from seceding and further enlarging the Confederacy.

Contraband of War

The notion of civil war was new to the United States, and the rules of engagement and operating procedures by which federal forces would act had to be defined as the conflict progressed. One of the key issues that appeared early in the conflict was the question of what to do with slaves who escaped to the federal lines and sought refuge under the protection of Union forces. It was unclear whether or not the Union army was going to function as an army of liberation since that was not the charge that was given to the military, nor was it deemed logistically feasible.

The purposes of the conflict were expressed by the U.S. Senate in a July 22 resolution that declared "this war is not waged . . . for any purpose . . . of overthrowing or interfering with the rights or established institutions of . . . southern States." The resolution further stated that the specific aim of the war was "to preserve the Union," not abolishing slavery in the southern states. Despite these assurances, it would prove extremely difficult for federal forces to march into the slaveholding South and not be perceived as liberators. How the government walked this fine line between preserving the Union but not abolishing slavery was a challenge of monumental proportions.

The Congress tried to clarify its position on slavery with respect to the aims of the war by passing the first Confiscation Act on August 6, 1861. Under the terms of this legislation, it was permissible to free those slaves who were in areas under Union army control, provided that they had been employed to aid the Confederate cause. Known as "contraband of war," these former slaves could then be put to work as wage laborers aiding the Union cause. Although the Congress was trying to be specific and only permit certain slaves to be emancipated under the terms of this legislation, the act was open to interpretation and many argued that all slaves in the southern states were beneficial to the Confederate war effort and thus should be liberated. Despite the theoretical sway of such an argument, the Lincoln administration was not prepared to support such a liberal interpretation of the Confiscation Act.

President Lincoln's views became clear in the summer of 1861 when he had to confront a serious challenge that had the potential of driving another state into the Confederacy. Acting on his own initiative and without the backing of officials in Washington, D.C., Major General John C. Frémont invoked martial law on August 30, 1861, and issued a proclamation that freed the slaves of all disloyal owners in Missouri. President Lincoln effectively nullified the order by asking Frémont to revise his proclamation so that it would not overstep congressional laws regarding emancipa-

tion. When the general refused to comply, Lincoln ordered him to do so and subsequently reassigned him to a different department.

An Uncertain Path

During the early months of the Civil War, Abraham Lincoln pursued his goal of preserving the Union without letting the issue of emancipation of the slaves cloud his judgment. Seeing himself torn between the demands of doing what was best for the nation and what would satisfy the abolitionist elements within the Republican Party, Lincoln always opted for the nation's best interests much to the chagrin of the abolitionists. He also realized that any decisions that he made with respect to slavery would have an impact on the Confederacy. Thus Lincoln had to view all decisions on matters relating to slavery in the strategic sense of how northerners would perceive of his action (or inaction) and how southerners would respond to his decisions.

In December 1861 Lincoln requested that Secretary of War Simon Cameron remove several controversial references to slavery from his annual report to the Congress. In the initial draft of the report, Cameron had advocated the use of emancipation as a wartime necessity that was related to the use of former slaves as military laborers and soldiers. Unwilling to contemplate either emancipation or the use of black troops as necessities in preserving the Union, Lincoln could not support the inclusion of these suggestions in the report. Shortly after this controversy, Lincoln removed Cameron from his position as secretary of war and appointed him as the U.S. minister to Russia.

Lincoln also had to respond to the efforts of General David Hunter who organized an all-black regiment without the approval of Union military authorities. The First South Carolina Volunteers, the first all-black regiment to be formed during the Civil War, had been organized in May 1862 in the South Carolina Sea Islands. In addition to putting the regiment together, Hunter also issued a proclamation that freed the slaves owned by all rebels in Georgia, Florida, and South Carolina. Enraged by the general's actions, Lincoln ordered that the black regiment be disbanded, and he revoked the emancipation edict that Hunter had issued.

In spite of these instances, President Lincoln did support certain initiatives related to slavery in the early years of the Civil War. He supported congressional efforts to end slavery in the District of Columbia through a system of compensated emancipation. One million dollars in federal support was provided to compensate owners of slaves who were thus emancipated, and $100,000 was provided to assist those emancipated slaves who opted to settle outside of the United States in locations such as Liberia or Haiti. In addition, Lincoln encouraged the border states to adopt a program of gradual, compensated emancipation that would be followed by colonization of freed blacks to locations outside of the United States, but officials in the border states rejected the president's proposal in July 1862.

The Burden of War

All hopes for a quick and easy victory in the Civil War faded during the summer of 1861 as Union and Confederate forces engaged in the first major battle of the war at the first battle of Bull Run in northern Virginia. Disorganized federal forces were routed and retreated toward Washington, D.C., and Confederate forces might have breached the perimeter of the nation's capital if they had pursued the fleeing Union troops. The reality of war was made manifest as the illusion of easy victory quickly vanished.

President Lincoln struggled to find able commanders who could lead Union forces to victory as he appointed several generals to lead the Army of the Potomac, but he was generally dissatisfied with their efforts. The burden of directing a war effort was made more difficult by the inability of Union forces to win the crushing victory that would signal the turning of the tide in the war. In addition, the ability to motivate a nation to fight exclusively for the preservation of the Union—an arcane theoretical concept—was increasingly difficult to sustain. It quickly became clear that reliance on volunteers alone would be insufficient to man the army that was needed to suppress the rebellion, and Lincoln had to initiate an unpopular draft to draw sufficient recruits into the Union army.

Vicious attacks were heaped upon the president, who was constantly second-guessed by those who considered him to be an inept leader. Even some of his own commanders found it difficult to take orders from a president whose only military experience had been brief service along the Illinois frontier during the Black Hawk War in 1832. He was criticized by northern abolitionists for not being a passionate supporter of the antislavery cause, while southerners and some disaffected northerners viewed him as a "Black Republican" who advocated emancipation, social leveling, and miscegenation. Members of Lincoln's own cabinet, which included some of the most prominent leaders of the Republican Party, believed themselves to be more capable of leading the country than the president.

Lincoln was constantly pressed to do more on behalf of the southern slaves. Republicans who had abolitionist leanings, like his friend Illinois congressman Owen Lovejoy, lobbied the president to consider emancipation as an act of wartime necessity that would irreparably weaken the fighting capacity of the South. The black abolitionist Frederick Douglass appealed to Lincoln to end slavery as a matter of common morality and urged the use of black troops to support the war effort. Some of the most scathing criticism of Lincoln came from *New York Tribune* editor Horace Greeley whose August 20, 1862, editorial "A Prayer of Twenty Millions" called for immediate emancipation of the slaves.

In a response to Greeley's editorial, Lincoln wrote: "My paramount object in this struggle is to save the Union, and it is not either to save or to destroy slavery. If I could save the Union without freeing any slave I would do it, and if I could save it by freeing all the slaves I would do it; and if I could save it by freeing some and leaving others alone I would also do that."

A Wartime Necessity

When Abraham Lincoln responded to Horace Greeley in August 1862, he did not reveal his true intentions to the newspaper editor. Earlier that summer Lincoln had drafted an emancipation proclamation that he first shared with his cabinet on July 22, 1862. Although the cabinet did not respond favorably to Lincoln's proposal, he determined that he would move ahead with his plans to make the proclamation public at an appropriate time. At the cabinet's urging, he agreed to wait until a significant Union victory had been achieved on the battlefield so that it would not seem that the proclamation was being issued as an act of desperation by the government. The president agreed with the suggestion.

Later in the summer the president met in the field with General George B. McClellan, the commander of the Army of the Potomac, and urged him to engage the enemy in battle. Lincoln was hoping that McClellan could secure the Union victory that would be necessary in order for the public announcement of the emancipation proclamation to be made. On September 17, 1862, McClellan's forces engaged a Confederate army in the battle of Antietam, in Maryland. The two armies combined suffered more than 25,000 casualties in what was the bloodiest single day of the Civil War, but Confederate forces withdrew at the end of the day and the Union army could claim a costly victory. Mc-Clellan had won the significant victory that Lincoln had requested, and the president was thus prepared to issue his preliminary emancipation proclamation.

On September 22, five days after the carnage at Antietam, President Abraham Lincoln made the preliminary emancipation proclamation public. It was stated that one hundred days hence, on January 1, 1863, the president intended to free all slaves residing in those areas that remained in rebellion against the government. It was stipulated that this power was given to the president in his official capacity as commander-in-chief of the armed forces of the United States since the abolition of slavery was viewed as a matter of wartime necessity. In keeping with this claim, it was necessary for the president to state that slaves in those areas that were no longer in rebellion and were effectively under Union control would not be set free by the proclamation. The September 22 reading of the proclamation was viewed as a preliminary announcement with the formal proclamation to be issued on January 1, 1863.

In addition to announcing his intention to emancipate the slaves of the South in areas that remained in rebellion, Lincoln's proclamation also called for the enlistment and training of black troops. This was one of the key points that black abolitionist Frederick Douglass had urged of the president from the earliest months of the Civil War. Many abolitionists believed that one of the most certain signs that could be used to justify the emancipation of the slaves was to permit black troops to fight and help win the freedom of their brethren who were held in bondage.

On January 1, 1863, the Emancipation Proclamation became effective, and all slaves were declared free except those in states, or parts of states, that were no longer in rebellion. The proclamation did not apply in the border states, nor did it apply in those areas that were already under control of the Union army. These areas included thirteen parishes in southern Louisiana (including New Orleans), the forty-eight counties that made up West Virginia, seven counties in eastern Virginia (including Norfolk), and the entire state of Tennessee.

The Balance Sheet

The Emancipation Proclamation must be viewed in the context of being a wartime necessity because that helps to explain the logic and motivation behind Lincoln's action. Although the document is one that has profound symbolic meaning and helped to fashion the mythic image of Lincoln as the Great Emancipator, it

is also a carefully crafted message that had strategic significance in possibly bringing an end to the Civil War before the end of 1862.

Some have argued that the Emancipation Proclamation was a hollow document in that it freed no slaves. In those areas that were still in rebellion against the federal government, Abraham Lincoln did not possess real power to emancipate anyone, and in the areas that were already under Union control, the places where Lincoln *could* have freed the slaves, he opted not to free them. Such a reading of the document also calls into question the necessity of a 100-day waiting period before emancipation would be effected. If Lincoln really wanted to free the slaves, some argue, he should have done so instantly in his preliminary announcement on September 22, 1862.

It may well be possible that Lincoln was trying to give the Confederacy a way to end the war and keep slavery. Knowing that slavery stood to be abolished if southern forces continued fighting and ended up losing the war, Lincoln hoped that Confederate leaders would consider their options and accept the certain preservation of slavery that would come from their decision to end the war during the 100-day waiting period that the proclamation provided. In any event, when southern leaders failed to take the bait and end the war according to Lincoln's time line, his promise of emancipation took effect and would subsequently be realized through a Union victory.

In addition, many legal scholars questioned whether or not Lincoln was within his rights as president to abolish slavery through executive decree. Recognizing that such action is more monarchical in character than is typically found in a constitutional republic, some believed that couching Lincoln's power to emancipate the slaves in a reading of the wartime powers of the president was a tenuous legal argument that might not survive careful judicial scrutiny. Accordingly, the Congress drafted language for a thirteenth amendment to the U.S. Constitution that would abolish slavery and submitted the matter to the states so that there would exist constitutional backing for the abolition of slavery.

Transformation

The Emancipation Proclamation's impact on the war effort was phenomenal. Rather than simply fighting a war for the theoretical preservation of the Union, the document transformed the war into a struggle that was designed to make men free. As a nation that was founded on the fundamental notion of freedom and liberty that stems from the natural rights of man, Lincoln was able to use the rhetoric of the Founding Fathers to justify the new birth of freedom that would come from emancipation of the slaves. This rhetorical style would be most evident in the Gettysburg Address that the president delivered in November of 1863.

In addition, the Emancipation Proclamation made it exceedingly difficult for foreign governments like Great Britain or France to consider offering diplomatic recognition to the Confederate States of America. The southern states had hoped that "King Cotton" diplomacy would work in their interests as foreign governments that relied on southern exports would be forced by economic necessity to support the southern cause. Once Lincoln turned the conflict into a war that would bring an end to slavery, it was impossible for the European powers to side with the Confederacy and work to preserve the onerous institution of slavery.

The Civil War was far from over when the Emancipation Proclamation took effect on January 1, 1863, but it became a conflict transformed by the president's actions. The battle to achieve emancipation had been effected, but the ongoing struggle to achieve liberty and true freedom for the former slave was just beginning.

RECONSTRUCTION: ARE LIBERTY AND JUSTICE FOR ALL?

If January 1, 1863, represented a new birth of freedom for the United States, it quickly became clear that the formative years of incipient liberty would pose many challenges to the nation. The Civil War was not yet concluded at the start of the new year in 1863, and the necessary Union victory on which emancipation was premised still seemed uncertain at the time. The nation had not yet learned of places like Little Round Top, Cold Harbor, and the Crater, and the lessons that would be learned in those future encounters was that liberty was a precious commodity that was purchased with the blood of thousands. The national bloodletting that was the Civil War would, in time, have a tremendous impact on how freedom and civil liberties were bestowed on the former slaves and how resistance to those efforts would materialize in the hearts and minds of those who, though vanquished, cherished the memory of the Lost Cause.

Abraham Lincoln had no illusions in 1863 that his decision to emancipate the slaves would bring a speedy end to the Civil War, but he did believe that the cause would add renewed energy to the Union war effort. In providing a very real focus to the effort by saying that it was a war about freedom, Lincoln hoped that the American people would recognize the moral nature of the calling and rally to the cause of liberating an estimated 4 million slaves who were held in bondage in the southern states. Yet even in his advocacy of emancipation, Lincoln did not harbor much confidence that the United States could exist as a multiracial society, and he privately confided that the freeing of the slaves would likely have to be followed by a massive national effort to colonize them elsewhere so that both white Americans and freed slaves could live harmoniously apart from one another.

In mid-August 1862 President Lincoln held a meeting with prominent black leaders in which he urged them to support a colonization plan that would have relocated freed blacks either to Central America or to Africa. Although this was the first time that an American president had sought the counsel of black leaders on a matter of public policy, many free blacks remained skeptical of the president's motives and were highly critical of his suggestions. On September 23, 1862, just one day after he announced the preliminary emancipation proclamation, Lincoln met with his cabinet to discuss the possible acquisition of new territory that the United States might use for the deportation of free blacks after the abolition of slavery.

It became clear to most Americans during the final years of the Civil War and in subsequent years that the task of ending slavery effectively was a national work in progress that lacked clearly defined goals, objectives, and strategies. Thus, lacking the resolution of a clearly defined approach, much of the burden of emancipation and incorporating freed slaves into the civic life of the nation would be influenced by the former slaves themselves. Given nothing but freedom, the former slaves would find a way to navigate the treacherous ground of proscribed liberties in a nation that was still defining the full meaning of freedom for all of its citizens.

Uniforms of Blue

By the end of the Civil War, 180,000 black troops were fighting in the Union army to win the emancipation of the slaves. The ability to participate as a soldier was an expression of manhood that had been denied to slaves and persons of color through the centuries, and the exploits of black troops made white Americans recognize their inherent humanity. It required tremendous courage and bravery for blacks to join the war effort, but the ultimate goal of destroying slavery was worth whatever sacrifices and deprivations might be required in order to secure it.

The Confederate government made clear that black troops would neither be recognized as soldiers on the battlefield nor extended the courtesies that war prisoners normally received. Believing that a black soldier was nothing more than a potential insurrectionist, Confederate policy permitted armed blacks to be summarily executed on the battlefield or enslaved—there was no such thing as a black prisoner of war in the minds of southerners. When considered in this context, the actions of black troops who donned uniforms of blue become even more extraordinary as the righteousness of their cause did not permit them to become dissuaded by the savage policies that the Confederate government had announced.

Organized into regiments in the United States Colored Troops (USCT), black soldiers continued to experience a world that was limited by racism and circumscribed opportunities. Only white officers were permitted to lead the black regiments that were created during the Civil War, and initially the pay that black troops received was less than that of their white counterparts. The training of black troops and the provisions they received were considered to be second-rate to that which white regiments received. Uncertain about their battle-readiness, Union army officials often hesitated to place black regiments in the thick of military engagements, preferring instead to use them as support troops who were perceived as having a subservient status. On certain occasions, when almost-suicidal missions were required, black troops were deployed so that they might become cannon fodder while preserving the fighting capacity of white regiments.

The Fifty-fourth Massachusetts Volunteers were perhaps the best known of all the black regiments that constituted the USCT. On January 26, 1863, Secretary of War Edwin M. Stanton authorized the governor of Massachusetts, John A. Andrew, to organize a company of black troops. The regiment that was formed included predominantly free blacks, including the sons of black abolitionist Frederick Douglass, and it was commanded by Colonel Robert Gould Shaw, a white officer with abolitionist sympathies. The Fifty-fourth Massachusetts Volunteers was the first black regiment to be raised in the North. Six months after it was formed, the Fifty-fourth Massachusetts led the federal assault on Fort Wagner at Charleston Harbor, South Carolina, on July 18, 1863. The heroism of the assault proved the mettle of black troops in battle as the fierce attack resulted in more than twelve hundred casualties.

Participation in the USCT also provided a training ground for leadership among the many African Americans who participated in the war effort. During the Reconstruction period that followed the Civil War, many African American political leaders emerged who had served in the military during the war years. Military service thus prepared a cadre of black leaders to assume roles in the political, civic, and commercial activities that were required to turn the new birth of freedom into a reality.

A Helping Hand

On March 3, 1865, in anticipation of the work that would have to take place after the Civil War ended, Congress authorized the creation of the Bureau of Refugees, Freedmen, and Abandoned Lands, a governmental agency that became the first public welfare program in the history of the United States. The Freedmen's Bureau, as it came to be known, was designed to assist freedmen and refugees as they made the difficult social and economic transformation from slavery to freedom after the war. The organization was placed under the leadership of General Oliver O. Howard.

The organization was instrumental in establishing a network of schools throughout the southern states that educated the children of former slaves and poor whites and even instituted adult literacy programs. The kinds of survival skills that were taught by the Freedmen's Bureau were essential to providing the helping hand that was necessary for former slaves to achieve success in their new lives in freedom. The Freedmen's Bureau also established a series of savings banks so that former slaves could establish a sense of economic security in their new status.

Considered a controversial program by those who believed that its mission and goals were contrary to the industriousness and virtuous self-help mentality that characterized American life, others opposed the Freedmen's Bureau because of blatantly racist assumptions. The program was never fully funded by the Congress, and it was short-lived.

During the Civil War years, the immediacy of present burdens occupied Abraham Lincoln as he sought wartime strategies that could most effectively conclude the war successfully for the Union cause. Still, Lincoln also pondered the momentous questions of what the United States would look like after the war and how a divided nation might be restored in a most harmonious fashion. Since the war, in Lincoln's view, had been extremely hard, it was essential that the peace not be punitive.

Lincoln's ideas about the postwar era coalesced around the idea of restoration rather than reconstruction as he envisioned a relatively easy path for the former Confederate states to rejoin the Union with as little delay as possible. In what came to be known as the "Ten Percent Plan," the president outlined a comparatively simple strategy that would require 10 percent of the registered voters of a southern state to sign an oath of allegiance to the United States government. The southern state would then need to draft a new state constitution that outlawed slavery. Once these basic requirements were met, the state would be readmitted to the Union.

Congress, too, had begun consideration of how the postwar years might be conducted most effectually and had drafted potential legislation that might outline procedures for such a strategy. Believing that the Confederate states had surrendered their statehood status through the act of secession, many within the Congress believed that the former Confederate states represented nothing more than conquered provinces, and as such, they had reverted back to territorial status. This theoretical framework was essential to the plans of the Congress since the U.S. Constitution specifically permitted the Congress to control all aspects of political life within the federal territories. If the former Confederate states remained states, then the president was free to act, but if they had reverted to territorial status, then their disposition would be an issue that fell under the purview of the Congress.

A tremendous amount of high-stakes political drama was associated with the pending battle between the Congress and the president over postwar policy. The extraordinary circumstances of fighting a civil war had permitted Abraham Lincoln, by necessity, to expand the powers of the executive branch of government, but this had been accomplished by concordantly reducing the power and influence of both the Congress and the federal courts. By 1864 it was becoming increasingly apparent that the Congress was willing to challenge the president on reconstruction policy as a means of reasserting some of its lost influence. Many believed that the president's wartime powers, which included initiating the draft, creating an income tax, suspending habeas corpus rights, and freeing the slaves, were executive decisions that represented an unchecked power grab, and the Congress was determined to challenge the president during the postwar years.

In July 1864 both houses of Congress approved the Wade-Davis Bill that outlined congressional plans for how postwar reconstruction was to be conducted in the South, but President Lincoln pocket vetoed the measure. In an extraordinary reply to the president's action that became known as the "Wade-Davis Manifesto," members of Congress made clear their intentions to challenge the president's authority to conduct postwar reconstruction policies exclusively as the prerogative of the executive branch of government. Although it was becoming evident that the Civil War itself was winding down, it was also clear that political battles lay ahead as plans for restoration and reconstruction were debated.

April 1865

Much of the military action in the final nine months of the Civil War centered on the siege of Petersburg, located just to the south of the Confederate capital of Richmond, Virginia. It was readily apparent to most that the Confederacy's dwindling resources, its inability to obtain diplomatic recognition from a foreign power, and the sustained impact of total war on the southern populace all indicated that a Union victory could be attained. Timing along with the prolonged loss of men and material were the only factors that characterized the conflict for both sides in its final months.

In April 1865 Confederate forces decided to abandon Richmond and make a desperate escape to the mountains of western Virginia where they hoped to regroup and continue the struggle. Many parts of the rebel capital were set ablaze as Confederate forces evacuated the city that they had unceasingly defended for nearly four years. Just days after the Confederate evacuation of Richmond, Abraham Lincoln visited the city and walked among its still-smoldering ruins. Visiting not as a conquering hero, but more as an emancipator, Lincoln was able to see firsthand the effects of emancipation as he pressed flesh with those whom he had liberated. It was an emotionally charged moment for the president.

Holy Week, as celebrated in the Christian calendar, fell during the second week of April 1865 and contained events of national importance. It was on Palm

Sunday that Confederate General Robert E. Lee surrendered his army to Union General Ulysses S. Grant in a private meeting held at Appomattox Court House, Virginia. Although sporadic fighting continued in other parts of the Confederacy into June 1865, Lee's surrender essentially marked the defeat of the southern cause. Five days later, on Good Friday, President Abraham Lincoln was assassinated while attending a play at Ford's Theater in Washington, D.C., and he died the following morning. The symbolism of Holy Week was readily apparent to many, but there was no comparable event to symbolize the Resurrection. America would need to struggle further to find the promise of redemption.

Vice President Andrew Johnson assumed the presidency on April 15, 1865, upon the death of Abraham Lincoln. As a southern Democrat from Tennessee, Johnson had been invited by Lincoln to run on the Union ticket of 1864 to symbolize the national unity that would be necessary to restore the Union in the postwar years. Although Johnson was always a staunch Unionist and had never supported the Confederate cause, his political rivals would characterize him as a tool of southern interests who sought to undermine all that was achieved on the battlefield by the blood and toil of Union forces.

Johnson hoped to carry out restoration policies as he believed that President Lincoln would have done by using the Ten Percent Plan. Assuming office in April 1865 with the Congress on an extended recess, Johnson immediately set in motion the plans to restore the former Confederate states to the Union according to the plan that Abraham Lincoln had drafted. Within the first eight months of his administration, Andrew Johnson had seen fit to restore seven of the former Confederate states to the Union, and he had begun the process of restoration in the four remaining southern states. It was Johnson's hope that he would soon preside over a nation restored, with the absence of slavery.

Congressional leaders were dismayed to learn of the new president's actions when they returned to the nation's capital in December 1865 to attend the next legislative session. Moreover, many northern politicians were horrified to discover that some of the states that Johnson had readmitted were sending delegations to the Congress that included high-ranking former Confederate leaders. Georgia, for example, was hoping to return former Confederate vice president Alexander Stephens to the U.S. Senate, and Louisiana voters had elected former Confederate General P. G. T. Beauregard to a seat in the House of Representatives. Utilizing the constitutional provision that allows the Congress to determine the fitness of its own membership, the Congress refused to seat these former Confederates and made clear that it disapproved of President Johnson's attempts to circumvent the Congress in implementing reconstruction policy.

It soon became apparent that Congress and the president were on a collision course regarding their views of what branch of government should direct reconstruction policy in the South. Believing that he was carrying out the mandate of the martyred president, Andrew Johnson continued to implement Lincoln's Ten Percent Plan, and he vetoed congressional measures that he considered a digression from that path. An emboldened Congress, sensing that Johnson was a weaker president than Lincoln had been, was determined to stymie his plans and restore power to the legislative branch that they felt had been weakened during the Civil War. Although this intense political battle was being played out in the nation's capital, more significant battles were taking place in locations large and small as multitudes of former slaves struggled to make the transition to true freedom.

A growing contingent within the Congress known as the Radical Republicans began to take control of congressional efforts to draft reconstruction policy. President Johnson tried to halt the growing influence of the Radical Republicans and campaigned against them vigorously during the midterm congressional elections of 1866, but his efforts failed to produce his desired results. The Congress that returned to the nation's capital in March 1867 contained even more Radical Republicans who held a "veto proof" majority of more than two-thirds of the seats in the Congress. For all intents and purposes, the crafting of reconstruction policy had shifted from the executive branch of government to the legislative branch.

Freedom and Nothing More

During the final months of the Civil War, some had speculated that the postwar era would be characterized by land reform in the former Confederacy as the federal government distributed confiscated plantation lands to the former slaves who had toiled there. The phrase "forty acres and a mule" had become a common description of the basic necessities that would be needed to transition former slaves to small independent farmers. In one brief experiment at Port Royal, South Carolina, former plantation lands were distributed to the ex-slaves who had worked the property, but this pattern was not replicated across the South as some had imagined. Essentially, what the former slaves received at the end of the Civil War was freedom and nothing more.

Although freedom was a tremendous gift, freedom alone could be quite problematic. Most of the former slaves in the South were illiterate, and they did not have the skills or training necessary to attain employment beyond the type of agricultural labor that most had pursued during the days of slavery. Moreover, many of the former slaves were made homeless when they were told to leave the plantations where they had labored as slaves. A large number purposefully left their old plantations and searched throughout the South to reconnect with a spouse or with children who had been separated in order to create the family life that the days of slavery had denied them. Without homes, jobs, and an income, many former slaves wandered almost aimlessly in many parts of the South, and hastily enacted vagrancy laws resulted in many of these individuals being arrested and jailed. Large numbers of freed slaves simply "vanished" during their first winter of freedom as the combined effects of destitution, homelessness, and vigilante justice in the form of revenge killings resulted in a high mortality rate for freedmen.

Black codes were developed in communities throughout the former Confederacy as a means of regulating the opportunities that would be permitted to the former slaves. Reminiscent of the slave codes that had existed on plantations in the antebellum era, the black codes covered a variety of measures ranging from where a freedman might live, what type of labor he might perform, and whether or not he could possess a firearm. Sometimes black codes included some type of community curfew stipulating the latest hour of the day that a freedman might be permitted to walk the streets. Freedmen who violated the terms of the black codes could be jailed; the number of blacks incarcerated in southern jails increased dramatically in the immediate aftermath of the Civil War.

Freedmen often found themselves the victims of community-sanctioned violence. In some cases this violence was carried out by organized groups like the Ku Klux Klan or the Knights of the White Camellia that sought to maintain white supremacy in the South, but the attacks on the freedmen also resulted from unorganized spontaneous mobs that carried out acts of vigilante justice with impunity. This behavior ranged from lynchings that occurred in the silence of the night to urban riots, like those that occurred in New Orleans, Louisiana, and Memphis, Tennessee, in broad daylight with the tacit approval of local police authorities. In addition, schools and churches that were working to help the former slaves make the transition to freedom were often targeted for arson.

Congressional Reconstruction

The rise of black codes and the continuing intransigence of white southerners were the principal reasons Congress felt the need to act in 1867 and implement new reconstruction policies to protect the rights of the freedmen. Congress passed the first Reconstruction Act over the veto of President Andrew Johnson. It established five military districts in ten of the former Confederate states (Tennessee was excluded), and it appointed a major general to command troops that were assigned to each district. The military was used to impose martial law in the region and provide oversight while the states in the district made their way toward carrying out the reconstruction policies that were demanded by the Congress. These policies included the drafting of new state constitutions and the ratification of the Thirteenth Amendment (abolishing slavery) and the Fourteenth Amendment (making blacks U.S. citizens) to the U.S. Constitution.

The success or failure of congressional reconstruction hinged on use of the military to make southerners obey federal law. Since the president of the United States was the commander-in-chief of the nation's armed forces, and Congress feared that President Johnson would do everything in his power to halt or prevent the effectiveness of congressional reconstruction, Congress passed two measures to limit the powers of the president. Shortly after it enacted the first Reconstruction Act, the Congress passed the Command of the Army Act and the Tenure of Office Act. The first of these measures required that general orders the president submitted to commanders in the field had to be cleared first through the Army chief of staff, who, at the time, was General Ulysses S. Grant. The Congress did not believe that General Grant would permit any orders that weakened federal law to be passed along to commanders in the field. The Tenure of Office Act was a measure specifically designed to protect Secretary of War Edwin M. Stanton, who was a friend of the Radical Republicans in Congress who had drafted the congressional reconstruction policy. Believing that Johnson might try to fire Stanton to appoint a new secretary of war who was less inclined to support congressional reconstruction policy, the Congress said that any federal officer whose position required Senate consent for hiring purposes would also require Senate consent for dismissal from office. Although both of these measures were likely unconstitutional, and both were intended to "trap" Andrew Johnson into violating a federal law, they were viewed as necessary by the Congress if the use of military forces in the South was to be maintained as part of congressional reconstruction policy.

When President Johnson took the bait and fired Secretary of War Stanton, the Congress voted to impeach the president for violating the Tenure of Office Act. Although he was spared removal from office by a margin of only one vote, a president with greatly diminished power and influence served out the remainder of his term until March 1869.

Congress revised its reconstruction policy to meet the changing circumstances that were occurring in the South. When it became clear that the voting rights of freedmen were not being honored in many parts of the former Confederacy, the Congress passed a Fifteenth Amendment to the U.S. Constitution granting black men the right to vote. The amendment was eventually ratified by the states and took effect in 1870.

A Dream Deferred

The rhetoric that supported the federal government's commitment to reconstruction policy was always greater than the reality that affected the lives of the former slaves. The United States devoted only a decade to the implementation of congressional reconstruction efforts, with federal troops being sent into the South in 1867 and the last troops being withdrawn in the spring of 1877. Since the government's removal of troops from the South was part of a political compromise engineered so that the Republicans could retain control of the presidency after the disputed election of 1876, the decision suggested that political expediency was a much greater concern than the government's true dedication to the success of its reconstruction efforts in the South.

Congress had implemented reconstruction policy through federal legislation, approved three new constitutional amendments to extend civil liberties to the freedmen, and enacted far-reaching Civil Rights Acts in 1867 and in 1875, but all of these measures fell short of achieving their desired goals. During the political scandals of the Grant administration, the constant stream of negative publicity emanating from the South made the federal reconstruction efforts there appear to be just another national outrage, and political leaders lost the will to continue enforcing what appeared to be bad policy. By 1877 many of the same leaders who had crafted reconstruction policy were willing to turn their backs to the freedmen and walk away from their previ-

ous pledge of support. Emboldened southern states crafted legislation that weakened the protections specified in the constitutional amendments. Slavery was abolished, but the rise of a nefarious convict-lease system that some considered worse than slavery took its place, and voting rights of black citizens were eventually restricted through the adoption of poll taxes and literacy tests. The courts also served to diminish the protections that were guaranteed to freedmen as the Civil Rights Act of 1867 was weakened by decisions in the *Slaughterhouse Cases* (1873) and *U.S. v. Cruikshank* (1875), and the Civil Rights Act of 1875 was later declared unconstitutional in the *Civil Rights Cases* (1883).

By the late nineteenth century, a code of strict racial segregation had descended upon the states of the former Confederacy as the so-called Jim Crow laws were adopted and enforced. Designed to keep the races in separate spheres and to diminish the social, economic, and political opportunities that were available to African American citizens, these laws remained in place until the civil rights movement of the 1950s and 1960s. When the U.S. Supreme Court decided the case of *Plessy v. Ferguson* (1896), which held that a "separate but equal" policy did not violate the equal protection clause of the Fourteenth Amendment, segregation in American society became seemingly institutionalized.

Making Do

Despite a bevy of federal laws that protected their civil rights, three new amendments to the U.S. Constitution, and the presence of federal military forces in the South, the freedmen had to devise much of their means of survival alone in the place where they found themselves. Since there was not a mass exodus of former slaves out of the South in the immediate aftermath of the Civil War, most of the freedmen remained where they had lived and labored in the years preceding the war. As largely illiterate agricultural laborers, many of the freedmen recognized that they faced a future of limited possibilities. Most would remain in the South as farmers.

White landowners faced a peculiar situation in the aftermath of the Civil War. Having lost their slave labor force, the planters still needed to have individuals work the agricultural lands of southern plantations and farms, but this was difficult since the region was economically depressed and cash-poor at the time. The freedmen and the planters essentially needed one another, but they had to find the means to navigate the social and economic boundaries that separated them from one another.

A system of sharecropping emerged in which freedmen along with poor white farmers found themselves making labor contracts with southern landowners who needed to find agricultural laborers. Provided with a cabin on the plantation or estate, the freedmen would farm a section of the planter's land accepting a portion of the crop as his annual income with a significant portion of the crop going directly to the landowner. In return, the landowners extended credit to the sharecroppers when they needed to purchase supplies before their crops came due at harvest. In most respects, the sharecropping system was exploitative of freedmen to the advantage of southern landowners, but it was a system in which many slaves found that they could "make do" and survive as free people.

A Better Day

One of the stellar accomplishments of the Reconstruction era was that African American leaders emerged who proved that a previously enslaved group of people could rise to great heights in the United States. A number of elected officials in states across the South demonstrated the capability of African Americans. Hiram Revels and Blanche K. Bruce both served in the U.S. Senate representing the state of Mississippi, and several African American congressmen were elected to the House of Representatives during the Reconstruction era. In Louisiana, P. B. S. Pinchback served that state as its acting-governor after political scandals had caused the removal of the elected governor.

A number of schools were established in the South to educate the children of former slaves, with some of the first such institutions being established under the auspices of the Freedmen's Bureau. In addition, a large number of northern educators, many of whom became branded by the epithet "carpetbagger." came to the South during the Reconstruction era to help the blacks move from the backwardness of slavery to a better day through the promise of education. Charitable organizations like the American Missionary Association and philanthropic groups like the Peabody Trust invested heavily in supporting the creation of schools in the former Confederacy that would help to create opportunities for African Americans. Within a few years historically black colleges and universities began to take shape as Fisk University, Atlanta University, and the Tuskegee Institute.

Black soldiers who had been given an opportunity to prove themselves during the final years of the Civil War continued to serve the nation in uniform. Regiments of black cavalry and infantry, who became known as the "Buffalo Soldiers," participated in the settlement of the western frontier during the late nineteenth century and distinguished themselves. Even though black soldiers remained confined to segregated units and had to serve under white officers, service in the military continued to be an avenue for African Americans to prove their abilities and to demonstrate their commitment to the ideals and values of American society.

In the years following the Civil War, the African American church played a fundamental role in the social and cultural survival of the freedmen. Living in a world of uncertainty where the terror of slavery transitioned into the new terror of community-sanctioned violence, a people who were rootless in so many respects found stability and permanence in the African American church. Through prayer and through song the church community found a common bond in the stories of the Hebrew people who stood up to the Pharaoh and made their way to freedom in a promised land. The spirituals they sang were grounded in the real experiences of a long-suffering people who held out hope for a better world and a better tomorrow.

Slavery: A Postmortem

The United States of America is the only nation in the history of the world that ever fought a civil war to end slavery. Did it have to happen that way? Societies have used slavery throughout human history, and the practice has appeared and disappeared generally on the basis of market forces in most of its settings. Some, including Abraham Lincoln, had believed that economic forces would lead to the end of slavery in the United States, but the onset of the Civil War and Lincoln's eventual decision to emancipate the slaves made the earlier prediction purely academic.

It is true that the Civil War was caused by a variety of reasons, of which slavery was just one, but as the war progressed the disposition of the slavery question increasingly became a central issue. Union forces quickly learned that it was impossible to enter a slaveholding region without causing hundreds of slaves to flee to the federal lines seeking freedom, and the awkward characterization of "contraband of war" did not suffice. Slaves were people and not property.

The United States ended slavery in a unique fashion. Neither the Emancipation Proclamation nor the Thirteenth Amendment to the U.S. Constitution incorporated any element of gradualism into the method that was used to abolish the institution of slavery. Slavery was abolished immediately. In spite of peculiar oddities, like the slaves in Galveston, Texas, not learning of emancipation until June 19, 1865, a date celebrated as "Juneteenth" since that time, emancipation came quickly once it was the established policy of the nation. No efforts to institute a transition period or a form of apprenticeship were even considered.

In addition, the emancipation that was effected in the United States was a form of uncompensated emancipation. Those southerners who owned the more than 4 million slaves who were set free earned no financial remuneration at the time of emancipation. Freedom for the slaves represented a financial loss of immense proportions for slaveholding southerners. Although one can question the morality of slaveownership itself and argue that no one who owned a fellow human being was entitled to any form of compensation, the financial loss to the slaveholders still remains. Having participated in what was until then a lawful enterprise, many southerners who had most of their wealth invested in slaves found themselves practically destitute because of emancipation.

Compensation was denied to both the slaveowner and the slave. In giving no financial assistance to the freed slaves, the United States was granting freedom but not opportunity for success. The idea of providing "forty acres and a mule" was much too socialistic a policy for lawmakers to advocate at the time, but even Congressman Thaddeus Stevens of Pennsylvania could not convince his fellow Radical Republicans to endorse a reparations bill that he introduced in the Congress in March 1867. If the United States was sincere about helping the former slaves to transition toward freedom, it seems extremely short-sighted that they were not given greater financial assistance in the immediate aftermath of the Civil War.

The path of slavery's demise was not well crafted in the United States, and much of the ill will created during the Reconstruction era served to create a racial divide in American society that has persisted into the modern era. Although the abolition of slavery was a noble achievement, the formation of a segregated society based on Jim Crow justice and institutional racism was an unfortunate consequence of emancipation and its aftermath. Only a renewed commitment by the Courts and by Congress during the civil rights movement of the twentieth century would begin to remedy the lingering influence that slavery and segregation held upon American society.

We cannot undo decisions today that were made in the 1860s, nor can we change the spiteful history that has taken place from the time of the Civil War to the present. It is all too easy to revert to the passive mantra "mistakes were made" to condemn historical forebears who did not have the vision or the capacity to see that their decisions might have long-term ramifications that would adversely affect the nation for subsequent generations. Slavery was and remains one of the central elements in our conflicted national history. We are all products of that history and we must all reckon with our past.

Entries

~ A ~

ABLEMAN V. BOOTH (1859)

Sherman M. Booth, the editor of a small antislavery newspaper, became the subject of several related legal cases resulting from the recapture (and subsequent escape) of a fugitive slave named Joshua Glover. The Supreme Court case (62 U.S. 506), decided in March 1859, followed in the wake of multiple cases flowing out of the conflict between the Wisconsin state courts and the federal courts, including *In re Booth,* 3 Wis. 1 (1854); *U.S. v. Rycraft,* 27 F. Cas. 918 (1854); *U.S. ex rel. Garland v. Morris,* 26 F. Cas. 1318 (1854); and *In re Booth and Rycraft,* 3 Wis 157 (1855).

Joshua Glover had fled his Missouri owner and resettled in Racine, Wisconsin. His owner, Benjamin Garland, found him in 1854 and tried to recapture him. Garland utilized the Fugitive Slave Law of 1850 to have a federal commissioner issue a warrant for Glover's arrest. When Glover was imprisoned, abolitionist forces surrounded the Milwaukee jail and clamored for his release. Racine's mayor issued a warrant for Garland's arrest for having kidnapped Glover. Meanwhile, a mob attacked the Milwaukee jail and freed Glover, who promptly fled to Canada. The supposed leaders of the mob, Booth and John Rycraft, were arrested and charged for their role in allegedly rescuing Glover.

As a result of differing attitudes toward runaway slaves, conflict between the Wisconsin state and U.S. federal courts was almost inevitable. Booth and Rycraft were convicted in federal trials for assisting a fugitive

slave but appealed to the state court for relief. The Wisconsin Supreme Court decided, in *In re Booth and Rycraft,* that the 1850 Fugitive Slave Law was unconstitutional, and ordered the release of Booth and Rycraft from jail. The state court's decision was appealed to the U.S. Supreme Court, which decided in *Ableman v. Booth* that federal courts could not be overruled by state courts: to do so "would subvert the very foundations of this Government." The case also upheld the constitutionality of the Fugitive Slave Law of 1850, which had been a portion of the Compromise of 1850, saying that, in Chief Justice Taney's words, "in all its provisions" the law was "fully authorized by the Constitution."

The Wisconsin court decision was part of a broader trend in which northern state courts obstructed the recapture of runaway slaves. Earlier cases, like *Prigg v. Pennsylvania* (1842), had relied on state-sponsored personal liberty laws, which placed stringent requirements on any person attempting to claim a fugitive slave. Combat between state and federal courts mirrored the increasing sectional tension felt in the late antebellum period. During the conflict, the Wisconsin Supreme Court went so far as to instruct its clerk not to send a copy of the *Ableman v. Booth* case to the U.S. Supreme Court, as had been requested after it pronounced the Fugitive Slave Act unconstitutional. Acts like this did much to damage relations between the North and the South in the period immediately preceding the Civil War. Only the Civil War resolved the differing interpretations between state and federal courts over the constitutionality of the Fugitive Slave Law of 1850.

— *Sally E. Hadden*

See also: Abolitionism in the United States; Compromise of 1850; *Dred Scott v. Sandford; Jones v. Van Zandt; Prigg v. Pennsylvania;* Taney, Roger B.; United States Constitution.

For Further Reading

Cover, Robert. 1975. *Justice Accused: Antislavery and the Judicial Process.* New Haven, CT: Yale University Press.

Finkelman, Paul. 1981. *An Imperfect Union: Slavery, Federalism, and Comity.* Chapel Hill: University of North Carolina Press.

Swisher, Carl. 1974. *History of the Supreme Court of the United States: The Taney Period, 1836–1864.* New York: Macmillan.

Taylor, Michael J. C. 2003. "'A More Perfect Union': *Ableman v. Booth* and the Culmination of Federal Sovereignty." *Journal of Supreme Court History* 28 (2): 101–116.

Wiecek, William E. 1978. "Slavery and Abolition before the United States Supreme Court, 1820–1860." *Journal of American History* 65: 34–59.

ABOLITIONISM IN THE UNITED STATES

The seeds of nineteenth-century abolitionism were planted in the eighteenth century, when the American Enlightenment intersected in time with the First Great Awakening (1720–1770). The first American Anti-Slavery Society was established in Pennsylvania in 1775, about the time that Lockean ideas were causing Englishmen in North America to identify their own status as one of "slavery." But if an ideological "window of opportunity" for abolishing slavery characterized the revolutionary era, it was never open very far or very long. By 1800, only New York, Pennsylvania, Massachusetts and a few other northern states had ended slavery, some gradually and via court opinions. State emancipation was unthinkable in the South, which rewarded black participation in the American Revolutionary War with promises of manumission (usually granted).

The problem with eighteenth-century abolitionism in the United States was less economic than ideological. A few patriots, such as Patrick Henry (who called plantation labor "inconvenient" without slavery) and Thomas Jefferson (who complained that debt prevented him from freeing his slaves), linked slavery's survival to financial factors. But even Jefferson expressed the kind of philosophical objections to the concept of an interracial nation that were widely shared in the North and South before the Civil War and that led to the most popular form of antislavery activity between 1800 and 1830: colonization. Jefferson wrote that blacks were equal in their capacity for moral sense but unequal in intelligence, creativity, courage, or imagination, and prone to insurrection with their justified (but dangerous) resentment.

Whether "north of slavery" or south, Americans believed that free blacks would have to be prepared for years before enjoying equality (if ever), and that segregation and disenfranchisement would have to be their lot for the foreseeable future. Colonization offered a way out of both slavery and inequality, and some of the nation's most renowned leaders (Henry Clay, John Marshall, James Madison, and Francis Scott Key) considered it to be the necessary precursor and handmaiden to abolition.

Historians have differed over the wellsprings of the militant, uncompromising, and urgent form of abolitionism that arose in America after 1830, associated with William Lloyd Garrison, editor of *The Liberator.* There is little doubt that Garrison's 1831 call for an immediate end to slavery (if necessary through violence and northern secession) reflected the confidence in human perfectibility redolent of nineteenth-century romanticism and the instrumentalist features of the Second Great Awakening (1790s–1830s). It is also possible that slavery offended northern Victorian feelings about hearth and home, especially after the most famous and popular antislavery polemic, Harriet B. Stowe's *Uncle Tom's Cabin* (1852), cast slavery as an assault on the integrity of the family.

But other candidates for the catalyst to militant antislavery have been proposed. According to David Donald in the 1950s, the abolitionists were financially strapped economic outsiders seeking material success from the launching pad of abolition. A generation later, Leonard Richards suggested that the abolitionists were upward bound in status and threatening to the best and the brightest of the local elites who led antiabolition mobs in opposition. More recently (2001), the argument has returned to religiosity and psychology as the motive. John Stauffer argues that abolition allowed some to construct a "performative self" as millennial outsider that belied their material success, a role that they wanted to fill as they waited for the Second Coming that they believed was at hand. Identifying with the outsider, white abolitionists argued that whites must adopt "black hearts" to gain the understanding that was a prerequisite for an interracial society.

The impact of the abolitionists on the coming of the Civil War can easily be exaggerated. Once *Uncle Tom's Cabin* moved the slavery issue to the center of the nation's political agenda, abolitionism began to recede as a potent political force. The antislavery movement was plagued by both a deep division within its ranks and an ugly racism, which kept surfacing as a divisive issue. In addition to Richards's antiabolition mobs, many northerners simply felt that the abolitionists' position was incompatible with the continuation of the Union and inconsistent with the Constitution. Abraham Lincoln and the Republicans certainly occupied this category.

In 1859 abolitionist John Brown attacked the federal arsenal at Harpers Ferry, Virginia, vowing to "purge" the nation's slavery "sins" in blood. Tied to the attack in leadership and financing, the abolitionists symbolically shared Brown's actual fate: they destroyed themselves as a force capable of accomplishing emancipation. The events at Harpers Ferry accelerated the slide toward war, but toward a war to destroy, or save, the Union—not to destroy slavery. The abolition movement contributed mightily to a sense of crisis that brought slavery to the forefront of the American people's attention. But when slavery was finally abolished, it was through the agency of the Civil War and the Thirteenth Amendment, not the abolitionist pen, press, or sword. Abolitionism could not write the coda to the Civil War era because it was too much a part of the painful story itself.

— *Richard A. Reiman*

See also: American Colonization Society; Brown, John; Garrison, William Lloyd; Harpers Ferry Raid.

For Further Reading

Donald, David, ed. 1956. *Lincoln Reconsidered: Essays on the Civil War Era.* New York: Alfred A. Knopf.

Filler, Louis. 1960. *The Crusade against Slavery.* New York: Harper.

McFeely, William. 1991. *Frederick Douglass.* New York. Simon and Schuster.

Perry, Lewis, and Michael Fellman, eds. 1979. *Antislavery Reconsidered: New Perspectives on the Abolitionists.* Baton Rouge: Louisiana State University Press.

Quarles, Benjamin. 1991. *Black Abolitionists.* New York: Da Capo Press.

Stauffer, John. 2001. *The Black Hearts of Men: Radical Abolitionists and the Transformation of Race.* Cambridge, MA: Harvard University Press.

JOHN QUINCY ADAMS (1767–1848)

The sixth president, son of the second president, and a statesman with a long and varied public service record, John Quincy Adams spent much of his postpresidential career opposing the institution of American slavery in numerous ways. As a congressman, he took a strong stance against the proslavery "gag rule," and as an attorney he argued for Africans' rights in the *Amistad* case before the Supreme Court.

Adams was president from 1825 to 1829, but the real beginning of his public antislavery efforts came after he lost his bid for reelection in 1828. All his life, Adams had

Ardently opposed to the institution of slavery, former president John Quincy Adams defended the *Amistad* captives by arguing their cause before the U.S. Supreme Court. (Library of Congress)

personally objected to slavery as immoral and repugnant to the republican tradition of America's founding, but he also realized that the issue was explosive enough to splinter the Union. In 1820, while serving as secretary of state, Adams watched apprehensively as Congress resolved the controversy surrounding Missouri's admission to the Union by dividing the United States into free and slaveholding territory. Privately, Adams remarked that "if the Union must be dissolved, Slavery is precisely the question upon which it ought to break" (Richards, 1986). Since he hoped to be president and knew that no candidate voicing such opinions could win election, Adams kept his convictions to himself until after his presidency. At that time, Adams did not retire quietly to his Massachusetts farm. Instead, he did what no other ex-president has done: he went to Congress in 1831 and represented the Plymouth, Massachusetts, district in the House of Representatives for the last seventeen years of his life. There Adams battled the notorious gag rule.

The gag rule was an attempt to silence one means of antislavery sentiment. It forbade the presentation of antislavery petitions, or written pleas for the demise of slavery signed by private citizens, to Congress. The antislavery petitioners were often women, free blacks, or even slaves, none of whom could vote; instead, they used petitions to participate in political life. Therefore, the gag rule not only stifled debate, but it barred segments of the American population from access to the political process and violated the First Amendment right to petition. On these grounds, Adams used his fabled eloquence and obstructionist tactics to attack the gag rule in the House of Representatives. Every week, he arrived at his desk with piles of antislavery petitions and rose to read them in spite of the insults, accusations, and censure to which other congressmen subjected him. Adams prevailed, and in 1844 the gag rule was revoked.

Adams further supported the antislavery cause by serving as counsel for the defense in the *Amistad* case (1841), a critical antebellum Supreme Court case. On June 28, 1839, the Spanish ship, the *Amistad,* sailed from Havana, Cuba, with a cargo of fifty-three Africans to be sold as slaves in Puerto Principe. Four nights later, the Africans freed themselves from their irons, mutinied, killed the ship's captain and cook, sent two crewmen overboard, and instructed two surviving crewmen to sail for Africa. The crewmen had other ideas, and the *Amistad* landed at Long Island, New York, on August 26. The Africans were jailed and charged with mutiny and murder. Meanwhile, the Spanish government claimed them as property and demanded their return. The case moved from district court to circuit court, arriving before the Supreme Court in late 1840. Antislavery advocates took an interest in the case and convinced Adams to defend the *Amistad* Africans. Adams hesitated, partly because he had not practiced law in years and partly because he was afraid his own heated emotions about the case would prevent him from carrying out the defense in a cool, rational manner. In his diary, Adams worried about how to "defeat and expose the abominable conspiracy" against *the Amistad* Africans, while simultaneously managing to "escape the imminent danger of . . . overheated zeal . . . and losing my self-possession" (Adams, 1874). Adams addressed the Court for over four hours on February 24, 1841, and again on March 1, presenting arguments that ranged from the minute wording of shipping laws to the ideals of the Declaration of Independence. On March 9, 1841, Chief Justice Roger B. Taney not only found the Africans innocent of murder and piracy, but he also ruled that they were free and should be allowed to

return to Africa. The Africans sailed for Sierra Leone in November 1841, to serve as missionaries.

With the *Amistad* case won, Adams devoted his efforts to his congressional duties, which he continued for the rest of his life. Adams was at his desk in the House of Representatives on February 21, 1848, when he suffered a stroke. He died two days later.

— *Chandra M. Manning*

See also: *Amistad* Case; Gag Resolution; Missouri Compromise; Taney, Roger B.

For Further Reading

Adams, Charles Francis. 1874. *Memoirs of John Quincy Adams Comprising Portions of His Diary from 1795 to 1848.* Philadelphia: Lippincott.

Cable, Mary. 1971. *Black Odyssey: The Case of the Slave Ship* Amistad. New York: Viking Press.

Miller, William Lee. 1996. *Arguing about Slavery: The Great Battle in the United States Congress.* New York: Alfred A. Knopf.

Remini, Robert V. 2002. *John Quincy Adams.* New York: Times Books.

Richards, Leonard L. 1986. *The Life and Times of Congressman John Quincy Adams.* New York: Oxford University Press.

AFRICAN BURIAL GROUND

The African Burial Ground, historically known as the Negro Burial Ground, is located in the Manhattan borough of New York City, New York. The burial ground was used primarily by the African population of colonial New York as a cemetery from approximately 1712 until 1795. It is estimated that some ten thousand to twenty thousand people were buried in this six-acre plot of land.

The African presence in New York was initiated in 1626 when the Dutch West Indies Company imported its first shipment of slaves, eleven men from today's Congo-Angola region of Africa, to New Amsterdam. By 1644, 40 percent of the colony's population consisted of enslaved Africans. In the mid-1770s New York had the second-highest number of enslaved Africans of any English colonial settlement and the highest ratio of slaves to Europeans of any northern settlement. Africans played a critical role in the foundation, building, and functioning of colonial New York.

New York City adopted a policy of mortuary segregation in November 1697, and thus blacks were forced to look for an alternative place rather than Lower Manhattan churchyards to bury their dead. An area of common land outside the city limits was chosen. The first known historical reference to Africans burying their dead in the common land is in a letter written by Chaplain John Sharpe in 1712. Soon after, the Negro Burial Ground began to appear on local maps and is referred to in contemporary land surveys.

In 1798 the African Methodist Episcopal Church was founded by Peter Williams, a black tobacconist and former sexton. African New York residents and their descendants now had a place to bury their dead on sacred soil. In the late eighteenth and early nineteenth centuries, the city's population growth led to a northward expansion, and the blocks overlying the burial ground were divided into lots for commercial and residential development. By the end of the nineteenth century, the burial ground was entirely paved or built over and all but forgotten, with the exception of notation in a few historical maps and documents.

In December 1990, the federal government purchased land from the city of New York to construct a thirty-four–story office tower. The environmental impact statement for the site identified the area as a section of the Negro Burial Ground. It was initially predicted that any archaeological remnants were destroyed by nineteenth- and twentieth-century construction. Archaeological testing began in May 1991 to determine if there were any remaining human burials. From September 1991 through July 1992, the remains of 419 individuals, approximately 93 percent African and 7 percent European and Native American, were excavated from a small section of the burial ground. This assemblage constitutes the earliest and largest collection of African American remains discovered during archaeological research to date.

Excavation of the site created an intersection of clashing philosophical, political, and ethical perspectives. A struggle ensued to determine whether the spiritual, historical, scientific, or business value of the property would be prioritized and who would control the destiny of the excavated remains and artifacts. An African-descendant community joined with politicians and other concerned citizens to gain control of the fate of the burial ground. Representatives teamed with scientists to create a research design. Four goals were outlined: origins of the population; physical quality of life; biological and cultural transition from African to African American identities, and modes of resistance (LaRoche and Blakey, 1997). Howard University scholars, directed by Dr. Michael Blakey, analyzed the physical remains.

Analysis of the physical remains revealed how socioeconomic conditions affected the health of the enslaved Africans and provided insight into their ethnic identities. Approximately 40 percent of the individuals excavated were children, many under two years old. Child and adult skeletons exhibited signs of malnutrition, disease, and hard labor. Arthritis, rickets, and anemia were common. Skull and spinal fractures and abnormalities from carrying heavy loads were also found. The children exhibited an abnormally high rate of birth defects (Mack and Hill, 1995). Dental problems, resulting from poor nutrition and a limited diet, were common. One female was found with a musket ball in her ribs, her death caused by the gunshot. One individual was recovered with an autopsied skull and may have been reinterred after an autopsy by local medical students who exhumed bodies from the burial ground for research in the late eighteenth century. As a whole, the physical remains point to physically demanding lives, poor nutrition, and premature deaths.

Many of the individuals were buried facing east, the direction of Africa and Mecca. Artifacts recovered from the burials were relatively few, probably reflecting the minimal economic standing of those who made use of the cemetery. Approximately five hundred sixty artifacts were found, consisting mostly of shroud pins. Artifacts consistent with traditional West African cultural practices, such as coins placed on eyelids, seashells to return the dead symbolically back across the seas, and glass beads were found in some burials. Some skeletons have filed teeth, which follows a contemporary coming-of-age ritual practiced in some West African cultures. In total, 155 beads were recovered at the burial ground. One adult female with glass and cowry waistbeads and a bracelet was found; dental modification suggests that she was probably born in Africa. A fired glass bead was found at another burial site; its discovery was highly significant because fired glass bead-making is an African tradition and the bead is one of very few artifacts excavated at a diasporal site that can be directly tied to Africa.

The African Burial Ground received National Historic Landmark status on April 19, 1993. The skeletons were reinterred on October 4, 2003. A memorial is located at the site.

— *Lori Lee*

See also: Arts and Crafts.

For Further Reading

Blakey, Michael. 1998. "The New York African Burial Ground Project: An Examination of Enslaved Lives, a

Construction of Ancestral Ties." *Transforming Anthropology* 7 (1): 53–58.

Hansen, Joyce, and Gary McGowan. 1998. *Breaking Ground, Breaking Silence*. New York: Henry Holt and Company.

Harrington, Spencer. 1993. "Bones and Bureaucrats: New York City's Great Cemetery Imbroglio." *Archaeology* (March/April): 28–38.

LaRoche, Cheryl, and Michael Blakey. 1997. "Seizing Intellectual Power: The Dialogue at the New York African Burial Ground." *Journal of Historical Archaeology* 31 (1): 85–96.

Mack, Mark E., and Cassandra Hill. 1995. "Pathologies Affecting Children in the African Burial Ground Population." *Newsletter of the African Burial Ground and Five Points Archaeological Projects* 1 (7): 4.

Pittman, Chandra. 1998. "If Bones Could Speak." *Transforming Anthropology* 7 (1): 59–63.

AFRICAN METHODIST EPISCOPAL CHURCH

The African Methodist Episcopal Church (AMEC) is the oldest black religious denomination in the United States. It includes more than eight thousand churches in twenty-nine countries, and its membership exceeds 3.5 million people. The AMEC dates from 1787 and grew out of the Free African Society, an altruistic self-help organization founded by Richard Allen and Absalom Jones. The history of the AMEC is testimony to the efforts of slaves in the United States to establish places of worship for themselves.

The African Methodist Episcopal (AME) Church became one of the most important social and cultural institutions within the free-black community in the United States, but its history also speaks of the virulent racism that often prevented white Christians from living their creed. In 1787 a small group of black Christians walked out of St. George Methodist Episcopal Church in Philadelphia, Pennsylvania, because newly imposed segregated practices forced blacks to sit in the balcony, away from white Christians. One November Sunday in 1787, Richard Allen and other black members of the congregation were being led to their segregated seats when the minister began praying. The group of blacks knelt to pray, but the usher tried to remove them from the area because it was reserved for whites. The indignant black people—Allen, Absalom Jones, Dorus Ginnings, William White, as well as Jane Ann Murray and Sarah Dougherty—walked out of the unwelcoming church.

After leaving the sanctuary of St. George Methodist Episcopal Church, Richard Allen and his associates formed the Free African Society, "a mutual-aid association with a participatory decision-making process [where] voting was the mechanism for making decisions" (Dodson, 2002). The society served as a catalyst for, but not as an example of, the church that would follow because the society was egalitarian, with women as voting and dues-paying members. Meetings were held at Dougherty's home. However, the men adopted the European American Methodist polity for the church, and this structure disempowered women.

In 1787 Allen purchased a plot of land from Mark Wilcox, a transaction that marks the oldest parcel of real estate owned continuously by black people in the United States. Future church buildings would be erected on this location at Sixth Street and Lombard. Allen also purchased an abandoned blacksmith shop for $35 from a man named Sims and hauled it with a team of six horses to the newly acquired lot. By 1794, the former slave Richard Allen had founded his own church, Bethel AME Church in Philadelphia. Born a slave in 1760 in that same city, he was owned by Benjamin Chews, chief justice of the Commonwealth of Pennsylvania, a Quaker lawyer who later sold Allen to a man named Stokley Sturgis in Dover, Delaware. Richard Allen purchased his own freedom in 1780 for two-thousand dollars, became a traveling preacher, returned to Philadelphia, and joined St. George's, where he was often permitted to preach an early morning service.

Paternalistic meddling in Bethel Church's affairs by the leaders of St. George, who apparently saw their church as the mother church, soon ended when Richard Allen solicited the help of Dr. Benjamin Rush, Robert Ralston, and attorney David Brown to secure a charter for him and his congregation. The request required a special act of the Commonwealth of Pennsylvania's legislature to obtain such a charter, but in 1796 Bethel became an independent organization and adopted the name African Methodist Episcopal Church. The congregation used the small church renovated from the blacksmith shop for eleven years until 1805 when a second church was erected. This new church was the site of the first AME convention held in April 1816. During this meeting, on April 11, 1816, Allen was ordained a bishop by his old friend Absalom Jones, now a priest in the Protestant Episcopal Church.

Bethel AME Church was the only institution for black Methodists in America until 1816. The example set by Allen and his congregation encouraged other black people who were insulted and rejected by white Christians, and in 1816 these groups began to withdraw from other Methodist Episcopal churches. The question of a separate independent church was the topic at the April 1816 convention, and those attending resolved that black people wanting to unite with the African Methodists could do so regardless of their location. They would become one body known as the African Methodist Episcopal Church.

The AME Church's constitution and bylaws have not always reflected the egalitarian principles on which it was founded. In 1809 the first woman to request a license to preach, Mrs. Jarena Lee, brought her petition to the mother church in Philadelphia. She was denied a license but returned in 1817, and received approval to carry on her activities but without formal recognition. She was free to hold prayer meetings. Women did not stop petitioning for equity. The question of licensing women to preach came before the 1844 Conference and again in 1848, 1852, 1864, 1868, 1874, 1888, 1893, 1896, and 1900. Each petition was denied; however, the churchmen recognized the power women, who constituted the majority of the congregations and provided invaluable services, represented. Thus they created stewardess positions in 1868 and posts for female evangelists in 1888, and authorized the Women's Missionary Mite Society in 1874. The male hierarchy refused to relinquish its power for as long as possible without losing the women's support. The tenacity of the women members forced amendments to the church structure. On March 5, 1953, the official name of the first church became Mother Bethel, and women were permitted to participate in the business of the corporation. On April 8, 1957, Mrs. Willie V. Simpkins was elected to the board of trustees, and on July 11, 2000, the election of the first woman, Vashti Murphy McKenzie, as AME bishop took place.

From its beginnings, the AMEC and its congregations worked for the freedom of African American slaves. During slavery in the United States, the AMEC was a voice for abolition, and Bethel became a waystation on the Underground Railroad, a covert network that helped slaves escape from the South. Bethel AME Church's basement sheltered many runaway slaves, and the congregation collected large sums of money to feed and clothe those seeking freedom. Prominent abolitionists, including Frederick Douglass and Lucretia Mott, denounced slavery from the church's pulpit.

Today the AMEC thrives, employing ninety people at its national headquarters in Washington, D.C., and managing a budget in excess of $5.8 million. A large portion of the budget goes toward education. The AMEC stood at the forefront of providing education to former slaves, establishing Wilberforce University, the first black private college in the United States in 1856, in Ohio; Edward Waters College (1866) in Jack-sonville, Florida; Allen University (1870) in Columbia, South Carolina; Paul-Quinn College (1872) in Waco, Texas; Morris Brown College (1881) in Atlanta, Georgia; Shorter College (1886) in North Little Rock, Arkansas; Western University (1881–1948) in Quindaro, Kansas; and Payne Theological Seminary (1884) in Wilberforce, Ohio. The AME Church's role in the fight against slavery and in the effort to educate and raise the status of former slaves is perhaps surpassed only by the American Missionary Association, a group with which AMEC worked closely.

— *Nagueyalti Warren*

See also: Abolitionism in the United States; Allen, Richard; American Missionary Association; Underground Railroad.

For Further Reading

Allen, Richard. 1983. *The Experience and Gospel Labors of the Right Reverend Richard Allen Written by Himself.* Ed. George Singleton. Nashville, TN: Abingdon.

Dodson, Howard. 2002. *Jubilee: The Emergence of African-American Culture.* Washington, DC: National Geographic.

George, Carol V. R. 1973. *Segregated Sabbaths: Richard Allen and the Emergence of Independent Black Churches 1760–1840.* New York: Oxford University Press.

Little, Lawrence S. 2000. *Disciples of Liberty: The African Methodist Episcopal Church in the Age of Imperialism, 1884–1916.* Knoxville: University of Tennessee Press.

Payne, Daniel Alexander. 1891. *History of the African Methodist Episcopal Church.* Nashville, TN: Publishing House of the AME Sunday School Union.

ALABAMA PLATFORM

The Alabama Platform, an important statement of the southern perspective on slavery in the territories, was first presented to the Alabama Democratic Party Convention in 1848. Facing attacks on the institution of slavery in the form of the Wilmot Proviso and the idea of popular sovereignty, Alabama Democrats set forth the southern view of the sanctity of slave property under the U.S. Constitution.

In an impassioned speech to the assembled delegates, Williams Lowndes Yancey outlined the principles of the Alabama Platform, in which he argued that no territory that outlawed slavery could prevent citizens from the slave states from settling with property, including slaves (Potter, 1976). Furthermore, Yancey believed that Congress had a constitutional responsibility to protect the property of slaveowners nationwide. Therefore, "territory acquired by common suffering, blood, and toil" could not be restricted by either Congress or territorial legislatures (Potter, 1976). If the national Democratic Party Convention did not support these principles, Yancey called for Alabama delegates to leave the convention. The platform gained wide support across the South, was officially supported by the Democratic conventions of Florida and Virginia, and was sanctioned by the Georgia and Alabama legislatures.

Sectional tensions were high at the Democratic Convention in Baltimore, and the party adopted a platform that did not directly address slavery. Yancey interpreted this silence to mean that party leaders were not concerned about southern interests. The convention also nominated Michigan Senator Lewis Cass, one of the foremost advocates of popular sovereignty, for the presidency. When that occurred, Yancey left the convention, but the remainder of the Alabama delegation remained, in defiance of its instructions.

At the 1860 Democratic Convention in Charleston, South Carolina, the Alabama Platform again contributed to internal party debates on the future of slavery. Again, Alabama Democrats, as well as those from the other Lower South states, had been instructed to leave the convention if a plank safeguarding slavery and slave property were not adopted in the platform. When the convention adopted a platform without such a provision, delegates from Alabama, Texas, Florida, Louisiana, Mississippi, Arkansas, Georgia, and South Carolina left in protest. In a subsequent convention, the southern wing of the party united behind John C. Breckinridge of Kentucky. Adherence to the Alabama Platform in 1860 split the Democratic Party and served as a warning to the nation that secession over the issue of slavery was imminent.

— *Richard D. Starnes*

See also: Popular Sovereignty; Wilmot Proviso; Yancey, William Lowndes.

For Further Reading
  Freehling, William. 1990. *The Road to Disunion.* New York: Harper and Row.
  Potter, David. 1976. *The Impending Crisis, 1848–1861.* New York: Harper and Row.

RICHARD ALLEN (1760–1831)

Born a slave in Philadelphia, Pennsylvania, Richard Allen grew up during the American Revolutionary War era. This period was directly influenced by philosophies promoting citizen's rights, religious freedom, and a burgeoning antislavery movement. After purchasing his freedom, Allen worked as a preacher, in addition to being a business and community leader. Ultimately he became founder, minister, and first bishop of the African Methodist Episcopal (AME) Church. Allen dedicated his life to the support of civil rights, racial equality, and the economic freedom of black people.

Richard Allen was born on February 14, 1760. His mother, father, and three siblings were owned by a Philadelphia lawyer named Benjamin Chew. In 1768 Chew sold the family to Stokely Sturgis, a plantation owner and farmer in Delaware. At the age of seventeen Allen and his brother, with the permission of Sturgis, began to attend Methodist meetings, leading Allen to join the Methodist Society and formally convert to Methodism in 1777.

At the society, Allen learned to read and write. He also began to preach at the society meetings. Other slaveowners feared that these assemblies where slaves embraced religion would make them less willing servants. Therefore Allen and his brother worked to ensure that their work in the fields was completed without interruption. Although Sturgis sold and divided his family at this time, he soon allowed Allen to hold Methodist meetings at his home. Influenced by these meetings, Sturgis also converted to Methodism in 1780, and he soon declared a moral opposition to owning slaves. He then offered Allen and his brother the chance to purchase their freedom for $2,000. They worked approximately five years as bricklayers, woodcutters, and wagon drivers to raise the money.

As he worked to pay for his freedom, Allen began a spiritual sojourn as an itinerant preacher, and he addressed black and white congregations at Methodist churches in Delaware, Pennsylvania, and Maryland. Although he lacked a formal education, he worked diligently to acquire and refine the social skills that would help him to solidify his leadership attributes.

In 1786, at the request of the white Methodist ministry, Allen accepted an invitation to preach at St. George's Church to a mixed-race congregation in Philadelphia. He quickly increased the church's black membership, resulting in the church elders agreeing to erect a balcony in the sanctuary. They also chose to limit the number of services that blacks could attend, and insisted that they be segregated to the balcony seating area. When Allen approached the elders about establishing a separate church for the black congregants, they opposed the idea.

On April 12, 1787, Allen and the Reverend Absalom Jones founded the Free African Society, a nondenominational association dedicated to the abolition of slavery and racial hatred. Allen's commitment to the prin-

Richard Allen with other early leaders of the African Methodist Episcopal (AME) Church.
(Library of Congress)

ciples of Methodism led him to eventually leave the society. During a service at St. George's, Reverend Jones decided to challenge the segregated seating plan by occupying the front of the church. In the middle of prayer the elders asked Jones to return to the balcony. Allen and the other members who were already seated in the balcony then left St. George's in unison.

The movement for a separate and independent black church was gaining momentum. In 1794 the Free African Society founded the African Church of Philadelphia. As a result of the treatment of blacks at the Methodist church, this group became part of the Protestant Episcopal Church. On July 29, 1794, a blacksmith shop owned by Allen in Philadelphia was officially dedicated as Bethel African Church (also called Mother Bethel). It is the oldest piece of land in the United States continuously owned by blacks.

Allen was soon named Bethel's deacon, and he began a fight with white Methodist leaders who tried to take control of the church. In 1807 the Pennsylvania Supreme Court ruled that since the congregation owned the land on which they worshiped, they had

the authority to decide who preached there. This ruling led to the formation of many African Methodist churches in the northeastern United States. The court granted Bethel independent status on January 1, 1816. At the convention of sixteen independent congregations later that year in Philadelphia, these churches united under the name African Methodist Episcopal (AME) Church. They now gained autonomy from white Methodist doctrines and jurisdiction. Allen was ordained an elder and became the first bishop of the new denomination on April 11, 1816.

Allen and the AME Church have played a crucial role in black history. The first members were poor people, and many were not able to read or write. Allen started night school classes in order to educate the local membership. The fundamentals of the African Society for the Education of Youth program that he founded and created still resonate today with the AME Church's operation of several colleges and universities throughout this country.

Frederick Douglass spoke against slavery from Bethel's pulpit. It also served as a stop on the Underground Railroad, providing comfort and shelter to fugitive slaves. Allen used his position to publish articles and deliver sermons against slavery, racism, and oppression. Other religious groups have historical origins related to ideological or theological ideals, but the AME Church was founded on the principles of nondiscrimination, social justice, and economic development for blacks in the United States.

The AME Church migrated to Haiti and Canada by 1830. Today membership is estimated at 1.2 million persons, with thousands of congregations in twenty-nine countries worldwide. Richard Allen remained pastor and bishop of Bethel AME Church until his death on March 26, 1831.

— *Anthony Todman*

See also: Absalom; African Methodist Episcopal Church; Underground Railroad.

For Further Reading

Barringer, James G. 1987. "The African Methodist Church: 200 Years of Service to the Community." *Crisis* 94 (June/July): 40–43.

Conyers, James L., Jr. 2000. *Richard Allen: An Apostle of Freedom.* Lawrenceville, NJ: Africa World Press.

Murphy, Larry, J. Gordon Melton, and Gary L. Ward, eds. 1993. *Encyclopedia of African-American Religions.* New York: Garland.

Nash, Gary B. 1989. "New Light on Richard Allen: The Early Years of Freedom." *William and Mary Quarterly* 46 (2): 332–340.

Salzman, Jack, David Lionel Smith, and Cornel West, eds. 1996. *Encyclopedia of African-American Culture and History.* New York: Macmillan Library Reference.

ALTON (ILLINOIS) *OBSERVER*

The Alton *Observer* was one of the most famous antislavery newspapers published in the Midwest, and its association with martyred publisher Elijah Parish Lovejoy (1802–1837) made the publication symbolic of freedom of the press in American life. Lovejoy published the *Observer* in Alton, a river town in Madison County, Illinois, from July 1836 until his death at the hands of an antiabolition mob in November 1837.

Before he moved his press to Alton, Lovejoy published the *Observer* in St. Louis, Missouri. The first edition appeared on November 21, 1833, to mixed reviews. As a Presbyterian minister turned editor, Lovejoy focused largely on religious themes in his newspaper, and the early issues of his weekly paper displayed a decidedly anti-Catholic bias. The focus of the *Observer*

shifted as did the editor's interests, and by 1835 it was clear that Lovejoy's publication had taken a strong antislavery stance.

The Midwest was certainly not a bastion of abolition sympathy in the 1830s, and operating an antislavery press in Missouri, a slave state, was a risky venture. Even though the mercantile and urbane interests of St. Louis proper did not rely solely on slavery, there were critics within the city who found Lovejoy's publications to be at odds with the community's standards. When Lovejoy took a two-week break from his duties to attend to business outside of St. Louis, the assistant editor of the *Observer* noted in the October 8, 1835, issue that the publication would not publish antislavery materials while Lovejoy was away.

Lovejoy was not unaware of the antipathy the *Observer* faced in St. Louis, but he believed that the larger principle of freedom of the press stood in the balance if he allowed himself to be silenced by the antiabolition mobs. In an editorial published on November 5, 1835, he wrote, "The truth is, my fellow-citizens, if we give ground a single inch, there is no stopping place. I deem it, therefore, my duty to stand upon the Constitution."

Lovejoy used the pages of the *Observer* to respond to his critics in St. Louis, but the growing litany of antiabolition sentiment convinced the editor that neither his publication nor his family was safe in Missouri. On July 21, 1836, Lovejoy announced his intention to move the *Observer* to Alton, Illinois, where he would continue the publication of the antislavery newspaper from the safe confines of a free state. Although Illinois was a free state, the southern portion of the state did contain a substantial number of proslavery sympathizers.

Despite the critics, the *Observer* did boast a significant number of subscribers in both Missouri and Illinois. By September 1837, Lovejoy claimed that more than twenty-one hundred subscribers received his weekly newspaper. Lovejoy believed that the community of Alton, which contained many pioneer settlers who had New England roots, would be a more supportive community from which one might openly espouse antislavery sympathies.

The move from St. Louis to Alton did not completely alleviate the problems that Lovejoy had faced from antiabolition critics. Essentially he had moved his press across the Mississippi River, but only about 30 miles upstream from St. Louis. The enemies that Lovejoy had accumulated during his time in St. Louis were still close enough to harass his press once it relocated to Alton, Illinois.

Lovejoy's press was destroyed on three occasions by antiabolition mobs that wanted to silence any criticism of slavery, but with the help of the Ohio Anti-Slavery Society, Lovejoy was able to replace each destroyed press with a new one. He vowed that he would not be silenced. In addition, Lovejoy's views as an abolitionist grew bolder. On July 6, 1837, he wrote an editorial calling for a statewide meeting to form the Illinois State Anti-Slavery Society, and by October 26 such an organization had been formed at a meeting held in Alton. This action proved to be too much for Lovejoy's critics.

Elijah Parish Lovejoy was murdered in Alton, Illinois, on November 7, 1837, as he defended the arrival of his fourth press. An armed mob stormed the warehouse where Lovejoy and about twenty supporters had gathered to defend the new press from the enemies who had vowed to destroy it.

After Lovejoy's death, the Alton *Observer* was published from December 28, 1837, to April 19, 1838, in Cincinnati, Ohio. The newspaper was edited by E. W. Chester, who also published the *Cincinnati Journal.*

— *Junius P. Rodriguez*

See also: Antiabolition Riots; Lovejoy, Elijah P.

For Further Reading

Beecher, Edward. 1965. *Narrative of the Riots at Alton.* New York: E. P. Dutton.

Mabee, Carlton. 1970. *Black Freedom: The Nonviolent Abolitionists from 1830 through the Civil War.* London: Macmillan.

Merideth, Robert. 1964. "A Conservative Abolitionist at Alton: Edward Beecher's *Narrative.*" *Journal of Presbyterian History* 42 (March and June): 39–53, 92–103.

Richards, Leonard L. 1975. *Gentlemen of Property and Standing: Anti-Abolition Mobs in Jacksonian America.* New York: Oxford University Press.

AMERICAN ANTI-SLAVERY SOCIETY

The American Anti-Slavery Society became the single largest and most influential organization against slavery up to the end of the Civil War. Arguing that slavery was a sin of national proportions, not just a southern one, the society drew support from a range of racial, social, and economic backgrounds and produced millions of newspapers, pamphlets, and books as part of its effort to abolish slavery. In addition to drawing heavily from interdenominational developments within the evangelical movement, the society published *The Emancipator* and the *National Anti-Slavery Standard.* It also had former slaves such as Frederick Douglass give speeches in an attempt to expose the wrongs of slavery.

Begun in Philadelphia on December 4, 1833, at a three-day organizational meeting, the American Anti-Slavery Society was a diverse, national organization that brought together sixty-three delegates from ten states and was exclusively devoted to promoting immediate emancipation. Led by William Lloyd Garrison, the meeting joined New Englanders such as John Greenleaf Whittier with financially successful, conservative abolitionists such as Arthur and Lewis Tappan and William Jay, men who were not necessarily in complete agreement with Garrison's notion of "immediatism" but who nevertheless joined its ranks. The society also included twenty-one Quakers, four women, and three black participants—James G. Barbadoes of Boston, Robert Purvis, and James McCrummell of Philadelphia. Although these three participants were involved in the proceedings and later signed various documents relating to the society's purpose and organization, they were not considered delegates.

The delegates to the Philadelphia conference opposed the colonization movement, which aimed at relocating blacks to Liberia, and denounced gradual antislavery movements as false or ineffective. As stated in the Constitution it drafted in Philadelphia, the primary object of the society was "the entire abolition of slavery in the United States" (AASS, 1833). Although the society recognized state's rights to legislate in regard to abolition, it nevertheless sought to effect the "immediate abandonment" of the practice and to influence Congress in constitutionally appropriate ways. In its "Declaration of Sentiments," delivered to the public on December 6, 1833, members of the society outlined the principles that informed the group's efforts to emancipate "one-sixth part of our countrymen" (AASS, 1833). As part of its moral and political imperatives, the society proposed organizing antislavery groups, sending forth individuals to raise the voice of "warning and rebuke," circulating "anti-slavery tracts and periodicals," and enlisting "the pulpit and the press in the cause of suffering and the dumb" (AASS, 1833). Although the document did not call for complete social equality, it declared that "all persons of color" should have the same "privileges" as whites (AASS, 1833). It also revealed the depths of Garrison's pacifism and his dislike for political abolitionism. The following year, at the society's annual convention in New York, Robert Purvis and eight fellow black abolitionists were elected to the Board of Managers, making up about 10 percent of its membership. Even though similar participation occurred in 1835, fewer blacks were appointed to leadership positions after 1837 because of efforts to streamline the society. During the rest of the decade, black attendance at the society's annual meetings was minimal.

Despite repeated acts of violence against supporters like Lewis Tappan, whose house in New York was vandalized, an indication that antislavery agitation had become more acceptable in American society was the decision by Reverend William Ellery Channing, a leader in the Unitarian Church, to publish *Slavery* (1835). His willingness to denounce the evils of slavery legitimized, especially for northerners, antislavery arguments and appeals. Indeed, such was the acceptance of antislavery sentiment that by 1838, the American Anti-Slavery Society had 1,350 affiliated societies throughout the states and a membership of about two-hundred-fifty-thousand. This was a clear signal that the antislavery movement in America had become more mainstream. Yet despite this increase in its ranks, there was also growing disagreement. Ideological controversy heated up between Garrison and his followers and less radical abolitionists like the Tappans and the Reverend William Goodell, who could not support the Garrisonians' statements that the clergy were proslavery.

The growing rift between Garrison and more conservative members of the society such as the Tappans became particularly evident at the New England Anti-Slavery Convention, which met in May 1838. Here, the "woman question" divided the abolitionist movement. Garrison's backing of Angelina and Sarah Moore Grimké, southern women who testified against the institution of slavery, reached a turning point at the annual meeting of the American Anti-Slavery Society in New York in 1840, when those aligned with Garrison nominated Abby Kelley for a position on the executive committee. Upset by the manner in which Garrison allowed his sympathies for women's rights to influence his politics and policymaking concerning abolition, a large contingent of the society (approximately three hundred people), led by Arthur and Lewis Tappan, Henry B. Stanton, and others, walked out of the convention and set up the short-lived American and Foreign Anti-Slavery Society. They later threw their support to the Liberty Party, which many consider the first political party based on antislavery.

Continued debate over the antislavery nature of the U.S. Constitution and dissent during the late 1840s and 1850s between Gerrit Smith, Lysander Spooner, and the Tappans, in one camp, and Garrison, in the other, prevented unity even as the Fugitive Slave Act (1850) was considered. Financial problems and dwindling numbers also hurt the society's cause. Black abolitionists criticized the actions of white abolitionists, who wrangled over nonresistance and other esoteric antislavery theories. Also, because black leaders continued to be marginalized in regard to leadership positions, many moved to rival societies, joined black-sponsored associations, or simply worked on their own. Douglass, for example, eventually went his own way, founding the *North Star* and, much to Garrison's dissatisfaction, embracing the political ideas of abolitionists from western New York. In a 1851 meeting of the American Anti-Slavery Society, Douglass shared his new views, which later prompted Garrison to denounce Douglass as "destitute of every principle of honor, ungrateful to the last degree and malevolent in spirit" (Garrison, 1851).

The American Anti-Slavery Society lasted through the Civil War, but even after the enactment of the Thirteenth Amendment, when Garrison's supporters attempted to discontinue the society, Wendell Phillips and others argued for keeping it so as to preserve black rights and freedom. In 1869, after Congress proposed the Fifteenth Amendment and submitted it to states for ratification, the society resolved at its annual meeting in May that in giving blacks the vote, the amendment represented "the capstone and completion of our movement; the fulfillment of our pledge to the Negro race" (AASS, 1870). The ratification process was completed in March 1870, and in April that same year the American Anti-Slavery Society held its last meeting, a move that other smaller societies quickly followed.

— *Mark L. Kamrath*

See also: Douglass, Frederick; Fugitive Slave Act (1850); Garrison, William Lloyd; Grimké, Angelina; Grimké, Sarah Moore.

For Further Reading

American Anti-Slavery Society. 1838. *The Constitution of the American Anti-Slavery Society.* New York: American Anti-Slavery Society.

American Anti-Slavery Society. 1870. *National Anti-Slavery Standard*, April 16.

Barnes, Gilbert Hobbs. 1933. *The Anti-Slavery Impulse, 1830–1844.* New York: Harcourt Brace.

Bracey, John H., August Meier, and Elliott Rudwick, eds. 1971. *Blacks in the Abolitionist Movement.* Belmont, CA: Wadsworth Publishing.

Brown, Ira V. "Pennsylvania, 'Immediate Emancipation,' and the Birth of the American Antislavery Society," *Pennsylvania History* 54 (1987) 54: 163–178.

Dumond, Dwight Lowell. 1961. *Antislavery: The Crusade for Freedom in America.* Ann Arbor: University of Michigan Press.

Friedman, Lawrence J. 1982. *Gregarious Saints: Self and Community in American Abolitionism, 1830–1870.* New York: Cambridge University Press.

Perry, Lewis. 1995. *Radical Abolitionism: Anarchy and the Government of God in Antislavery Thought.* Knoxville: University of Tennessee Press.

Indigenous village in Liberia established by the American Colonization Society, c. 1822. (Library of Congress)

AMERICAN COLONIZATION SOCIETY

During the nineteenth century, the American Colonization Society (ACS) was the principal institution promoting the resettlement of black Americans to Africa as a solution to problems associated with slavery and race in the United States. The idea of colonization dated from the late eighteenth-century work of Virginians like Thomas Jefferson, James Madison, and James Monroe. The British provided an early model for the ACS by establishing a refuge in Sierra Leone for poor blacks from London's slums in the 1780s. In the United States, Robert Finley, Ralph R. Gurley, Francis Scott Key, and Charles Fenton Mercer were especially important in promoting colonization.

The ACS was founded in 1816, and in 1822 the organization established the West African settlement of Liberia to receive colonists. By 1899 the ACS had settled 15,386 colonists in Liberia, a tiny portion of the African American population in the United States. Life initially was precarious in the colony, and before 1842, 41.3 percent of the colonists died within six years of settling there. Those who survived domi-

nated the surrounding Africans, and Liberia experienced long-standing class tensions between the descendants of the colonists and the original inhabitants of Liberia. The ACS played a significant role in governing the colony until 1847, when Liberia became an independent nation.

The society drew support from groups with remarkably diverse motives, and to prevent controversy among potential supporters, the ACS avoided the issue of slavery. The ACS officially endorsed only the idea of resettling free blacks, not slaves, in Africa. Despite the caution of the society's program, some opponents of slavery hoped the ACS would encourage the emancipation of slaves.

Several abolitionist leaders, including Arthur and Lewis Tappan, James G. Birney, and Gerrit Smith, were initially prominent colonizationists. They believed that slaveholders would gladly emancipate their slaves if offered a plan for freeing their slaves without increasing the number of free blacks in America. Indeed, just over half of the African Americans colonized by the ACS before the Emancipation Proclamation of 1863 were slaves freed specifically for the purpose of colonization. The remainder of the colonists were free people. Ironically, many Southern colonizationists saw the ACS as a means for making slavery more secure, and they believed the colonization of free blacks would remove people who allegedly corrupted the morals of slaves and encouraged them to escape.

Many of the colonizationists, regardless of their views on slavery, believed that removing free blacks would promote national progress and safety. Because free blacks were denied equality with whites, it was claimed that free blacks lacked ambition, a work ethic, and other inducements to good behavior. They seethed with anger regarding their oppressed condition and posed an internal threat to the United States. Some colonizationists argued that removing free blacks to Africa would remove them from the ill effects of white prejudice. Blacks would be placed in an environment where they could exercise their talents and abilities, and some colonizationists hoped that blacks from the United States would plant Christianity in Africa.

Given the large diversity of motives for supporting colonization, it was a popular solution to racial problems in the United States. The ACS was endorsed by the U.S. Congress and a dozen state legislatures, several of which joined Congress in funding the ACS. Even bitter political enemies like Andrew Jackson and Henry Clay united to support the ACS.

So great was the popularity of colonization during the 1810s–1820s that the ACS faced competition from rival colonization plans. Charging that the great distance to Africa made Liberian colonization expensive and impractical, critics sought a closer location for black resettlement—perhaps Central America, the island of Haiti, or even the western territories of the United States. The leadership of the ACS, however, insisted that African Americans should be resettled in Africa, where their American education, democratic ideals, and Christian religion would transform the continent, thereby repairing some of the damage done to Africa by the slave trade.

Ironically, the Americans who most strongly objected to colonization were African Americans themselves. Even slaves who were offered freedom in exchange for colonization sometimes refused the offer. Seeing through the prejudice that undergirded the ACS, blacks were skeptical of the claims that colonization would improve their condition and were reluctant to leave their families and homes. The ACS typically had more funds available to send out colonists than they had persons willing to be colonized.

Some African Americans did believe that colonization provided a means of escaping prejudice and white domination. Shortly before the founding of the ACS, a black merchant and sea captain, Paul Cuffee, took a group of blacks to Africa. Alexander Crummell, Daniel Coker, Lott Cary, and Colin Teague were prominent blacks who migrated to Liberia as missionaries. Martin R. Delany, Henry Highland Garnet, and Lewis Woodson promoted emigration as a way for African Americans to assert control over their lives. Black colonizationists often had ambivalent attitudes toward the ACS. They were wary of its motives and suspicious of its control but jealous of its resources.

Support for the ACS peaked about 1832, when the society sent 796 emigrants to Liberia and there were 302 local and state branches of the ACS. After that year, the ACS faced serious defections. Repelled by racial prejudice and proslavery attitudes within the ACS, many former supporters of the society became abolitionists, favoring immediate emancipation without colonization. Their actions were galvanized by the pamphlet *Thoughts on African Colonization* (1832) written by the former colonizationist William Lloyd Garrison. In response, many proslavery colonizationists withdrew their support from the ACS as they became suspicious of a society that was the breeding ground for abolitionism.

During the financial panic of 1837, contributions to the ACS dried up and Americans took a critical look at the society's record. The ACS's plan seemed overly complex, expensive, and impractical, since comparatively few blacks had been settled in Liberia. The ACS subsequently experienced two brief periods of revival. Amid the increasingly virulent racism of the 1850s and the growing movement in both northern and southern states to expel free blacks from their boundaries, some white Americans took a renewed interest in colonization as a method of black removal. Following the Civil War and the abolition of slavery, some white Americans likewise hoped colonization might relieve the nation of the difficult transition from slave to free labor. The ACS experienced its greatest success in sending out emigrants during the years 1848–1857 and 1865–1872—more than half of the colonists sponsored by the ACS emigrated during these seventeen years—but the ACS never recovered the high levels of popularity and political influence it had enjoyed in the 1810s–1820s.

The ACS continued to function until 1963, but lacking public support, it worked mostly to promote Liberian and African American educational causes. When the society disbanded, its remaining funds went to the Phelps-Stokes Fund to help support African and African American education.

— *Harold D. Tallant*

See also: Delany, Martin R.; Garrison, William Lloyd; Liberia.

For Further Reading

Campbell, Penelope. 1971. *Maryland in Africa: The Maryland State Colonization Society 1831–1857.* Urbana: University of Illinois Press.

Frehling, William W. 1994. *The Reintegration of American History: Slavery and the Civil War.* New York: Oxford University Press.

Miller, Floyd J. 1975. *The Search for a Black Nationality: Black Colonization and Emigration, 1787–1863.* Urbana: University of Illinois Press.

Shick, Tom W. 1971. "A Quantitative Analysis of Liberian Colonization from 1820 to 1843 with Special Reference to Mortality." *Journal of African History* 12: 45–59.

Staudenraus, Philip J. 1961. *The African Colonization Movement, 1816–1865.* New York: Columbia University Press.

Tallant, Harold D. 2003. *Evil Necessity: Slavery and Political Culture in Antebellum Kentucky.* Lexington: University Press of Kentucky.

AMERICAN FREEDMEN'S INQUIRY COMMISSION

The American Freedmen's Inquiry Commission was one of the first federal investigations of its kind. Reports and recommendations generated by this commission led to the creation of the Freedmen's Bureau in 1865, the first federal agency entrusted with a social responsibility, granting citizenship to 4 million ex-slaves in the South.

Created by the War Department in 1863, the American Freedmen's Inquiry Commission was charged with assessing the condition of slaves in the South. Three abolitionists, Samuel Gridley Howe, James McKaye, and Robert Owens, were chosen. They spent several months listening to testimony from blacks and whites, traveling through the South, and investigating the conditions of slaves before issuing several findings.

Commission members wrote two lengthy reports, and Owens and McKaye published findings on the condition of ex-slaves who had migrated to Canada. Through their investigations, commission members found blacks in desperate if not destitute condition. Slaves often told of harsh treatment, separation from family and kin, and a lack of food, clothing, and shelter as well as medical care.

These and other details by commission members reflected their strong desire for federal intervention. They were, however, challenged by those who did not

see a need for federal assistance to slaves and later ex-slaves. Proponents and opponents of federal aid to blacks debated throughout the period between 1863 and 1864. Commission members suggested that without help, thousands of slaves would likely die. Federal guardianship, they argued, would ensure that blacks might survive the coming winter. In addition to social and political equality, McKaye, perhaps the most radical commission member, pressed for the redistribution of land to blacks. Commission members also supported limited federal aid.

In its final report, the American Freedmen's Inquiry Commission recommended to Congress that it create a Bureau of Emancipation to take control of helpless blacks in the South. Between 1863 and 1865, Congress argued their findings. Generally, Republicans in Congress supported the agency, while southern Democrats were strongly opposed to any such assistance, especially from the federal government. On March 3, 1865, Congress created the Bureau of Refugees, Freedmen, and Abandoned Lands, commonly known as the Freedmen's Bureau. This agency, in existence for nearly twelve years, did much to integrate ex-slaves into American society.

The tireless work of Howe, Owens, and McKaye finally gained fruition when Congress split over not only the very existence of the Freedmen's Bureau but also the severity of conditions indicated by commission members. Upon reading these reports, many congressmen and others could not imagine the degree of misery and deprivation experienced by some 4 million blacks in the South. Some even questioned the veracity of the findings, doubting that such conditions could exist in the United States.

Perhaps the first of its kind, the American Freedmen's Inquiry Commission left an indelible mark on the history of the period. Their recommendations and the subsequent creation of the Freedmen's Bureau, led to the uplift of 4 million ex-slaves in the South and demonstrated a federal commitment to assisting ex-slaves, even if brief and tenuous.

— *Jackie R. Booker*

See also: Freedmen's Bureau.

For Further Reading

Fields, Barbara J. 1985. *Slavery and Freedom on the Middle Ground.* New Haven, CT: Yale University Press.

Foner, Eric. 1988. *Reconstruction: America's Unfinished Business, 1863–1877.* New York: Harper and Row.

Howe, Samuel G. [1864] 1969. *Report to the Freedmen's Inquiry Commission.* New York: Arno Press.

McPherson, James. 1982. *Ordeal by Fire: The Civil War and Reconstruction.* New York: Alfred A. Knopf.

AMERICAN MISSIONARY ASSOCIATION

The American Missionary Association (AMA), which formed on September 3, 1846, was preceded by four other missionary organizations that merged to become one. The Holmes Missionary Society formed in 1839 when abolitionist members created a committee to provide legal assistance to fifty-four Africans charged with mutiny on the *Amistad*, a Spanish schooner that had been seized in American waters. The Africans were freed and returned to their own country accompanied by three missionaries. The other groups to merge into the AMA were the Union Missionary Society, the Committee for West India Missions, and the Western Evangelical Missionary Society. The AMA consisted of two sections, the Foreign Field and the Home Department. Its stated purpose was to protest the inactivity of northern churches against slavery. It became the first organization to begin efforts in the South for the education and religious instruction of the slaves.

The AMA, a predominantly white abolitionist society led by Arthur Tappan and later by his brother Lewis, was unique in its time. It included African Americans as voting members and as members of the executive board. The first African American members were Theodore S. Wright, Samuel Ringgold Ward, James Pennington, and Charles Bennett Ray. Not only were the officers of the AMA an integrated group, but also they were ministers or lay members of racially mixed congregations. The schools and colleges established by the AMA were not designated for African Americans only but were open to all without regard to race, gender, religion, or class. Berea College in Kentucky, founded in 1855, is one example. It enrolled its first African Americans in 1866, and maintained an integrated student body in the then-segregated South.

The abolitionist movement, often characterized as a political reform movement and secular in nature, was, in fact, a movement of "liberal Protestantism" and is part of religious history. Clara DeBoer argues convincingly that William Lloyd Garrison was a "Christian abolitionist" (DeBoer, 1994). Nonetheless, there were significant differences between Garrison's American Anti-Slavery Society and the AMA. In 1865, Garrison called for the dismantling of the American Anti-Slavery Society because he felt that with the end of the Civil War its mission had been accomplished. At the same time, the work of the AMA shifted into establishing schools and colleges in the South and providing teachers to educate the newly freed. Garrison's more limited goal was to eliminate slavery. The AMA and its group of evangelical abolitionists intended to eradicate racism, hatred, classism, greed, and all the sins that had produced slavery in the first place.

The AMA professed to stand on the tenets of pure Christianity in that it saw slavery as a fundamental sin against God and humanity that endangered the mortal souls of both slaveowners and slaves and poisoned all southern institutions, including the home, church, and school. Thus the AMA members advocated a religious revival. Their goal was to reform American Protestant Christianity and to eliminate caste based on race, class, or color. They believed that southern Christianity affirmed a "diluted message that denied African Americans humanity" (DeBoer, 1994) and that this perverted message was necessary in order to maintain the institution of slavery. To tolerate slavery, the North also had to depart from the basic tenets of Christianity. The AMA, though political, recognized the limits of political action in changing the hearts and minds of people. Therefore, instead of using the speaker's podium and lecture circuit in their effort to abolish slavery and injustice, the AMA, under the direction of Lewis Tappan and George Whipple, organized churchmen in the fight against prejudice and ignorance.

The Reverend John G. Fee was a pioneer in the religiopolitical movement. Born in Kentucky the son of a slaveowner, Fee was so outspoken in his objection to slavery that his father disinherited him. Fee organized a group of nonslaveholding men and formed a church. He applied to the American Missionary Association for a commission, and the AMA commissioned him on October 10, 1848. Reverend Fee established Sunday schools and started what is now Berea College in Kentucky.

The AMA was nonsectarian and ecumenical. Primary among its leadership were Lewis Tappan who helped to form the *Amistad* Committee, George Whipple, D.D., the first corresponding secretary of the AMA, and General Samuel Chapman Armstrong, who became the first president of Hampton Normal and Industrial Institute (now Hampton University). The AMA assisted Japanese and Chinese immigrants on the West Coast of the United States, worked for and with Native Americans and poor whites in Appalachia, and established schools for Eskimos in Alaska. It sent teachers to Puerto Rico and maintained education there until public education was established, and it also opened schools for Mexican Americans in New Mexico. In 1861 the AMA was the first organization to send agents into the South. Many of the teachers and missionaries were women. Appeals were made to the Christian women of the North to work among the newly freed. By 1877 the church women had organized a women's meeting, and in 1883 the Bureau of

Woman's Work was formed. The Women's Bureau was an effective agency for producing teachers and raising funds for mission schools.

By 1864 there were 250 AMA missionaries in the southern and border states, and by 1868, there were 532. These missionaries helped the newly freed African Americans acquire land, demand their political rights, establish schools and churches, and lobby for a system of public education. The AMA worked assiduously during the years of Reconstruction to establish educational institutions for freed slaves. Between 1866 and 1869, it opened Fisk University (1866) in Nashville, Tennessee; Atlanta University (1865) in Georgia; Talladega College (1867) in Talladega, Alabama; Straight (now Dillard University, 1869) in New Orleans, Louisiana; Tillotson (now Houston-Tillotson College, 1877) in Austin, Texas; LeMoyne (now LeMoyne-Owen College, 1870) in Memphis, Tennessee; Hampton Institute (1868) in Hampton, Virginia; and Tougaloo College (1869) in Tougaloo, Mississippi. The AMA also assisted in the founding of Howard University in Washington, D.C., in 1867. The southern schools for blacks started by the AMA, once scoffed at and called unrealistic, are now eminent institutions.

In 1868, the terror of the Ku Klux Klan, which the AMA labeled "the Thugs of America" (Whipple, 1876), spread throughout the South. African Americans were denied employment, assaulted by mobs, shot down in the streets, prevented from attending political meetings, and dragged from their homes in the night to be murdered in cold blood. The AMA, under these increasingly dangerous conditions, sent more missionaries than in any other year. The number reached 532.

As Joe Richardson (1986) stated, the AMA had its shortcomings. Even as it gave valuable assistance to African Americans with respect to health, education, and welfare, it suffered from blatant paternalism, cultural imperialism, and perhaps an unrealistic belief that education could eradicate prejudice and racism. In light of its high and noble ideals and the contribution it made in the training of African American teachers, ministers, lawyers, and other leaders, its flaws seem but minor. The AMA disbanded in 1890, after institutional "Jim Crow" legislation made it increasingly difficult for the association to achieve its objectives.

— *Nagueyalti Warren*

See also: Pennington, James.

For Further Reading

DeBoer, Clara Merritt. 1994. *Be Jubilant My Feet: African American Abolitionist in the American Missionary Association, 1839–1861*. New York: Garland.

DeBoer, Clara Merritt. 1995. *His Truth Is Marching On: African Americans Who Taught the Freedmen for the American Missionary Association, 1861–1890*. New York: Garland.

Richardson, Joe M. 1986. *Christian Reconstruction: The American Missionary Association and Southern Blacks, 1861–1890*. Athens: University of Georgia Press.

Stanley, A. Knighton. 1979. *The Childrening: Congregationalism among Black People*. New York: Pilgrim Press.

Whipple, Rev. George. 1876. *History of the American Missionary Association*. New York: 56 Reade Street AMA.

AMERICAN PARTY (KNOW-NOTHING PARTY)

A political party in the United States during the 1850s, the American Party, generally nicknamed the Know-Nothing Party, focused on the perceived threat that Roman Catholics and recent immigrants posed to American political and cultural values. The American Party was the political manifestation of a nativist movement that included numerous secret organizations such as the Order of the Star-Spangled Banner and the Order of United Americans.

In the late 1840s and early 1850s, unprecedented numbers of European immigrants, primarily from Ireland and Germany, flooded the United States, bringing new cultural traditions and greatly increasing the nation's Roman Catholic population. As these immigrants became eligible to vote, many older-stock Americans, particularly in the northeastern states where immigration had its greatest impact, were concerned about their loss of cultural and political power. Urban laborers in particular felt threatened by increased economic competition posed by low-paid, unskilled immigrants. Secret nativist organizations were organized to combat this "menace" through tougher immigration laws, longer residency requirements for citizenship, and a proscription on foreign-born citizens holding political office. Since most immigrants voted for the Democratic Party and the Whig Party was collapsing under the weight of sectional disputes over slavery, these nativist, anti-Democrats created a new political organization called the American Party and ran candidates successfully in several northern states in the early 1850s.

The American Party also had political support in southern states where former Whigs saw it as a natural political platform to continue opposing the Democratic Party. Many southern Know-Nothings also hoped that anti-immigration could be used to divert political attention from the sectional issue of slavery. As long as the American Party was active only at the

Nativists of the Know-Nothing Party tried to move the nation away from the divisive issue of slavery by focusing on other controversial issues such as the rapid influx of new immigrants. (Library of Congress)

state and local level, slavery posed few problems; southern Know-Nothings could be proslavery and anti-Democratic, while northern Know-Nothings could be antislavery and anti-Democratic. Attempts at national political activity proved to be problematic. Just as the Whig Party had discovered, national parties had to reconcile conflicting sectional stances on slavery, especially after the controversial Kansas–Nebraska Act (1854).

In the American Party's national convention in 1855, southern delegates controlled the meeting and pushed for the adoption of a report endorsing the repeal of the Missouri Compromise (1820) and passage of the Kansas–Nebraska Act, which opened western territories to the expansion of slavery. When the report was endorsed over staunch northern opposition, the entire delegations of all the northern states except New York bolted the convention and denounced this attempt to validate slavery's expansion. In 1856 southerners again dominated the national meeting, which endorsed the Kansas–Nebraska Act and nominated former president Millard Fillmore for president. Angered by this support of slavery, the bulk of northern Know-Nothings

bolted the party and supported the Republican candidate, John C. Frémont. Although Fillmore and the Americans ran well throughout the country, garnering over 21 percent of the popular vote, they only managed to win Maryland's electoral votes. Following this disaster, most northern Know-Nothings rapidly abandoned the party for the Republicans. In the South, the American Party continued to run state and local candidates in some areas, but it too collapsed within five years. Like the Whig Party that it tried to replace, the American Party found sectional differences over slavery to be impossible to reconcile.

— *James L. Sledge, III*

See also: Cobb, Howell.

For Further Reading

Beals, Carleton. 1960. *Brass-Knuckle Crusade: The Great Know-Nothing Conspiracy, 1820–1860.* New York: Hastings House.

Carey, Anthony G. 1995. "Too Southern to Be Americans: Proslavery Politics and the Future of the Know-Nothing Party in Georgia, 1854–1856." *Civil War History* 41: 22–40.

Holt, Michael F. 1992. *Political Parties and American Political Development from the Age of Jackson to the Age of Lincoln.* Baton Rouge: Louisiana State University Press.

Leonard, Ira M., and Robert D. Parmet. 1971. *American Nativism, 1830–1860.* New York: Van Nostrand Reinhold Company.

Levine, Bruce. "Conservatism, Nativism, and Slavery: Thomas R. Whitney and the Origins of the Know-Nothing Party." *Journal of American History* 88 (2): 455–89.

Maizlish, Stephen E. 1982. "The Meaning of Nativism and the Crisis of the Union.

"The Know-Nothing Movement in the Antebellum North." In *Essays on American Antebellum Politics, 1840–1860.* Ed. Stephen E. Maizlish and John J. Kushma. College Station: Texas A & M University Press.

AMERICAN REVOLUTION. *See* Black Loyalists; Crispus Attucks.

AMISTAD CASE (1841)

In July 1839, a slave mutiny occurred aboard the Spanish slaver *Amistad* off the Cuban coast. On June 28, 1839, the *Amistad,* commanded and owned by Ramón Ferrer, had departed Havana for Puerto Principé in east-central Cuba with six crew members and fifty-four illegally imported African slaves belonging to José Ruiz and Pedro Montez. On the fourth night at sea, one of the slaves, Joseph Cinqué, led a mutiny in which the ship's captain and cook were killed. For fifty-seven days, the *Amistad* skirted the eastern coast of the United States until August 26, when a U.S. Coast Guard brig commanded by Lt. Thomas Gedney seized it.

Gedney's seizure of the *Amistad* raised questions. First, did the *Amistad's* cargo and slaves still belong to Ruiz and Montez? Second, what crimes had the slaves committed in mutinying, and by what means and where would they be punished for those crimes? Third, would the U.S. government return the *Amistad* and the "*Amistad* captives" to Spanish authorities under Pinckney's Treaty (1795), which had outlined terms of trade relations between the United States and Spain, or would it free them according to Anglo-American agreements outlawing the slave trade?

The U.S. State Department recommended that the Spanish minister take custody of the *Amistad* and its cargo, but when the mutineers were indicted for piracy, Lewis Tappan and other abolitionists established the *Amistad* Committee to raise money for their defense. Committee attorneys prepared arguments that Ruiz and Montez had violated international law by purchasing slaves that had been smuggled illegally into Cuba.

On January 8, 1840, a U.S. district court ruled that all the slaves except one, Antonio, Ferrer's Creole cabin boy, who was deemed a legally-held slave, were entitled to their freedom and that the United States should transport them to Africa. When the U.S. district attorney appealed the lower court's decision, former president John Quincy Adams agreed to serve as the slaves' counsel before the U.S. Supreme Court.

Adams presented the Africans' case in February 1841. On March 9, 1841, Justice Joseph Story affirmed the lower court's decision and granted the captives their freedom. In November 1841, the *Amistad* Committee, aided by Yale University's Divinity School, returned the thirty-five *Amistad* survivors (excluding the cabin boy) to Africa. The committee naively expected the captives to proselytize Christianity and serve as positive examples for the American Colonization Society.

The *Amistad* case remained a contentious point in antebellum U.S–Spanish relations. From 1844 until 1860, when Spain abandoned its claims in the *Amistad* case, every president suggested that the U.S. government should indemnify Spain and mentioned the *Amistad* case in state-of-the-union addresses. Ironically, two years after the Supreme Court had ruled on the *Amistad* case, the *Creole* case presented the U.S. State Department with a quandary similar to the one Spain had faced in the *Amistad* case.

— *John Grenier*

See also: Adams, John Quincy; American Colonization Society; Cinqué, Joseph; Illegal Slave Trade.

For Further Reading

Cable, Mary. 1971. *Black Odyssey: The Case of the Slave Ship* Amistad. New York: Viking Press.

Jones, Howard. 1987. *Mutiny on the* Amistad: *The Saga of a Slave Revolt and Its Impact on American Abolition, Law and Diplomacy.* New York: Oxford University Press.

McClendon, R. Earl. 1933. "The *Amistad* Claims: Inconsistencies of Policy." *Political Science Quarterly* 48: 386–412.

SUSAN BROWNELL ANTHONY (1820–1906)

Although Susan B. Anthony is best remembered for her leadership in the female suffrage movement, she was also an ardent, active Garrisonian abolitionist and radical egalitarian, rigorously committed to universal equality. Anthony grew up in a climate steeped in antislavery sentiment. Her father Daniel Anthony, a Hicksite Quaker, espoused the liberal antislavery beliefs integral to that sect. After relocating to Rochester, New York, in 1846, the Anthony family became closely associated with a group of Hicksite Quakers involved in temperance, antislavery, and woman's rights reforms. Through the late 1840s and early 1850s the Anthonys hosted gatherings that included abolitionist notables such as Frederick Douglass, William Ellery Channing, Samuel J. May, William Lloyd Garrison, and Wendell Phillips.

Despite Anthony's regular attendance at antislavery meetings, her efforts to educate herself on abolitionist issues, and her longing to be a Garrisonian, she began her reform career working in the temperance movement in 1848. Even a week of antislavery lecturing with Abby Kelley Foster and Stephen Foster in upstate New York in 1851 did not dispel her notion that she lacked the knowledge and the oratorical skills required of Garrisonians.

In 1856, following many successes as a temperance and women's rights organizer and lecturer, Anthony eagerly accepted a post as New York agent for the American Anti-Slavery Society. From this point on, she worked indefatigably for the abolitionist cause. For ten dollars a week plus expenses, she organized antislavery meetings throughout New York State and directed a large, constantly changing group of speakers. Antiabolitionist sentiment increased steadily throughout the late 1850s, changing typically antagonistic

Susan B. Anthony, one of the most significant leaders of the woman's suffrage movement, also lent her support to the antislavery cause. (Library of Congress)

American men and all women. In fact, she was one of the first abolitionists to insist that African Americans be given the franchise. Following the suggestion of abolitionist and independent editor Theodore Tilton, both Anthony and Stanton were instrumental in leading the battle for universal suffrage by helping to form the American Equal Rights Association (AERA) in 1866. Both women remained key players in the AERA until 1869, when it became clear that their male abolitionist colleagues, in their scrambling to secure the franchise for African American males through the Fifteenth Amendment, could not be persuaded to reconsider their decision to withdraw their decades-long commitment to woman suffrage. Because of this failure, Anthony and Stanton left the AERA to form the National Woman Suffrage Association.

— *Judith E. Harper*

See also: American Anti-Slavery Society; Foster, Abigail Kelley; Women and the Antislavery Movement.

For Further Reading

Anthony, Katharine. 1954. *Susan B. Anthony: Her Personal History and Her Era.* Garden City, NY: Doubleday.

Barry, Kathleen. 1988. *Susan B. Anthony: Biography of a Singular Feminist.* New York: New York University Press.

Harper, Ida Husted. 1899. *The Life and Work of Susan B. Anthony.* Indianapolis, IN: Bowen-Merrill.

Harper, Judith E. 1998. *Susan B. Anthony: A Biographical Companion.* Santa Barbara, CA: ABC-CLIO.

Venet, Wendy Hamand. 1991. *Neither Ballots Nor Bullets: Women Abolitionists and the Civil War.* Charlottesville: University Press of Virginia.

crowds into violent, egg-throwing, knives-flashing mobs in 1860 and early 1861. Frequently abandoned by overstressed speakers, Anthony was often left alone to confront audiences with her vituperative rhetoric. Referring to the South as "the Hydra monster," she declared in one of her few surviving speeches from this period, "He sucks his lifeblood from the unpaid and unpitied toil of the slaves and can only die when those bleeding backs and breaking hearts are wrested from his gory lips" (Anthony, 1954).

In 1863 Anthony and her fellow activist and friend Elizabeth Cady Stanton, both impatient with women's nonparticipatory role in the Civil War, formed the Women's National Loyal League out of the conviction that a Thirteenth Amendment to the Constitution was essential to guarantee the freedom of African Americans. Anthony, with Stanton's support, directed the project that collected and presented to Congress 400,000 signatures supporting a Thirteenth Amendment.

In the final months of the Civil War and after, Anthony recognized the urgent need to continue the struggle to secure civil and political rights for African

ANTIABOLITION RIOTS

Antiabolition mobs and riots became an important feature of the social landscape of Jacksonian America. Such mobs represented the most violent reaction to abolitionism, a movement that gained strength throughout the 1830s and 1840s, and most of the behavior occurred in the North because the abolitionist movement never took firm root in the South. There were episodes in the South, however, when opponents of slavery found themselves dunked in water, ridden out of town on a rail, or tarred and feathered. Such crowd actions shared the ritualized violence of the charivari (raucous European peasant celebrations) with their northern counterparts, but there was less destruction of property than there was in the North, such as in the New York City riot of 1834. In the South, such actions represented punishment for those people who transgressed lines of family honor and questioned the institution of slavery. Southerners thus responded with the creation of "lynch law" and vigilance committees that controlled the expression of dissent by antislavery southerners and ejected northern abolitionists. There was little physical violence; rather, the ritualized violence served to maintain racial solidarity among whites, protect slavery from criticism, and prevent servile rebellion.

Antiabolition riots occurred in the North between 1833 and 1845, especially in New England, New York, and Ohio, which were areas of sustained abolitionist activity. Opposition to the antislavery movement in the North occurred for several different reasons. Antiabolitionists from the propertied classes feared that antislavery activities might disrupt the Union because of the anger that the abolitionist movement created in the South. Those opposed to the abolitionist movement, especially merchants and factories, also feared the loss of profitable southern business, such as exporting southern agricultural products or acting as middlemen or agents for such products. Finally, antiabolitionists from the working classes often disliked blacks and feared they would take jobs from whites; such fears became acute during hard economic times, such as the depression that followed the Panic of 1837. Whites also feared that interaction with blacks would lead to miscegenation and the amalgamation of the races. These racist fears suffused the antiabolition movement and were especially prominent among the working classes, who lived nearest to the free black communities in the North.

The most common form of antiabolition mob action in the North was rioting. Paul Gilje defines a riot as "any group of twelve or more people attempting to assert their will immediately through the use of force outside the normal bounds of law" (Gilje, 1996). Mobs sought to enforce their will through "coercion or compulsion based upon violence, or based on the threat of violence" (Gilje, 1996). They blocked entrances to halls used by abolitionists, threw eggs, paint, and ink at abolitionists, and played drums and horns to drown out abolitionist speakers. Greater destruction of property took place when mobs attacked the presses of abolitionist newspapers and destroyed machines, threw away type, and burned buildings. Occasionally, mobs stoned or clubbed abolitionists, but such physical violence was rare. An example of this brutal, but rare, sort of attack was the killing of Elijah P. Lovejoy, an outspoken abolitionist editor, by an enraged mob in Alton, Illinois in 1837. The mob attacked Lovejoy's printing press, the fourth such attack, and when he attempted to defend it, with a firearm, the mob set fire to the building that housed his press and shot him. The worst violence usually occurred in race riots such as that in New York City during July 4–12, 1834, when white mobs attacked black sections of the city and destroyed homes, churches, and a school.

There is still much debate about who composed the antiabolition mobs. Leonard Richards asserts that most mobs consisted of "gentlemen of property and standing" (Richards, 1970), that is, merchants, lawyers, doctors, bankers, and politicians. In his study, Richards demonstrates that over 70 percent of each mob came from the commercial and professional ranks, whereas fewer than 20 percent came from the ranks of tradesmen and manufacturers. The mobs tended to be native-born and attracted sizable percentages of Episcopalians. Their members differed greatly from the abolitionists (who attracted far fewer numbers of high-ranking professional or commercial men and Episcopalians) and were more often made up of foreign-born men from the ranks of tradesmen and manufacturers. Thus antiabolitionists often perceived the abolitionists as threats to their elite status, moral leadership, and values and traditions. Antiabolitionists also feared miscegenation and amalgamation should southern slaves be freed and head north. Paul Gilje, in contrast, sees antiabolition mobs as tradesmen expressing opposition to black encroachment into their professions and to the de-skilling of labor, which was a side effect of the industrialization of the North. David Grimsted's study of antiabolition mobs revealed a pattern where the mobs often included men from slightly less prominent socioeconomic standing than the abolitionists and an affiliation with the Democratic Party.

Antiabolition rioting began to decrease dramatically after 1845 as northern newspapers began to decry the destruction of property and lawless behavior of the mobs. Abolitionists pointed to southern vigilance committees as the first step toward the loss of free speech for northern white men, and mob action against northern antislavery efforts led more people into the antislavery movement because of the perceived threat to northern civil liberties. There was also a growing concern that the mobbing of abolitionists only served to gain them sympathy for their cause and led to the creation of more abolitionists.

— *James C. Foley*

See also: Democratic Party; Episcopal Church; Lovejoy, Elijah P.

For Further Reading

Gilje, Paul. 1996. *Rioting in America.* Bloomington: Indiana University Press.

Grimsted, David. 1998. *American Mobbing,*

1828–1861: Toward Civil War. New York: Oxford University Press.

Kerber, Linda. 1967. "Abolitionists and Amalgamators: The New York City Race Riots of 1834." *New York History* 48 (January): 28–39.

Nye, Russel. 1949. *Fettered Freedom: Civil Liberties and the Slavery Controversy, 1830–1860.* East Lansing: Michigan State College Press.

Richards, Leonard. 1970. *Gentlemen of Property and Standing: Anti-Abolition Mobs in Jacksonian America.* New York: Oxford University Press.

Wyatt-Brown, Bertram. 1982. *Southern Honor: Ethics and Behavior in the Old South.* New York: Oxford University Press.

ANTILITERACY LAWS

Slaveowners in the South thought they had ample reason to curtail the spread of literacy among slaves. Literate slaves might forge passes, read newspapers, or communicate conspiratorial plans. Thus, in 1740, after the Stono Rebellion of 1739, the colonial government of South Carolina enacted a ban on educating slaves, and Georgia soon followed suit.

The nineteenth century brought new black antiliteracy laws. Immediately after David Walker published his revolutionary *Appeal* in 1829, Georgia applied the slave antiliteracy law to free black residents, and Savannah, Georgia's largest city, had a similar law. By 1834, after a series of published attacks on slavery, other states also enacted antiliteracy laws. Antiliteracy laws never became universal across the slave South, however; Tennessee and Kentucky, for example, never enacted them. Of the four states that maintained such laws from the 1830s through the Civil War, three— North Carolina, South Carolina, and Georgia— banned anyone from teaching any African American, whether slave or free, to read or write. Virginia banned schools for blacks but not private tutoring.

In Norfolk, Virginia, Margaret Douglass, a white seamstress, spent a month in jail in 1854 for violating Virginia's antiliteracy law by running a school for free black children. Across the South, teaching an occasional slave or free black to read or write took place in the private sphere, whatever the law. But so did the punishment of slaves' efforts to learn to read or write. Antiliteracy laws would have been unnecessary had there been no efforts to teach slaves or free blacks reading and writing, but opposition to slave literacy did not require the force of law to be quite effective.

In pre–Civil War America, literacy was a badge of liberty, a symbol of citizenship, and a tool for achievement. While various states, northern and southern alike, were launching new efforts to establish common schools, some southern states enacted new restrictions on black residents' access to literacy. The fact that those restrictions targeted free blacks as well as slaves displayed an effort to narrow the meaning of black freedom. In the antebellum North, the pattern was ragged, yet most communities permitted black schools, many jurisdictions invested public funds in black schools, and by the 1850s Boston's public schools had been racially integrated.

The South's antiliteracy laws died when slavery did. In summer 1865—after the surrender at Appomattox but before ratification of the Thirteenth Amendment—Freedmen's Bureau and American Missionary Association schools sprouted across the southern landscape. No legislature had yet repealed an antiliteracy law, but every such law had become a dead letter. When the Black Codes of 1865–1866 mentioned literacy, they specified that the masters of apprentices should see that their charges learned to read and write. Hosts of black southerners, of all ages albeit especially young people, sought literacy as a badge of emancipation.

In the 1870s, every southern state created a system of public schools that, on a segregated basis, might provide all children access to literacy. Moreover, new institutions of higher education for African Americans—including Hampton Institute, Howard University, Fisk University, and Atlanta University—emerged soon after emancipation. Not only were such institutions now legal, but some received public funds, either state or federal, and each trained black teachers for the new black elementary schools.

Most former slaves entered freedom illiterate, and the impediments of illiteracy—a legacy of slavery— long undermined full freedom, whether because contracts might be misleading, veterans' pension applications might be disregarded, or literacy could be required of voters. Many members of the postwar generations of black children, however, had a strikingly different experience. A rapid rise in literacy among young people brought a substantial decline in overall black illiteracy.

— *Peter Wallenstein*

See also: Stono Rebellion; Walker, David.

For Further Reading

Cornelius, Janet Duitsman. 1991. *"When I Can Read My Title Clear": Literacy, Slavery, and Religion in the Antebellum South.* Columbia: University of South Carolina Press.

Foner, Philip S., and Josephine F. Pacheco. 1984. *Three Who Dared: Prudence Crandall, Margaret Douglass,*

Myrtilla Miner—Champions of Antebellum Black Education. Westport, CT: Greenwood.

Fort, Bruce. 1999. "The Politics and Culture of Literacy in Georgia, 1800–1920." Ph.D. dissertation, University of Virginia.

Wallenstein, Peter. 2004. "Higher Education and Civil Rights: South Carolina, 1860s–1960s." *History of Higher Education Annual* 23: 1–22.

Webber, Thomas L. 1978. *Deep Like the Rivers: Education in the Slave Quarter Community, 1831–1865.* New York: Norton.

Woodson, Carter Godwin. 1968. *The Education of the Negro Prior to 1861.* New York: Arno Press.

"APPEAL OF THE INDEPENDENT DEMOCRATS"

The "Appeal of the Independent Democrats," issued in January 1854 by northern antislavery Democrats, was a protest against the terms of the Kansas–Nebraska bill. In late 1853, Senator Stephen A. Douglas of Illinois introduced a seemingly innocuous bill to organize the Nebraska Territory, which lay along the proposed route for a transcontinental railroad to be built from Chicago to San Francisco. According to the Missouri Compromise of 1820, which prohibited slavery in the Louisiana Purchase above 36°30', Nebraska was to be free territory. A junta of proslavery southern politicians, however, coerced Douglas into amending his bill so as to create two territories—Kansas and Nebraska—and to provide for the repeal of the 36°30' restriction. The new bill organized the territories according to the principle of popular sovereignty, meaning that the territorial residents would decide the status of slavery for themselves, without interference from the national government. The issue erupted into a bitter conflict over slavery expansion. Southern Democrats and Whigs alike backed the bill, while northern Whigs and Free Soil Party members fought the measure. Northern Democrats, meanwhile, including President Franklin Pierce, generally bowed to pressure from leading southerners and supported the bill.

A few free soil Democrats, however, broke party ranks and opposed lifting the 36°30' ban on slavery. Calling themselves Independent Democrats, these anti-Nebraska dissenters counted among their leaders Senators Salmon P. Chase of Ohio and Charles Sumner of Massachusetts as well as Representatives Gerrit Smith of New York and Joshua R. Giddings of Ohio. In January 1854 these congressmen and two colleagues published the "Appeal of the Independent Democrats" protesting the Kansas–Nebraska proposition. Mostly Chase's work, the appeal warned the nation of a great "slave power" conspiracy bent upon grafting slavery into territories previously consigned to freedom. It assailed the Nebraska bill as "a criminal betrayal of precious rights; as part and parcel of an atrocious plot" to convert Nebraska into "a dreary region of despotism, inhabited by masters and slaves" (Foner, 1970). The Independent Democrats attributed this plot not only to a cabal of sinister southern slavemongers but to their northern "doughface" accomplices as well. The appeal singled out Douglas for especially harsh treatment, accusing him of pandering to the southern slavocracy to advance his own political fortunes.

The "Appeal of the Independent Democrats" failed to prevent the passage of the Kansas–Nebraska Act, which became law in May 1854. Nevertheless, the protest deserves a prominent place among the list of speeches, tracts, and events that galvanized northern public opinion against the proliferation of slaveholding territory. Equally important, the appeal prefigured the coalescence of "Conscience" Whigs (northern Whigs who opposed slavery), Free Soilers, and anti-Nebraska Democrats into a single antislavery party—the Republican Party, which took shape in the wake of the Kansas–Nebraska controversy.

— *Eric Tscheschlok*

See also: Douglas, Stephen A.; Free Soil Party; Giddings, Joshua; Kansas–Nebraska Act; Missouri Compromise.

For Further Reading

Blue, Frederick J. 1987. *Salmon P. Chase: A Life in Politics.* Kent, OH: Kent State University Press.

Foner, Eric. 1970. *Free Soil, Free Labor, Free Men: The Ideology of the Republican Party before the Civil War.* New York: Oxford University Press.

Gienapp, William E. 1987. *The Origins of the Republican Party, 1852–1856.* New York: Oxford University Press.

Potter, David M. 1976. *The Impending Crisis, 1848–1861.* New York: Harper and Row.

AN APPEAL TO CHRISTIAN WOMEN OF THE SOUTH (1836)

Angelina Grimké wrote the abolitionist pamphlet *An Appeal to Christian Women of the South,* and it was published by the American Anti-Slavery Society of New York in 1836. The work aroused such intense disfavor in the South that southern postmasters intercepted and destroyed copies of it to prevent its distribution. In the North, the pamphlet sparked interest in abolitionism and quickly increased Grimké's standing in the abolitionist movement.

In the pamphlet, Grimké addressed southern women

as a woman born and raised in the South herself. As such, she thought she could reach and influence the thinking of other southern women. The women, in turn, could persuade their brothers, fathers, and husbands to change the laws. She called upon women as sisters, wives, and mothers and urged them to try to understand that slavery violated natural law, Christianity, and human law. God, she argued, created all human beings in His image; therefore, no one could be treated as a "thing" the way southerners treated slaves. Using the Bible, she showed that slavery in the South was not at all like biblical slavery, for southern slaves lost all of their rights as human beings. Pointing to the Declaration of Independence, she appealed to southern women to recognize the equality of slaves as human beings with a natural right to freedom.

As Grimké saw it, southern women could do more than just understand the injustice of slavery; they could pray over it, speak about it, and act against it by freeing any slaves they owned, educating them, and paying them wages. She also asked women to send petitions to their state legislatures demanding an end to slavery. She argued, "Speak to your relatives, friends, acquaintances, be not afraid . . . to let your sentiments be known. . . . Try to persuade your husband, father, brothers and sons that slavery is a crime against God and man." She even advised southern women to stand firm against "wicked laws" that dehumanized people. She wrote, "slavery must be abolished . . . there are only two ways in which it can be effected, by moral power or physical force, and it is for you to choose which of these you prefer."

Grimké's *Appeal* was not unique in its content; many abolitionists used similar arguments when writing against slavery. Her *Appeal* was unique, however, because it was the first and only abolitionist tract written by a southern woman to southern women. Grimké's family name was well known in Charleston, South Carolina, where she was born and raised, and that fact made her *Appeal* even more controversial among southern women. When copies of her pamphlet reached Charleston as part of a mass mailing of abolitionist literature ("the great postal campaign" of 1835–1837), the postmaster publicly burned them. Charleston police even advised Grimké that she would not be permitted to visit the city ever again, and she never did.

— *Mary Jo Miles*

See also: Abolitionism in the United States; Grimké, Angelina; Grimké, Sarah Moore.

For Further Reading
Ceplair, Larry. 1989. *The Public Years of Sarah and Angelina Grimké: Selected Writings, 1835–1839.* New York: Columbia University Press.
    Lerner, Gerda. 1964. *The Grimké Sisters from South Carolina.* Boston: Houghton Mifflin.

HERBERT APTHEKER (1915–2003)

Herbert Aptheker, the author of the definitive *American Negro Slave Revolts* (1943), was born in Brooklyn, New York, on July 31, 1915. After receiving his Ph.D. from Columbia University in 1943, Aptheker began a scholar-activist sojourn that would help shape and change how the field of African American history is understood. Aptheker's career achievements include the editing and/or writing of over eighty books, of which over forty volumes consist of the personal letters and scholarly works of the American educator and writer W. E. B. DuBois. His wife Fay, whom he married in 1942, ably assisted him in these scholarly efforts.

Although Aptheker was born of affluent Russian immigrants, he said that a black woman and nursemaid, Angelina Corbin, helped elevate his racial horizons as a young man. Aptheker reflected that "Annie raised me as much as mother. I loved her and mother loved her" (Aptheker Interview, 1995). He fondly remembers seeing his mother and Angelina, appearing almost like sisters, sitting and talking, in long stretches, at the kitchen room table. His intellectual curiosity was challenged by Ulysses S. Grant's biography, which asserted that American slaves were accurately portrayed by the stereotyped sambo image. Reflecting on the strength of character of Annie, Aptheker said of this historical interpretation, "It can't be true. It was impossible that her people were like that." His social consciousness was further pricked, in 1932, after traveling in the Depression-era South and seeing how the "barbarism" of peonage and Jim Crow degraded the black populace. In his words, "white people were starving and black people were starving to death" (Interview).

Aptheker recalled an incident that would be seared in his mind for the rest of his life. His father's car had mechanical problems, and while his father attended to the problem, young Herbert walked up to a nearby shanty and offered a comparable youngster of his age a cookie. The young black kid literally "reached for the cookie, like a dog would, and bit a piece as I held it in my hand." Years later, when Aptheker, recalled this story, tears would well up in his eyes as he mumbled "incredulous" (Interview).

Returning to New York City, young Herbert began

to write scholastic stories in the school paper entitled "The Dark Side of the South" exposing the racial injustices he witnessed. This was his first venture into the muddy waters of political activism.

Aptheker believed that these early experiences led to his interest in African American resistance to oppression. Searching for historical truth, Aptheker wrote a master's thesis that analyzed Nat Turner's rebellion and was eventually published in 1966. His dissertation was a comprehensive interpretation of American Negro slave revolts. He also published two essays with the same title as his dissertation in successive issues of *Science and Society* in 1937. Two years later, he published "Maroons Within the Present Limits of the United States" in the *Journal of Negro History*. International publishers continued publishing his work on slave resistance with *The Negro in the Civil War* (1939) and *Negro Slave Revolts in the United States, 1526–1860* (1939). When his dissertation was published in 1943, it became a watershed in the historiography of slavery.

In that work, Aptheker tried to address and refute the racist assumptions of Ulrich B. Phillips and others, who stated that "slave revolts and plots very seldom occurred in the United States" and that the slaves themselves were mentally defective, docile, and submissive. In *American Negro Slave Revolts,* Aptheker challenged "the racism of the dominant historical profession and of the society it mirrored and served . . . [but also] further substantiated its thesis, that the African-American people, in slavery forged a record of discontent and of resistance comparable to that marking the history of any other oppressed people." Aptheker defined a revolt as "a minimum of ten slaves involved; freedom as the apparent aim of the disaffected slaves; contemporary references labeling the event as an uprising, plot, insurrection" (Aptheker, 1943).

The impact of the book on the historical profession was a polar one, with white historians generally rejecting its thesis while black historians praised the author and his scholarship. A favorable review in 1944 noted that the book was scholarly, penetrating, and scientific, whereas a negative critique in 1951 argued that the research was so subjective that it did not deserve to be defined as history. The polarity of these two reviews reflected Aptheker's leftist politics and the onslaught of the Cold War, which further divided the historical profession on clear ideological grounds. One historian who had pro–civil rights sympathies recalled that this work "was the single most effective antidote to the poisonous ideas that Blacks had not a history of struggle" (Bracey, 1993). By the 1970s, most historians accepted Aptheker's thesis either by incorporating or modifying its assumptions in their work. George Rawick would agree that

slaves "fought back in constant struggle," and Eugene Genovese accepted the "slaves' rebellious spirit." John Blassingame and Mary Berry argued that "slaves engaged almost continuously . . . in . . . conspiracies, rebellions"; Leslie H. Owen thought that "again and again bondsmen attacked slavery"; Peter Wood's and Gerald Mullin's book affirmed Aptheker's premise; and Vincent Harding's book presented a wide pattern of multilayered resistance within slave culture (Shapiro, 1984). Aptheker's book forced historians to see rebellion as an essential characteristic of those held in bondage and illuminated a tradition of which all Americans can be proud.

The activism of scholarship did not take a back seat to the activism of struggle. Dr. Aptheker always lived his life according to the motto "study and struggle." In 1939 he joined the American Communist Party, which then was in the vanguard of the struggle against racism and class oppression. Aptheker began to work with many blacks who also were on the left or members of the party. One interesting and brave instance of activism, took Aptheker to Olgethorpe, Kentucky, during the 1930s to help black exploited workers escape the "debtor prison" of southern peonage. The Peonage Abolition Act of 1867 made it illegal to coerce labor from a person because of debt. By the third decade of the twentieth century, approximately 4 million black sharecroppers had been reduced to a state of peonage. On the advice and direction of the black communist William Patterson, Aptheker traveled to Olgethorpe County, Kentucky, posing as an insurance salesman with the name of H. Beal. His goal was to help these workers to escape, via a neo-Underground Railroad, to the North. Dr. Aptheker, in relating this story in the late 1990s was still animated about the danger so many years later, stating that if he had been discovered by the Kentucky authorities, he would have surely been murdered by "persons unknown" (Interview).

Another proud highlight of his activism was his involvement as a major and commander of an all-black artillery regiment during World War II. He deliberately requested this command because blacks were not allowed the status of commanding officers. Aptheker and his troops were stationed in Louisiana near the town of Pollock, whose city sign proclaimed, "Nigger, don't let the sun set on you in Pollock," Aptheker devised a plan to challenge this image of white supremacy. He took his men on a long march that went through the town and at an agreed-upon moment, his men sang "John Brown's Body" (Interview). Laughingly, Dr. Aptheker said he was sure the whites thought they were being invaded.

After the war was over and Cold War tensions

developed between the Soviet Union and the United States, Aptheker continued his involvement in struggles on the left. He testified for the defense of fellow communist members being prosecuted under the Smith Act in the early 1950s, and he became a widely requested speaker on campuses in the 1960s. His public activism continued until the 1970s when, as a senatorial candidate in New York, he was attacked and severely beaten. Aptheker remembers that his attacker did not take his wallet but only a letter addressed to him to prove to his co-conspirators that this reactionary deed was accomplished. His commitment to the Soviet Union ended in 1992 when he left the Communist Party in disagreement with Gorbachev's *perestroika* and *glasnost* policies. Much of the antagonism toward him faded in the later years of his life.

Aptheker's most cherished memories are of his shared office with Dr. W. E. B. DuBois, who became a lifetime friend. As a fellow traveler, DuBois became a muse for Aptheker's continued research in African American history. It was during this period that Aptheker began his singular voluminous *Documentary History of the Negro People*. His friendship with DuBois was so deep and abiding that DuBois asked Aptheker to become the literary executor of his letters and scholarship. As late as 1996, Aptheker and his wife Fay recalled how they barely saved volumes of DuBois's work from a rain-soaked cellar in their home.

Aptheker's work in African American history was rediscovered during the Black Power movement of the 1960s. His *American Negro Slave Revolts* provided a sense of continuity with those who had resisted racial oppression in the past.

— *Malik Simba*

See also: DuBois, W. E. B.; Sambo Thesis.

For Further Reading

Aptheker, Herbert. 1943. *American Negro Slave Revolts*. New York: International Publishers.

Aptheker, Herbert. 1995. Private interview conducted in the subject's home by Malik Simba. San Jose, CA: May–June.

Bracey, John. 1993. "Foreword." in *American Negro Slave Revolts*. New York: International Publishers.

Shapiro, Herbert. 1984. "The Impact of the Aptheker Thesis: A Retrospective View of American Negro Slave Revolts." *Science and Society* 48: 52–73.

ARTISANS

Slave artisans represented a major component of the colonial and early American skilled labor force. Typically male, American-born, and English-speaking, slave artisans worked in countless occupations throughout the colonies and much of the United States. Although there were slave artisans of Native American descent during the colonial period, the overwhelming majority of enslaved skilled labor was of African descent. This steady pool of skilled slave labor helped give a young American economy plagued by chronic labor shortages the necessary ingredient for it to grow, diversify, and ultimately industrialize.

Slave artisans served two primary functions within the American economy. First, they provided urban centers with a captive and capable labor supply that their fledgling industries desperately needed and could readily exploit. Second, slave artisans enabled rural plantation managers to improve and diversify the productive capacity of their operations by increasing the range of money-saving or cash-producing activities that took place on site. Thus the labor of slave artisans helped transform plantations into increasingly efficient, self-sufficient units of production. Because of their productivity, slave artisans were highly valued and commanded top prices. For example, in 1780, joiners in New Orleans were valued between 750 and 800 pesos, while unskilled slaves commonly sold for 400 pesos. Similarly, by 1840, the owner of a Louisiana mechanic and carpenter named Sandy appraised his slave's value at $3,000, a sum far exceeding the value of fieldhands.

An abbreviated list of slave artisan occupations helps to illustrate the importance of this diverse labor source for both urban and rural localities. Slave artisans worked as barbers, blacksmiths, carpenters, cooks, coopers, draftsmen, hatters, joiners, potters, printers, seamstresses, shipbuilders, shoemakers, silversmiths, weavers, and wood carvers. Historians believe that the tradition of skilled artisan in Africa augmented this wide range of occupations both quantitatively and qualitatively as African knowledge meshed well with the demands of familiar tasks in the New World. The fine ironwork of slave-built antebellum homes in Charleston, South Carolina, and New Orleans, Louisiana, attests to this historic transfer of talent.

The slave artisans' value to master and community often allowed these skilled individuals greater autonomy and privileges than were allowed average slaves. Many slave artisans worked without daily supervision or the constant threat of physical coercion, and the demands of skilled occupations such as printing gave them greater access to the empowering tool of literacy. For example, an Edgefield, South Carolina, slave, "Dave the Potter," boldly demonstrated his literacy by inscribing his stoneware storage jars with poetry, biblical verses, and whimsical sayings. Masters of valued slave artisans like

Dave often permitted them to hire out their own time within the community on condition that the master receive a designated percentage or specified amount of the money earned. Particularly industrious slaves could receive material incentives to find extra work. For example, masters might permit slave artisans to retain the surplus portion of money earned in excess of an agreed amount. In addition to using these earnings to improve their material conditions, many such artisans set aside this money to buy their own or a family member's freedom. Appreciation for a slave artisan's skill could also, in rare cases, earn them their freedom as in the case of carpenter and master mason Emperor Williams who was freed when he successfully orchestrated the placement of a cornice on a New Orleans building.

The ability to negotiate and improve the conditions of their bondage elevated many artisans to positions of leadership within the slave community. Occasionally, slave artisans like Gabriel Prosser used their leader status to organize and incite rebellion against the institution of slavery. Frederick Douglass used the autonomy and literacy he gained as a caulker in Baltimore to escape from bondage forever. For these reasons as well as their success in competing against free artisans, the white community often viewed slave artisans with suspicion and resentment. Accordingly, cities like Philadelphia and Charleston sought to limit the number and activities of slave artisans through restrictive legislation.

— *Daniel L. Fountain*

See also: Arts and Crafts; Douglass, Frederick; Prosser, Gabriel.

For Further Reading

DuBois, W. E. B., ed. 1902. *The Negro Artisan.* Atlanta, GA: Atlanta University Press.

Newton, James, and Ronald Lewis, eds. 1978. *The Other Slaves: Mechanics, Artisans, and Craftsmen.* Boston: G. K. Hall.

Patton, Sharon. 1995. "Antebellum Louisiana Artisans: The Black Furniture Makers." *The International Review of African American Art* 12 (3): 15–23, 58–64.

Peek, Phil. 1978. "Afro-American Material Culture and the Afro-American Craftsman." *Southern Folklore Quarterly* 42 (2–3): 109–134.

Vlach, John M. 1991. *By the Work of Their Hands: Studies in Afro-American Folklife.* Ann Arbor, MI: UMI Research Press.

ARTS AND CRAFTS

The institution of slavery robbed African Americans of their freedom, but it did not strip them of their creativity and artistic abilities. From the beginning of their forced migration from Africa until emancipation, African American slaves made significant contributions to the American tradition of arts and crafts. Indeed, a select cohort of slave artists left a memorable legacy within the fine and decorative arts, while even greater numbers of their enslaved brethren created functional yet equally beautiful pieces of art within the craft tradition. Much of the artwork produced by slaves exhibits both African and European characteristics and thus reflects the cultural diversity and synthetic nature that defines African American culture.

Slave contributions to the fine and decorative arts mostly reflect the significant role played by slave artisans within colonial America and the early United States economy. Slave artisans produced a wide range of luxury items that required the delicate blend of the craftsman's skillful hand and the artist's eye. The slaves' refined artistic abilities appear in the gold and silver work, furniture, wood carvings, and ironwork produced by their hands. The wrought iron fences and balconies of Charleston, South Carolina, and New Orleans, Louisiana, are an excellent example of the slaves' considerable talent for high art. However, slave contributions to the fine and decorative arts were not limited to the work of artisans. Small numbers of slaves also demonstrated their artistic abilities through portraiture. In fact, the notable American painter Gilbert Stuart drew early inspiration from watching Neptune Thurston, a slave, sketch faces on barrels. Similarly, the work of the slave painter Scipio Morehead inspired African American poet Phillis Wheatley to dedicate a poem to his ability as an artist.

Although some slaves exhibited their artistic talents through high art, a far greater percentage of them revealed similar skills through handicrafts. Unlike the luxury items created by slave artisans, the artistic items produced by the typical slave were not purchased primarily by white consumers but remained within the creator's community where they served day-to-day needs. The most common handicrafts produced by slaves were woodcarvings, baskets, quilts, musical instruments, and pottery. Each of these slave craft forms reveals the persistence of African culture within the slave community as age-old skills combined with New World circumstances to create articles of utility and beauty.

Slaves used their carving skills to create useful items such as bowls, spoons, forks, drums, fifes, and walking sticks out of wood and bamboo. These items often featured anthropomorphic images that resembled decorative forms used in Africa; African cultural continuity also appears through the variety of split wood, palmetto, and grass baskets made by slaves. Used in fanning rice, picking cotton, and storing food, the baskets strongly resembled forms found throughout the continent of Africa. In addition to keeping people warm inside the drafty slave quarters, slave-made quilts maintained African decorative and textile traditions through their creators' use of similar colors, patterns, and iconography. Finally, slave-made pottery forms such as face jugs and Colono Ware (low-fired handmade pottery) resemble West African ceramic styles and may demonstrate the continuation of African religious beliefs in America. More specifically, X-shaped designs carved into Colono Ware bowls may reflect cosmograms, depictions of the universe, based on Bakongo religious beliefs. Similarly, some scholars argue that face jugs could have also served a spiritual function in relation to conjure practices.

— *Daniel L. Fountain*

See also: Artisans.

For Further Reading
Burrison, John A. 1978. "Afro-American Folk Pottery in the South." *Southern Folklore Quarterly* 42 (2–3): 175–199.

Ferguson, Leland. 1992. *Uncommon Ground: Archaeology and Early African America, 1650–1800.* Washington, DC: Smithsonian Institution Press.

Fry, Gladys-Marie. 1990. *Stitched from the Soul: Slave Quilts from the Ante-bellum South.* New York: Dutton Studio Books.

Peek, Phil. 1978. "Afro-American Material Culture and the Afro-American Craftsman." *Southern Folklore Quarterly* 42 (2–3): 109–134.

Vlach, John M. 1978. *The Afro-American Tradition in Decorative Arts.* Cleveland, OH: Cleveland Museum of Art.

Vlach, John M. 1991. *By the Work of Their Hands: Studies in Afro-American Folklife.* Ann Arbor, MI: UMI Research Press.

ATLANTIC ABOLITIONIST MOVEMENT

By the 1770s Western cultural developments converged with transatlantic imperial crises to provide society with the language and opportunity for collective opposition to slavery and the slave trade. Natural rights philosophy, the Enlightenment critique of traditional authority, British Protestantism's emerging faith in the individual's capacity for virtue, and new economic theories suggesting that free labor and free trade best promoted economic progress all undermined older justifications for slavery. American Quakers revitalized their moral opposition to warfare during the Seven Years' War (1756–1763), extended their critique

of violence to include slavery itself, and dedicated themselves to eliminating slaveholding within their own ranks. The American and French Revolutions, fought for liberty and equality, encouraged others to join the abolitionist movement.

Fearing that radical experimentation might undermine the social order, early Anglo-American and French abolitionists supported modest measures for eliminating slavery. They generally favored ending the slave trade, emancipating slaves gradually, and compensating slaveholders for their losses. In the newly independent United States, Quakers, evangelicals, and several revolutionary leaders established the first state abolition societies to promote these aims. Between 1780 and 1808, abolitionists secured legislation preventing slavery's expansion into the Northwest Territory, freeing the children of slaves in the northern states after apprenticeships of approximately twenty years, and prohibiting U.S. participation in the transatlantic slave trade.

Inspired by antislavery advocates in the United States, Quaker and evangelical abolitionists in England campaigned against British participation in the transatlantic slave trade, hoping that a diminished slave supply would encourage West Indian planters to treat their slaves more humanely and ease the transition to free labor. Operating through the Society for the Abolition of the Slave Trade (1787), they won the patronage of influential figures in Parliament. But despite a massive public campaign far surpassing that of their U.S. counterparts, they failed to overcome powerful slave-trading interests until 1807. This year marked the beginning of their efforts against foreign participation in the transatlantic slave trade as well, but justifiable international suspicion of British motives limited their success.

In 1788, following the example of Anglo-American abolitionists, the French reformer Brissot de Warville organized a group of enlightened nobles and *philosophes* into the *Société des Amis des Noirs.* During the 1789 meeting of the Estates General in Paris, the *Société* condemned slavery but limited their immediate goals to supporting colonial mulatto representation and abolishing the slave trade. Planter and merchant representatives easily suppressed the initiatives of the sanguine and poorly organized group.

Insurrectionary slaves, rising in rebellion when Spanish and English troops invaded the French colony of St. Domingue (modern Haiti), eclipsed the *Amis's* moderate efforts. Desperate to secure the loyalty of insurrectionists, French commissioners issued a decree freeing loyal slaves in 1793, and the Convention in Paris abolished slavery in 1794. Napoleon forcibly reinstituted slavery in the colonies but failed to subdue the revolutionaries in St. Domingue, who represented 80 percent of France's former colonial slave population. The resulting relative marginality of French colonial slavery opened the way for its eventual abolition in 1848.

Anticolonial nationalism, not abolitionism, led to the emancipation of most Latin American slaves. Revolutionaries like Simon Bolívar granted freedom to slaves willing to join the military campaigns for independence. But most nationalist leaders, many of whom owned large landholdings and numerous slaves, supported such measures only reluctantly. Though willing to endorse freedom for slaves who would assist them in the war effort, they balked at full-scale, immediate emancipation. The newly independent mainland Latin American republics along the Atlantic seaboard eventually passed legislative gradual emancipation acts, beginning with Argentina in 1813 and ending with Venezuela in 1854. Spanish Cuba and independent Brazil, however, resisted this trend toward emancipation.

Following legislative prohibition of both British and U.S. participation in the transatlantic slave trade, antislavery advocates explored new moderate measures to promote emancipation. British abolitionists proposed registering all West Indian slaves to ensure their protection from flagrantly exploitative abuses and to set a legal precedent for more substantial parliamentary intervention. In the United States, the American Colonization Society (1816) popularized the idea of emancipating southern slaves and colonizing them in Africa, thereby eliminating the potential threat of a much reviled free African American population. But planter intransigence and the expansion of slavery into new U.S. territories led Anglo-American abolitionists in the 1820s to reject gradualism and demand more radical, immediate action. Religious developments reinforced this tactical shift. Evangelicals seeking to hasten the millennium, became less willing to tolerate compromise with slaveholding sinners. This later generation of abolitionists also benefited from the more active participation of middle-class white women who increasingly viewed slavery as an affront to new domestic family ideals.

British abolitionists, armed with new conviction and organizational strength, and pointing to the recent slave revolts in Barbados, Demerara, and Jamaica, convinced Parliament to pass the Emancipation Act (1833).Not entirely pleased with the statutory provisions to compensate slaveholders and the apprenticeships required of slave children, abolitionists successfully supported legislation to eliminate lengthy work requirements in 1838. Having promoted the emancipation of seven hundred fifty thousand British West Indian slaves, abolitionists turned their attention toward slavery and the slave trade elsewhere. They organized the World Anti-Slavery Conventions of 1840 and 1843 to encourage emancipation in the southern United States, they scored significant successes in curtailing the slave trade by advocating mutual search of European vessels, and later helped secure British diplomatic support for the Union during the Civil War.

Parliamentary supremacy over its distant colonies simplified the task of British abolitionists, but a decentralized federalist political system granting great autonomy to slaveholding states hampered U.S. antislavery advocates. In 1833 William Lloyd Garrison established the American Anti-Slavery Society, a group that condemned the racial prejudice implicit in the colonization movement and called for immediate, uncompensated emancipation. Members of the society grew to consider the U.S. Constitution a proslavery document and preferred dissolution of the Union over compromise with slaveholders.

Garrison's strict stance, and his support for other controversial issues like women's suffrage, alienated some of his followers. In 1840, these critics formed the Foreign and American Anti-Slavery Society, most of whom viewed the Constitution as an antislavery blueprint giving the federal government a right to dismantle slavery. Black abolitionists—particularly fugitives from the slave South like Frederick Douglass and William Wells Brown—played an important role in healing some of the rifts, eloquently reminding contending factions in both Britain and the United States to combat dogmatism and tackle the immediate problem of slavery. Despite the conflicts between various abolitionist groups, they managed to convey to southerners that their ideas were widely held by the northern public. In this sense, they helped fuel the sectional animosity that resulted in both Civil War and the eventual emancipation of 4 million southern slaves.

Independent Brazil and Spanish Cuba remained the last major bastions of slavery in the Americas. In both areas, the dramatic recent example of U.S. abolition, British successes at effectively ending the transatlantic slave trade, the efforts to attract European immigrants, and the rebellious activities of slaves facilitated emancipation. Only in Brazil did there exist an organized abolitionist movement. The lawyer and parliamentarian Joaquim Nabuco led a small group of secular-minded abolitionists from northeastern Brazil where slave-based sugar production was in serious decline. In 1871, despite the opposition of new coffee planters in southwestern Brazil, the government passed a gradual abolition law requiring lengthy indentures for former slaves. An emancipation law offering current slaves immediate freedom passed in 1888, but by this time slaves had already begun to take matters into their own hands by fleeing their masters in large numbers. In Cuba a gradual abolition law was passed in 1880, and full emancipation came in 1886.

After slavery was abolished in the West Indies, British antislavery advocates directed their attention to emancipation in Africa. To reinforce their goal, they supported a naval squadron along the African coast to enforce abolition of the transatlantic slave trade, promoted the "legitimate trade" in tropical staples, and encouraged missionary activity to spread Christianity. But this campaign also served to legitimate Britain's growing imperial ambitions in the region.

British naval power effectively prohibited the transatlantic trade in the late nineteenth century, but it also challenged the sovereignty of African nations. Although New World markets for tropical staples offered Africans an alternative to the international traffic in slaves, the growing labor employed in the production of such commodities was often indistinguishable from domestic slavery. Missionary explorers, discovering the great extent to which Africans utilized slaves, became key proponents of greater colonial authority. International antislavery agreements, like those contained in the Brussels Act (1890), authorized direct intervention to end domestic slavery and the slave trade. But the fine line distinguishing domestic slavery from other profitable forms of labor exploitation was drawn with an eye toward promoting economic benefits. Such ventures met only minimal success, though they did much to expand European colonial power in Africa.

Various forms of human bondage—though often difficult to classify definitively as slavery—continue to this day. The United Nations, the Working Group of Experts on Slavery, the London-based Anti-Slavery International (ASI), and other organizations have challenged exploitative labor contracts, forced relocation, pawning of individuals for debt, betrothal of children, convict labor, and prostitution.

— *Anthony A. Iaccarino*

See also: Abolitionism in the United States; American Colonization Society; Brown, William Wells; Child, Lydia M.; Compensated Emancipation; Douglass, Frederick; Emancipation Proclamation; Free African Society; Garrison, William Lloyd; Grimké, Angelina; Grimké, Sarah Moore; Immediatism; Quakers; Truth, Sojourner; Weld, Theodore Dwight.

For Further Reading

Azevedo, Celia M. 1995. *Abolitionism in the United States and Brazil: A Comparative Perspective.* New York: Garland.

Blackett, R. J. M. 1989. *Building an Antislavery Wall: Black Abolitionists in the Atlantic Abolitionist Movement, 1830–1860.* Ithaca, NY: Cornell University Press.

Davis, David Brion. 1975. *The Problem of Slavery in the Age of Revolution, 1770–1823.* Ithaca, NY: Cornell University Press.

Davis, David Brion. 1984. *Slavery and Human Progress.* New York: Oxford University Press.

Fladeland, Betty. 1972. *Men and Brothers: Anglo-American Antislavery Cooperation.* Urbana: University of Illinois Press.

Frey, Sylvia R. 1999. *From Slavery to Emancipation in the Atlantic World.* London: Frank Cass.

ATLANTIC SLAVE TRADE, CLOSING OF

Efforts to end the Atlantic slave trade began in the late eighteenth century, but the trade continued well into the late nineteenth century. The main goal of antislave trade policies was the suppression of the West African slave trade, which involved the transportation of slaves to the major slave nations of the Western Hemisphere such as the United States or Brazil. Great Britain undertook a concerted effort to end the trade, but only after the United States adopted stringent antislave trade legislation was the trade suppressed.

In 1792 Denmark became the first major European state to abolish the slave trade. Nonetheless, from the abolition of the slave trade within the British Empire in 1807 until the essential end of the international trade in African slaves at the close of the nineteenth century, Great Britain was the primary force behind the suppression of the African slave trade. Prior to abolition of the trade, Great Britain was the trade's largest actor. British slave traders shipped Africans to the British colonies in the West Indies, the various states of South and Central America, and the southern United States. Although efforts to abolish the trade began in Parliament in the 1780s, the British slave traders and the West Indian plantation owners who depended on slave labor presented a powerful, economic block that was able repeatedly to defeat abolitionist legislation. It was not until 1807 that Thomas Clarkson and William Wilberforce were able to convince Parliament to pass legislation to abolish the slave trade within the empire. In 1811, Parliament followed its abolition act with another law that made involvement in the slave trade a felony for British citizens.

As part of the legislation, the British government offered to pay a bounty for captured slave ships and for each slave that was captured while being transported. The captured slaves were to be freed and transported to the colony of Sierra Leone. Sierra Leone, in fact, became the center of Britain's efforts to end the West African trade. Its capital, Freetown, became the major base for the British naval units involved in suppressing the trade and the home for the courts that would try slavers.

In 1808 two British naval ships were sent to Africa with orders to intercept slave vessels. The end of the Napoleonic Wars in 1815 freed up more naval resources and the British steadily increased the size of the antislave squadron. The British also carried out a diplomatic offensive to end the trade by negotiating with other nations to end their involvement and, more importantly, to allow the British navy to stop, search, and, if necessary, arrest non-British citizens engaged in the slave trade. For instance, in 1815 Portugal agreed to end its involvement in the slave trade north of the equator and to allow the British to stop suspected slave ships. In 1817 British courts decided in the *Le Louis* case that foreign ships suspected of being slave traders could only be stopped and searched with the permission of their national government. The British government then embarked on a broad diplomatic campaign to secure agreements with the major European powers and the United States. By the 1820s, most nations, with the notable exception of the United States, had granted the British the right to search and capture vessels involved in the trade.

The British were able to insert "equipment clauses" in most of these treaties, which allowed the British to seize empty slave ships if those ships were rigged to transport slaves. Some nations, including France and eventually the United States, also stationed antislavery squadrons along the West African coast. By the 1830s these naval squadrons were capturing, on average, approximately thirty slave ships and freeing approximately five thousand slaves per year. Nonetheless, the eighty thousand to ninety thousand slaves who continued to be transported to the Americas dwarfed these numbers.

The United States was the major impediment to attempts by the major European powers to suppress the trade. Although the U.S. government had passed numerous laws to curtail the slave trade, these regulations were only sporadically enforced. For instance, in 1794 Congress had enacted legislation that banned the building or equipping of ships for the slave trade, and in 1800 a law was passed that prohibited U.S. citizens from engaging in the slave trade between two foreign countries. However, neither piece of legislation was vigorously enforced. The United States itself banned the slave trade in 1807; nonetheless, the trade between

West Africa or the Caribbean and the southern states continued.

The United States refused to grant other nations the right to stop and search U.S. ships. As a result, slavers from other nations would sail under the U.S. flag to escape from the antislavery squadrons. Under pressure from southern politicians, successive administrations in Washington pressed the British to provide restitution for Americans involved in the trade whose slaves were set free by the Royal Navy patrols.

The Americans also provided the bulk of the slave ships. By the 1850s, two out of every three slave ships captured had been outfitted in U.S. ports. Nonetheless, substantial progress in curtailing the trade was accomplished. By the 1830s all of the major European powers backed British efforts to end the trade, even including the "equipment clause" in the Quintuple Treaty (1841). When Texas became an independent country, its national government also agreed to grant the British permission to stop and search suspected slavers sailing under the Texan flag. Often, mixed-prize courts (special naval tribunals) were established with both British and officials from other nations to adjudicate cases. For instance, mixed courts were established in Sierra Leone and Havana to try cases involving suspected Spanish slave traders.

In 1819 the United States enacted laws that equated participation in the slave trade with piracy and made such engagement punishable by death. The following year, the United States dispatched a small four-ship flotilla to Africa to help suppress the slave trade. The squadron was recalled after four years when negotiations between Great Britain and the United States on a treaty to suppress the trade failed after the U.S. Senate weakened the proposed treaty through amendments. In 1837 the British invited France and the United States to form a tripartite naval antislavery squadron, but the United States refused. The French did cooperate, however, and joint patrols between the two countries were established.

Beginning in the 1840s, the British also began efforts to cut off the supply of slaves by either offering subsidies to native rulers to end their involvement in the trade or taking direct military action against those who refused to cooperate. For instance, the British military conquered the territory of Lagos when its king refused to end the kingdom's prolific slave trade. The British instituted a tight naval blockade of Dahomey for the same reasons. The British also purchased the former slave colonies of Denmark in 1850.

Diplomatic efforts to involve the United States in the suppression of the trade proved successful when a portion of the Webster-Ashburton Treaty (1842)

pledged that the United States would dispatch a small naval squadron to patrol with the British so that suspected slave ships flying the U.S. flag could be stopped without incidence. Known as joint cruising, this effort proved to be more symbolic than effective. U.S. officials refused to act upon British intelligence information about suspected slave ships, and even as late as 1860, some twenty slave ships were outfitted in the port of New York alone, without any interference from U.S. customs officials.

The United States further insisted on a clause in the treaty to provide restitution for freed slaves. The British initially balked, but then compromised and agreed to compensate owners for slaves freed when a slave ship was wrecked on British territory. In return, the United States accepted a provision in the treaty for extradition.

The Civil War and the subsequent Union blockade of southern ports effectively ended the large-scale transport of West African slaves. From 1860 to 1864, the number of slaves transported to the Western Hemisphere dropped from approximately twenty-five thousand to seven thousand. The Washington Treaty (1862) further strengthened abolition efforts between the United States and Great Britain by finally allowing the British to seize suspected slave ships, sailing under the U.S. flag. The treaty also established mixed courts in New York, Capetown, and Sierra Leone to try cases of suspected trafficking in slaves. Significantly, there was no right of appeal for the courts. Throughout the Civil War, Union warships also vigorously sought out slave ships or other vessels suspected of bringing supplies to the Confederacy.

Despite the fact that slavery continued in Cuba until 1886 and in Brazil until 1888, the expanded ability of the British antislavery squadron to stop and search suspected slave ships convincingly ended the Atlantic slave trade by the 1870s. The imposition of European prohibitions on the slave trade as the European powers carved Africa into colonies during the period known as the Scramble for Africa more or less ended the external African slave trade by the early 1900s, although as late as 1920 a slave ship was discovered in the Persian Gulf and the internal slave trade in Africa would continue. In the end, only the formal abolition of slavery as an accepted institution throughout Africa effectively ended the slave trade.

— *Tom Lansford*

For Further Reading

Alpers, Edward. 1975. *Ivory and Slaves.* Berkeley: University of California Press.

Lovejoy, Paul. 2000. *Transformations in Slavery: A History of Slavery in Africa.* New York: Cambridge University Press.

Mannix, Daniel, and Malcolm Cowley. 1962. *Black Cargoes: A History of the Atlantic Slave Trade.* New York: Viking.

Miers, Suzanne. 1975. *Britain and the Ending of the Slave Trade.* New York: Longman.

Northrup, David, ed. 2002. *The Atlantic Slave Trade.* Boston: Houghton Mifflin.

Ward, William. 1969. *The Royal Navy and the Slavers.* New York: Pantheon.

CRISPUS ATTUCKS (C. 1723–1770)

Crispus Attucks, a mulatto and former slave of African and Native American descent, is noted as the first person killed in the Boston Massacre, but little else about him is certain. Apparently, Attucks was once the slave of Deacon William Browne of Framingham, Massachusetts, until November 1750, when he escaped at the age of twenty-seven. As a free black in colonial America, Attucks worked on a whaling ship where he met other American colonists who disapproved of Britain's colonial policies. His life ended on March 5, 1770, when he became the first person to fall at the hands of the British soldiers stationed in Boston.

Although his background remains obscure, Attucks played an important role in the event that caused his death. Court records and the testimonies of several other participants in the melee indicate that Attucks led a mob of fifty to sixty men to the Boston Custom House on King Street. The jeering crowd pressed forward and began to throw snow and ice at the British soldiers stationed at the Custom House, and according to one eyewitness, Andrew, a slave of Oliver Wendell, Attucks struck at a soldier. Colonial essayist Samuel Adams later told the court a different story claiming that Attucks was not the person who started the riot.

Whatever Attucks did that night, a violent episode ensued between the mob and the British soldiers under Captain Thomas Preston's command. Several shots were fired, and five civilians were killed, including Attucks, and his conduct during the event played a prominent role in the trial that followed. The documents used to indict the British soldiers for the massacre identified Attucks as the first individual upon whom the soldiers fired. The same documents accused the soldiers of participating in an unprovoked altercation with uncontrollable force and malice. Responding to the plaintiffs tactics, John Adams, the British soldiers' defense attorney, focused on Attucks's actions. Adams argued that Attucks was the person who formed the mob and led the attack on the soldiers.

Roth, James Michael. 1999. "The Many Faces of Crispus Attucks: The Symbolism of Crispus Attucks in the Formation of American Identity." M.A. thesis, Department of History, University of New Hampshire. Durham, New Hampshire.

Simmons, William, J. 1968. *Men of Mark: Eminent, Progressive and Rising.* New York: Arno.

Crispus Attucks, a former slave who became the first victim of the Boston Massacre, was an inspiring symbol of freedom during the American struggle for independence. (Library of Congress)

Eventually, the court found two British soldiers guilty of manslaughter, and they were branded and given clemency.

After his death and the end of the War of Independence, Attucks's name continued to receive much attention. Throughout the antebellum period, several African American military regiments named themselves the Attucks Guard. Between 1858 and 1870, many of Boston's African Americans held annual Crispus Attucks Day celebrations. In 1888 an Attucks memorial was constructed on the Boston Common. His name became a symbol of courage for all Americans, particularly African Americans.

— *Eric R. Jackson*

For Further Reading

Fisher, Ruth Anna. 1942. "Manuscript Materials Bearing on the Negro in British America." *Journal of Negro History* 27 (1): 83–93.

Lanning, Michael Lee. 1997. *The African-American Soldier: From Crispus Attucks to Colin Powell.* Secaucus, NJ: Carol Publishing.

Livermore, George. 1970. *An Historical Research Respecting The Opinions of the Founders of the Republic on Negroes as Slaves, as Citizens, and as Soldiers.* New York: Augustus M. Kelley.

Quarles, Benjamin. 1961. *The Negro in the American Revolution.* New York: Norton.

AUTOBIOGRAPHIES

Autobiographies by slaves in the United States served as a principal means by which the victims of the peculiar institution and abolitionists could offer an alternative perspective on slavery. For abolitionist groups like the Massachusetts Anti-Slavery Society, they provided eyewitness accounts that contradicted owners' claims of a paternalistic and even beneficent institution. They offered a vision of a nightmare society, filled with violence, torture, and promiscuity, where all members both black and white were degraded through the uncontrolled exercise of power. Because of this potential, abolitionist societies published dozens of narratives between 1760 and 1865. They were one of the most popular early nineteenth-century literary forms, especially among northern white female readers.

For the writers, these autobiographies presented an opportunity to tell their experiences in their own words. In doing so, they were able to claim an identity and selfhood that slavery had denied them. But this privilege came at a price. The authors could not assume that the audience would accept the story's veracity or even the narrator's humanity. Various devices had to be employed to validate both the writers and their experiences. One such device was the authentication letter, a statement from one or more prominent whites that they knew the author, that he or she was a trustworthy person, and that they had good reason to believe that the story was true. The author was put in a position of dependence on whites, much as he or she had been in slavery; the writer's word alone counted for little.

Another technique for engaging the reader was to indicate the inhumanity and even sadism of the treatment experienced under slavery; the slave narratives went into great detail about the cruelties inflicted on innocent victims. Whippings were shown not merely as straightforward punishment, but as arbitrary acts resulting from the immoral character of masters. Such people enjoyed drawing blood and eliciting screams. Drawings were often included of torture devices, with explicit directions on how they were used. Such detail substantiated the writers' claims.

One convention of the genre was to show the lengths to which slaves would go to gain their freedom. Henry "Box" Brown nailed himself in a shipping crate and was sent to the North as goods. Much of his narrative relates to the suffering he endured during the transportation. William and Ellen Craft were able to escape because she was light enough to pass for white. They dressed her as a master, with William as her servant. They managed to travel overland to freedom by making her appear to have a broken arm (because she could not write) and a toothache (because her speech would give them away). Despite a number of close calls, they reached the North. Interestingly, the narratives that are now considered the most important give relatively little attention to the important role that the fugitives played in effecting their own freedom .

The most important means by which narrators made themselves and their stories convincing was through their self-presentation as people very similar to their readers. In one of the earliest and most important narratives, Olaudah Equiano presents himself as an English gentleman. The engraved image of Equiano from the 1789 edition of his *Narrative* shows a figure indistinguishable in dress and manner from his intended audience; the difference comes in skin color and hair texture. This identification is reinforced in the text as he depicts the culture and people of his African childhood. His Africans display close parallels in family structure, moral probity, diligence in work, and spirituality to the British. Equiano himself is the model of the hard-working entrepreneur who deals honestly with everyone. The flawed characters in his autobiography are those whites whose association with slavery and the slave trade have made them greedy, cruel, and generally uncivilized. He directs his narrative specifically to members of the British Parliament and clearly seeks to present himself as a worthy subject. He called on them, out of common humanity, to end slavery.

Equiano's work is international in its frame of reference, but two major U.S. texts focus on national and local issues. Frederick Douglass became famous as a result of his 1845 *Narrative*. He had managed to escape seven years earlier and by 1841 had become a successful lecturer on the abolitionist circuit. The *Narrative* was written to counter charges that one so articulate could not have been a slave. In his story Douglass gives particular attention to what Robert Stepto (1979) has asserted is the principal theme of the narratives: the link between literacy and freedom. Douglass's story of how he came to be able to read and write, though it was against the law and against his master's explicit orders, is connected to his sense of self and desire for freedom.

The escape from a slave mentality is for him more important than the physical escape, about which he says nothing in this first version of his autobiography.

Harriet Jacobs, in *Incidents in the Life of a Slave Girl* (1861), provides a distinct perspective as she describes what it means to be a young woman in a social order in which white men have no limits on the exercise of their power. Her master constantly tries to seduce her, and, because of this, Jacobs is subject to his wife's jealous rage. Her appeal is to the understanding of virtuous white women who have not had to face the kinds of pressures imposed on slave women. Both she and Douglass, more than other narrators, demand recognition of their equality with the audience.

The slave narrative tradition did not end with the Civil War. Some sixty-five narratives were published by ex-slaves from 1870 to 1930. During the Depression, the collection of oral histories was a project of the Federal Writers Project. Over twenty-five hundred narratives were collected in seventeen states. About six thousand narratives exist in one form or another, offering the voices of one group of victims of history. The tradition has been continued in literature with fictional versions, such as Ernest Gaines's *The Autobiography of Miss Jane Pittman* (1971) and Toni Morrison's *Beloved* (1987).

— *Keith Byerman*

See also: Brown, Henry "Box"; Craft, William and Ellen; Douglass, Frederick; Jacobs, Harriet Ann; Works Progress Administration Interviews.

For Further Reading

Andrews, William. 1986. *To Tell a Free Story: The First Century of Afro-American Autobiography, 1760–1865.* Urbana: University of Illinois Press.

Davis, Charles T., and Henry Louis Gates, Jr. 1985. *The Slave's Narrative.* New York: Oxford University Press.

Sekora, John, and Darwin Turner, eds. 1982. *The Art of Slave Narrative: Original Essays in Criticism and Theory.* Macomb: Western Illinois University Press.

Stepto, Robert B. 1979. *From Behind the Veil: A Study of Afro-American Narrative.* Urbana: University of Illinois Press.

↬ B ↬

GAMALIEL BAILEY (1807–1859)

Gamaliel Bailey was an important American antislavery journalist during the antebellum period. After receiving his M.D. in 1827, he spent the next three years as a ship's doctor on a vessel employed in the China trade. In 1830 he went to work for a Methodist newspaper in Baltimore, Maryland, but he returned to medicine the following year to help fight a cholera epidemic in Cincinnati, Ohio. He remained in Cincinnati after the epidemic to lecture on physiology at Lane Theological Seminary.

In 1832 Bailey became involved in Lane's famous debate over slavery, which convinced him that voluntary emancipation was the best way to end slavery. In 1835 he cofounded and became secretary of the Cincinnati Anti-Slavery Society. The following year he became corresponding secretary of the Ohio Anti-Slavery Society and assistant editor of the *Philanthropist,* the first abolitionist newspaper in Ohio. In 1837 he became the paper's coeditor. In this capacity he continued to espouse voluntary emancipation via moral suasion, but he also began promoting political action against slavery by calling on abolitionists to vote only for antislavery candidates. He further demanded that the federal government outlaw slavery in the District of Columbia and federal territories and stop enforcing the Fugitive Slave Act of 1793. On three separate occasions, his office was attacked by proslavery mobs, and once the entire establishment, including the printing press, was destroyed.

In 1838 Bailey joined the ranks of the immediate abolitionists. He began to formulate the "slave power" theory by arguing that proslavery forces controlled both major political parties and the federal government; consequently, they threatened the liberties of nonslaveholders as well as slaves and must be opposed through both political and moral means. He insisted that the best way to end slavery was to eliminate the slave power influence in the federal government, after which he believed the people of the South would repeal slavery once they discovered how inefficient it was. To this end, he called for the creation of a third party devoted to immediate abolition. His call was partly responsible for the creation of the Liberty Party, which ran a candidate for president in the elections of 1840 and 1844.

In 1847 Bailey moved to Washington, D.C., to become editor-in-chief of the weekly *National Era* the official organ of the American and Foreign Anti-Slavery Society. He appealed to a wide readership by printing national and international news items as well as literary pieces, articles on religion, and cogent abolitionist editorials. The general tone of the editorials was that abolitionism was a class struggle, not a sectional one, and he appealed repeatedly to nonslaveholding southerners to throw off the oppression of slave power.

The paper's moderate tone, necessitated in large part by its being the only abolitionist paper published in slave territory, drew constant criticism from radical abolitionist editors safely ensconced in the North. However, it also made the *National Era* one of the country's most influential antislavery papers. By 1850 the paper had gained enough of a national readership that the proslavery *Southern Press* was started in Washington that same year to counter the *National Era*'s influence. Undaunted by criticism or competition, Bailey continued to publish the *National Era* until his death in 1859.

Of all the items that Bailey published, the most influential was Harriet Beecher Stowe's *Uncle Tom's Cabin*. It was originally scheduled to appear in serial form in ten issues in 1851, but its immediate popularity caused Stowe to lengthen it significantly so that it ran well into 1852. *Uncle Tom's Cabin* greatly enhanced the *National Era*'s reputation and helped increase circulation to its mid-1853 peak of twenty-eight thousand. However, Bailey's main purpose for running Stowe's serial was to teach nonslaveholders in the South in a nonthreatening way that slavery was evil.

— *Charles W. Carey*

See also: Stowe, Harriet Beecher; *Uncle Tom's Cabin.*

For Further Reading
Harrold, Stanley C., Jr. 1976. "Forging an Antislavery Instrument: Gamaliel Bailey and the Formation of the Ohio Liberty Party." *Old Northwest* 2 (December): 371–387.
Harrold, Stanley C., Jr. 1977. "The Perspective of a Cincinnati Abolitionist: Gamaliel Bailey on Social Reform in America." *Bulletin of the Cincinnati Historical Society* 35 (Fall): 173–190.
Harrold, Stanley C., Jr. 1986. *Gamaliel Bailey and Antislavery Union.* Kent, OH: Kent State University Press.

CHARLES BALL (B. 1780)

Charles Ball was the author of *Slavery in the United States: A Narrative of the Life and Adventures of Charles*

Ball (1837), which was first released anonymously as *The Life and Adventures of a Fugitive Slave* (1836). This antebellum slave narrative, viewed by some literary scholars as an archetype of African American literature, was used by abolitionists to dramatize the immorality of southern slavery because of its sometimes symbolic presentation of the plight of individual slaves. Like Charles Ball, most successful slave runaways were adult males; thus male slaves wrote most of the slave narratives. It is clear that traditional antebellum gender roles, although they did not altogether trump racial biases, nevertheless sometimes permitted black male slaves certain benefits that black female slaves were more frequently denied because of their gender. For example, Charles Ball and numerous other black male slaves were allowed to hire themselves out and work for other owners much more often than female slaves, sometimes traveling from one farm to another on their own using a pass. This freedom to gather "intelligence" about the lay of the land as well as the habits of whites on other farms doubtless aided slaves like Ball, who were able to use such information later to escape slavery successfully.

For abolitionists, the critical component of all slave narratives was their firsthand recitation of the evils of slavery per se. However, the narratives universally point to the importance of "literacy, identity, and freedom" for antebellum slaves; indeed, the inclusion of these three points in most narratives is a convention of the slave narrative form.

For slaves, attaining literacy was linked to both personal identity and freedom, and obviously, without it, no narrative would have been possible. Various criticisms were directed at the slave narratives: abolitionists were accused of appropriating slaves' lives in ways similar to those used by slaveowners themselves, and skeptical readers considered some of the narrative prose too polished or sophisticated to have been written by slaves. Nevertheless, most were proved to be authentic. Ball's own narrative has been compared with other contemporary accounts of events, agriculture, landmarks, and local types in South Carolina.

Ball's narrative addressed several questions concerning the slave's life, including how black slaves felt about white owners. He distinguished among his several owners as a slave in South Carolina, Georgia, and Maryland, criticizing one for being arbitrary in dispensing punishment although he also conceded that he had loved that particular master very much. Thus both the "intimacy" and ambivalence produced by slavery were shown. Ball also recalled that he noticed a clear difference between African-born and native-born American slaves—Africans resisted slavery more, he reported.

Apparently, Ball was familiar with African ideas because his own grandfather was a pure African who taught him certain African religious perspectives and especially cautioned him about the hypocrisy of white Christians, whose version of Christianity, he said, was "false" and really "no religion at all." Ball's relationship with his grandfather may have prepared him for the environment in which he found himself when he was sold to an owner from South Carolina: there, he had the experience of living among Africans who practiced both African folk religions and Islam. Historians have noted that the retention of African mores was facilitated when large numbers of Africans were able to live together in close proximity; and Ball recounted the practice of African rituals and mores in the slave quarters, such as burial practices based on certain West African beliefs that the deceased returned to the African homeland after death, or, at the very least, to a Christian heaven that would allow for retribution by slaves. Slave Christians, according to Ball, believed fervently in the idea that they would change places with whites in the world to come and that the last would become first.

— *Dale Edwyna Smith*

See also: Autobiographies; Narratives; South Carolina.

For Further Reading

Davis, Charles T., and Henry Louis Gates, Jr., eds. 1985. *The Slave's Narrative.* New York: Oxford University Press.

Frey, Sylvia R. 1991. *Water from the Rock: Black Resistance in a Revolutionary Age.* Princeton, NJ: Princeton University Press.

Kolchin, Peter. 1993. *American Slavery, 1619–1877.* New York: Hill and Wang.

Nichols, Charles H. 1963. *Many Thousand Gone: The Ex-Slaves' Account of Their Bondage and Freedom.* Bloomington: Indiana University Press.

Raboteau, Albert J. 1978. *Slave Religion: The "Invisible Institution" in the Antebellum South.* New York: Oxford University Press.

BENJAMIN BANNEKER (1731–1806)

Benjamin Banneker was an eighteenth-century rationalist who was also a self-taught mathematician, astronomer, author, surveyor, humanitarian, and inventor. Born the free son of a mulatto mother and a black father, Banneker learned some skills from his grandmother, Molly Welsh, a Quaker schoolteacher who taught him the rudiments of an elementary education, and another Quaker, George Ellicott, loaned him as-

Benjamin Banneker, born a free African American in Maryland, became a self-taught mathematician, scientist, astronomer, and almanac maker. (North Wind Picture Archives)

tronomy books. Banneker combined his limited education with an unusual mathematical ability and earned a reputation for remarkable innovation.

Because clocks and clock makers were rare, Banneker as a young man had seen only two timepieces—a sundial and a pocket watch—but at the age of twenty-two he constructed a wooden clock, using the pocket watch as a model. First he drew a diagram of the watch's internal mechanism, and then he converted the diagram into three-dimensional parts. Built almost entirely of hand-carved, hard-grained wood wherever possible, the clock not only kept the time but also struck the hour.

In the late 1750s Banneker began studying astronomy. After mastering astronomical concepts through books loaned by Ellicott, Banneker predicted eclipses and calculated the cycle of the seventeen-year locust. Later dubbed "the black Poor Richard," Banneker published more than ten annual farmers' almanacs for the Mid-Atlantic states beginning in 1792. Finding that no publisher would take on an unknown black man's almanac, he wrote a twelve-page letter on August 19, 1791, and sent a copy of his 1792 almanac to Thomas Jefferson, then secretary of state under President George Washington, refuting the pervasive belief that "blacks were inferior to whites." Jefferson responded by sending a copy of the almanac to the French Royal Academy of Sciences in Paris and Britain's House of Commons, and Banneker's 1792 almanac became the first scientific book published by a black American.

Banneker later participated in a historical survey of the future District of Columbia. He brought to the project a knowledge of astronomy and related instruments as well as a familiarity with surveying. As the first black presidential appointee in U.S. history, he assisted Major Andrew Ellicott during the preliminary survey from February to April 1791 and helped establish lines for some of the major points in the city. Accounts of Banneker's contributions include the legend that he played a pivotal role in saving the city, but Silvio A. Bedini's exhaustive search of surviving documents challenged the legend that Ellicott was able to reconstruct master city planner L'Enfant's proposals for the city from Banneker's memory.

Banneker was dedicated to exploring and applying natural law for the betterment of the human race. He proposed a federal government office entitled "Secretary of the Peace" and wrote *Plea of Peace* (1793). He supported public education, the prohibition of capital punishment, and the abolition of the militia. Antislavery organizations highlighted his achievements in science as an example of what African Americans can achieve.

— *Yolandea Wood*

For Further Reading
Allen, Will W. 1971. *Banneker: The Afro-American Astronomer.* Freeport, NY: Libraries Press.
Bedini, Silvio A. 1972. *The Life of Benjamin Banneker.* New York: Charles Scribner's Sons.
Green, Richard L., ed. 1985. *A Salute to Black Scientists and Inventors.* New York: Empak.

EDWARD BEECHER (1803–1895)

A noted preacher, abolitionist, and educator, Edward Beecher was the third child, and second son, of Lyman and Roxanna Beecher. He was born on Long Island in East Hampton, New York, and when Edward was seven, his family moved from East Hampton to Litchfield, Connecticut. In his early years, Edward received religious instruction in orthodox Protestant Christianity, taught to him by his father Lyman, and these early lessons greatly influenced the future direction of Edward's life.

In 1818 Edward Beecher began his education at Yale College. Four years later in 1822, he graduated from Yale as valedictorian. For Beecher, 1822 was a year filled with momentous occasions, of which his conversion may have been the most significant. It was also in 1822 that Beecher became the headmaster of the Hartford Grammar School, a position he held for two years. After tiring of his efforts to impart knowledge to unwilling young boys at the Hartford Grammar School, Beecher decided he was ready to become a minister and enrolled in Andover Theological Seminary in 1824. Discontented with the Andover curriculum, he stayed there only a short time, but he soon accepted a tutorship at Yale.

In 1826 Beecher accepted the pastorship at the Park Street Church in Boston, which was widely recognized for its strict adherence to orthodoxy. Beecher spent four years at Park Street before he was dismissed from his post by parishioners who were not satisfied with his preaching. Beecher then accepted an invitation to become president of Illinois College, in Jacksonville, Illinois, in 1830.

The 1830s saw Beecher thrust into the abolition movement. He was an advocate of abolition but supported gradual emancipation or African colonization. Events witnessed by Beecher in the mid-1830s, however, convinced him that gradual emancipation was not the answer to slavery. Rioting mobs comprised of leading citizens often violently attacked vocal supporters of abolition. Beecher established a close relationship with the militant abolitionist Elijah Lovejoy and eventually became a staunch supporter of those who advocated immediate emancipation. In spite of his eventual support of immediate emancipation, Beecher continued to view William Lloyd Garrison and his supporters as extremists.

Over the next few years Beecher worked closely with Lovejoy in his efforts to spread the abolitionist message. In November 1837, Lovejoy was murdered by rioters protesting his outspoken stance on slavery. Several years later in 1844, worn out from his antislavery efforts and having neglected his theological work, Beecher returned to Boston, this time as the pastor of the Salem Street Church. Beecher spent the next several decades of life engaged in both theological work and antislavery activities.

— *Beverly Bunch-Lyons*

See also: Antiabolition Riots; Immediatism; Lovejoy, Elijah P.

For Further Reading

Merideth, Robert. 1964. "A Conservative Abolitionist at Alton: Edward Beecher's *Narrative*." *Journal of Presbyterian History* 42 (March and June): 39–53, 92–103.

In 1840 and 1844, the Liberty Party—the first antislavery party to form in the United States—nominated James G. Birney as its presidential candidate. (Library of Congress)

Merideth, Robert. 1968. *The Politics of the Universe: Edward Beecher, Abolition and Orthodoxy.* Nashville, TN: Vanderbilt University Press.

Rugoff, Milton. 1981. *The Beechers: An American Family in the Nineteenth Century.* New York: Harper and Row.

JAMES G. BIRNEY (1792–1857)

An abolitionist and third-party presidential candidate in 1840 and 1844, James G. Birney won pivotal votes that had the unintended effect of helping to elect proslavery candidate James K. Polk in the 1844 election. Born into a Kentucky slaveholding family, Birney became a slaveholder when he was six, yet he never advocated the institution, both because of his family and because of his education. He studied at Transylvania University and later at Princeton, and after studying law in Philadelphia, he returned to Danville, Kentucky, to practice law. His father favored emancipation despite being a slaveholder himself, and in Philadelphia, Birney was further introduced to antislavery sentiment. Despite these factors, Birney gained ownership of even more slaves through his marriage in 1816.

In 1818 he moved to northern Alabama's Madison County, where he entered state politics, ignored his plantation, and increased his visibility as an attorney. As a member of the Alabama Constitutional Convention (1819), Birney was largely responsible for a constitutional provision prohibiting the introduction of slaves to the state for sale. Compensated emancipation was also provided upon an owner's consent. Elected to the state legislature in 1819, Birney was a founder of the University of Alabama. Birney was noted for his antislavery views, and after he opposed the state's support of Andrew Jackson's presidential candidacy, he was not reelected. By 1823 he had a lucrative law practice in Huntsville, Alabama. One of his more prominent clients was the Cherokee Nation, and he increasingly became an advocate for the Cherokee and an opponent of slavery. Raised an Episcopalian, he converted to Presbyterianism in 1826 and started supporting gradual emancipation.

During the next decade, Birney gained notoriety as an opponent of slavery but was not yet an abolitionist. In August 1832, he became an American Colonization Society agent, traveling across the South lecturing on the society's objective—to encourage black Americans to emigrate. Birney believed that Kentucky was an ideal state in which to advocate his antislavery sentiments, and he promoted his views in lectures and letters to newspapers and friends. Gradually recognizing that colonization was not the answer to slavery, in 1834 he wrote his "Letter on Colonization," first published in the Lexington, Kentucky, *Western Luminary* and reprinted in other newspapers and as a pamphlet. He attempted to justify his resignation from the Kentucky Colonization Society, and this added to his standing among antislavery forces.

Living in Danville, Birney helped found a state antislavery society and planned to publish a newspaper advocating his views. After being personally threatened and having his mail interrupted, Birney moved across the Ohio River to New Richmond, Ohio (near Cincinnati), and published his paper. Birney had become an abolitionist, and his pamphlet, *The American Churches, the Bulwarks of American Slavery* (1835), was an established abolitionist tract. In 1839 he emancipated his twenty-one slaves at an estimated cost to him of twenty thousand dollars.

In January 1836 Birney's inaugural issue of the *Philanthropist* attacked slavery, Democrats, and Whigs, and advocated political action for abolitionists. The publication added to the distrust of and opposition to Birney's ideas and his public appearances were frequently threatened with violence. He remained in Ohio until September 1837, when he moved to New York to become executive director of the American Anti-Slavery Society. In his belief in abolishing slavery by constitutional or legal means, Birney differed from the followers of William Lloyd Garrison, the best-known abolitionist in the country. Birney's philosophy, which was based on using political action to end the peculiar institution, increased his national visibility.

In 1840 an Albany, New York, antislavery convention nominated Birney as the newly formed Liberty Party's candidate for president. He garnered 7,100 popular votes. Four years later he had a determining impact on the presidential election. Running once again as the Liberty Party's nominee, Birney won 62,300 votes nationally, but more significant were his 15,812 votes in New York. Without Birney on the ballot, these votes would probably have gone to Whig candidate Henry Clay; instead, Democrat Polk won New York's electoral votes and the election. Polk and his party defended slavery and, if anything was learned politically from the election of 1844, it was the power of the vote in the attempt to end slavery.

In 1845 Birney suffered a crippling fall from a horse and remained partially paralyzed for the rest of his life. He continued writing in opposition to slavery through pamphlets, letters, and other antislavery tracts, but late in life he became a bitter recluse. Birney died in New Jersey on November 25, 1857, a unique figure in the antislavery movement who proved difficult to label or characterize—a slaveowner who opposed slavery. As strident as other abolitionists in his antislavery views, Birney advocated a constitutional end to bondage. Through his writing, public speaking, and presidential candidacy, Birney was an important figure in the American antislavery movement.

— *Boyd Childress*

See also: Compensated Emancipation; Gradualism.

For Further Reading
Birney, William. 1969. *James G. Birney and His Times: The Genesis of the Republican Party.* New York: Bergman.
Fladeland, Betty. 1955. *James G. Birney: Slaveholder to Abolitionist.* Ithaca, NY: Cornell University Press.
Strong, Douglas M. 2001. *Perfectionist Politics: Abolitionism and the Religious Tensions of American Democracy.* Syracuse, NY: Syracuse University Press.

BLACK BELT

A geographical region spreading across much of the cotton-growing area of the southern United States, the Black Belt was a stronghold of the South's agricultural heartland and slavery. At first glance, the region seems to defy an accurate description. Two lines of thought define the Black Belt: one defines it as a distinct southern geographic region, and the other, used by sociologists, describes the same region's demographic characteristics.

Geographically, the Black Belt is the crescent-shaped 300-mile area stretching from central Alabama to northeastern Mississippi and even into Tennessee. It is an unusually flat region about twenty to twenty-five miles wide and is situated between 200 and 300 feet below the upland areas lying north and south. The region includes 5,000 square miles, 75 percent of which is in Alabama. The region drains primarily into the Alabama and Tombigbee river systems. Long considered one of the most desirable southern agricultural regions, the Black Belt takes its name from the rich black soil—calcareous soil formed from large deposits of Selma chalk. With its fertile soils, the region was ideal for cultivating cotton.

The presence of a large slave population to tend cotton planting and production led sociologists and historians to use the term *Black Belt* to describe the plantation society that emerged. This social science definition stems from the large black population that tilled the rich soil, as at the zenith of "King Cotton" in the South, blacks constituted over two-thirds of the region's population. Some historians concluded that many white planters and farmers even avoided the region.

Throughout history, the Black Belt has been generally identified with Alabama. A Creek cession of land in 1816 opened Alabama's Black Belt for settlement, and by the 1820s, cotton and corn were the major crops farmed in the region. Only the Mississippi River Valley produced more cotton than the Black Belt. More extensive settlements had developed by the 1830s, and the region remained a dominant cotton area until the end of the century when the boll weevil invaded the South and caused agricultural diversification and an emphasis on livestock production. Between 1830 and 1860, Alabama's Black Belt was easily the state's most productive region—it was home to the greatest number of slaves and was the stronghold of the state's Whigs. The region claimed three of the state's five capitals, including the current capital of Montgomery, and a significant number of plantations. With water travel available on a number of rivers, including the Alabama and Tombigbee, there was not much rail development. That fact helped preserve the region during the Civil War, as Union armies made few invasions into the area. Even by 1880, cotton production was still the major occupation of Black Belt residents.

Tenancy became a way of life in the region after cotton declined; thus the area became nearly synonymous with poverty. In *Let Us Now Praise Famous Men* (1936), James Agee and Walker Evans depicted this poverty through text and vivid photography. Although little attention is paid to the Black Belt today, in history the region is still as distinct and recognizable as the Carolina Piedmont and the Virginia Tidewater.

— *Boyd Childress*

See also: Short-Staple Cotton.

For Further Reading
Odum, Howard W. 1936. *Southern Regions of the United States.* Chapel Hill: North Carolina University Press.
Wimberley, Ronald C., and Libby V. Morris. 1997. *The Southern Black Belt: A National Perspective.* Lexington: TVA Rural Studies and University of Kentucky Press.

BLACK LOYALISTS

Black loyalists were African Americans who served the British forces in various capacities during the American Revolution. Lured by proclamations promising manumission in return for service to the Crown (and by the republican ideology of liberty, equality, and fraternity), many blacks (some free, some indentured, most enslaved) declared their independence from slavery, joined the British, and toiled as victualers, laborers, and aides-de-camp. They served as auxiliaries to British, Hessian, and Loyalist militia, and they organized into formal military units like the Black Pioneers and the Ethiopian Regiment. Scholars estimate that perhaps one hundred thousand black Loyalists (and perhaps an equally large number of enslaved blacks) were evacuated, along with white counterparts, when peace was declared.

Loyalist communities began forming soon after the Revolution began. The British shifted and moved these Loyalists from one location to another as military activities unfolded in Massachusetts, Pennsylvania, and New York and later in Georgia, South Carolina, and the West Indies. Populations in Savannah, Georgia; Charles-Town, South Carolina; and New York swelled as refugees, both black and white, migrated to British-controlled areas. The single largest black community formed in and around New York City. The city's population began increasing soon after the

British occupation, and it expanded to over twenty-five thousand by 1783. Black folk lived in "Negro quarters," barrack-like domiciles converted from housing seized, confiscated, and leased from Americans.

Some indication of the black community's size and viability is evidenced by evacuation returns and by firsthand accounts of black festivities. *The Book of Negroes,* a listing by name, age, gender, place of origin, and so on, of black people transported on British ships, shows an aggregate total of just over three thousand. Besides providing services to the Crown, blacks formed free communities. Eyewitness accounts of "Ethiopian balls," black festivities attended by whites, attest to the importance of such events in both the black and the white communities.

Despite proclamations assuring their liberty, the black Loyalist's plight was insecure and negotiations concerning their disposition assumed top priority as the Revolution ended. Sir Guy Carleton, hoping to honor British proclamations, interpreted Article Seven of the Treaty of Versailles (1783) to mean that blacks within British-controlled areas as of a given date were free. Despite this effort, military correspondence is replete with accounts of former slaveowners entering British-controlled areas to reclaim what they considered their property—slaves. Both sides confiscated slaves and the British or British-affiliated agents engaged in illicit trade to the West Indies throughout the Revolution.

The transport and relocation of black Loyalists constituted one of the largest Diasporas in the Atlantic region. Between July 1782 and November 1783, the British evacuated Wilmington, Delaware; Savannah, Georgia; Charles-Town, South Carolina; and New York City. Britain had estimated that 50,000 tons of shipping would be necessary to remove the military, the Loyalists, and their baggage, so with less than 30,000 available at any one time, Carleton opted for a series of mini-evacuations. Four separate convoys left Savannah in July 1782: the largest went to New York, the second to Charles-Town, the third to St. Augustine, and the fourth to Jamaica. Three convoys sailed in December 1782 from Charles-Town: the first and largest went to New York, the second to Jamaica, and the third went to England. New York was the last and largest port evacuated. A small number of blacks left in June 1783 for Jamaica, a larger convoy departed for the Bahamas in August and October, while another group went to Canada in November 1783.

Organizing convoys resolved transportation issues but not relocation. It was one thing to offer a home away from home for white Loyalists and quite another

for blacks. Most blacks were transported to the Canadian Maritimes where they established communities in Nova Scotia and New Brunswick. Dissatisfied with Canada, substantial numbers opted for transport to England, and, finding life in England little better, they later left for Sierra Leone in West Africa. A small, but influential, number of blacks opted for transport to Jamaica. Among the more notable of these were Moses Baker and George Liele, folk or itinerant preachers who laid the basis for the island's practice of Afro-Christianity. The history of black Loyalists remains one of the untold stories. Although investigations into their Diaspora have been undertaken, we know little concerning their plight and future in the Old World or the New.

— *John W. Pulis*

See also: Dunmore, John Murray, Fourth Earl of.

For Further Reading

Clifford, Mary Louise. 1999. *From Slavery to Freetown: Black Loyalists after the American Revolution.* Jefferson, NC: McFarland.

Hodges, Graham, ed. 1996. *The Black Loyalist Directory: African Americans in Exile after the American Revolution.* New York: Garland.

Pulis, John W. 1997. "Bridging Troubled Waters: Moses Baker, George Liele, and the African-American Diaspora to Jamaica. " In *Moving On: Black Loyalists in the Afro-Atlantic World.* New York: Garland.

Pulis, John W. 1999. *Moving on: Black Loyalists in the Afro-Atlantic World.* New York: Garland.

Quarles, Benjamin. 1960. *The Negro in the American Revolution.* Chapel Hill: University of North Carolina Press.

Wilson, Ellen. 1976. *The Loyal Blacks.* New York: Capricorn Books.

BLACK NATIONALISM

Black Nationalism is a complex concept. Because of its multiple dimensions, there is no universally acclaimed definition for the term. Scholars have approached Black Nationalism from varying perspectives. Generally, it is based on the conviction that blacks share a common ethnic background, cultural identity, worldview, and historical experience. Nationalist consciousness among black Americans can be traced to the very dawn of enslavement. Drawn together by the experiences of slavery and discrimination, blacks, both in the United States and other parts of the world, began to espouse nationalist ideas and consciousness. The underlying goal has been the search for freedom and equality.

Racial/ethnic solidarity is perhaps the leitmotiv of Black Nationalism. The forging of this solidarity is often geographically exclusive, being confined to a particular location—the United States, Africa, or the Caribbean. Sometimes it is geographically unifying, embracing several regions where peoples of African descent are found. This is the Pan-African dimension. This transatlantic thrust is both a reaction to, and a reflection of, the historical practice of justifying black subordination on the basis of Africa's alleged barbaric and heathenish condition. The practice of mobilizing black consciousness against domination, oppression, and exploitation, and in pursuit of justice, gives Black Nationalism the character of a resistant phenomenon. This has often led to the mistaken projection of Black Nationalism as essentially antiestablishment and countercultural.

Black Nationalism has assumed varied forms throughout its history. "Integrationism" affirms black values, and integrationists evince a determination to belong, to become accepted as an integral element of a state or nation. "Emigrationism," or separatism, entails the search for a new national identity external to the oppressive state or nation. At times, emigrationism has been aimed at effecting relative isolation—either spatial or cultural—from the oppressor state's material and cultural influences, albeit within the same geographical confines. Spatial isolation is often described as "internal statism." Black Nationalists who favor cultural isolation advocate the construction of race and ethnically based institutions and values as defensive mechanisms against the destructive influences of the hegemonic group with whom they share territory. Black cultural nationalists vigorously affirm the unique cultural and historical identity of blacks and insist on the intrinsic essence and validation of their heritage.

The history of Black Nationalism in the United States exhibits all of the aforementioned dimensions. Since Black Nationalism originated with slavery and oppression, the earliest expressions of Black Nationalism were the slave revolts/plots, and antislavery organizational efforts of free blacks in the North. Slavery induced a consciousness of shared experience and group solidarity. By the mid-nineteenth century, this consciousness, particularly the underlying experience of deprivation and dehumanization, had led to a determined struggle to define and assert an identity.

Blacks mobilized their resources in demanding an end to bondage and the granting of full citizenship. Nationalists such as Lott Cary and Paul Cuffee proposed colonization as a strategy meant to enhance the cause of racial and social elevation, within both the United States and Africa. Cooperative efforts of free blacks in New York, Philadelphia, Boston, and Ohio from the late eighteenth century to the first half of the nineteenth represented the greatest expression of national consciousness up to that time. These blacks clearly manifested a desire to end slavery and discrimination and to become fully integrated as Americans. Their failure to achieve integration unleashed an emigrationist consciousness and movement that mobilized black solidarity toward the assumption of an external national identity in Africa or the Caribbean

The passage of the Fugitive Slave Act in 1850 heightened emigrationist consciousness. Led by Martin R. Delany and Henry H. Garnet, emigrationists proposed creating an independent black nationality abroad, and they urged blacks to build their own nation where they could develop their potential unburdened by slavery and racism. In the second half of the nineteenth century, Africa became the focus of this independent black nationality. The plan of the nationalists was to initiate a successful cotton-producing economy in Africa that they hoped would rival and outsell American slave-grown cotton on the international market. This, they believed, would render slavery unprofitable, resulting in its demise. The outbreak of the Civil War in 1861 temporarily halted this trend as blacks, including emigrationists, became optimistic that the war would ultimately destroy slavery. For blacks, the Civil War was a war for freedom and the realization of the elusive American national identity. This expectation was only temporarily realized during the war itself and the Reconstruction period that followed (1861–1877). The end of Reconstruction brought about a revival of Black Nationalism. With their aspirations betrayed and threatened by a renewed southern offensive, many blacks embraced emigration in both its external and internal dimensions. Some sought a new beginning in Africa; others looked toward Haiti; and still others turned to the lands of the West and Southwest, in the direction of Oklahoma and Kansas.

By the early twentieth century, Black Nationalism had coalesced into a strong Pan-African movement. Knowledge and consciousness of shared historical experiences of slavery, colonial exploitation and domination, and racism's pervasive and ubiquitous character compelled blacks in the United States, the Caribbean, and Africa to forge a common front. The ethos of shared experience, identity, and cultural and historical heritage created and sustained the solidarity that Pan-Africanism represented. Marcus Garvey was most forceful in projecting this consciousness in the first two decades of the twentieth century. The Pan-African consciousness is deeply rooted in black history. However, it was not until the early twentieth century that Pan-Africanism became a sustained movement on a global scale, directed against the forces of colonialism and racism. Essentially, Pan-Africanism developed from consciousness into a movement that galvanized resistance against colonialism in Africa and worldwide racism by the mid-twentieth century . Black cultural nationalism was most pronounced and productive during the Harlem Renaissance of the 1920s, when black artists, musicians, and writers used their talent and vocations to express, define, and project a consciousness of identity and nationalism.

The civil rights movement of the 1960s in the United States witnessed the flowering of Black Nationalism and consisted of a curious mixture of integration and separatist values—from the moderate approaches of Martin Luther King, Jr., and the Southern Christian Leadership Conference to the militant traditions of Malcolm X, Black Power, the Black Muslims, and the Black Panthers. Attempts by blacks to exercise control over their communities and such vital sectors and resources as education, religion, economics, and culture, and to wrest these vital aspects of their lives from the control and influence of forces and agents deemed hostile, represent enduring expressions of nationalism.

Within the United States today may be heard loud echoes of past traditions of Black Nationalism. Integrationism shapes the consciousness of many black conservatives who harbor faith in "the American dream," and the notion of progress through industry and self-help. They strongly believe in the perfectibility of the American order. Cultural nationalistic and separatist aspirations and values inform the visions of the Black Muslims, proponents of Afrocentric projects, and the "hyper politicized" nationalism of black aesthetics and hip hop culture. They evince skepticism about the future of blacks in America, and they are bitterly critical of American institutions, values, and orientations.

— *Tunde Adeleke*

See also: Delany, Martin R.; Garnet, Henry H.

For Further Reading

Bell, Howard H. 1959. "The Negro Emigration Movement, 1849–1854: A Phase of Negro Nationalism." *Phylon* 20 (Summer): 132–142.

Bell, Howard H. 1962. "Negro Nationalism: A Factor in Emigration Projects, 1858–1861." *Journal of Negro History* 47: 42–53.

McAdoo, Bill. 1983. *Pre–Civil War Black Nationalism.* New York: David Walker Press.

Miller, Floyd J. 1971. "The Father of Black Nationalism." *Civil War History* 17 (December): 310–319.

Pinkney, Alphonso. 1976. *Red, Black, and Green: Black Nationalism in the United States.* Cambridge, England: Cambridge University Press.

Robinson, Dean R. 2001. *Black Nationalism in American Politics and Thought.* Cambridge, England: Cambridge University Press.

Udom, Essien. 1969. *Black Nationalism: A Search for Identity in America.* New York: Dell.

BLACK SLAVEOWNERS

Slavery in the United States has traditionally been portrayed as an institution that was based on race. Generally speaking, this conviction is correct, but its propagation has led to the almost universal belief that all slaveowners were white and that all slaves were of African descent. In reality, although there were no white slaves, there were black slaveowners from the colonial period to the Civil War. Census records, deeds of sale, wills of free blacks providing for the disposition of slaves, and records of freedom suits brought by slaves against free blacks attest that there were numerous black masters in the United States. Black slaveowners, as did white owners, obtained slaves by inheritance, gifts, and purchase.

Records identify Anthony Johnson as perhaps the earliest black slaveowner, for Johnson, a former slave himself, acquired John Casor, a slave, in the 1650s. A local court sanctioned the right of free blacks to own slaves when it ruled not to give Casor his freedom when he sued Johnson for it. Another noteworthy case involving a freedom suit was initiated by Sarah, a slave, against Mary Quickly in the 1660s. Again, no claim was made that Quickly, being a black woman, had no right to own a slave, and the grounds for the suit were unrelated to the color of the defendant. Although some colonies initiated legislation forbidding blacks from owning slaves, none became law. A 1670 Virginia law specifically stated that blacks were not barred from buying any of "their own nation." Later, some states restricted free blacks' ability to own slaves. After 1832, Virginian blacks could no longer acquire slaves except spouses, children, parents, or those gained by inheritance or through descent.

In 1830 approximately thirty-seven hundred free African Americans, mostly in the Lower South, owned nearly twelve thousand slaves. According to the 1830 census, slightly more than 2 percent of the free black population in the southern and border states owned slaves. In Louisiana and Virginia, black slaveowners numbered more than nine hundred. Maryland and South Carolina ranked third and fourth, with 653 and 464 black owners, respectively. Black slaveownership was not confined to the southern states. In 1830 both Pennsylvania and Rhode Island reported twenty-three black masters. New York and New Jersey followed, with twenty-one and sixteen, respectively.

Some black masters held many slaves. In 1830 over 200 black owners held ten or more slaves. The largest black slaveowners resided in Louisiana, South Carolina, and Virginia where ten or more black owners held more than twenty slaves each. Antoine Decruir and Martin Donatto owned seventy-five and seventy slaves, respectively. A Louisiana colony of free Creoles, descended from an eighteenth-century French settler and an African slave, contained 411 free persons who owned 276 slaves by 1860. One free black Virginian held seventy-one slaves, and two free blacks in South Carolina each owned eighty-four slaves. Two African-born mulatto brothers owned rice plantations in South Carolina worked by 100 slaves, and William Ellison, also of South Carolina, owned over 60 slaves prior to the Civil War. William Johnson, son of a white father and a mulatto woman, operated three barber shops in Natchez, Mississippi, owned 1,500 acres of land, and had at least fifteen slaves.

There were two kinds of black masters and black slaveowning. Most black slaveowners had some personal interest in their property. State policy toward manumission was often responsible for this type of slaveholding, as black slaveowners had purchased husbands, wives, or children and were not able to emancipate them under existing state laws. Phil Cooper, a slave in Virginia, became the chattel property of his wife in 1828 when she purchased him from his master, and Ermana, a slave woman, was the property of her husband—neither could legally be freed by the spouse. There were, moreover, some affluent free blacks who purchased relatives or friends, thus rescuing them from the worst features of slavery, if not bondage. This was a benevolent form of slaveholding in which the slaves were not seen as, nor treated as, slaves per se by their black masters but were merely technically enslaved. Despite the benevolent nature of such slaveowning, the relationship was still legally that of master and slave, and there were inherent dangers for the slave. Even ownership by one's relative was insecure. There was always the possibility of misuse since the power and control resided in the owner. A free black shoemaker in Charleston, for instance, purchased his wife for $700, but, having decided she was unsuitable, he sold her a few months later, reaping $50 in profit. Dilsey Pope owned her husband but sold him after he offended her in some manner.

The second type of black master was of a much different nature. There were some black masters who most assuredly did not practice a benevolent form of slaveownership. These masters considered their blacks as chattel property; bought, sold, mortgaged, willed, traded, and transferred fellow blacks; demanded long hours in the workshops and fields; severely disciplined recalcitrant blacks; and hunted down escaped slaves. Major black owners sought slave property in part as an effort to conform to the dominant white pattern and to elevate themselves to a position of respect and privilege. For these free black masters, slaveholding was neither a philanthropic gesture nor a strategy for uniting family members. In these instances, free black masters had a real economic interest in the institution of slavery and owned slaves to improve their own economic status. Most black owners in this category were planters like Jacob Sampson, whose eleven slaves worked his 500-acre Virginia plantation.

It is impossible to determine how many black owners held slaves for profit and how many owned slaves for benevolent reasons. Raw census figures provide only hints as to the nature of black ownership of slaves. The number of slaves held was not necessarily indicative of the nature of that ownership. Although it can logically be presumed that the majority of those blacks who owned ten or more slaves held them for economic motivations, the reverse cannot be said. The ownership of a small number of slaves may indicate a benevolent purpose to the slaveownership, but it is not prima facie evidence of benevolence or philanthropy. Artisans and tradesmen were apt to own between one and three slaves. Gilbert Hunt, for instance, was a free black artisan in Richmond, Virginia, who ran his blacksmith shop with the help of two slaves.

Although slaveowning was spread across the economic spectrum of the free black community, it was concentrated near the top. In 1860, almost half of the free blacks with real estate worth $2,000 or more owned slaves, and owning more than two or three slaves was confined to the economic elite since, whatever their desires, few free blacks could afford to own any slaves at all. Two of the wealthiest free blacks, Justus Angel and Mistress L. Horry, each owned eighty-four slaves. Cyuprian Ricard, who purchased an estate with ninety-one slaves in Louisiana, and Charles Rogues and Marie Metoyer, who had forty-seven and fifty-eight slaves, respectively, were all members of the elite black class. Their need for labor, skilled and unskilled, drew them to the institution, as it was the only viable source of labor in the South. Furthermore, one of the best capital investments in the South, besides land, was slaves.

Wealthy free blacks drew distinctions between themselves and poorer free blacks and slaves. The fact that free blacks in the South owned slaves underscores the distance that freedom placed between the free and the enslaved. Black masters were often trying to fit in with white society, and because they lived in a society in which more than 90 percent of the black population was slave, their principal goal was to preserve their freedom. To avoid slipping backward into bondage, they had to give their freedom substance, and one way to do that was to become a slaveholder. The Civil War and emancipation removed from these free blacks their labor force, a significant capital investment, a means of belonging to white society, and often, their economic status.

— *Sharon A. Roger Hepburn*

See also: Ellison, William.

For Further Reading

Hogan, William, and Edwin Davis, eds. 1951. *William Johnson's Natchez: The Antebellum Diary of a Free Negro.* Baton Rouge: Louisiana State University Press.

Koger, Larry. 1985. *Black Slaveowners: Free Black Slave Masters in South Carolina, 1790–1860.* Jefferson, NC: McFarland.

Schwarz, Philip J. 1987. "Emancipators, Protectors, and Anomalies: Free Black Slaveowners in Virginia." *The Virginia Magazine of History and Biography* 95 (July): 317–338.

Schweninger, Loren. 1997. *Black Property Owners in the South, 1790–1915.* Chicago: University of Illinois Press.

Schweninger, Loren. 1990. "John Carruthers Stanly and the Anomaly of Black Slaveholding." *North Carolina Historical Review* 62 (April): 159–192.

Whitten, David O. 1981. *Andrew Dunnford: A Black Sugar Planter in Antebellum Louisiana.* Natchitoches: Northwestern Louisiana State University Press.

Woodson, Carter G. 1925. *Free Negro Owners of Slaves in the United States in 1830.* Washington, DC: Association for the Study of Negro Life and History.

BLAIR EDUCATION BILL

According to an 1880 survey of the United States, seven out of twelve children and one voter out of seven could not read or write, with the southern regions having disproportionally higher numbers of illiterates. To ameliorate this national crisis, Chairman of the Senate Education and Labor Committee, Henry W. Blair, a Republican from New Hampshire, introduced the Blair Education Bill. The proposed legislation was intended to distribute federal funds equally for the instruction of African American and white children. Although it did not deal with the issue of segregation, minimum standards of fairness toward newly freed African Americans were required since "separate but equal" public educational systems were to be instituted.

First presented to Congress in 1881, the bill suggested a ten-year commitment of federal money, beginning with $15 million in the first year and decreasing by $1 million each successive year. Approximately 75 percent of the money would have gone to the South because aid was to be allotted in proportion to state illiteracy rates. In its various incarnations, the bill was passed by the Senate in 1884, 1886, and 1888, but it never reached the floor of the House of Representatives. By 1890, interest in the Blair Education Bill disappeared completely. Had it been passed, this legislation would have allowed southern states to expand their dilapidated school systems and to make education available to impoverished white children. It would have been particularly valuable for newly freed African Americans, 47.7 percent of whom were illiterate in 1883 compared to the 6.96 percent national average for their white counterparts.

From the beginning, the bill was controversial and hotly debated, especially in the South. Worried that too many were "growing up in absolute ignorance of the English alphabet" and arguing that "ignorance is slavery," Blair sought equal access to education for all, especially African Americans. He hoped to eradicate one of the legacies of slavery that continued to keep freedmen in bondage in spite of legal emancipation. His supporters viewed universal education as a prerequisite for solving moral degeneration, economic lethargy, and uninformed voting in the post–Civil War (1861–1865) era since an intelligent and industrious citizenry could better promote financial and political stability. Northern and southern educators, southern independents and Republicans, and African Americans, among others, strongly endorsed the Blair Education Bill.

Ultimately, party politics, long-held racial beliefs, and suspicions of federal intervention in education defeated the bill. Many Democrats suspected that the legislation was politically motivated, designed to use up a tax surplus that resulted from high protective tariffs that the Republican Party favored. Although proponents of the bill argued that it was the nation's responsibility to help the overburdened South, opponents believed that federal encroachment was unconstitutional and would result in the usurpation of states' rights since education was a power reserved for local governments. Furthermore, many perceived the Blair Education Bill to be a costly and futile ploy to uplift African American southerners, the majority of whom were deemed to be incapable of learning. Others worried that too much schooling would "spoil a good plow-hand" and enable educated African Americans to compete economically and politically with northern and southern whites. Northern Republicans, who nominated the bill but were then seeking reconciliation with the South after the Civil War, did not aggressively promote the legislation and essentially abandoned the freedmen. In the end, the failure of the Blair Education Bill reflected the divisive racial and political climates that continued to plague the nation in the era after Reconstruction (1863–1877).

— *Constance J. S. Chen*

See also: Education.

For Further Reading
Crofts, Daniel W. 1971. "The Black Response to the Blair Education Bill." *Journal of Southern History* 37 (1): 41–65.

Going, Allen J. 1957. "The South and the Blair Education Bill." *Mississippi Valley Historical Review* 44 (2): 267–290.

Woodward, C. Vann. 1971. *Origins of the New South, 1877–1913.* Baton Rouge: Louisiana State University Press.

JONATHAN BLANCHARD (1811–1892)

Firmly entrenched in the ideals of reform and social progress, Jonathan Blanchard strove to correct the ills of American society as abolitionist, pastor, and educator. Although his life is intertwined with common names of history, he remains unknown—in part because of history's oversight, but also because of Blanchard's self-recognized difficult personality. Writing to Thaddeus Stevens on May 12, 1847, he said, "I can see that my zeal is mixed with vehemence, my firmness with stubbornness, and, like Sampson, perhaps, my attempts against God's enemies shaded with the spirit of revenge" (Blanchard Papers).

Blanchard grew up in meager conditions, but through hard work he was able to finish preparatory studies at Chester Academy in Vermont. He then attended Middlebury College (1828–1832) where he learned debate and parliamentary procedure as a member of the Philomathesian Literary Society. At this time he began *The Undergraduate,* one of several newspapers he would establish.

After Middlebury, Blanchard became the head of an academy in Plattsburgh, New York. It was there that he assumed the mantle of an abolitionist. He did not call for repatriation of slaves to Africa or gradual emancipation, but advocated for the immediate abolition of slavery. This would be the focus of his career for the next three decades.

After experiencing a conversion while at Middlebury, Blanchard felt called to the ministry and began theological studies at Andover Seminary (1834–1836). While at the seminary he heard Theodore Dwight Weld's call for itinerant lecturers for the American Anti-Slavery Society. He heeded Weld's call, becoming one of Weld's "Seventy" (key abolitionist agents who were sent out to recruit new members to the movement). He was assigned to Pennsylvania and traveled throughout the region for the cause of abolition.

After a year of mobs, threats, beatings, and successes, Blanchard returned to his theological training in 1837 at Lane Seminary in Cincinnati, Ohio. As a student he was called to preach temporarily at the Sixth Presbyterian Church, after his ordination he became its full-time minister. Two important figures at his ordination were Lyman Beecher and Calvin Stowe.

In addition to his continued antislavery work in Cincinnati, in 1843 Blanchard was a delegate to the second World's Anti-Slavery Convention in London and was elected a vice president. The following year he journeyed to Quincy, Illinois, to deliver the commencement address to Dr. David Nelson's abolitionist Mission Institute. During his time in the region, he took the opportunity to visit Knox College in Galesburg, which had offered him its presidency, and in 1845 he was installed as president, a position he held until 1858. Just prior to leaving Cincinnati for Knox, Blanchard debated Dr. Nathan Lewis Rice for four days on whether slaveholding was a sin.

Though removed from the fray of abolitionist work in rural Illinois, Blanchard made strong attempts to maintain his abolitionist activities. He publicly challenged Stephen A. Douglas on his congressional voting record on slavery-related matters, and in 1850 he wrote an open letter to Douglas concerning the Fugitive Slave Act that spanned seven newspaper columns. On October 13, 1854, in Knoxville, Illinois, Blanchard debated Douglas, a debate in which Douglas sought to show Blanchard as an extremist.

Blanchard's abolitionist fervor eventually caused problems with Knox College founder George W. Gale, and so he left in 1858. A year later he became president of the Illinois Institute, and Blanchard restructured the board of trustees, nominating Owen Lovejoy, younger brother of famed abolitionist martyr Elijah P. Lovejoy, to the board.

Blanchard has been called a "minority of one," and

his self-recognized vehemence and sublimated tendency for vengeance seemingly kept him from rising into the inner-circle of American abolitionism. Though his mind was keen, his work devoted, his spirit strong, and his acquaintances were numerous, his demeanor created barriers that distanced him from others, limiting him to regional importance.

— David B. Malone

See also: American Anti-Slavery Society; Douglas, Stephen A.; Immediatism; Weld, Theodore Dwight.

For Further Reading
Blanchard, Jonathan. Papers. Wheaton College Library, Wheaton, Illinois.
Blanchard, Jonathan, and Rice, N. L. [1846] 1970. *A Debate on Slavery: held in Cincinnati, on the first, second, third, and sixth day of October, 1845, upon the question: Is slave-holding in itself sinful, and the relation between master and slave, a sinful relation?* New York: Negro University Press.
Kilby, Clyde S. 1959. *Minority of One.* Grand Rapids, MI: Eerdmans.
Taylor, Richard S. 1977. "Seeking the Kingdom: A Study in the Career of Jonathan Blanchard, 1811–1892." Ph.D. dissertation, Department of History, Northern Illinois University, DeKalb, Illinois.
Taylor, Richard S. 1981. "Beyond Immediate Emancipation: Jonathan Blanchard, Abolitionism, and the Emergence of American Fundamentalism." *Civil War History* 27 (September): 260–274.

BLEEDING KANSAS.
See Border War (1854–1859).

BLUFFTON MOVEMENT (1844)

The Bluffton movement led by secessionists and former nullifiers (South Carolina political figures who tried to nullify federal laws in the 1830s) like Robert Barnwell Rhett and Governor James Henry Hammond, was a short-lived attempt to make South Carolina provoke disunion. It began when Rhett gave a fire-eating speech at Bluffton, South Carolina, on July 31, 1844 (hence the name of the movement) calling for nullification or secession. The "Bluffton boys" sought to nullify the Whig tariff of 1842, called for the annexation of Texas as a slave state, and threatened to secede from the Union if southern demands were not met. "Texas or disunion" became a popular phrase in the state, and as during nullification debates, the tariff was portrayed as part of a northern antislavery plot. The repeal of the gag rule against abolitionist petitions in

Congress in 1844 further aggravated the secessionist-minded slaveholding Carolinian aristocracy. Moreover, during the same year, Samuel Hoar ventured into this stronghold of slavery to remonstrate against the unjust treatment of African American citizens of Massachusetts under South Carolina's notorious Negro Seamen's Act. Hoar was summarily expelled from the state and barely escaped the ire of the Carolina slave oligarchy with body intact. The Bluffton movement received added support from Governor Hammond, who in his annual message recommended state action to address southern grievances.

John C. Calhoun, who dominated state politics, headed off the revolt by Rhett and Hammond and nipped the movement in the bud. His faithful lieutenants, Francis W. Pickens and Franklin Harper Elmore, together with former unionists like Benjamin F. Perry and Christopher G. Memminger, led the counterattack against the Bluffton boys. The ill-fated Bluffton movement was, according to most historians, a victim of Calhoun's plans to win the Democratic Party presidential nomination. The Carolinian leader, after the bitter experience of nullification, was probably also convinced of the inadvisability of precipitous and lone action by his state. More important, for Calhoun, through much of the 1840s, southern redemption lay not in secession but in his own elevation to the presidency.

Rhett and the Bluffton boys, unlike many before them, emerged unscathed from their temporary falling out with Calhoun. He along with Elmore, the president of the Bank of South Carolina, had led the Calhoun political machine, which controlled the state after nullification. In fact, Rhett quickly reemerged as a Calhoun confidant and was enlisted to check local criticism of Calhoun's advocacy of internal improvements on the Mississippi. On the other hand, Pickens, who helped Calhoun contain the Bluffton movement, soon became estranged from him over the issue. Moreover, some of Calhoun's closest followers, George McDuffie and Armistead Burt, had flirted with Blufftonism. Calhoun's private correspondence reveals that he, like the Bluffton boys, was acutely suspicious of the Van Buren northern wing of the Democratic Party and saw northern opposition to the annexation of Texas as extremely dangerous for the future of the slave South. Calhoun also played an instrumental role in fulfilling one of the major demands of the Bluffton movement, namely, the annexation of Texas. The Carolina leader differed with the Bluffton boys in policy but not in principles.

— Manisha Sinha

See also: Calhoun, John C.; Fire-Eaters; Hammond, James Henry; Nullification Doctrine.

For Further Reading

Boucher, Chauncey S. 1919. "The Annexation of Texas and the Bluffton Movement in South Carolina." *Mississippi Valley Historical Review* 4 (June): 3–33.

Rayback, Joseph G. 1948. "The Presidential Ambitions of John C. Calhoun, 1844–1848." *Journal of Southern History* 14 (3): 331–356.

Sinha, Manisha. 1994. "The Counter-Revolution of Slavery: Class, Politics and Ideology in Antebellum South Carolina." Ph.D. dissertation, Department of History, Columbia University, New York, New York.

BORDER WAR (1854–1859)

The rising tensions over the issue of slavery in the United States first produced a violent combustion in the remote territory of Kansas in the mid-1850s. The border war of 1854–1859, also known as Bleeding Kansas, was a preview of the Civil War but preceded the national conflict by seven years. The fighting in Kansas over the issue of whether or not slavery would be allowed in the territory turned into a bloody partisan conflict that foreshadowed conflict in the border states during the Civil War. The Kansas–Missouri border erupted into armed combat and reduced the likelihood that the debate over slavery could be peacefully contained. The border war was a dress rehearsal for the Civil War.

The long-term causes of the border war were rooted in the westward expansion of slavery and the Missouri Compromise of 1820. The compromise had allowed Missouri to enter the union as a slave state but prohibited slavery from any future states in Louisiana Purchase territory above the 36°30' line, the southern border of Missouri. Although the agreement seemed to quell the sectional tensions of 1820, it only delayed the growing debate over slavery. The development of industry in the northern states and the rise of abolitionism, among other factors, in the next three decades polarized the nation over the issue.

In the short term, the border war was the product of the Kansas–Nebraska Act of 1854. That act organized two territories west and northwest of Missouri, and the bill's author, Illinois Senator Stephen A. Douglas, invoked the doctrine of popular sovereignty, which meant that the status of slavery in each territory would be decided by a vote of the citizens of the territories. Since these territories lay north of the 36-degree 30-minute line, the act effectively nullified the Missouri Compromise. The bill narrowly passed Congress but raised the ire of the increasingly antislavery North.

Out of this dispute rose the Republican Party, a sectional party dedicated to stopping the expansion of slavery in the territories. The Republicans gathered membership from the defunct Whig Party, the nativist American (Know-Nothing) Party, and the growing number of Democrats alienated by what they saw as the southern domination of their party. The reversal of the Missouri Compromise was further evidence for these northerners of the southern slaveholders' ability to exercise a disproportionate share of political influence over the country's affairs. The slaveholding South had now given slavery a chance in a place where, for the last generation, slavery had been banned.

Many people saw popular sovereignty as a panacea for the ills of sectionalism, but events in Kansas Territory soon destroyed that illusion. When the territory was officially opened for settlement in mid-1854, many of the early inhabitants were nonpartisans who cared little for the slave issue, but outsiders saw Kansas as the next great battleground over slavery. In the territorial elections of March 1855, several thousand proslavery Missourians, called "border ruffians," flooded across the boundary to cast fraudulent votes. Even though free soil settlers were in the majority, they lost by a count of 5,247 to 797. It was later determined that 4,968 of the proslavery votes were fraudulent, but the proslavery forces had the territorial government thoroughly intimidated.

The dispute soon erupted into violence. A November 1855 killing of a free soil settler by a proslavery man triggered a series of events that led to the formation of large partisan bands that resembled armies. In May 1856 a federal marshal gathered a posse of seven hundred proslavery men to arrest some free soil officials at their headquarters in Lawrence. The posse went well beyond the arrests and looted the town, destroying two presses belonging to antislavery newspapers and burning the Free State Hotel. The "sack of Lawrence" led to a series of violent reprisals. John Brown, the man who later tried to incite a slave insurrection on the eve of the Civil War, led his sons in a brutal attack along Pottawatomie Creek in which five men were taken from their homes in a small proslavery community and hacked to death with broadswords.

Some two hundred men died in Kansas during 1856 alone, and the violence continued unabated. The national press covered each murder and skirmish with intense scrutiny, fueling sectional tensions. The Missourians' hopes of making Kansas a slave state were ultimately swamped by a sea of settlers from the free states. The instability of the territory made the prospect of taking slaves there a very risky proposition, and for many people the Kansas prairie seemed to represent the natural limits of the institution of slavery. By 1857, the Free State Party was in firm control of territorial political life, and in 1859, the Topeka Convention drafted a free soil constitution. Still, Kansas did not enter the Union until after the first southern states had seceded in the winter of 1860–1861.

The Border War signaled the end of popular sovereignty as a useful method for deciding the issue of slavery in the territories. The conflict technically ended in 1859, but the local fighting was merely subsumed by the larger Civil War. The Kansas–Missouri border area witnessed some of the most brutal guerrilla conflict as the border ruffians and the antislavery supporters (jayhawkers) continued their bitter contest. In many ways, the climax to the violence that began in 1855 did not come until August 20, 1863, when southern raiders under the command of William Clarke Quantrill struck Lawrence again. The town, which had been the center of the free state movement during the border war, was burned and 200 men and boys killed. The violence on the Kansas–Missouri border between 1855 and 1865 was a microcosm of the larger conflict over slavery.

— *Richard D. Loosbrock*

See also: Brown, John; Jayhawkers; Lecompton Constitution.

For Further Reading

Etcheson, Nicole. 2004. *Bleeding Kansas: Contested Liberty in the Civil War Era.* Lawrence: University Press of Kansas.

Monaghan, Jay. 1955. *Civil War on the Western Border, 1854–1865.* Boston: Little, Brown.

Nichols, Alice. 1954. *Bleeding Kansas.* New York: Oxford University Press.

Rawley, James A. 1969. *Race and Politics: "Bleeding Kansas" and the Coming of the Civil War.* Philadelphia: J. B. Lippincott.

BOSTON FEMALE ANTI-SLAVERY SOCIETY (1833–1840)

The Boston Female Anti-Slavery Society associated itself with both the American Anti-Slavery Society and the New England Anti-Slavery Society and supported both organizations with financial contributions. The Boston Female Anti-Slavery Society, much like the Philadelphia Female Anti-Slavery Society, included both white and black women in its membership. More importantly, the Boston organization consisted of two diverse religious groups: evangelicals—those belonging to Baptist, Presbyterian, and Congregational denominations—and liberals—including primarily the Quaker and Unitarian members. Initially, a coalition of these two divergent groups constituted the Boston organization. Both evangelicals and liberals were drawn to antislavery by their religious commitment to emancipation, and despite their differences, the women worked well together and made great strides toward their goals.

In its brief seven-year history, the Boston Female Anti-Slavery Society conducted three national women's conventions, organized a multistate petition campaign, brought suit against southerners bringing slaves into Boston, organized elaborate and profitable fund-raisers to keep male antislavery organizations financially solvent, and sponsored the Grimké sisters' lecture series throughout New England.

The society organized annual antislavery fairs at which handmade items and luxury items donated from European antislavery societies were sold. These fairs quickly became the social event of the Christmas season for Boston residents. In addition, the society published fifteen volumes of *The Liberty Bell*, a literary annual first published in 1839. Marie Weston Chapman served as editor, and each volume included poetry, reflective essays, biographical sketches, and short stories written by distinguished political and literary figures. The sale of these books provided both fund-raising and moral suasion opportunities for the society.

Religious differences finally split the society in 1840 after several years of bitter fighting between the factions that began in 1837. Although it officially disbanded in April 1840, Maria Weston Chapman led the liberal faction in declaring the dissolution illegal based on the society's original constitution and continued to operate the organization under the same name. In addition to its religiously liberal membership, the Chapman-run faction closely allied itself to William Lloyd Garrison and his antislavery beliefs. This society existed on paper into the 1850s, and its primary activity was the annual antislavery fair. The evangelical women formed a new society in 1840, the Massachusetts Female Emancipation Society, but this group had disappeared by the mid-1840s.

Prominent members of the Boston Female Anti-Slavery Society included liberal members Maria Weston Chapman, Lydia Maria Child, Anne Warren Weston, Henrietta Sargent, Caroline Weston, and Thankful Southwick, as well as evangelical members Mary Parker, Martha Ball, Lucy Ball, and Catherine Sullivan. Despite appearances, the evangelical women held a majority in the society, but the liberal members' names appeared in the antislavery literature more frequently as they were more outspoken than their evangelical sisters.

— *Sydney J. Caddel-Liles*

See also: Child, Lydia M.; Grimké, Angelina; Grimké, Sarah Moore; Women and the Antislavery Movement.

For Further Reading

Boylan, Ann M. 1994. "Benevolence and Antislavery Activity among African American Women in New York and Boston, 1820–1840." In *The Abolitionist Sisterhood: Women's Political Culture in Antebellum America*. Ed. Jean Fagan Yellin and John C. Van Horne. Ithaca, NY: Cornell University Press.

Chambers-Schiller, Lee. 1994. "'A Good Work among the People': The Political Culture of the Boston Antislavery Fair." In *The Abolitionist Sisterhood: Women's Political Culture in Antebellum America*. Ed. Jean Fagan Yellin and John C. Van Horne. Ithaca, NY: Cornell University Press.

Hansen, Debra Gold. 1993. *Strained Sisterhood: Gender and Class in the Boston Female Anti-Slavery Society*. Amherst: University of Massachusetts Press.

Stearn, Bertha-Monica. 1932. "Reform Periodicals and Female Reformers, 1830–1860." *American Historical Review* 3 (July): 678–699.

BREEDING OF SLAVES

Because the slave population in the United States was unique in that it reproduced itself, the question of whether slaveowners there utilized a deliberate breeding strategy has long been debated. A combination of historical circumstances no doubt contributed to a gradual but consistent increase in the native-born black slave population of the United States after the American Revolution, including the acquisition of the Louisiana Territory in 1803 and then the lands gained in the war with Mexico, both of which resulted not only in the westward expansion of the United States but also in the westward expansion of slavery. In 1808 the constitutional ban on African importations went into effect, and although importations had been deliberately increased in anticipation of the ban in the decades immediately preceding it, the market demand for slaves after the ban went into effect had to be met solely by the natural increase of native-born slaves. At the same time, technological innovations in agriculture resulted in an antebellum cotton boom, which added to the increased demand for black slaves.

Initially, so-called surplus slaves from the older settled areas of the South were moved westward, both with their owners and alone after being sold. From 1810 through 1860, approximately five hundred thousand black slaves made the involuntary migration from Virginia and the Carolinas to Kentucky, Tennessee, Alabama, Mississippi, and other Deep South states. Of particular interest for people who are inclined to conclude that slave breeding was at least a consideration of slaveowners is the fact that, unlike the strategy utilized during the colonial period, slave women and men were equally in demand in the old Southwest and sales of women and men were roughly equal. At least one historian has suggested that the odds of a slave couple being separated by sale were one in three, and slave women in their childbearing years were rarely allowed to remain without a mate, whether it was one of her own choosing or one selected by her master. Slave women almost invariably recalled being forced into sexual relationships, both with other slaves and with whites, including the owner. Heart-rending tales of the violent dissolution of slave marriages by slaveowners made indelible impressions on slave children, who recalled these scenes to Works Projects Administration interviewers many years later. "Encouragement" to reproduce often included rewards of leisure time, colorful cloth for dresses, and even cash. Occasionally, an owner might promise a particularly fertile slave woman her freedom after she had produced a certain number of healthy children. Despite continual interference, slave marriages tended to be long-lived, and families tended to be stable.

The flourishing internal trade in slaves suggests that the so-called surplus was constant over a period of five decades. In addition, larger commercial brokerages operating in southern coastal cities were responsible for acquiring, auctioning, and transporting hundreds of slaves annually. Additional slaves were also purchased and sold along the southwestern internal slave trade route, either overland or by sea via New Orleans. Some historians have insisted that slave traders were despised in a society that, nevertheless, used the acquisition and possession of slaves as an indicator of wealth and status.

The birthrate of Africans in the United States steadily increased, and the death rate decreased after the American Revolution. Indeed, native-born slaves had begun to outnumber Africans even before that. It is possible that tropical diseases in the West Indies and in South America contributed to the continued low birthrate of Africans in those countries, but in their own words, former slaves recounted to interviewers hired by the federal government during the 1930s the deliberate, artificial, and forced creation of slave "marriages" or even more temporary sexual liaisons for the clear purpose of producing offspring.

Women singled out for their fertility were referred to by the slaves themselves as "breed women," and women who failed to reproduce recalled being sold. When slaveowners had many more female than male slaves, "breeding males" or "stockmen" were sometimes hired specifically to impregnate slave women. In other situations, a favored male hand might be allowed to take more than one wife at a time as a kind of reward. Thus former slaves recalled pairings of slaves by the white owner, the exertion of "influence" of one kind or another in order to pair a particular slave couple, rewards offered and given for producing offspring, the sale of women who did not reproduce after a period of time (although one historian has suggested that slave women might have used abortion techniques since documentary evidence has been found to show that some slave women who were considered infertile did in fact reproduce after emancipation), the "renting" of stud males, or the male owner himself impregnating females. It seems clear that the slaveowners strongly supported both promiscuity among the slaves and at least a version of polygamy for slaves. In addition, antebellum criminal court records contain evidence that slave women did occasionally violently resist being forced into sexual situations by slave men or by white slaveowners, resulting in the injury to or death of those men.

Slavery was meant to be a profit-making venture. Because slaves were sold as a hedge against inflation or bankruptcy, to mortgage property, or as collateral for loans; bequeathed in wills; and used as an indicator of social status as well as laborers, slaveholders strongly encouraged the "production" of slave infants either by "wedded" couples (keeping in mind that marriage between slaves was not recognized by law and was recognized by slaveholders only when it was expedient for them to recognize such a connection) or by slaves placed together arbitrarily for that purpose.

— *Dale Edwyna Smith*

See also: Domestic Slave Trade; Franklin and Armfield; Narratives.

For Further Reading

Escott, Paul D. 1979. *Slavery Remembered: A Record of Twentieth-Century Slave Narratives.* Chapel Hill: University of North Carolina Press.

Johnson, Walter. 1999. *Soul by Soul: Life Inside the Antebellum Slave Market.* Cambridge, MA: Harvard University Press.

McLaurin, Melton A. 1991. *Celia: A Slave.* New York: Avon.

Rawick, George P. 1972. *The American Slave: A Composite Biography.* Westport, CT: Greenwood Press.

Sutch, Richard. 1975. "The Breeding of Slaves for Sale and the Westward Expansion of Slavery." In *Race and Slavery in the Western Hemisphere.* Ed. Stanley L. Engerman and Eugene D. Genovese. Princeton, NJ: Princeton University Press.

BROOKS–SUMNER AFFAIR

The Brooks–Sumner Affair was a brutal attack that occurred on May 22, 1856, on the U.S. Senate floor against Massachusetts Senator Charles Sumner by South Carolina Representative Preston Brooks. The assault was one incident in a series of events in the 1850s connected with the debate on slavery.

On January 23, 1854, Democratic Senator Stephen A. Douglas of Illinois, an advocate of westward expansion and a potential candidate for the presidency, introduced the Kansas–Nebraska bill in the U.S. Senate. The bill called for creating two territories from part of the Nebraska territory. One territory to the west of Iowa would become Nebraska, and the other to the west of Missouri would become Kansas. Both territories would have the right of popular sovereignty to decide whether they would be free or slave states.

Douglas, hoping to gain support from southern legislators for his bill, supported the principle of popular sovereignty as established in the Compromise of 1850, which effectively voided the line between free and slave territory established in the Missouri Compromise (1820). After lengthy debate, Congress finally passed the Kansas–Nebraska bill. Antislavery forces in Congress, Massachusetts Senator Charles Sumner included, argued that passage of the measure represented a conspiracy of proslavery forces to expand slavery. Sumner, an avid abolitionist who was one of the most vocal congressional opponents of slavery, believed that if slavery could be prevented from expanding to new territories it would eventually fade away.

The Kansas–Nebraska Act's passage placed the focus of the slavery question in the new territories, especially Kansas, where political and moral questions would be addressed violently in the upcoming months. In March 1855, fraudulent voting in Kansas helped elect a proslavery territory legislature. This proslavery legislature, based in Lecompton, dismissed the few antislavery delegates and enacted slave codes. Later that summer, antislavery forces called their own meeting in Topeka and established an extralegal antislavery legislature that passed laws prohibiting slavery and made formal application that Congress admit the Kansas territory as a free state. President Franklin Pierce condemned the antislavery Topeka legislature, recognized the proslavery legislature, and showed his support for the territorial administration by sending troops and appointing proslavery judges in Kansas.

Antislavery forces, especially the New England Emigrant Company, which organized to promote the movement of antislavery settlers to Kansas, appealed to Sumner to champion the cause of preventing

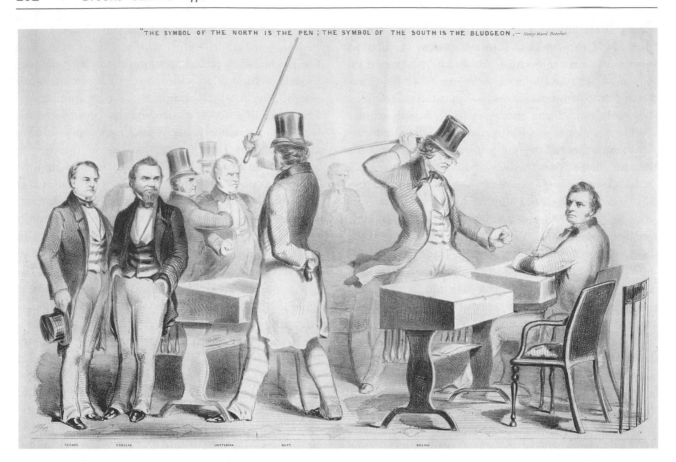

"THE SYMBOL OF THE NORTH IS THE PEN; THE SYMBOL OF THE SOUTH IS THE BLUDGEON.— *Henry Ward Beecher.*

The Brooks–Sumner Affair was an indication of both the growing hostility between anti and proslavery forces and an increasing sectional and political rivalry that eventually led to the Civil War. (Library of Congress)

Kansas from becoming a slave state. Sumner realized that Kansas's request for statehood would be a topic on the Senate floor over which antislavery and proslavery forces would clash. In March 1856, when Douglas condemned Kansas's antislavery forces, Sumner defended antislavery attempts to make Kansas a free state.

On May 19, 1856, Sumner began a two-day speech titled "The Crime Against Kansas." In the speech, which was meant to arouse northern sentiment against the Kansas violence and the growing influence of proslavery forces in Congress, Sumner first recognized that in Congress the main agents of slavery were Senators Stephen A. Douglas of Illinois and Andrew Butler of South Carolina. Sumner then detailed the crime committed against Kansas. It was allowing the slavery forces to invade the once secure free territory. Only restoring the Missouri Compromise line, continued Sumner, could ameliorate the crime committed by the Congress and proslavery advocates.

Sumner also condemned President Pierce for supporting the illegally elected Kansas proslavery government, reprimanded U.S. senators who supported slavery, and then, in a series of personal attacks, focused

his anger on South Carolina Senator Andrew Butler. Sumner informed the crowded Senate chamber that Butler had taken up with "the harlot, slavery," ridiculed Butler's inability to control his drooling, and accused him of being an incompetent fool. Sumner also maligned South Carolina by making trivial the importance of the state's contribution to American society. Southern congressmen reacted vehemently with threats and insults, but Sumner refused any special protection from his supporters.

South Carolina Congressman Preston Brooks, determined to protect the honor of Butler, his relative, and the state of South Carolina, and to strike a blow against the antislavery forces in Congress, planned his response. Since Brooks considered Sumner to be a social inferior, the southern code of honor prevented him from challenging Sumner to a duel. Instead, Brooks decided to teach Sumner a lesson. On May 22, just two days after the "Crime Against Kansas" speech, Brooks and his cohort South Carolina Representative Lawrence M. Keitt, who stood nearby to prevent anyone from interfering, entered the Senate chamber soon after the day's session ended and approached Sumner who was seated at his desk. Brooks informed Sumner that his "Crime against Kansas" speech was libelous against the state of South Carolina and demeaned the honor of Senator Butler, who happened to be a close relation. Without waiting for Sumner to respond, Brooks began beating Sumner with his walking cane.

The attack was so vicious that Brooks's hollow cane broke into pieces from the impact of the blows. Sumner, unable to avoid the blows because he was trapped at his desk, which was bolted to the floor, finally tore the desk from the floor and collapsed bloody and unconscious on the Senate floor. Keitt, who kept onlookers from interfering with the attack, ended the attack by warning Brooks that if he continued the beating Sumner might die.

After the attack, Brooks received hundreds of canes from southern proslavery sympathizers. The injuries Sumner sustained in the attack prevented him from returning to the Senate for three years. Massachusetts reserved his Senate seat until he was well enough to return. In the House of Representatives legislators failed to pass a recommendation expelling Brooks. Soon after the vote, Brooks defended his attack on Sumner and tendered his resignation. South Carolina voters immediately returned Brooks to Congress by an overwhelming vote. Brooks's beating of Sumner helped sway many conservatives to the Republican Party and to take up a strong antislavery stance.

— *Craig S. Pascoe*

See also: Border War (1854–1859); Kansas–Nebraska Act; Lecompton Constitution.

For Further Reading
Blue, Frederick J. 1994. *Charles Sumner and the Conscience of the North.* Arlington Heights, IL: Harlan Davidson.
Donald, David Herbert. 1960. *Charles Sumner and the Coming of the Civil War.* New York: Alfred A. Knopf.
Potter, David M. 1976. *The Impending Crisis, 1848–1861.* New York: Harper and Row.
Sewell, Richard H. 1988. *The House Divided: Sectionalism and Civil War, 1848–1865.* Baltimore, MD: Johns Hopkins University Press.
Sinha, Manisha. 2003. "The Caning of Charles Sumner: Slavery, Race, and Ideology in the Age of the Civil War. " *Journal of the Early Republic* 23 (2): 233–262.

BROWN FELLOWSHIP SOCIETY

The rules and regulations of the Brown Fellowship Society record that the organization was established on November 1, 1790, by five "free brown" men (James Mitchell, George Bampfield, William Cattel, George Bedon, and Samuel Saltus) who sought to relieve "the wants and miseries" and promote "the welfare and happiness" of the free mulatto population of Charleston, South Carolina, by founding a charitable and benevolent association. As the earliest and the "preeminent mulatto organization in antebellum Charleston" (Johnson and Roark, 1982) the society restricted its membership to fifty of the city's wealthiest free mulatto (brown) men. Perhaps as a consequence of such self-conscious class and complexional exclusivity, several other free black and free mulatto mutual aid societies later formed in Charleston, most notably the Humane Brotherhood and the Friendly Moralist Society.

The Brown Fellowship Society levied a sizable $50 initiation fee and regular monthly dues to insure members for times of illness and indigence, providing "a decent funeral for any deceased member who did not leave in his estate sufficient funds for that purpose" (Harris, 1981), and furnishing financial support for widows and educating any remaining children when necessary. The purchase of a lot to be used as a burial ground was achieved soon after the society's formation, a necessity no doubt made more urgent by the difficulties of burying brown bodies in such a color-conscious Christian city. Although the Brown Fellowship Society included affluent tailors, carpenters, shoemakers, a nationally known hotelier (Jehu Jones, Sr.), and even some slaveholders, its relatively well-heeled members were not shielded from the growing force of racially oppressive and proscriptive white supremacist legislation. In the wake of Denmark Vesey's conspiracy (1822), Nat Turner's revolt (1831), and the growing sectional crisis, the free black and free mulatto populations of Charleston found themselves facing new controls on their education and mobility, which added to the burden of special "capitation" taxes and subaltern status under South Carolina's "Negro law," which restricted the rights of the state's free black population.

Questions of status and identity have been the key issues occupying most scholarly analyses of Charleston's free mulatto aristocracy and its organizations. Although most historians agree that the free brown elite managed to occupy a middle ground between the broader free black and slave populations and the city's white residents, there has been some dispute as to the degree of exclusivity, color consciousness, or caste discrimination as evidenced by the correspondence and official records of mulattoes affiliated to self-help groups such as the Brown Fellowship Society. In addition to the organization's name having often been taken too "literally by many scholars as prima facie evidence of mulatto exclusiveness" (Harris, 1981), perhaps too little has been made of the achievement of the free brown elite's mindful policy of public accommodation and simultaneous exploitation of the personalism of the dominant culture (Johnson and Roark, 1984). Although members of the Brown Fellowship Society did not enjoy the dubious comforts of the third racial space occupied by the mulattoes of New Orleans, they successfully maintained their organization beyond the difficult years of the Civil War by judiciously excluding political controversy and by carefully cultivating white patronage. Just when the society disbanded is uncertain, but it continued to own the burial ground until 1957.

— *Stephen C. Kenny*

See also: South Carolina.

For Further Reading

Harris, Robert L., Jr. 1981. "Charleston's Free Afro-American Elite: The Brown Fellowship Society and the Humane Brotherhood." *South Carolina Historical Magazine* 81: 289–310.

Johnson, Michael P., and James L. Roark. 1982. "'A Middle Ground': Free Mulattoes and the Friendly Moralist Society of Ante-bellum Charleston." *Southern Studies* 21 (3): 246–265.

Johnson, Michael P., and James L. Roark, eds. 1984. *No Chariot Let Down: Charleston's Free People of Color on the Eve of the Civil War.* Chapel Hill: University of North Carolina Press.

Wikramanayake, Marina. 1973. *A World in Shadow: The Free Black in Ante-bellum South Carolina.* Columbia: University of South Carolina Press.

HENRY "BOX" BROWN (C. 1815–1878)

Henry Brown gained fame through an extraordinary escape to freedom. Born a slave in Louisa County, Virginia, Brown was sent to work in the city of Richmond at about the age of thirteen when his master died. At about the age of twenty he met and married another Richmond slave, Nancy, and they lived as happily as possible under slavery for about twelve years. In August 1848, she and their three children were suddenly sold to a Methodist preacher from North Carolina.

No longer deterred from seeking to escape slavery—as Brown later noted, now "my family were gone" (Stearns)—he conceived an approach that, though dangerous, might work. He had a carpenter make a wooden box, 2 feet by 2 1/2 feet by 3 feet, and took it to a white friend, Samuel A. Smith, a shoe dealer, and

Smith's free black employee, James Caesar Anthony Smith. Asked what the box was for, Brown exclaimed, to "put Henry Brown in!" The two Smiths marked the box "right side up with care"; addressed it to William A. Johnson, Arch Street, Philadelphia; and on March 29, 1849, shipped it by Adams Express.

Brown took with him a container of water and had three small holes for air, yet he thought he would die when, for parts of the journey, he traveled in the crate upside down. But the trip ended at last—after twenty-seven hours—and like Lazarus from the dead, Brown rose from the box when four men (including William Still, a black abolitionist, and James Miller McKim, a white one) from the Philadelphia Vigilance Committee, a group associated with the Underground Railroad and the Pennsylvania Anti-Slavery Society, collected the box and opened it. As for Samuel Smith, he went to the Virginia penitentiary for attempting again in May 1849 to ship two boxes, each containing a slave man, north to freedom.

Henry Brown took the name Henry "Box" Brown and, after moving to Boston, became active in the abolition movement as a witness to the horrors of slavery even at its best. He told crowds his tale, and abolitionist Charles Stearns published Brown's narrative, *Narrative of the Life of Henry Box Brown* (1849), "written from a statement of facts made by himself." In January 1850, Brown attended a giant antislavery convention in Syracuse, New York. Also at the Syracuse meeting was James Caesar Anthony Smith, who, having made his way north after Samuel Smith's conviction in Richmond, now assumed the moniker "Boxer" for his role in boxing up Brown. Some people in Boston painted a panorama, "Mirror of Slavery," that depicted scenes from slavery and Brown's flight, and "Box" Brown and "Boxer" Smith toured the Northeast with the panorama and the famous crate.

On August 30, 1850, slave catchers nearly kidnapped Brown. In order to put himself beyond their reach and that of the new Fugitive Slave Act, Brown left for England. In subsequent years, he told his compelling story to people in Great Britain. In England he also published another version of his story, *Narrative of the Life of Henry Box Brown, Written by Himself* (1851). Although slavery in the United States came to an end in 1865, Brown continued to perform on stage in England and Wales until as late as 1875, when he returned to America.

Accompanying Brown on his return to the United States were his second wife, whom he had married in the late 1850s, and their teenaged daughter. Having largely left behind the panorama that he had performed in his early years as a showman, Brown more

THE RESURRECTION OF HENRY BOX BROWN AT PHILADELPHIA.
Who escaped from Richmond Va in a Box 3 feet long 2½ ft deep and 2 ft wide

Henry "Box" Brown devised one of the most ingenious means of making his way to freedom in Philadelphia. (Library of Congress)

often performed magic tricks on stage. The historical record of Henry "Box" Brown fades in 1878, when he would have been about sixty-three years old.

— *Peter Wallenstein*

See also: Abolitionism in the United States; Fugitive Slave Act (1850); Underground Railroad.

For Further Reading
Brown, Henry Box. 2002. *Narrative of the Life of Henry Box Brown, Written by Himself.* New York: Oxford University Press.
Ripley, C. Peter, ed. 1985. *The Black Abolitionist Papers: The British Isles, 1830–1865.* Chapel Hill: University of North Carolina Press.
Ruggles, Jeffrey. 2003. *The Unboxing of Henry Brown.* Richmond: Library of Virginia.
Schwarz, Philip J. 2001. *Migrants against Slavery: Virginians and the Nation.* Charlottesville: University Press of Virginia.

Stearns, Charles. 1849. *Narrative of Henry Box Brown.* Boston: Brown and Stearns.
Still, William. 1872. *The Underground Railroad.* Philadelphia: Porter and Coates.

JOHN BROWN (1800–1859)

John Brown was a radical religious abolitionist whose die-hard commitment to the destruction of slavery in the Harpers Ferry Raid prefaced the American Civil War. Brown was born on May 9 in Torrington, Connecticut, and was one of six children reared under the strict supervision of Calvinist parents Ruth and Owen Brown. The family relocated to Hudson, Ohio, in 1805. Owen, a tanner and shoemaker by trade, was also a successful land speculator. He was zealous in his commitment to the liberation of blacks and evangelical abolitionism. This commitment was reflected in his

Captured during his failed attempt to seize the federal arsenal at Harpers Ferry, Virginia, the radical abolitionist John Brown soon became a martyr to the antislavery cause. (Library of Congress)

support for antislavery educational establishments, including Western Reserve College and Oberlin College in Ohio. Reared in this reformist environment, the young Brown imbibed strict discipline, religious faith, and antislavery convictions.

By the time he was twenty, Brown's path was set. A skilled tanner, student of mathematics and surveying, Brown sought business success in order to realize his primary objective of abolition. On June 21, 1820, Brown married Dianthe Lusk, a member of a New York family who had relocated to Hudson. They were to have eight children, but frontier life, childbirth, and infant mortality eroded Dianthe's health and she died at thirty-one. An earlier move to Crawford County, in western Pennsylvania, in 1823, where Brown went into joint tannery business with Seth Thompson, proved unsuccessful and Brown returned to Ohio in 1836. Despite his hard work and obvious skills, Brown was often unsuccessful in his business ventures. One recent

biographer points to "wrong turns, dead ends, failed attempts, lawsuits, and grinding debts" (DeCaro, 2002). In 1846, the Brown family moved to Springfield, in western Massachusetts.

These failures coincided with his burgeoning public commitment to antislavery. During the 1840s, Brown was in touch with Quaker abolitionists and antislavery leaders Gerrit Smith and Frederick Douglass. On January 15, 1851, Brown helped found the League of Gileadites. It attracted forty-four members, many of whom were free blacks, fugitive slaves, and working citizens of Springfield. The primary aims of this group were to promote physical resistance to the Fugitive Slave Act (1850) and to protect runaway slaves from pursuing slaveowners and federal agents. By the mid-1850s, this organization had declined, but Brown's commitment to antislavery increased.

The Kansas–Nebraska Act (1854) opened up the possibility of the western expansion of slavery. Brown followed his sons to Kansas, settling along the Osawatomie River. The future status of this territory—whether it would enter the Union as a free or slave state—was in fierce dispute. After one failed attempt to destroy Lawrence, a free state town, proslavery forces attacked again on May 21, 1856, and destroyed it. Three days later, Brown and his sons Owen, Frederick, Oliver, and Salmon and son-in-law Henry Thompson, along with free state men Theodore Weiner and Townsley, executed five proslave settlers along the Pottawatomie Creek with short broadswords.

During this period, Brown became known as "Osawatomie Brown" or "Old Osawatomie." For some abolitionists, he came to symbolize a holy crusade against slavery; to many proslavery supporters and southern sympathizers, he became a hated figure. This difference of opinion helped to clarify the complex nature of growing sectional divisions in the antebellum United States.

By the mid-1850s, Brown had planned a raid on the federal armory at Harpers Ferry in northern (now West) Virginia. The place was well stocked with arms and was strategically well situated for easy access to the slave South down the Appalachian Mountain range. In early 1858, while visiting with Frederick Douglass at Rochester, New York, Brown wrote *Provisional Constitution and Ordinances for the People of the United States.* Consisting of forty-eight articles, the document condemned slavery, envisioned a mountain-based community, and outlined a political structure based on the U.S. Constitution. Later that year, Brown traveled to Chatham, Canada West, which was home to black communities, to drum up support for his planned raid. By summer 1859, Brown had secured financial backing from a secret six (Gerrit Smith, Samuel G. Howe, Franklin Sanborn, Theodore Parker, George L. Stearns, and Thomas W. Higginson). His twenty-one followers included two former slaves (Shields Green and Dangerfield Newby); three black activists (Osborne P. Anderson from Chatham and Oberlinites John Copeland, Jr. and Lewis Leary); and an assortment of religious abolitionists, antislavery activists, and Brown family members. The youngest follower, twenty-year-old William H. Leeman, explained the nature of the plan in a letter to his mother: "We are now all privately gathered in a slave state, where we are determined to strike for freedom, incite the rebels to rebellion, and establish a free government" (Oates, 1970).

The twenty-two-man army began its raid on the federal arsenal late Sunday evening, October 16 1859. Thirty-six hours later, and after fifteen deaths including Brown's sons, the raid was over. Brown had failed to accomplish his stated objective of slave insurrection. The bodies of the black rebels were sliced and diced by students at Winchester Medical School. After a brief examination, short imprisonment, and show trial, Brown was convicted for treason against the state (although his was legally a federal offense). On December 2, 1859, John Brown was hanged. His corpse was later transferred to his family's farm near Lake Placid in upstate New York.

Many northerners praised Brown's principles even if many of them disagreed with his methods. Southerners condemned the event even as they used it to galvanize popular support for their cause. On October 25, 1859, the *Richmond Enquirer* wrote: "The Harpers Ferry Invasion advanced the cause of Disunion more than any other event." Most importantly, the raid served as the opening shot of the Civil War. As Brown scrawled on a small note the day of his execution: "I John Brown am now quite certain that the crimes of this guilty land: will never be purged away; but with Blood" (Oates, 1970). At a eulogy held for Brown in New York City the same day, Henry Highland Garnet spoke of "the dreadful truth written as by the finger of Jehovah—For the sins of this nation there is no atonement without the shedding of blood." This was less a prophecy than a direct recognition that only warfare would abolish American slavery.

The historical significance of John Brown has been debated ever since. Was he a dangerous antislavery fanatic or a principled freedom fighter? Although slaveholders, northern Democrats, and moderate abolitionists thought the former, radical abolitionists and generations of African Americans believed the latter. Did the plan fail because it was poorly planned, or because slaves did not want to engage in insurrection? Clearly, the raid was well planned if poorly executed. Perhaps Brown should have taken to the hills Spartacus-like and incited the slaves. Alternatively, the slaves would probably not have followed him because of the blunt power of the slave regime. When this regime began to collapse a few years later, however, slaves did self-emancipate themselves, fight for the Union, and help destroy slavery. From whence arose Brown's passionate antislavery beliefs? Some biographers make much of his commitment to black people. Others insist the basis of this commitment was his fierce desire to eradicate the evil system of slavery through doing God's work. The historical jury remains out on several of these issues, but there are some irrefutable points. Brown's racial solidarity has always kindled greater respect among Americans of African descent than among whites. And Brown's raid and its consequences portended the underlying reality of the antebellum sectional crisis—namely, slavery.

— *Jeffrey R. Kerr-Ritchie*

See also: Harpers Ferry Raid.

For Further Reading

Brown, John. 1969. *Provisional Constitution and Ordinances for the People of the United States.* Ed. Boyd Sutler. Weston, MA: M&S Press.

DeCaro, Louis A., Jr. 2002. *Fire from the Midst of You: A Religious Life of John Brown.* New York: New York University Press.

DuBois, William E. B. 1909. *John Brown.* Philadelphia: G.W. Jacobs.

Finkelman, Paul, ed. 1995. *His Soul Goes Marching On: Responses to John Brown and the Harpers Ferry Raid.* Charlottesville: University of Virginia Press.

Oates, Stephen B. 1970. *To Purge This Land with Blood: A Biography of John Brown.* New York: Harper and Row.

Quarles, Benjamin. 1974. *Allies for Freedom: Blacks and John Brown.* New York: Oxford University Press.

JOHN MIFFLIN BROWN (1817–1893)

The abolitionist, educator, and eventually the eleventh bishop of the African Methodist Episcopal (AME) Church, John Mifflin Brown was born in Cantwell's Bridge (currently known as Odenta), Delaware, on September 8, 1817. Details of his early life are sketchy, but his future close involvement with the AME church was probably due to the influence of his mother and grandfather, both of whom were Methodists.

Prior to reaching his teens, Brown left Cantwell's Bridge for Wilmington, Delaware, where he resided with the Quaker family of William A. Seals. While in Wilmington, Brown attended Sunday School and church services at the Presbyterian church, where he and all other blacks were forced to sit in black pews located in the gallery of the church. Unwilling to accept this seating arrangement, Brown began attending Sunday School at the Roman Catholic church, where he was welcomed. The next few years of Brown's life were spent serving as an apprentice, first to attorney Henry Chester and then to Frederick H. Hinton, a barber.

In January 1836, Brown became a member of the Bethel AME Church in Philadelphia. After working as a barber in New York for a short while, Brown enrolled in Wesleyan Academy in Wilbraham, Massachusetts, in order to prepare for college, but failing health forced him to return to Philadelphia in summer 1840. During the fall of 1841, he enrolled at Oberlin College but did not complete a degree. Brown was an avid supporter of Oberlin, an institution that was known for its abolitionist tradition and a place where Brown found an environment that welcomed abolitionist lecturers and activists. Brown praised Oberlin College for its liberal tradition and encouraged blacks to attend because of this tradition and because of its reasonable tuition. In 1844 Brown opened the first school for black children living in Detroit, Michigan, and during that same year, he began serving as acting minister of the AME church there, a position he held until 1847.

After joining the Ohio Conference in 1849, Brown was given the pastorship of the AME church in Columbus, Ohio. That same year, he was appointed principal of Union Seminary, the first school owned and operated by the AME Church. Although enrollment at Union Seminary grew dramatically under Brown's leadership, the future of the school was tenuous, and in 1856 the assets from the then-defunct Union Seminary were merged with the newly established Wilberforce University.

As a result of his commitment to abolition and spreading the gospel, Brown was imprisoned on several occasions for allowing slaves to attend worship services. In 1858 he became the pastor of Bethel AME Church in Baltimore, where he was instrumental in increasing church membership and also raising significant funds to remodel the building. In 1868 Brown was elected bishop, was consecrated, and was assigned to the Seventh Episcopal District, which included several southern states. Brown was instrumental in organizing conferences and increasing church membership. He died at his Washington, D.C., home on March 16, 1876.

— *Beverly Bunch-Lyons*

See also: African Methodist Episcopal Church.

For Further Reading
Angell, Stephen Ward. 1992. *Bishop Henry McNeal Turner and African-American Religion in the South.* Knoxville: University of Tennessee Press.
Murphy, Larry G., J. Gordon Melton, and Gary Ward, eds. 1993. *Encyclopedia of African American Religions.* New York: Garland.

WILLIAM WELLS BROWN (C. 1814–1884)

An abolitionist and writer, William Wells Brown was born a slave, and his father was a white slaveholder. As a youth he was taken to St. Louis, Missouri, where he lived and worked for three different owners. He was hired out for various jobs: a farmhand, a servant in a tavern, for a brief time a handyman in Elijah P. Lovejoy's printing office, a worker on Mississippi River steamboats, an assistant in his owner's medical office, and a handyman for James Walker, a slave trader who took him along on three trips to New Orleans. Brown's work in the doctor's office inspired him later to study and practice medicine, while his work in a tavern led to his later activism in the temperance movement. His various work experiences provided a wealth of information for him to draw on when he became an antislavery activist.

Since childhood, Brown had thought of escaping from slavery, and when his last owner, a St. Louis commission merchant and steamboat owner, took him to Cincinnati as a servant he seized his chance. Traveling on his own and falling ill, he chanced on Wells Brown, an Ohio Quaker who housed and fed him for about a week until he was able to continue his journey. Assuming the status of a free person, Brown took his benefactor's name and was thereafter known as William Wells Brown. Later he dedicated the first edition of his narrative to Wells Brown.

Brown lived for several years in Cleveland, and then in Buffalo for nine years before moving close to Rochester, New York. During much of that period, he worked on Lake Erie steamers, taking advantage of the opportunity to help other fugitives reach Canada. Largely self-educated, he lectured on temperance and in 1843 became a lecturer for the Western New York Anti-Slavery Society. In 1847 he moved to Boston where he lectured for both the Massachusetts and American Anti-Slavery societies. William Lloyd Garrison recognized Brown's talents as a speaker, and he and other New England abolitionists sponsored Brown's tours. For his part, Brown was loyal to the Garrisonians, continuing to work with them when many other antislavery advocates had shifted their support to electoral politics or free soil tactics.

In 1848 Brown represented the American Peace Society at the Peace Congress in Paris, where he met Victor Hugo and other European reformers. While he was abroad, Congress enacted the new Fugitive Slave Act (1850), which made it much more dangerous for him to return to the United States. He traveled and lectured extensively in Britain, joining fellow black abolitionists William and Ellen Craft at some public meetings and at others exhibiting a panorama to add a visual dimension to his lectures on slavery. The panorama was not well received, but Brown's lectures were always impressive. He and other former slaves had the stamp of authenticity in speaking of the peculiar institution. Many who would not listen to a white abolitionist were moved by Brown's forceful presentation. Yet he wished to return to his native country and finally agreed, reluctantly, to permit British abolitionists to purchase his freedom.

After returning to the United States, Brown devoted himself to antislavery work with another series of lecture tours. As the North became more free soil in sentiment, Brown met a much warmer reception from audiences. He also wrote more than a dozen books, pamphlets, and plays, beginning with the *Narrative of William W. Brown, A Fugitive Slave, Written by Himself* (1847), which quickly became a best-seller. The 3,000-copy first edition sold out within six months. Three more editions followed, reaching a total of 10,000 copies sold in two years. It was one of only a few slave narratives that were written by the subject rather than having been dictated to abolitionists.

By 1856 Brown supplemented his lectures by reading one of his works, a three-act antislavery drama entitled *Experience; Or How to Give a Northern Man a Backbone.* Although he never published his first play, it met an enthusiastic response. By the end of 1856 he planned a second drama, *The Escape; Or a Leap for Freedom,* the first known play to be published by an African American. Brown often read it, too, during his extensive travels in the antislavery cause.

Although his lectures and dramatic readings were based primarily on his personal experiences as a slave, it was his novel *Clotel: Or, The President's Daughter* (1853), which became his most controversial work. Published in London, *Clotel* was based on the rumor that Thomas Jefferson had fathered a slave daughter by his personal servant Sally Hemings. As a novel it was flawed, parts of it being virtually lifted from Lydia Maria Child's story "The Quadroons." Yet as one of the earliest novels published by an African American,

it adds to Brown's significance as a pioneer writer for his race. *Clotel* did not appear in the United States during Brown's lifetime, though he wrote three variations on its theme for domestic readers.

Another of Brown's innovations was a travel book, *Three Years in Europe; or, Places I Have Seen and People I Have Met* (1852), written from the perspective of a former American slave. Its contents included articles and letters Brown contributed to the London press and American antislavery papers during his European sojourn. In contrast to other travel accounts, Brown's book compared the freedom he found in Britain with the slavery he had suffered in his native land. In a letter to his last owner, Brown wrote of his affection for America but his hatred for "her institution of slavery."

Brown pioneered in yet another area, writing a history of African Americans. Although he was not a trained historian, he called attention in his four books to the contributions of African Americans in the American Revolution and in the Civil War. Later editions of *The Black Man; His Antecedents, His Genius, and His Achievements* (1863) and *Rising Son; Or the Antecedents and Advancement of the Colored Race* (1874) included biographical sketches of more than one hundred African American men and women whom Brown believed represented the best in their race.

Brown recruited for the Union army during the Civil War and continued his efforts for civil rights. He also undertook the practice of medicine, combining it with lecturing and writing. Temperance remained one of his major concerns. Late in life Brown traveled through the South, writing of that experience in his last book, *My Southern Home: Or, the South and Its People.* Brown, who rose from slavery by his own efforts, produced more than a dozen publications and broke ground for later African American writers in several fields, was a significant American writer.

— *Larry Gara*

See also: Craft, William and Ellen; Fugitive Slave Act (1850); Garrison, William Lloyd; Underground Railroad.

For Further Reading

Brown, Josephine. 1856. *Biography of an American Bondman, By His Daughter.* Boston: R. F. Walcutt.

Brown, William Wells. 1847. *Narrative of William W. Brown, A Fugitive Slave, Written by Himself.* Boston: Anti-Slavery Office.

Farrison, William Edward. 1969. *William Wells Brown: Author and Reformer.* Chicago: University of Chicago Press.

Yellin, Jean Fagan. 1972. *The Intricate Knot: Black Figures in American Literature, 1776–1863.* New York: New York University Press.

JAMES BUCHANAN (1791–1868)

As the fifteenth president of the United States, James Buchanan did much to inflame sectional passions and to exacerbate controversies over slavery. A Pennsylvania native, Buchanan began practicing law after graduating from Dickinson College in 1809. Election to his state's legislature in 1812 began a long political career that kept Buchanan in public office almost continuously until 1861. He entered Congress in 1820 as a Federalist, though by the end of his decade-long tenure in the House of Representatives he had become baptized into the Jacksonian faith. After a brief stint as minister to Russia (1832–1833), Buchanan spent ten years in the U.S. Senate (1835–1845), where he showed traces of being a "doughface"—a northerner who sided with the South on slavery questions. Buchanan viewed such concessions as necessary for preserving the integrity of the Democratic Party as a unified national institution. Hence, he supported the annexation of Texas as a slave state in order to mollify the southern wing of the Democracy and thus to maintain party solidarity.

Buchanan left the Senate to join President James K. Polk's cabinet as secretary of state (1845–1849). In this post he showed skill and tact in handling diplomatic crises, but at the same time his pro-southern tendencies came into sharper focus. He supported Polk's aggression against Mexico and joined southerners in opposing the Wilmot Proviso, which aimed to bar slavery from all territory acquired as a result of the Mexican War (1846–1848). Instead, to resolve the question of slavery in the West, Buchanan advocated extending the Missouri Compromise line—which applied only to the old Louisiana Territory—to the Pacific Coast, thereby dividing the Mexican Cession into clearly delineated free and slaveholding spheres. But Democratic chieftains rejected this formula and instead hitched their party's platform to the doctrine of popular sovereignty—that is, to the idea of territorial self-determination of the slavery question. Largely for this reason, in 1848 the Democrats declined to run Buchanan for the presidency, an office he desired keenly, preferring rather the candidacy of Michigan senator Lewis Cass, the reputed "Father of Popular Sovereignty."

After again failing to win his party's presidential nomination in 1852, Buchanan joined President Franklin Pierce's administration as minister to Great Britain (1853–1856). In this station he became involved in an imbroglio concerning American plans for acquiring Cuba. In 1854 Buchanan and two other diplomats endorsed the Ostend Manifesto. The brainchild of Pierre Soulé, a fiery proslavery annexationist from Louisiana and head of the American legation in

James Buchanan, the fifteenth president of the United States, did little to prevent southern states from seceding from the Union and forming the Confederate States of America. (Library of Congress)

Madrid, the Ostend Manifesto proposed that the United States should seize Cuba by force if Spain refused to sell the island. This action endeared Buchanan to southern slavery expansionists, who coveted Cuba as an additional slave state, but it earned him the wrath of northern free soilers, who became convinced that Buchanan was a minion of the "slave power." Nevertheless, the Ostend fracas paled in comparison to the Kansas–Nebraska controversy, which also exploded in 1854 and which helped make Buchanan the Democratic presidential nominee in 1856. Rising anti-Nebraska sentiment in the party caused Democratic leaders to pass over Buchanan's chief rivals, the incumbent Pierce and Stephen A. Douglas of Illinois, both of whom figured prominently in passing the Kansas–Nebraska Act. Buchanan secured the party's candidacy because he was overseas when the Nebraska trouble broke and thus seemed untainted by the affair. With solid southern backing, he won the election of 1856.

Sectional discord over slavery plagued Buchanan throughout his term, and he did much to fuel the antagonisms. Tensions began mounting days after his inauguration when the Supreme Court issued its decision in the *Dred Scott* case (1857), decreeing that the Constitution did not recognize black people, slave or free, as citizens, while denying the authority of Congress or territorial legislatures to exclude slavery from the territories. Seeing the ruling as a final resolution to the territorial conundrum, Buchanan endorsed it wholeheartedly. Privately, in fact, the president committed a serious breach of constitutional ethics by pressuring one of the Court's northern Democratic justices to side with the Court's southern majority in handing down a proslavery judgment. Buchanan's southern supporters appreciated his stance, but it undermined the northern wing of his party because, since 1848, northern Democrats had embraced popular sovereignty as their formula for dealing with slavery in the territories. Yet, in disavowing the ability of territorial governments to regulate slavery, the *Dred Scott* decision seemed to invalidate that doctrine and to do so with the president's blessing. Buchanan thus helped precipitate a sectional rift in his own party.

Buchanan shattered his party completely during the debates over Kansas statehood in 1857–1858. As part of the original Louisiana Purchase lying north of the 36°30' line, Kansas Territory fell within the slave-free zone established under the Missouri Compromise of 1820. In 1854, however, Congress reorganized the region on the basis of popular sovereignty, thereby opening the door for the possible introduction of slavery into Kansas. Though most Kansans supported the free soil cause, a militant pro-southern minority used rigged elections, voter fraud, and similar artifices to elect a proslavery constitutional convention. Meeting at Lecompton in 1857, this bogus assembly drafted a slave-state constitution and submitted it to Congress in application for statehood. Buchanan fully endorsed the Lecompton Constitution, despite its questionable legitimacy, and pushed hard for the immediate admission of Kansas into the Union as a slave state. He hoped that a speedy admission, even under dubious auspices, would bring closure to the matter and eliminate the source of sectional agitation. Once again, however, he failed to see the consequences of his blatantly pro-southern policies. Led by Stephen Douglas, numerous anti–Lecompton Democrats broke with the administration in 1858 and joined Republicans in denouncing the Lecompton Constitution as a sham and a subversion of popular will in Kansas. Buchanan's course, therefore, split the northern Democrats and all but ensured a Republican presidential victory in 1860.

The election of Abraham Lincoln in that year triggered the secession of the Lower South. Buchanan approached this crisis with equivocation. He denied the right of any state to leave the Union, but he simultaneously denied the power of the federal government to coerce states to remain in the Union. He spent his final days in the White House attempting to avert civil war, happily transferring the reins of government to Lincoln in early 1861. He retired to Pennsylvania, where he died in 1868. Unapologetic to the last, Buchanan went to his grave blaming the dissolution of the Union and the ensuing Civil War on the zealotry of fanatical abolitionists and uncompromising "black" Republicans, who placed their devotion to the black race above the preservation of the republic itself.

This, of course, was hardly an accurate assessment. The former president himself bore a heavy burden of responsibility for the sectional apocalypse. Well before the Civil War erupted, Buchanan had earned the nickname "Old Public Functionary," a reference to the many offices he held during his long civic career. Yet, for all his political experience and insight, Buchanan confronted the sectional conflicts of the 1850s with considerable ineptitude. Indeed, his policies helped sunder the Union to which he had devoted his life.

— *Eric Tscheschlok*

See also: Border War (1854–1859); Civil War; *Dred Scott v. Sandford;* Lecompton Constitution; Popular Sovereignty.

For Further Reading

Klein, Philip S. 1962. *President James Buchanan: A Biography.* University Park: Pennsylvania State University Press.

Nichols, Roy F. 1948. *The Disruption of American Democracy.* New York: Macmillan.

Potter, David M. 1976. *The Impending Crisis, 1848–1861.* New York: Harper & Row.

Smith, Elbert B. 1975. *The Presidency of James Buchanan.* Lawrence: University Press of Kansas.

ANTHONY BURNS (C. 1830–1862)

Anthony Burns ranks near Frederick Douglass and Harriet Tubman among the more famous fugitive slaves in U.S. history. Born in the early 1830s in Stafford County, Virginia, Burns had a hand mangled in a sawmill accident, but he learned how to read and write, and in his teens he became a Baptist preacher. Employment in Richmond, Virginia, in 1853 offered him a realistic opportunity to escape, and in February 1854 he stowed away on a ship bound for Boston by way of Norfolk.

On May 24, eleven weeks after arriving in Massachusetts, Burns was on his way home from his job at a

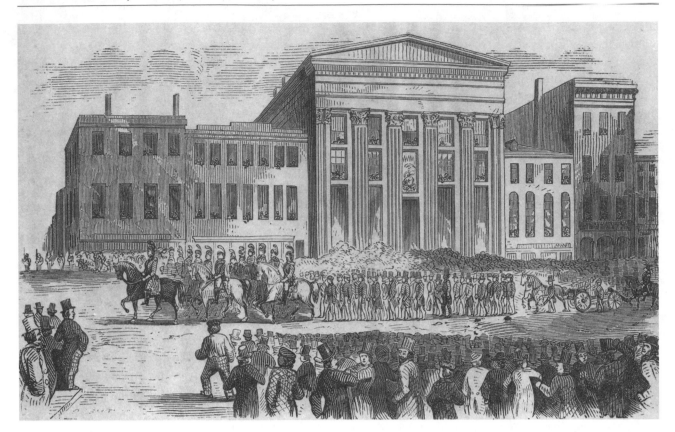

Officials in Boston provoked public discontent by returning the fugitive slave Anthony Burns to Virginia, even though their actions complied with the terms of the Fugitive Slave Act of 1850. (Library of Congress)

clothing store when he was arrested on a false charge of robbery, taken to the federal courthouse, and confronted by his Virginia owner, Charles F. Suttle. The next morning, Burns was taken before the fugitive slave commissioner, Judge Edward G. Loring, for what was intended as a quick hearing under the Fugitive Slave Act of 1850 and a quiet return to slavery in Virginia. But a failed rescue effort on May 26 led to the death of a jailer. Continued intervention by Burns's black pastor, Leonard A. Grimes, a white lawyer, Richard Henry Dana, and other Bostonians drew the procedure out until June 2. Judge Loring then determined that Burns was indeed the fugitive slave being sought. Hundreds of state militia and more hundreds of federal soldiers ushered Burns to the docks for his return to Virginia.

At enormous cost, the federal act had been enforced—a situation that inflamed passions over slavery on both sides. Northerners who had considered slavery a distant phenomenon saw the system's political power reach into their own region—and just as a furor over the Kansas–Nebraska Act erupted as well. Opposition grew toward slavery, along many dimensions, whether because of what it did to so many blacks or what it did

and threatened to do to whites. White northerners, that is, even if they had little interest in what slavery did to the enslaved in the South, might respond, as did one Massachusetts newspaper, "We are the slaves and vassals of the South" (Von Frank, 1998, p. 258). Yet proslavery southerners could see that the Fugitive Slave Act might not be worth much; as the *Richmond Enquirer* put it, "A few more such victories, and the South is undone" (Schwarz, 2001, p. 54). The Anthony Burns case propelled the nation toward secession, Civil War, and emancipation.

As for Anthony Burns himself, in despair after his capture, he had regarded quiet cooperation with the slave catchers as the safest way to behave, but the fracas associated with his being rendered back to slavery also led to his eventual freedom. For months following his return to Richmond on June 12, 1854, he was kept manacled in a filthy jail cell. Suttle then sold him to David McDaniel, a slave trader and planter from Rocky Mount, North Carolina. Burns managed to write letters to Boston, and black Bostonians soon learned of his new whereabouts. McDaniel agreed on a purchase price that would permit Burns to return to the North, this time as a free man. Burns arrived back in Boston one year after he had stepped off the steamer that carried him out of slavery the first time.

Burns's wish to study to become a trained preacher took him to Oberlin College in Ohio in summer 1855 and to Fairmont Theological Seminary in Cincinnati. Sales of his biography helped finance his education. He served briefly as the minister of a black church in Indianapolis, and in 1860 he became the pastor of a congregation of fugitive slaves, Zion Baptist Church, in St. Catherines, on the Canadian side of Lake Ontario. Still weak from his 1854 ordeal, Burns died of tuberculosis a year and a half after moving to his new home.

— *Peter Wallenstein*

See also: U.S.–Canadian Relations on Fugitives; Fugitive Slave Act (1850)

For Further Reading
Boston Slave Riot, and Trial of Anthony Burns. 1854. Boston: Fetridge and Company.

Finkelman, Paul. 1996. "Legal Ethics and Fugitive Slaves: The Anthony Burns Case, Judge Loring, and Abolitionist Attorneys." *Cardozo Law Review* 17 (May): 1793–1858.

Pease, Jane H., and William H. Pease. 1975. *The Fugitive Slave Law and Anthony Burns: A Problem in Law Enforcement.* Philadelphia: Lippincott.

Schwarz, Philip J. 2001. *Migrants against Slavery: Virginians and the Nation.* Charlottesville: University Press of Virginia.

Stevens, Charles Emery. 1856. *Anthony Burns: A History.* Boston: John P. Jewett and Company.

Von Frank, Albert J. 1998. *The Trials of Anthony Burns: Freedom and Slavery in Emerson's Boston.* Cambridge, MA: Harvard University Press.

WILLIAM BYRD (1674–1744)

The second William Byrd of Virginia, one of that colony's most prominent slaveholding planter aristocrats, distinguished himself as a lawyer, colonial official, and writer. He inherited a large James River plantation, its slaves, and the family home, Westover, from his father, William Byrd (1652–1704), who had obtained part of his fortune through land speculation and the traffic in African slaves. The son William Byrd later acquired more land and slaves, which allowed him an elegant and cultivated lifestyle.

Byrd owned over two hundred African slaves and several Native Americans. On occasion he imported Africans directly; others he acquired when he took over the Mount Folly estate of his deceased father-in-law, Daniel Parke. Byrd, like many Virginia planters, occasionally sold his slaves to pay his creditors.

Although Byrd attempted to be a kind master, referring to his slaves and servants as "my family," his paternalism also had a harsh side. His *Secret Diary* details how he often talked with his slaves, listened to their troubles, advised them on personal matters, and prescribed cures for their illnesses. He made sure that his slaves had adequate clothing, and as a strict observer of the Sabbath, he tried to minimize their Sunday work. On more than one occasion he prevented his hot-tempered first wife, Lucy Parke Bryd, from brutalizing household slaves. However, he personally whipped slaves whose behavior displeased him, or he might induce an unruly slave to vomit, which he found to be an effective punishment. He ordered others to be tied by the leg or fastened with a bit in their mouth, but he never branded them, relying on threats, not punishment to maintain discipline. Occasionally a slave escaped, but this occurred less frequently at Westover than at other Virginia plantations.

Though intensely religious, Byrd possessed elastic morals, which stretched to the slave quarters. He appreciated the beauty of black women and lusted for them. His *Histories of the Dividing Line* recounted an encounter with a "Dark Angel," and his *Commonplace Book* contained raunchy jokes about blacks and whites together. His *Diary* referred to "tawny nymphs," kissing black women, and fondling the breasts of a "Negro girl" who "resisted a little." He also composed verses to "Ebonia with an Olive Skin," but apparently he refrained from sexual relations with his female slaves until after 1720, when he began to make visits to slave quarters in search of female companionship.

Byrd gradually came to disapprove of slavery as unchristian. He advocated prohibition of slavery in the new Georgia colony and once expressed the hope that Virginia would prohibit the chattels altogether. He claimed that slavery contributed to moral degeneracy and laziness among whites, who disdained work "for fear it should make them look like slaves." He felt uncomfortable with the inhumanity of slavery and regretted the cruelty it engendered. But severity was necessary, he conceded, because the vast numbers of slaves made them insolent. His greatest concern, however, was the possibility of a servile revolt that would tinge Virginia's rivers with blood. Byrd also had great contempt for self-righteous New Englanders who carried rum and slaves up Virginia's rivers, once characterizing them as "felons." Despite Byrd's reservations about slavery, he recognized the institution as an economic necessity.

— *Charles H. McArver, Jr.*

See also: Women and the Antislavery Movement.

For Further Reading

Berland, Kevin, Jan Kirsten Gilliam and Kenneth A. Lockridge, eds. 2001. *The Commonplace Book of William Byrd II of Westover.* Chapel Hill: University of North Carolina Press.

Hatch, Alden. 1969. *The Byrds of Virginia,* New York: Holt, Rinehart and Winston.

Lockridge, Kenneth A. 1987. *The Diary, and Life, of William Byrd II of Virginia, 1674–1744.* Chapel Hill: University of North Carolina Press.

Mariambaud, Pierre. 1971. *William Byrd of Westover.* Charlottesville: University of Virginia Press.

Sobel, Mechal. 1987. *The World They Made Together: Black and White Values in Eighteenth-Century Virginia.* Princeton, NJ: Princeton University Press.

Wright, Louis B., and Marion Tinling, eds. 1941. *The Secret Diary of William Byrd of Westover, 1709–1712.* Richmond, VA: Dietz Press.

JOHN C. CALHOUN (1782–1850)

Although he served as vice president and cabinet officer in two presidential administrations, John C. Calhoun is most remembered as a staunch supporter of slavery and states' rights. No southern politician of the antebellum period was more widely experienced than South Carolina's Calhoun. As congressman, senator, cabinet member, and vice president, he was as powerful and influential as any American before his death in 1850. Yet, despite his national stature, history recognizes him more as the strategist who engineered the antebellum defense of slavery.

Calhoun was a significant slaveholder, and not surprisingly, he viewed slavery as an economic good. He was interested in agriculture and scientific farming, and he had mining interests in northern Georgia. His largest landholdings were near Pendleton, South Carolina, where he owned a 1,000-acre cotton plantation named Fort Hill. He owned another cotton plantation in Alabama's Black Belt in Marengo County. Calhoun owned over 150 slaves at the two operations combined, and he also utilized slave labor at his gold mine located near Dahlonega, Georgia. Calhoun added several large land grants to his already considerable interests, but in his later years, he went into serious debt with land investments and several poor harvests.

Calhoun grew up with slaves and was considered a good and fair master. The historical record shows that his slaves were rather fond of their master. He was convinced of blacks' inferiority and found them incapable of freedom. He defended slavery on moral and economic grounds and rejected the "necessary evil" defense, convinced that the institution was the foundation of a southern society based on agriculture. Over the last two pivotal decades of his life, Calhoun did not waver in his belief that slavery was a "positive good" that was benevolent to the inferior race.

Calhoun saved his most vitriolic attacks for northerners who were critical of slavery, especially abolitionists. Calhoun charged that northern contentions that slavery was a sin and immoral were baseless, and he did not mince words when provided a public audience. Unlike several of his more enlightened southern colleagues, Calhoun opposed emancipation, but, to the satisfaction of many of his fellow slaveowners, his was one major defining voice defending the existence of slavery.

Calhoun was born on March 18, 1782, near the Abbeville community in South Carolina. In fall 1802, he left South Carolina for Yale and returned two years later a graduate and a Unitarian. Calhoun began the study of law in Charleston and graduated from Connecticut's Litchfield Law School in 1806. His early years practicing law proved unfulfilling, and he entered politics in 1808. His early experience led to Calhoun's election to Congress in 1811 where he served until 1817, when he was appointed President James Monroe's secretary of war. A war hawk in Congress, Calhoun served eight years in the cabinet, reorganizing the War Department and overseeing its significant growth. Aspiring to the presidency, Calhoun settled for the vice presidential post under John Quincy Adams. As the Democratic Party emerged with the meteoric rise of Andrew Jackson, Calhoun found the party's states' rights platform compatible with his doctrine of nullification, and when Jackson easily carried the presidency in 1828, Calhoun was again elected vice president.

The year 1828 was pivotal for Calhoun—he anonymously penned the so-called South Carolina Exposition, thus continuing the states' rights stand. Calhoun introduced his interpretation of the doctrine of interposition, arguing that a state had the right to veto any federal legislation that it found to be unconstitutional. The entire argument centered on opposition to the protective tariff of 1828, and Calhoun and South Carolina led the charge. As a split developed between

John C. Calhoun, a staunch supporter of slavery and states' rights, served as vice president and cabinet officer in two presidential administrations. (Library of Congress)

Jackson and Calhoun, South Carolina nullified the tariffs of 1828 and 1832, and threatened secession. The volatile Calhoun was elected to the Senate in December 1832, and he then resigned from the vice presidency. In time, a lower tariff measure passed as a compromise and the secession crisis was averted.

From the Senate, Calhoun further developed his defense of slavery as a positive good and opposed the growing national antislavery movement. As a rather large slaveowner, Calhoun moved away from defending the institution as a necessary evil for southern economic development. Confronting abolitionists at every turn, Calhoun defended the South's right to protect its constitutional guarantee to own slaves, a defense that further projected his position as a national political figure. He briefly considered a run for the presidency in 1844 and was appointed secretary of state under President John Tyler in April 1844. Again slavery became an issue for Calhoun, as he pushed for allowing slavery in the annexed Texas territory. He left the State Department when James K. Polk was elected, but once again returned to the Senate in late 1845. One final time Calhoun rose to defend states' rights, this

time over the Compromise of 1850 and California statehood. Seeing the South being pushed into a minority position on slavery, Calhoun argued against the compromise. Too weak to read his own speech, Calhoun heard his words read for him on the Senate floor. He appeared in the Senate for the final time on March 13, 1850, and died on March 31. Like so many other southerners who fought to defend states' rights and thus slavery, Calhoun never strayed from his views.

— *Boyd Childress*

See also: Compromise of 1850; Democratic Party; *Disquisition on Government* (Calhoun); Nullification Doctrine; *South Carolina Exposition* and *Protest*.

For Further Reading

Bartlett, Irving. 1993. *John C. Calhoun: A Biography.* New York: Norton.

Bolt, William K. 2004. "Founding Father and Rebellious Son: James Madison, John C. Calhoun, and the Use of Precedents." *American Nineteenth Century History* 5 (3): 1–27.

Calhoun, John C. 1957–. *The Papers of John C. Calhoun.* Ed. Clyde N. Wilson. Columbia: South Carolina University Press.

Coit, Margaret L. 1950. *John C. Calhoun,* American Portrait. Boston: Houghton Mifflin.

Scribner, David. 1997. "A Study of the Antecedents, Argument, and Significance of John C. Calhoun's South Carolina Exposition." Ph.D. dissertation, Department of Political Science, University of Houston, Houston, Texas.

CANADA. *See* United States–Canadian Relations on Fugitives.

LUCRETIA "PATTY" HANLEY CANNON (C. 1764–1829)

Patty Cannon led the nineteenth century's most successful kidnapping ring in the abduction of free blacks. Cannon's gang, which included over thirty white thugs and a black confederate, terrorized African Americans from Philadelphia, Pennsylvania, to Accomac, Virginia. Responsible for sending countless numbers of free blacks into slavery, Cannon's operation illuminates the dangers that freed slaves and freeborn people living within a slave nation faced.

Much of Lucretia Hanley Cannon's life remains a mystery. Born in about 1764 possibly in Canada, the black-haired, brown-eyed, and buxom woman nicknamed "Patty" spent most of her life in Delaware. Large and powerful with a rowdy disposition, she reputedly had the ability to fling a man to the ground by his hair, She married Jesse Cannon and produced several children, one of whom she later confessed to strangling three days after its birth. Jesse, killed by poison, also figured among Cannon's eleven acknowledged murder victims.

One of her daughters married Joe Johnson, and he did much of the gang's kidnapping work. Cannon supervised blacks imprisoned in the two Cannon–Johnson homes, each located in the heavily wooded Johnson's Crossing (now Reliance, Maryland) at the intersection of Dorchester and Caroline counties along Delaware's southern border with Maryland near the Nanticoke River. In these houses, chained African Americans were held captive in attics, basements, and hidden rooms. They would be transported in covered wagons to Johnson's Ferry (now Woodland's Ferry) for shipment to plantations. Johnson captained the ships and led the bands taking captives to the South. With easy access to the Chesapeake Bay, the gang operated by both land and water for years.

In the United States, free blacks risked being kidnapped and sold into slavery. Although kidnapping occurred throughout the nation, residents of states bordering the Mason–Dixon line were in greatest jeopardy, and Delaware was a good site for the Cannon–Johnson gang. On the Chesapeake's eastern shore peninsula, whites viewed freeborn and emancipated blacks, who by 1819 already outnumbered slaves, as a threat. Antikidnapping laws could not be enforced in such a hostile climate, and newly opened cotton country in the old Southwest created a huge demand for slaves just after the African slave trade had been abolished. Kidnapping could be a highly lucrative and relatively safe occupation. In abducting slaves, kidnappers risked death at the hands of angry slaveholders, but by abducting freeborn or emancipated blacks, kidnappers faced only slight risk since the victims and their families had little legal recourse and few powerful supporters.

The exact number of Cannon's kidnapping victims is unknown but is estimated to be over two dozen. Slave testimony collected in Delaware's Federal Writers' Project shows that while Quakers sent runaway slaves north into freedom, Cannon shipped free blacks south into slavery.

In the late 1820s, a farmer working land near the Cannon–Johnson property discovered several buried skeletons. The remains were eventually linked to Cannon. Arrested in 1829 for killing a slave trader, she confessed to murdering eleven people and admitted to playing a role in twelve other deaths. She committed suicide in jail on May 11, 1829, in Georgetown, Delaware, by taking poison. At a posthumous trial in October 1829, the Delaware court, refusing to allow justice to be thwarted, convicted Cannon of the murder of three children and sentenced her to hang.

In subsequent years, Cannon acquired immortality in print. Featured in both George Alfred Townsend's 1884 collection, *The Entailed Hat,* and R.W. Messenger's 1926 novel, *Patty Cannon Administers Justice,* Cannon has become a nightmarish legend and as such, part of American folklore.

— *Caryn E. Neumann*

See also: Free Persons of Color.

For Further Reading
Miller, M. Sammy. 1975. "Legend of a Kidnapper." *Crisis* 82 (April): 118–120.
Wilson, Carol. 1994. *Freedom at Risk: The Kidnapping of Free Blacks in America, 1780–1865.* Lexington: University of Kentucky Press.

SLAVE CATCHERS

Slave catchers were persons engaged in locating and capturing slaves who attempted to escape a condition of servitude (as in the United States), or in capturing persons who subsequently became commodities in slave commerce (as in Africa). Slave catchers were important members of all slaveholding societies throughout recorded history. Babylonian Laws 17–20 defined the responsibilities and expectations of such a profession (searching), as did Hittite Laws 22–23 and 61. Elaborate Roman legislation categorized slave types and processes applicable in retrieving fugitive slaves, and attempted to remove opportunities for collusion between fugitive slaves and catchers/entrepreneurs. The Romans commonly used branding as a technique for identifying runaways, and officials regularly detained branded persons for collection by owners, even before owners reported them missing. Muslim-influenced African societies appealed to Islamic law (Sura 47) to define an employer's obligations to slave catchers and to legitimize slave catching. Africa's animistic societies appealed to indigenous law.

In the Americas, various slave-catching (retrieving) traditions applied. In the United States, the Fugitive Slave Act (1793) permitted slaveowners to apply to federal court officials for an order to return fugitive slaves to the state from which they had fled, but that act did not provide for enforcement of the court's decision within the state of discovery or establish procedures for returning fugitive slaves legally to owners. In 1818 Congress considered a new proposal designed to give force to earlier legislation and to satisfy both slaveowners and antislavery sentiments, but Congress failed to reach consensus or compromise sufficient for passage. Consequently, the 1793 act remained the principal law (however flawed) regarding slave retrieval until when, in the Compromise of 1850, Congress passed a new Fugitive Slave Act as part of the Compromise of 1850.

Between 1793 and 1850, sentiments of both slaveowners and antislavery advocates changed dramatically, and the slave-catching/searching/retrieving profession also changed. In 1793 significant numbers of settlers and slaves were under a service obligation/contract, and society respected the professional catcher. After 1793, numbers of free-based indentures in the North declined significantly, leaving a preponderance of catchers employed in locating and retrieving fugitive slaves who crossed from slaveholding to nonslaveholding states. Until 1850, federal law complicated slave catching/searching/retrieving within northern states since it provided no binding process for enforcement. In addition, state laws, state courts, and state officials confounded the process by obstructing legitimate slave catchers. Abolitionist opposition and successes in blocking lawful retrievals encouraged the slaveowners' increasing willingness to sanction extralegal means to retrieve property. Slave catchers consequently changed search-and-return methods. Rather than risking opposition and time-consuming involvements of northern courts, catchers increasingly avoided the legal process altogether, simply seizing fugitive slaves and secretly transporting them to a place that sanctioned slavery. Contemporary abolitionist literature characterized such persons as bounty hunters or kidnappers, often accusing them of kidnapping free African Americans to replace financial losses suffered by slaveowning employers.

The Fugitive Slave Act of 1850 was part of a larger compromise between northern and southern states and was designed to remedy the defects of previous legislation. Unfortunately, this act did not halt the excesses of catchers who were accustomed to working outside legal processes. It effectively legalized and sanctioned slave catching in the North, protecting by federal law and enabling federal marshals and other federal officials to enforce it. Abolitionists interpreted the law as significantly failing to meet its antislavery objective and a victory for slaveowners who pursued fugitive slaves both by legal means (protected by the federal government) and illegal means (kidnapping).

Slave catching as it relates to capturing people for the purpose of enslaving them mainly applied to Africa in modern times, although slave catching was practiced by others and in other areas much earlier. Wars have always produced winners and losers, and losers often became booty or compensation for the costs of fighting the war. This was particularly true in Greek and Roman societies, and to a lesser degree in Spanish territories during the Reconquista (the reconquering of the Iberian Peninsula from the Muslims, 711–1492) and subsequent conquest of the Americas. In Africa, people became captives in various ways. Some African states (Oyo, Abomey, Asanti, Kongo, Benin) waged wars of expansion, often to produce captives, which they then sent to coastal purchasers of slaves in exchange for European/American merchandise or goods that could be obtained only on the coast. In some areas, such as the Fula Empire (Guinea-Conakry), powerful ethnic groups considered others as inferior or infidel and subject to periodic culling or harvesting; those harvested persons (perhaps age or gender specific) then became commodities in the transatlantic slave trade. In other areas (the Gambia and Sierra Leone), interior raids by coastal peoples produced captives, who became coastal commodities.

Generally, accepted wisdom along the west coast of Africa specified that European buyers needed to pay a fair price and a tax for each slave exported from the coast. Failure to do so would inevitably result in retaliation against other Europeans visiting the coast. As a practice, slave catching became increasingly counterproductive for Europeans and threatened the coastal industry of purchasing slaves and selling manufactured goods. Thus, by 1750, most slaves leaving the west coast of Africa were captives of Africans who sold them to European/American buyers for transport across the Atlantic. The significant decrease in transatlantic slave trading after 1830 did not end the slave catching profession on the continent. Legal indigenous slavery continued throughout Africa into the twentieth century, as did active slave raiding and wars fought for purposes of collecting slaves.

— *Bruce L. Mouser*

See also: Fugitive Slave Act (1850); Fugitive Slave Acts, State.

For Further Reading

Campbell, Stanley W. 1970. *The Slave Catchers*. Chapel Hill: University of North Carolina Press.

Daube, David. 1952. "Slave-Catching." *The Juridical Review* 64: 12–28.

Grace, John. 1975. *Domestic Slavery in West Africa*. New York: Barnes & Noble.

Watson, Alan. 1987. *Roman Slave Law*. Baltimore, MD: Johns Hopkins University Press.

ELIZABETH BUFFUM CHACE
(1806–1899)

Elizabeth Buffum Chace was a leader of the antislavery movement in Massachusetts and Rhode Island. She became an abolitionist largely because of her family's involvement in the movement. Her father, Arnold Buffum, cofounded and served as president of the New England Anti-Slavery Society in 1832. Her grandfather, as a member of the Rhode Island Society for the Gradual Abolition of Slavery, had helped runaway slaves from New York reach freedom in Canada before New York abolished slavery in 1827. A devout Quaker, Chace had no doubt that slavery was evil, and in the early 1830s she became an active abolitionist. Despite her extreme reluctance to speak before anyone other than family members, in 1836 she cofounded and served as vice president of the Ladies' Anti-Slavery Society of Fall River, Massachusetts. The following year she became the society's president, and in 1838 she represented the society at the Female Anti-Slavery Convention in Philadelphia, Pennsylvania.

Chace was not a fiery leader like William Lloyd Garrison, editor of the abolitionist newspaper, the *Liberator,* whom she greatly admired. Rather, she led her group by quietly hosting meetings in her home, which contained a small lending library of antislavery material. She also circulated petitions demanding that the state legislature grant more civil rights to blacks, and she contributed goods that she had sewn to proabolition fund-raising events.

In 1839 Chace moved to Valley Falls, Rhode Island, where her husband had opened a new business. She became the unofficial secretary for Rhode Island abolitionists; she organized meetings across the state and made most of the arrangements for a Sunday lecture series in Providence that focused on abolition. She also began writing articles for the *Liberator* while continuing to raise money and to circulate petitions to the state legislature.

Shortly after relocating to Valley Falls, Chace and her husband turned their home into a station on the Underground Railroad. Many runaway slaves were able to make their way to Cape Cod by sneaking aboard a ship bound for Boston from a southern port, but once on the Cape they still needed help to get to Canada and freedom. Fortunately for them, a number of abolitionists lived on the Cape, and whenever they happened upon a runaway they sent the fugitive to the Underground Railroad station in New Bedford, Massachusetts. From there, the runaways were sent to Fall River, where Chace's sister and brother-in-law operated a station in their home. From Fall River, runaways were sent to Valley Falls, where the Chaces would put them on the train to Worcester, Massachusetts. In Worcester, an abolitionist conductor made sure the runaways got on a train headed north through Vermont to Canada.

Chace was so devoted to abolitionism that in 1843 she gave up her beloved Quaker faith. The occasion for this momentous decision was the yearly meeting of New England Friends, which refused to allow abolitionists, many of whom were Quakers, to hold their gatherings in Quaker meetinghouses. That same year she heeded Garrison's call to all abolitionists to refuse to vote in federal elections, on the grounds that voting supported the federal government, which in turn supported slavery. In 1860 she served as vice president of the New England Anti-Slavery Convention. From 1865 to 1870 she served as vice president of the American Anti-Slavery Society, which continued to function after the demise of slavery in an effort to help freed people gain economic and political equality.

— *Charles W. Carey*

See also: Garrison, William Lloyd; Underground Railroad.

For Further Reading

Salitan, Lucille, and Eve Lewis Perera, eds. 1994. *Virtuous Lives: Four Quaker Sisters Remember Family Life, Abolitionism, and Women's Suffrage.* New York: Continuum.

Stevens, Elizabeth C. 2003. *Elizabeth Buffum Chace and Lillie Chace Wyman: A Century of Abolition, Suffragist and Workers' Rights Activism.* Jefferson, NC: McFarland.

Wyman, Lillie Buffum Chace. 1903. "Reminiscences of Two Abolitionists." *New England Magazine* (January): 536–550.

JOHN CHAVIS (1763–1838)

As a free black conservative teacher and preacher, the Reverend John Chavis announced that the abolition of slavery would add to the problems of his enslaved brethren, and in 1831 he referred to Nat Turner's revolt as an "abominable insurrection" (Hudson, 1976). Concern for his own personal welfare outweighed his concern for and identification with enslaved blacks, as the Turner rebellion had made it impossible for Chavis to continue his life's work when North Carolina's frightened whites nearly expelled all free blacks from the state.

Chavis was born near Oxford in Granville County, North Carolina, at a place known locally as the Reavis

Cross Roads in 1763. In 1832 Chavis described himself as "a free born American [who] saw service in the Revolutionary War" (Hudson, 1976). Chavis managed to receive an extraordinary education. An 1802 court record shows that he had regularly attended Washington Academy (now Washington and Lee University). According to some sources, Chavis attended but did not graduate from the College of New Jersey (now Princeton University). He was sent to college as an experiment to see if black people could learn the same as whites, and the experiment obviously succeeded—Chavis excelled in both classics and rhetoric.

The records of a meeting of the Presbytery of Lexington, Virginia, in October 1799, indicate that Chavis was eligible for a license to preach provided he passed the trials. The trials included an exegesis in Latin and a homily on the decree of Election. In 1801 the Presbyterian Church licensed Chavis to preach; thus he became the first ordained black preacher and theologian in the Presbyterian Church. He worked as a missionary in southern Virginia, and in 1805 he returned to North Carolina and joined the Orange Presbytery where for more than twenty years he preached in Granville, Orange, and Wake counties.

By 1808 Chavis had married a woman named Frances and settled in Raleigh where he opened a private integrated school, but he was forced to separate his black and white students. He taught the white children in the day school, charging them $2.50 for tuition, and the blacks in the night school from sundown until 10 P.M. He charged black families $1.75 tuition (probably per year). Chavis was described in later years by his former students as black in complexion, immaculate in his dress, somewhat corpulent, and about five feet six or seven inches tall.

Vigorously involved in the politics of the 1800s, Chavis identified himself as a Federalist. He opposed Andrew Jackson's election, stating that Jackson was a backwoods countryman without benefit of "blood or training" (Knight, 1930). Clearly, Chavis favored the aristocracy, and perhaps even thought himself a part of it, until 1835 when the North Carolina General Assembly stripped him of the vote, deciding that blacks, including freemen, could not cast ballots.

On June 13, 1838, Gales and Son published a pamphlet written by Chavis entitled *Letter Upon the Atonement of Christ,* the sale of which provided income for Chavis and his wife; in addition, the Presbyterian Church voted to support them for the remainder of their lives. Chavis and his wife resided with his brother, Mark Chavis, a prosperous millwright with land 6 miles north of Oxford. For years after his death, Chavis's work as a minister and an educator seemed

forgotten, but after fifty years of obscurity, Charles Lee Smith, an educator, resurrected the name and had a large park and housing project in Raleigh, North Carolina, named in Chavis's honor.

— *Nagueyalti Warren*

See also: Turner, Nat.

For Further Reading
Cooper, Richard. 1985. *John Chavis: To Teach a Generation.* Raleigh, NC: Creative Productions.

Hudson, Gossie. 1976. "John Chavis." In *Dictionary of Negro Biography.* Ed. Rayford W. Logan and Michael R. Winston. New York: Norton.

Knight, Edgar W. 1930. "Notes on John Chavis." *North Carolina Historical Review* 7: 326–345.

Othow, Helen Chavis. 2001. *John Chavis: African American Patriot.* Jefferson, NC: McFarland.

CHEROKEE SLAVEOWNERS

The Cherokee, one of the Five Civilized Tribes whose territory once extended from North Carolina southwest into Alabama, became slaveowners in their attempt to assimilate into white planter society. The Cherokees who adopted the plantation culture of their white neighbors, which included slave-based agriculture, did so in the hopes of assimilating into white society. Many Cherokee were already of mixed heritage as from the time of European settlement, they had intermarried with whites; by the 1830s many of the Cherokee tribal leaders came from families with mixed Cherokee/white blood. For them, adopting white culture was another step toward assimilation.

As slaveowners, the Cherokee tended to treat their slaves less harshly than did white southern planters, although recent scholarship disputes this belief. Traditionally, the Cherokee had enslaved their prisoners of war, but enslavement was not always permanent: some prisoners were later adopted into the tribe. Before Europeans settled in the southeastern part of the United States, chattel slavery did not exist in Cherokee tribal society because the accumulation of wealth was not important to them. However, after they accepted some aspects of white culture, including a centralized government, commerce, and increased productivity, the Cherokees began to use slave labor.

In 1828 the Cherokee established their own republic with its capital at New Echota in north Georgia. The constitution they created was similar to that of the United States. However, their slave code, a series of laws regarding the control of black slaves within Cherokee lands, predated their constitution. Little of the slave code dealt with slave rebellion or insubordination, and most punishments were reserved for the master rather than the slaves. Cherokees who married slaves, bought merchandise from them, or sold them liquor were punished. These Cherokee slave codes were influenced more by their own tradition than by white custom.

The new Cherokee republic was largely run and organized by slaveholding Indians. By the 1830s their prosperity and status had brought them respect both within the tribe and in white society. Most Cherokee slaveholders spoke English and were part white. They farmed more acres and owned more businesses; mainly mills, taverns, and ferries, than nonslaveholders. As a group, the Georgia Cherokee had considerably more wealth than the North Carolina Cherokee, who followed traditional ways and owned relatively few slaves.

Although editorials in the *Cherokee Phoenix* (the newspaper of the Cherokee Nation, founded in 1828) favored abolition with compensated emancipation by 1839, most Cherokee probably accepted their white neighbors' views on slavery and regarded blacks as inferior. Cherokee law excluded blacks and mulattoes from voting or holding office in the Cherokee republic, and free blacks who moved onto Cherokee land were regarded as unwelcome intruders and had to obtain a residence permit. The Cherokee were forbidden by law to marry slaves, but they could marry free blacks and the 1835 census listed a small number of Cherokee with African blood.

Slaves owned by the Cherokee were allowed to establish chapters of the African Benevolent Society, an outgrowth of the American Colonization Society within the republic. Missionaries who proselytized among the Cherokee converted more blacks than Indians. The Moravians, first to preach in the Cherokee republic, established a mission school at Spring Place (near present-day Chatsworth), the home of James Vann a wealthy Cherokee slaveowner. Their church services were integrated, as were those of the American Mission Board, which followed the Moravians into Cherokee territory and established several schools and churches for the Cherokee. Slaves were allowed to attend both church services and mission schools. This soon became a problem because Georgia state law forbade the instruction of blacks. Although the Cherokee may have treated their slaves better than white owners did, they still considered slaves to be property or chattel, just as the white owners did. Because Cherokee law protected property, slaves were sold in payment of debt or to settle estates.

Despite their successful adoption of white culture, when gold was discovered in Georgia, the state government demanded the Cherokee be removed to Indian Territory in Oklahoma. Although they won their case before the Supreme Court of the United States, the Cherokee were forced to leave their Georgia land. Many took their slaves with them to Oklahoma. Henry Bibb, a slave owned by a Cherokee in Oklahoma, was quoted as saying, "If I must be a slave, I had by far, rather be a slave to an Indian, than to a white man" (Mails, 1992).

— *Elsa A Nystrom*

See also: Seminole Indians

For Further Reading

Mails, Thomas E. 1992. *The Cherokee People: The Story of the Cherokees from Earliest Origins to Contemporary Times.* Tulsa, OK: Council Oaks Books.

Miles, Tiya. 2005. *The Story of an Afro-Cherokee Family in Slavery and Freedom.* Berkeley: University of California Press.

Perdue, Theda. 1979. "The Development of Plantation Slavery before Removal." In *The Cherokee Indian Nation: A Troubled History.* Ed. Duane H. King. Knoxville: University of Tennessee Press.

Wilkins, Thurman. 1988. *Cherokee Tragedy.* Norman: University of Oklahoma Press.

CHARLES WADDELL CHESNUTT (1858–1932)

Charles Chesnutt confronted the perils of slavery and its reaches first through imaginative literature and then through political action. An artistic innovator, he combined fiction with social history in the hope of awakening white Americans and attaining social justice; he produced a distinctive genre of American literature. Disappointed in his purpose, however, he turned to other literary categories—biography, letters, essays, articles, speeches—and to politics. He became a foremost expository protagonist for African Americans and a formidable antagonist of racism in the United States.

Although he could have passed as a white person, Chesnutt determined to honor his black heritage and to throw his talents into the balance. His collections of short stories (*The Conjure Woman and Other Conjure Tales, The Wife of His Youth and Other Stories*) established him as a superlative writer of short fiction. His novels (*The House Behind the Cedars, The Marrow of Tradition, The Colonel's Dream*) drew themes from his own experience and that of his ancestors, as well as from the drama being played out in the long shadow of black slavery in the United States. The novels examine "passing" (blacks passing for white), race riots, and the lingering powers of the landed families of the antebellum era. Critics as eminent as William Dean Howells applauded Chesnutt's work; but because the South was rushing toward white supremacy, his books never reached a substantial public.

Turning to expository writing and political action, Chesnutt addressed subjects of concern to African Americans and to white contemporaries. He wrote a life of Frederick Douglass, the black abolitionist–orator–journalist born in slavery. Through many publications and speeches he confronted racial issues of American experience: laws affecting former slaves and reinstating limits on their opportunities; problems of lynching and race rioting; political alignments that reinstituted slave conditions; and African American civil rights, their abrogation, and the consequences to the nation of their denial. He corresponded with figures of influence in the white world.

Chesnutt conducted extensive dialogues with Booker T. Washington and W. E. B. DuBois, African American leaders who, in the wake of American slavery, set courses for interracial relations. In widely read articles, Chesnutt delineated a third racial posture: Washington believed that vocational education and the interlacing of black energy with white business would eventually achieve resolutions; DuBois believed that militant insistence on every right, especially education, would bring results. Chesnutt thought that the vote should be secured immediately regardless of education or previous servitude. He concluded that in the end, intermarriage of the races would prove the only answer to the cruelties attendant on slavery.

— *Frances Richardson Keller*

See also: Literature; Passing.

For Further Reading

Andrews, William L. 1980. *The Literary Career of Charles W. Chesnutt.* Baton Rouge: Louisiana State University Press.

Chesnutt, Helen. 1952. *Charles Waddell Chesnutt: Pioneer of the Color Line.* Chapel Hill: University of North Carolina Press.

Crisler, Jesse S., Robert C. Leitz, III and Joseph R. McElrath, Jr., eds. 2002. *An Exemplary Citizen: Letters of Charles W. Chesnutt, 1906–1932.* Palo Alto, CA: Stanford University Press.

Keller, Frances Richardson. 1978. *An American Crusade: The Life of Charles Waddell Chesnutt.* Provo, UT: Brigham Young University Press.

McWilliams, Dean. 2002. *Charles W. Chesnutt and the Fictions of Race.* Athens: University of Georgia Press.

Render, Sylvia Lyons. 1979. *Charles Waddell Chesnutt:*

Eagle with Clipped Wings. Washington, DC : Howard University Press.

LYDIA MARIA CHILD (1802–1880)

Coupling an eighteenth-century sensibility with a nineteenth-century radical's passion to free the slaves, Lydia Maria Child was one of the antislavery movement's most brilliant essayists. From her *Appeal in Favor of That Class of Americans Called Africans* (1833) to *Romance of the Republic* (1867), Child was a tireless and accomplished advocate of black Americans' human rights. Clear-sighted in her analyses of southern slavery, Child discerned its links to the social lot of white women and also found time to investigate comparative religions.

Child's first book, *Hobomok* (1824), treated the shocking subject of miscegenation (marriage or cohabitation between a white person and a member of another race), yet literary Boston welcomed this novel and its author with open arms. Soon, Child was writing essays and short stories to popular acclaim, and editing *The Juvenile Miscellany,* an enormously popular children's magazine. Finding belles lettres insufficiently lucrative, Child turned her energy and talent to domestic guides like *The Frugal Housewife* (1829) and *The Mother's Book* (1831).

Both of the last-named books sold extremely well until Child published her exhortatory *Appeal;* after that, she was labeled a radical and ostentatiously shunned. Undeterred, Child joined the Boston Female Anti-Slavery Society, accompanied George Thompson on his U.S. tour, and published *Authentic Accounts of American Slavery* (1835), *The Evils of Slavery, and the Cure of Slavery* (1836), and an *Anti-Slavery Catechism* (1836).

Although dismayed by the antislavery movement's dissent over the role of women in abolition, Child continued to oppose the South's peculiar institution. In the early 1840s, she edited the *National Anti-Slavery Standard* and published short stories and essays opposing slavery. Yet in 1843, after separating her finances from her husband's, Child stepped out of the antislavery limelight, exhausted by the internecine quarrels that plagued the movement at the time.

In the 1850s and 1860s, her energy renewed, Child attended antislavery gatherings and asked permission to nurse John Brown in prison. She also helped to raise funds for the families whose sons and fathers had died in the raid on Harpers Ferry, engaged in a letterwriting campaign with Virginians who were outraged at Brown's supposed treachery, and composed antislavery treatises like *The Patriarchal Institution* and *The Duty of Disobedience to the Fugitive Slave Law* (1860). In addition, Child penned pro-emancipation articles that were printed anonymously, and edited Harriet Ann Jacobs's *Incidents in the Life of a Slave Girl* (1861), a slave narrative that focuses on the sexual exploitation of women born as slaves. A section of the last book reappeared in Child's *Freedmen's Book* (1865), a compendium intended to instill racial pride in people long subjugated to the lash. When that work appeared, Child was lobbying for the redistribution of confiscated plantation lands.

In 1870 she attended the closing meeting of the Massachusetts Anti-Slavery Society and the last antislavery festival. Nine years later, she wrote her last article, a tribute to William Lloyd Garrison.

— *Barbara Ryan*

See also: Jacobs, Harriet Ann.

For Further Reading

Karcher, Carolyn L. 1994. *The First Woman in the Republic: A Cultural Biography of Lydia Maria Child.* Durham, NC: Duke University Press.

Meltzer, Milton, and Patricia G. Holland, eds. 1982. *Lydia Maria Child: Selected Letters, 1817–1880.* Amherst: University of Massachusetts Press.

CHRISTIANA RIOT (1851)

The most violent incident of African American resistance to the Fugitive Slave Act of 1850 occurred on September 11, 1851, near Christiana, Pennsylvania. That morning, Maryland slaveowner Edward Gorsuch, six of his relatives, and three U.S. marshals bearing federal warrants arrived at the tiny Quaker village of Christiana and surrounded the house of William Parker, a local black farmer.

The posse demanded the surrender of Nelson Ford and Joshua Hammond, two slaves who had run away from the Gorsuch farm in 1849 and were hiding inside the Parker home. Parker's wife sounded a horn, and dozens of neighbors—both black and white—responded. Two Quakers advised the posse to retreat, but Gorsuch refused, declaring, "My property I will have, or I'll breakfast in hell" (Slaughter, 1991). After a heated verbal exchange, shots were fired and, when the confusion subsided, Gorsuch lay dead and three members of his party were nursing serious wounds.

The affair quickly assumed national importance. Southern proslavery newspapers and the abolitionist press waged a fierce propaganda battle, each attempting to use the incident to sway public opinion. The proslavery papers viewed the riot as a breach of southern property rights under the U.S. Constitution and saw abolitionist provocation as the cause. The abolitionist press blamed slaveholding interests and cast the rioters in the liberty-loving tradition of the heroes of the American Revolution.

Fearing political repercussions, President Millard Fillmore dispatched a company of U.S. Marines and some forty Philadelphia policemen to Christiana to apprehend those involved. Nearly forty blacks and six whites, some with tenuous links to the incident, were arrested. But the five blacks who were most responsible for Gorsuch's death—including Parker, Ford, and Hammond—escaped to Canada West (now Ontario), where requests for their extradition went unheeded.

Federal prosecutors sought to make examples of the rioters and charged them with treason. A grand jury indicted and imprisoned thirty-six blacks and two whites until they could be tried before the U.S. circuit court in Philadelphia. The trial of Castner Hanway, a white miller alleged to have directed the rioters in their attack on the posse, became the test case on which the fate of the other thirty-seven rested. But his trial, which ironically convened on the second floor of Independence Hall, only served to show the weakness of the government's case. The available evidence proved insufficient to substantiate the charges and after Hanway was acquitted in early December, the prosecution waived all remaining indictments and the rioters were released.

The incident at Christiana, and its aftermath, demonstrated the difficulty of enforcing the Fugitive Slave Act. It also polarized public opinion regarding the law. Southerners were outraged that none of the rioters were convicted. At the same time, federal efforts to punish the rioters increased sympathy for the abolitionists in the North. As a result of the riot, sectional tensions increased, and the nation moved closer to civil war.

— *Roy E. Finkenbine*

See also: Fugitive Slave Act (1850); Slave Catchers.

For Further Reading

Forbes, Ella. 1998. *But We Have No Country: The 1851 Christiana, Pennsylvania, Resistance.* Cherry Hill, NJ: Africana Homestead Legacy.

Nash, Roderick W. 1961. "The Christiana Riot: An Evaluation of Its National Significance." *Journal of the Lancaster County Historical Society* 64: 66–91.

Nash, Roderick W. 1961. "William Parker and the Christiana Riot." *Journal of Negro History* 46 (January): 24–31.

Slaughter, Thomas. 1991. *Bloody Dawn: The Christiana Riot and Racial Violence in the Antebellum North.* New York: Oxford University Press.

JOSEPH CINQUÉ (C. 1811–C. 1852)

The man who came to be known as Joseph Cinqué was the leader of a successful revolt in which thirty-eight slaves under his command seized the slave ship *Amistad* and attempted to return to Africa. When U.S. authorities thwarted that plan, northern abolitionists pursued legal appeals on behalf of Cinqué and his colleagues, appeals that eventually led to their release and repatriation to Africa.

Cinqué was born Sing-gbe in a region of West Africa now known as Sierra Leone. The year of his birth is generally accepted as 1811, although some sources claim he was born in 1817. Sing-gbe, a member of the Mende tribe, was captured by slave traders in 1837 or 1838 and forcibly removed to the infamous Portuguese slave factory on the island of Lomboko off the coast of West Africa. He left behind a wife and three small children. On Lomboko, Portuguese slavers called him "Cinqué," a phonetic approximation of Sing-gbe, and prepared him for transportation to the slave market in Cuba. The voyage aboard the Portuguese slaver, *Tecora*, was exceptionally harsh even by the grim standards of the usual transatlantic voyage in a slave ship. More than half of the men, women, and children who left Lomboko did not live to see Havana. Since the importation of slaves to Cuba was illegal, slavers gave incoming Africans Christian names and falsely listed them as Cuban-born. Sing-gbe was thereafter known as Joseph Cinqué.

Two Spanish planters, José Ruiz and Pedro Montez, bought Cinqué and thirty-eight other slaves in Havana and loaded them and some other slaves aboard a 120-ton schooner, the *Amistad,* for the short run up the Cuban coast to Puerto Príncipe. The slaves were connected by a long chain threaded through their neck rings and fastened to the inside of the wooden hull of the *Amistad* in the cramped, dark hold of the ship. For two days and nights they pitched and rolled in terror as the *Amistad's* crew fought an unexpected storm that drove them far off course.

Using a rusted nail pried from the floor planks of the hold, Cinqué methodically worked at the bracket that anchored the slaves' chain to the hull. Once freed, the slaves broke into the cargo hold where they armed themselves with cane knives. Then, under cover of darkness on the first night of calm, Cinqué led the slaves out of the hold. On deck they found an ex-hausted captain and crew asleep, with only one man awake at the helm. Within minutes the deck of the *Amistad* was awash with the blood of the captain, Ramón Ferrer, and his crew. Two of the crew members were killed; four survived. Two of the survivors evaded the slaves and slipped off the ship in a lifeboat. They eventually reached the port of Havana and told the story of the *Amistad* mutiny. The other two survivors, Ruiz and Montez, were spared because Cinqué needed their navigational skills to pilot the Amistad to its new destination—Africa.

For sixty-three days, Ruiz and Montez, who were expert seamen, deceived Cinqué by setting a northeasterly course by day and turning hard north by night. Ruiz and Montez intended the zigzag path to lead them, not to Africa, but to the United States, where slavery was legal and the rights of slaveholders were recognized and protected. The land they eventually spotted, which Cinqué assumed to be an island off the African coast, was Long Island off the coast of New York City. The *Amistad* was intercepted by a U.S. Coast Guard cutter and escorted under arms to the port of Montauk, New York, where Cinqué and his compatriots were arrested and imprisoned.

When the news of the *Amistad's* capture reached Havana, Spanish and Cuban authorities demanded the return of the ship and its slave cargo. The penalty for slave insurrection in Cuba was burning at the stake, the fate that awaited Cinqué and his band if they were returned to Havana. U.S. president Martin Van Buren, eager not to offend the powerful slavery interest in Congress, ordered their return to Spanish authorities. Northern abolitionists, however, filed a lawsuit in federal court to block Van Buren's action.

For almost two years, a protracted legal battle played out in the federal court system. At stake were both the lives of Cinqué and his fellow Africans and the important legal principle of a human being's right to resist enslavement forcibly. Although the highly publicized case proceeded through the appellate process, with the abolitionists winning at each level and the appeal carried to the next level by the government, Cinqué, free on bond posted by wealthy New England abolitionists, lived comfortably in Farmington, Connecticut. A powerful speaker with a charismatic physical presence, Cinqué took to the lecture circuit, and the fees he earned helped pay the mounting legal bills. Although he spoke only in Mende, Cinqué's speeches were translated into English and widely distributed throughout the North.

Cinqué's cause won the support of former president John Quincy Adams, an ardent abolitionist and respected elder statesman. Adams, who was also a skilled litigator, personally pleaded the case for the *Amistad* insurgents before the U.S. Supreme Court in 1841. The Court ruled in Cinqué's favor, declaring that he and his fellow mutineers were free to return to Africa. Joseph Cinqué returned home in 1842.

His subsequent life is not clearly documented. Some accounts claim he died barely a decade after his return to Africa; others contend he lived until 1879 and was buried on the grounds of the American Missionary Association compound in Sierra Leone.

Regardless of his ultimate fate, Joseph Cinqué remained an important symbolic presence for slaves in the United States and, after the abolition of slavery there, for African Americans. In 1939, on the centennial anniversary of the Amistad mutiny, a major artwork was unveiled. The *Amistad Murals* by noted African American artist Hale Woodruff commemorated Joseph Cinqué's seizure of freedom.

— *Frederick J. Simonelli*

See also: Adams, John Quincy; *Amistad* Case.

For Further Reading
Barber, John W. 1840. *A History of the* Amistad *Captives.* New Haven, CT: E. L. and J. W. Barber.

Cable, Mary. 1971. *Black Odyssey: The Case of the Slave Ship* Amistad. New York: Viking Press.

Hoyt, Edwin. 1970. *The* Amistad *Affair.* New York: Abelard-Schuman.

CIVIL WAR (1861–1865)

The Civil War in the United States began after decades of discord between the northern and southern states. Various economic, political, and social issues led to disagreements between the states, yet slavery seemed to be at the heart of each problem. Since slavery predominated in the South, southerners felt increasingly isolated and threatened by attempts to hinder or ban slavery. Whereas slaveholders had earlier seen slavery as a necessary evil that was inconsistent with the ideals of the American Revolution, by the 1830s southerners believed slavery to be a positive good.

This change in attitude was partially a result of slavery's benefits. Unlike the more industrialized North, slaves were the principal form of wealth in the agricultural South; by 1860, the 4 million slaves had a market value of $3 billion. Slavery, however, was not only a means of providing a large labor force, but it also served as a way to preserve white supremacy. This aspect was especially important for some people whose sole claim of superiority came from the color of their skin.

Slaveholders also became much more defensive of slavery as the antislavery movement intensified and produced more abolitionists, like William Lloyd Garrison, who called for an immediate end to slavery without compensation to slaveowners. As a result, the South became a dangerous place to express antislavery sentiments.

During the 1840s, the national debate dealt more with slavery's expansion into the western territories than with the actual abolition of slavery. Southerners believed that it was their constitutional right to take their slaves into the territories with them and that Congress lacked the power to prevent them from doing so. Northerners opposed the expansion of slavery, some on moral grounds and others for economic reasons. Despite opposing the expansion of slavery into the new territories, many northerners did not oppose the institution of slavery in areas where it already existed, as they feared that if slavery ended, emancipated slaves would flock to the territories and take land that could be used by whites.

After several heated debates in Congress, Senator Henry Clay of Kentucky proposed a compromise bill in 1850. The bill included five measures:

1. The admission of California as a free state

2. The creation of the New Mexico and Utah territories, in which residents would be allowed to choose whether or not to permit slavery

3. The payment of Texas's debts in return for that state's promise not to seek to widen its western border

4. The end of the slave trade in Washington, D.C.

5. The creation of a new fugitive slave law, which required that runaway slaves be returned to their masters and authorized the use of federal power to enforce the law.

Congress ultimately approved Clay's bill, which became known as the Compromise of 1850. Despite widespread acceptance of the Compromise, it soon became obvious that it offered only a temporary solution to the problem, as its vague language left much open to debate. One tragedy of the Compromise was that under the Fugitive Slave Law, a number of free blacks were captured and sent south without an opportunity to prove that they were not runaway slaves. However, the greatest problem with the Compromise of 1850 was its failure to confront the issue of the expansion of slavery directly. Instead, Congress placed a seal of approval on the theory of popular sovereignty—that is,

Bombardment of Fort Sumter in Charleston Harbor, South Carolina, on April 12-13, 1861. The Battle of Fort Sumter was the first armed action of the American Civil War. It ended when Major Robert Anderson's Union forces surrendered after thirty-three hours of continued shelling by the Confederate army. (Library of Congress)

allowing settlers to choose whether or not they wanted slavery. Consequently, Congress sent out mixed signals to people on both sides of the debate.

In 1854 Congress passed the Kansas–Nebraska Act, which established Kansas and Nebraska as territories and ruled that popular sovereignty should settle the issue of slavery in these two areas. Conflict erupted almost as soon as President Franklin Pierce signed the bill into law in May 1854. When Missouri slaveowners moved into Kansas Territory, they immediately clashed with antislavery settlers. Soon the conflict, known as Bleeding Kansas, turned deadly, and fighting continued for four years until antislavery forces emerged as the victors.

The slavery issue split both the Whig and Democratic parties down sectional lines, causing northern Whigs and Democrats to take sides against their southern counterparts. At the same time, several political groups joined to form the Free Soil Party to oppose slavery's expansion. However, the major disintegration of the political parties came with passage of the

Kansas–Nebraska Act. Many northern Democrats left their party, as did northern Whigs, and most of these men, along with members of the Free Soil Party, created the new Republican Party, which took a firm stance against the expansion of slavery.

As tensions grew between North and South, so did the antislavery movement. Southerners were outraged at the publication of the novel *Uncle Tom's Cabin* (1852), which sold 500,000 copies and strengthened the antislavery movement in the North. Written by the northern abolitionist Harriet Beecher Stowe, *Uncle Tom's Cabin* told of the horrors of slavery; it was banned in the South.

Yet some southerners also criticized slavery. Although slavery was immensely profitable for some, others argued that slavery would ultimately ruin the South. In his book *The Impending Crisis of the South* (1857), North Carolinian Hinton Rowan Helper argued that slavery was an inefficient system that stunted the South's economic growth and hurt the nonslaveowning majority. He believed that by focusing on agriculture and ignoring natural resources and industry, the South was becoming "a cesspool of ignorance and degradation." Most of all, Helper expressed his hatred of the rich planter class, whose arrogance and greed prevented poor whites from prospering.

The book was banned by southern states, and people found to own a copy of the book were fired from their jobs, arrested, or even executed. However, Helper's ideas did receive support. Not only did his book appeal to poor whites in the South, but it was also used as a propaganda tool by Republicans, who distributed 100,000 edited copies in 1858.

Despite attacks from antislavery supporters, southerners still had a powerful voice in national politics, a power that was reflected in the Supreme Court decision in the *Dred Scott* case. In this case a slave, Dred Scott, argued that since his master had moved him from Missouri to free territory, he was a freeman. In 1857 the U.S. Supreme Court ruled that since slaves were not U.S. citizens, they could not sue in federal courts. Chief Justice Roger B. Taney wrote that slaves could be moved anywhere, as they were the property of their owner, and he found the Missouri Compromise, or any other attempt by Congress to limit slavery's expansion, to be unconstitutional.

Although southerners were jubilant following that court decision, their excitement turned to fear following John Brown's raid on Harpers Ferry, Virginia, in 1859. Brown, a lifelong abolitionist and participant in the struggles of Bleeding Kansas, planned to end slavery through force. With a small band of men, including runaway slaves, Brown took control of the U.S. arsenal at Harpers Ferry. Ultimately, Brown was hanged for his actions, thus becoming a martyr for the abolitionist movement and proving to southerners the importance of political power.

Relations between North and South deteriorated rapidly after 1859. At the 1860 Democratic National Convention, southerners pushed for a platform that included a federal slave code for the territories. When northern Democrats refused to accept the idea, southern Democrats left the convention, thus splitting the Democratic Party and allowing the Republican candidate for president, Abraham Lincoln, to win the election of 1860.

In December 1860, South Carolina and seven other slave states seceded from the Union and formed the Confederate States of America. In an attempt to appease the eight slave states that remained in the Union, Kentucky Senator John J. Crittenden offered a compromise that stressed the protection of slavery below the Missouri Compromise line of 36°30' and promised compensation to owners of runaway slaves. Lincoln opposed the Crittenden Compromise, and the measure was defeated. Although Lincoln hoped to appease the remaining eight slave states, his promises not to interfere with slavery or the Confederacy could not stop the war. Soon after the Confederate attack on Fort Sumter in April 1861, four more slave states seceded, and only the border states of Missouri, Kentucky, Maryland, and Delaware remained, precariously, in the Union.

Whereas the South went to war to protect slavery and southern sovereignty, Lincoln's initial desire was to protect the Union. Lincoln did not wish to interfere with the institution of slavery, and he even ordered his generals to return any slaves who escaped behind Union lines and to help prevent slave rebellions.

Organized slave rebellions were not, however, common during the war. Instead, many slaves simply refused to cooperate with their masters, especially when the slaveowners went to war and left their wives in control of the plantations. Slaves often took this opportunity to work at a slower pace or to leave their work altogether. Home guards were established to maintain order and to prevent slaves from running away. Since the presence of the Union army led many slaves to cross Union lines to freedom, slaveowners told their slaves stories about the cruelty of Union soldiers in an attempt to frighten the slaves into staying on the plantation.

Many slaves did remain on the plantations out of loyalty or fear of the unknown. Others ignored the warnings of their masters and fled across Union lines, providing the Union army with information about Confederate activities. Although slaves were at first returned to their masters, the confiscation acts of 1861–1862 ruled that slaves who crossed Union lines should be considered contraband of war and freed from slavery. Behind Union lines, the escaped slaves found life to be almost as harsh as plantation life. Those who remained with the Union troops labored with little or no compensation and lived in crowded camps with inadequate shelter, food, and clothing. Others moved into urban areas, where they faced poverty, overcrowding, and disease. Fortunately, the former slaves received some help from sources such as the Freedmen's aid societies and missionary societies, which provided them with supplies and educational opportunities. At the same time, the escaped slaves formed tightly-knit communities and began to demand equal rights.

The slaves who remained behind played an important role in the Confederate war effort. In the absence of white workers, slaves were put to work in factories, mines, and on the railroads; others served in home guard units, replacing the white men who went off to war. The use of slaves in the home guard was especially prominent in Louisiana, where slaves formed almost half of the state's population. Slaves also often accompanied the Confederate army to help carry supplies and build forts. This work was unpopular among slaves and slaveowners alike because slaves found it to be particularly difficult work and slaveowners disliked sending their best slaves to the front. Owners thus reserved this work for their most uncooperative slaves.

As the war continued, Lincoln realized the need to redefine the Union's war goals. Although Lincoln's original goal was to preserve the Union, he faced criticism from abolitionists who wished to make the war one to end slavery. He also faced problems abroad as European nations seemed increasingly sympathetic to the South's claims that the Confederacy was fighting for its independence. Fearing that Europe would intervene economically or militarily on the South's behalf, Lincoln realized that freeing the slaves must become a priority. This was a difficult decision for Lincoln, for while he personally opposed slavery, he was not convinced that blacks and whites could ever live together peacefully. However, he believed that emancipation might be the only way to quiet his critics and preserve the Union.

Lincoln began to draft a document that would order an end to slavery but did so secretly since he was concerned that outside observers might take his decision as a sign that the Union was wearing down after a series of Confederate victories. Although not a Union victory per se, the battle of Antietam (or Sharpsburg) repelled a Confederate invasion of the North and provided Lincoln with the opportunity to announce the emancipation proclamation on September 22, 1862. In the final Emancipation Proclamation, which became law on January 1, 1863, Lincoln ordered that all slaves in areas under rebellion were free as of that date. The proclamation did not apply, however, to slaves in the four border states or slaves in areas occupied by Union troops.

Technically, the Emancipation Proclamation did not legally free any slaves, for such an action required a constitutional amendment. Symbolically, however, the Emancipation Proclamation had a significant impact on the northern war effort. It appeased abolitionists, and it also prevented foreign intervention by making it a war for slavery's abolition rather than one of northern aggression against the Confederacy. Moreover, the Emancipation Proclamation encouraged the thousands of slaves who remained in the South, giving them hope that freedom was just around the corner.

Following the announcement of the Emancipation Proclamation, Lincoln approved the use of black troops in the Union Army. Although many Union soldiers disagreed with Lincoln's decision, the need for more men was greater than the prejudice of individuals. Sadly, black soldiers were not treated as equals. At first denied the opportunity to fight, when necessity did demand that black soldiers enter battle, they often went in without adequate training or supplies. Until 1864, black soldiers received less pay than their white counterparts and had few opportunities for advancement.

In spite of this discrimination, black soldiers played a vital role in the Union victory. The Fifty-fourth Massachusetts Regiment, formed primarily of northern free blacks, gained fame for their courageous but ill-fated attack on Fort Wagner, South Carolina, on July 18, 1863. Despite losing over 250 men during the attack, the Fifty-fourth went on to participate in other battles in South Carolina, Georgia, and Florida. The First South Carolina Volunteers, which consisted entirely of fugitive slaves, had a reputation not only for bravery and skill in battle, but also for its ability to recruit large numbers of slaves into their regiment. In all, two hundred thousand blacks served in the Union armed forces, making up 10 percent of the total Union enlistment. Of these two hundred thousand black men, approximately one-third gave their lives for the cause of freedom.

When the war ended, Lincoln had met his goal of preserving the Union, but he would not live to see the painful process of the reconstruction. Lincoln also achieved a second goal, one he had not intended: the end of slavery. In 1865, the Thirteenth Amendment to the Constitution abolished slavery throughout the United States. This would be the first step on the road to equality for black Americans.

— *Jason H. Silverman*

See also: Confiscation Acts; Contrabands; Emancipation Proclamation; Lincoln, Abraham.

For Further Reading
Gerteis, Louis S. 1973. *From Contraband to Freedom: Federal Policy Toward Southern Blacks, 1861–1865*. Westport, CT: Greenwood.

Glatthaar, Joseph. 1990. *Forged in Battle: The Civil War Alliance of Black Soldiers and White Officers*. New York: Free Press.

Potter, David M. 1976. *The Impending Crisis, 1848–1861*. New York: Harper and Row.

Quarles, Benjamin. 1953. *The Negro in the Civil War*. Boston: Little, Brown.

HENRY CLAY (1777–1852)

Henry Clay's efforts to defuse sectional tensions earned him acclaim as the "Great Compromiser," but his statecraft made little impact on the elimination of slavery.

At the age of twenty, Clay moved from his native Virginia to Kentucky and emerged a leading politician and plantation owner. Clay first gained national acclaim in 1812 as a leading "War Hawk," concluding that war with Britain was necessary to maintain American commercial and political sovereignty. His primary political concerns were development of the Whig Party and pursuit of the presidency. The Whig Party, formed in opposition to the principles of Andrew Jackson, advocated Clay's "American System" with a national bank, a protective tariff, and the government offering economic aid for internal improvements. His leadership, resulting in five unsuccessful presidential efforts, helped define national policies for over four decades but failed to preserve the solidarity of the Union.

Throughout his career Clay opposed slavery; he argued against it but practiced it on a large scale. He believed slavery was an evil institution and knew slaves lived in physical and mental anguish. Nonetheless, he bought, sold, and leased slaves for his Ashland estate and firmly believed slaves were unprepared to succeed as free men because they lacked education. He concluded that emancipation would be injurious to the slave, the master, and result in a bloody racial war.

His solution was removal of African Americans to colonies in Africa. He also contended that slaveowners must be compensated for their loss of property. From 1836 until his death in 1852, Clay served as the president of the American Colonization Society. Although the effort colonized former slaves in Liberia, it failed to gain support of the state or federal government and Clay turned to politics in an effort to solve the problem.

Though a nationalist and a proponent of a vigorous federal government, Clay deferred to the states on the issue of emancipation. Maintaining public opinion would eventually result in the elimination of slavery, he urged Congress to solve the dilemma with the Missouri Compromise (1820). His proposal resulted in Maine entering the Union as a free state and Missouri as a slave state. Still, sectional strife continued. Southerners argued that Congress had no authority to regulate slavery, and northerners abhorred the introduction of slaves into the areas acquired by the Louisiana Purchase.

In 1844 Whigs nominated Clay for president, but he was defeated by the lesser-known Democratic nom-

Henry Clay, the "Great Compromiser," was instrumental in securing passage of the Missouri Compromise and the Compromise of 1850. (Library of Congress)

inee, James Polk. As a result of Clay's opposition to the annexation of Texas, a republic that permitted slavery, the South refused to support his candidacy. During the hostilities between Mexico and the United States, Clay denounced the Polk administration and predicted that any territories acquired from the war with Mexico would challenge the solidarity of the nation. He criticized Polk's prosecution of the "most unnecessary and horrible war," claiming that the war was too costly—in both lives and dollars (Remini, 1991). He also maintained that Polk had exceeded the bounds of the executive office. Aiming for the presidency in 1848, Clay claimed that if he had been elected in 1844, war would have been averted.

Returning to the Senate in 1849, Clay hoped to forge a lasting compromise that would defuse the arguments in Congress regarding the western territories and slavery. Concerned about Senator John C. Calhoun and other intemperate southern politicians who favored disunion if slavery were banned in the territories, Clay drafted a compromise calling for the admission of California as a free state, the organization of

New Mexico as a territory without restrictions on slavery, and the payment of the debts incurred by the Republic of Texas in exchange for a significant reduction of eastern lands claimed by the state. The compromise, however, passed only as separate measures, revealing the disparate interests of North and South. After leaving the Senate, Clay briefly returned home before returning to Washington to speak about the need to curb sectional strife. He did not witness the turbulence of the Civil War as tuberculosis claimed him on June 29, 1852, at his Washington residence.

Clay's compromises in 1820 and 1850 proved inadequate, but remarkably, his principles shaped the nation from 1810 through Reconstruction. Although Clay never enjoyed the public approval of his rival Andrew Jackson, the Republican Party later adopted his vision for the future of the United States, and Abraham Lincoln declared Clay the ideal statesman and his guiding influence.

— *Dallas Cothrum*

See also: Compromise of 1850; Missouri Compromise.

For Further Reading

Baxter, Maurice G. 2000. *Henry Clay: The Lawyer.* Lexington: University Press of Kentucky.

Eaton, Clement. 1957. *Henry Clay and the Art of American Politics.* New York: Little Brown and Company.

Peterson, Merrill. 1987. *The Great Triumvirate: Webster, Clay, and Calhoun.* New York: Oxford University Press.

Remini, Robert. 1991. *Henry Clay: Statesman of the Republic.* New York: Norton.

Shankman, Kimberly C. 1999. *Compromise and the Constitution: The Political Thought of Henry Clay.* Lanham, MD: Lexington Books.

Van Deusen, Glyndon G. 1979 [1937]. *The Life of Henry Clay.* Westport, CT: Greenwood.

HOWELL COBB (1815–1868)

A proponent of southern Unionism, Howell Cobb was elected speaker of the U.S. House of Representatives in 1849 and held that position during the hotly debated Compromise of 1850, playing a key role in its passage. Born in Jefferson County, Georgia, Cobb was reared in Athens, Georgia. Attending Franklin College (now the University of Georgia), he graduated with a bachelor's degree in 1834. He studied law for two years and gained admittance to the Georgia bar in 1836. Using the family's political influence, he secured a position as solicitor general of Georgia in 1837. Always attracted to

Howell Cobb was elected Speaker of the U.S. House of Representatives in 1849 and held that position during the debate over the Compromise of 1850. (Library of Congress)

politics, he ran successfully for a congressional seat in 1842, representing a pro-Union district in northeast Georgia.

While serving in Congress from 1843 to 1851 and 1855 to 1857, Cobb supported Texas annexation, the Mexican War, and slavery's expansion into the territories. Despite his position on these issues, he was regarded as a moderate among national Democrats. Though a slaveowner, Cobb found the states' rights doctrine and secessionist views of John C. Calhoun anathema. During his tenure as speaker of the House, the debate over California's admission as a free state threatened the Union. Cobb, much to the chagrin of many southerners, supported the Compromise of 1850. Under its provisions, California became a free state, but the South received a stronger federal Fugitive Slave Law.

Passage of the Compromise of 1850 preserved the

Union but created a major upheaval in southern politics that did not spare Cobb's home state. The weakening of the national Whig Party created chaos in Georgia politics, as did a split among Georgia Democrats. Georgia Whigs and Democrats realigned themselves into two factions—the States' Rights Party representing secessionist sentiments and the pro-Union, Constitutional Union Party. Resigning from Congress, Cobb returned to Georgia to lead the forces of the Constitutional Union Party as its gubernatorial candidate in 1851.

Cobb served a successful two-year term as governor, but he had national political ambitions, and campaigned vigorously for the 1856 Democratic presidential nominee, James Buchanan. When Buchanan became president, Cobb won a cabinet appointment as secretary of the treasury. Exerting great influence in the administration, Cobb was once described as "the president as much as if he were sworn in" (Simpson, 1973).

As 1860 approached, Cobb desired the Democratic presidential nomination but failed to win it and instead witnessed the disintegration of the national Democratic Party. He resigned from the cabinet after the election of Republican candidate Abraham Lincoln. Returning to Georgia, he supported the immediate secession of his state from the Union—joining his antebellum political foes and reversing his previous positions on several issues. In February 1861, he presided over a convention of seceded states in Montgomery, Alabama, which created the Confederate States of America. Disappointed at not securing the Confederate presidency, he organized a regiment and fought in several major Civil War engagements in the eastern theater. Following the war he practiced law in Macon, Georgia, until his death in 1868.

—*Mary Ellen Wilson*

See also: Compromise of 1850.

For Further Reading
Cook, James F. 1995. *The Governors of Georgia, 1754–1995.* Macon, GA: Mercer University Press.
Greene, Helen Ione. 1946. "Politics in Georgia, 1853–1854: The Ordeal of Howell Cobb." *Georgia Historical Quarterly* 30 (2): 185–211.
Simpson, John Eddins. 1973. *Howell Cobb: The Politics of Ambition.* Chicago: Adams Press.

CODE NOIR

In 1682, French King Louis XIV's prime minister Colbert appointed a commission to draft a code for the French colonies, where slaves and free blacks, in something of a legal vacuum, lived at the mercy of owners and local officials. Signed by the king in March 1685, the *Code Noir* became the centerpiece of legislation regulating the status of slaves and freedmen in the French Antilles and, later, Louisiana. Louis made his intentions clear in the preamble, declaring that the Code was to "maintain the discipline of the . . . Roman Church and to regulate the state and quality of slaves in our said Islands." In proclaiming the supremacy of Roman Catholicism in the colonies, he anticipated the revocation of the toleration espoused in the Edict of Nantes later that year. More importantly for basic material and social conditions, the Code established the legal framework of master–slave relations and the status of freedmen in the French colonies until the final abolition of slavery in 1848.

Slaves were defined as movable property and treated accordingly. As valuable assets necessary for the plantation economy, they were often involved in trials over financial disputes, so the Code outlined legal procedures to be followed. Although the main purpose of these regulations was to safeguard the colonial economy, for example, by preventing the separation of slaves from their plantation during debt litigation, they also provided a modicum of protection for the slaves. Legally seized slave couples and children, for example, could not be separated. Still, slaves enjoyed no civil rights and could own no property. Precluded from public office, they could neither appear as a party nor be admitted as witnesses in court, and slave depositions could only be used to aid judges seek evidence elsewhere.

Discipline for a potentially rebellious slave population was harsh and designed to protect the socioeconomic status quo, though codification perhaps did prevent the most flagrant abuses. First, the Code targeted slave violence. Slaves were forbidden to carry arms and to congregate. Violence against free persons was penalized severely, if necessary by death. Even minor theft was typically punished by beating and branding with the fleur-de-lis. Fugitive slaves were liable to have their ears cut off and shoulder branded; repeat offenders were hamstrung—or executed. In previous regulations, by comparison, runaways had been shot on sight. Second, slaves were forbidden to trade valuable commodities. The sale of sugarcane was expressly forbidden, on pain of whipping for the slave and a 10 livres fine for both his master and the buyer of the cane.

Numerous articles of the Code stipulated minimal standards of care. Slaves were to be given weekly rations of 2 1/2 pots of manioc flour and 2 pounds of salt beef, or similar provisions, and provided with two outfits of clothes per year. Masters were required to care for physically incapacitated slaves. Torture was outlawed, though chaining or beating was accepted. Masters and overseers who killed would be brought to court. Finally, abused slaves could (in theory) appeal to the royal authorities.

The Code contained liberal provisions for manumission. Masters aged twenty and above were granted complete powers of enfranchisement, and freedmen could not be forced to work for former masters. In theory, at least, freedmen were considered citizens with full civil rights.

The Roman Church was firmly established as an expression of Louis XIV's aggressive Catholic absolutism, exemplified in the watchwords "one king, one law, one faith." Slaves were to be baptized and instructed in Catholicism. All subjects were ordered to observe Sundays and Church holidays. Interracial sexual relations—practically impossible to eradicate in a rude colonial society with a paucity of white women—were highly regulated. Free (married) subjects who had children with slave concubines were condemned; but an unmarried free man might marry his slave concubine in church, legitimizing and enfranchising his wife and children in one stroke. Slave marriages required the consent of the master. However, masters were prohibited from forcing slaves to marry. Masters were responsible for burying deceased baptized slaves in designated cemeteries; unbaptized slaves were buried at night in a convenient field.

The Code also served as a blueprint for the *Code Noir* of French Louisiana (1724). Compared to the original, the revised version significantly tightened the provisions regulating manumission, the status of free blacks, and miscegenation. In the words of Sala-Molins, the original Code's "latent" racism had now become "patent" (Sala-Molins, 2003).

Judging from follow-up legislation, enforcement was difficult, and archival research shows that masters were very rarely condemned in court for having contravened the Code. Furthermore, many of the relatively liberal provisions, for example, for manumission, were largely voided by subsequent regulations. Indeed, by the time of the French Revolution, French planters were known as the most efficient slaveowners in the region. On balance, therefore, the Code was probably motivated less by humanity than by an interest in the maintaining of public order and plantation profitability. Thus articles establishing minimal levels of nourishment were probably intended mainly to prevent theft and illicit trading, and those articles mandating the care of old and infirm slaves appear designed to prevent vagabondage. Even the articles enjoining religious instruction, at least one scholar, George Breathett, has maintained, were intended more to make slaves submissive through fear of damnation than to convert souls. Scholarship then, is divided on the extent of the Code's humanitarianism, as on its implementation, because gauging the real conditions of slave life has been difficult given the variety of actual experiences. George Breathett called it "one of the most significant humanitarian developments in the history of colonial Haiti" (1988); yet Joan Brace argued that "it did almost nothing to improve the slaves' human and civil status" (1983). Sala-Molins termed it quite simply "the most monstrous legal text of modern times."

Briefly abolished with slavery in 1794 (though only on paper, for the French revolutionaries never actually applied the abolition decree), the Code was reintroduced by Napoleon in 1802 and maintained under the Restoration (1814–1848). King Louis-Philippe dismantled part of it, passing legislation during 1830–1832 to guarantee the civil rights of free people of color in the colonies, though slavery itself still remained until final abolition in 1848.

— *William L. Chew III*

See also: Louisiana.

For Further Reading

Brace, Joan. 1983. "From Chattel to Person: Martinique, 1635–1848." *Plantation Society* 2 (1): 63–80.

Breathett, George. 1988. "Catholicism and the Code Noir in Haiti." *Journal of Negro History* 73 (1–4): 1–11.

Louis XIV. 1998. *Le Code Noir. Introduction and notes Robert Chesnais.* Paris: L'Esprit frappeur.

Roach, Joseph. 1998. "Body of Law: The Sun King and the Code Noir." In *From the Royal to the Republican Body: Incorporating the Political in Seventeenth- and Eighteenth-Century France.* Ed. Sara E. Melzer and Kathryn Norberg. Berkeley: University of California Press.

Sala-Molins, Louis. 2003. *Le Code Noir ou le calvaire de Canaan.* Paris: Presses universitaires de France.

Stein, Robert Louis. 1988. *The French Sugar Business in the Eighteenth Century.* Baton Rouge: Louisiana State University Press.

LEVI COFFIN (1789–1877)

Abolitionist and Underground Railroad operator, Levi Coffin was born and spent his youth in North Carolina where his Quaker family's antislavery views influenced his attitude toward the institution. His views deepened at the age of seven upon observing a coffle of

Levi Coffin was an Indiana Quaker merchant. His home served as a haven for slaves who used the Underground Railroad to escape from the South before the Civil War. (North Wind Picture Archives)

shackled slaves being transported. Later he saw a slave physically attacked without provocation, and at age fifteen he helped liberate a free African American who had been kidnapped into slavery.

In 1821 Levi and his cousin Vestal organized a school for African Americans, but local slaveholders forced its closure. Coffin also helped organize a local manumission society that favored gradual emancipation. When the moderate organization voted to support the forced removal or colonization of freed slaves, Coffin resigned. Like many North Carolina Quakers, he found it difficult to espouse antislavery in a slave state.

In 1826 Coffin and his wife Catherine moved to Newport (now Fountain City) in Wayne County, Indiana. Learning that fugitive slaves occasionally traveled through Newport, where assistance was improvised and sometimes ineffective, Coffin made it known that his home was open to fugitive slaves. Soon he was providing temporary shelter, food, and clothing to fugitives and transportation to antislavery workers further north. He established a network of Underground Railroad workers that served about one hundred refugees per year. None was ever captured. Coffin's position as a prosperous businessman provided a degree of protection since he was open about his antislavery activity. While in Indiana he became known as "President of the Underground Railroad."

Coffin also helped African Americans living in the Newport area. He served on a Quaker committee that provided schools for black children, visited their homes, and provided aid as needed. He was also active in the temperance movement, but his abolitionist views were most controversial, even among Quakers. Even though they purged themselves of slavery, many Friends objected to William Lloyd Garrison's call for immediate emancipation, favoring instead a program of gradual emancipation and colonization. In 1843 Coffin helped establish a separate Indiana Yearly Meeting of Anti-Slavery Friends. The two yearly meetings remained separate for thirteen years, until a growing northern free soil sentiment made abolitionism more acceptable to conservative Quakers.

In 1844 Coffin and another Quaker abolitionist visited Canadian settlements of former slaves, who had found a haven within the British Empire. There he contacted many whom he had helped on their journey north. The two also visited schools for black children and encouraged refugees to acquire as much education as possible. Although many of the former slaves were in better condition than had been reported, some new arrivals were in desperate need of clothing and other essentials. After returning home, Coffin raised money and collected clothing for the refugees. It was the first of several trips he made to visit black settlements in Canada.

Coffin also played a major role in the free labor movement. As a merchant, he became increasingly uncomfortable about dealing in cotton and other merchandise dependent on slave labor for its production and distribution. Influenced by John Woolman's example of refusing to wear fabrics dyed by slave labor, and by a growing free labor movement among abolitionists, Coffin in 1847 reluctantly agreed to move to Cincinnati to manage a wholesale depository of free labor goods. In his new position, Coffin traveled to eastern cities to observe free labor stores and factories that bought cotton and other supplies from mostly small-scale southern farmers who did not own slaves. Abolitionists purchased a cotton gin and moved it to Mississippi to be operated with free labor. Coffin traveled south to locate cotton planters using only free labor, and there he spoke freely of his antislavery views; his nonconfrontational approach and his southern background enabled him to do so without serious consequences. His free labor business was highly successful, and the move to Cincinnati proved to be permanent.

Arriving in Cincinnati, the Coffins feared that their Underground Railroad work was over, but they soon learned that it was more needed than ever, for fugitive slaves passing through the city found little aid on which they could count. Coffin quickly organized a similar network as he had established in Newport, and once again his home became the center of such activity. The Coffin home was also the meeting place for the Anti-Slavery Sewing Society, which provided essential clothing for fugitives traveling through Cincinnati. Demands on Coffin's time were especially heavy after passage of the Fugitive Slave Law (1850), when increasing numbers of slaves left Kentucky and other southern states, and many of Cincinnati's African Americans fled to Canada to avoid kidnapping.

It was in Cincinnati where Coffin received national attention for his work with fugitives. The character Simeon Halliday, a Quaker abolitionist in Harriet Beecher Stowe's *Uncle Tom's Cabin,* was a composite of Coffin and Thomas Garrett of Wilmington, Delaware. Eliza Harris, another of Stowe's characters, was modeled after a fugitive whom Coffin had assisted. Some years after the Civil War, Charles T. Webber depicted Coffin and his wife in the famous painting of the Underground Railroad.

Coffin considered the Civil War divine punishment for slavery. As a Quaker nonresistant, he did not openly support the Union military cause, but he nursed the wounded and provided supplies for those preparing to defend Cincinnati against threatened Confederate raids. He traveled extensively to work with former slaves, called contrabands, within the Union lines. He helped organize the Western Freedman's Aid Commission and traveled to England to raise money for its work. In 1867 he attended an International Anti-Slavery Conference in Paris. Coffin's autobiography, published in 1876, remains one of the more reliable accounts of the Underground Railroad by a participating abolitionist.

Larry Gara

See also: Garrett, Thomas; Quakers; Stowe, Harriet Beecher; Underground Railroad.

For Further Reading
Coffin, Levi. 1876. *Reminiscences of Levi Coffin, Reputed President of the Underground Railroad.* Cincinnati, OH: Western Tract Society.

Haviland, Laura S. 1881. *A Woman's Life-Work: Labors and Experiences of Laura S. Haviland.* Chicago: Publishing Association of Friends.

Mabee, Carlton. 1970. *Black Freedom: The Nonviolent Abolitionists from 1830 Through the Civil War.* New York: Macmillan.

Siebert, Wilbur H. 1898. *The Underground Railroad from Slavery to Freedom.* New York: Macmillan.

EDWARD COLES (1786–1868)

Edward Coles's role in slavery is intriguing. Born into an Albemarle County, Virginia, slaveowning family, he is best known for his opposition to slavery, and he represented Thomas Jefferson's hope that slavery would be removed in a generation after the American Revolution.

Coles decided slavery was immoral during his education at the College of William and Mary in Virginia (1805–1806). He agonized for over a decade about how to put his belief into effect, and during that time, he conducted a correspondence with Jefferson trying to convince him to lead a campaign against slavery. Coles's conviction that slavery was immoral stemmed from his understanding of natural rights and laws; his perception that Jefferson shared these beliefs, and Jefferson's status, made him the obvious leader in Coles's mind.

Disillusioned by Jefferson's refusal, Coles decided to leave Virginia and free his own slaves. In 1819 he finally went to Illinois, emancipating his slaves along the way. Coles's delay illustrates the practical problems connected with manumission in the United States. He worried about maintaining his own livelihood without a slave labor force, the well-being of his slaves after emancipation, and the economic burden of posting bond for the manumitted slaves. His move to Illinois solved each of these problems.

In Illinois, he took a leading role in the opposition to a movement to allow slavery. In 1824, while governor, he worked to prevent the calling of a constitutional convention that would have written a constitution allowing the introduction of slavery. As part of the Northwest Territory, slavery had been forbidden, but after statehood, Illinois, Indiana, and Ohio all debated the legality of introducing slavery. Coles's role in Illinois was important because he threw into the opposition his status as governor and his past relationships with fellow Virginians Jefferson and James Madison. Coles's opposition played a significant part in the defeat of the group that supported a convention, and his actions helped maintain the integrity of the nonslave Midwest.

Coles's beliefs reveal the paradoxes of early nineteenth-century antislavery efforts. Although he opposed slavery for moral reasons, he believed that emigration was the best option for African Americans. He was an early member of the American Colonization

Society, which established Liberia as a removal destination, and as late as the mid-1850s, he was offering to pay the expenses of his former foreman to scout in the Caribbean for a suitable removal site. Coles was shocked when the former slave declined the offer, arguing that he was an American and had no wish to leave. That incident revealed the extent to which antislavery and an acceptance of diversity could be separated. Although professing a belief in the equality of African Americans, Coles was unable to imagine the United States as a multiracial nation.

In 1833 Coles moved from Illinois to Philadelphia, at which point his visible role in the antislavery movement ended. His family split during the Civil War, with one son fighting for the Union and the other for the Confederacy. Coles's life illustrates the essential dilemmas posed by slavery for many white Americans in the nineteenth century.

— Kurt E. Leichtle

See also: Jefferson, Thomas; *Notes on Virginia.*

For Further Reading

Finkelman, Paul. 1989. "Evading the Ordinance: The Persistence of Bondage in Indiana and Illinois." *Journal of the Early Republic* 9: 21-52.

Fishback, Mason McCloud. 1904. "Illinois Legislation on Slavery and Free Negroes, 1818–1818." Illinois State Historical Society *Transactions* 9: 414-32.

Ress, David. 2006. *Governor Edward Coles and the Vote to Forbid Slavery in Illinois, 1823–1824.* Jefferson, NC: McFarland.

Washburne, E. B. 1969 [1882]. *Sketch of Edward Coles, Second Governor of Illinois, and the Slavery Struggle of 1823-4.* New York: Negro Universities Press.

SOUTHERN COMMERCIAL CONVENTIONS (1852–1859)

Until 1852, commercial conventions in the South were loosely organized gatherings of economic and political elites who met to discuss ways to strengthen the region's economic infrastructure and to show solidarity for the institution of slavery. Beginning in 1852, the commercial conventions became more organized, and from 1852 to 1859, conventions were held in New Orleans, Baltimore, Memphis, Charleston, Richmond, Savannah, Knoxville, Montgomery, and finally Vicksburg. Convention participants discussed ways to improve the southern economy by promoting the introduction of nonslave industry into the region, while simultaneously maintaining the slave-based economy.

Early supporters, like James Dunwoody Brownson

DeBow, intended to keep the conventions focused primarily on the development of the South's commercial and economic infrastructure and attempted to avoid political debates and sectional rivalries. But with the growing sectionalism between the North and South in the 1850s, and a growing antislavery sentiment in the North, these meetings of the South's economic and political elites increasingly focused on protecting the South's slave economy. The conventions also became the vehicle for a debate over reopening the African slave trade, a debate that grew in intensity as northern antislavery forces and sectional rivalries increased.

At the 1857 convention in Knoxville, delegates focused almost exclusively on discussing the importance of preserving the slave economy and defending the institution from what they believed was a dangerous threat to its existence from northern interests. Radical proslavery interests at the conventions insisted that slavery ensured domestic order, provided a satisfactory economic system, and, most important, was the South's right to maintain.

By the 1859 convention in Vicksburg, all pretense of keeping political questions off the convention floor disappeared. Delegates passed resolutions to repeal federal laws that prohibited the slave trade, to negotiate a treaty with Canada that would provide slaveowners with a way to retrieve runaway slaves, and to promote the protection of slavery in Cuba and Central America. Members of this convention also passed resolutions that emphasized the rights of slaveholders to settle in western territories and, in a move to support the growth of slavery in the new territories, called for slaveholders to move to Kansas to aid slaveholding interests there. The development of the extreme proslavery position of the southern commercial conventions demonstrates how southerners increasingly supported efforts in the 1850s to defend slavery from northern antislavery forces.

— Craig S. Pascoe

See also: Abolitionism in the United States; DeBow, J. D. B.; Proslavery Argument.

For Further Reading

Johnson, Vicki Vaughn. 1992. *The Men and the Vision of the Southern Commercial Conventions, 1845–1871.* Columbia: University of Missouri Press.

Jordon, Weymouth T. 1958. *Rebels in the Making: Planters' Conventions and Southern Propaganda.* Tuscaloosa, AL: Confederate Publishing.

Shore, Laurence. 1986. *Southern Capitalists: The Ideological Leadership of an Elite, 1832–1885.* Chapel Hill: University of North Carolina Press.

Wender, Herbert. 1930. *Southern Commercial Conventions, 1837–1859.* Baltimore, MD: Johns Hopkins University Press.

COMMONWEALTH V. JENNISON (1783)

For many scholars, this case represents the proverbial "last nail in the coffin" that buried, and thus abolished, slavery in Massachusetts. A few years earlier, several Massachusetts towns had complained about the state's constitution because it did not contain an antislavery clause; subsequently, the state constitution of 1780 in a Declaration of Rights declared that "all men are born free and equal, and have certain natural, essential, and unalienable rights." The age of revolutionary fervor created an atmosphere that favored freedom over slavery throughout Massachusetts and in many other colonies. Also, because of the early proliferation of white labor in Massachusetts and a numerically small slave population, merchants and farmers had turned to immigrant white labor to meet their labor needs; thus slavery never solidified its economic stranglehold on this state. It is from this historical and economic context that *Commonwealth v. Jennison* was decided.

Quock Walker's (also known as Quo, Qwack) pursuit of his freedom began when he took flight from one Nathaniel Jennison, who claimed to be Walker's master. Walker's flight took him to the nearby farm of Seth and John Caldwell, whose brother was, at one time, Walker's legal master. Their brother passed away, and his widow married Jennison, thus creating the legal dilemma when her property, that is, Quock Walker, became his.

Seeking to reclaim his property by marriage, Jennison, along with several cohorts, accosted Walker, beat him severely, and returned him to the condition of bondage. The Caldwells, in turn, hired the noted lawyer, Levi Lincoln, who became Walker's lawyer when Walker sued Jennison for assault and battery. This first case of *Quock Walker v. Jennison* was heard in June 1781 with the jury listening to Levi Lincoln's argument that the higher law of God almighty should take precedence over the positive law of man. Lincoln strongly urged the jury to understand that man is free within the law of nature, which is also God's law, and that ethereal law is against slavery. This jury agreed with the line of reasoning and decided in favor of Walker, awarding him 50 pounds sterling, and declared that he was a "Freeman." When Jennison sued the Caldwell brothers on the grounds that they had "seduced Quock Walker for plaintiff service," another jury contradicted the first and in *Jennison v. Caldwell*, found in favor of Jennison and awarded him 25 pounds sterling for loss of his slave's service.

The last case involving these litigants occurred in April 1783, when state authorities indicted and charged Jennison with assault and battery on Walker. In *Commonwealth v. Jennison,* the state attorney general, Robert Paine, claimed that one of Massachusetts's free citizens had been unlawfully attacked. To Paine, Walker was a free citizen because of a verbal contract of manumission made to him by his deceased master, which was renewed by his widow.

Refuting proslavery arguments by Jennison, Chief Justice William Cushing, referring to the 1780 constitutional "Declaration of Rights" and the ideological basis of the American Revolution, which favored freedom, declared that the accused was guilty of assault and battering a free man with "rights and privileges wholly incompatible and repugnant to its [slavery] existence." Cushing quoted the 1780 state constitution that said "that all men are born free and equal; and that every subject is entitled to liberty and to have it guarded by the laws as well as his life and property." The jury followed Cushing's dicta and convicted Jennison of assault and battery. Many citizens of this state including Cushing had accepted African bondage up until the American Revolution; however, as Cushing noted in his decision, "Sentiments more favorable to the natural rights of mankind . . . without regard to complexion . . . have prevailed since the glorious struggle for our rights began." In favor of freedom rather than slavery defined the American Revolution and created the social and political context for Cushing and his fellow citizens to abolish slavery by sentiment and law. What initially began as a slave case between the Caldwell brothers and Jennison over who would have the rights to the labor of Quock Walker ended up establishing the philosophical basis for antislavery for public opinion and as the public policy of the state of Massachusetts.

— *Malik Simba*

See also: Black Loyalists; Free Persons of Color.

For Further Reading

Cushing, John D. 1961. "The Cushing Court and the Abolition of Slavery in Massachusetts: More Notes on the Quock Walker Case." *American Journal of Legal History* 5: 118–119.

Higginbotham, A. Leon, Jr. 1978. *In the Matter of Color.* New York: Oxford University Press.

O'Brien, William. 1961. "Did the Jennison Case Outlaw Slavery in Massachusetts?" *William and Mary Quarterly* 3d ser 17 (April): 219–241.

Spector, Robert M. 1968. "The Quock Walker Cases (1781–83)—Slavery, Its Abolition, and Negro Citizenship in Early Massachusetts." *Journal of Negro History* 53 (January): 12–32.

Zilversmit, Arthur. 1967. *The First Emancipation: The Abolition of Slavery in the North.* Chicago: University of Chicago Press.

COMPARATIVE SLAVERY: RECENT DEVELOPMENTS

Since the 1980s, scholars have increasingly looked at slavery in the United States as a phenomenon comparable to other forms of unfree labor outside the New World. The appearance of Peter Kolchin's monograph *Unfree Labor* (1987) and Shearer Davis Bowman's monograph *Masters and Lords* (1993) has marked the beginning of a new subfield in comparative slavery studies. Both books compare the antebellum American South with roughly contemporaneous European societies, offering new interpretations of the nature of slavery in the United States and questioning previous assumptions. Indeed, debate has started on the relationship between slavery, serfdom, and capitalism and on the definition of unfree labor in the context of Old World and New World history.

Although Kolchin and Bowman support strikingly different views of American slavery, both—in different ways and degrees—refer to Immanuel Wallerstein's "modern world-system" approach; Wallerstein's studies have been enormously influential in redefining the concept of unfree labor. According to Wallerstein, during the sixteenth century a complex interrelation of factors, most importantly demographic and geographic expansion and price increase, created a European economy that from the beginning was characterized by a capitalist mode of production.

The single most important consequence of this process was the "discontinuity between economic and political institutions" (Wallerstein, 1979). Within the global economy of the capitalist world system, there grew a distinction between stronger regions in the "core" and weaker regions in the "semiperiphery" and "periphery." Core regions and semiperipheral and peripheral regions differed substantially in regard to how labor was "recruited and recompensed in the labor market" (Wallerstein, 1979). In core regions, wage labor was the norm, while in semiperipheries and peripheries, sharecropping and various forms of coerced labor, ranging from serfdom to slavery, were widespread. Therefore wage labor became associated with diversified agricultural and industrial activities within core regions, where workers were employed in the production and trade of finished products. Conversely, unfree labor became synonymous with monocultural agriculture within peripheral regions, where workers were forced to participate in the process of production and exportation of raw materials to core regions.

Wallerstein's model links the emergence of slavery and serfdom to the spread of global capitalism, thereby questioning the orthodox Marxist assumption that holds that capitalism is based exclusively on wage labor. Historians of slavery have recognized an important implication: the range of societies with which to compare slave systems increases enormously if we follow Wallerstein's suggestions. Conceptualizing these suggestions has been a necessary step in moving away from the idea of strict comparative slavery, and several historians have started looking at New World slavery as one of the many forms coerced labor took in peripheral economies. Not all historians agree with Wallerstein's view, of course, but they have incorporated it in looking for new directions of comparison.

Kolchin's and Bowman's monographs give precise ideas of two different reactions to Wallerstein's model and of two different ways of using it. Since both comparisons involve the American South and Eastern Europe, they explore potentially the same kinds of issues: the rise and demise of unfree labor systems, the ideology of landed elites, and the defense of conservatism from external threats. However, Kolchin's comparison of slavery in the United States and serfdom in Russia focuses on labor relations, control, and management, while Bowman's comparison of the American South and Prussia considers almost exclusively the worldview of elites. Inevitably, both works compare elements considered common to each case with different results in the end. Still, their points of departure are similar: the rise of unfree labor systems in Old World and New World peripheries is clearly linked in both studies to the expansion of the European economy on a global scale.

Bowman's *Masters and Lords* acknowledges its debt to Wallerstein's model by treating the "consolidation of Junkerdom and then planterdom as peripheral landed elites" (Bowman, 1993) actively involved in producing and exporting raw materials to the world's core regions. He considers the American South and East Elbia (in Prussia) as "relatively backward peripheries" that, nevertheless, played an important role in transforming the United States and Germany from semiperipheries to core regions in the nineteenth century.

That view is essential to his central argument, according to which Junkers (members of the Prussian landed aristocracy) and planters functioned as capitalist entrepreneurs engaged in production for the world market. By the first half of the nineteenth century, only a mild form of serfdom existed in East Elbia, making comparison with the American South's slave system difficult to support if Bowman did not share Wallerstein's view on the relation between types of labor and capitalism. In fact, Bowman elaborates this idea, stating that "although capitalist development since the fifteenth century has furthered proletarianization in core areas by promoting greater reliance on free wage labor in conjunction with technological advances, this does not mean that only a free-labor economy qualifies as capitalist" (Bowman, 1993). In other words, the conservative, reactionary, and antimodern ideologies of planters and Junkers rested on different, but related, systems of labor control, which were part of a global capitalist mode of production.

In stark contrast with Bowman's work, Kolchin's *Unfree Labor* is heavily influenced by Eugene Genovese's approach to slavery in the United States. Kolchin's monograph may be seen as a way of reinforcing the strength of Genovese's approach by transferring it to a comparative context. Kolchin views American planters and Russian landowners essentially as behaving in a "paternalistic" way toward their subjects. Like Genovese, he sees paternalism as being incompatible with capitalistic production, so that in the end both the antebellum South and pre-1860 Russia share a status as "pre-bourgeois" societies. Interestingly, this general rejection of the link between capitalism and slavery/serfdom does not prevent Kolchin from acknowledging his intellectual debt to Wallerstein.

Although in a milder form than Bowman, Kolchin recognizes that "the concept of a European core versus periphery to the east and west" (Kolchin, 1987) is important in his comparative analysis of the rise of unfree labor systems at the two extreme ends of the European world economy. He sees American slavery as a particular labor system born in a process similar and related to the rebirth of serfdom at the periphery of Early Modern European settlements. Without a hint of the role of the two peripheries in the world market or of the link between this role and the form coerced labor took in the American South and Russia, there is enough to make one wonder how far one can argue—as Kolchin does—that slavery and serfdom are related and comparable phenomena without acknowledging a similarity in origins and structure between the various types of unfree labor employed in the peripheral areas of the world economy.

In fact, following the above suggestion, one can easily envision that one of the next steps in studying comparative slavery will be to engage in a more comprehensive comparison between slavery and other forms of labor control and management that developed outside Wallerstein's core regions of the world system. In his latest monograph—*Servitude in the Modern World* (2000)—Michael L. Bush provides a sweeping comparative survey of slavery and serfdom in the context of the evolution of different systems of coerced labor, or servitude. Although Bush's work is but a general

treatment, it hints at very important issues that deserve consideration in future studies of comparative slavery. Among them certainly the most important is the relativity of the definition of unfree labor. Bush goes well beyond the conventional limits of comparative slavery, linking in a sort of historical continuum coerced labor systems as diverse as slavery, serfdom, indentured servitude, and concentration camp labor in an analytical treatment that covers the entire period from the late Middle Ages to the present and its modern forms of servitude.

Bush's work synthesizes the results of generations of scholarship. At the same time, he shows how the task of historians of comparative slavery has become far more complicated than it used to be, since they can no longer assume that slavery and unfree labor are synonymous categories related to specific working conditions. Indeed, servitude is a category that continues to be subject to scrutiny and redefinition as comparative study of societies based on different types of unfree labor proceeds.

Another, equally important and strictly related, step in the study of comparative slavery is likely to be the inclusion of an increasing number of geographical areas characterized by specific features into the subfield of comparative history of the nineteenth-century American South. Students of comparative slavery have long seen comparative history of the nineteenth-century American South as a privileged field of studies for scholarship at the forefront of historical comparison. Presently, comparative history of the nineteenth-century American South is more than ever at the center of the attention of scholars of comparative slavery, as both Kolchin's and Bowman's comparative monographs testify.

Expanding his horizon well beyond the confines of comparison with Czarist Russia that characterized unfree labor, in his latest work—*A Sphinx on the American Land* (2003)—Peter Kolchin has taken the nineteenth-century American South as both a paradigm and an ideal case study in all the topics—above all, slavery—that engage the efforts of comparative historians. Kolchin has also set much of the agenda for future comparative studies, outlining three basic types of comparison that focus on the American South: comparison between the South and the North, or "un-South"; comparison between the "many souths" that form the South; and comparison between the South and other regions of the world, or "other souths." The third type of comparison not only includes all the studies on comparative slavery, but also implies that there are virtually endless possibilities of comparison between the nineteenth-century American South and other regions of the world. Naturally, these regions should share some similarities with the American South in regard to either particular features (such as slavery or other forms of unfree labor) or general historical processes (such as emancipation or even nation-building)—a point with which, even though coming from a different perspective, Immanuel Wallerstein would certainly agree.

In this respect, one of the most promising areas of research for comparative slavery studies is comparison between the nineteenth-century American South and the nineteenth-century Italian South, or Mezzogiorno, one of several "other souths" with which the American South shared interesting features and from which it differed in a number of important respects. On the one hand, both the nineteenth-century American South and the Mezzogiorno were characterized by preeminently agrarian economies and were located at the periphery of Wallerstein's world system. On the other hand, even though the Mezzogiorno—including both Prussia and Russia—had a monarchy and a hereditary nobility, southern Italian peasants were legally free after the beginning of the nineteenth century. This makes the comparison with American slavery particularly intriguing.

Yet, as Enrico Dal Lago points out in his monograph *Southern Elites* (2004), it is in the realm of elite ideology that comparison between the American South and the Mezzogiorno yields particularly valuable insights. Although American slaveholders and southern Italian landowners supervised labor forces that were exploited in radically different ways because of the absence of racial slavery in the Mezzogiorno, they were equally preoccupied with maintaining their power in a nineteenth-century world that was increasingly dominated by liberal ideas. To this end, they promoted modernization only insofar as it helped them to both justify and strengthen their economic and social privileges, and they supported nationalism only as an ultimate means of resisting state centralization and governmental interference in their authority on local affairs.

Unlike other types of comparative projects that focus exclusively on slavery, comparison between the nineteenth-century American South and the Italian Mezzogiorno yields particularly valuable insights in regard to the connection between slavery and the Civil War. This is especially the case when seen in comparative perspective with contemporary European nationalist movements, such as the Italian Risorgimento, and the role that the elites played in them. In this respect, it is hoped that an increasing number of studies will focus not just on comparative slavery, but also on comparison between the Civil War—which culminated with the slaves' emancipation—and other, equally revolutionary, transformations that occurred in other regions of the world, especially Europe, at approximately the same time.

— *Enrico Dal Lago*

For Further Reading

Bowman, Shearer Davis. 1993. *Masters and Lords: Mid-19th Century U.S. Planters and Prussian Junkers.* New York: Oxford University Press.

Bush, Michael L. 2000. *Servitude in the Modern World.* Cambridge, England: Polity.

Dal Lago, Enrico. 2004. *Southern Elites: American Slaveholders and Southern Italian Landowners.* Baton Rouge: Louisiana State University Press.

Kolchin, Peter. 1987. *Unfree Labor: American Slavery and Russian Serfdom.* Cambridge, MA: Belknap Press.

Kolchin, Peter. 2003. *A Sphinx on the American Land: The Nineteenth-Century South in Comparative Perspective.* Baton Rouge: Louisiana State University Press.

Wallerstein, Immanuel. 1979. *The Capitalist World-Economy: Essays by Immanuel Wallerstein.* Cambridge: Cambridge University Press.

COMPENSATED EMANCIPATION

Compensated emancipation programs compelled slaveholders to free their slaves but offered them restitution through the labor of the ex-slaves (euphemistically called apprenticeship), monetary payment, or both. Depending on the compensation terms, freedom for the slave could be immediate and unconditional, or gradual with full freedom for the slave, delayed long enough for the owner to recoup as much of his or her investment as possible.

Debates over compensated emancipation focused foremost on whether to free the slaves. After examining the religious, economic, and ideological grounds for emancipation, the debate shifted to the question of compensation. At issue was the protection of slaveowners' property rights, specifically whether the state had the right to deprive owners of their property without compensation. For those who considered slavery evil, the critical question remained whether slaveowners deserved restitution for participating in an immoral institution.

The total cost and the compensation terms varied from place to place. Some compensated emancipation plans spread the expense between taxpayers, slaveholders, and the slaves, but other programs, seeking to free nonslaveholders and the state from any financial burden, placed the full cost on the owners and the slaves. Slaveowners bore part of the burden of compensation, for they lost the legal right to own the slave's life-long labor. Where governments used state funds to recompense owners, the expense fell on taxpayers, both slaveowners and nonslaveowners. The slaves, typically required to serve years of apprenticeship before receiving complete freedom, paid for a portion of their emancipation with their labor.

Compensated emancipation plans ranged from those that freed only the unborn, leaving all living slaves still enslaved, to those programs that freed and compensated owners for the youngest and oldest slaves while deferring freedom for slaves in their prime years. Typically, compensated emancipation programs offered free-born status to all children born on or after a specified date, with the manumission being either unconditional or delayed until satisfaction of an apprenticeship.

Usually, few of the principal characters involved in compensated emancipation programs—the state, slaveholders, and the slaves—expressed full satisfaction with the policy. Frequently, slaveowners bemoaned the compensation level and many did not receive the promised restitution. Slaves facing gradual emancipation often found the terms unacceptable, and many chose to escape from their apprenticeship. The high cost of financial compensation proved too burdensome for many nations, leading, in some instances, to revised legislation that ended slavery without the benefit of compensation.

The northern part of the United States inaugurated the trend toward compensated emancipation during the late eighteenth century. During the early nineteenth century, European nations instituted compensated emancipation programs in their colonies. Great Britain enacted its policy in 1833, France and Denmark issued compensated emancipation decrees in 1848, and the Dutch followed in 1863. With the exception of Cuba and Brazil, Latin American and Caribbean nations ended slavery and compensated owners during the 1850s and 1860s. Cuba in 1870 issued a free-birth decree and in 1880 passed a law freeing the remaining slaves after an eight-year apprenticeship. In 1871 Brazil enacted a free-birth law that provided both gradual emancipation and compensation for owners.

The case of the United States and Great Britain in its colonies illustrates the varieties of compensated emancipation programs. During the American Revolution, the states in the northern United States enacted laws repealing the legal basis of slavery within their respective state boundaries. Acknowledging the legal rights of owners to their slave property, the gradual abolition laws freed no living slave; instead they only conferred partial freedom on the future issue of slave mothers and deferred full freedom for these free children until they served apprenticeships that typically lasted till their mid- or late twenties. The plans confirmed owners' property rights to living slaves, relieved the state and nonslaveholder citizens of the financial burden of compensation, and split the fiscal responsibility between the owners (who lost the right to the life-long labor of the free-born children) and free children, who paid for their emancipation with years of unpaid labor.

Amid the chaos of the Civil War, President Abraham Lincoln attempted to introduce a plan for compensated emancipation. Hoping to remove the cause of dissension and war between North and South and thereby restore the divided nation, Lincoln in 1862 proposed to free the slaves in the remaining slave states in the Union, pay partial compensation to the owners for their property losses, and remove the freed slaves through colonization. Unlike the northern gradual abolition laws, Lincoln's proposal, which never became law, would have used national funds to compensate slaveholders and to colonize the freed slaves.

In the British colonies, taxpayers, slaveowners, and slaves bore the cost of compensating slaveowners. Britain's 1833 Emancipation Act abolished slavery throughout its colonies, freeing all slaves—immediately and unconditionally for children under age six, gradually for the others—and indemnified slaveowners for their loss. The state allocated a fund of £20 million to pay direct monetary compensation to slaveowners. Slaveholders assumed partial costs, for they lost their rights to the life-long labor of their slaves and, as some complained, received less than the full market value for their slaves. Slaves over age six paid a portion of the cost of their emancipation with apprenticeships of up to six years. In 1838, following loud complaints about abuses suffered under the emancipation act, Britain enacted a new law freeing all remaining slaves unconditionally.

— *Patience Essah*

See also: Gradualism; Immediatism; Lincoln, Abraham.

For Further Reading
Blackburn, Robin. 1988. *The Overthrow of Colonial Slavery, 1776–1848*. London: Verso.

Davis, David Brion. 1975. *The Problem of Slavery in the Age of Revolution, 1770–1823*. Ithaca, NY: Cornell University Press.

Fogel, Robert William. 1989. *Without Consent or Contract: The Rise and Fall of American Slavery*. New York: Norton.

Shepherd, Verene. 2002. *Working Slavery, Pricing Freedom: Perspectives from the Caribbean, Africa and the African Diaspora.* New York: Palgrave.

COMPROMISE OF 1850

The Compromise of 1850 emerged out of President Zachary Taylor's attempt to resolve the problems related to territorial expansion and slavery following the Mexican War (1846–1848). When Taylor was inaugurated in 1849, four compelling issues faced the nation. First, the rush of some eighty thousand miners to California qualified that territory for admission to the Union, but California's entry as a free state would upset the balance between slave and free states in the Senate that had prevailed since 1820.

The unresolved status of the territory acquired from Mexico in the Southwest posed a second problem. The longer the area was left unorganized, the louder local inhabitants called for an application of either the Wilmot Proviso, which prohibited slavery in the newly acquired territories, or the Calhoun doctrine, which protected the extension of slavery. The boundary between Texas and New Mexico Territory was also in dispute, with Texas claiming lands all the way to Santa Fe. This claim increased northern fears that Texas might be divided into five or six slave states. A third problem was the existence of slavery and slave trading in the nation's capital, one of the largest slave markets in North America. Fourth, southerners resented lax federal enforcement of the Fugitive Slave Act of 1793 and called for a stronger act that would end the protection northerners gave runaway slaves.

President Taylor attempted to sidestep the conflict over slavery in the territories by inviting California and New Mexico to bypass the territorial stage and apply immediately for statehood, presumably as free states. The residents could then decide the slavery question for themselves without embarrassment to Congress. Southerners, seeing that California had already prohibited slavery and expecting New Mexico to do the same, realized that Taylor's plan was as effective as Wilmot's Proviso in keeping slavery out of that area. When they protested, Taylor drew a firm line, threatening to use force if necessary to preserve the Union.

The southerners decided that Taylor had betrayed them, and in late 1849, sixty-nine congressmen and senators from the South convened a special caucus in Washington, D.C. John C. Calhoun emerged as leader of the caucus and accused the North of committing numerous "acts of aggression" against the South. According to Calhoun, and the forty-eight congressmen who eventually signed the caucus petition, the North was out to destroy the South's way of life. As proof he cited the laws prohibiting slavery in various territories and the problems southerners were having in recapturing fugitive slaves in the North. Calhoun insisted that the only way out of the impasse was to restore to southerners their Fifth Amendment property rights, which he interpreted as meaning that slaveowners should be able to take their slaves anywhere in the United States and should be afforded adequate legal assistance in repossessing escaped slaves.

The main spokesman for northern antislavery forces was William H. Seward of New York. Seward and those who sided with him in the long and heated debate insisted that the former Mexican territories should not be surrendered to slavery, that the Fugitive Slave Law could not be enforced, and that the agitation in the North against slavery was impossible to suppress. With disunion threatening, the aged Senator Henry Clay of Kentucky, author of the famous Missouri Compromise of 1820, offered a compromise that he hoped would settle for good the territorial crisis and other disputed issues between the two sections of the country. Clay's plan, which was introduced in Congress in January 1850 as an omnibus bill, contained five key provisions: immediate admission of California as a free state; organization of the rest of the area acquired from Mexico into two territories, Utah and New Mexico, without restrictions on slavery, the matter to be decided by the constitutions of the territories; assumption of the Texan national debt by the federal government; abolition of the slave trade in the District of Columbia: and a tough new Fugitive Slave Law. When Clay's package of compromise measures came to a vote, opponents of the individual measures defeated it. His bill and his health in ruins, Clay withdrew into retirement.

Stephen A. Douglas of Illinois assumed Clay's place in steering the compromise through Congress. Douglas devised a new strategy of introducing Clay's measures separately, relying on sectional blocs and a few swing votes to form majorities for each of the separate laws, which became known as the Compromise of 1850. The first was the Texas and New Mexico Act of September 9, 1850, which established the borders of Texas and a payment of $10 million to that state. The act provided that when New Mexico entered the Union, the state would make its own decision on slavery. The Utah Act of September 9, 1850, provided that this territory, too, should decide for itself the legal status of slavery within its borders. On that same date, California was admitted as a free state. The District of Columbia Act of September 20, 1850, abolished the slave trade, but not slavery, in that area. The slaveholders won their most cherished victory with the passage of the Fugitive Slave Act in September 1850. This act, far more stringent than the 1793 law, authorized slaveholders to pursue runaways into other states and imposed heavy fines on people who aided runaway slaves.

The immediate response to the Compromise of 1850 was an enthusiastic welcome with celebrations held in many cities, but events soon revealed that the compromise had settled nothing at all. Rather, it had only delayed more serious sectional conflict. In its aftermath, political parties appeared to realign more along sectional lines. In addition, northerners, in response to the Fugitive Slave Act, increased Underground Railroad activity and passed personal liberty laws, which prohibited the use of state officials and institutions in recovering fugitive slaves.

— *Michael Washington*

See also: Clay, Henry; Douglas, Stephen A.; Fugitive Slave Act (1850); Wilmot Proviso.

For Further Reading

Holt, Michael F. 1978. *The Political Crisis of the 1850s.* New York: Norton.

Miller, William Lee. 1996. *Arguing about Slavery: The Great Battle in the United States Congress.* New York: Alfred A. Knopf.

CONFISCATION ACTS (1861–1862)

Congress passed the confiscation acts during the Civil War, and this legislation authorized military authorities to appropriate permanently any property owned by Confederate citizens, including slaves. The two confiscation acts were the first small steps taken to erode the legal foundations of slavery in the United States.

Union forces advancing southward immediately confronted the problem of what they could legally do with captured Confederate property. Since Lincoln's administration insisted that Confederates were rebellious insurgents rather than foreign belligerents, the laws of war giving nations the right to seize enemy aliens' property might not apply. Some specific legislative act was necessary in order to allow the North to legally seize and retain the South's war-making matériel. On August 6, 1861, Congress therefore passed with little debate the First Confiscation Act allowing military forces to keep any rebel war-making property.

Did this "property" include slaves? If so, the first Confiscation Act might easily become a de facto emancipation proclamation. Southerners certainly understood it as such. Angrily referring to the northern law as an emancipation act, they passed their own harsh confiscatory legislation to exact revenge against what they saw as the Union's poorly concealed declaration of war against their slave "property."

Slaves performed essential military service throughout the Confederacy, and some northerners like General Benjamin Butler believed that slaves should be considered "contraband of war that had been seized and kept, with the same justification the Union army might use to keep a captured Confederate musket or cannon. The First Confiscation Act's authors therefore specifically provided that slaves directly employed in aiding the Confederate military effort could be confiscated, but it made no provisions for deciding whether these individuals might subsequently be emancipated. As a result, the army was flooded with thousands of runaway slaves whose legal status remained in limbo.

The ambiguity of this and other provisions caused Congress to pass a Second Confiscation Act in July 1862. This act authorized the government to seize any property owned by rebellious southerners. Sponsored by more radical antislavery congressmen, many northerners understood it to be a first step toward total emancipation, treating the slaves of rebel owners as "captives of war" and unequivocally declaring them "forever free."

The Second Confiscation Act did not resolve the basic legal confusion over whether the Confederates were rebels or foreign enemies. It referred to rebels as "traitors," implying they were simply wayward U.S. citizens who might nevertheless possess certain basic rights in a court of law, such as a hearing to determine whether their property might be taken from them. But using the phrase "captives of war" to describe confiscated slaves suggested that Confederate slaveowners were waging a war as foreign belligerents. This afforded the Confederacy indirect legal recognition as a foreign nation, a status Lincoln's administration very much wished to avoid conferring on the South.

Lincoln had so many doubts about these and other matters that he took the unprecedented step of sending a message to Congress stating his objections to the bill and indicating he would veto it if certain changes were not made. He believed the law incorrectly implied that Congress could end slavery in a state, and he suggested that the wording should be altered to give the national government ownership of confiscated slave "property" prior to freeing those slaves. Lincoln took pains to indicate that he had no objections to liberating slaves as such. Even as he wrote this opinion, he was working on a preliminary draft of the Emancipation Proclamation.

Congress took Lincoln's suggestions for changing the bill's wording, and it became law in fall 1862. In the final analysis, both the First and Second Confiscation Acts were relatively ineffective with regard to slavery, for just six months after passage of the second act, Lincoln freed the slaves using his powers as commander-in-chief. Yet the laws set certain precedents. They marked the first congressional attempt to address the issues of emancipation and slavery's legal status during the Civil War, and they implied that such issues were national rather than local in scope. The Confiscation Acts are best remembered for their symbolic value, as milestones on the difficult road northerners took from fighting a war for the Union to fighting a war to end slavery.

— *Brian Dirck*

See also: Abolitionism in the United States; Civil War; Contrabands; Emancipation Proclamation; Lincoln, Abraham.

For Further Reading

Cimbala, Paul A., and Randall M. Miller, eds. 2002. *An Uncommon Time: The Civil War and the Northern Home Front.* New York: Fordham University Press.

Frederick, Duke. 1966. "The Second Confiscation Act: A Chapter of Civil War Politics." M.A. Thesis, Department of History, University of Chicago, Chicago.

Hamilton, Daniel W. 2004. "A New Right to Property: Civil War Confiscation in the Reconstruction Supreme Court." *Journal of Supreme Court History* 29 (3): 254–285.

Siddali, Sylvana R. 2005. *From Property to Person: Slavery and the Confiscation Acts, 1861–1862.* Baton Rouge: Louisiana State University Press.

Syrett, John. 1971. "The Confiscation Acts: Efforts at Reconstruction during the Civil War." M.A. Thesis, Department of History, University of Wisconsin, Madison, WI.

Syrett, John. 2005. *The Civil War Confiscation Acts: Failing to Reconstruct the South.* New York: Fordham University Press.

CONSTITUTION.
See United States Constitution.

CONTRABANDS

In a general sense, warriors throughout history have recognized all goods and property seized during a conflict to be the contraband of war if such items are deemed to aid and abet the enemy's ability to continue to make war. The Civil War is a unique conflict because often the assets that were considered contraband included human beings as southern plantations were liberated by advancing Union forces and as many slaves sought self-emancipation by rushing toward the advancing Union lines. The question of what to do with these individuals, ostensibly the chattel property of Confederate sympathizers, and also the status of these liberated persons, were perplexing issues that often faced Union commanders in the field. The mixed signals and miscues between the Lincoln administration and the U.S. Army suggest that no clear policy regarding former slaves as contrabands had been developed at the onset of the Civil War and that the formulation of such policy was a work in progress during the first months of the conflict.

Since Abraham Lincoln did not issue the Emancipation Proclamation until September 22, 1862, a carefully crafted veil of discomfiture shrouded the question of emancipation during the first year and a half of the conflict. Faced with the dilemma of keeping the proslavery border states of Missouri, Kentucky, Maryland, and Delaware in the Union, the Lincoln administration believed that any rash action toward wholesale emancipation might drive these states toward secession, thus augmenting the Confederacy and extending its ability and resources to make war. In such a world of high-stakes realpolitik, all policies regarding the status of slaves as contrabands of war were viewed as profound decisions that could affect the conduct of the war.

On May 24, 1861, only six weeks after the opening shots were fired at Fort Sumter, Union General Benjamin F. Butler reported to authorities in the War Department that he had put a group of fugitive slaves to work at Fortress Monroe, Virginia. In his dispatch, Butler described the fugitives as "contraband of war," and stated that some were employed on construction projects while others picked cotton.

Although the fugitive slaves were not considered to be legally emancipated, they were effectively free, and they did receive a small wage (usually 25 cents per day plus rations) from the federal treasury for the labor that they performed for the Union forces. Among northern abolitionists the catchphrase "contraband of war" became almost synonymous with emancipation. This practice became increasingly common after Congress passed the First Confiscation Act on August 6, 1861. This measure authorized the freeing of slaves in areas that were already under Union army control and who had previously been employed to aid the Confederate cause.

Even with these policies in place, President Lincoln still proceeded very cautiously on the issue of emancipa-

Contrabands, slaves who sought refuge with Union troops during the Civil War, accompanied William Tecumseh Sherman's march through Georgia. (Library of Congress)

tion. In September 1861, he ordered General John C. Frémont to revise a proclamation of martial law that he had issued. Frémont's initial proclamation had freed the slaves of all disloyal slaveowners in Missouri. In December 1861 Lincoln convinced Secretary of War Simon Cameron to delete several controversial passages in his annual report to Congress. It was Cameron's wish to urge emancipation as a wartime necessity and to advocate the use of former slaves as military laborers and as soldiers. Shortly after Cameron submitted the revised report, Lincoln removed him from the War Department by naming him minister to Russia.

For many former slaves, their role as "contraband of war" was part of the transition from slavery to freedom. The role of emancipation and contrabands was always closely linked, and when freedom finally came to the slaves in the South, Union lines swelled as tens of thousands of the newly free joined the camps and eventually the ranks of their liberators. Coping with the demands of vast contraband camps that were teeming with displaced persons was a taxing obligation to the War Department and represents one of the first social welfare efforts sponsored by the U.S. government. The provision of basic supplies of food, shelter,

and clothing, the furnishing of rudimentary health services, and the establishment of schools were not skills traditionally associated with the military. As the war progressed, however, efforts to assist the wards of the government in the contraband camps became more systematic. Not surprisingly, when the Congress created the Bureau of Refugees, Freedmen, and Abandoned Lands in March 1865, the agency was placed under the auspices of the War Department, and General Oliver Otis Howard was appointed its first director.

— *Junius P. Rodriguez*

See also: Confiscation Acts.

For Further Reading

Buker, George E. 1993. *Blockaders, Refugees, and Contrabands: Civil War on Florida's Gulf Coast, 1861–1865.* Tuscaloosa: University of Alabama Press.

Eaton, John. 1907. *Grant, Lincoln, and the Freedmen: Reminiscences of the Civil War, with Special Reference to the Work for the Contrabands and Freedmen of the Mississippi Valley.* New York: Longmans, Green, and Co..

Swint, Henry L., ed. 1966. *Dear Ones at Home: Letters from Contraband Camps.* Nashville, TN: Vanderbilt University Press.

ANNA JULIA COOPER (C. 1858–1964)

Anna Julia Cooper became a controversial educator who demanded standards of excellence as well as equal opportunity for black schools. Late in life she headed one of the first community colleges, Freylingshuysen University in Washington, D.C. An early black feminist, Cooper lectured widely on behalf of the "doubly enslaved" black woman, while insisting on a right to higher education for all women. In the nineteenth century, she became a founder and supporter of the National Association of Colored Women's Clubs and other organizations. As a crowning achievement, her 1925 Sorbonne doctoral thesis expressed a seminal interpretation of international slavery and its repercussions (L'Attitude de la France a l'egard de l'esclavage pendant la revolution [Slavery and the French Revolutionists]).

Anna Cooper's mother was Hannah Stanley, a slave, the property of Dr. Fabius J. Haywood. Haywood was Cooper's owner and probably her father. Along with Mary Church Terrell and Ida A. Gibbs, Cooper stood among the first women to receive the bachelor's degree from Oberlin College; in 1887 she received the master's degree. Thirty-eight years later she received the doctorate from the Sorbonne in Paris, France.

In 1892 Cooper published her first book, *A Voice from the South by a Black Woman of the South*. In this feminist work she discussed the discouragements she had encountered in growing up in the post–Civil War South. For much of her life she wrote and lectured on women's rights and on justice for the former slaves. For many years she taught Latin and Greek and mathematics to students at the M Street Colored High School in Washington, D.C. A gifted linguist, she later translated from ancient to modern French a classic epic, *Le Pelerinage de Charlemagne* (The Pilgrimage of Charlemagne).

Cooper's least known and probably most important work is her study of the relations between the assemblies of the French Revolution and the slaves of France's richest colony, San Domingue (Haiti). Cooper believed that slavery anywhere affected slavery everywhere, that it encapsulated a world labor problem, that slave labor thus became a matter of international concern. She thought that denial of freedom to the slaves of San Domingue severely limited the freedom of the French and that it negated hope of democratic progress through the French Revolution. She thus showed the inevitable involvement of darker peoples with the Western world. Cooper wrote this study in French when she was sixty-seven years old, and the Sorbonne published it. Until 1988 it was never published in any language in her native land, but toward the end of her 105 years, Cooper lived to see major scholars advance the issues that she had raised in her scholarship.

—*Frances Richardson Keller*

See also: Education; Literature.

For Further Reading

Cooper, Anna Julia. 1988. *Slavery and the French Revolutionists (1788–1805)*. Translated from the French with introductory essay by Frances Richardson Keller. Lewiston, NY: Edwin Mellen Press.

Cooper, Anna J. 1998. *The Voice of Anna Julia Cooper: Including "A Voice from the South" and Other Important Essays, Papers, and Letters*. Ed. Charles C. Lemert, Esme Bhan, et al. Lanham, MD: Rowman & Littlefield.

Hutchinson, Louise Daniel. 1981. *Anna J. Cooper: A Voice from the South*. Washington, DC: Smithsonian Institution Press.

Nash, Margaret. 2004. "'Patient Persistence': The Political and Educational Values of Anna Julia Cooper and Mary Church Terrell." *Educational Studies* 35 (2): 122–136.

COTTON. *See* Long-Staple Cotton; Short-Staple Cotton.

COTTON GIN

The cotton gin is a device for separating cottonseed from the fiber. In the United States, the first profitable variety of cotton produced consisted of long fibers grown in the Sea Islands and coastal South Carolina, Georgia, and Florida. Introduced for cultivation in 1786, the cotton gin made cotton's black seeds easier to separate from its lint. This made it cost-effective for landowners to use African and African American slaves to process the fiber. Environmental factors, however, prevented this variant's inland cultivatation.

In the southern uplands, a plant with short fibers and green seeds grew abundantly, but the extreme difficulty of extracting the seeds from the fibers made it unprofitable to process. Gins used for separating black seeds from the long-staple cotton proved ineffective when applied to the shorter fibers. Those gins were patterned on a device used for centuries in India consisting of two grooved wooden rollers that rotated conversely when turned by a handle. The grooves captured the seeds of the long-staple cotton as it was pulled through the rollers, thereby cleaning it for spinning. The seeds from the upland variety, however, clung so tightly to the fiber that the rollers could not remove them.

Planters in Georgia brought this problem to the attention of Eli Whitney (1765–1825), a mechanically in-

The cotton gin, introduced in 1793, is a device for separating cottonseed from the fiber. Its development made it cost-effective for landowners to use African and African American slaves to process the fiber. (Library of Congress)

clined graduate of Yale University from Massachusetts. In 1792 Whitney accepted a position as tutor for a family in South Carolina. On his journey south, he met Catherine Littlefield Greene (1755–1814) and accepted an invitation to stay at her plantation in Georgia. Following discussions with Greene and others regarding the problems of ginning upland cotton, Whitney chose not to proceed to South Carolina. Instead, he remained at Greene's plantation and worked on a means of separating green seeds from the upland cotton.

Whitney constructed a model for a cotton gin in ten days in November 1792 and then spent six months building a working machine, which he finished in April 1793. Whitney based his design on the gins used in cleaning lowland cotton, but his apparatus consisted of one roller with iron pins attached that pulled the lint through a metal grid, which caught the seeds and dropped them into a box below. A second cylinder rotated a brush that removed the fibers from the toothed roller. Supposedly, it was Greene who sug-

gested employing the brush, which solved the problem of how to prevent the lint caught in the pins from accumulating and choking the gin.

Whitney's device cleaned fifty times more fiber than could be accomplished by hand and made it profitable to put slaves to work picking short-staple cotton, thereby encouraging the expansion of slavery throughout the southeastern United States. The gin also enabled the United States to become the world's leading producer of cotton by 1825. The boom in the production of cotton encouraged white southerners to demand the removal of Native Americans from their lands so that planters could acquire more land for cultivation.

Whitney profited little from his invention. Although he and a business associate received a federal patent, other mechanics easily varied the basic design, which allowed for the proliferation of gins while making it nearly impossible for Whitney to collect either damages or royalties.

— *Dan R. Frost*

For Further Reading

Green, Constance McLaughlin. 1956. *Eli Whitney and the Birth of American Technology.* Boston: Little, Brown.

Mirsky, Jeannette, and Allan Nevins. 1952. *The World of Eli Whitney.* New York: Macmillan.

Ogilvie, Marilyn Bailey. 1986. *Women in Science: Antiquity through the Nineteenth Century.* Cambridge, MA: MIT Press.

HANNAH PEIRCE [PEARCE] COX (1797–1876)

As an abolitionist and a partner in operating the first Underground Railroad station in Pennsylvania, Hannah Peirce (variously spelled Pearce) Cox is considered one of America's premier abolitionists. She grew up on her family's farm in Pennsylvania, part of the fifth generation of her family to be born in America. Her Quaker upbringing shaped her sympathy for people held captive by slavery, and her marriage to John Cox, a like-minded Quaker, served to reinforce her antislavery beliefs.

Hannah Cox was reportedly stirred by reading William Lloyd Garrison's *Liberator* and by attending a lecture at which John Greenleaf Whittier's poem "Our Fellow Countrymen in Chains" was read. She became an ardent supporter of immediate emancipation and felt the idea of a gradual extermination of slavery to be ridiculous. She agreed with fellow abolitionists like Garrison that gradual release of slaves was "to tell a man to moderately rescue his wife from the hands of the ravisher, or tell the mother to gradually extricate her babe from the fire" (Smedley, 1969). The burning of Philadelphia's Pennsylvania Hall in 1838 by proslavery advocates further spurred her activity in the antislavery cause.

Hannah and John Cox eagerly joined the Underground Railroad, providing their home as the first station north of Wilmington, Delaware, on the way to the Canadian border. Their children also aided in the almost nightly activities: feeding everyone, clothing those who needed clothes, conveying people to the next safe house along the route, or giving them directions for their flight northward. The Coxes carried on these duties quietly and for many years. Slaves were not the only people welcomed at the Cox home. Fellow abolitionists Lucretia Mott, William Lloyd Garrison, Sarah Pugh, Abby Kelley, Lucy Stone, John Greenleaf Whittier, and many others always found comfort at the Cox homestead.

Over the years, Hannah and John Cox were frequently chosen as delegates to antislavery state and national conventions, and from the antislavery movement, Hannah Cox went on to support many other social causes. She died in her home in Pennsylvania, the same house where she had been born and lived her entire life.

— *Maria Elena Raymond*

See also: Underground Railroad.

For Further Reading

Hanaford, Phebe A. 1883. *Daughters of America, or Women of the Century.* Augusta, ME: True and Company.

Hersh, Blanche Glassman. 1978. *Slavery of Sex: Feminist-Abolitionists in America.* Urbana: University of Illinois Press.

Malone, Dumas and Allen Johnson, eds. 1930. *Dictionary of American Biography.* New York: Charles Scribner's Sons.

Smedley, R.C. 1969. *History of the Underground Railroad.* New York: Arno Press.

WILLIAM (1827–1900) AND ELLEN (C. 1826–1890) CRAFT

William and Ellen Craft gained national attention because of the circumstances of their escape from slavery in 1848. The two married in Macon, Georgia, while both were slaves, and later decided to flee the South in search of freedom. William, a cabinetmaker whose master allowed him to work independently, used his earnings to buy disguises and to pay for travel costs, and the two obtained passes to leave Macon during the Christmas season.

Ellen, the daughter of a former master, wore dark glasses and a muffler to hide her face while posing as an elderly and ailing master, with William playing the part of a faithful servant. With her right arm in a sling, the illiterate Ellen was able to avoid signing hotel registers or other documents. They traveled by train and steamer without incident until they reached Baltimore, Maryland, the last slave city on their journey. Maryland law required masters to sign and post bond for slaves accompanying them to the North. William's plea for his master's urgent need of medical care persuaded the railroad agent to waive the requirement. On the train they met a free African American who directed them to a Philadelphia abolitionist.

After resting briefly in Philadelphia, the Crafts continued to Boston accompanied by former slave and abolitionist William Wells Brown. They had a second wedding in Boston, where they remained for two years.

There William worked as a cabinetmaker and Ellen trained as a seamstress, and they were both active in the antislavery movement. In October 1850, when agents of their masters appeared in Boston with warrants for their arrest under the new Fugitive Slave Law, the Crafts fled the United States. Assisted by other abolitionists they went first to Nova Scotia, then to Britain.

The Crafts attended British antislavery meetings and attracted attention upon visiting the Crystal Palace Exhibition of 1851. Their five children were born in Britain, where they lived until after the Civil War. In 1868 they returned briefly to Boston and then moved to Georgia to manage an industrial school financed by British and American abolitionists. After the Ku Klux Klan burned the school, the Crafts supervised a similar project located on a Bryan County, Georgia, plantation. That site later became the Craft Family plantation.

The Crafts frequently spoke publicly about their dramatic escape, which relied solely on their ingenious plan. While in Britain they told their story in the book *Running a Thousand Miles for Freedom, or the Escape of William and Ellen Craft from Slavery* (1860). Their use of the Underground Railroad was typical of many other escapes from slavery. Although they eventually received valuable assistance, it was only after reaching the North that they received any help beyond their own resources.

—Larry Gara

See also: Brown, William Wells; Fugitive Slave Act (1850); Underground Railroad.

For Further Reading

Blackett, R. J. M. 1978. "Fugitive Slaves in Britain: The Odyssey of William and Ellen Craft." *Journal of American Studies* 12: 41–62.

Craft, William and Ellen. 1860. *Running a Thousand Miles for Freedom, or the Escape of William and Ellen Craft from Slavery*. London: William Tweedie.

Still, William. 1883. *The Underground Railroad*. Philadelphia: William Still.

Tiffany, Nina Moore. 1890. "Stories of the Fugitive Slaves, I: The Escape of William and Ellen Craft." *New England Magazine* 1: 528.

Woodson, Carter G., ed. 1926. *The Mind of the Negro as Reflected in Letters Written During the Crisis, 1800–1860*. Washington, DC: Association for the Study of Negro Life and History.

PRUDENCE CRANDALL (1803–1889)

Prudence Crandall became famous in 1833 when she defied northern racial prejudice by accepting black students into her Canterbury, Connecticut, female boarding school. Abolitionist leaders seized on Crandall's action and Connecticut's violent reaction as a means of promoting antislavery and demonstrating to white northerners the danger slavery and prejudice posed to their own civil liberties. When Sarah Harris, the daughter of a local black farmer and abolitionist, asked to attend the all-white school so that she could learn enough to teach black children, Crandall could not say no. The school's board of visitors demanded that Crandall remove Harris; if she did not, they would remove the white pupils. Crandall refused and then took her stand against racism further: she dismissed the white students and announced she would take only black students. The school for black girls opened on April 1, 1833.

The town's attack proceeded on two fronts: in the courts and the state legislature and through intimidation. Urged by a prominent member of the board of visitors, the Connecticut state legislature passed a "black law" in 1833 requiring local approval for schools to admit out-of-state black students and instituting onerous fines for those who violated the new policy. The authorities arrested Crandall, and when she would not post bond, the town was forced to jail her, an action abolitionist leaders eagerly publicized. Her trial in August 1833 ended in a hung jury, but she was found guilty in October by the state supreme court. That decision was overturned on appeal because of a technicality.

All this time Crandall continued her school, which endured boycotts by the town's storekeepers, churches, and doctors. Townspeople smashed windows and dumped manure in the well; they insulted Crandall and the black students on the street; and they threw manure and dead animals at them. One student was arrested for vagrancy and threatened with public whipping. The terrorism continued after the court decisions—including an arson attempt while Crandall, her husband, and the students were sleeping, and a midnight attack on September 9, 1834, by a mob that smashed windows and downstairs rooms with clubs and iron bars. The mob attack convinced Crandall that the danger was extreme, and she reluctantly closed the school.

After Crandall gave up her school, she dropped from the public eye. In the mid-1870s a regiment of black soldiers raised money to assist her, and several of her black students did become teachers. Although her antislavery stand occurred during only a small portion of her life, Crandall's principles and her sufferings on behalf of those principles placed her in the community of martyrs who were admired and publicized by aboli-

A CURE FOR REPUBLICAN LOCK-JAW

Crittenden Compromise: The seven amendments that made up the Crittenden Compromise were proposed during the 1860–1861 session of Congress by Kentucky Senator John Crittenden. The compromise was a last-ditch attempt to avert the Civil War. (Library of Congress)

tionist speakers and newspapers throughout the antebellum period.

— *Andrea M. Atkin*

For Further Reading

Foner, Philip. 1984. "Prudence Crandall." In *Three Who Dared: Prudence Crandall, Margaret Douglass, and Myrtilla Miner—Champions of Antebellum Black Education*. Ed. Philip S. Foner and Josephine F. Pacheco. Westport, CT: Greenwood.

Fuller, Edmond. 1971. *Prudence Crandall: An Incident of Racism in Nineteenth-Century Connecticut*. Middletown, CT: Wesleyan University Press.

CRITTENDEN COMPROMISE

On December 18, 1860, in an effort to avoid destroy-ing the United States over the unresolved issues of slavery and states' rights, Kentucky senator John Jordan Crittenden presented several proposals to the U.S. Senate, including six possible amendments to the Constitution and four resolutions.

Crittenden's proposals included the following stipulations. One, in lands already in the possession of the United States (or yet to be acquired north of 36°30'), slavery would be prohibited; south of the line, slavery would be protected as property. Two, Congress could not abolish slavery in areas under federal control in the slave states. Three, Congress could not abolish slavery in the District of Columbia without compensation to the owners and the consent of the states of Maryland and Virginia. Four, Congress could not interfere with the interstate transportation of slaves. Five, Congress would have to compensate owners of fugitive slaves.

And six, Congress should not have the power to interfere with slavery where it already existed by the passage of constitutional amendments that would alter the Fugitive Slave Law or interfere with slavery in the states.

Crittenden's compromise also included the following four resolutions. First, the Fugitive Slave Law was constitutional, and therefore it should be enforced. Second, any state laws (personal liberty acts) that conflicted with the Fugitive Slave Law were to be null and void and should be repealed by the states. Third, Congress should amend the Fugitive Slave Law to remove certain passages that were offensive to northern citizens. Fourth, Congress should enforce and further strengthen laws forbidding the foreign slave trade.

The Senate appointed a committee of thirteen, and the House a committee of thirty-three to review Crittenden's plan. On December 22, 1860, the Senate committee rejected the plan because President-elect Lincoln and the Republicans refused to compromise on the extension of slavery into the territories. In February and March 1860, Congress passed a resolution to prohibit interference with slavery in the states by the federal government, but it was not ratified by the states.

The rejection of these proposals was a terrible blow to those hoping for a peaceful solution to the nation's problems. Crittenden received approbations from many Americans for his efforts to reach an agreement between North and South, and moderates from both sections of the nation earnestly hoped for an acceptable alternative to the specter of disunion. A convention of the states of the Upper South held in Washington, D.C., on February 4–27, 1861, endeavored to modify the Crittenden Compromise but failed to satisfy either section of the country and eventually only added to the confusion and distrust between the two regions. The Crittenden Compromise was a desperate effort to salvage a disintegrating Union. By rejecting that effort, the U.S. government faced the grim reality of not only the breakup of the Union but, ultimately, civil war.

— *Ron D. Bryant*

See also: Peace Convention (1860–1861).

For Further Reading

Coleman, Chapman, Mrs. 1871. *The Life of John J. Crittenden.* Philadelphia: J.B. Lippincott.

Keene, Jesse Lynn. 1961. *The Peace Convention of 1861.* Tuscaloosa, AL: Confederate Publishing.

Kirwan, Albert D. 1962. *John J. Crittenden: The Struggle for the Union.* Lexington: University of Kentucky Press.

JAMES DUNWOODY BROWNSON DEBOW (1820–1867)

James D. B. DeBow is well known among historians of the Old South as a proslavery advocate and eloquent editor of *DeBow's Review*—the only antebellum southern commercial magazine. Historians consider him one of the prominent "fire-eaters," a label assigned to those outspoken southerners who were engaged in a "persistent advocacy of southern independence" (Walther, 1992). In defending the institution of slavery, proslavery ideologues commonly denied not only the logic but also the existence of modern industrial relations in the South's racial structures. Compared to other proslavery advocates, DeBow was more "liberal" in his outlook on the South's economic development based on the progress of commerce and industry.

DeBow was a respectable journalist both in the South and among commercial and publishing enterprises in New York and Boston. Thus he was better informed about the political and economic issues of the nation than many of his colleagues. Since he tried to establish *DeBow's Review* for all southerners, not just for particular groups or individuals, he was in a good position to receive and consider different opinions from diverse sections of the South. From its early days, the magazine claimed "active neutrality" in politics. Its editorial policy and viewpoints on politics and economics were moderate except for DeBow's personal belief that the North could not really understand the South and its perspective on slavery. By the mid-1850s, DeBow could no longer keep silent about the intensified sectional conflict, especially as it concerned questions of slavery and southern states' rights. From then on, DeBow actively disseminated proslavery arguments and ideas, pushing commercial conventions for reopening the African slave trade and, after Lincoln's election in 1860, spearheading the secessionist movement. After Fort Sumter, DeBow was appointed to the Produce Loan Bureau of the Confederate government. The task of the bureau was to secure revenue for the Confederacy through sales of commodities loaned to it by planters.

DeBow was born in Charleston, South Carolina, on July 10, 1820. Educated exclusively in South Carolina, first in Charleston public schools and later at the Cokesbury Institute of the Methodist Church in Charleston, he graduated from the College of

Charleston as valedictorian of his class in 1843. De-Bow then read law and was admitted to the South Carolina bar in 1844. Dissatisfied with practicing law, he found a new career in journalism and remained a journalist throughout his life. At the age of twenty-five, after serving briefly as assistant editor of the *Southern Quarterly Review,* DeBow moved to New Orleans and started his own magazine, *Commercial Review of the South West,* later to be better known as *DeBow's Review.*

He was one of the founders of the Louisiana State Historical Society in 1847, which eventually merged into the Academy of Science. In 1849 DeBow was appointed professor of political economy at the newly founded University of Louisiana; in the same year, he was appointed head of the Bureau of Statistics in Louisiana. Four years later, he became superintendent of the Seventh Census of the United States. After the Civil War, he resumed publication of *DeBow's Review* but only until 1867.

In 1853 DeBow married Caroline Poe of Mobile, Alabama, who died in 1858. They had two children, Mary and James Dunwoody Brownson. James died as an infant; Mary died at sixteen. In 1860 DeBow married Martha E. Jones of Nashville, Tennessee, and this marriage produced four children. He died of pleurisy in New Jersey on February 27, 1867, at the age of forty-six.

DeBow was a good example of a southern intellectual whose ideas were shaped and informed by the increasingly hostile social systems within the antebellum United States. As a good southerner, he embraced the radical proslavery ideology in the final period of sectional conflict, believing that slavery, as ordained by God, was an institution that was suitable for the South. The typical argument among southerners was that blacks as a naturally inferior race could exist in an advanced society only through "union with whites in an unequal relation." In order to defend the slave system successfully, he needed to show that there was no fundamental conflict between slavery and the economic development of the South. In so doing, he adjusted and modified classical political economy to suit the conditions of the Old South, proposing that slave labor could become efficient industrial labor.

DeBow's early proslavery ideas were based on biblical arguments and Enlightenment philosophy that maintained that slavery was a "natural" institution. His later proslavery ideas were influenced by the increased North-South sectional conflict and expanded to incorporate the scientific and racial arguments that defended slavery as the best state of social organization.

DeBow believed that given its natural resources and a slave labor system under the guidance of enlightened masters, the South could regain its dominance in national politics and improve its economy based on agriculture, commerce, and manufacturing. With a strong and progressive economy, the South could defend its institutions, especially slavery, from northern attacks. His economic ideas were basically informed by the economic ideas of merchant capital: progress and the prosperity of society were based on commodity exchanges rather than on the production process.

Proslavery ideas conveniently allowed southern intellectuals to place blacks in a barbarous stage in a linear social development and to justify their guidance and protection by civilized men and societies. Accordingly, slavery brought blacks into the modern world order and also perfected and harmonized the natural hierarchical social order. Ultimately, southern intellectuals defended slavery as a social system that was ordained by God and justified by history as the most suitable system for an inferior and unequal race.

DeBow's economic ideas stressed the "industrial revolution" of the South and the sustainability of slavery, which resulted in his arguing for the reopening of the African slave trade. For southern political economists, the security of the institution of slavery depended on a prosperous and strong South, which, in turn, relied on its capability to diversify its economy based on a balance of agriculture, commerce, and manufacturing. For these economists, the successful defense of slavery presupposed an adequate rate of economic growth. DeBow was aware that the single-crop agriculture of the South was inadequate to sustain the rapid growth of the South's economy in the competitive world market, so his advocacy of an "industrial revolution" in the South was a logical outcome of his peculiar economic theory.

Like other southern political economists, however, DeBow's ideas on the promotion of manufacturing, and the diversification of surplus slave labor, were contradictory and impractical. His vision of industrialization was grounded on a view of society as functioning like a working body or organism and the idea that men were responsible for each other. This made possible the unity between capital and labor on the condition that the labor system would consist exclusively of black slaves while capital was owned by white southerners. Ultimately, he denied the existence of class conflict within the South and on the eve of the Civil War argued that nonslaveholders also benefited from having slavery as a main labor system in the South. For him, economic development was a precondition for a defense of slavery. The paradox of DeBow's economic ideas thus lay mainly in his commitment to the defense of slavery.

— *Thanet Aphornsuvan*

See also: Fire-Eaters; Proslavery Argument.

For Further Reading

Aphornsuvan, Thanet. 1990. "James D.B. DeBow and the Political Economy of the Old South." Ph.D. dissertation, History Department, Binghamton University. Binghamton, New York.

Ashworth, John. 1995. *Slavery, Capitalism, and Politics in the Antebellum Republic.* Cambridge: Cambridge University Press.

Hall, Mark. 1982. "The Proslavery Thought of J.D.B. DeBow: A Practical Man's Guide to Economics." *Southern Studies* 21 (Spring): 97–104.

Shore, Lawrence. 1986. *Southern Capitalists: The Ideological Leadership of an Elite, 1832–1885.* Chapel Hill: University of North Carolina Press.

Skipper, Ottis Clark. 1958. *J. D. B. DeBow: Magazinist of the Old South.* Athens: University of Georgia Press.

Walther, Eric H. 1992. *The Fire-Eaters.* Baton Rouge: Louisiana State University Press.

MARTIN R. DELANY (1812–1885)

Martin R. Delany was the son of a free mother and a slave father. Throughout his lifetime, he always claimed that he was descended from West African native chieftains. In 1822 his family moved to Chambersburgh, Pennsylvania, and in 1831, Delany left Chambersburgh for Pittsburgh where he spent the next twenty-five years of his life. Upon his arrival in Pittsburgh, he worked first as a barber while attending a school run by the Reverend Lewis Woodson, a black Methodist minister. During his time in Pittsburgh, Delany participated in the abolitionist movement, newspaper editing, moral reform, and the practice of medicine.

From 1843 to 1847 Delany edited *Mystery,* one of a few black newspapers of the period, and from late 1847 until the middle of 1849 he coedited the *North Star* with Frederick Douglass. In 1852 he published one of the most important books to be written by a free black in the nineteenth century—*The Condition, Elevation, Emigration, and Destiny of the Colored People of the United States, Politically Considered.* This is the text that established Delany's later reputation as the "father of black nationalism." During the Civil War years and thereafter, Delany served as a major over "colored troops." In that capacity, he actively recruited blacks into the Union army. Later he was appointed subassistant commissioner of the Bureau for the Relief of Refugees, Freedmen, and of Abandoned Lands.

Delany's *Condition* is a compelling text for any number of reasons, not the least of which is the context that produced it. Published only two years after passage of the Fugitive Slave Act of 1850, *The Condition* represents a direct response to the political ramifications of that law. Prior to the 1850s, moral suasion had been the primary political strategy for defeating slavery. In fact, Delany himself had been a great proponent of moral suasion. The logic was that if blacks could demonstrate—through education, industry, and thrift—that they were capable of citizenship with whites, then that fact would, over time, make possible the end of slavery. That was the popular ideology of the 1830s and 1840s. However, passage of the Fugitive Slave Act confirmed that whites and the government had not been acting in good faith. It was not the condition of black people that kept them from being considered the equals of whites, it was race and racism.

Delany's *Condition* is a rhetorically sophisticated and politically astute response to that realization. The text outlined and argued for the tenants of emigration (which Delany had taken great pains to distinguish from colonization—a policy of the proslavery forces begun in 1817 to colonize blacks outside the United States). The book also argued for black self-determination, which was dependent on black economic independence. That aspect met with sharp opposition from the black churches, which believed in providential determinism, but the rhetorical sophistication of Delany's argument for materialism as sanctioned by God is noteworthy. Delany was aware of the complexity of the discursive terrain he was embarking on in the text. That awareness is one of the qualities that makes the book one of the most interesting and important documents written by a free black in the United States.

Fusing an unusual blend of black self-determination with the contemporary black emigration movement, Delany favored the concept of "a nation within a nation." He worked actively to establish an African American nation in Africa and saw this move as the cornerstone of the liberation and elevation of black people. Although the mass of blacks never adopted Delany's rather elitist ideas for racial uplift or his campaign for African emigration, twentieth-century thinkers such as Booker T. Washington and Marcus Garvey were deeply influenced by his philosophy.

Although Delany is still widely regarded as the "father of black nationalism," historian Floyd Miller was among the first to take issue with this appellation. Miller contends that it was Lewis Woodson, Delany's teacher in Pittsburgh, who was the real father of black nationalism and who served as the source of Delany's emigrationist and nationalistic ideology. In a 1971 essay, "'The Father of Black Nationalism': Another Contender," Miller demonstrates that most of Delany's ideas about emigration and racial uplift were first published as letters by Lewis to the *Colored American* in the July 1, 1837, issue under the pseudonym "Augustine."

The years 1859–1862 saw the first publication of Delany's work of fiction, *Blake, or the Huts of America*. The first attempt to publish the novel in serial form was made in the *Anglo-African Magazine* from January–July 1859. For unknown reasons (though perhaps because Delany went out of the country), publication was halted after twenty-six chapters had been printed. It was not until 1861–1862 that the entire novel was printed in the *Weekly Anglo-African*—from November 26, 1861, until May 24, 1862. The novel differs from much of nineteenth-century African American literature in two important respects: first, the hero of the text was an unapologetic black revolutionary thinker; and second, the hero was also a man of unmixed African blood, "a pure Negro," and not a tragic mulatto figure as in the works of William Wells Brown, Charles W. Chesnutt, and James Weldon Johnson. In many respects, Delany's hero is much like the author himself—a thinker and a man of action who was proud of his heritage.

— *Dwight A. McBride*

See also: American Colonization Society, Brown, William Wells; Douglass, Frederick; *North Star*.

For Further Reading
Delany, Martin R. 1852. *The Condition, Elevation, Emigration and Destiny of the Colored People of the United States, Politically Considered.* Philadelphia: Martin R. Delany.
Griffith, Cyril F. 1975. *The African Dream: Martin R. Delany and the Emergence of Pan-African Thought.* University Park: Penn State University Press.
Levine, Robert. 1997. *Martin R. Delany, Frederick Douglass, and the Politics of Representative Identity.* Chapel Hill: University of North Carolina Press.
Painter, Nell Irvin. 1988. "Martin R. Delany: Elitism and Black Nationalism." In *Black Leaders of the Nineteenth Century.* Ed. Leon Litwack and August Meier. Urbana: University of Illinois Press.

DEMOCRATIC PARTY

The Democratic Party was one of the two major political parties in the pre–Civil War United States. Although historians debate whether the party came into being to protect the interests of slaveholding southerners, by 1860 the party had become identified as the staunch defender of slavery. The Democratic Party, which for so long had supported the right of slaveholding southerners to move their property into the disputed western territories, wound up a casualty of the sectional discord that engulfed the nation in 1860. In that year, the party split into two wings, northern and southern, with each wing running its own presidential candidate. The last national political party, and the last bond of union between the sections, had broken into two.

The Democratic Party came into being around 1826. Its principal architect was the veteran New York politician Martin Van Buren, and the principal reason for the creation of this party was to elect Andrew Jackson president in 1828. In lining up newspaper editors in various states, which offered Jackson the opportunity to spread his message to potential voters, Van Buren laid the groundwork for the first mass political party in the United States. Though not explicitly formed to protect slavery, this new party, with a Tennessee slaveholder as its first presidential candidate did not offend any slaveholder, nor did it threaten the right to hold slave property; Democratic Party ideology reinforced this sense of security among slaveholders. The party carried on the Jeffersonian tradition by advocating a national government limited in the scope of its powers, promoting states' rights, and making the primary tasks of the national government the maintenance of order and the protection of private property. The Democratic Party, particularly its southern wing, viewed the ownership of slaves not only as the right to own constitutionally protected property but also as an example of liberty for whites.

From 1830 to 1860, the Democratic Party upheld the rights of slaveholders as the abolitionist movement gained strength in the North. In 1835 President Jackson responded to the burning of abolitionist literature that had been seized from a South Carolina post office by instructing Amos Kendall, his postmaster general, not to forward this type of material to the South. Jackson viewed such abolitionist tactics as threats to the sanctity of the Union. In 1836 the Democratic Party-controlled House of Representatives approved the gag rule, which laid aside, without opportunity for debate, abolitionist petitions sent to Congress. The gag rule lasted until 1844, when the House repealed the measure. Thus, to a large degree, the politics of slavery negated freedom of speech and the right to petition one's representatives.

In 1846 the first sign of a split in party unity appeared. During the Mexican War, David Wilmot, a freshman representative from Pennsylvania, introduced a resolution that would have forbidden the introduction of slavery into any territory acquired from Mexico as a result of the war. Although the House repeatedly passed the proviso, the Senate never approved the measure, and so Wilmot's proposal died in Congress. The Compromise of 1850 resolved the issue, though neither satisfactorily nor for very long. With the admission of California as a free state, the North now had numerical superiority in both houses of Congress, and the South became a political minority within the Union.

The issue of the expansion of slavery into the territories introduced a North-South sectional division not only into American politics generally but also into the Democratic Party. The Fugitive Slave Act of 1850 proved to be highly unpopular in the North and strengthened the abolitionist movement. In 1854 Congress approved the Kansas–Nebraska Act, the brainchild of Democratic Senator Stephen A. Douglas of Illinois. This act effectively repealed the Missouri Compromise of 1820. Slavery could now spread to the territories if the residents of a territory, through popular sovereignty, decided to allow slavery in that territory. A sense of outrage swept across the North, and in 1854 voters in that section elected not to return most Democrats to the House of Representatives. The number of northern Democrats in the House fell from ninety-one to twenty-five. As a result, southern Democrats dominated the party in the national government, and northerners began increasingly to identify the Democratic Party as the party of the South and slavery.

New political parties that favored the exclusion of slavery from the territories, such as the American (Know-Nothing) Party, the Free Soil Party, and the Republican Party, fostered such a policy through their campaign rhetoric, while abolitionists and their political allies accused northern Democrats who supported southern interests of being tools of the slave power. By 1860 the breach between the two wings of the Democratic Party had become irreparable, and the party split at the conventions held in Charleston, South Carolina, and Baltimore, Maryland, with each section running a candidate agreeable to its position on slavery. The northern wing ran Stephen A. Douglas while the southern wing nominated John Breckinridge. The divided Democratic vote allowed Abraham Lincoln and the Republican Party to emerge victorious in 1860.

— James C. Foley

See also: Douglas, Stephen A.; Free Soil Party; Whig Party; Wilmot Proviso.

For Further Reading

Cooper, William. 1978. *The South and the Politics of Slavery, 1828–1856.* Baton Rouge: Louisiana State University Press.

Freehling, William W. 1990. *The Road to Disunion, Volume 1: Secessionists at Bay, 1776–1854.* New York: Oxford University Press.

Holt, Michael. 1978. *The Political Crisis of the 1850s.* New York: John Wiley and Sons.

Nichols, Roy Franklin. 1948. *The Disruption of American Democracy.* New York: Macmillan.

Potter, David. 1976. *The Impending Crisis, 1848–1861.* New York: Harper and Row.

Remini, Robert. 1951. *Martin Van Buren and the Making of the Democratic Party.* New York: Columbia University Press.

JAMES DERHAM (B. 1762)

James Derham, the first registered African American physician in the United States, began life as a slave, bought his own freedom, and went on to establish a successful medical practice in New Orleans, Louisiana.

Derham was born in Philadelphia, Pennsylvania, but very little is known of his early years, except that he was a slave of Dr. John Kearsley who taught him to compound medicines and to assist in treatment of patients. After Kearsley's death, Derham was sold possibly several times, eventually becoming the slave of Dr. George West, surgeon of the Sixteenth British Regiment during the American Revolution, who gave him additional training in medicine. At the end of the war, New Orleans physician Dr. Robert Dove bought Derham and made him an assistant in his practice.

In 1783 Derham purchased his freedom from Dr. Dove for 500 pesos, a practice known as *coartación* in Spain's New World colonies. In the act of emancipation, written in Spanish, Derham was given his freedom, as well as all rights and privileges with respect to buying and selling, appearing in court, entering into contracts, and performing acts, judicial or otherwise, that free persons might perform. Self-emancipation in the Spanish New World had its roots in Spain's *Siete Partidas,* which regulated slavery in Spain and became a part of the *Código Negro Español* in the Americas. Once the process of *coartación* began, it took precedence over the relationship between master and slave and despite an owner's objections could not be revoked. The number of slaves taking advantage of *coartación* in Louisiana increased steadily during the Spanish colonial period (1763–1800), with approximately two hundred slaves in New Orleans purchasing their freedom during the first decade of Spanish rule. Over time, New Orleans's free people of color population included teachers, musicians, artists, skilled workers, inventors, and writers.

Speaking English, French, and Spanish, Derham established his own medical practice, specializing in throat disorders and diseases related to climate. By 1800 he had become a well-known New Orleans physician serving people of all races, and is said to have netted an annual income of $3,000 from his work. Like the majority of individuals who entered medicine at the time, Derham's preparation had come through apprenticeship rather than university education.

On a trip to Philadelphia in 1788, Derham met Dr. Benjamin Rush, noted physician, author, and signer of the Declaration of Independence. In commenting on James Derham to the Pennsylvania Abolition Society, Benjamin Rush wrote: "I have conversed with him upon most of the acute and epidemic diseases of the country where he lives and was pleased to find him perfectly acquainted with the modern simple mode of practice on these diseases. I expected to have suggested medicines to him; but he suggested many more to me" (Miller, 1916).

Details concerning Derham's date of death and burial are unknown. In his honor, New Orleans established the James Derham Middle School in 1960.

— *Claude F. Jacobs*

For Further Reading
Miller, Kelly. 1916. "The Historic Background of the Negro Physician." *Journal of Negro History* 1 (2): 99–109.
Morais, Herbert M. 1969. *The History of the Negro in Medicine.* New York: Publishers Company.
Tureaud, A. P., and C. C. Haydel. 1935. *The Negro in Medicine in Louisiana. National Medical Association Souvenir Program.* New Orleans: Amistad Research Center.

THOMAS RODERICK DEW (1802–1846)

Thomas Dew grew up in a planter family in the Tidewater region of Virginia, taught at the College of William and Mary from 1826 to 1846, and gained wide influence with his essays on public issues. He gained particular notice in the early 1830s with his essays on slavery, in which he proclaimed the institution's merits and rejected as impractical the Virginia General Assembly's enactment of any kind of legislation designed to end slavery in the Old Dominion.

In the 1831–1832 legislative session, the Virginia House of Delegates conducted a searching debate as to whether, in the wake of Nat Turner's slave uprising in Southampton County in August 1831, the state should inaugurate some program of gradual emancipation of slaves, coupled with the deportation of black Virginians. Dismayed by the debate, Dew rushed a lengthy essay, "Abolition of Negro Slavery," to publication in the *American Quarterly Review* of September 1832. He also published an expanded version, *Review of the De-*

bate in the Virginia Legislature of 1831 and 1832 (1832). That work reached a wide readership at the time and was selected after Dew's death for inclusion in *The Pro-Slavery Argument as Maintained by the Most Distinguished Writers of the Southern States* (1852).

Dew lectured in *Review of the Debate* against "the crude, undigested theories of tampering legislators." Politicians' "passion for legislation" against slavery, he warned, intruded upon "dangerous and delicate business" and threatened to do "irretrievable" damage to Virginia. Dew sought to demonstrate why no good, and much evil, would come from legislative interference.

Dew demonstrated "the impossibility of colonizing the blacks." How could deportation be financed, he asked, and where would the emigrants go? Drawing on historical analogies, such as Europeans migrating to the Caribbean or to North America, he contended that African Americans, if they went to Africa, would die of disease in droves and would occasion great hostilities with their neighbors. No matter how conceived, the costs of forced colonization would be too great for everyone affected.

Nor could emancipation be accomplished without deportation. Virginia's slaves, whether from nature or nurture, were unfit for freedom in Virginia, he claimed. They would work only under compulsion. And white Virginians, with their customs and prejudices, would not permit black freedom in Virginia. Dew rejected, as irrelevant to Virginia, the models of successful abandonment of slavery in Europe or the North. The North had had few slaves to free, and European societies had developed a middle class that could gradually absorb slaves as free people. The South had far too many slaves for its middle class to absorb and, unlike European societies, had an unfree population that differed in physical appearance: A black southerner, said Dew, "forever wears the indelible symbol of his inferior condition."

Dew saw three options, two of which—emancipation and deportation—he rejected. Having disposed of the arguments for emancipation, whether with or without deportation, he proceeded to adopt a proslavery stance—"to demonstrate . . . the complete justification of the whole southern country in a further continuance of . . . slavery." He denied that most slaves suffered from either discontent or poor treatment: "A merrier being does not exist on the face of the globe than the negro slave of the United States." For Dew, Nat Turner better symbolized why whites should desist from collective action than why they should feel an urgency to act: "But one limited massacre is recorded in Virginia history; let her liberate her slaves," and it "will be almost certain to bring down ruin and degradation on both the whites and the blacks."

As one support for his position, Dew reached for a biblical justification of slavery. In the Old Testament the "children of Israel were themselves slave-holders," and in the New Testament, though slavery in the Roman Empire was "a thousand times more cruel than slavery in our own country," Christ himself never challenged slavery.

According to Dew, slavery rather than being incompatible with republican liberty, was basic to it, for slavery fostered "the perfect spirit of equality so prevalent among the whites of all the slave-holding states." Even more important, Dew could not compromise on the sanctity of property, regardless of whether it was in slaves. He called on "Western Virginia and the non-slave-holders of Eastern Virginia, not to be allured" by arguments that the state could properly interfere in such property holding. For Dew, the French Revolution demonstrated why no legislature should be so wantonly foolish as to "tamper" with "the fundamental relations of society."

Then, however, Dew's rhetoric veered from proslavery to antislavery. If only the legislature would leave slavery alone—and especially if it would foster improvements in transportation, whether roads, canals, or railroads—Virginia would emulate Maryland in gradually abandoning slavery through social and economic evolution. Towns would emerge in rural eastern Virginia, and plantations would become farms. Let the slave trade to the Deep South continue. Free labor would replace slave labor in Virginia, as white immigrants displaced black emigrants.

Looking far down the road, Dew could envision an all-white, free-labor Virginia. Not only was a legislative emancipation scheme incapable of accomplishing such an outcome, but it would make things far worse for everyone rather than any better for anyone. "In due time," Dew forecast, "abolitionists will find" that this natural process was "working to their heart's content, increasing the prosperity of Virginia, and diminishing the evils of slavery without those impoverishing effects which all other schemes must *necessarily* have."

The political economist Dew, a devotee of free trade but not of laissez faire, assigned government at each level, national and state, a particular role as regarded slavery. He blamed the federal government and its high tariff, not slavery, for the South's economic malaise. The federal government's tariff policies damaged Virginia; so would the state if it embraced an emancipationist scheme. The state government should protect, not challenge, wealth invested in slaves, and its actions should foster economic growth and development through banking and transportation improvements.

Dew died young, in the 1840s, so he did not live to observe or write about later developments in the struggle over slavery. The challenges to legislating the system away had seemed to force Dew to conclude that the system must persist for the foreseeable future. Subsequent proslavery theoreticians built on Dew's work, but they ignored his talk of "the evils of slavery." Similarly, historians have tended to characterize Dew as proslavery, when in fact his writings reveal a powerful ambivalence regarding the institution.

— *Peter Wallenstein*

See also: Proslavery Argument; Virginia's Slavery Debate.

For Further Reading

Faust, Drew Gilpin. 1979. "A Southern Stewardship: The Intellectual and the Proslavery Argument." *American Quarterly* 31 (Spring): 63–80.

Freehling, William W. 1990. *The Road to Disunion: Secessionists at Bay, 1776–1854.* New York: Oxford University Press.

Goodson, Susan H., et al. 1993. *The College of William and Mary: A History.* 2 vols. Williamsburg, VA: King and Queen Press.

Harrison, Lowell. 1949. "Thomas Roderick Dew: Philosopher of the Old South." *Virginia Magazine of History and Biography* 57 (October): 390–404.

Stampp, Kenneth M. 1942. "An Analysis of T.R. Dew's *Review of the Debate in the Virginia Legislature.*" *Journal of Negro History* 27 (October): 380–387.

DIASPORA. *See* Atlantic Slave Trade, Closing of; Illegal Slave Trade; Middle Passage; Triangular Trade.

DIET

One of the most significant factors in the life and labor of slaves in the United States was the quantity, quality, and variety of the foodstuffs they consumed. Generally speaking, the slave's diet was ordinarily low in protein and just barely contained the minimum daily needs of vitamins, caloric intake, and fiber. As a result, most slaves were not necessarily malnourished, but they were undernourished, and this contributed to a host of problems including fatigue, dizziness, weakened immunity to disease, and lower-than-average life expectancies as compared to free blacks and whites.

Since slaves were largely beholden to their owners for the provision of foodstuffs, and owners sought to keep overhead costs down to maximize profits, the quality and quantity of food provided for the slave diet was marginal at best. Meat was generally provided to the slave in the form of salted pork, and it always consisted of the lesser-cuts. Slaves generally received a ration of corn meal each day. Occasionally, various types of beans and peas provided additional nourishment in a carbohydrate-rich diet. Some slaves found ways to supplement their rations through theft, but most supplemented their diet by cultivating personal "provision grounds"—small patches of produce grown for their own consumption.

The primary function of the provision ground was to grow enough produce to sustain or to supplement the slave's diet. The slave gardens usually included corn, okra, beans, squash, sweet potatoes, onions, and various types of "greens" (mustard, collards, and turnip). Aside from the beans that were grown, there was very little to add protein to the slave's diet, and the foodstuffs grown in the provision grounds were heavy in carbohydrates and limited in dietary fiber. It was rare to find slaves who regularly attained the 2.000 calorie per day minimum regimen deemed necessary to sustain health. The slave's limited diet and lack of medicine and healthcare made slavery all the more brutal.

Few slaves were permitted to keep livestock, which limited the likelihood that meat would constitute an extensive part of their diet. On occasion some slaves tried to trap or kill small game in order to supplement their diet and add variety to their foodstuffs. Slaves commonly ate rabbit and squirrel, and less-favored game, including racoons and opossum, were also trapped in order to expand the dietary menu. When slaves had access to livestock—or to discarded carcasses of cattle or pigs—they regularly seized upon the find to make secondary and sometimes tertiary cuts, leaving nothing to go to waste. The dietary practice of eating beef tripe, chitterlins, and all imaginable pork remnants has its cultural antecedents in the days of slavery. Such practices are a reminder that "necessity is the mother of invention" and suggest the extent to which individuals will respond when faced with the perils of hunger.

A limited diet was especially dangerous for pregnant slave women. Having to sustain oneself was difficult on meager rations, and the burden of pregnancy only exacerbated this situation for women of childbearing age. The death of women during a difficult childbirth was not uncommon, and the burdens of nursing newborn children weakened already marginally nourished mothers. Not surprisingly, infant mortality rates among slave populations was high during the antebellum era.

The slave's limited diet was one of the primary factors leading to the cultural development of cooking known as "soul food" within the African American community. It became common to use spices and herbs to enhance the taste of otherwise bland nutrients. Family recipes, some dating back to slavery days, are a cultural reminder of how the slaves managed to sustain themselves and their kin within so desperately wretched a system.

— *Junius P. Rodriguez*

See also: Provision Grounds.

For Further Reading
Hilliard, Sam B. 1972. *Hog Meat and Hoecake: Food Supply in the Old South, 1840–1860.* Carbondale: Southern Illinois University Press.

Kiple, Kenneth F., and Virginia H. King. 1981. *Another Dimension to the Black Diaspora: Diet, Disease, and Racism.* Cambridge: Cambridge University Press.

Moore, Stacy Gibbons. 1989. "'Established and Well-Cultivated': Afro-American Foodways in Early Virginia." *Virginia Cavalcade* 39: 70–83.

Westmacott, Richard. 1992. *African American Gardens and Yards in the Rural South.* Knoxville: University of Tennessee Press.

DISQUISITION ON GOVERNMENT (CALHOUN)

John C. Calhoun began writing his *Disquisition on Government* in spring 1845. It was the first of his two major philosophical inquiries into the nature and character of representative government in general and on the United States government in particular. The *Disquisition* was to have been a preliminary "inquiry into the elements of political science, preliminary to a treatise on the Constitution of the U. States" (Spain, 1951). The second work was *A Discourse on the Constitution and Government of the United States.* He did not live to see either book in print.

The underlying themes of both works was how best to secure and safeguard the interests and the way of life of a minority against the will of democratic majorities. It was in his *Disquisition* that Calhoun redefined and developed his doctrine of the "concurrent majority," which he first described during the Nullification Movement of the late 1820s.

It was Calhoun's hope that his political works would be considered among the great philosophical books of his century. In the *Disquisition* he argued that the nature of man was such that he was a social being. Mankind was physical and moral, and Calhoun assumes that man is inherently self-centered. This self-centeredness led to self-preservation and, therefore, "implies an unusual excess of the individual over the social feelings" (Post, 1953). He further concluded that man cannot exist without government of some sort and that representative government is the best government.

He argued that true representative government would be sympathetic to all points of view and thus must provide adequate protection for every minority: region, district, class, and economic level. It was the ideal of the protection of the minority that underscores the philosophy of the present work. It was here that Calhoun's ideas were fully developed. He believed that the Framers of the Constitution so worried about the tyranny of the majority that they insisted on the Bill of Rights. He was trying to carry that concept to a higher level.

The actual impact of the *Disquisition on Government* is difficult to measure. The book itself was largely ignored by a country on the brink of Civil War. Although Calhoun's views on southern politics and particularly his views on economics and slavery were well known and documented, some of the views expressed in this writing were less known. The most important result seems to have been its use in a conference on reforming Maryland's constitution held during the winter of 1850–1851, where delegates from the Eastern Shore (which was the strongest slaveholding district in the state) claimed that the state's constitution was a compact. They used Calhoun's views as expressed in the *Disquisition* to show that the compact was designed to protect the minority from the "ruthless actions of the majority" (Green, 1930). Calhoun would have agreed with those delegates that the compact idea made more sense than the fundamental law theory, which was being hotly debated at the time.

The principal value in Calhoun's *Disquisition on Government* lies in its defense of the minority, an argument that goes well beyond that of any of his contemporaries and one in which recent history sees as becoming increasingly important in a democratic society.

— *Henry H. Goldman*

See also: Nullification Doctrine.

For Further Reading

Bancroft, Frederic. 1928. *Calhoun and the South Carolina Nullification Movement.* Baltimore: Johns Hopkins University Press.

Green, Fletcher M. 1930. *Constitutional Development in the South Atlantic States, 1776–1860: A Study in the Evolution of Democracy.* Chapel Hill: University of North Carolina Press.

Post, C. Gordon, ed. 1953. *A Disquisition on Government and Selections from the Discourse.* New York: Liberal Arts Press.

Spain, August O. 1951. *The Political Theory of John C. Calhoun.* New York: Bookman Associates.

DISEASES AND AFRICAN SLAVERY IN THE NEW WORLD

Diseases played a pivotal role in the economic history of African slavery in the Americas as well as in the experiences of Europeans in both Africa and the New World. The trade in African peoples caused the unforeseen exchange of pathogens that changed the path of history. The Old World pathogens brought to the Americas by both Africans and Europeans irreversibly changed the disease environment across the various climatic and geographic regions of the New World.

Diseases evolved in specific environments and locations, and humans residing in those environments developed resistance, both innate and acquired, to pathogens native to their locales. Evolutionary biology indicates that human populations that have survived for generations and millennia in a specific disease environment will be less susceptible to the diseases that predominate in their region and be more susceptible to diseases from different areas. Populations that lived in distinct locations endowed with different climates and geographies would develop different genetic endowments.

Diseases cull from populations those individuals whose genetic inheritance makes them susceptible to diseases that exist in their homelands. Genes that confer relative resistance to the pathogens of a location give humans that possess them a better chance of reproducing and, consequently, passing their genes on to future generations. The result is that those genes become more frequent in the population. An increased exposure to a variety of pathogens leads to greater genetic (inborn) resistance to a larger number of diseases in the population. In addition to developing innate resistance, endemic diseases result in acquired childhood immunities in the afflicted populations. Consequently, people of different origins have disparate reactions to a given pathogen because they have different acquired and innate immunities to diseases native to their places of birth and residence.

The nature of diseases and the reasons for their differential impact on different peoples were not understood during the centuries that the African slave trade and African slavery existed in the New World. Upon contact with peoples of other origins, Africans and people of African descent were less susceptible to pathogens that were "African" (endemic to Africa) and more susceptible to pathogens that were "European" (endemic to Europe). Conversely, Europeans and people of European descent were less susceptible to European pathogens and more susceptible to African pathogens. When people of African (European) descent were exposed to disease pathogens endemic to Europe (Africa), they experienced substantially higher rates of morbidity and mortality than did people who were native to that disease environment.

A number of diseases affected the economic history of Africans and Europeans in the Americas and Europeans in Africa. The "European" diseases that played an important role are regarded today as primarily cold-weather and/or childhood diseases such as upper-respiratory lung infections, tuberculosis, chicken pox, measles, mumps, pleurisy, influenza, pneumonia, and whooping cough. The important "African" diseases are primarily of tropical West African origin. They are malaria, yellow fever, dengue fever, hookworm, schistosomiasis, and other fevers and worm infections. Smallpox, which probably affected the greatest number of people, is in a class by itself.

Europeans involved in the slave trade came into contact with pathogens for which they had little or no prior exposure. Their susceptibility to pathogens from tropical West Africa (the area that supplied the vast majority of African slaves to the Americas) was so extraordinarily high that the papal ambassador to Portugal considered it a death sentence, and a violation of the concords that the papacy had with the Portuguese, if Catholic prelates were sent into exile there. Since Africa was a "white man's graveyard," direct contacts and trade in African slaves, especially in the interior of Africa, were carried on by African intermediaries, people of mixed African and European backgrounds, and the few hardy and lucky Europeans who survived the onslaught of African pathogens.

We have a number of reliable estimates for European mortality in Africa during Europe's involvement in the African slave trade. These estimates during the Europeans' first year in residence in tropical West Africa in the late seventeenth and early eighteenth centuries range from a low of 540 deaths per thousand per year to a high of 667 deaths per thousand. The estimated mortality rate for European sailors during the loading of African slaves off the coast of Africa in the late eighteenth century is 238 per thousand sailors per year; the comparable estimate for the enslaved Africans during loading is only 45.3 per thousand Africans. Estimates of the annual mortality rates for European troops in the British army stationed in West Africa during the early nineteenth century range from 483 to 683 per thousand European troops; the comparable estimate for African troops in the British army stationed in West Africa is only 32 deaths per thousand African troops. The reason for these mortality differences is the ethnically disparate reactions to diseases.

We have no reliable historical data for morbidity before the middle of the nineteenth century. However, present-day data on morbidity combined with historical data on mortality and our knowledge of the disease environment allow some well-founded conjectures about morbidity rates in the past. Some diseases, such as malaria and hookworm, had low case mortality rates but were virtually hyperendemic in Africa and parts of the New World. This means that the mortality rate would be an unrealistically low estimate for the incidence of these diseases. People were sickened by hookworm and malaria, but they were not killed by them.

The migrations of Africans and Europeans to the Americas set in motion interchanges of human and nonhuman organisms that fundamentally altered the ecology of the various climatic and geographic regions of America. Prior to contact with the Old World, the Americas were relatively disease free; after contact, the disease environments of the various climatic and geographic regions of the New World resembled their Old World counterparts. The imported diseases decimated the Amerindian populations who had little resistance to Old World pathogens. Tropical America became infested with pathogens from tropical West Africa, while the temperate regions of the New World were infested with the diseases of temperate Europe. The regional specificity of pathogens also affected the patterns of settlement in the New World. The eventual predominance of Africans in the tropics, and their greater relative numbers in the semitropical areas of the New World, and the predominance of Europeans in the temperate regions, were due to the altered biological environment.

Once the diseases reached beyond a critical threshold, the New World regional environments began to change. As one traveled further north in the Northern Hemisphere, or further south in the Southern Hemisphere, the disease environments evolved into one of predominantly cold-weather European diseases. Further south in the Northern Hemisphere (or further north in the Southern Hemisphere), the disease environment evolved into a mixture of cold-weather European and warm-weather African diseases. In the American tropics, the disease environment became "African," and, relative to Europeans, Africans lived longer and healthier lives in the tropics of the Americas. This made African labor economically more valuable than European labor in the tropics because it increased its lifetime productivity relative to Europeans. Over time, Africans and their descendants became the predominant source of unskilled agricultural labor in tropical America.

Once European pathogens became endemic to the temperate regions of the Americas, relative to Africans, Europeans lived longer and healthier lives there. This increased their lifetime productivity in the temperate regions, making European labor more economically valuable than African labor in those regions. Accordingly, Europeans and their descendants became the predominant source of unskilled agricultural labor in the temperate regions. In the American South, Europeans lived longer but less healthy lives than Africans. Africans were less susceptible to malaria and hookworm (both warm-weather diseases) relative to Europeans. These diseases struck during the economically critical (for agriculture) warm-weather months. Thus Africans were more productive and more valuable to planters in the U.S. South the longer the summer weather prevailed. The changed disease environment in the South created an environment that led to the concentration of African slavery there.

The growth of African slavery as a predominant source of labor in the South during the eighteenth century indicates that substantial differences in regional productivity between Africans and Europeans emerged during this period. Estimates of the mortality rate for Africans and African Americans (blacks) and Europeans and Euro-Americans (whites) indicate that blacks lived shorter and less healthy lives the further north they resided in the British mainland colonies. In Philadelphia, estimated annual mortality rates are 67 deaths per thousand for blacks and 46 deaths per thousand for whites. In Boston, the rates are 80 deaths per thousand for blacks and 32 deaths per thousand for whites. In the summer months in Philadelphia however, estimated annual mortality rates are 36 per thousand for blacks and 60 per thousand for whites. Mortality estimates for only cold-weather diseases are 88 per thousand for blacks and 47 per thousand for whites. For only warm-weather diseases, estimated rates are 59 deaths per thousand for blacks and 52 deaths per thousand for whites. Estimated mortality rates for troops in the British army stationed in the Caribbean during the early nineteenth century show similar ethnic differences. Again the reason for the differences is the disparate reactions to diseases.

A somewhat paradoxical result of African slavery is that it cursed both the enslaved Africans and the European migrants to the Americas. It was only after a significant African slave trade was established that the New World disease environment began to resemble that of the Old World. The changed environment made the American South a pesthouse and the New World tropics a graveyard for Europeans.

— *Philip R. P. Coelho and Robert A. McGuire*

For Further Reading

Coelho, Philip R. P. and Robert A. McGuire. 1997. "African and European Bound Labor in the British New World: The Biological Consequences of Economic Choices." *Journal of Economic History* 57 (March): 83–115.

Curtin, Philip D. 1968. "Epidemiology and the Slave Trade." *Political Science Quarterly* 83: 90–216.

Kiple, Kenneth F., and Virginia Himmelsteib King. 1981. *Another Dimension to the Black Diaspora.* New York: Cambridge University Press.

McNeill, William H. 1977. *Plagues and Peoples.* New York: Anchor Books.

DOMESTIC SLAVE TRADE

The domestic slave trade in the United States was the internal movement of slaves from the Upper South and eastern seaboard states to the cotton- and sugar-producing regions of the old Southwest. The trade's golden age followed the abolition of the international slave trade by Britain in 1807 and by the United States in 1808 and the subsequent expansion of the cotton region following the War of 1812 between Great Britain and the United States. From the 1790s through the 1820s, there was a gradual increase of slave trading southward from the Chesapeake Bay area and the Carolinas, with transportation of forty to fifty thousand slaves in the 1790s and one hundred fifty thousand by the 1820s.

As the South's slave system expanded into the old Southwest, the domestic trade moved south and west to accommodate it. Some states, and regions within states, changed from being net importers to net exporters of slaves. Georgia, which had imported slaves until the 1830s, became a net exporter of slaves in the 1850s. The 1830s through the 1850s witnessed further expansion of the trade, averaging nearly a quarter of a million movements, or 10 percent of the Upper South's slave population, each decade. Over 1 million American-born slaves were transported via the domestic trade.

The mechanisms for the domestic trade were well developed. Slave-trading firms (e.g., Franklin and Armfield) specializing in mass purchases of slaves operated throughout the South, but professional slave traders, operating independently of the trading firms, purchased either individually or in small groups most of the slaves transported in the trade. After purchasing

A father is separated from his family after being sold into slavery. (Library of Congress)

slaves in summer and early autumn, traders usually transported them south during fall and put them on the market in early winter at New Orleans, Louisiana, and Natchez, Mississippi, the major entrepôts for trade into the old Southwest. En route to their new homes, most slaves were transported in overland coffles, some containing three hundred slaves. In addition, an active water-borne trade flourished between the eastern seaboard ports (Baltimore, Alexandria, Norfolk, Richmond, and Charleston), and along the Mississippi River and its tributaries to the New Orleans and Natchez markets.

The domestic trade was one of the most hotly debated issues of the antebellum period. Abolitionists attacked the trade and its destruction of slave families as the penultimate evil of the South's slave system. They charged that the change from tobacco to wheat cultivation in the Chesapeake Bay region had revealed the unprofitable nature of slavery and led slaveowners in the Upper South to switch from plantation agriculture to slave breeding. Proslavery apologists countered that plantation owners treated their slaves paternalistically and encouraged the formation of slave families; most

interregional movements of slaves resulted from planter migrations west to more fertile lands; planters sold slaves only when economic hardships required them to do so; the trade was unprofitable; and most important, slave traders were pariahs within southern society.

Historians' examinations of the trade have challenged the abolitionists' contention that the Upper South was a breeding ground for slaves. Since most slaves were sold after age eight, it was unprofitable, and thus unlikely, that slaveowners bred their slaves solely for the purpose of selling them. However, abolitionists were correct in arguing that the trade destroyed slave families: in fact, nearly 20 percent of all slave marriages in the Upper South were destroyed by it. In addition, the number of slave families sold and transported as a unit accounted for less than 2 percent of the total trade. Between 1820 and 1860, slaveowners in the Upper South sold 10 percent of that region's teenage slave population to slave traders, the very age group necessary for the formation of slave families.

The proslavery defense of the domestic slave trade has not withstood the scrutiny of historical inquiry, as is demonstrated by Michael Tadman's *Speculators and Slaves* (1996). Tadman contends that the scale of the domestic slave trade destroyed black families more than any paternalistic sentiments toward encouraging families could have hoped to accomplish. The proslavery argument that most slaves were part of planter migrations was also specious; from the 1810s and 1820s on, 60 percent of the slaves transported to the Lower South were sold to slave traders. In addition, slaveowners willingly speculated in the domestic slave trade. Tadman argues that only 4 to 5 percent of slaves sold to traders were sold out of economic necessity. He notes that from the 1830s on, the sale of slaves to traders resulted in windfall profits for the seller, while profits from the resale of slaves often made traders some of the wealthiest men in their communities. As such, slave traders gained positions of influence, power, and respect within southern society and were hardly the pariahs proslavery apologists contended they were.

Historians continue to grapple with the significance of the domestic slave trade in the United States. Several historians, including Robert Fogel and Stanley Engerman, in *Time on the Cross* (1974), have discounted both the scale and significance of the trade, but Tadman's groundbreaking work convincingly argues that the domestic slave trade was a central characteristic of the antebellum South's slave system and offers profound insight into the functioning of that system.

— *John Grenier*

See also: Breeding of Slaves; Franklin and Armfield; Paternalism.

For Further Reading
Caldehead, William. 1972. "How Extensive Was the Border State Slave Trade? A New Look." *Civil War History* 18 (1): 42–55.

Kotlikoff, Laurence J., and Sebastian Pinera. 1977. "The Old South's Stake in the Inter-Regional Movement of Slaves, 1850–1860." *Journal of Economic History* 37 (2): 434–450.

Tadman, Michael. 1996. *Speculators and Slaves: Masters, Traders, and Slaves in the Old South.* Madison: University of Wisconsin Press.

Wesley, Charles H. 1942. "Manifests of Slave Shipments along the Waterways, 1808–1864." *Journal of Negro History* 27 (2): 155–174.

DOUGHFACES

During the antebellum era in the United States, the Democratic Party was the only true national political party that had broad-based appeal in both the North and the South. Both the Whig Party and the Republican Party, the respective rivals of the Democrats in consecutive periods, were largely recognized as regional political groups with singular interests. Whigs tended to be pro-commerce in their orientation as they ascribed to Henry Clay's "American System," and they supported the national bank, protective tariffs, and the use of federal dollars to support the internal improvements needed to fashion a commercial and industrial infrastructure for the young nation. When the Republican Party formed in 1854, it adopted the commercial provisions of the Whigs but combined this with a free soil view—a clear denunciation of supporting the spread of slavery into the newly acquired western territories.

Southern Democrats were unapologetic supporters of the institution of slavery, and they fought all congressional measures that might halt or limit the institution's existence and potential expansion. Although northern Democrats were less vociferous in their support of slavery, they did fear that the issue was so divisive it might tear the Union asunder. As a result, they generally voted with their southern brethren to defeat measures that might negatively impact the institution of slavery. For these reasons, Democrats, both southern and northern, supported the imposition of the infamous congressional "Gag Resolution" that effectively silenced debate on slavery concerns for eight years (1836–1844). The coalition did seem to break in 1846 as Congressman David Wilmot, a freshman Democrat from Pennsylvania, introduced a measure that would have prevented the expansion of slavery into any western lands that might be acquired from the then-ongoing war with Mexico. The Wilmot Proviso was never enacted, but it was a strange admixture of southern Democrats and so-called cotton Whigs alike who came together to oppose the measure.

The pejorative term *doughface* was used during the antebellum era to identify those northern politicians, particularly northern Democrats, who tended to have southern sympathies with respect to the issue of slavery. Reputedly, the term derived from statements that Virginia senator John Randolph of Roanoke made during the congressional debate concerning passage of the Missouri Compromise (1820). Randolph minced no words in decrying the pliable nature of his colleagues who supported the admission of Missouri as a slave state.

Historian Leonard L. Richards has identified more than three hundred northern congressmen who consistently voted with proslavery tendencies, thus exhibiting doughface leanings. The vast majority of this group consisted of northern Democrats. Although the term was used to identify *any* northern politician who held such views, the nickname was most often applied to the northern Democrats who served as president of the United States—especially Martin Van Buren, Franklin Pierce, and James Buchanan. Even Millard Fillmore, a northern Whig, was identified as a doughface for his support of the Compromise of 1850, which included passage of the notorious Fugitive Slave Act (1850).

When Congress approved the Compromise of 1850 legislation, the abolitionist poet Walt Whitman published "Song for Certain Congressmen" in the New York *Evening Post.* The poem was later published with the revised title of "Dough-Face Song." Whitman included the scathing lyrics:

*"We are all docile dough-faces,
They knead us with the fist,
They, the dashing southern lords,
We labor as they list."* (Whitman, 1892).

In 1856 the Republican supporters of John C. Frémont sang the raucous campaign song, "We Loathe Your Doughface Fillmore," to criticize the former president who was then seeking to return to the presidency as a candidate of the American (Know-Nothing) Party. Slavery had become such a politically charged issue by the mid-1850s that Fillmore's presumed pro-southern, proslavery leanings could not escape attention during the heat of the political campaign. Unfortunately, in an odd twist of fate, the 1856 campaign produced the election of James Buchanan—a more blatant doughface than Fillmore had ever been.

In 1854, Illinois Senator Stephen A. Douglas, chairman of the important Committee on Territories, used the concept of popular sovereignty as the basis of the controversial Kansas–Nebraska Act. The act allowed individual territories to determine whether or not they would allow slavery. (Library of Congress)

The proslavery tendencies of presidents Franklin Pierce and James Buchanan were readily apparent during the debate and passage of the Kansas–Nebraska Act (1854) and the subsequent unrest in "Bleeding Kansas" as factions did battle during the popular sovereignty campaign that would determine the status of slavery within the territory. Buchanan's eventual endorsement of the proslavery Lecompton Constitution demonstrated clearly that he favored the expansion of slavery into the formerly free territory of Kansas. During the final months of Buchanan's presidency, the southern states began to secede from the Union and the nation drifted toward civil war.

During the 1850s many abolitionists and their sympathizers began to charge that there existed a "Slave Power Conspiracy" in the United States that held undue power and influence within the highest reaches of the government. Adherents of this view believed that the northern doughface politicians had lost touch with their regional sensibilities and been swayed to accept an institution that was anathema to American national values. Although the charge of an organized conspiracy was dubious, it is certainly true that proslavery interests were well-served by the consistent voting patterns of those northern politicians who found it easier to condone slavery than to confront it.

— *Junius P. Rodriguez*

See also: Buchanan, James; Compromise of 1850; Democratic Party; Gag Resolution; Whig Party; Wilmot Proviso.

For Further Reading
LeMaster, J. R., and Donald D. Kummings, eds. 1998. *Walt Whitman: An Encyclopedia*. New York: Garland.
Richards, Leonard L. 2000. *The Slave Power: The Free North and Southern Domination, 1780–1860*. Baton Rouge: Louisiana State University Press.
Silbey, Joel. 2002. *Martin Van Buren and the Emergence of American Popular Politics*. Oxford, England: Rowman and Littlefield.
Whitman, Walt. 1963. *Prose Works*. Edited by Floyd Stovall. New York: New York University Press.

STEPHEN A. DOUGLAS (1813–1861)

Despite his small stature, Stephen A. Douglas cast a long shadow in the tumultuous political period before the American Civil War. Intelligent, charismatic, and politically astute, Douglas believed in the indissolubility of the U.S. Constitution, and the importance of political compromise in order to preserve the Union placing him at the forefront of the debate over slavery in the United States.

Born on a farm in Brandon, New York, on April 23, 1813, Stephen Arnold Douglas had a very typical childhood for youth of the period, even though his father, a physician, died shortly after Stephen's birth and his mother was forced to move in with her brother. As a child, he did farm chores, attended the local common school, and aspired to a better, more secure future. At fifteen, he apprenticed himself to a local cabinetmaker, a trade he practiced for two years before physical disability and a love of politics led him in new directions. He entered the Canandaigua Academy in 1830 and obtained a classical education at his own expense. He began to read law, recognizing that that profession was the traditional route to political office, but stringent requirements for the New York bar and rumors of opportunity in the West led him to Illinois in 1833. Once there, he was quickly admitted to the bar and became active in Democratic Party politics.

An avid Jacksonian, Douglas was more adept at politics than at law. In rapid succession, he was elected a state attorney, legislator, secretary of state, and superior court judge, and all the while, he honed his oratorical skills and strengthened his political connections. Elected to the U.S. Congress in 1843, he soon became a powerful force in national politics. He was dubbed "the little giant," a dual reference to his powerful oratory and his small stature. Douglas's most common political theme was popular democracy: he fervently believed in the ability of the people to make proper decisions through the electoral process. By the end of the Mexican War (1846–1848), he realized that slavery's westward expansion was the most volatile issue in American politics. In 1846, he voted against the Wilmot Proviso, which would have banned slavery in territory acquired from Mexico, because he believed that the question of whether or not to exclude slavery would be best made by voters through their territorial legislatures. This, according to Douglas, was the most democratic and least divisive way to cope with the issue.

Thus popular sovereignty, as the concept was called, came to dominate, and in some ways to haunt, Douglas's political philosophy for the rest of his life. Initially, this position gave him widespread popularity, as many voters and politicians were ambivalent on the issue of slavery expansion and appealing to the democratic ethos of the electorate seemed to be the best and least divisive solution. In 1854 Douglas, as chairman of the important Committee on Territories, used this principle as the basis of the controversial Kansas–Nebraska Act, which allowed each individual territory to determine its slave status. Although the debates surrounding the bill were bitterly divisive, the Kansas–Nebraska Act passed by a narrow margin. Through this important legislation, Douglas repealed the Missouri Compromise, which had regulated slavery's expansion since 1820. Douglas argued that popular sentiment, not accidents of geography, should determine the future of slavery in a newly admitted state.

That faith in democracy worked well in theory but poorly in practice. Nebraska voted to remain free, but Kansas erupted in civil war. The conflict in Kansas between free and slave-state advocates resulted in the destruction of property, many deaths, and two different constitutions. Slavery proponents produced the controversial Lecompton Constitution, which legalized slavery in Kansas, and soon gained the support of President James Buchanan and southern Democrats in Congress. Douglas, however, opposed the Lecompton Constitution, believing correctly that it did not represent the majority of Kansans. This stand tarnished Douglas in the eyes of many southern Democrats.

Although the crisis in Kansas occupied much of his time, Douglas faced political opposition at home. Free soil Democrats criticized Douglas for what they perceived as a willingness to sacrifice morality in pursuit of higher office. To them, popular sovereignty was a veiled mechanism to protect slave interests. In Illinois, the Republican Party quickly gained political power after 1856, uniting former Whigs and Free Soil Democrats to fight slavery's expansion, and Douglas became the target of the Republicans during the legislative race of 1858. The Senate seat, which the legislature would fill, became an important campaign issue, and candidates actively sought the office. This unusual campaign for the seat pitted Republican Abraham Lincoln against Douglas, and the issue of slavery defined the race. In a series of seven debates, the two candidates offered opposing views of slavery and slavery expansion. Lincoln favored restricting slavery's westward movement, realizing that the institution would eventually die out. Douglas held firm to the theory of popular sovereignty as the most democratic means to address slavery expansion. Although Lincoln condemned slavery on moral grounds, Douglas refused to do so, hoping to revive his reputation among disaffected southern Democrats. Douglas returned to the Senate, but the issue remained in the forefront of his activities.

In 1860 Douglas sought the Democratic presidential nomination. His opposition to the proslavery Lecompton Constitution made southerners suspicious of his true beliefs, however, and so they nominated John C. Breckinridge for the presidency while northerners backed Douglas. This sectional split destroyed Democratic hopes and allowed the Republican Abraham Lincoln to win the election. Douglas's belief in popular sovereignty as a remedy for slavery expansion, while true to his belief in popular democracy, dashed his hopes for national office. He died in 1861, shortly after Lincoln's inauguration.

— *Richard D. Starnes*

See also: Border War (1854–1859); Kansas–Nebraska Act; Lecompton Constitution; Lincoln–Douglas Debates; Popular Sovereignty; Wilmot Proviso.

For Further Reading
Johannsen, Robert. 1973. *Stephen A. Douglas.* New York: Oxford University Press.

Johannsen, Robert. 1989. *The Frontier, the Union, and Stephen A. Douglas.* Urbana: University of Illinois Press.

FREDERICK DOUGLASS (C. 1817–1895)

The most famous and influential former slave in the United States in the nineteenth century, Frederick Douglass rose from being a slave in Maryland to being a popular abolitionist lecturer, narrator of slavery, newspaper publisher, president of the Freedmen's Bank, and author of *Lessons of the Hour* (1892), a denunciation of lynching. The story of his confrontation with a "slave-breaker" is a classic moment in the literature of southern slavery, but Douglass's greater importance lies in the work he did after fleeing bondage in 1838.

Neither the fame nor the power could have been predicted from Douglass's origins as Frederick Bailey, house slave. But when he learned to read, while serving in a Baltimore home, he was inspired by a dialogue in the *Columbian Orator* that denounced the injustice of owning human beings. Determined to win his freedom, even while he was a fieldhand and caulker who was obliged to turn over his wages to his master, the intrepid "Fred" borrowed the free papers of a black sailor and went to Massachusetts. There, he was joined by his wife, took a new name, and joined the abolitionists around William Lloyd Garrison.

Though admired, Douglass was always controversial. His assurance and intelligence angered some whites—later, he and Garrison would be estranged by political differences—and he tangled with the "holiness" militant, Sojourner Truth, on religious grounds. Outstanding among fugitive and former slaves for his literary skills and the power of his address, Douglass was even charged with faking the role of former slave. These attacks persuaded him to commit his life story to print as the *Narrative of the Life of Frederick Douglass, an American Slave: Written by Himself* (1845).

With the publication of the book, Douglass grew famous but endangered. He sailed to Great Britain, where his power and insights were acclaimed, to lecture in England, Ireland, and Scotland. In 1846 English friends purchased Douglass from his legal master so that he could continue his campaign to establish racial justice in the United States. A year later, Douglass returned to the land of his birth and began a publishing career with the help of fellow activist, Martin Delany.

In Douglass's newspaper—first called the *North Star*, after the astronomical signpost to the free states, and later *Frederick Douglass' Paper*—the country's most famous former slave excoriated the practice of owning and trading in human beings and advocated women's rights. He also stoutly opposed the exclusion of blacks from white churches and the segregation of public

Frederick Douglass, a former slave, became the most influential African American leader in the abolitionist movement. (Library of Congress)

schools in the United States and analyzed the theory of separate accommodations for blacks and whites. In 1855 he rewrote and expanded his life story as *My Bondage and My Freedom* in order to distance himself from the white "handlers" who had limited his participation in the abolitionist cause.

Too brilliant to go unnoticed, Douglass was attacked for the *Narrative*'s harsh words about the Christianity of slaveholders; his dark view of racial justice in the United States, both before and after the slaves were freed; and his second marriage, to a white woman, in 1884. Verbally gifted and tirelessly dedicated, Douglass rode out such attacks to become the century's most feted black man. His important essays include "What to the Slave Is the Fourth of July?" (1852), which has been called the greatest abolitionist address, and "The Claims of the Negro, Ethnologically Considered" (1854).

Persuaded of the need for violent resistance by passage of the Fugitive Slave Act in 1850, Douglass was privy to John Brown's plans to initiate insurrection in the slave states. Douglass welcomed the onset of civil war and helped to recruit black troops with essays like

"Men of Color, To Arms!" (1863). Two of his four children served in the famous Massachusetts Fifty-fourth Regiment, but Douglass would come to scorn the injustices that the Union army meted out to black volunteers. "No war," he demanded, in 1864, "but an Abolition war; no peace but an Abolition peace; liberty for all, Chains for none; the black man a soldier in war, a laborer in peace; a voter at the South as well as at the North; America his permanent home, and all Americans his fellow-countrymen" (Foner, 1964). In August of the same year, Douglass proposed that black federal agents infiltrate the slaveholding states in order to incite the bolder slaves to revolt. Lincoln was apprized of the scheme, but it was never tried.

Douglass continued to fight for social reforms following emancipation. In the essay "We Are Not Yet Quite Free" (1869), he informed Americans: "We have been turned out of the house of bondage, but we have not yet been fully admitted to the glorious temple of American liberty. We are still in a transition stage." He concluded, "and the future is shrouded in doubt and danger" (Foner, 1964). Douglass defended the new rights of blacks during Reconstruction, remonstrated with Andrew Johnson for his pro-South policies, and cheered the passage of the Fifteenth Amendment, which gave black men the right to vote.

Douglass served as marshal of and recorder of deeds for the District of Columbia, minister-resident and consul-general to Haiti, and chargé d'affaires for Santo Domingo when its annexation to the United States was under discussion. In 1892 Haiti appointed him to represent the country at the Columbian Exposition in Chicago, and he used the opportunity to distribute copies of the pamphlet he cowrote with Ida B. Wells, "Why the Colored American Is Not in the World's Columbian Exposition." At the end of his life, when Douglass was asked what course young black Americans should follow, he replied: "Agitate! Agitate! Agitate!"

— *Barbara Ryan*

See also: Abolitionism in the United States; Autobiographies; Brown, John; Delany, Martin R.; Garrison, William Lloyd; Narratives; *North Star;* Truth, Sojourner.

For Further Reading
Douglass, Frederick. 1845. *Narrative of the Life of Frederick Douglass, an American Slave: Written by Himself.* Boston: American Anti-Slavery Office.
Douglass, Frederick. 1855. *My Bondage and My Freedom.* New York: Miller, Orton.
Foner, Philip S. 1964. *Frederick Douglass: A Biography.* New York: Citadel.
Quarles, Benjamin. 1968. *Frederick Douglass.* New York: Oxford University Press.

DRED SCOTT V. SANDFORD (1857)

Universally condemned as the U.S. Supreme Court's worst decision, *Dred Scott v. Sandford* emerged amid deep political crisis. Renewed sectional conflict over slavery's extension shattered the relative calm that accompanied the Compromise of 1850. With Kansas erupting into bloody conflict and South Carolina Representative Preston Brooks viciously assaulting Massachusetts Senator Charles Sumner, spring 1856 saw the slavery issue flare up once again and threaten the nation. In this political setting, the Supreme Court heard the first of two oral arguments in the *Dred Scott* case. In response to heightening tensions, Chief Justice Roger Taney sought to impose his own judicial solution to the problems posed by slavery's extension.

The case centered on whether a slave named Dred Scott became a free man by residing in free territory, and whether he had standing as a Missouri citizen to make that claim in federal court. What the case represented was something much different: The Court's 7-2 decision came to symbolize the danger of judicial ambition exceeding its grasp and reminds us that not all constitutional conflicts are amenable to judicial resolution.

The lawsuit arose from two series of events: the travels of Dred Scott with his owner, Dr. John Emerson, and congressional efforts to prevent slavery's expansion into western territories. Buying Scott in 1833, Emerson, an assistant surgeon in the U.S. army took him from St. Louis, Missouri, to Fort Armstrong in Illinois, a free state, where Emerson was stationed. Emerson, who complained repeatedly of his physical ailments and his military postings, was transferred to Wisconsin territory, in what is now Minnesota. Because of the Missouri Compromise (1820), the Wisconsin Territory (later called the Iowa Territory) was free of slavery.

During his stay in free territory, Scott married Harriet Robinson, but subsequently followed Emerson to Louisiana, and then back to Minnesota, as Emerson continued requesting transfers. Emerson married Eliza Irene Sanford in 1838 during his brief sojourn to Louisiana. In 1840 Mrs. Emerson, along with Dred and Harriet Scott, returned to St. Louis while her husband served in Florida during the Seminole War. Emerson's duties lasted two years before he was honorably discharged. Returning north, he tried establishing a private medical practice in Iowa but died shortly after leaving the army, possibly of syphilis.

In 1846 Dred and Harriet Scott first filed suit for freedom against Mrs. Emerson in St. Louis, claiming that their travels and residence (on two occasions) in

NOW READY:

THE

Dred Scott Decision.

OPINION OF CHIEF-JUSTICE ROGER B. TANEY,

WITH AN INTRODUCTION,

BY DR. J. H. VAN EVRIE.

ALSO,

AN APPENDIX,

BY SAM. A. CARTWRIGHT, M.D., of New Orleans,

ENTITLED,

"Natural History of the Prognathous Race of Mankind."

ORIGINALLY WRITTEN FOR THE NEW YORK DAY-BOOK.

THE GREAT WANT OF A BRIEF PAMPHLET, containing the famous decision of Chief-Justice Taney, in the celebrated Dred Scott Case, has induced the Publishers of the DAY-BOOK to present this edition to the public. It contains a Historical Introduction by Dr. Van Evrie, author of "Negroes and Negro Slavery," and an Appendix by Dr. Cartwright, of New Orleans, in which the physical differences between the negro and the white races are forcibly presented. As a whole, this pamphlet gives the *historical*, *legal*, and *physical* aspects of the "Slavery" Question in a concise compass, and should be circulated by thousands before the next presidential election. All who desire to answer the arguments of the abolitionists should read it. In order to place it before the masses, and induce Democratic Clubs, Democratic Town Committees, and all interested in the cause, to order it for distribution, it has been put down at the following low rates, for which it will be sent, free of postage, to any part of the United States. Dealers supplied at the same rate.

Rather than settle the sectional debate on slavery and its possible expansion into the territories, the *Dred Scott* decision intensified sectional animosity. (Library of Congress)

free territory had removed the condition of slavery. Legal precedent existed in Missouri to support their argument, and in 1850, after initial legal wrangling, a state judge declared Dred Scott (and by extension, his wife) free. But by this time, Mrs. Emerson had moved to Massachusetts, leaving her affairs in the care of her brother, John F. A. Sanford. Sanford appealed the ruling to Missouri's Supreme Court that overturned the lower court in 1852.

Shortly thereafter, Scott filed another suit, this time in federal court, against Sanford, claiming diversity ju-

risdiction because of Sanford's residence in New York. (The case is entitled *Dred Scott v. Sandford* because a clerk misspelled Sanford's name in the court records.) Sanford's attorneys claimed that Scott had no standing to sue in federal court quite simply because, being a slave, he was not a Missouri citizen. The judge ruled that Scott had standing to sue, but the jury nonetheless returned a verdict against him. Scott appealed the verdict to the U.S. Supreme Court.

The issues present before the Supreme Court were threefold: the question of Dred Scott's citizenship; the status of slaves living on free soil; and the constitutionality of federal legislation prohibiting slavery in the territories. Clearly, Taney did not have to rule on all three; he could have narrowly interpreted these issues and confined his ruling to Scott's standing to sue in federal court. But Taney wanted to impose a judicial solution on this intractable political problem. He hoped to resolve the constitutional status of slavery in the territories by deciding the issue in favor of southern interests, but in doing so, he solved too much and established the logical framework for the Civil War.

What, then, did Taney rule? First, he declared that blacks were not citizens of the United States, nor could states bestow U.S. citizenship on them. In a gross historical distortion, Taney claimed that blacks never had been citizens, nor could they ever become citizens. According to Taney, blacks, whether free or slave, were not part of the original popular sovereignty that created the United States. At the founding, wrote Taney, only whites were citizens. Moreover, states could not expand their definitions of citizenship to include free blacks because naturalization was a federal responsibility. Accordingly, no black had standing to sue as a U.S. citizen in federal courts.

This ruling, alone, ended Dred Scott's claim, but Taney, propelled by a need to resolve larger political issues, continued. He ruled, second, that slavery was a property right recognized by the Constitution. Therefore, Congress could not outlaw slavery in territories, nor could territories exclude slaveholders. As a consequence, the Missouri Compromise (1820) was unconstitutional. In short, all territories were slave territories. They were, Taney ruled, the common lands of the United States and therefore their governments must recognize the property rights of all U.S. citizens, including slaveholders.

Taney's decision drew on two important impulses within American political ideology: a doctrine of racial superiority and a doctrine of limited government. The first dimension of Taney's decision is obvious, but the second merits further attention. Taney argued that Congress cannot destroy through legislative action property that is recognized as legitimate throughout much of the nation. Because congressional powers are limited, their scope cannot be exceeded without violating the Founders' first concern, the protection of liberty. A government of limited powers is a government that protects liberty, but Taney transformed that doctrine by linking it with the defense and preservation of slavery. A popular sovereignty committed to slavery at the local level necessarily meant slavery at the national level if congressional powers were as limited as Taney claimed they were. For Taney, slavery was a necessary outcome of the conjunction of popular sovereignty and congressional limitations, and that linkage soon spurred major historical events.

Taney's decision lit a fire in the North. It dramatically fueled the Republican Party's growth and convinced its members that slavery, in addition to being morally wrong, was an assault on the North and the cause of liberty. Rather than resolving the contradiction between slavery and liberty that lay at the heart of the American founding, Taney's decision propelled the nation headlong into a bloody struggle to redefine the terms of that bitter compromise. In the wake of the Civil War, the nation overturned Taney's decision by ratifying the Thirteenth and Fourteenth Amendments, which ended slavery throughout the United States, explicitly created national citizenship, and provided for the equal protection of the laws for all persons.

John F. A. Sanford died in an insane asylum less than two months after the decision came down, and Dred Scott was manumitted shortly thereafter. He lived only sixteen months as a free man, before dying of tuberculosis.

— *Douglas S. Reed*

See also: Brooks–Sumner Affair; Compromise of 1850; Missouri Compromise; Taney, Roger B.

For Further Reading

Allen, Austin. 2004. "The Political Economy of Blackness: Citizenship, Corporations, and Race in Dred Scott." *Civil War History* 50 (3): 229–260.

Ehrlich, Walter. 1979. *They Have No Rights: Dred Scott's Struggle for Freedom.* Westport, CT: Greenwood.

Fehrenbacher, Don E. 1978. *The Dred Scott Case.* New York: Oxford University Press.

Whittington, Keith E. 2001. The Road Not Taken: Dred Scott, Judicial Authority, and Political Questions. *Journal of Politics* 63 (2): 365–391.

SYLVIA DUBOIS (C. 1768–1889)

Known for her quick tongue and aggressive behavior, Sylvia Dubois secured freedom from slavery through physical resistance, an avenue rarely available to women. Her militant stance against slavery demonstrates the multiple forms of resistance employed by slave women. In addition, her experience in slavery suggests the dynamic relationship between African American women slaves and their mistresses.

Dubois was born a slave on New Jersey's Sourland Mountain sometime between 1768 and 1789. Her mother, Dorcas Compton, purchased her freedom with financing from Dominicus Dubois when Sylvia was two years of age. When Compton failed to repay the loan, however, she and her children became Dubois's slaves. In her efforts to secure her freedom, Compton was forced to leave her children with Dubois in Great Bend, Pennsylvania, as she sought work elsewhere.

Left without her mother's protection, young Sylvia suffered incredible abuse from her mistress, Mrs. Dubois, who used a variety of tools to abuse the young girl. Sylvia asserted, "She'd level me with anything she could get hold of—club, stick of wood, tongs, fire-shovel, knife, axe, hatchet, anything that was handiest" (Larison, 1988). Yet, after enduring years of torture, Sylvia maintained her will and eventually triumphed over Mrs. Dubois.

As a young girl, Sylvia determined to defend herself physically from her mistress's abuse when she became older and stronger. Sylvia finally seized her opportunity when Mrs. Dubois struck her publicly. Sylvia recognized the advantage offered by an audience and struck her mistress in return. Both Mrs. Dubois and the onlookers were stunned by her action. Sylvia then warned the crowd against attacking her, declaring, "I smacked my fist at 'em, and told 'em to wade in if they dared and I'd thrash every devil of 'em" (Larison, 1988). Sylvia realized the crowd would be cautious of a black woman who was courageous, or insane, enough to strike her mistress in public. The fact that she was not attacked and escaped to the next town proved her surmise correct.

When Sylvia's master learned of her resistance and flight, he summoned her back to Great Bend and freed her on the condition that she take her child and leave the area. She moved to Flagtown, New Jersey, and worked until she inherited land on Sourland Mountain upon her father's death. She died on the mountain in 1889.

Although the date of Sylvia's birth is unclear, she was an expressive and articulate centenarian when she related her life story to Dr. Cornelius Wilson Larison in 1883. Sylvia Dubois related her experiences in humorous language that displays her ability—common to many slave women—to view and represent past experiences with wit and levity. Unfortunately, many depictions of slave women produced by white writers are absurd and so hold slave women up to ridicule and diminish their humanity. Contrarily, Dubois's narrative humor substantiates her authority and celebrates resistance. Rather than detract from the seriousness of the situation, this humorous attitude reinforces her agency and triumph, and allows readers to laugh with, rather than at, black women.

— *Do Veanna S. Fulton*

For Further Reading

Larison, Cornelius Wilson. 1988. *Sylvia Dubois: A Biografy of the Slav Who Whipt Her Mistres and Gand Her Freedom.* Edited by Jared C. Lobdell. New York: Oxford University Press.

W. E. B. DUBOIS (1868–1963)

William Edward Burghardt DuBois was the first professionally trained African American historian to examine slavery "scientifically." He devoted his life as a historian, sociologist, editor, and polemicist to explaining slavery's long-term negative influence on blacks and whites and race relations in the United States.

Raised among only a handful of blacks in western Massachusetts, as a youth W. E. B. DuBois had little firsthand contact with ex-slaves, their history, or their culture. It was when he was studying at Nashville's Fisk University in the 1880s that he became familiar with and intrigued by the folk traditions of the former slaves. After studying historical methods at the University of Berlin (1892–1894), he finished his doctorate at Harvard University under Albert Bushnell Hart, completing what became his landmark dissertation, *The Suppression of the African Slave-Trade to the United States of America, 1638–1870,* in 1896. The dissertation was the first volume published in the series, Harvard Historical Studies.

In that study, DuBois argued that the white Founding Fathers, both northern and southern, never were seriously committed to ending the Atlantic slave trade in 1808. Driven by economic self-interest and racism, whites imported more than two hundred fifty thousand Africans into the United States between the congressional prohibition on slave importations and 1862. The 1808 prohibition, DuBois noted with sarcasm, was "probably enforced as the people who made it wished it enforced." Coastal slave patrollers performed their tasks loosely, especially in the 1850s when some southern partisans were lobbying to reopen the At-

African American historian W. E. B DuBois examined slavery and its long-term effects on blacks, whites, and on race relations in the United States. (Library of Congress)

lantic slave trade. According to DuBois, the lax control of slave smuggling was part and parcel of white Americans' persistent "bargaining, truckling, and compromising" with slavery and its proponents.

Although DuBois exaggerated the number of Africans brought surreptitiously into the United States after 1808 and undervalued the natural rate of reproduction among slaves, his use of West African port records and other primary sources set a high standard for later studies of the transatlantic slave trade. He was also the first scholar to emphasize the broad panic that Toussaint L'Ouverture's 1791 Haitian slave revolt caused throughout the Atlantic rim. Alone among contemporary works, DuBois's path-breaking *Suppression of the African Slave-Trade* sympathized openly with the plight of the expatriated Africans. He viewed with scorn white racism and the complicity of white officials at every level in the transatlantic slave trade.

In his many other writings, DuBois both explored particular features of American slavery and underscored slavery's direful legacy for race relations in the

United States. In *The Philadelphia Negro* (1899), he remarked that the powerful, polygamous slave family, "with all its shortcomings," provided more protection for black women than "the promiscuous herding" of the U.S. slave plantation.

In an article published in *Southern Workman* in 1901, DuBois uncovered important connections between African building design and technology and the first homes of American slaves. They shared an essential form, he insisted, which meant windowless huts with woven walls and thatched roofs positioned around four posts. As "the cold brutality of slavery" increased, however, the slave cabins came to reflect the harshness of the institution.

In his classic work, *The Souls of Black Folk* (1903), DuBois analyzed the African contributions to African American slave religion. The slaves, DuBois explained, drew upon "the resources of Heathenism"—exorcism, witchcraft, Obi worship, spells, and blood sacrifices—to resist their captivity. The slave drew upon religion as a weapon to resist "the dark triumph of Evil over him." The slave preacher, according to DuBois, provided a vital cultural link between the slaves' African background, their ability to survive the hardships of slavery, and their preparation for the afterlife. The slaves, DuBois said, also drew upon their African-derived cultural forms, especially music, to withstand the horrors of enslavement.

In his popular book *The Negro* (1915), DuBois also championed the cultural achievements of past and contemporary Africans in art, industry, political organization, and religion. Three years later, DuBois attacked Ulrich B. Phillips, who then reigned as the master of slave historiography. According to DuBois, Phillips's *American Negro Slavery* (1918) was "curiously incomplete and unfortunately biased." DuBois attacked Phillips both for his inability to treat blacks as "ordinary human beings" and for his unwillingness to see growth and change in blacks from the fifteenth to the twentieth centuries.

In later books, articles, and editorials, DuBois missed few opportunities to identify slavery as the source of the "veil" of racism that envelops society in the United States. For over six decades, DuBois eloquently and powerfully condemned slavery for denying the descendants of the slaves true freedom and justice.

— *John David Smith*

See also: Phillips, Ulrich Bonnell.

For Further Reading

Byerman, Keith E. 1994. *Seizing the Word: History, Art, and Self in the Work of W. E. B. DuBois.* Athens: University of Georgia Press.

Lewis, David Levering. 1993. *W. E. B. DuBois: Biography of a Race.* New York: Henry Holt.

Smith, John David. 1991. *An Old Creed for the New South: Proslavery Ideology and Historiography, 1865–1818.* Athens: University of Georgia Press.

Zamir, Shamoon. 1995. *Dark Voices: W.E.B. DuBois and American Thought, 1888–1903.* Chicago: University of Chicago Press.

JOHN MURRAY, FOURTH EARL OF DUNMORE (1730–1809)

On November 14, 1775, Virginia governor John Murray (fourth earl of Dunmore) offered freedom to slaves and indentured servants willing to desert rebel masters and join "his Majesty's troops . . . for more speedily reducing the Colony to a proper sense of their duty" (Selby, 1977). The proclamation was tactical, not humanitarian. Lord Dunmore needed soldiers and hoped to awe colonists into obedience; he did not wish to enact general emancipation.

Nonetheless, hundreds of slaves sought and obtained liberty by responding to his call. Dunmore reinforced the slaves' belief that a British victory provided the best hope for liberty. Consequently, his actions galvanized slave resistance on the eve of the American Revolution and alarmed and angered slaveholders. Like no previous measure, it alienated the southern colonies and spurred their drive for independence from Great Britain.

The decision to arm slaves itself reflected the collapse of imperial authority in Virginia, which Dunmore had exacerbated by seizing gunpowder from the public magazine in Williamsburg in April 1775 and weeks later taking refuge on a man-of-war stationed in the York River. Dunmore had exploited the colonists' fear of a slave revolt during the crisis by threatening to arm blacks and Indians if colonists resisted British rule and by receiving on board his fleet nearly one hundred escaped slaves in the fall of 1775.

After defeating colonial militia at Kemp's Landing outside of Norfolk on November 14, Dunmore published his proclamation, declaring the colony in rebellion and calling upon all Virginians, including the rebels' slaves, to rally to the King's standard. Three hundred slaves joined Dunmore within a week of the proclamation; he may have recruited as many as fifteen hundred in succeeding months. The threat of punishment and the difficulty of reaching the flotilla from land discouraged others. Most who reached Dunmore were employed as soldiers in his "Ethiopian Regiment," with many dressed in uniforms bearing the inscription Liberty to Slaves.

The Ethiopian regiment met a tragic end. Defeat at Great Bridge in December 1775, where black soldiers composed nearly half of his troops, drove Dunmore to the James River, away from provisions and access to loyalists. Smallpox then decimated Dunmore's troops in the spring and summer of 1776 at Tucker's Point and Gwynn Island. The 300 remaining black troops went with Dunmore to New York in 1776, and some emigrated as free persons to Nova Scotia and England in 1783.

Dunmore's initiative had varied consequences. In arming slaves, the governor had acted on his own, and the controversial measure never received official approval, although slaves would figure significantly in British military strategy in the American Revolution. Commanders later granted liberty to slaves who defected from rebels, and more than ten thousand escaped to British lines during the American Revolution. They were then employed as pioneers and military laborers, and the British army honored some of the fugitives' claim to freedom at the conclusion of the war.

In 1782, after Cornwallis's surrender at Yorktown, Dunmore and British offices in South Carolina proposed to recruit 10,000 black troops for service in the low country areas of coastal Georgia and the Carolinas and the Floridas. The British government, however, would not authorize the establishment of black regulars until the Haitian Revolution and the Napoleonic Wars more than a decade later.

— *Christopher L. Brown*

See also: American Revolution; Black Loyalists.

For Further Reading

Frey, Sylvia. 1991. *Water from the Rock: Black Resistance in a Revolutionary Age.* Princeton, NJ: Princeton University Press.

Quarles, Benjamin. 1961. *The Negro in the American Revolution.* Chapel Hill: University of North Carolina Press.

Selby, John. 1977. *Dunmore.* Williamsburg, VA: Virginia Independence Bicentennial Commission.

ANDREW DURNFORD (1800–1859)

As the son of a white man and a free woman of color, Andrew Durnford held a complex place in the society of antebellum Louisiana. In 1828 he purchased a large piece of property in Plaquemines Parish on a bend of the Mississippi River about 33 miles from New Orleans and built the St. Rosalie sugar plantation. St. Rosalie would become the home of Andrew; his wife Marie Charlotte Remey, a free woman of color; their children, Thomas, Rosema, and Andrew, Jr.; and more than seventy-five black slaves.

The notion of a black slaveholder in antebellum Louisiana strikes us today as an oddity, but in reality it was not that uncommon. In one parish in Louisiana there were eight black planters who owned a total of 297 slaves, and in that region of the state in 1830 one out of every four free black families owned slaves. The free black population in Louisiana was rather sizable, but of those who did own slaves, most tended to own only one or two, and these were often members of their own family. Few had the relative wealth that Durnford had.

Very little is known about Durnford's early life, and most of what we do know of him is derived from letters written to his friend and mentor John McDonogh, a wealthy white businessman who held, for his time, enlightened views regarding race and slavery. McDonogh was a close friend of Thomas Durnford, Andrew's father, and when Thomas died, his friendship was extended to Andrew. Through McDonogh, Durnford remained informed of the American Colonization Society's activities and was introduced to the British abolitionist Elliot Cresson. Durnford's letters to McDonogh are numerous and provide information about St. Rosalie's operations and insights into the psychology of a man who disliked the institution of slavery, yet maintained and profited from his position as a mulatto plantation master.

Although there is every indication that Durnford was relatively humane in the treatment of his slaves, he was first and foremost a businessman, and his letters reveal the pressures of successfully operating St. Rosalie. Durnford mentions an occasion when he severely threatened his slaves in order to get them to do their duties. He also revealed anger over a runaway slave and the flogging of another. Although Durnford appears to have been conscientious in seeing to his slaves' material needs, he was not above using coercion to ensure the plantation's profitability.

Perhaps in order to come to grips with his place in society, Durnford developed an interest in philosophy. A letter to McDonogh dated January 12, 1844, provides this telling statement on Durnford's view of society: "I think society is made up of two distinct parts. On the one hand wolves and foxes, and on the other hand lambs and chickens providing food for the former. In the forest a lion recognizes another lion, tiger does not make another tiger its prey" (Whitten, 1981). Believing the abolition of slavery to be an unattainable goal in his lifetime, Durnford suppressed his idealism and used the existing system for his own benefit.

— *Mark Cave*

See also: American Colonization Society; Black Slave-owners; Louisiana; Mulattoes.

For Further Reading

Schweninger, Loren. 1990. "Prosperous Blacks in the South, 1790–1880." *American Historical Review* 95: 31–56.

Sterkx, H. E. 1972. *The Free Negro in Ante-Bellum Louisiana.* Cranbury, NJ: Fairleigh Dickinson University Press.

Whitten, David O. 1981. *Andrew Durnford: A Black Sugar Planter in Antebellum Louisiana.* Natchitoches: Northwestern State University of Louisiana.

EDUCATION

On the issue of slave education, southern whites were of divided mind. Prominent leaders such as James Henry Hammond and John C. Calhoun warned of dire consequences for white southern society if slaves were taught to read and write. Despite these warnings, and for various social, economic, and religious reasons, some whites chose to teach their slaves. Slave education, perhaps more than any other issue, represented the ideological duplicity of the South's slaveowning class. Slaves themselves recognized the importance of education, perhaps because it was normally kept from them. For those in bondage, knowledge represented empowerment and a type of freedom they did not enjoy in their daily lives.

Organized efforts at slave education began as early as the seventeenth century. A minority of masters, realizing that a literate slave would be more useful and worth more in the event of sale, took a keen interest in teaching slaves to read and write. Others had more altruistic motivations. Christian missionaries, usually Anglicans, believed that education was a key component of a slave's religious salvation. Unless slaves were educated, they could not read the Bible, understand and appreciate the liturgy, and never be truly saved. Through organizations like the Society for the Propagation of the Gospel in Foreign Parts, Anglican missionaries established schools, trained slave teachers, and taught hundreds of slave students basic literacy and the tenets of the Christian faith. Such efforts met with some success. One such school in Charleston had an enrollment of seventy slaves in 1755 and enjoyed the support of several prominent leaders despite legal prohibitions against such activities. Other denominations shared Anglican views on slave education. Puritans in New England and Quakers in Pennsylvania agreed that literacy was a key component in the religious indoctrination of slaves and made some organized attempts to educate them. Therefore, before the American Revolution, some masters and religious leaders called for the education of slaves, but these whites were definitely in the minority.

Still, the majority of slaveowners thought such efforts were at best a waste of time because they believed that slaves lacked the ability to absorb formal education. African slaves were viewed as ignorant, primitive, and unworthy to receive formal education, and by educating them, masters believed they were acknowledging that slaves were more than chattel to be bought and sold like livestock. Slaves, in their view, were meant for work and little else, and a life of the mind was unnecessary in the rice, cotton, and tobacco fields. Moreover, many people feared that literacy would make slaves more difficult to control, for it was feared that educated slaves would become leaders in the slave quarters and would use their skills to foment rebellion.

The 1739 Stono Rebellion in South Carolina led to severe restriction of slave activities in that colony. The colonial assembly passed laws that prohibited slaves from assembling, traveling without written permission, possessing firearms, and engaging in other actions that were, from the perspective of many whites, threatening. Teaching slaves to read and write was also outlawed, though this section of the law was enforced only sporadically. Georgia enacted a similar law against slave education in 1770, and all southern states had followed suit by 1803. In some ways, whites were justified in fearing the effects of educated slaves on the social order. Many of the future leaders of slave rebellions, such as Denmark Vesey and Nat Turner, were literate, and literate slaves often held positions of responsibility on plantations and elsewhere.

Slaves themselves thirsted for knowledge and the intellectual liberation literacy provided, but relatively few slaves were afforded the opportunity to learn to read. Masters most frequently taught favorite slaves, usually house servants, and often they taught their own mulatto children. White children, who received instruction from private tutors or at local academies, might also impart their newly found knowledge to slave playmates. Such cases were the exception, however, as only about 5 percent of the southern slave population was functionally literate. Usually, slaves were educated if it was in the master's economic interest to do so. This small cadre of educated slaves provided ministers, artisans, and other leaders to the slave community. In some cases, slaves kept account books, tracked crop production, and managed plantations, tasks they were delegated because of their literacy. After 1865, these educated slaves emerged as the first generation of black politicians.

Despite the relatively small number of literate slaves, virtually all desired to learn to read. Religion was one of the most important forces driving this quest for literacy. Religion, as historians such as Eugene Genovese and John Blassingame have demonstrated, was one of the key elements of life in the slave community. Although slave preachers were sometimes literate, many were not, and they wanted to be able to read the Bible so as to better minister to their congregations. The laity wanted to read the Bible for themselves in order to partake of God's word firsthand. Literacy allowed blacks to free themselves from a theology imposed by whites and to interpret the Scriptures for themselves.

There was more to slave education than basic literacy. More slaves acquired vocational skills as a result of the work their masters assigned them. Male slaves became forge operators, blacksmiths, woodworkers, tanners, and stockmen as well as other skilled and semi-skilled trades. Women had more limited opportunities, but many became seamstresses, weavers, or midwives. This type of vocational education allowed some slaves to earn cash with which to purchase their freedom, and to develop trades that would help them adapt to harsh economic realities following emancipation.

— *Richard D. Starnes*

See also: American Missionary Association; Hammond, James H.

For Further Reading

Blassingame, John. 1972. *The Slave Community: Plantation Life in the Antebellum South.* New York: Oxford University Press.

Cornelius, Janet. 1991. *"Where I Can Read My Title Clear?" Literacy, Slavery, and Religion in the Antebellum South.* Columbia: University of South Carolina Press.

Genovese, Eugene. 1974. *Roll, Jordan, Roll: The World the Slaves Made.* New York: Pantheon Books.

Webber, Thomas. 1978. *Deep Like the Rivers: Education in the Slave Quarter Community, 1831–1865.* New York: Norton.

STANLEY M. ELKINS (B. 1925)

Born in Boston, Massachusetts, in 1925, Stanley M. Elkins earned his Ph.D. at Columbia University in

1959 and published one of the most provocative works on slavery, *Slavery: A Problem in American Institutional and Intellectual Life,* in the same year. The book stimulated debate among historians of slavery throughout the 1960s.

Influenced by the pathbreaking works of Gilberto Freyre and Frank Tannenbaum, and dissatisfied with Kenneth M. Stampp's method in *The Peculiar Institution* (1956), Elkins presented a richly comparative, analytical, and thought-provoking book. In his opinion, "Stampp, locked in his struggle with Ulrich Phillips," proved unable "to disengage his mind from the debate of which he, Phillips, and [James Ford] Rhodes, were all a part and which they had taken over from the proslavery and antislavery debaters of ante-bellum times." Distancing himself from the old debate, Elkins looked beyond questions of slavery's morality and racial inferiority and considered what he deemed slavery's deleterious psychological damage on African Americans. To do so, Elkins used interdisciplinary approaches, including comparative history, role psychology, and interpersonal theory.

Elkins argued that slaves in Spanish and Portuguese America experienced a milder, more "open" enslavement than those in British America. This difference resulted, he said, from the Catholic and hierarchical traditions of Latin America as contrasted with the Protestant, locally autonomous, and "unrestrained" capitalist orientation of British America. Slaves in British North America lived in a "closed" system, one in which "virtually all avenues of recourse for the slave, all lines of communication to society at large, originated and ended with the master."

So oppressive and so brutal was slavery in British America that slaves there often developed "Sambo" personalities. White southerners defined "Sambo" as "docile but irresponsible, loyal but lazy, humble but chronically given to lying and stealing; his behavior was full of infantile silliness and his talk inflated with childish exaggeration."

In one of his more controversial statements, Elkins argued that the slaves' "Sambo" personality was analogous to behavior exhibited by Nazi concentration camp inmates during World War II. In his opinion, both slaves and death camp dwellers suffered psychic shock and became both dependent and infantilized. "The individual, consequently, for his very psychic security, had to picture his master in some way as the 'good father,' even when, as in the concentration camp, it made no sense at all. But why should it not have made sense for many a simple plantation Negro whose master did exhibit, in all the ways that could be expected, the features of the good father who was really 'good'?"

Elkins's provocative *Slavery* sparked much criticism in the 1960s, criticism that was directed at the author's method and conclusions. Though richly theoretical, suggestive, and imaginative, the book lacked thorough grounding in the blacks' day-to-day lives and variety of responses to their enslavement. Elkins also failed to recognize that slaves might have had more than one significant person in their lives. Nor did Elkins come to grips satisfactorily with the notion that what he deemed "Samboization" might have been the slaves' simple manipulation of the system that kept them in chains. Stampp, for instance, remarked in 1952 that "there were plenty of opportunists among the Negroes who played the role assigned to them, acted the clown, and curried the favor of their masters in order to win the maximum rewards within the system" (Lane, 1971).

But it was Elkins's concentration camp analogy that drew the most fire. According to the historian John W. Blassingame, Hitler's death camps "differed significantly from the plantation." "If," he added, "some men could escape infantilism in a murderous institution like the concentration camp, it may have been possible for the slave to avoid becoming abjectly docile in a much more benign institution like the plantation" (Lane, 1971). Still other critics faulted Elkins's thesis that Latin American institutions protected the slaves from the victimization that sealed their fate in British North America.

The debate over Elkins's book ignited a spirited discourse that, according to Peter J. Parish, represents "the supreme example of a book which has exercised a profound influence, not by the persuasiveness of its arguments, but above all through the questions it raised, the massive critical response it elicited, and the new work it stimulated" (Parish, 1989). Determined to refute Elkins, many historians of the 1970s examined the various slave responses to oppression, including overt and covert resistance, community formation, familial solidarity, and folk and cultural expression, and some scholars probed the nature of slave treatment by examining other comparative systems of unfree labor. Elkins's book, then, redirected the attention of historians away from the behavior of the masters toward the ways the slaves withstood and overcame their captivity.

— *John David Smith*

See also: Phillips, Ulrich Bonnell; Sambo Thesis; Stampp, Kenneth M.

For Further Reading

Gilmore, Al-Tony, ed. 1978. *Revisiting Blassingame's The Slave Community: The Scholars Respond.* Westport, CT: Greenwood Press.

Kolchin, Peter. 1993. *American Slavery, 1619–1877.* New York: Hill and Wang.

Lane, Ann J., ed. 1971. *The Debate over Slavery: Stanley Elkins and His Critics.* Urbana: University of Illinois Press.

Parish, Peter J. 1989. *Slavery: History and Historians.* New York: Harper and Row.

WILLIAM ELLISON (1790–1861)

A cotton-gin maker and southern planter, William Ellison was born April Ellison in South Carolina. His mother was a slave and his father a white man, probably his first owner, Robert Ellison. For the first twenty-six years of his life, April was a slave. Perhaps because of his parentage, he was apprenticed to a trade rather than sent to the fields, and the training he received making and repairing cotton gins served him well. During his apprenticeship, which extended over fourteen years, April learned to read and write and acquired basic bookkeeping and managerial skills.

In April 1816, April Ellison appeared in the Fairfield District Courthouse with his owner to formalize his freedom, purchased with money he saved while working for the cotton-gin maker to whom he had been apprenticed. Shortly after his emancipation, Ellison moved to Stateburg, South Carolina, and established his own cotton-gin business. Within a year, Ellison had purchased the freedom of his wife and daughter; their subsequent children were born free. In 1820 April Ellison legally changed his name from April to William, symbolizing his passage from slave to freeman.

Also in 1820, William Ellison purchased the first of his many slaves. Ownership of slaves attached him and his family to the dominant class of the South and helped to preserve his family's greatest asset, their freedom. By becoming a planter and a slaveowner, William Ellison was conforming to the ways and norms of that particular era. His slaves were said to be the worst fed and worst clothed in the vicinity, and he had a reputation as a harsh master. Evidence strongly suggests that Ellison sold young slave girls, probably because they were of little use to his cotton-gin business, to raise the money needed to buy more adult slaves and additional land. He employed slave-hunters to recapture escaped slaves, and he never freed any of his slaves. Interestingly, all of Ellison's slaves were listed in the records as black; none was ever listed as mulatto, creating a distance between his family and his slaves. Color differentiated the master from his slaves.

William Ellison ruled his extended family with complete patriarchal authority. All four Ellison children brought their spouses home to live in their father's household. In 1850 the sprawling family compound contained sixteen family members spanning three generations. His sons did not own the houses they lived in or the shops where they worked. William Ellison gave his sons only a token of economic independence; they had little opportunity to accumulate their own wealth. Although the children expected to inherit their father's wealth, until then they lived and worked almost entirely under their father's direction.

When William Ellison died on December 5, 1861, he was the wealthiest free black in South Carolina and one of wealthiest free blacks in the South. Indeed, by 1835, Ellison was prosperous enough to purchase the home of Stephen D. Miller, former governor of South Carolina, which Ellison named Wisdom Hall. Ellison owned approximately sixty-three slaves and more than 900 acres of land. He had gained the respect of his white neighbors, symbolized when the Church of the Holy Cross permitted the Ellison family a pew on the main floor of the church, behind the rows of white worshipers and below the gallery where other free blacks and slaves sat.

During the American Civil War, the Ellisons made efforts to prove themselves loyal to the Confederate cause. They converted their land entirely to food production, offering corn, fodder, and bacon to the Confederate army. They purchased treasury notes and Confederate bonds. In 1863 William Ellison's grandson, John Wilson Buckner, enlisted in the Confederate army. He was wounded in action on July 12, 1863 at Battery Wagner.

For the Ellisons, emancipation resulted in the loss of their labor supply and slave capital. This loss affected them much as it did white southern planters. The subsequent breakdown of the plantation system further impacted members of the Ellison family and they never recouped their losses or regained their prosperity or stature after the war. In 1879 the Ellisons harvested a mere six bales of cotton. The value of their land plunged, and they were forced to sell off much of their once large landholdings.

— *Sharon A. Roger Hepburn*

See also: Black Slaveowners.

For Further Reading

Berlin, Ira. 1974. *Slaves without Masters: The Free Negro in the Antebellum South.* New York: Pantheon Books.

Johnson, Michael P., and James L. Roark. 1984. *Black Masters: A Free Family of Color in the Old South.* New York: Norton.

Johnson, Michael P., and James L. Roark, eds. 1984. *No Chariot Let Down: Charleston's Free People of Color on the Eve of the Civil War.* New York: Norton.

1864 engraving of the "Proclamation of Emancipation" had an eagle and U.S. flags over a portrait of Abraham Lincoln and a composite of seven slavery scenes. President Lincoln issued the Emancipation Proclamation on January 1, 1863. (Library of Congress)

Wikramanayake, Marina. 1973. *A World in Shadow: The Free Black in Antebellum South Carolina.* Columbia: University of South Carolina Press.

EMANCIPATION PROCLAMATION

On January 1, 1863, President Abraham Lincoln issued the Emancipation Proclamation freeing all slaves in territories still rebelling against the federal government of the United States. The decision to proclaim slaves of the Confederate States free took years of agonizing deliberations and debates. In fact, from the onset of the Civil War, there were speculations about the possibility of emancipating slaves. Abolitionists, black and white, who supported the Republican Party's antislavery platform, envisaged the abolition of slavery, but northern Democrats proved hesitant and reluctant. Despite his antislavery sentiments, Lincoln himself was not enthusiastic about making slavery the focus of a war he saw as essentially meant to protect and preserve the Union. Cautious about emancipation, he was also uncertain if his executive authority gave him jurisdiction over slavery. And, too, he was concerned about the loyalty of such border states as Maryland, Kentucky, and Missouri. Consequently, Lincoln prevaricated, and opposed and reversed decisions of Union officers who had emancipated the slaves who flocked to their command.

When Lincoln eventually decided on emancipation, he proposed two plans. The first was for gradual emancipation with compensation to slaveowners for their property losses. The second was a plan to colonize free blacks, believing that the two races could not coexist on the basis of equality and freedom. In fall 1861 Delaware rejected Lincoln's plan for gradual emancipation with compensation. In spring 1862 he sent a resolution to Congress recommending government cooperation with, and assistance to, any state willing to adopt a gradual-emancipation-with-compensation plan. He pleaded unsuccessfully for the support of congressional delegates from Maryland, Delaware, West Virginia, Kentucky, and Missouri.

In April 1862 Lincoln recommended emancipation in the District of Columbia, with limited compensation and a provision for voluntary colonization of free blacks in Haiti or Liberia. This recommendation became law, and $100,000 was earmarked for colonizing blacks of the District of Columbia. That same month, Lincoln summoned a delegation of prominent blacks to discuss colonization. The outcome is unclear, but Lincoln indicated that the delegates seemed favorably disposed toward his plan. On June 17, 1862, Lincoln signed a bill freeing slaves who joined the Union side. Two days later, another bill abolished slavery in the territories. Between July 21 and 22, he presented the cabinet with the draft of a proposal freeing all slaves, to take effect from January 1, 1863.

Public opinion developed in favor of emancipation. White abolitionists urged Lincoln to regard emancipation as the consummation of his party's antislavery platform. Prominent black leaders, including Frederick Douglass and Martin Delany, implored him to adopt emancipation on moral, humanitarian, and military grounds. In fact, both Delany and Douglass, on different occasions, met with Lincoln and tried to persuade him that proclaiming universal emancipation would guarantee a speedy crippling of the rebellion. But others advised waiting for an opportune moment. The Union victory at Antietam on September 17, 1862, finally prompted Lincoln to act. Five days later, he issued a preliminary draft, suggesting the possibility of compensated emancipation with voluntary colonization. The draft proclaimed that with effect from January 1, 1863, "all persons held as slaves within any state or, designated part of a state, the people whereof shall be in rebellion against the United State, shall be, thenceforward, and forever free," and pledged government support for protecting the freedom of such persons. The government also promised not to do or act in any manner that would jeopardize such persons in the exercise of their freedom.

The draft enraged many northerners, who felt that it committed the nation to a cause that was not the war's original intent. Abolitionists, however, applauded it. The presentation of the draft prompted debates and suggestions for modification in the months ahead, and Lincoln held several deliberative and discursive sessions with his cabinet before completing the final draft on the morning of January 1, 1863. He immediately signed it into law.

Lincoln underlined the proclamation's strategic importance. He issued it "upon military necessity" because it was "a fit and necessary war measure" designed to end the rebellion. He had come to realize how vital slaves were to the South's economy and war efforts. In fact, by January 1863, the southern economy was heavily dependent on slave labor, and rebels were also tapping into slave resources to carry out noncombatant war tasks such as fortifications and constructions. Emancipation provoked widespread jubilation and celebrations among blacks across the nation. As one authority argued, "the newly emancipated slaves inherited a variety of slave holiday rituals, which they drew from in molding their freedom celebrations . . . from somber, religious thanksgiving to exuberant, carnal good times . . . . Some slaves chose to celebrate the news of their freedom with religious thanksgiving. . . . In east Texas, the slave ancestors of Mr. Booker T. Washington Hogan celebrated their initial Juneteenth in 1865 with religious songs and prayers of thanksgiving" (Wiggins, 1987). Blacks in the North hailed the emancipation, and celebrated with prayers, barbecues, and thanksgiving. For blacks January 1, 1863, has since remained a defining moment in their struggle for equality. For the entire nation, the proclamation was a milestone in the tortuous journey toward obliterating the cancer of slavery and racism.

Despite the applause and celebration it evoked, the proclamation did not free all slaves. It affected only slaves of the rebellious territories and left untouched the more than eight hundred thousand slaves in the border states; thirteen parishes of Louisiana, including the city of New Orleans, the state of West Virginia; and seven counties in eastern Virginia, including Norfolk and Portsmouth. The proclamation had the desired effect of crippling the South's war effort, however. The Confederates almost immediately lost control of their slave population, and there were mass desertions.

The proclamation transformed the war from a struggle to preserve the Union to a crusade for human freedom. It gave the Union cause a moral and humanitarian complexion, which generated worldwide support, and it established Lincoln's reputation among blacks as "the Great Emancipator." It has since given an added significance to New Year's Day, and many blacks celebrate January 1 as a day of commemoration by reading the proclamation. Reaction to the document today is mixed. As one authority suggested, "Even when the principles it espoused were not universally endorsed and even when its beneficiaries were the target of mistreatment of one kind or another, the Proclamation somehow retained its hold on the very people who saw its promises unfulfilled" (Franklin, 1995). Many blacks and whites continue to view the proclamation positively as a shining example of the nation's accomplishment, while others remember it differently as a living testimony to the unfulfilled national aspiration. During the 1960s, many statesmen and politicians invoked the Emancipation Proclamation as proof of the nation's commitment to freedom and equality and as a reminder of its "unfulfilled promises." Such sentiments fed the flames of the civil rights movement.

— *Tunde Adeleke*

See also: Douglass, Frederick; Juneteenth; Lincoln, Abraham.

For Further Reading

Cox, LaWanda. 1981. *Lincoln and Black Freedom: A Study in Presidential Leadership.* Columbia: University of South Carolina Press.

Franklin, John Hope. 1995. *The Emancipation Proclamation.* Wheeling, IL: Harlan Davidson.

Franklin, John Hope, and Mass A. Alfred. 1994. *From Slavery to Freedom: A History of African Americans.* New York: McGraw-Hill.

Quarles, Benjamin. 1962. *Lincoln and the Negro.* New York: Oxford University Press.

Wiggins, William H. 1987. *O Freedom! Afro-American Emancipation Celebrations.* Knoxville: University of Tennessee Press.

THE *EMANCIPATOR*

Published monthly in Jonesborough, Tennessee, from April to October 1820, the *Emancipator* was the second newspaper in the United States devoted solely to the abolition of slavery. The paper was a one-man effort,

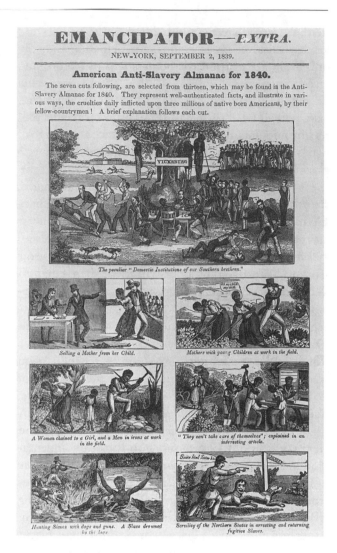

Illustrated front page of an 1839 issue of the *Emancipator.* (Bettmann/Corbis)

written by and funded by Quaker Elihu Embree (1782–1820), but its subscription list of over two thousand carried it beyond Tennessee. It succeeded Embree's earlier weekly, *Manumission Intelligencer,* established in Jonesborough; *Manumission* was probably the first American antislavery periodical and had ceased publication in December 1819. With Embree's death, combined with the fiscal difficulties of the iron business in which he had been involved, the *Emancipator* ceased publication. Another abolitionist newspaper, *The Genius of Universal Emancipation,* might not have been published had Embree's father, Thomas, been successful in convincing abolitionist editor Benjamin Lundy to continue publishing the *Emancipator* after Elihu's death.

In the *Emancipator,* Embree sought to encourage manumission by applying Christian principles and exposing the behavior of slaveowners. Embree advocated neither immediate manumission nor the use of violence; instead he urged gradual emancipation and colonization. He distributed the paper to legislators, advised antislavery voters to use the ballot, and encouraged petitions. He also celebrated the slaveowners who had freed their slaves; published pertinent letters from one individual to another; traced the history of slavery, declared that northern farms were more prosperous than southern farms; published the speeches of people who opposed slavery; and argued that slavery was not economically advantageous, that it destroyed family ties, and that it fostered unrepublican attitudes among slaveowners and the general populace.

Embree complained that unsympathetic postal workers interfered with distribution of his paper. When he sent complimentary copies to several southern governors, for example, the copies were returned in a manner that required him to pay postage. Embree had his detractors: Governor George Poindexter of Mississippi, for one, denounced him as a paid stooge of northern agitators.

Embree resigned from the Manumission Society of Tennessee because he believed that its constitution might interfere with the publication of his paper. The eleventh article of the society's constitution required that an inspection committee approve the publications of members, but the irregular gatherings of the society would have made it difficult for Embree to publish his writings regularly. Ironically, Embree had written the society's articles in 1815 to ensure consensus decision making. Despite his resignation, he regularly published the society's addresses, proceedings, and tracts. Above all, he believed that God would punish the unjust. In the second issue of the *Emancipator* he declared: "My creed is universal and equal liberty," and I "endeavor to know what is right, and do it, dreading no consequences."

In 1813 or 1814, Embree was converted to abolition after having been compelled to sell a family of slaves to cover a debt, but he remained a slaveowner until his death. In his will, he freed his "faithful servant and slave black Nancy together with her children Frames a yellow boy or young man Abegil & Sophea her two black daughters and Mount her yellow daughter and John her son nearly black" (Blassingame and Henderson, 1980). Not only did he free Nancy's children, but he made provisions for their education as well.

Charles D'Aniello

For Further Reading

Blassingame, John W., and Mae G. Henderson, eds. 1980–1984. *Antislavery Newspapers and Periodicals, Volume I (1817–1845): Annotated Index of Letters in the Philanthropist, Emancipator, Genius of Universal Emancipation, Abolition Intelligencer, African Observer, and the Liberator.* Boston: G.K. Hall.

Embree, Elihu, and Robert H. White. 1932. *The Emancipator.* Nashville, TN: B. H. Murphy.

Goodheart, Lawrence B. 1982. "Tennessee's Antislavery Movement Reconsidered: The Example of Elihu Embree." *Tennessee Historical Quarterly* 41 (3): 224–238.

EMPLOYMENT. *See* Hiring of Slaves.

STANLEY L. ENGERMAN (B. 1936)

Stanley L. Engerman's most influential book, *Time on the Cross: The Economics of American Negro Slavery* (1974), coauthored with Robert William Fogel, ignited a crucial historical debate over the nature of slavery. Critics initially responded to the first volume with favorable comments. The ensuing dialogue, which centered on the nature of antebellum slavery and spanned more than two decades, would call into question Fogel and Engerman's methodology, their conclusions, and even their personal intentions. The avalanche of responses came from critics in every corner of the United States and as far away as Finland, Sweden, Holland, Russia, and France.

Fogel and Engerman provided a new methodological paradigm. They followed a tradition—begun by Alfred Conrad and John Meyer in the late 1950s—that used statistical evidence to examine slavery's profitability and sparked a debate over southern growth rates and the importance of slavery to the southern economy. No longer could historians intuitively interpret documents without facing serious criticism. Fogel and Engerman's statistical methods, fully explicated in their second volume, *Time on the Cross: Evidence and Methods—A Supplement,* offered a more systematic approach to large bodies of quantifiable data in the hopes of producing some definitive answers to historical questions. They sought to correct previous interpretations concerning the slave economy of the antebellum South and described the ten most common misconceptions about slavery in their prologue.

Their statistical evidence suggested that slavery had been a flexible, highly developed form of capitalism. The future of this productive, efficient, and profitable system looked bright in the eyes of slaveholders and could only have been destroyed by some event as devastating as the Civil War. They argued that slavery stimulated economic growth in the South and provided slaves with a measure of economic security not enjoyed by many free urban, industrial workers in the North. Twenty-five percent of slaves held skilled or semiskilled jobs and received goods and food as compensation, placing them above the subsistence level. Capitalist developments made slavery ever more profitable, and they simultaneously encouraged slaves to become achievement-oriented, hard workers. Moreover, Engerman and Fogel argued that slave families were relatively stable and headed by husbands, and it was from these families that slaves cultivated a distinctively black culture.

Some critics claimed that Fogel and Engerman were self-righteous racists bent on resurrecting old notions about slavery's benevolent qualities. Historians like Herbert G. Gutman chose to focus on the authors' selection and use of quantifiable data questioning their calculations, samples, and assumptions. Gutman, in *Slavery and the Numbers Game* (1975), charged them with underrepresenting the large plantations, incorrectly calculating data, and then making erroneous assumptions based on their misinterpretation of the evidence. More generally, he insisted that they completely ignored racism and that they asked and answered the wrong historical questions. Gutman countered Fogel and Engerman's assertions of stable slave families by arguing that they were fragile at best and not merely because of the selling of family members.

Other critics, like Richard Sutch, Paul A. David, and Peter Temin, followed suit, suggesting that Fogel and Engerman had underestimated the issues of general welfare, psychic well-being, and brutality in slave life. Some things, according to this view, could not be understood in numerical terms, and these critics recognized the limited usefulness of statistics.

Engerman and Fogel, both together and separately, have replied to critics in writings following *Time on the Cross*. It is significant that historians continue to address the arguments and methodology presented in their two volumes. Yet Engerman has also made new and important contributions to slave history, including his work on the growth of the world economy and the Atlantic slave trade with books like *The Atlantic Slave Trade* (1992) and *Race and Slavery in the Western Hemisphere* (1975), coedited with Joseph Inikori and Eugene Genovese, respectively. In addition, Engerman has delved into the slave history of other colonies, including the West Indies in *The Lesser Antilles in the Age of European Expansion* (1996), coedited with Robert Paquette.

— *Debra Meyers*

See also: Historiography.

For Further Reading

David, Paul, et al. 1976. *Reckoning with Slavery: A Critical Study in the Quantitative History of American Negro Slavery.* New York: Oxford University Press.

Fogel, Robert. 1989. *Without Consent or Contract: The Rise and Fall of American Slavery.* New York: Norton.

Fogel, Robert, and Stanley Engerman. 1974. *Time on the Cross: The Economics of American Negro Slavery* and *Time on the Cross: Evidence and Methods—A Supplement.* Boston: Little, Brown and Company.

Gutman, Herbert. 1975. *Slavery and the Numbers Game: A Critique of* Time on the Cross. Urbana: University of Illinois Press.

THE ENLIGHTENMENT

The single most important philosophical development of the Enlightenment was, perhaps, that of "natural rights" discourse. In the eighteenth century, when much of learned European and American society was consumed with the systematization and structure of knowledge, the rise of empiricism, Denis Diderot's *Encyclopedia* project, and the measure and quantification of the world as a way of knowing it, it is not surprising that attention would turn to one of the most discussed, volatile, and morally important issues of the day—slavery. All of the rhetorical and philosophical force of the Enlightenment came to bear on the question of African humanity, which lay at the center of the question of slavery itself. There had to be a way of justifying slavery that made it morally permissible. Otherwise, Charles Louis Montesquieu's prophecy would return to haunt the slaveowners: "If they [African slaves] are, indeed, human, then we [whites] are not Christian" (Tiainen-Anttila, 1994).

Literacy was a very important issue in discussions of slavery during the Enlightenment era. Proslavery advocates argued that Africans were suited to be slaves because they could not reason. The visible sign of reason during the Enlightenment, as Henry Louis Gates, Jr. (1987) has argued, was the ability to read and to write (especially creatively). Since blacks were unable to produce poets and artists, they were not considered to be of the same variety of humanity as whites. Of course, the literary accomplishments of figures like Phillis Wheatley, Jupiter Hammon, and George Moses Horton flew in the face of such racist claims and went far to demonstrate that Africans shared the same "natural rights" as whites.

Hence, any consideration of the Enlightenment and slavery must necessarily take into account the circulation and influence of the language of "natural rights" and "natural laws" in the eighteenth and nineteenth centuries. Robert M. Cover, in *Justice Accused: Antislavery and the Judicial Process* (1975), analyzes the ways in which the judicial and political discourses of the period (particularly the decisions of justices sitting on the bench) aided and abetted the system of slavery. He begins his analysis with a discussion of "natural law" and "natural rights." These concepts have sources as disparate as Thomas Hobbes's *Leviathan* (1651), Montesquieu's *The Spirit of the Laws* (1752), Jean-Jacques Rousseau's *Discourse on Inequality* (1761) and *The Social Contract* (1762), Thomas Paine's *Rights of Man* (1791–1792) and Thomas Jefferson's *Notes on the State of Virginia* (1781–1782), among others.

Concomitant with the rise of natural rights philosophy and rhetoric was the development of the "master–slave dialectic." The dominant articulations of this idea can be traced most usefully, perhaps, through the philosophy of Hobbes's *Leviathan,* Georg Wilhelm Friedrich Hegel's *Phenomenology of Spirit* (1807), Karl Marx's *Grundrisse* (1850), and Friedrich Wilhelm Nietzsche's *Beyond Good and Evil* (1885). Each of these works provided a discussion of the relationship between master and slave that influenced the intellectual and public debates surrounding slavery well into the nineteenth century.

Similarly, since the primary progenitors of these discourses of natural rights that so profoundly influenced social and political thought in Britain and the United States were French (primarily Montesquieu and Rousseau), it is important to remember that these discourses also animated the discussions of French slavery and colonialism. The support that American intellectuals like Thomas Jefferson, Benjamin Franklin, and Thomas Paine offered the French Revolution is well documented.

Jefferson, for example, spent much time in France; in fact, he was there in 1787 when the U.S. Constitution was drafted. Not only was he greatly influenced by John Locke's philosophy of knowledge (especially his *Essay Concerning Human Understanding* [1690]), but also by the natural rights philosophies of Montesquieu and Rousseau.

Thomas Paine was involved in revolutionary activity in the United States, France, and England. In fact, he was in London in 1775 when he met Benjamin Franklin, whose letters of introduction allowed Paine to go to Philadelphia where he worked as a journalist. It was during that time that Paine wrote his attack on U.S. slavery, "African Slavery in America" (1775), and the anonymously published *Common Sense* (1776), which encouraged American colonists to declare independence from Britain. *Common Sense* was enormously successful in both the United States and France. While back in London in 1791, Paine joined the pamphlet war over the French Revolution with his *Rights of Man* (1792), written in response to Edmund Burke's conservative *Reflections on the Revolution in France* (1790).

Such transatlantic concern and writing led to the political debate between the recently defeated British and the Americans over the rights of man, with Burke and Paine squaring off as the representative interlocutors. This kind of political and intellectual cross-fertilization again demonstrates the need to recognize the triangular relationship among the three nations which framed the political and moral philosophical discourses that gave rise to the Enlightenment and later ushered in romanticism. In light of such compelling evidence, the connections between slavery and the Enlightenment are undeniable.

— *Dwight A. McBride*

See also: *Notes on Virginia* (Jefferson); Romanticism and Abolitionism; Wheatley, Phillis.

For Further Reading
Cover, Robert. 1975. *Justice Accused: Antislavery and the Judicial Process.* New Haven, CT: Yale University Press.

Gates, Henry Louis, Jr. 1987. *Figures in Black: Words, Signs and the "Racial" Self.* New York: Oxford University Press.

Hume, David. 1987. "Of National Characters." In *Essays: Moral, Political, and Literary.* Ed. David Hume. Indianapolis, IN: Liberty Classics.

Pieterse, Jan Nederveen. 1992. *White on Black: Images of African and Blacks in Western Popular Culture.* New Haven, CT: Yale University Press.

Tiainen-Anttila, Kaija. 1994. *The Problem of Humanity: Blacks in the European Enlightenment.* Helsinki: Finnish Historical Society.

EPISCOPAL CHURCH

The history of the American Episcopal Church and slavery is conflicted. Although some church leaders denounced the institution and fought for its abolition, others remained silent as many wealthy slaveholders, dependent on the economic status quo, were Anglican or Episcopalian. The church took virtually no stand on the issue at the national level.

The history of slaves and the Anglican Church began in the early colonial era. Most black Christians in America were Anglicans because most slaveowners in the middle and southern colonies belonged to the Church of England and church leaders viewed captive peoples as fertile ground for missionary work. The Society for the Propagation of the Gospel in Foreign Parts, established in England in 1701, made a concerted effort to convert slaves. Although the society enabled many slaves to learn to read and write, to acquire instruction in catechism, and to marry in the church, blacks were usually segregated into slave galleries or even separate buildings during worship services. Religious instruction was almost always under the control of a white priest or bishop.

After the American Revolution, the Church of England in the United States was reorganized, becoming the American Episcopal Church in 1787. Instructing and evangelizing slaves became prominent issues from this time until the Civil War. Slaveowners paternalistically felt it their Christian duty to provide religious instruction, arguing that Christianized blacks were more honest, truthful, moral, well-behaved, and devoted to their masters than those who were not so instructed. Slaveowners believed that providing religious instruction to slaves would convince northerners that the slave system was not so evil after all and argued that the effect of the black preacher—who often acquired influence independent of the slaveowner—must be minimized by "proper" religious teaching. Slaveholders who argued against providing religious instruction feared that separate black churches, though necessary in places where white church buildings were overcrowded, might incite insurrection. They also feared that slaves could misinterpret the gospel message itself—"freedom in Jesus" might be interpreted as political freedom and opposition to slavery.

Abolitionist forces in the United States pressured Christian leaders, including Episcopal slaveholders, to dismantle the system. Although few U.S. bishops were on this side of the issue—a Bishop Onderdonk of New York did address the Episcopal Convention in 1843 in powerful antislavery language—several Church of England bishops did speak out, and their abolitionist sermons were distributed widely in North America.

Meanwhile, many blacks sought to establish themselves as Africans within the church. Absalom Jones, born a Delaware slave, eventually bought his own freedom and became a leader of Philadelphia's free black community, the largest urban community of former slaves in the postrevolutionary period. Jones became the first minister of St. Thomas's African Episcopal Church in 1794 and, with his ordination to the priesthood in 1804, the first black Episcopal priest.

In Jones, the Episcopal Church found one of its few eloquent spokesmen against slavery. In 1797, he helped organize the first petition of African Americans against slavery, the slave trade, and the Fugitive Slave Act of 1793. From the pulpit, he preached pride and self-respect to blacks, especially newly enfranchised males. Jones taught in schools established by the Pennsylvania Abolition Society and helped found the Society for the Suppression of Vice and Immorality.

During the Civil War, southern bishops formed a group that was welcomed back into the national church at the war's end, and southern black Episcopalians had the unfortunate choice of acquiescing to this arrangement or leaving the church. Most left and became aligned with Methodist or Baptist congregations. By this time, blacks had already been leaving the Episcopal Church for several reasons: exclusion from membership, the ministry, and convention proceedings; the church's rejection of African and evangelical traditions; and literacy requirements related to the Episcopal/Anglican liturgy and catechism.

In recent years, priests and laypeople of the Episcopal Church have labored to combat the tragic legacy of slavery and its ugly offspring, racism. The Union of Black Episcopalians, founded in 1968 as the Union of Black Clergy and Laity, is dedicated to justice and the ministry of blacks in the Episcopal Church. In 1940 the church published the first denominational hymnal to contain a hymn of African American origin, "Were you there when they crucified my Lord?" In 1981 the official hymnal supplement, *Lift Every Voice and Sing: A Collection of Afro-American Spirituals and Other Songs,* was published and is now in use throughout the country. The hymnal's title derives from the hymn of the same name, written by James Weldon Johnson and his brother, J. Rosamond Johnson, in 1900 and known widely as the black national anthem.

The consecration in 1989 of Barbara C. Harris as suffragan (assistant) bishop of Massachusetts was historic not only because she was the first woman bishop in the Anglican Communion (and in any of the liturgical churches worldwide in modern times), but also because she was the direct descendant of a slave. Twenty years earlier the Diocese of Massachusetts had made history by electing John Burgess as the first black bishop to head an Episcopal diocese in the United States. When he was first consecrated in 1962 as suffragan bishop in Massachusetts, Burgess became the first black anywhere to serve as an Episcopal bishop of white congregations. In 2002 Bishop Harris retired and was succeeded by another African American woman, Gayle E. Harris.

The battle against the effects of slavery continues. In 1994 the church's bishops felt the need to issue a strong pastoral against racism. Currently, only 3.4 percent of priests in the United States (excluding bishops) and 4 percent of bishops are African American. The church is making progress, but it still has a long way to go.

— *Valerie Abrahamsen*

See also: African Methodist Episcopal Church.

This commemorative montage depicts the May 19, 1870, parade in Baltimore that celebrated the passage of the Fifteenth Amendment. The amendment was adopted by the U.S. Congress on February 26, 1869, and protected the voting rights of African American men. (Library of Congress)

For Further Reading

Bennett, Robert A. 1974. "Black Episcopalians: A History from the Colonial Period to the Present." *Historical Magazine of the Protestant Episcopal Church* 43 (September 3): 231–245.

Edwards, Lillie Johnson. 1996. "Episcopalians." In *Encyclopedia of African-American Culture and History.* Ed. Jack Salzman, David Lionel Smith, and Cornel West. New York: Macmillan.

Hayden, J. Carleton. 1971. "Conversion and Control: Dilemma of Episcopalians in Providing for the Religious Instruction of Slaves, Charleston, South Carolina, 1845–1860." *Historical Magazine of the Protestant Episcopal Church* 40 (June 2): 143–171.

Jay, William. 1853. "Introductory Remarks to the Reproof of the American Church Contained in the Recent History of the Protestant Episcopal Church in America, by the Bishop of Oxford." In *Miscellaneous Writings on Slavery.* Boston: John P. Jewett.

Mohler, Mark. 1926. "The Episcopal Church and National Reconciliation, 1865." *Political Science Quarterly* 41 (December): 567–95.

∾ F ∾

FIFTEENTH AMENDMENT

The Fifteenth Amendment to the U.S. Constitution, ratified in 1870, represents one portion of the unprecedented legislation passed by the radicals in Congress during Reconstruction guaranteeing every male citizen the right to vote. Many people considered this amendment the culmination of the work begun by the radicals with the Fourteenth Amendment, which focused on establishing equal civil and political rights for freedmen by limiting the authority of state governments with the threat of federal intervention. Congress thought it necessary to initiate the later legislation because, at least in part, it saw the political advantage of ensuring black male suffrage that the Fourteenth Amendment had merely encouraged.

In 1868, when Republican Ulysses S. Grant garnered 3 million popular votes compared to Democrat (and former New York governor) Horatio Seymour's 2.7 million, it became clear just how valuable the Republican black vote could be. Republican leaders recognized that black suffrage had won them several states and they had lost others when states denied freedmen the right to vote. Most southern states, under federal pressure during Reconstruction, ratified the new amendment quickly, as did the northern states.

The Fifteenth Amendment further abridged states' rights, a process begun by the Fourteenth Amendment, by prohibiting disenfranchisement based on "race, color, or previous condition of servitude," with the threat of federal enforcement if states chose to ignore the new provisions. With this amendment (supplemented by the Enforcement Acts of 1870 and 1871), Congress sought to prevent states from encroaching upon the federal rights of black men, but it did nothing to prevent individuals, like Ku Klux Klan members, from injuring, killing, or destroying the property of black Americans. To address that problem, Congress passed an unprecedented act in April 1871, aimed at Klan members, that called for placing individuals under federal jurisdiction if a state failed to punish their criminal acts of terrorism.

With the ratification of the Fifteenth Amendment, many reformers, like William Lloyd Garrison and members of the American Anti-Slavery Society, felt their job was done. Having grown weary of Reconstruction in general and believing they had accomplished their goals by ensuring the black man's political participation, and thus his ability to protect himself against exploitation, Americans focused their attentions on other issues.

Ex-Confederate leaders gained political power during the 1870s, and Democrat "Redeemers" sought to reestablish white supremacy in the South. Their success meant a dramatic decline in black rights. Property qualifications, poll taxes, and literacy tests, not specifically prohibited in the Fifteenth Amendment, effectively disenfranchised southern black men. Subsequently, southern states passed Jim Crow laws, which stripped the freedmen of their right to vote while legalizing racial segregation, and thus effectively nullifying the Fifteenth Amendment.

— *Debra Meyers*

See also: Fourteenth Amendment.

For Further Reading

Foner, Eric. 1989. *Reconstruction: America's Unfinished Revolution, 1863–1877.* New York: Harper and Row.

Fridlington, Robert. 1995. *The Reconstruction Court, 1864–1888.* Danbury, CT: Grolier.

Linden, Glenn. 1970. "A Note on Negro Suffrage and Republican Politics." *Journal of Southern History* 36 (August): 411–420.

Wesley, Charles. 1970. *The Fifteenth Amendment and Black America, 1870–1970.* Washington, DC: Associated Publishers.

FILIBUSTERS

The U.S. acquisition of the vast Southwest after the Mexican War (1846–1848) led many expansionists to advocate the conquest or liberation of other foreign territories, and the idea was directly related to the slavery issue. During the 1850s, thousands of citizens openly defied the Neutrality Act (1818) by participating in several private military expeditions against Mexico and other Central American or Caribbean nations. These adventures were popularly known as "filibusters," a term derived from the Dutch *vrijbuiter* (freebooter), which was first applied to Caribbean buccaneers.

The major filibustering expeditions of the era were Narciso Lopez's forays against Cuba in 1850–1851 and William Walker's invasions of Mexico, Nicaragua, and Honduras between 1853 and 1860. Motivated by the aggressive spirit of manifest destiny and the lure of adventure, many filibusters were also influenced by the rising controversy over slavery, as many southern expansionists believed that the acquisition of new territory would maintain the political balance of power between slave and free states.

The conspiracy of Mexican War hero and former Mississippi governor, John A. Quitman, to invade Cuba between 1853 and 1855 was largely influenced by southern fears that Spain planned to abolish slavery on the island. In 1853 Juan de la Pezuela, a known abolitionist, was appointed captain-general of Cuba. He issued orders freeing all Africans imported illegally from the United States since 1835, permitting marriage between black women and white men, and allowing freedmen to serve in the militia.

Pezuela's measures alarmed southern expansionists who dreamed of bringing Cuba into the Union as new slave territory. Furthermore, the island's proximity to the Gulf Coast states led many southerners to regard Cuban emancipation as a direct threat to southern society and institutions. Many were convinced that news of Cuban events would spark slave rebellions throughout the South.

Filibusters associated with William Walker rest in their quarters after a battle in Nicaragua in 1856. (Library of Congress)

Backed by Cuban associates of the ill-fated Narciso Lopez, Quitman, an ardent advocate of Cuban annexation, was preparing to lead a major invasion of the island at the time of Pezuela's appointment. The Mississippian regarded the possible emergence of what he called a "Negro" or racially mixed "mongrel empire" in the Caribbean as a serious threat to the "whole social fabric of the Southern states" (May, 1985). Motivated by the desire to prevent the "Africanization" of Cuba, leading southerners helped Quitman gather men, arms, and ships for the expedition.

Besides widespread southern support, Quitman apparently obtained assurances from members of President Franklin Pierce's cabinet that the administration would not intervene to thwart his invasion plans. Pezuela's seizure of a U.S. vessel in early 1854 produced a crisis that might have assured government support of Quitman's enterprise. However, the filibuster chief continued to delay, explaining to his Cuban backers that he would not move until he had sufficient men, an armed steamer, and adequate funds.

Although the reasons are not entirely clear, spring 1854 saw a shift in official policy that boded ill for Quitman's venture. One factor might have been a desire to avoid the overwhelming criticism that could result from government support of a proslavery invasion of Cuba. Whatever the true motive, the Pierce administration determined to withdraw support for filibustering and to acquire Cuba by purchase.

Instructing his minister in Madrid to offer $130 million to the Spanish government, Pierce blocked efforts in the U.S. Senate to repeal the neutrality laws. He also issued a proclamation warning that the government would prosecute any violators. Quitman, while protesting what he regarded as a violation of his understanding with the administration, continued to prepare for the invasion.

In June 1854 a federal grand jury in New Orleans compelled Quitman to enter a recognizance in the sum of $3,000 to observe the neutrality laws for nine months. Quitman promptly postponed his expedition until spring 1855, but the delay only worsened his prospects. In early 1855 Spanish authorities arrested over one hundred of the filibuster chief's Cuban supporters, thus destroying all hopes of revolutionary support on the island.

In early spring 1855, President Pierce met personally with Quitman in Washington, D.C., and offered convincing evidence that Cuba was virtually invulnerable to attack. This factor, coupled with the knowledge that Cuba's new captain-general did not share Pezuela's zeal for emancipation, led Quitman to disband his private army on March 15. Although Quitman formally severed ties with his Cuban backers on April 30, he continued to support other filibustering schemes, including William Walker's Nicaraguan venture.

The abortive Quitman expedition was followed by another failed filibuster venture, the plot of the Knights of the Golden Circle, a secret, proslavery society in the United States, to invade Mexico in 1859–1860, before the outbreak of the Civil War brought an end to large-scale filibustering activities. Although filibustering cannot be regarded solely as a manifestation of southern expansionism, the expeditions of Lopez, Walker, and others received widespread support in the South, particularly among people who advocated the annexation of additional slave territory. Besides being regarded by the international community as a symbol of U.S. imperialism, filibustering contributed to the sectional discord that led to the Civil War.

— *James M. Prichard*

See also: Quitman, John; Knights of the Golden Circle; Lopez, Narciso; Walker, William.

For Further Reading
Brown, Charles H. 1980. *Agents of Manifest Destiny: The Lives and Times of the Filibusters.* Chapel Hill: University of North Carolina Press.

May, Robert E. 1973. *The Southern Dream of a Caribbean Empire 1854–1861.* Baton Rouge: Louisiana State University Press.

May, Robert E. 1985. *John A. Quitman: Old Southern Crusader.* Baton Rouge: Louisiana State University Press.

FIRE-EATERS

A small but powerful group of antebellum southern politicians, the fire-eaters were an important force during the sectional crisis in the United States. Although they represented a minority of southern leaders, the fire-eaters were vocal, articulate advocates for their region and the cause of states' rights.

Fire-eaters believed that by the 1840s, the South's social, political, and economic interests were under attack by outside forces. Vocal northern abolitionists seemed to wield significant influence in both houses of Congress, and more important, the abolitionists had begun to attack the character and morality of slaveowners, not simply the institution itself. By the 1850s proposals like the Wilmot Proviso and agreements like the Compromise of 1850 led many southern leaders to conclude that the South's interests would no longer be protected by the national government. In fact, to many fire-eaters, the government itself appeared to be doing the bidding of northern abolitionists by attempting to legislate slavery—and thereby the social and political organization of southern society—out of existence.

Faced with these apparent attacks, a minority of southern politicians began actively to champion the cause of states' rights. Drawing on Thomas Jefferson's ideological legacy, this group, called the fire-eaters by people of both the North and the South, went beyond traditional rhetoric concerning state sovereignty. These leaders believed that the U.S. Constitution represented a compact of states that had agreed to unite in 1787 for certain purposes. The federal government established by this compact was charged with national defense, international diplomacy, regulation of interstate commerce, and very little else.

Fire-eaters such as John C. Calhoun, like Jefferson before him, believed that the powers of the federal government were limited to those specified by the Constitution, with all remaining powers reserved for the states or individual citizens. These reserved powers included the power to regulate slavery. Furthermore, they believed that the Union existed to protect the interests and rights of individual states. Over time, the Union had been transformed, gradually assuming more power, and according to the fire-eaters, this transformation had led to federal policies that were contrary to southern interests. Therefore, as southern rights were no longer being honored and protected, the slave states should dissolve the bonds that held them in the Union. This belief went beyond earlier notions of interposition and nullification. Through secession, the fire-eaters reasoned that the southern states would retain their sovereignty and protect their slave-based economic system. Secession was a panacea designed to protect what the fire-eaters viewed as the fundamental social, political, and economic underpinnings of southern society.

Fire-eaters were most powerful in South Carolina, Alabama, and Mississippi and existed in smaller numbers in other southern states. United in their belief in immediate secession as a way to protect southern rights and slavery, the fire-eaters had few other things in common. Most were political leaders in their respective states with a gift for oratory, and they were almost universally from planter families or had risen to such status through their own labor. Though small in number, several fire-eaters were particularly influential. Robert Barnwell Rhett edited the bombastic *Charleston Mercury,* which became the voice of the fire-eater cause. John A. Quitman, though born in Ohio, served as military governor of Mexico and as governor of Mississippi. A vocal proponent of states' rights, Texan Louis T. Wigfall later became a severe critic of Jefferson Davis and the Confederate government. Agriculturalist and editor Edmund Ruffin of Virginia fired the first shot at Fort Sumter and subsequently committed suicide after Appomattox. In Alabama, William Lowndes Yancey articulated the fire-eaters' position in the Alabama Platform and generally served as the faction's most eloquent orator in Congress and at Democratic Party conventions.

Although the fire-eaters did not cause the dissolution of the Union in 1861, their ardent defense of states' rights and protectionist attitudes toward slavery certainly helped create a political climate in which secession could be considered. Ironically, many went on to criticize the Confederate government for usurping the rights of individual states. These vocal defenders of states' rights and slavery, though representing an extreme minority view in the South, wielded tremendous influence and helped lead the nation to Civil War.

— *Richard D. Starnes*

See also: Alabama Platform; Calhoun, John C.; Quitman, John A.; Ruffin, Edmund; Yancey, William Lowndes.

For Further Reading

Heidler, David. 1994. *Pulling the Temple Down: The Fire-Eaters and the Destruction of the Union.* Mechanicsburg, PA: Stackpole Books.

Potter, David. 1976. *The Impending Crisis, 1848–1861.* New York: Harper and Row.

Walther, Eric. 1992. *The Fire-Eaters.* Baton Rouge: Louisiana State University Press.

GEORGE FITZHUGH (1806–1881)

George Fitzhugh was one of the most vociferous, and radical of the proslavery southern polemicists in the United States. He married nearly Marxist critiques of European and northern capitalism to an impassioned defense of feudal-style patriarchy in two major antebellum books, *Sociology for the South or the Failure of Free Society* (1854) and *Cannibals All! or, Slaves without Masters* (1857).

In these books, and in numerous articles in the *Richmond Examiner* and *DeBow's Review,* Fitzhugh characterized the capitalism of Europe and the northern part of the United States as a form of slavery in which, unlike southern plantation society, the industrialist had no motive to care for his labor force's well-being. Fitzhugh rejected the notion of human equality and liberty advanced by John Locke and Thomas Jefferson. He argued that ancient slave patriarchies like Rome and Greece were more compassionate than the so-called modern democracies. Western society had declined, he suggested, after post-Luther philosophers extended the Protestant Reformation's ideas to promote notions of individualism and personal liberty.

Heavily influenced by Thomas Carlyle's philosophical attack on economic liberalism, Fitzhugh believed that competition spawned by the emerging capitalist order resulted in wealth for few and misery for many. Humans, he stated, are by nature social creatures, like ants and bees, and all people are not created equal. In an unequal world, he argued, to require "inferior" individuals such as women, children, African Americans, and poor whites to compete with "superior" white male elites was cruel. In industrial society, the inferior and incompetent were slaves to capital rather than to human masters. Unlike the well-fed plantation slave, industrial workers were left to starve and were denied civilizing contact with Christian masters.

Fitzhugh suggested that northern capitalism was ultimately doomed, and, anticipating Frederick Jackson Turner's "frontier thesis," he contended that only the open frontier and the opportunity it gave white industrial workers to escape wage slavery and become landholders suppressed class violence north of the Mason–Dixon line. Fitzhugh's writings provoked a storm in the North, and quotes were taken from his books out of context to suggest that he favored the enslavement of white industrial workers and the poor.

Despite his fondness for the master–slave relationship, Fitzhugh never suggested the extension of slavery to white laborers in the United States. In fact, he called for mass education among the South's working class and poor whites as a way of winning the nonslaveholders' loyalty to plantation elites. Nevertheless, Fitzhugh's writings provided fodder for abolitionists, who warned of southern slaveholders plotting to enslave northern workers. Fitzhugh's rhetoric proved influential even among slavery opponents. Abraham Lincoln, in particular, was inflamed by Fitzhugh's prediction in *Sociology for the South* that slavery would later be "everywhere abolished" or "everywhere reinstituted"; a more famous restatement of this idea appeared in Lincoln's 1858 "house divided" speech.

Fitzhugh was largely self-taught and his reading tastes were not always sophisticated, but he was widely exposed to French and English socialist thought, and occasionally his wording suggested that he had read Karl Marx. His writings exhibit some understanding of Marxist theories on surplus value, and some ringing phrases in *Cannibals All!*, such as when Fitzhugh described the industrial poor as "continually forging new chains for themselves," sound as if they were lifted directly from the *Communist Manifesto* (published nine years earlier in 1848). Other aspects of Fitzhugh's economic analysis foreshadowed twentieth-century leftist thought.

His description of the handicaps agricultural regions like the antebellum South suffer in world trade, and the damaging effects of unequal exchange on an agricultural economy when competing with industrial centers, are reminiscent of the arguments of dependency theorists like Arghiri Emmanuel, Immanuel Wallerstein, Fernando Cardoso, and Enzo Faletto. Despite his flirtation with socialism, Fitzhugh neither conceded the extent to which African American slaves were exploited nor fully acknowledged that the plantation culture he so vigorously defended might have played a part in the region's economic dependency.

Fitzhugh has typically been portrayed as a southern anomaly. He vigorously attacked Jefferson's ideas of human equality enshrined in the Declaration of Independence, and he asserted that the American Revolution was no battle for human liberty but merely a struggle of local elites to achieve political independence. He bitterly denounced free trade, laissez faire, and the liberal economic thought of classical economists like Adam Smith while praising pre-Reformation feudalism.

These notions may have placed Fitzhugh outside the mainstream of southern thought, and planters must have winced when Fitzhugh declared plantation slavery as the "beau ideal of Communism" or when he bitterly depicted the "vampire capitalist class" of Europe and the northern portion of the United States. Yet, Mitchell Snay's research suggests that Fitzhugh was less iconoclastic than has traditionally been suggested. Snay argues that Fitzhugh's depiction of man as naturally social, his argument that patriarchy produces a harmonious society of mutual obligations, and his view of the master–slave relationship paralleling that of God and humanity reflect ideas common among antebellum southern clergy.

Ironically, despite his vociferous defense of southern planters, Fitzhugh's family had lost its farm at auction in 1825, and for much of his career, Fitzhugh was a mediocre lawyer depending largely on the property of his wife, Mary Brockebrough, in Virginia's Caroline County. Despite his relatively humble status, he became perhaps the most famous propagandist for the planter class. For all his occasional prescience, however, Fitzhugh's writings were highly repetitive and disorganized, symptomatic of his lack of formal schooling. "We are no regular built scholar," as Fitzhugh acknowledged in *Cannibals All!* (Fitzhugh, 1960), and even his supporters were forced to acknowledge his intellectual eccentricity. If Fitzhugh's ideology was not exactly embraced by southern elites, he was seized upon as a spokesman for southern ideology and in the North symbolized the threat that attitude posed to the working class throughout the Union.

— *Michael Phillips*

See also: Jefferson, Thomas; Wage Slavery.

For Further Reading
Fitzhugh, George. 1960. *Cannibals All! Or, Slaves without Masters.* Cambridge, MA: Belknap Press.
Perskey, Joseph. 1992. "Unequal Exchange and Dependency Theory in George Fitzhugh," *History of Political Economy,* 24 (1, Spring): 117–128.
Snay, Mitchell. 1989. "American Thought and Southern Distinctiveness: The Southern Clergy and the Sanctification of Slaves." *Civil War History,* 35 (4, December): 311–328.
Wish, Harvey, ed. 1960. *Antebellum: Writings of George Fitzhugh and Hinton Rowan Helper on Slavery.* New York: Capricorn Books.

FLORIDA

Florida was the second-to-last slaveholding state to be admitted to the Union. When Florida joined the Union on March 3, 1845, the United States consisted of twenty-seven states, of which thirteen were free and fourteen were slave states. The admission of Florida, and subsequently of Texas, in 1845 made it more urgent for antislavery advocates to support the creation of new states in the northern and northwestern territories of the United States to counter the growing political influence of the proslavery lobby.

The history of slavery in Florida, like that of Texas and Louisiana, was influenced largely by the region's complicated colonial history. For most of the colonial period Florida was ostensibly a colony of Spain, though the level of royal authority and control waned considerably over time. For a brief period (1763–1783), Florida came under British control in the aftermath of the French and Indian War. Although the United States officially acquired Florida from Spain in 1819,

American military forces had already been occupying large parts of the territory prior to the official diplomatic transfer. As a result of shifting ownership and the absence of effective governance, the area of Florida was often viewed as an inviting region where fugitive slaves might escape and find succor amid the anarchic state of affairs there.

Slavery in the lands that eventually formed the United States can trace its beginnings to Florida. The Spanish established the colonial outpost of St. Augustine, Florida, in 1565, and this community holds the distinction of being the oldest continuously settled town in the United States. The founding of St. Augustine followed a failed attempt just two years prior to establish a French Huguenot refuge in the same vicinity at Fort Caroline, near modern-day Jacksonville. Slaves were used in both the Fort Caroline and St. Augustine settlements. Pedro Menédez de Avilés, the Spaniard who established the St. Augustine settlement, had permission to introduce 500 slaves within the first three years of the colony's existence, and evidence shows that slaves were used there as early as 1565.

When the English began to establish colonies on the eastern seaboard of North America, particularly the settlement of the Carolinas in the 1660s, Spanish authorities became concerned about the perceived encroachment upon their territory in Florida. The frontier between the poles of English and Spanish colonial hegemony was marked by contention, and this prompted the settlement of Georgia by the British in 1733 to act as a buffer between its more valuable tobacco colonies to the north and the threat of Spanish Florida to the south. Spanish authorities in Florida continued to incite unrest in the region by encouraging slaves to run away from their British colonial masters and escape to Florida where they could obtain emancipation and find sanctuary.

Florida, as geographically defined during the colonial era, consisted of two parts—East and West Florida. East Florida corresponds largely to the region comprising the present-day state, but West Florida was a narrow strip of Gulf coastal territory that extended across portions of present-day Alabama, Mississippi, and Louisiana until reaching the Mississippi River at Baton Rouge, Louisiana. During the era when the British held Florida, a substantial number of planters relocated to West Florida where they established plantations that cultivated tobacco and cotton using slave labor.

It was the joint presence of political instability and the Seminole Indians in Florida that prompted the United States to take extralegal action in the aftermath of the War of 1812. General Andrew Jackson led a foray of U.S. military into Spanish Florida to restore order to an area that was destitute with anarchy. Jackson's actions, including the declaration of martial law and the execution of two British nationals who were living in Florida, received international condemnation, but the blunt use of power was enough to force the hand of Spain to relinquish possession of Florida by 1819. The pacification of the Seminole would prove more difficult. Essentially an amalgamation of fugitive slaves and disaffected Creeks who had crossed into Florida after the Creek Indian War, the Seminole Indians presented a formidable threat along the Georgia border where they regularly raided plantations of supplies and slaves.

Pacification of the Seminole Indians would not be effected until the conclusion of the Second Seminole War (1837–1845). The so-called Black Seminoles played a significant role in this conflict as black leaders like John Horse, Alligator Sam Jones, and Wild Cat fought against regular forces of the U.S. military. As a result of that conflict, most of the Seminole were removed to reservation land in Oklahoma, but some members of the tribe did resist and remained in Florida's swamps and marshes living lives as isolated outliers.

Cotton cultivation did develop in post–1845 Florida, thus leading to a substantial increase in the area's slave population. In the 1840 census, the territory of Florida recorded a slave population of 26,526, but by the eve of the Civil War, this population had increased to 61,750 slaves—nearly 44 percent of the state's population. Perhaps slavery's greatest impact on Florida during this era involved its role in the domestic slave trade. Because of its position along the Gulf Coast and with an abundance of navigable rivers and streams, the Florida Panhandle became one of the busiest regions of commerce in the domestic slave trade. Ships carrying slaves from portions of the Upper South regularly arrived at St. Marks, and from there slaves would be taken to Tallahassee where they would be sold at auction. Slaves introduced through the Florida slave market made their way to the cotton plantations of the Black Belt region in Alabama and Georgia.

Florida became the third state to secede from the Union and join the Confederate States of America when its legislature adopted a secession resolution on January 10, 1861. The state suffered economically from the naval blockade that the Union imposed to quarantine southern ports. The effects of the blockade were especially hard on Jacksonville and Tampa Bay. Florida territory remained relatively untouched by the physical ravages of the Civil War, but the social and economic changes wrought by emancipation and the Reconstruction era would leave scars that would linger for subsequent generations.

— *Junius P. Rodriguez*

See also: Domestic Slave Trade; Seminole Indians.

For Further Reading
Colburn, David R., and Jane L. Landers, eds. 1995. *The African American Heritage of Florida.* Gainesville: University Press of Florida.

Jones, Maxine D., and Kevin M. McCarthy. 1993. *African Americans in Florida.* Sarasota, FL: Pineapple Press.

Rivers, Larry Eugene. 2000. *Slavery in Florida: Territorial Days to Emancipation.* Gainesville: University Press of Florida.

Shofner, Jerrell H. 1974. *Nor Is It over Yet: Florida in the Era of Reconstruction, 1863–1877.* Gainesville: University Press of Florida.

Smith, Julia Floyd. 1973. *Slavery and Plantation Growth in Antebellum Florida, 1821–1860.* Gainesville: University Press of Florida.

ELIZA LEE CABOT FOLLEN
(1787–1860)

Eliza Lee Cabot Follen, abolitionist, writer, and church organizer, was born to Sally Barrett and Samuel Cabot in Boston, Massachusetts. She was one of thirteen children in the family. Cabot's mother made sure Eliza focused her interests on religious and social problems. Long before Eliza Cabot's marriage on September 14, 1820, to Dr. Charles Follen, she was already well connected to Boston society and known for her determination and support of her social convictions.

Many of Follen's female friends went on to establish themselves as well-known abolitionists. Although Follen is often considered as more of a footnote in the abolition movement, it would be a mistake to overlook her contributions. In the early 1830s, Follen was one of a group of men and women who organized the Unitarian Federal Street Church in Boston and taught Sunday School classes at the church. When Follen's husband was removed as a professor at Harvard University because of his antislavery views, the Follens moved to Roxbury, Massachusetts. Eliza earned money by writing religious tracts and books. Among her works was *The Christian Teachers' Manual* (1828 and 1830). By the late 1830s, it was clear to true abolitionists that the Federal Street Church was no more supportive of the antislavery movement than most churches, and it ap-

pears that Follen's connection with the church ended during that time.

During the 1830s Follen was also instrumental in creating the Boston Female Anti-Slavery Society. The mixture of members included middle-class African American women, some of the wealthiest white women in the city, and self-supporting women abolitionists and activists who had jobs in the religious community or within other social reform movements. Follen was among the members who voted to send regular monetary support to a Boston school for young black girls in 1833. The Boston school eventually lost the support of radical abolitionists and closed in 1839. Through her extensive travels in Britain and France, Follen was able to strengthen ties with foreign abolitionists. It was a move that extensively aided the antislavery movement both in the United States and abroad.

By the early 1840s the Boston Female Anti-Slavery Society started to deteriorate following an internal struggle over the society's methods of operation. Follen, however, continued her activities in support of abolitionism. Her writing of children's books increased. One of her most noted books was *The Child's Friend* (1843, 1850). She edited the American edition of *Grimms' Fairy Tales* in 1840, and continued to write children's books until approximately 1855.

Follen also served on the executive committee of the American Anti-Slavery Society and was a counselor of the Massachusetts Society. Her fame as an antislavery writer increased with the publication of *Anti-Slavery Hymns and Songs* and *A Letter to Mothers in the States.* After the decline of the Boston Female Anti-Slavery Society, Follen focused her energies on the American Anti-Slavery Society. Before her death in Brookline, Massachusetts, she published a five-volume series on the work of her husband entitled *The Works: A Memoir of His Life.* She died in Brookline on January 26, 1860, of typhoid fever during the occasion of the American Anti-Slavery Society's annual meeting.

— *Maria Elena Raymond*

See also: American Anti-Slavery Society; Boston Female Anti-Slavery Society; Women and the Antislavery Movement.

For Further Reading
Hansen, Debra Gold. 1993. *Strained Sisterhood: Gender and Class in the Boston Female Anti-Slavery Society.* Amherst: University of Massachusetts Press.

Schlesinger, Elizabeth Bancroft. 1965. "Two Early Harvard Wives: Eliza Farrar and Eliza Follen." *New England Quarterly* 38 (June): 141–167.

Sterling, Dorothy. 1991. *Ahead of Her Time: Abby Kelly and the Politics of Antislavery.* New York: Norton.

CHARLOTTE FORTEN (1837–1914)

Charlotte Forten was active in U.S. abolitionist, women's rights, intellectual, and art circles from the antebellum years through the post-Reconstruction period. As a diarist, her record of the thought and activities of northern free blacks of the antebellum and post-Reconstruction periods has contributed significantly to an understanding of the evolution of free black ideologies and culture.

Forten was part of the fourth generation of a prominent, free black family in Philadelphia, Pennsylvania. She served as a link between slave and free persons and based her antislavery activity on an antebellum free black philosophy of racial "uplift" and self-help. As such, Charlotte Forten provided an important model for blacks and women of the period, and her story is still important in African American, and indeed American, history. Forten attended a private girls' school in Salem, Massachusetts, because her father objected to Philadelphia's racially segregated schools. While in Massachusetts, Forten witnessed the capture of a runaway slave, who was then returned to slavery. This event, along with the example of her family's activism, encouraged her own participation in antislavery and other social reform movements. At the age of seventeen, Forten joined the Salem Anti-Slavery Society.

Her grandfather, James Forten, had made a fortune as a sailmaker and as an entrepreneur by patenting a device used on sailing vessels. Forten's boldly acerbic criticism of racism in America distinguished him even among the tiny and vocal activist free black community of his day and provided an indelible example for his granddaughter, Charlotte. Her father, Robert Forten, though less successful as a businessman, was also a model of social activism and belonged to both local and national abolitionist societies. Many of Charlotte Forten's associates and models were white, including *Liberator* publisher William Lloyd Garrison and Theodore Parker, although black women who were Forten's contemporaries, such as fellow *Liberator* contributor Maria W. Stewart and Isabella Van Wagenen—more famously remembered as Sojourner Truth—were also active in antislavery and women's rights activities of that time. It has been suggested that Forten herself shunned the spotlight of a public career in activism, perhaps because the credo of her genteel background urged women to stay within the proscribed "domestic circle of true womanhood" (Peterson, 1995). Forten was briefly a teacher at the Salem Normal School; however, her delicate health forced her to curtail many physical activities. A meticulous recorder of contemporary events in her diaries, Forten also tried her hand at poetry; although most literary critics have found her poetry to be merely adequate, Garrison published her poems, which contained antislavery messages, in the *Liberator.*

In 1862, during the Civil War, Forten traveled to South Carolina's Sea Islands to teach freed children, and her memoirs of her experiences there were published in the *Atlantic Monthly.* Her essays convey both her sincerity and her dedication to the cause of black freedom, while they also reveal the confusion of a sheltered black daughter from a privileged background when confronted with blacks whose life experiences were so different from her own.

In 1878 Forten married Francis J. Grimké, the son of a slave woman named Nancy Weston and her white slaveowner. Though disowned by their southern relatives, Francis Grimké and his brother had been taken in by their father's sister, Angelina Grimké Weld, a northern aunt who was well known in antislavery circles. Francis J. Grimké earned degrees in law and theology before taking a pulpit in Washington, D.C. He and Charlotte Forten had only one child, who died in 1880. Forten herself died in 1914.

— *Dale Edwyna Smith*

See also: Garrison, William Lloyd; Sea Islands; Stewart, Maria W.; Truth, Sojourner.

For Further Reading
Billington, Ray Allen. 1953. *The Journal of Charlotte L. Forten.* New York: Collier.
Birnbaum, Jonathan, and Clarence Taylor, eds. 2000. *Civil Rights Since 1787: A Reader on the Black Struggle.* New York: New York University Press.
Curry, Leonard P. 1981. *The Free Black in Urban America, 1800–1850: The Shadow of the Dream.* Chicago: University of Chicago Press.
Hine, Darlene Clark, Elsa Barkley Brown, and Rosalyn Terborg-Penn, eds. 1993. *Black Women in America, An Historical Encyclopedia.* Brooklyn, NY: Carlson.
Lapsansky, Emma Jones. 1989. "Feminism, Freedom and Community: Charlotte Forten and Women Activists in Nineteenth-Century Philadelphia." *Pennsylvania Magazine of History and Biography* 113: 3–19.
Peterson, Carla L. 1995. *"Doers of the Word": African-American Women Speakers and Writers in the North (1830–1880).* New York: Oxford University Press.

Sterling, Dorothy, ed. 1984. *We Are Your Sisters: Black Women in the Nineteenth Century.* New York: Norton.

Stevenson, Brenda, ed. 1988. *The Journals of Charlotte Forten Grimké.* New York: Oxford University Press.

JAMES FORTEN, SR. (1766–1842)

Noted for his work as an abolitionist and sailmaker, James Forten was one of the eighteenth century's most distinguished African American leaders and the grandfather of the abolitionist Charlotte Forten. Born in Philadelphia, the son of Thomas and Sarah Forten, James was a mulatto whose ancestors were free for at least two generations. In 1773, when Forten was seven years old, his father died. James briefly attended a local school for Philadelphia's free blacks established by Anthony Benezet, a Quaker abolitionist and philanthropist. In 1775, when he was nine, Forten left school to go to work at a local grocery store to help support his family.

In 1781, Forten became a powder-boy on the *Royal Louis,* a vessel commanded by Stephen Decatur. During the American Revolution, when the British vessel *Amphion* captured the *Royal Louis,* Forten anticipated being sold into slavery. His future was altered when he was sent to Great Britain where he met many prominent abolitionists, including Granville Sharp. After his seven-month imprisonment, Forten returned to the United States and became an apprentice to Robert Bridges, a prominent sailmaker in Philadelphia.

In 1786 Forten became a supervisor. When Bridges died twelve years later, Forten took ownership of the firm. The business flourished, and by 1832, he had acquired a fortune of about $100,000. This made him one of Philadelphia's wealthiest African Americans. With his newly found resources, Forten was able to maintain a large country home and a city dwelling for his wife and family of eight children.

Forten, along with Richard Allen, pastor of the African Methodist Episcopal Church, and Absalom Jones, founder of the African Episcopal Church, gradually became prominent leaders within Philadelphia's African American community. In 1797 they organized the city's first African American Masonic Lodge. During the War of 1812, they recruited nearly twenty-five hundred African Americans to build fortifications around Philadelphia to protect the city after the British had burned parts of Washington, D.C.

During the early nineteenth century, Forten, Allen, and Jones began directing their attention to ending slavery. In 1800 they petitioned Congress to pass a law to end slavery through gradual emancipation. These three leaders, in 1817, created a public forum to protest creation of the American Colonization Society that intended to send many free black Americans back to Africa. In 1830 Forten, Allen, and Jones sponsored the first national convention that focused on the problem of colonization within the interracial abolition movement.

Forten's success as an abolitionist and entrepreneur makes him one of the eighteenth century's outstanding African American pioneers. His leadership skills, respect within early Philadelphia's African American community, and the many people who attended his funeral on February 22, 1842, all illustrate the wide acclaim of this exceptional African American.

— *Eric R. Jackson*

See also: Allen, Richard; American Colonization Society.

For Further Reading

Billington, Ray Allen. 1953. *The Journal of Charlotte L. Forten.* New York: Dryden.

Douty, Esther M. 1968. *Forten the Sailmaker: Pioneer Champion of Negro Rights.* Chicago: Rand McNally.

Feldman, Lynne B., and John N. Ingham, eds. 1994. *African American Business Leaders: A Biographical Dictionary.* Westport, CT: Greenwood.

Winch, Julie. 2002. A *Gentleman of Color: The Life of James Forten.* New York: Oxford University Press.

ABIGAIL KELLEY FOSTER (1811–1873)

Better known as Abby Kelley, Abigail Foster was an extraordinarily effective lecturer, fund-raiser, and organizer for women's rights, nonresistance, and antislavery. She was notorious both for her radical abolitionism and for her willingness to speak before "promiscuous assemblies" of men and women. Only Maria Stewart and Sarah and Angelina Grimké preceded her on the lecture platform. Like Angelina Grimké, Kelley married a prominent abolitionist, but unlike Grimké she did not let marriage or motherhood stop her antislavery work. The emancipation of the slaves and the end of racial prejudice came first, and Kelley endured years of misogynist attacks, illness, and frequent separation from her husband, Stephen Symonds Foster, and her daughter to achieve these goals—without accepting any pay.

Kelley's deep belief in women's equality brought her to the center of the 1840 split in the abolitionist movement when the followers of William Lloyd Garrison broke with the "new organization" abolitionists led by Lewis Tappan and Amos Phelps over the role of women in the American Anti-Slavery Society and other philosophical and strategic differences. When Kelley, a Garrisonian, was elected to an important committee at the 1840 convention and insisted on speaking, the Tappanites and Garrisonians separated. Kelley had begun lecturing in 1838 and was becoming well known, but the fight within the American Anti-Slavery Society brought her to new prominence. In particular, she inspired women to become abolitionists and cultivated a number of young women to travel the antislavery lecture circuit, most prominent among them being Lucy Stone, Susan B. Anthony, Sallie Hollie, and Sarah Redmond, the sister of Charles Redmond.

Kelley was an organization woman, fiercely promoting Garrison's radical brand of antislavery and the Massachusetts and American Anti-Slavery Societies. For twenty years she lectured, raised money, and planned lecture and propaganda campaigns throughout New England, Pennsylvania, New York, and the Midwest. She also helped found Ohio's *Anti-Slavery Bugle.* Other abolitionist leaders relied on her abilities as a shrewd organizer and administrator. In an 1859 meeting of the New England Anti-Slavery Society, Garrison accused Kelley of fraudulently obtaining funds for the abolitionist movement. Kelley broke with Garrison, who refused to apologize, and withdrew from her prominent role in abolitionist organizations. Their disagreements continued during the Civil War and afterward, for Kelley was skeptical of Lincoln and the Republican Party's commitment to emancipation and to the civil rights of the freed slaves. After the Fifteenth Amendment was ratified in 1870, Kelley turned her attention to the issues of temperance and women's rights.

— *Andrea M. Atkin*

See also: Anthony, Susan B.; Garrison, William Lloyd.

For Further Reading
Pease, Jane H. 1969. "The Freshness of Fanaticism: Abby Kelley Foster." Ph.D. dissertation, Department of History, University of Rochester, Rochester, New York.
Sterling, Dorothy. 1991. *Ahead of Her Time: Abby Kelley and the Politics of Anti-Slavery.* New York: Norton.

FOURTEENTH AMENDMENT

The U.S. Constitution's Fourteenth Amendment, ratified by three-fourths of the states in 1868, represented a radical move on the part of Congress during the Reconstruction period. Submitted to the states for approval in 1866, this amendment significantly reduced state powers, attacked the southern black codes, defined citizenship, and granted considerable political rights to freedmen. With its passage, states could no longer legally enforce laws like the black codes that stood in opposition to federal legislation.

Reacting to Reconstruction, southern states instituted these codes aimed at controlling the labor of freed blacks after emancipation. The legal restrictions placed on ex-slaves differed from state to state, but all essentially denied freedmen the rights mandated by the first eight amendments: namely, their rights to free speech, bear arms, obtain a trial by an impartial jury, have protection against cruel or unusual punishment, and not to be subject to unwarranted search and seizure. Moreover, the black codes regulated the relationships between white landowners and black laborers, limiting workers' ability to rent land in certain areas and to negotiate wages as well. The codes and the punishments meted out for their violation, like whipping and forced labor, essentially permitted slavery to continue in the South after emancipation. With the passage of the Fourteenth Amendment, the federal government could now prevent states from enforcing black codes if the states chose to "deprive any person of life, liberty, or property, without due process of law."

The first clause declares that everyone "born or naturalized in the United States, and subject to the jurisdiction thereof, are citizens of the United States." Congress believed that by admitting freedmen into the political community as citizens with rights, the ex-slaves could protect and defend themselves from exploitation. Besides legally defining citizenship, the Fourteenth Amendment stipulated that the right to suffrage was reserved for men twenty-one years old or older.

The freedman's political rights were not assured, however. By basing a state's congressional representation on the number of enfranchised men, the second clause encouraged, but did not require, states to grant freedmen the right to vote. The final three clauses attempted to conclude some of the issues with which Congress had been grappling during Reconstruction. Hoping to fill the U.S. House of Representatives with loyal unionists, clause three barred ex-Confederate leaders from holding state or national offices unless two-thirds of Congress voted to grant a pardon. The fourth clause repudiated the Confederate debt, and the fifth empowered Congress to enforce the amendment's provisions with any legislation it found necessary.

Congress initiated the Fourteenth Amendment for at least three reasons: its members wanted to guarantee ex-slaves equality before the law at the federal level, and they sought to secure black Republican

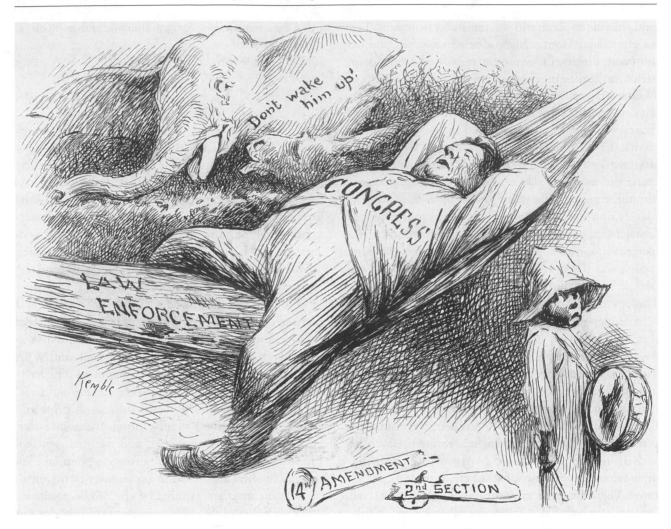

Cartoon criticizing authorities' failure to enforce the Fourteenth Amendment. (Library of Congress)

support, at the same time they legally defined the right to vote for males. Because this amendment failed in its mission to allow the freedmen to defend themselves against white southern Democrats, the Republican-dominated Congress began the ratification process of the Fifteenth Amendment that would, at least for a time, bar states from preventing black males from voting.

—*Debra Meyers*

See also: Fifteenth Amendment; United States Constitution.

For Further Reading

Antieau, Chester James. 1997. *The Intended Significance of the Fourteenth Amendment.* Buffalo, NY: W. S. Hein.

Maltz, Earl M. 2004. The *Fourteenth Amendment and the Law of the Constitution.* Durham: Carolina Academic Press.

Nelson, William Edward. 1995. *The Fourteenth*

Amendment: From Political Principle to Judicial Doctrine. Cambridge, MA: Harvard University Press.

Perry, Michael. 1994. *The Constitution in the Courts: Law or Politics?* New York: Oxford University Press.

ELIZABETH FOX-GENOVESE (1941–2007)

Elizabeth Fox-Genovese—Eléonore Raoul Professor of the Humanities, professor of history, until 1991 founding director of the Institute for Women's Studies at Emory University, Atlanta, and the author of several books and numerous articles—is among the most prolific writers on slavery and on women in the southern United States. She studied at Bryn Mawr College and at Harvard, where she completed her Ph.D. in 1974, focusing on social and economic changes in eighteenth-century France. As an assistant professor at the University of Rochester from 1973 to 1976, she became involved in the Marxist debate on merchant capitalism and the role of slavery in the transition from feudalism to capitalism. From a Marxist perspective, she and her husband, Eugene D. Genovese, published a series of articles on European slave economies, on the origins of Western capitalism, and on the economic and social relations in the slaveholding societies in the United States. Fox-Genovese participated in the vigorous academic debate following the publication of Robert Fogel and Stanley Engerman's *Time on the Cross* (1974), which portrayed southern slavery as a successful rational and capitalist system. She criticized the book's analysis of slavery as a simple matter of economics and suggested instead that one should see the peculiar institution as a paternalistic, precapitalist economic and social system, which was based essentially on personal relations and should be analyzed with research tools taken from psychology, anthropology, sociology, and economics.

Fox-Genovese's own interests became increasingly focused on aspects of gender and women's history. In her award-winning book *Within the Plantation Household* (1988), she discussed issues of gender, race, and class in the antebellum South. Drawing on women's diaries, letters, and memoirs, as well as on interviews of the Works Progress Administration (WPA), she reconstructed the lives of southern black and white women, which revolved around a system of household labor. In her meticulous description of southern women based on psychological as well as anthropological analysis, class and race rather than gender were the dominant categories to define women's identity and behavior within the system, which differed fundamentally from life in the North. In her more recent studies on feminism and American individualism in the United States (*Feminism Is Not the Story of My Life* [1996]; *Hidden Histories of Women in the New South* [1994]), she argues that the lives of African American women are still defined by the experience of slavery and racial discrimination.

In recent years Fox-Genovese became increasingly interested in issues of family and faith. She died in Atlanta, Georgia in January 2007.

— *Raingard Eßer*

See also: Genovese, Eugene.

For Further Reading

Fox-Genovese, Elizabeth. 1988. *Within the Plantation Household.* Chapel Hill: University of North Carolina Press.

Fox-Genovese, Elizabeth. 1991. *Feminism without Illusions.* Chapel Hill: University of North Carolina Press.

Fox-Genovese, Elizabeth, ed. 1992. *Southern Women: Histories and Identities.* Columbia: University of Missouri Press.

Fox-Genovese, Elizabeth, ed. 1994. *Hidden Histories of Women in the New South.* Columbia: University of Missouri Press.

Fox-Genovese, Elizabeth, and Eugene D. Genovese. 1983. *Fruits of Merchant Capital.* New York: Oxford University Press.

FRANKLIN AND ARMFIELD

Franklin and Armfield was a major slave-trading firm created by the partnership of Isaac Franklin and John Armfield, Franklin's nephew by marriage, on February 28, 1828. The company engaged in a long-distance domestic slave trade, with Franklin's offices in Natchez, Mississippi, and Armfield's in Alexandria, Virginia. A junior partner, Rice C. Ballard, later joined the firm.

The partnership enjoyed a favorable reputation in a commercial area frowned upon even by advocates of slavery. Abolitionist E. A. Andrews reported that Virginia slaves, aware of their impending sale, often requested to be sold to Franklin and Armfield. The firm's positive image derived from two perceptions. First, Franklin and Armfield appeared to treat their subjects humanely. According to all reports, their slaves appeared healthy, well groomed, and well fed. Second, the firm had a reputation for preserving families. Although the firm cultivated this reputation, when profitable, they separated families by sale and by purchase.

Franklin and Armfield transported slaves to Natchez overland via coffles and by sea on coastal brigs. The firm sent one annual coffle of 100 or more slaves in late summer when travel conditions were best for walking. More frequently, they shipped their slaves by sea. The partners owned several brigs, including the *Uncas,* the *United States,* the *Tribune,* and the *Isaac Franklin,* each of which could transport 150 slaves. Such a capacity allowed the firm to ship slaves belonging to migrating planters and other traders for additional profit.

The ships unloaded at New Orleans, where a few slaves were sold, and the remaining slaves went to Natchez by steamboat. At the apex of the firm's operation in the early 1830s, Franklin and Armfield sent a boatload of slaves every two weeks. Contemporary estimates that the firm sold one thousand to twelve hundred slaves annually in Mississippi are probably accurate. The firm's income reportedly rose from $33,000 in 1829 to $500,000 in 1834.

Franklin and Armfield was the largest of the slave-trading firms in Natchez, but not the only one. Although observers attributed responsibility to Isaac Franklin for most of the slaves in Mississippi, at least thirty other slave traders operated in Natchez by the

1830s. Nonetheless, Franklin and Armfield was the dominant and most influential firm in the area. Indicative of its influence is that after the firm relocated its Natchez stockade outside of town in 1834, the new stockade, Forks in the Road, became the chief Natchez slave market for the remainder of the antebellum period.

The partnership's charter expired in November 1841, but owing to a Mississippi legislative ban on the importation of slaves as merchandise, Franklin and Armfield had ceased operations in 1837. Isaac Franklin retired from the trade and became a respected planter in Tennessee. John Armfield continued in the trade, managed Franklin's Louisiana operations, and oversaw the firm's remaining affairs into the 1840s.

— *David J. Libby*

See also: Domestic Slave Trade.

For Further Reading

Andrews, E. A. 1836. *Slavery and the Domestic Slave-Trade in the United States.* Baltimore, MD: Light and Stearns.

Bancroft, Frederick. 1931. *Slave-Trading in the Old South.* Baltimore: J. H. Furst.

Stephenson, Wendell. 1938. *Isaac Franklin: Slave Trader and Planter of the Old South.* Baton Rouge: Louisiana State University Press.

Tadman, Michael. 1989. *Speculators and Slaves: Masters, Traders, and Slaves in the Old South.* Madison: University of Wisconsin Press.

FREE AFRICAN SOCIETY

Founded in April 1787 by Richard Allen (1760–1831) and Absalom Jones (1737–1818), both free blacks in Philadelphia, the Free African Society was a benevolent organization started to promote the positive treatment of people of color. The society espoused moral reform, self-help, self improvement, and black unity. The Free African Society members believed in making the United States hospitable to blacks, advocated abolition, and condemned prevalent repatriation schemes. Although the membership maintained close ties to both the Methodist Church and to the Quakers, the Free African Society was nondenominational. Members of the society insisted on the humanity and equality of blacks, and on their right to fair treatment. They petitioned both state and federal governments and issued broad appeals to the white community and to enslaved and freed blacks to end the inhumane practice of slavery in the United States.

Members contributed money to the general treasury that was then used to help widows and orphans and others in need, they attended regular meetings, and they were further required to adhere to the society's articles of association. These articles were guidelines for sobriety, decorum, and good moral conduct. Infractions of the rules were judged by a committee of members, and anyone found guilty was either fined or suspended.

During the Philadelphia yellow fever epidemic of 1793, members responded to the public solicitation for colored people to help care for the sick. Under the guidance of Absalom Jones and William Gray, and encouraged by the belief that people of color were not liable to succumb to the infection, black people from the Free African Society visited over twenty families a day, removed the dead bodies that whites refused to touch, buried corpses, administered to the needs of the dying, and even fulfilled duties such as bloodletting for white physicians.

Meetings of the society, which were held for the first year at 150 Spruce Street in the home of Richard Allen and for three years subsequent at the Willings Alley School House, were used in part to plan for the establishment of an independent African church. The free black community in Philadelphia was rudely awakened to the necessity of establishing their own church when they were forced to sit in segregated areas, behind the pews, in St. George's Methodist Episcopal Church, where there was a growing number of black worshipers. After several black worshipers were forcibly removed by white deacons while kneeling in prayer in the church, the black community withdrew its membership completely from the church. Afterward, the Free African Society as an organization became increasingly hostile to Methodism and began showing a tendency toward Quaker thought. Among other reforms, they adopted a simple, Quaker-like marriage ceremony and began each meeting by observing fifteen minutes of silence. Richard Allen maintained, however, that the Quaker message of detachment and introspection was not as relevant to the needs of free blacks as Methodism. He therefore broke with the society in the spring of 1789, leaving its leadership in the hands of the less dynamic but also less confrontational Absalom Jones.

Absalom Jones and members of the Free African Society began a public subscription to raise money for a church building that on July 17, 1794, became the African Episcopal Church. At the same time, Richard Allen and several former members of the society created a Methodist society and worked to establish their own church. They began public worship services by the end of June 1794 and secured a charter from the

Pennsylvania legislature in 1796 for the Mother Bethel Church, the African Methodist Episcopal church that later played an active role in the Underground Railroad and the abolition movement. With the increasing attention to African churches, the Free African Society disbanded in the early 1790s.

— *Jennifer Margulis*

See also: Allen, Richard.

For Further Reading

Allen, Richard. 1983. *The Life Experience and Gospel Labors of the Rt. Rev. Richard Allen.* Nashville, TN: Abingdon Press.

DuBois, W. E. B. 1899. *The Philadelphia Negro.* Philadelphia: University of Pennsylvania Press.

George, Carol V. R. 1973. *Segregated Sabbaths: Richard Allen and the Emergence of Independent Black Churches, 1760–1840.* New York: Oxford University Press.

Nash, Gary B. 1988. *Forging Freedom: The Formation of Philadelphia's Black Community, 1720–1840.* Cambridge, MA: Harvard University Press.

FREE LABOR. *See* Transition from Slave Labor to Free Labor.

FREE PERSONS OF COLOR

Occupying a position somewhere between "slaves without masters" and the highest ranks of the master class, freedpersons have formed a part of every slave society in history. In the United States, they experienced some of the harshest restrictions of any society in the Americas. Nevertheless, free people of color made significant contributions in all regions of the country. Slave systems based on race, such as that in the United States, were fundamentally threatened by the mere existence of free blacks because they presented the spectacle of people of the subordinate race who were less than fully subordinate. At the same time, free blacks were essential for the system to function, both because they could do jobs that whites would or could not do, and because the possibility of manumission offered slaves an inducement to cooperate with the system.

In the British colonies of North America, and subsequently in the independent United States, the role of free people of color in society was restricted by contrast to that of free black populations in other colonies in the Americas. In most places, free blacks were essential because there was a shortage of white labor. In addition, new slaves were reasonably cheap because of plentiful imports, reducing the cost to the slaveowner of replacing labor lost though manumission. In the United States, there were relatively few imports of slaves at any time, and slave importation was cut off by law in 1807 (and illegal importations were insignificant) before the large expansion of the cotton industry in the Deep South. Although slaves in the United States had more children than slaves in other slave societies, their birth rates and child survival rates were lower than those of American whites. Unlike most other slave societies in the Americas, the United States experienced significant white immigration. As a result, many whites were available for the subaltern jobs of the plantation economy: overseers, technical specialists, small craftspeople, small farmers producing food for the plantation, intermittent laborers, and providers of various services to whites. Long before formal "Jim Crow" segregation was established in society, many occupations were restricted to whites either by custom or even by law.

In *Slave and Citizen* Frank Tannenbaum clearly expresses the traditional view of differing racial attitudes in the Americas. Tannenbaum's hypothesis, briefly, attributes much of the difference to the cultural, historical, and legal background of the European colonizer. He points out that the Iberian countries had the longest historical tradition of rule over an alien working class, dating back to Spain's experience with Jews and Moors during the *Reconquista.* In addition, Catholicism gave them a set of universalist values—though admittedly applied imperfectly in practice—which at least prepared them to consider the person of color as a fellow human and even potential citizen.

Tannenbaum contrasts the situation of people of color in the Iberian colonies to that in the northern European (British, French, Dutch, and Danish) colonies. He suggests that a lack of historical experience in dealing with aliens within the society, the lack of legal provisions for slavery in the home country, and the relative weakness of the moderating influence of universalist Catholic teachings were responsible for the harsher treatment of people of African descent there. England in particular, Tannenbaum noted, had an unfortunate history with subordinate aliens in its adventure in Ireland. The lessons learned in Ireland were applied in destructive ways in the British North American colonies.

The 1992 edition of Tannenbaum's work includes an introduction by Franklin Knight, who points out that Cuba, the Spanish colony that received the largest number of slaves, had a very harsh slave regime in the nineteenth century. At the same time, historian of the British Antilles Michael Craton has pointed out that treatment of persons of color varied quite remarkably from Jamaica to the Bahamas—both of which were within the supposedly harsh British colonial world.

Knight offers the alternative explanation that economic conditions, especially the strength of the plantation system, and the demography of the colony, drove changing attitudes toward people of color. In places where the plantation complex was not highly developed, free blacks were often socially almost indistinguishable from their white neighbors, and slaves were often very similar to free laborers or peasants.

Interestingly in this regard, in colonial Virginia, African slaves were at first treated no differently than white indentured servants. It was only when tobacco planting became extremely profitable in the late seventeenth century that new slave codes made slavery a permanent and heritable condition, and set conditions for manumission.

A person of color might become free through several avenues. Running away was the most direct. The Underground Railroad flourished only from the 1840s on. Prior to this time, most runaways quietly fit into American society, living "as free" with phony papers, often in marginal or frontier areas, or drifting to the north through porous borders, as did Frederick Douglass. Formal manumission was common, but difficult, as most states significantly restricted the practice. Manumissions of more than a small percentage of any master's work force were typically prohibited. For example, George Washington's will provided for the freedom of his entire workforce, but the will was modified on the request of the heirs as contrary to public policy. Masters were often required to provide for the support of their freedmen and/or move them out of the state. The white elite's desire to rid slave societies of free blacks led to the movement to send them "back" to Africa (this despite the fact that almost all freedmen were native-born Americans). Spurred by the missionary impulse of the times, many African Americans cooperated enthusiastically, forming the modern nation of Liberia and a few short-lived colonies in the Americas before 1863.

In most slave societies in the Americas, one important reason for manumission was the existence of a family relationship between master and slave. Particularly in the Roman Catholic colonies, Iberian and French, the white father of a mixed-race slave was obliged by custom to free at least his child, if not the mother. In British North America, despite the frequency with which masters had sexual relations with their slaves, Puritan ideas about sexual morality, a strict color line, and a large white female population meant that this "mulatto escape hatch" was less open to the mixed-race children of slaves. The proportion of mixed-race slaves in the United States was much higher than in other colonies, where most were freed.

However, famously, Thomas Jefferson bucked the cultural mores by freeing the children born, perhaps, from his relationship with Sally Hemings.

Other, less prominent masters also bucked the system as best they could in order to help slaves they felt had deserved well of them for whatever reason. Self-purchase by slaves was forbidden by law. Masters had to get permission from the authorities (local judges or state legislatures) to free slaves in most states, alleging some prosocial act on the part of the slave as justification. These authorities were often concerned that self-purchase encouraged slaves to steal, prostitute themselves, or engage in other antisocial activities to raise their purchase price. Nonetheless, for the master, self-purchase was often the most profitable market for surplus slaves, and so they engaged in all sorts of deceptions. States with declining plantation economies, like those in Virginia and Maryland in the nineteenth century, saw high rates of manumission.

Despite all the roadblocks placed in the way of manumission, all southern states in 1861 had significant free populations of color. The largest proportions were found in the Old South areas of the Chesapeake and the Carolinas and the frontier areas of Florida, Texas, Arkansas, and Missouri. Even in the heart of the Cotton Belt, though, it would not be uncommon to find a free black artisan or peasant living on the outskirts of the plantation, next door to poor whites and often working alongside them at the same tasks (albeit usually for less pay).

The Northeast had a substantial free black population by 1863. This population owed its origin to the role of the northeastern ports in the slave trade. Persons of color were important subalterns in the slave-trading system, as interpreters, seamen, and commercial contacts on the African coast. Crispus Attucks, one of the victims of the Boston Massacre, was a member of this community. Small numbers of slaves were imported into the northeastern colonies, mostly as domestic servants. The immediate postindependence era saw the abolition of slavery in all the states north of the Mason–Dixon line. Subsequently, some free blacks (including runaways) from the South migrated here. The free black population of Boston, in particular, was large and relatively wealthy, while in New York and Philadelphia, free blacks competed with recent immigrants for working-class jobs. The free black community of New York was a primary target of the mob in the New York City Draft Riots of 1863.

Free blacks filled a number of roles in southern society, from humble artisan or peasant to slaveholding plantation owner. Local cultural practices, especially notable in (formerly French and Spanish) Louisiana or frontier conditions, as in early Virginia, permitted free blacks greater integration into white-dominated society. Free blacks were highly marginalized in the core areas of the Cotton Belt, though, and it was there that the risk of reenslavement was highest. Grants of manumission were often either explicitly or implicitly conditional on "good" behavior by the freedperson. Freedpeople were required to be deferential to whites, and "uppity" behavior could result in judicial reenslavement. Kidnapping was also not unknown, and the fact that all states in the South refused free blacks access to their courts made it difficult for a freedperson to prove their status as against a master who claimed them. These difficulties encouraged outmigration by free blacks even if it was not officially required by state law. In any case, the need for free black labor was greater in frontier areas.

The American myth of a predominantly white West, promulgated by Hollywood, ignores the enormous role played by people of color, from Meriwether Lewis's (slave) companion York to Jean-Baptiste Pointe du Sable, the first settler of Chicago, to many cattle hands and mountain men and the Reconstruction-era Exodusters. In more settled areas, free blacks were an important intermediate class, either as direct subordinates of the white masters—overseers, rural police, slave-catchers, small agriculturists supplying the plantations—or at least as a living example to the slaves of the rewards possible for faithful service.

— *Stewart King*

See also: Douglass, Frederick; Mulattoes; Octoroons; Quadroons; Artisans; Underground Railroad.

For Further Reading

Berlin, Ira. 1974. *Slaves without Masters: The Free Negro in the Antebellum South.* New York: Pantheon Books.

Cohen, David, and Jack Greene. 1972. *Neither Slave nor Free.* Baltimore: Johns Hopkins University Press.

Johnson, Michael P., and James L. Roark. 1984. *Black Masters: A Free Family of Color in the Old South.* New York: Norton.

Tannenbaum, Frank. 1992. *Slave and Citizen.* Introduction by Franklin W. Knight. Boston: Beacon Press.

FREE SOIL PARTY

The Free Soil Party's significance far outshines its brief existence on the antebellum political scene. As the first antislavery party attracting widespread support from members of the major parties, the Free Soil Party ushered in a new era of sectionalism and set the stage for the political crises of the 1850s.

Salmon Chase was a founder of the Free Soil Party, and he later served as senator and governor of Ohio, U.S. treasury secretary under Abraham Lincoln, and chief justice of the United States. Chase coined the slogan "Free Soil, Free Labor, Free Men." (Library of Congress)

Officially christened in Buffalo in August 1848, the national Free Soil Party was an amalgam of disgruntled Democrats, northern Whigs, and Liberty Party men. Advocating a broad array of (mostly Democratic) reforms such as free homesteads and cheap postage, the party made the restriction of slavery its fundamental issue. The extension of slavery became the nation's preeminent political issue during the Mexican War (1846–1848), when acquisition of vast new western territories forced Americans to consider the future of the "peculiar institution." Northerners believed that extending slavery into the West would threaten the development of that region as a haven for family-sized farms, while southerners generally advocated opening the territories to slave labor. The issue crystallized with the Wilmot Proviso, which was introduced in Congress in 1846, attempted to bar slavery from territories gained during the Mexican War.

Although the Wilmot Proviso never passed in the Senate, the slavery issue remained at the center of national politics as the 1848 election approached. In 1847 the South Carolina Democrat and slaveholder John

C. Calhoun formulated a strong "southern rights" position, which affirmed the slaveowners' constitutional right to take their human chattel into any territory. This direct challenge to the Wilmot Proviso convinced many northern Whigs and Democrats that slaveholders intended to spread the institution throughout the new territories.

The antislavery Liberty Party, which attracted few votes in 1840 and 1844, responded to Calhoun by endorsing the Wilmot Proviso and nominating former Democratic congressman John P. Hale of New Hampshire for the presidency. The Democrats, severely split over the slavery extension issue, attempted to prevent a formal rift by excluding the issue from the platform. This was too much for an antislavery faction of New York Democrats (and Martin Van Buren supporters) known as "Barnburners," who walked out of the convention, vowing to adhere to the Wilmot Proviso. Similarly, part of the Whig Party known as "Conscience Whigs" bolted their party when it nominated the slaveholding Mexican War General Zachary Taylor for president. Under the brilliant coalition-building of Ohio Liberty Party men Salmon P. Chase and Gamaliel Bailey, Conscience Whigs and Barnburners combined with the Liberty Party to form a new, broad-based antislavery party.

Thousands of northerners streamed into Buffalo for the carnivalesque Free Soil convention, which nominated former president Martin Van Buren and ex-Whig Charles Francis Adams (the son and grandson of presidents, respectively) on a platform of "no more slave states and no more slave territories." During the 1848 campaign, both major parties tried to bury the slavery issue, but pressure from the many Free Soil papers that sprang up across the North kept it in the national spotlight. On election day, the Free Soilers polled 14 percent of the northern vote (most of it coming from former Democrats) and essentially threw the election to Taylor and the Whigs. Still, the Free Soil Party had increased the number of antislavery votes from 62,300 in 1844 to 291,263 in 1848.

Although the party won no electoral votes in 1848, the Free Soil Party did make significant gains. Nine Free Soil congressmen were sent to Washington from states like New York, Massachusetts, Ohio, and Indiana. In addition, political realignments secured the election of two famous Free Soil senators—Salmon P. Chase in Ohio and Charles Sumner in Massachusetts. Also, the 1848 election reflected a restructuring of U.S. politics at national, state, and local levels. Insurgencies at each level severely damaged both major parties and encouraged development of a far-reaching national political realignment in the 1850s and 1860s. Northerners,

fearing slavery's expansion, abandoned their old parties in growing numbers, presaging the new Republican coalition in the North.

In 1852 the Free Soil Party became the Free Democratic Party, and nominated John P. Hale for the presidency. It polled fewer votes than in 1848, but with the Kansas–Nebraska Act (1854), most former Free Soil adherents entered the new Republican Party. Former Free Soil leaders like Chase, Sumner, and Preston King helped launch the new party at every level and founded its large and enduring radical wing.

— *Jonathan Earle*

See also: Democratic Party; Wilmot Proviso.

For Further Reading
Blue, Frederick J. 1973. *The Free Soilers: Third Party Politics, 1848–54.* Urbana: University of Illinois Press.
Foner, Eric. 1965. "Politics and Prejudice: The Free Soil Party and the Negro, 1849–1852." *Journal of Negro History* 50 (October): 239–256.
Mayfield, John. 1979. *Rehearsal for Republicanism: Free Soil and the Politic of Antislavery.* Port Washington, NY: Kennikat Press.
Rayback, Joseph G. 1971. *Free Soil: The Election of 1848.* Lexington: University Press of Kentucky.

FREEDMEN'S BUREAU

Starting in about 1862, the U.S. Congress had been planning to take part in determining the terms of Reconstruction of the nation once the Civil War ended, and on March 3, 1865, Congress passed an act to establish a Bureau of Refugees, Freedmen and Abandoned Lands. Subsequently known as the Freedmen's Bureau Act, the agency it created was to focus on issues that distressed a torn nation. Designed to provide relief and medical attention, to establish schools, and to aid former slaves and white refugees in the exigencies of their situations, the bureau functioned influentially but precariously. Until then, such services as were available had been furnished more or less haphazardly by a few groups, some public, some private. In its brief existence, the Freedmen's Bureau operated as the federal government's first broadly conceived welfare program.

A compelling need for such a program had arisen when at the termination of hostilities and without preparation 4 million black slaves were released from bondage and when many white persons were wounded or displaced. Lands had been "abandoned" or seized. The need for medical attention had become urgent. Education had been forbidden for slaves and neglected for whites, just as industrial advance had recom-

Harper's Weekly illustration characterizing the Freedmen's Bureau as a peacemaker. (Library of Congress)

menced. Yet no agency had been designated to deal with the desperate social problems that ensued.

The bureau also emerged out of the trail of consequences that followed the introduction of human slavery in Virginia in 1619. From the acceptance of the Articles of Confederation in 1783 to the military conclusion of the Civil War in 1865, struggles over the reaches of slavery characterized the republic. States were admitted or rejected according to arrangements regulating legal black bondage. In 1865, as many freedmen and freedwomen joined the ranks of the displaced, the question of whether the federal government should assist all Americans who lacked survival resources became acute. The Freedmen's Bureau bill was intended to address this problem, the largest part of which resulted from black slavery.

While, as some argued, the bureau represented a mere beginning in meeting the needs of former slaves and white clients, it did bring substantial, if often temporary, relief. During its four-year existence, the bureau distributed 21 million parcels of food to former slaves and white refugees, or 140,000 rations per day. It set up more than forty hospitals, and it treated four hundred fifty thousand ill and wounded persons. As

many as thirty thousand displaced persons were assisted in resettling. The bureau achieved its most lasting success in areas of education. In 1866 and 1867, it established twelve hundred new day and night schools, and it found seventeen hundred teachers, many from the North. All of the schools met crucial needs, especially the needs of former slaves, and many have become important institutions.

It had taken two years, however, to secure passage of the first bureau bill; the agency was conceived as a wartime measure, situated in the War Department, and designed to last for one year after the close of hostilities. Congress allowed no operating appropriation; it intended that the bureau would be financed by returns from the sale of abandoned lands. Upon the finding of a joint committee of Congress that the work of the bureau was indeed valuable, a second bill was introduced and passed into law in 1866, this time with some arrangement for financial supports.

President Lincoln chose Union General Oliver O. Howard to administer the agency. From the start, General Howard and the agents of the bureau experienced difficulties of every description with the governments that were being established in the states of the former

Confederacy. Appeals to southern Union supporters proved useless, nor could the bureau's efforts bring about any degree of cooperation.

The bureau's activities also produced disturbing harbingers of continued racial alienation. Supporters had intended that the agency would work in behalf of the blacks; the bureau had little success, however, in promoting civil rights for all or in dealing with the state governments that President Andrew Johnson favored. According to George Bentley's early *History of the Freedmen's Bureau* (1955), in point of fact the sponsors cared only to furnish the North some economic benefits through constructing the new state governments and through securing votes. But more recently William McFeely has provided a less censorious interpretation in *Yankee Stepfather: General O. O. Howard and the Freedmen's Bureau* (1968).

Whatever the reasons for establishing a federal agency, it is nearly impossible to portray the extreme opprobrium heaped upon the bureau, its agents, and its northern teachers in bureau schools. People were ostracized; persecuted; driven from the South; some were even lynched. This aspect of the bureau's efforts is sensitively treated in Charles W. Chesnutt's little-known but poignant short story, "The Bouquet," and in William Faulkner's novel, *Light in August.*

President Johnson opposed the second Freedmen's Bureau bill. He rendered the first of his many vetoes; he thus brought to Congress's attention the connected issues of welfare for the destitute and civil rights for all Americans. The president argued that federal programs for aid were unconstitutional and that they ought to be considered, if at all, at state levels of government. Johnson, a southerner, said the bill would establish military control over the defeated territories, something southerners vehemently denounced. He insisted that the framers of the Constitution never contemplated federal aid for destitute persons. He concluded that the positions of the former slaves were not desperate because their labor was necessary and would function as a bargaining tool. The president's refusal to modify these positions led in part to his impeachment. His confrontation with the nation's representatives over welfare and civil rights implications of the Freedmen's Bureau act and the repeated resurgence of these issues demonstrate that these issues bear connections to historical precedents.

— *Frances Richardson Keller*

For Further Reading

Bentley, George. 1955. *A History of the Freedmen's Bureau.* Philadelphia: University of Pennsylvania Press.

DuBois, W. E. B. 1995. *Black Reconstruction in America.* New York: Simon and Schuster.

Franklin, John Hope. 1994. *Reconstruction after the Civil War.* Chicago: University of Chicago Press.

Litwack, Leon. 1979. *Been in the Storm So Long: The Aftermath of Slavery.* New York: Vintage Books.

Lowe, Richard. 1993. "The Freedmen's Bureau and Local Black Leadership." *Journal of American History* 80 (3): 989–998.

McFeely, William S. 1968. *Yankee Stepfather: General O. O. Howard and the Freedmen.* New Haven: Yale University Press.

Woodward, C. Vann. 1966. *Reunion and Reaction: The Compromise of 1877 and the End of Reconstruction.* Boston: Little, Brown.

FREEPORT DOCTRINE

Like many other "doctrines" throughout history, Stephen Douglas's Freeport doctrine was the result of political expediency. But despite its humble origins, the Freeport doctrine illuminates a great deal about Abraham Lincoln's political ascent in the late 1850s and Douglas's decline. Douglas's reply to Lincoln's question about the future of slavery in the territories during the debate of August 27, 1858, speaks volumes about the breakdown of national consensus at that time.

Stephen Douglas and Abraham Lincoln's second debate of the 1858 Senate campaign took place at Freeport, Illinois, a town close to the Wisconsin border. Most accounts agree that Lincoln had been placed on the defensive during the first debate, and in order to regain momentum, he decided to ask Douglas several questions at Freeport, including Douglas's opinion on whether residents of a territory could decide to prohibit slavery before a state constitution was drafted. This ostensibly straightforward question was based on the background of the Kansas–Nebraska Act, the recent turmoil in Kansas, and the *Dred Scott* decision. Lincoln hoped to portray Douglas as a leader preaching a contradiction between the popular sovereignty philosophy behind the Kansas–Nebraska Act and the proslavery attitudes of James Buchanan and the Supreme Court. However Douglas replied, his stand would cost him much needed political support. To oppose slavery in the territories would lose southern support for Douglas; to support *Dred Scott* and the proslavery Lecompton Constitution in Kansas would cause northern Democrats to desert him. Douglas opted for consistency and denied that *Dred Scott,* presidential pressure, or any other obstacle would keep people in a territory from prohibiting slavery.

Douglas's reply became known as the Freeport doctrine, despite the fact that he had frequently taken the same stand in several previous public speeches. The exchange may have won Lincoln some momentum, although the heavily Republican composition of the crowd may have accounted for much of it, but Lincoln still lost the election to Douglas despite the points he had scored getting his opponent to commit to the Freeport doctrine.

While Lincoln was still alive, a heated debate about his motives in getting Douglas to state the Freeport doctrine arose, and the debate continued into the twentieth century. Lincoln admirers developed an elaborate legend that Lincoln asked a question of minimal interest to Illinois voters because he intended to run for president in 1860. Lincoln scholars have meticulously debunked the legend, but its persistence is a tribute to Americans' compulsion to posthumously endow great leaders with superhuman powers of foresight.

A balanced historical understanding of the Freeport doctrine should place it in the context of the debate strategies of Lincoln and Douglas. For Lincoln, the goal was to focus on slavery and to prevent Douglas from dodging the issue. For Douglas, the goal was to portray Lincoln as a Black Republican (i.e., he was proabolitionist) committed to legal and political equality with white Americans. Both candidates hammered away at these issues during the 1858 debates, and it was only in retrospect, when viewed by people who knew the outcome, that Douglas's remarks at Freeport were elevated to the status of a doctrine.

All debunking aside, the Freeport doctrine still offers valuable insights into what was happening in the United States at that time. What happened at Freeport was part of each candidate's strategy to portray himself as a moderate on the divisive issue of slavery. Unfortunately, by 1858 moderation was no longer admired or emulated in American politics, and it would take more than a series of debates to confront the legal and moral implications of slavery for the Union.

— *Michael Polley*

See also: Douglas, Stephen A.; *Dred Scott v. Sandford;* Lincoln, Abraham; Lincoln–Douglas Debates; Popular Sovereignty.

For Further Reading

Donald, David, Jr. 1995. *Lincoln.* New York: Simon and Schuster.

Fehrenbacher, Don E. 1987. *Lincoln in Text and Context: Collected Essays.* Palo Alto, CA: Stanford University Press.

Holt, Michael. 1978. *The Political Crisis of the 1850s.* New York: Norton.

FUGITIVE SLAVE ACT (1850)

Certainly the antebellum era's most controversial legislative measure, the Fugitive Slave Act (1850) polarized the already-strained relationship between the antislavery North and the proslavery South. Many southerners viewed the measure as a natural affirmation of their constitutional right to recapture all fugitives from labor who sought to escape from the chattel slavery that defined southern institutional life. For the slaveholders and the slave catchers that they employed, the right to recapture fugitive slaves was an obvious extension of common law property rights long considered essential to free market capitalism. For many northerners, the Fugitive Slave Act was an assault upon the integrity of freedom, an appalling contradiction for a society with cherished origins as a land of liberty. Abolitionists and their supporters decried the measure on moral grounds and mounted sustained efforts to render it useless by encouraging acts of civil disobedience.

When the states ratified the U.S. Constitution in 1789, they instituted a document that included a fugitive slave clause (Article IV, Section 2), which stipulated the return of criminal fugitives and fugitives from labor, but the clause neither stated who was responsible for conducting this action nor described the process of recovering fugitives. Congress enacted the Fugitive Slave Act (1793) to clarify the vague provisions of how this constitutional guarantee should function, but many northerners remained dissatisfied with specific internal weaknesses of this measure. Many believed that the 1793 act did not do enough to protect the civil liberties of free blacks who might be falsely accused of being fugitive slaves. Others balked at the act's recognition of the right of recapture, the common-law provision that southern slaveowners maintained gave them the right to recapture their property without the burden of using the court system. Between 1780 and 1850, fourteen states enacted "personal liberty laws" to protect the rights of free blacks within their jurisdictions by imposing a judicial hearing before a suspected fugitive could be removed from the state.

The internal weaknesses of the Fugitive Slave Act (1793) were recognized by the courts, and the measure's effectiveness plummeted with time. In the case of *Prigg v. Pennsylvania* (41 U.S. 539 [1842]) the U.S. Supreme Court struck down an 1826 Pennsylvania personal liberty law that had added additional hindrances to the process of recapture that were in violation of the Fugitive Slave Act (1793). The Pennsylvania law had required that slave catchers obtain a "certificate of removal" from a local magistrate before removing a

An 1850 illustration condemns the Fugitive Slave Act. The act increased federal and free-state responsibility for the recovery of fugitive slaves. (Library of Congress)

suspected fugitive from the state. The Supreme Court's ruling was a rather hollow victory for proslavery forces in that it asserted the constitutional right of recapture, but also stated that while local and state officials should enforce the Fugitive Slave Act, the national government could not mandate such compliance. In the wake of the *Prigg* decision, local and state officials began to refuse to cooperate with slave catchers, and this systematic noncompliance marked the effectual demise of the Fugitive Slave Act (1793).

Southern political leaders demanded that a new and stronger Fugitive Slave Act was needed in order to force compliance upon northern magistrates whose efforts had made recapture more difficult. The push for such legislation became the chief agenda item of the South's congressional caucus. Many feared that if the Congress failed to act on such a measure, some proslavery states might consider seceding from the Union. Hoping to defuse the growing sectional crisis through effective compromise, Kentucky Senator Henry Clay included such a fugitive slave measure in his Omnibus Bill, but that legislative package failed to

win Senate approval in 1850. Illinois Senator Stephen A. Douglas was able to repackage the provisions of Clay's measure into five separate bills that each won approval as shifting coalitions consolidated in the so-called Compromise of 1850.

The Fugitive Slave Act (1850) was harsher than the 1793 measure, for it specifically forbade states from interfering with recapture. It also authorized federal marshals and specially-appointed commissioners to sign warrants for arrest and certificates for removal of suspected fugitives. Although the new act made it easier for recapture to occur, most northern states maintained personal liberty laws and urged noncompliance with what they perceived as an unjust law.

A wave of outrage and righteous indignation swept the North upon the passage of this measure and fanned the flames of antislavery sentiment. Massachusetts citizens deemed Senator Daniel Webster a traitor for having supported the measure, and adding his own vitriol, abolitionist poet John Greenleaf Whittier immortalized Webster's fall from grace in the poem "Ichabod." In 1851 Harriet Beecher Stowe began publishing portions of *Uncle Tom's Cabin* in serial form, and when the entire book was released in 1852, it galvanized northern opposition to slavery and its apologists. Antislavery sentiment and opposition to the Fugitive Slave Act grew so strong in the North that in 1854 the U.S. government had to spend $100,000 to cover the costs associated with returning the fugitive slave Anthony Burns from Boston to the South. It required hundreds of Massachusetts militia and 2,000 federal troops to escort Burns from his jail cell to the dock where he boarded the vessel that carried him back to Virginia.

In 1855 Wisconsin's Supreme Court declared the federal Fugitive Slave Act to be unconstitutional in the case of *In re Booth and Rycraft* (3 Wis. 157 [1855]), but the U.S. Supreme Court later ruled in *Ableman v. Booth* (62 U.S. 506 [1859]) that state courts could not subvert federal law. The U.S. Supreme Court decision also upheld the constitutionality of the Fugitive Slave Act (1850).

Although the Fugitive Slave Act (1850) made life more difficult for those slaves who attempted to escape from bondage, the measure truly had little effective consequence in stemming instances of escape or in raising aggregate rates of recapture. Even though passage of the measure may have salved the consciences of southerners who demanded affirmation of the proslavery position, the act's effective response did much more to galvanize the antislavery position of the abolitionists and their supporters.

— *Junius P. Rodriguez*

See also: Burns, Anthony; Compromise of 1850; Fugitive Slave Acts, State; Personal Liberty Laws.

For Further Reading

Campbell, Stanley W. 1968. *The Slave Catchers: Enforcement of the Fugitive Slave Law, 1850–1860.* Chapel Hill: University of North Carolina Press.

Gara, Larry. 1961. *The Liberty Line: The Legend of the Underground Railroad.* Lexington: University of Kentucky Press.

Nye, Russell B. 1963. *Fettered Freedom: Civil Liberties and the Slave Controversy, 1830–1860.* East Lansing: Michigan State University Press.

Pease, Jane H., and William H. 1975. *The Fugitive Slave Law and Anthony Burns: A Problem of Law Enforcement.* Philadelphia: J.B. Lippincott.

FUGITIVE SLAVE ACTS, STATE

Beginning with Virginia in 1660 and continuing until the American Civil War, colonial assemblies and state legislatures in the South passed hundreds of fugitive slave acts to aid in the orderly and effective recovery of runaway bondsmen, especially those within their jurisdictions. These statutes established procedures for the capture and return of escaped slaves and mandated punishments for runaways and people who encouraged and assisted them in their escape. Historians in the United States have usually concerned themselves with the federal fugitive slave acts of 1793 and 1850; "almost completely missing," as Philip Schwarz has noted, "is an understanding of slave states' laws concerning runaways and fugitives, the first line of defense on which owners relied" (Schwarz, 1996). But state acts were an omnipresent, and often important, element in the effort to control slave behavior.

Fugitive slave acts in the colonial South defined runaways as outlaws in rebellion against their masters. Outlawry mandated harsh punishments, ranging from whipping, maiming, cropping of ears or noses, and branding with an R on the cheek to permitting pursuers to kill fugitive slaves on sight. A 1705 Virginia law authorized justices of the peace to issue proclamations against runaways and directed sheriffs to raise forces to track them. Under the law, if a fugitive failed to surrender, he or she could be killed by any white. If captured alive, runaways could be maimed or dismembered as punishment for their flight. Similar statutes were drafted in Maryland, North Carolina, and South Carolina.

By the late eighteenth century, most southern states had ended outlawry and its harsher punishments. What remained were statutes outlining a legal procedure for the recovery of fugitive slaves. Most antebellum state acts stated that individuals capturing runaways should deliver them to a justice of the peace, who would then have the slave jailed. If the owner were known, he or she could immediately claim the slave. If the owner were unknown, the slave's capture would be advertised in local newspapers. If not claimed after a specified period of time, the slave could be sold. Some of these statutes provided that slaves could be hired out until claimed or sold.

State fugitive slave acts were a moderately effective means of protecting the economic interests of southern slaveholders, but many barriers worked against their complete enforcement. One was the problem of recovering fugitive slaves beyond state lines. Southern state legislatures responded in several ways. They pressed for federal fugitive slave acts; they set substantial compensation amounts for individuals apprehending and returning fugitives from other states, including northern states; and they tightened control of state boundaries. Virginia even created a system of inspection commissioners in 1856 to search for runaways on every boat leaving one of the state's ports.

A second barrier was those whites (especially Quakers) and free blacks who helped or encouraged slaves to escape. All of the state statutes provided punishments for harboring fugitives. Slaves were to be whipped; all free persons—whether black or white—received fines or imprisonment. Only one state, Texas, actually defined the offense of harboring as the "act of maintaining and concealing a runaway slave; a person so harboring having knowledge of the fact that the slave is a runaway."

A related offense was to entice slaves to run away from their masters (also called inveigling). An 1816 Georgia law prescribed a year in prison and sale as a slave for any free black found guilty of this crime. By midcentury it was also a serious criminal offense for whites in most southern states. Mississippi and Kentucky, for example, mandated two to twenty years in prison for anyone found guilty of slave enticement. Although enforcement varied, many southerners were punished for violating state fugitive slave acts. An 1860 list of inmates of the Virginia Penitentiary listed fifteen whites and free blacks who were serving sentences for encouraging or participating in slave escapes.

The onset of the Civil War further hampered the enforcement of state fugitive slave acts as southern slaves fled by the thousands to the safety of Union lines. Even so, Confederate state and local courts continued to prosecute violations of these laws throughout the conflict. Such efforts, though strenuous, proved fruitless in stopping the flood of runaways from southern cities and plantations. State acts concerning fugitive slaves were effectively nullified in 1865 by the passage of the Thirteenth Amendment.

—*Roy E. Finkenbine*

See also: Fugitive Slave Act (1850).

For Further Reading

Morris, Thomas. 1996. *Southern Slavery and the Law, 1619–1860.* Chapel Hill: University of North Carolina Press.

Schwarz, Philip J. 1996. *Slave Laws in Virginia.* Athens: University of Georgia Press.

GAG RESOLUTION

The adoption of the "gag resolution" in the U.S. House of Representatives in 1836 indicated the shrill level to which the antislavery debate had risen in the U.S. Congress. Many believed that the use of such self-imposed censorship to stifle debate on a vital issue of the day was anathema to the democratic principles on which the United States was founded. Supporters of the measure maintained that the primary role of the Congress—to conduct the people's business—could not be accomplished if the legislative body was constantly embroiled in pointless debate over each abolitionist petition and memorial that was addressed to the Congress. The resolution was another sign of growing resistance to the abolitionist movement, as the measure was approved at the same time that antiabolition riots were taking place in many northern cities.

South Carolina Congressman Henry L. Pinckney first proposed the gag resolution in the House of Representatives on May 18, 1836. Pinckney hoped that the measure would alleviate discord in the Congress by automatically tabling all antislavery petitions upon arrival without having them read aloud in the House. The measure produced a vehement discussion in the House of Representatives and indirectly gave renewed urgency to antislavery supporters in the United States.

Pinckney's resolution stated, "Resolved, that all petitions, memorials, and papers touching the abolition of slavery or the buying, selling or transferring of slaves in any state, district, or territory of the United States be laid upon the table without being debated, printed, read, or referred and that no further action whatever shall be had thereon" (Miller, 144).

The U.S. Congress adopted and began using the so-called gag rule on May 26, 1836. The rule effectively prevented the reading and circulation of all antislavery petitions and memorials that were received by the Congress. As a parliamentary maneuver, the House of Representatives had to renew the gag rule at the start of every year's congressional session until the rule was eventually repealed in 1844.

Former president, and Whig congressman from Massachusetts, John Quincy Adams, had not been a vocal opponent of slavery before passage of the gag rule, but this measure moved him toward solidarity with the antislavery advocates. Adams believed that the measure was "a direct violation of the Constitution of the United States (Amendment I), of the rules of this House and of the rights of my constituents" (Miller, 210). One of the most basic civil liberties of a free people, the right to petition their government for a redress of their grievances, was being denied to all who shared antislavery sentiments. Despite all appeals by his political opponents that he remain silent, Adams fought relentlessly for repeal of the gag rule.

On February 15, 1838, Congressman Adams introduced 350 antislavery petitions in defiance of the gag rule that the House of Representatives had instituted. The petitions opposed slavery and the annexation of Texas. Adams continued to be one of the most vocal congressional opponents of the gag rule. Ohio congressman Joshua R. Giddings, the first abolitionist to be elected to the U.S. Congress, took his seat in the House of Representatives on December 3, 1838, and he too became a vocal opponent of the gag rule.

The House of Representatives voted to renew the gag rule on December 11, 1838. The measure had been introduced by Congressman Charles G. Atherton, a New Hampshire Democrat, and the policy thereafter became known as "the Atherton gag." Despite the unpopularity of the measure, the gag rule continued to win support, and it remained in effect for eight years.

The gag rule did not stop antislavery supporters from addressing petitions and memorials to the Congress. Under the direction of the American Anti-Slavery Society, a sustained effort in 1837–1838 produced more than one hundred thirty thousand petitions to the Congress calling for the abolition of slavery within the District of Columbia. The magnitude of this campaign made proslavery congressmen confident that they had acted wisely by prohibiting any consideration of these proposals.

Despite intense protests against the policy, in 1840 the House of Representatives made the gag rule even more restrictive. It was modified to state that Congress would no longer accept antislavery petitions. Although the measure was never challenged in the courts, it appears to have been a legislative attempt to restrict constitutionally protected First Amendment rights to a significant portion of the American population.

On December 3, 1844, after years of difficult enforcement, the House of Representatives lifted the gag rule, which had prohibited the discussion of antislavery petitions received by the Congress. The resolution calling for repeal of the gag rule passed by a vote of 108 to 80. The resolution that repealed the gag rule was authored by Congressman John Quincy Adams.

During the years it was in effect, the gag rule applied only to the House of Representatives and not to the Senate, which had rejected such an option. Despite the concerns of some congressmen that they could not conduct the people's business without the presence of the gag rule, the Senate seemed to function normally without resorting to such self-imposed censorship. Yet even without a gag rule, Senate procedures did not permit the automatic reading of antislavery proposals that were received by that body.

It is almost inconceivable that self-imposed censorship in the U.S. House of Representatives prohibited consideration of materials related to the slavery question from 1836 to 1844. Issues ranging from the proposed annexation of Texas to the *Amistad* case all had a direct bearing on the institution of slavery, and the gag rule made it impossible for the rich debate that is the hallmark of democracy to occur during this era.

— *Junius P. Rodriguez*

See also: Adams, John Quincy; Antiabolition riots; Giddings, Joshua R.

For Further Reading
   Miller, William Lee. 1996. *Arguing about Slavery: The Great Battle in the United States Congress.* New York: Alfred A. Knopf.

HENRY HIGHLAND GARNET (1815–1882)

A noted fugitive slave, abolitionist, clergyman, diplomat, and political activist, Henry Highland Garnet was one of the nineteenth century's most elusive and provocative African American leaders. His grandfather was a leader in West Africa's once powerful Mandingo Empire, and Henry was the son of George and Henny (Henrietta) Garnet, who later changed her name to Elizabeth.

He was born a slave on a plantation in New Market, Kent County, Maryland, but when he was nine, his family, assisted by Quakers, escaped and moved to Pennsylvania. In 1826 the family moved to New York, and Garnet entered the famous African Free School No. 1 that the New York Manumission Society had established in 1787. Afterward Garnet enrolled in the Noyes Academy in New Canaan, New Hampshire, a school that was constructed during the height of intense racial agitation. In summer 1835, a mob of nearly three hundred men, with perhaps one hundred oxen, tore the building apart, leaving it in ruins.

Garnet continued his education at Oneida Theological Institute, near Utica, New York. There, under the tutelage of Reverend Theodore S. Wright, a Presbyterian minister, Garnet obtained his intellectual skills and spiritual framework. His friendship with Wright greatly influenced Garnet's later career as an abolitionist and a minister.

Completing his theological training in 1840, Garnet moved to Troy, New York, where he became the minister of a local African American Presbyterian church, and he rapidly developed into an ardent abolitionist for the American Anti-Slavery Society. From 1842 to 1860, he was a very influential and powerful African American abolitionist. In 1843, Garnet delivered a speech at a national convention of free black Americans in Buffalo, New York, in which he called for African slaves to rebel against their masters. This speech frightened the audience greatly, and many attending the convention refused to support Garnet's radical ideas. Frederick Douglass, a prominent leader in the African American community and Garnet's chief critic, was in attendance. Douglass disagreed with several major points in the speech and specifically disapproved of Garnet's call for African slaves to use violence to end slavery.

This convention signaled the beginning of Garnet's decline as a prominent African American abolitionist and stimulated Douglass's rise as the new African American abolitionist leader. Still, Garnet did not give up his antislavery efforts entirely, and he even traveled overseas to promote the cause. In August 1850, he delivered an emotional speech as a delegate to the World Peace Congress, in Frankfurt, Germany, and in 1851, he gave several antislavery speeches to abolitionist organizations in England and Scotland.

As his abolitionist status declined, Garnet began devoting most of his energy to spreading the gospel. From 1843 to 1848, he was the minister of the Liberty Street Presbyterian Church in Troy, New York. In 1852 the United Presbyterian Church of Scotland sent him to Jamaica to spread Christianity, and in 1853, he became pastor of Jamaica's Stirling Presbyterian Church. A few years later, upon the death of Reverend Wright, Garnet returned to the United States to become the new pastor of New York's Shiloh Presbyterian Church.

During the Civil War, Garnet demanded that President Abraham Lincoln enlist the services of African Americans in the Union army, and he continued expressing this viewpoint despite the 1863 New York City race riot, which threatened his own safety. In 1864, Garnet moved to Washington, D.C., to become the pastor of the Fifteenth Street Presbyterian Church. On several occasions, his sermons attracted enormous biracial audiences. Having a pulpit in Washington, D.C., encouraged Garnet to reactivate his antislavery message, and he traveled throughout the Northeast to deliver inspirational sermons to battle-weary African American troops. In winter 1863–1864, Garnet gave an emotional sermon to several African American regiments stationed in New York City. On February 12, 1865, he delivered a sermon in the House of Representatives to celebrate passage of the Thirteenth Amendment.

After the Civil War, Garnet held an administrative position with the Freedmen's Relief Association. This privately funded association, which was separate from the government-sponsored Freedmen's Bureau, sought to build schools and shelters in local African American communities in the United States. These facilities were designed to help African Americans adjust to their new status as free men and women.

In Washington, D.C., alone, the Freedmen's Relief Association had built four schools and twelve shelters by late 1865, and Garnet played an active role in developing one of these—the African Civilization Society School. Eventually, he became dissatisfied with the association's position on the role of African American teachers and withdrew his support.

Disillusioned by declining race relations within the United States, Garnet began to express an interest in Africa in the later years of his life. He had opposed colonization vigorously throughout the antebellum and Civil War years, but gradually, his views began to change. Undoubtedly, his change of heart stemmed partly from continuing racial problems within the United States and partly from the inability of African Americans to move up the socioeconomic ladder during the Reconstruction era.

In 1881 President James Garfield appointed Garnet the minister and counsel general to Liberia. In January 1882, Liberian president Edward Wilmot Blyden sponsored a dinner to honor Garnet. Many high-ranking government officials attended the celebration, and Garnet praised the many achievements of the Liberian people in the speech he gave at the ceremony. His health declined very soon thereafter, and on February 13, 1882, Garnet died in his sleep.

— *Eric R. Jackson*

See also: Abolitionism in the United States; Liberia.

For Further Reading
   Brewer, W. M. 1928. "Henry Highland Garnet." *Journal of Negro History* 13 (1): 36–52.
   Holmes, James Arthur. 1997. "Black Nationalism and Theodicy: a Comparison of the Thought of Henry Highland Garnet, Alexander Crummell, and Henry McNeal Turner." Ph.D. dissertation, Department of Religion, Boston University, Boston, Massachusetts.

Pasternak, Martin B. 1995. *Rise Now and Fly to Arms: The Life of Henry Highland Garnet.* New York: Garland.

Schor, Joel. 1977. *Henry Highland Garnet: A Voice of Black Radicalism in the Nineteenth Century.* Westport, CT: Greenwood.

Stuckey, Sterling. 1988. "A Last Stern Struggle: Henry Highland Garnet and Liberation Theory." In *Black Leaders of the Nineteenth Century,* edited by Leon Litwack and August Meier. Urbana: University of Illinois Press.

THOMAS GARRETT (1789–1871)

An ardent abolitionist, Thomas Garrett made major contributions to the antislavery cause through his work with fugitive slaves. Tradition traces his concern for slaves to 1813 when kidnappers attempted to sell a female servant into slavery from the family home in Pennsylvania. The incident led Garrett to a prolonged period of volunteer service on behalf of escaping slaves. Building on his Quaker family's antislavery sentiment, Garrett provided skilled leadership, time, and money to the abolition movement's Underground Railroad efforts.

Although most Quakers held moderate antislavery views, Garrett allied with William Lloyd Garrison and his confrontational approach to the issue. After 1822 Garrett lived and worked in Delaware, a border state whose population held mixed views on slavery. He asserted that there was as much antislavery sentiment in Delaware as in Boston, but only a few citizens were willing to join Garrett in his work with fugitives. He organized a small group of accomplices who provided food, transportation, and temporary shelter to escaping slaves. This endeavor was so successful that it later contributed to a legend of a nationally organized network of Underground Railroad operatives.

Garrett claimed to have assisted twenty-seven hundred men and women to escape slavery. He worked closely with William Still, the African American chairman of the Philadelphia Vigilance Committee, which was an arm of the Pennsylvania Anti-Slavery Society. On several occasions Harriet Tubman escorted escaped slaves to Garrett's home, though he himself neither entered southern states nor enticed slaves to leave their masters. Garrett's commitment to nonviolence did not prevent his advising fugitives to join the Union army. To a friend he wrote: "Am I naughty, being a professed nonresistant, to advise this poor fellow to serve Father Abraham?" (McGowan, 1977).

As a successful businessman, Garrett was largely immune from public criticism and physical attack, but not entirely. On one occasion he was nearly thrown from a train while trying to keep a woman from being sold into slavery. In 1848 Garrett and his coworker, John Hunn, were sued for damages for helping several slaves to escape. Roger B. Taney was one of two judges who heard the case, finding both defendants liable for $54,000 in damages. An often-repeated story suggests Garrett's total impoverishment as a result. Actual court records show a compromise settlement of $1,500, enough to reduce Garrett's resources seriously but not enough to impoverish him. In 1860 Maryland's legislature proposed offering a $10,000 reward for Garrett's arrest, though the action was largely symbolic.

Following emancipation Garrett worked for civil rights, woman suffrage, and temperance. After ratification of the Fifteenth Amendment to the Constitution, African Americans drove Garrett through Wilmington's streets in an open carriage under a banner that proclaimed "Our Moses." Upon learning of Garrett's death, William Lloyd Garrison observed: "His rightful place is conspicuously among the benefactors, saviors, martyrs of the human race" (McGowan, 1977).

— *Larry Gara*

See also: Quakers; Still, William; Tubman, Harriet; Underground Railroad.

For Further Reading

Drake, Thomas E. n.d. "Thomas Garrett, Quaker Abolitionist," In *Friends in Wilmington, 1738–1938.* Ed. Edward P Bartlett. Wilmington, OH.

McGowan, James A. 1977. *Station Master on the Underground Railroad: The Life and Letters of Thomas Garrett.* Moylan, PA: Whimsie Press.

Still, William. 1883. *The Under-Ground Railroad.* Philadelphia: William Still.

Thompson, Priscilla. 1986. "Harriet Tubman, Thomas Garrett, and the Underground Railroad." *Delaware History* 22 (September): 1–21.

WILLIAM LLOYD GARRISON (1805–1879)

William Lloyd Garrison was the most significant U.S. champion of immediate abolitionism. Born into poverty and abandoned by his father at the age of three, Garrison had a lifelong empathy with the disadvantaged and oppressed. He was apprenticed to a printer at thirteen and worked at various reform newspapers in New England until 1829, when he became coeditor of the newspaper *Genius of Universal Emancipation* in Baltimore, Maryland. Garrison's fervid antislavery editorials roused the anger of the local

With the help of philanthropist Arthur Tappan, William Lloyd Garrison started the antislavery paper the *Liberator* on January 1, 1831. (National Archives)

slaveholding elite, and in January 1830, he was jailed for libeling a slave trader. His plight caught the attention of philanthropist Arthur Tappan, who bailed him out of jail and provided partial financial support for Garrison to start a new antislavery paper, the *Liberator*, on January 1, 1831.

In the *Liberator*, Garrison abandoned the gradualist approach of most earlier opponents of slavery and embraced the new doctrine of abolitionism. Denying that slavery was a social and an economic problem of such great complexity that it might take years to abolish, Garrison said slavery was a matter of personal morality that could be remedied on an individual basis instantly. Slavery wrongfully denied blacks certain rights, and slaveholders should be asked to free their slaves immediately in the same way that they would be asked to immediately stop any other immoral action. Slaveholders should not be financially compensated for abandoning sin. The effort to colonize manumitted slaves in Africa reflected white prejudice and should be abandoned. Garrison proposed that blacks be given the same civil and political rights as white citizens of the United States.

The *Liberator* spoke to a generation of antislavery activists who were unhappy with the moral compromises involved in the old gradualist approach to emancipation. Soon after the *Liberator* began publication, abolitionism burst onto the scene with a suddenness that shocked Americans and alarmed slaveholders. Garrison played the leading role in galvanizing and organizing the new immediatists. Garrison's pamphlet, *Thoughts on African Colonization* (1832), rallied antislavery forces against the American Colonization Society; he also helped found the New England Anti-Slavery Society in 1832 and the American Anti-Slavery Society (AAS) in 1833.

Garrison endorsed several other controversial reforms that affected the antislavery movement. Embracing the doctrine of nonresistance, Garrison rejected the use of violence and coercive force and argued that many human relationships were, like slavery, based on violent coercion. Garrison believed that the power of religious denominations to compel adherence to creeds was a kind of slavery, and by the late 1830s, he rejected organized religion.

Garrison also believed that government was an example of coercive force. Rejecting the moral authority of governments, Garrison argued that Christians needed no law but the higher law of God, and he refused on principle to vote. Understanding that most abolitionists would not follow his nonresistant principles, Garrison continued to speak out in the *Liberator* on political issues, telling others how to exercise the franchise if they believed in voting. Nevertheless, Garrison argued that it was tactically wrong for abolitionists to concentrate their reform activities on the political world. The role of the abolitionist was not to organize political parties, but to practice moral suasion, holding forth the standard of right and exhorting others to follow it.

Garrison applied his beliefs about human equality to gender relationships and encouraged the efforts of abolitionist women such as Sarah and Angelina Grimké to carve out a public role for themselves in the abolitionist movement. Such actions shocked the conventional morality of the nineteenth century and helped split the American Anti-Slavery Society in 1840. Members of the society argued about whether women should be able to vote and hold office within the AAS and whether abolitionists should organize a political party to accomplish their goals.

Ultimately, Garrison himself became an issue. Some abolitionists believed potential supporters were driven off by his positions on nonresistance and women's rights and by his increasingly unorthodox religious ideas and harsh denunciations of opponents. When

Garrisonian abolitionists emerged with a majority from the society's convention in 1840, Garrison's opponents, led by Arthur and Lewis Tappan and James G. Birney, left the AAS and formed a rival organization, the American and Foreign Anti-Slavery Society.

Although other abolitionists worked in the 1840s and 1850s to end slavery through political parties and religious organizations, Garrison played the roles of prophet and agitator. He remained a lonely voice crying out for truth and justice as he saw it and urging others to follow him. In 1843 Garrison proclaimed the U.S. Constitution a "Covenant with Death, an Agreement with Hell" (*Liberator*, March 17, 1843). Arguing that the Constitution protected slavery, Garrison urged northerners to secede from the Union. Believing that slavery could not survive without the support of the federal government, Garrison believed that the disruption of the Union would strike a deathblow to slavery.

Although often remembered today as a divisive figure with a contentious personality, Garrison had a much different image among his closest followers, for whom he served as a kind of father figure. "Father Garrison," as he was affectionately known, acted as trusted advisor, peacemaker, and encourager for his followers, creating an almost familial closeness among them. Seeking to overcome the family insecurity of his youth, Garrison also became a doting father to his own children and an affectionate husband to his wife, Helen Benson. Living his reform principles at home, Garrison drew his family into the world of social reform, and his children who survived to adulthood—George, William, Wendell, Fanny, and Frank—would continue to play important roles in such diverse causes as women's suffrage, international peace, anti-imperialism, tax reform, and civil rights into the early twentieth century.

The outbreak of the American Civil War caused a change in Garrison's views and public standing. Heartened by the North's stand against the South, Garrison believed northerners had been converted to antislavery, and he supported the effort to preserve the Union. Abraham Lincoln's decision to issue the Emancipation Proclamation prompted Garrison to violate his no-voting principle by casting a ballot for Lincoln's reelection in 1864. During the war, Garrison was transformed in the public's mind from crank to hero. At the end of the fighting, he was the government's guest of honor at the ceremony raising the U.S. flag over Fort Sumter. Believing his abolitionist work was largely done, Garrison ceased publication of the *Liberator* and resigned from the AAS in 1865. This decision estranged Garrison from his longtime friend and collaborator Wendell Phillips, who argued that the AAS must continue its activities in order to secure equal rights and economic security for former slaves. Until his death, Garrison continued to lecture occasionally and to write essays for the *New York Independent* newspaper on various social reforms, including the rights of freed people.

— *Harold D. Tallant*

See also: Abolitionism in the United States; American Colonization Society; The *Liberator*.

For Further Reading

Alonso, Harriet Hyman. 2002. *Growing up Abolitionist: The Story of the Garrison Children*. Amherst: University of Massachusetts Press.

Kraditor, Aileen S. 1969. *Means and Ends in American Abolitionism: Garrison and His Critics on Strategy and Tactics, 1834–1850*. New York: Pantheon Books.

Mayer, Henry. 1998. *All on Fire: William Lloyd Garrison and the Abolition of Slavery*. New York: St. Martin's Press.

Merrill, Walter M. 1963. *Against Wind and Tide: A Biography of William Lloyd Garrison*. Cambridge, MA: Harvard University Press.

Stewart, James Brewer. 1992. *William Lloyd Garrison and the Challenge of Emancipation*. Arlington Heights, IL: Harlan Davidson.

Thomas, John L. 1963. *The Liberator: William Lloyd Garrison*. Boston: Little, Brown and Company.

GEECHEE

The word "Geechee" is the name of a unique African ethnic group that exists in the southeastern portion of the United States of America. Geechee (which has often been incorrectly spelled "Geechie") is thought to be derived from an island in the Sierra Leone region of West Africa called "Kissee" or "Kissi" but pronounced "geechee." The Gizzis, Kissis, or Giggis were kidnapped form the forest belt along Africa's windward coast (modern-day Sierra Leone and Liberia) during the transatlantic slave trade. They were subsequently brought to and heavily populated the Sea Islands, which extend from the area that is now Jacksonville, North Carolina, southward to Jacksonville, Florida.

The word "Gullah" is thought to be derived from the Gola peoples of the same region of Africa from whence Geechee comes. Both Geechee and Gullah share many linguistic influences with the Fula, Mende, upper Guinea coast, and Gambia River areas.

Some Georgia residents have mistakenly believed that the name "Geechee" derived from the Ogeechee River, which empties into the Atlantic Ocean near Savannah. This river still bears the name that the indigenous Americans of the area used for it. The people who live along this river have often nicknamed themselves "Geechee," which is not the historically accurate reason for use of the term in reference to the people of African descent of the area.

The word "Gullah" is often used to describe the people of the Georgia Sea Islands and the mainland of the Carolina/Georgia low country region that speak a dialect of the Gullah language and share similar traditions as those of the South Carolina Sea Islands who are referred to as "Gullah." In addition, this word has been used as a derogatory term for southern people of African descent who ate rice for many years. However, scholarly research over the years has revealed that this is a unique oral expression system that has a relationship to other languages spoken throughout the African Diaspora.

The people of the Sea Islands and low country of the United States that share the African heritage that has come to be known as "Gullah" and "Geechee" have come together to be recognized as one people and are known as the Gullah/Geechee Nation. On July 2, 2000, they had an official ceremony for this designation at which they presented their governing principles and flag. The Gullah/Geechee Nation Constitution states that "Gullah includes the people, history, language, and culture and Geechee is the 'descendant' of this. Gullah is the native tongue and pure language. Geechee is the creolization of the language in which loan words from other languages are used as the Gullah/Geechee people continue to interact with those that speak other languages."

— *Marquetta L. Goodwine*

See also: Gullah; Rice Cultivation and Trade; Sea Islands.

For Further Reading
Goodwine, Marquetta L. 1998. *The Legacy of Ibo Landing: Gullah Roots of African American Culture.* Atlanta, GA: Clarity Press.

Joyner, Charles W. 1989. *Remember Me: Slave Life in Coastal Georgia, 1750–1860.* Atlanta: Georgia Humanities Council.

Kemble, Frances Anne. 2000. *Journal of a Residence on a Georgia Plantation in 1838–1839.* Ed. Catherine Clinton. Cambridge, MA: Harvard University Press.

Pollitzer, William. 1999. *The Gullah People and Their African Heritage.* Athens: University of Georgia Press.

Turner, Lorenzo Dow. 1974. *Africanisms in the Gullah Dialect.* Ann Arbor: University of Michigan Press.

Works Progress Administration, Georgia Writers Project. [1940] 1986. *Drums and Shadows; Survival Studies Among the Georgia Coastal Negroes.* Athens: University of Georgia Press.

GENIUS OF UNIVERSAL EMANCIPATION

During the 1820s, under Benjamin Lundy's editorship, the *Genius of Universal Emancipation* was the nation's major antislavery newspaper and linked together abolitionist groups across the nation. It was first published in Lundy's hometown of Mount Pleasant, Ohio, in January 1821. Elihu Embree's father had hoped that Lundy would continue the *Emancipator* after Elihu's death in 1820 and move to Jonesborough, Tennessee, but Lundy moved to Greeneville, Tennessee, a few months later instead. However, the *Genius of Universal Emancipation* was continued using the same printing equipment as the earlier newspaper. Then, in the summer of 1824, the paper was moved to Baltimore, where a Baltimore slave-dealer, Austin Woolfolk, assaulted Lundy in 1827 because of comments published in the paper. The paper was moved to Washington, D.C., in 1830, where it was published until 1834. Between 1835 and 1836, publication of the *Genius of Universal Emancipation* ceased, and Lundy began publishing another newspaper in Philadelphia, the *National Enquirer,* which opposed the annexation of Texas. This paper became the *Pennsylvania Freeman* in 1838. That May, Lundy lost all his papers in a mob attack on Pennsylvania Hall, and he moved to Illinois and reestablished the *Genius of Universal Emancipation.* The twelve issues that preceded his death had the dateline of Hennepin, Illinois, but they were actually printed in Lowell, Illinois.

Lundy is credited with bringing William Lloyd Garrison into the national spotlight. In 1829 Garrison became associate editor after Lundy had met him during a six-month lecture tour, but Garrison's militancy led to a separation with Lundy. In 1830, while Lundy was away, Garrison libeled a Newburyport, Massachusetts, slave dealer in the paper, and both he and Lundy were sued and physically attacked. Garrison even spent seven weeks in jail for the libel. In 1831 Garrison moved to Boston and founded the *Liberator,* a paper that quickly replaced the *Genius of Universal Emancipation* as the nation's major antislavery newspaper. As early as 1829, Garrison had openly recanted "gradual abolition" in the *Genius of Universal Emancipation,* which he noted in the prospectus for the *Liberator.*

Lundy's approach was different as he advocated a gradualist voluntary approach to abolition. He believed that demonstration of the productivity of free black labor would lead to the gradual extinction of slavery through voluntary manumission. Although he believed free blacks had a right to stay in the United States, he thought it would be easier for them to prove the superiority of their labor in emigrant colonies. To find a suitable location for a colony for freed blacks, he traveled to Haiti (1825 and 1829), Upper Canada (1832), and Mexico's Texas (1830–1831, 1833–1834, 1834–1835). He published both evangelical appeals, expressed largely by southerners, and secular arguments against slavery, and he condemned only violence as a means for ending the institution. Lundy denounced slavery for nurturing aristocratic and undemocratic attitudes among slaveowners. Ahead of his time, he advocated political action as an appropriate antislavery strategy. The types of material he published included reports of law cases, proceedings of abolition societies, biographical and historical sketches, and summaries of pertinent foreign and domestic news.

— *Charles D'Aniello*

See also: The *Emancipator;* Garrison, William Lloyd; The *Liberator.*

For Further Reading

Blassingame, John W., and Mae G. Henderson, eds. 1980–1984. *Antislavery Newspapers and Periodicals, Volume I (1817–1845): Annotated Index of Letters in the Philanthropist, Emancipator, Genius of Universal Emancipation, Abolition Intelligencer, African Observer, and the Liberator.* Boston: G.K. Hall.

Dillon, Merton L. 1966. *Benjamin Lundy and the Struggle for Negro Freedom.* Urbana: University of Illinois Press.

Dillon, Merton L. 1986. "Benjamin Lundy: Quaker Radical." *Timeline* 3 (3): 28–41.

EUGENE GENOVESE (B. 1930)

Eugene Genovese is a scholar of American history and an author of numerous important monographs on the nineteenth-century United States. More than any other historian he has used Marxian theory to analyze American slavery and the antebellum South.

With Herbert Aptheker and Raimondo Luraghi, Genovese argues that the slave labor system was the Old South's distinguishing feature. Slavery retarded capitalism's development, created a powerful planter elite, and inevitably led to the American Civil War. "Slavery," Genovese writes in his first work, "gave the South a social system and a civilization with a distinct class structure, political community, economy, ideology, and a set of psychological patterns and that, as a result, the South increasingly grew away from the rest of the nation and from the rapidly developing sections of the world" (Genovese, 1983, 3).

A graduate of Brooklyn College and Columbia University, where he earned a Ph.D. under the super-

vision of Richard B. Morris, Genovese almost single-handedly challenged much of the accepted wisdom on the antebellum South. Where historians had increasingly focused on the similarities between North and South, arguing that the Civil War had been the ghastly mistake of a "blundering generation," Genovese elaborated the striking contrasts between the two sections. In his path-breaking *The Political Economy of Slavery: Studies in the Economy and Society of the Slave South* (1965), Genovese explored how "slavery gave the South a special way of life" (Genovese, 1965, 3) that made it a distinct section of the nation. Borrowing from the so-called Hegelian Marxism of Antonio Gramsci, Genovese explained southern planter control over both black slaves and the white yeomanry as a result of cultural hegemony. The yeomanry "went against its apparent collective interests" in large measure because the planter class disguised its domination behind a mask of race solidarity. Some whites might have nothing but freedom, but they were not slaves.

Genovese's conviction that slavery proved the great distinguishing characteristic of the Old South led him to undertake highly focused studies on both slaves and slaveowners. In *Roll, Jordan, Roll: The World the Slaves Made* (1974), he asserts that slaves "laid the foundations for a separate black national culture while enormously enriching American culture as a whole" (Genovese, 1974, xv). This pioneering work incisively demonstrates how slaves responded to an odious and oppressive system in imaginative and resourceful ways. With a mixture of accommodation and resistance, including petty theft and arson, slaves succeeded in maintaining at least some measure of human dignity in the face of great hardship, while simultaneously establishing autonomous black cultural institutions. Meticulously researched, *Roll, Jordan, Roll,* offers an extraordinarily detailed panorama of black, religious, linguistic, and familial cultural formations. Genovese concludes that for all its African roots, "separate black national culture has always been American" (ibid, xv).

Genovese's description of planter "paternalism," a precapitalist, protective stance toward slaves is one of his most important contributions to the field and has gained wide acceptance among historians. His claims about the planter class and its hegemony, however, have drawn good deal of criticism, as has his rather generous view of the paternalistic slaveowner. In works remarkably reminiscent of Ulrich B. Phillips in the early twentieth century, Genovese has offered a surprisingly sympathetic portrait of the anticapitalist, patrician planter class. More remarkably still, in recent years Genovese has maintained his admiration for the planter elite while simultaneously renouncing his former Marxist convictions.

Spanning four decades, the work of Eugene Genovese has contributed enormously to our understanding of the American antebellum South. By documenting in rich detail the remarkable, uniquely American, and deeply complex development of masters and slaves, slavery and freedom, Genovese has forcefully demonstrated the centrality of slavery to the history of the American South.

— *Peter S. Field*

See also: Aptheker, Herbert; Fox-Genovese, Elizabeth; Phillips, Ulrich Bonnell.

For Further Reading:

Aptheker, Herbert. 1943. *American Negro Slave Revolts.* New York: Columbia University Press.

Frederickson, George. 1981. *White Supremacy: A Comparative Study in American and South African History.* New York: Oxford University Press.

Fox-Genovese, Elizabeth. 1988. *Within the Plantation Household.* Chapel Hill: University of North Carolina Press.

Fox-Genovese, Elizabeth. 1991. *Feminism without Illusions.* Chapel Hill: University of North Carolina Press.

Fox-Genovese, Elizabeth, ed. 1992. *Southern Women: Histories and Identities.* Columbia: University of Missouri Press.

Fox-Genovese, Elizabeth, ed. 1994. *Hidden Histories of Women in the New South.* Columbia: University of Missouri Press.

Fox-Genovese, Elizabeth, and Eugene D. Genovese. 1983. *Fruits of Merchant Capital.* New York: Oxford University Press.

Genovese, Eugene D. 1965. *The Political Economy of Slavery; Studies in the Economy and Society of the Slave South.* New York, Pantheon Books.

Genovese, Eugene D. 1966. *The Legacy of Slavery and the Roots of Black Nationalism.* Boston: New England Free Press.

Genovese, Eugene D. 1971. *In Red and Black; Marxian Explorations in Southern and Afro-American History.* New York: Pantheon Books.

Genovese, Eugene D. 1974. *Roll, Jordan, Roll: The World the Slaves Made.* New York: Pantheon Books.

Luraghi, Raimondo. 1978. *The Rise and Fall of the Plantation South.* New York: New Viewpoints.

Morgan, Edmund. 1975. *American Slavery, American Freedom: The Ordeal of Colonial Virginia.* New York: Norton.

GEORGIA

Georgia was the last of the thirteen British colonies to be established on the Atlantic seaboard of the North American continent during the early eighteenth century. When it was founded in 1733 as a royal colony dedicated to the philanthropic ideals of its founder, James Oglethorpe, the colony became the only British colony that specifically prohibited slavery. Oglethorpe's altruism did not necessarily apply to abolitionist notions as he had previously been a slaveholder in the Carolinas and served as deputy governor of the Royal Africa Company, a British firm that was heavily involved in the transatlantic slave trade. As early as 1739 settlers were petitioning to have slavery introduced, and by 1749 the trustees of the Georgia Colony repealed the prohibition against the importation of slaves into the colony.

The colony of Georgia was originally established to provide a buffer zone between the more economically prized tobacco colonies to the north and Spanish Florida to the south. Some of the early colonial settlers were individuals who were released from British jails after having been imprisoned as debtors. Their early settlements were recognized as the first line of defense between the largely Anglo-Saxon Protestant settlements to the north and the Spanish Roman Catholic settlements of Florida. The tenuous nature of this boundary, especially with relation to slavery, was the effort by South Carolina slaves to foment insurrection during the Stono Rebellion (1739) and make their way to Spanish Florida where they had been promised emancipation and sanctuary.

Colonial Georgia consisted of a small geographic region that included Savannah, one of the few planned cities in the Americas, and its surrounding hinterland counties. The population was small, and it supported limited economic pursuits that were associated primarily with sustaining the colony. There was some agricultural development of rice and indigo in the coastal areas, and a small amount of long-staple Sea Island cotton was produced as well. None of these ventures developed into a "cash crop" as tobacco had sustained the colonies to the north, and as a result, the colony struggled financially.

Slightly more than four decades separated Georgia's founding from the coming of the American Revolution (1775–1783) that sought to separate the North American colonies from Great Britain. By relative comparison to the other colonies, many settlers in Georgia still maintained close cultural and familial ties with their British kinsmen, and as a result, there was a relatively high incidence of persons with Loyalist (Tory) sympathies during the years of the American Revolution. In addition, a significant number of fugitive slaves and free blacks congregated in areas, like Savannah, that came under British control during the Revolution. Many of these so-called Black Loyalists were removed from North America between July 1782 and November 1783 as Sir Guy Carleton conducted a series of mini-evacuations to remove these individuals to other locations including Canada, the Bahamas, and Sierra Leone.

Postrevolutionary Georgia continued to develop the limited agricultural pursuits that had sustained the region during the colonial era. Additional economic activity, specifically in the area of shipbuilding and naval stores, began to emerge in the region. By 1790, the population of Georgia was 82,548, and this figure included a slave population of 29,264, or 35.4 percent of the state's inhabitants.

In 1792 Eli Whitney arrived in Savannah to study law and to tutor the children of General Nathanael Greene, a hero of the American Revolution. While living in Mulberry Grove, Georgia, the Massachusetts native recognized the problems inherent with cultivating cotton in the area—particularly the difficulty of removing cotton seeds from cotton fiber by hand. Whitney's ingenious solution to this problem—the development of the cotton gin—would do much to transform the agricultural economy not only of Georgia but also of the entire antebellum South. In addition, the expansion of cotton cultivation would trigger an insatiable demand for slave laborers throughout the region.

Essentially the cotton gin made possible the large-scale cultivation of short-staple upland cotton in regions that had been previously considered marginal lands. Unlike long-staple Sea Island cotton, the short-staple variety could practically grow anywhere, but its production had been limited by the time-consuming effort needed to remove the seeds from the fiber. Even though the quality of short-staple cotton was viewed as being second-class to long-staple cotton, the product was ideally suited to a world of cotton gins and protoindustrial textile plants that were beginning to emerge both in Britain and in the northern states. The cotton gin facilitated the expansion of a cotton economy, and by necessity, a slave-based agricultural regime in the South.

The primary obstacle to the expansion of cotton cultivation and slavery in Georgia was the abundant expanse of land within the state that was recognized by treaty as belonging to the Native American tribes that inhabited it. The vast acreage belonging to the Cherokee, Creek, and, to a lesser extent, Seminole, nations was perceived by Georgia planters as an impediment to progress, and efforts were made at the state level to renegotiate treaty arrangements. Not until the passage of the Indian Removal Act (1830) and the presidency of Andrew Jackson did the state of Georgia find a friendly accomplice in federal efforts to remove the "Five Civilized Tribes"—the Cherokee, Creek, Seminole, Choctaw, and Chickasaw peoples—from the lands they inhabited in the southeastern United States.

Once Indian Removal had been effected (by the late 1830s), thousands of planters and yeoman farmers acquired land in the newly opened lands of northern, western, and southwestern Georgia. During the 1840s this cotton-boom land rush continued unabated, and by the 1850s a distinct cultural demographic region began to take shape. The so-called Black Belt region began to form in an area that made a southwestward swath from Athens to Columbus and then continuing onward into central Alabama. This red-clay region of the antebellum South became one of the most productive areas where short-staple upland cotton was cultivated; correspondingly, the region had some of the highest per capita rates of slaveownership in the South.

From the 1830s onward toward the Civil War (1861–1865), Georgians cultivated a reputation as some of the most vociferous defenders of the institution of slavery. In 1831 the Georgia legislature went so far as to issue a reward of $5,000 to anyone who might capture the abolitionist William Lloyd Garrison and turn him over to Georgia authorities. By 1835 the legislature had enacted a measure authorizing the death penalty for anyone who distributed abolitionist literature within the state. Not surprisingly, many of the "fire-eaters"—the most vocal defenders of slavery and the southern way of life—were individuals like William Lowndes Yancey who had Georgia roots.

Georgia became the fifth southern state to secede from the Union when its legislature voted to do so on January 19, 1861. One month later, Alexander Stephens of Georgia was named vice president of the Confederate States of America when representatives of the seceded states convened in Montgomery, Alabama, to organize their government. Stephens affirmed on that occasion that the Confederacy "rests upon the great truth that the Negro is not equal to the white man, that slavery, subordination to the superior race, is a natural and normal condition . . . our new Government, is the first in the history of the world, based upon this great physical, philosophical, and moral truth" (Schott, 1988).

Georgia witnessed much hardship during the Civil War, particularly during 1864. After the fall of Chattanooga, Union forces entered Georgia and made a sustained push toward Atlanta as Confederate forces under General John Bell Hood constantly retreated. Following the fall of Atlanta, General William Tecumseh Sherman began his "March to the Sea" that brought total war to the plantations and farms of east-central

Georgia. By December 1864 Union forces had reached Savannah.

Having been staunch defenders of antebellum slavery, white Georgians did not readily accept the civil rights that were bestowed upon freedmen in the aftermath of the Civil War. During the Reconstruction era Georgians used black codes and other extralegal measures to stymie the freedmen's efforts to acquire the protections guaranteed by federal Civil Rights Acts and the passage of the Thirteenth, Fourteenth, and Fifteenth amendments to the U.S. Constitution.

— *Junius P. Rodriguez*

See also: Black Belt; Georgia Code; Sea Islands; Stono Rebellion (1739); Whitney, Eli.

For Further Reading

Flanders, Ralph B. 1933. *Plantation Slavery in Georgia.* Chapel Hill: University of North Carolina Press.

Lane, Mills, ed. 1993. *Neither More Nor Less Than Men: Slavery in Georgia: A Documentary History.* Savannah, GA: Beehive Press.

Mohr, Clarence L. 1986. *On the Threshold of Freedom: Masters and Slaves in Civil War Georgia.* Athens: University of Georgia Press.

Schott, Thomas E. 1988. *Alexander H. Stephens of Georgia: A Biography.* Baton Rouge: Louisiana State University Press.

Smith, Julia Floyd. 1985. *Slavery and Rice Culture in Low Country Georgia, 1750–1860.* Knoxville: University of Tennessee Press.

Wood, Betty. 1984. *Slavery in Colonial Georgia, 1730–1775.* Athens: University of Georgia Press.

GEORGIA CODE (1861)

Georgia was the first jurisdiction in the United States to codify the common law. Although Dakota Territory (1866), California (1872), and Montana (1895) later adopted codes, and other states (notably Massachusetts and New York) debated codification proposals, the Georgia Code (1861) represents the only systematic attempt to incorporate slavery into the legal framework of a common law jurisdiction. (Louisiana based its code on the French civil law system rather than common law.)

In December 1858 the Georgia legislature created a three-member commission with a broad mandate to compile all laws of the state, whether based on statute or common law, into a code covering political organization, private law, penal law, and rules of procedure. The commissioners began preparing a code "which should embody the great fundamental principles of our jurisprudence, from whatever source derived, together with such Legislative enactments of the State as the wants and circumstances of our people had from time to time shown to be necessary and proper."

Thomas R. R. Cobb, a leading Athens attorney and University of Georgia law professor, drafted the code's private and penal law sections. Having written A *Historical Sketch of Slavery from the Earliest Period* (1858) and a digest of Georgia's common law, Cobb was well suited to integrate slavery systematically into private law. He was also a prominent member of the Confederate Constitutional Convention, served as a brigadier general in the Confederate army, and died in the battle of Fredericksburg. David Irwin and Richard H. Clark, the other commissioners, were primarily responsible for the remaining portions of the code.

The Georgia legislature passed the code on December 19, 1860, to take effect on January 1, 1862. Georgia's secession in 1861 required an extensive revision of the code and accounts for the code's name. Irwin revised the code again in 1867 to take into account the end of the Confederacy and of slavery. Comparing the 1861 and 1867 versions of the code shows the effect of the end of slavery on private law.

The foundation of the code's view of slavery is its classification of all persons into five categories: citizens, residents who are not citizens, aliens, slaves, and free persons of color. The code defined a slave as "one over whose person, liberty, labor and property another has legal control." The code made slavery the default status of blacks: all "negros and mulattos" were "prima facie slaves" and required to prove their free status if they claimed they were not slaves. Slaves could not legally hold property or make contracts independent of their masters. Slaves were a form of chattel property, and the rules governing such property applied to them "except where the nature of the property requires a modification of the ordinary rule." The "state of slavery" did not eliminate the natural right to life and limbs.

The code's provisions concerning free persons of color contained an implicit justification of slavery based on an assumption of the mental inferiority of blacks. An extensive set of laws governed free persons of color, requiring that they have legal guardians, restricting their ability to make contracts, and requiring their registration with the county in which they resided. The only legal difference between a free person of color and a slave was that the free person of color was "entitled to the free use of his liberty, labor and property, except so far as he is restrained by law." All laws concerning slaves also applied to free persons of color unless specifically exempted.

Although free persons of color over age twenty could sell themselves into slavery, the code barred manumission within Georgia except by legislative act. (Masters could send slaves out of state to be freed.) Provisions in wills and other agreements that attempted to free a deceased's slaves were void, and title to the slaves concerned passed as if the provisions were not present.

The code contained comprehensive provisions for the direct regulation of slavery. It also provided detailed rules governing private law areas such as contracts for the hiring of slaves, treatment of slaves during life tenancies, will provisions concerning slaves, gifts of slaves, and torts (wrongful acts) committed by slaves. Because of its systematic approach to private law based on common law, the Georgia Code offers a unique opportunity to study slavery's effect on private law.

— *Andrew P. Morris*

See also: Georgia.

For Further Reading

The Code of the State of Georgia. 1861. Prepared by R. H. Clark, T. R. R. Cobb, and D. Irwin.

The Code of the State of Georgia. 1867. Revised and Corrected by David Irwin.

Morriss, Andrew P. 1995. "'This State Will Soon Have Plenty of Laws'—Lessons from One Hundred Years of Codification in Montana." *Montana Law Review* 56: 359–450.

Smith, Marion. 1930. "The First Codification of the Substantive Common Law." *Tulane Law Review* 4: 178–189.

GERMAN COAST UPRISING (1811)

In January 1811 the worst nightmare of Louisiana's planter class became reality. A massive slave revolt occurred in St. Charles and St. John the Baptist parishes, an area located about forty miles upriver from New Orleans. The region was known as the German Coast because of its initial European settlers. Estimates of the number of slaves involved in the revolt vary from 150 to perhaps 500, but regardless of the number, the event caused widespread panic in the Territory of Orleans and warranted worldwide attention.

On the evening of January 8, slaves on Manual Andry's Woodlawn plantation attacked Andry and his son, killing the son and wounding Andry. The slaves then began marching downriver, pillaging, burning buildings, and recruiting more slaves as they went. White residents in the region were terrified. Many sought refuge in New Orleans while others hid in the woods as the mob approached their homes. Only two white people were killed, Andry's son and Jean-Francois Trepegnier, who was killed while confronting the mob

at his plantation. The beginning of the revolt seemed well planned, with leaders on horseback directing its movement, but organization deteriorated as the revolt grew. Evidence suggests one primary leader—Charles Deslondes, a mulatto slave, possibly of St. Domingue origin, who was temporarily in the service of Andry.

After surviving the attack on his plantation, Manual Andry notified U.S. authorities of the insurrection and within twenty-five hours had organized a militia of nearly eighty men and set out after the slaves. The governor of the Territory of Orleans, William C. C. Claiborne, was informed, and he immediately dispatched General Wade Hampton, commander-in-chief of the U.S. troops in the southern division, who was by coincidence visiting New Orleans at the time. An additional force of 200 regular soldiers was sent from Baton Rouge under the command of Major Homer Virgil Milton. The forces led by Andry, Hampton, and Milton converged on the slaves on the morning of January 11 near Francois Bernard Bernoudi's plantation. The result was more a massacre than a battle. Armed only with cane knives, axes, and a few small arms, the slaves were no match for the well-armed militia that surrounded them. Estimates of casualties vary, but at least sixty slaves were killed and countless others wounded.

On the afternoon of January 13, the trial began for the slaves who were captured. Held at the nearby Destrehan plantation, the proceedings were directed by St. Charles Parish judge Pierre Bouchet St. Martin. For the next two days the court listened to testimony from thirty of the accused. Twenty-one were found guilty and were sentenced to death. As a brutal example to others who might disturb the social order, their corpses were beheaded and the heads placed on posts along the German Coast. On January 14, 1811, Governor Claiborne wrote to Secretary of State Smith: "The Insurrection among the negroes is quelled; and nearly the whole of the insurgents either killed or taken. The prompt and judicious movement of Genl. Hampton contributed very much to the public safety: and the ardour, activity, and firmness of the Militia have made an impression upon the Blacks that will not (I suspect) for a length of time be effaced" (Rowland, 1917).

From the trial testimony it is difficult to ascertain a specific cause for the insurrection other than the slaves' obvious hatred of the system that held them captive. Perhaps the idea of rebellion had been imported to the region in 1809 when more than nine thousand refugees from St. Domingue settled in Louisiana. They had been expelled from Cuba in reaction to the war between France and Spain and had witnessed the successful St. Domingue slave revolt in 1791. Among the nine thousand refugees were three thousand slaves and over three thousand free people of color. In addition, some evidence suggests that the leaders of the rebellion had been influenced by runaway slaves, often referred to as "outlyers," who lived by their own means on the fringes of the plantations.

In response to the insurrection, the territorial legislature completely reorganized the militia, something Governor Claiborne had been urging since 1806, in the hope that it would be more responsive to internal threats. To strengthen security in the territory further, the federal government stationed a regular army regiment at New Orleans and sent three gunboats to add to the existing naval force in the region. Perhaps the revolt's most important outcome was that it intensified the state of tension brought about by the slave economy and raised doubts in the minds of many people as to whether or not that type of economy could be maintained.

— *Mark Cave*

See also: Louisiana.

For Further Reading
Dormon, John H. 1977. "The Persistent Specter: Slave Rebellion in Territorial Louisiana." *Louisiana History* 18: 389–404.

Rodriguez, Junius Peter, Jr. 1992. "Ripe for Revolt: Louisiana and the Tradition of Slave Insurrection, 1803–1865." Ph.D. dissertation, Department of History, Auburn University, Auburn, Alabama.

Rowland, Dunbar, ed. 1917. *Official Letter Books of W. C. C. Claiborne 1801–1816.* Jackson, Mississippi: State Department of Archives and History.

JOSHUA REED GIDDINGS (1795–1864)

A powerful opponent of slavery for twenty-one years in the U.S. House of Representatives, Joshua Reed Giddings possessed an uncompromising attitude on slavery that earned him the title "lion of Ashtabula" (the name of the county in Ohio from where he came). Giddings went to Congress from one of the nation's most fervent abolitionist strongholds, Ohio's Western Reserve (northeastern Ohio), and never one to be obsessed with party regularity, Giddings did not compromise on principle.

Giddings fought against slavery on the basis of its denationalization; that is, efforts to remove the federal government from the slavery controversy by leaving the matter entirely up to the states. He argued that all states should cherish the right not to support slavery by law or federal appropriation. From the official protection of slavery in the District of Columbia (1795) to

Joshua Reed Giddings of Ohio was an influential opponent of slavery in the U.S. House of Representatives. (Library of Congress)

the *Dred Scott* decision (1857), the federal government sought to protect slavery, but Giddings believed that the great expense and moral blight upon the nation wrought by this policy was staggering. He made his mark in Congress during his first term when, in partnership with John Quincy Adams, he tried to circumvent the infamous gag rule, which prohibited any discussion of slavery or petitions against it on the floor of the House.

The greatest expression of Giddings's opposition to slavery and the federal government's protection of it came as a result of the *Creole* case (1841). Several slaves aboard the brig *Creole* bound for New Orleans from Virginia mutinied and killed the owner of thirty-nine of the slaves aboard. The ship docked in the Bahamas, and the British gave the mutineers (except for the murderers) haven. The southern leadership wanted the slaves returned for trial. On March 21–22, 1842, to solve the *Creole* crisis, Giddings offered in the House of Representatives the "municipal theory," comprising nine resolutions written largely by Theodore Dwight Weld. The House interpreted his resolutions as justification for slave rebellion and murder. Giddings was censured for his efforts and resigned the next day, but he was returned to the Congress by an overwhelming margin the following month.

When the Whigs nominated slaveowner Zachary Taylor for president in 1848, Giddings bolted and joined the Free Soil Party, and when the Kansas–Nebraska Act passed in 1854, he helped organize the new Republican Party. Whatever party Giddings was affiliated with, he was always its most radical member. Though many admired him, scores of legislators avoided him.

In his later years he was known as "father Giddings" by his admirers. As the years passed and slave power became more entrenched in the federal government, Giddings grew more radical. Abandoning his trust in political abolition, he now espoused "higher law" ideas and declared that "powder and ball" should be issued to the slaves if they were ever to be free.

Giddings's influence on Abraham Lincoln was considerable. Lincoln listened intently to Giddings's impassioned speeches regarding the Mexican War during the congress of 1847–1849, and Giddings had Lincoln's ear during and after the campaign of 1860. Giddings died in Montreal while serving as U.S. consul to Canada on May 27, 1864.

— *Jim Baugess*

See also: Adams, John Quincy; Giddings Resolutions; Weld, Theodore Dwight.

For Further Reading
Gamble, Douglas A. 1979. "Joshua Giddings and the Ohio Abolitionists: A Study in Radical Politics." *Ohio History* 88 (1): 37–56.

Miller, William Lee. 1996. *Arguing about Slavery: The Great Battle in the United States Congress.* New York: Alfred A. Knopf.

Stewart, James Brewer. 1970. *Joshua Giddings and the Tactics of Radical Politics.* Cleveland, OH: Case Western University Press.

GIDDINGS RESOLUTIONS (1842)

Joshua Giddings, an antislavery congressman from Ohio's Western Reserve (northeastern Ohio), secured a place in history by offering controversial resolutions in the House of Representatives on March 21–22, 1842. He paid a substantial political price for presenting the resolutions, but in doing so, he began to destroy the infamous gag rule, which denied discussion of (or the presentation of) antislavery petitions on the floor of the House of Representatives.

The occasion for presenting the resolutions was the *Creole* incident of 1841 in which nineteen slaves aboard the brig *Creole* mutinied, murdered the owner of thirty-nine of the slaves, and wounded two crew members. The mutineers commandeered the ship into Nassau in the Bahamas on the morning of November 9, 1841, and sought sanctuary.

The politicians of the American South were appalled at the British response to the *Creole* incident (the British agreed to give the mutineers sanctuary) and argued that the response encouraged both slave rebellion and murder. John C. Calhoun agreed but further stated that the British had also violated national honor and property rights. Northern abolitionists, however, wanted the British to stand their ground and neither indemnify the slaveowners nor return the slaves to the United States.

During the period of delicate negotiations over the *Creole* incident and other Anglo-American issues, Giddings offered his resolutions in the House. The congressman proposed nine resolutions (written largely by the committee's researcher, Theodore Dwight Weld) that presented the state theory of slavery's status as it applied to international law. Giddings argued that if some states could elect to support slavery, then free states could elect not to support it as well. He declared that prior to the adoption of the U.S. Constitution, the states exercised "full and exclusive" jurisdiction over slavery within their territory, and they could continue or abolish it at will. The moment a ship left the area where slavery was law, the people on board ceased to be under the subjection of those state laws and were governed "in their own relations to each other by, and are amenable to the laws of the United States" (Miller, 1996).

Southern congressmen were outraged because they believed that Giddings was supporting mutiny, slave rebellion, and murder. The House reacted by censuring Giddings by a vote of 125–69, with all Democrats and most Whigs voting against him. Giddings resigned the next day but was returned by his district in a landslide reelection victory the following month. Nevertheless, his arguments remained part of the slavery discussion until the adoption of the Emancipation Proclamation in 1863. His view was that slavery may be legal but not moral; he also felt that the true state of nature for all humanity was that of freedom and liberty.

The remaining slaves on the *Creole* were freed, except for the two murderers, who were executed by British authorities in the Bahamas. Twelve years later, the British, valuing peaceful relations with the United States, paid the slaveowners $110,330 for their loss of "property." After Giddings returned to the House of

Representatives, he boldly offered his resolutions in a long speech, but he was not censured. The resolutions marked the beginning of the end for the gag rule, and they exposed the slavery issue as both a national and an international problem.

— *Jim Baugess*

See also: Giddings, Joshua Reed.

For Further Reading
Gamble, Douglas A. 1979. "Joshua Giddings and the Ohio Abolitionists: A Study in Radical Politics." *Ohio History* 88 (1): 37–56.

Miller, William Lee. 1996. *Arguing About Slavery: The Great Battle in the United States Congress.* New York: Alfred A. Knopf.

Savage, Sherman W. 1938. "The Origins of the Giddings Resolutions." *Ohio Archaeological and Historical Quarterly* 48 (October): 28–39.

Stewart, James Brewer. 1970. *Joshua Giddings and the Tactics of Radical Politics.* Cleveland: Case Western University Press.

GOLD COAST. *See* Atlantic Slave Trade, Closing of; Illegal Slave Trade; Middle Passage; Triangular Trade.

GRADUALISM

Abolitionists in the United States were never of a single mind on the most appropriate means of bringing an end to slavery. More radical antislavery advocates supported the notion of instant emancipation, or immediatism, but other more conservative abolitionists favored a more moderate notion of emancipation over time, or gradualism. Several varieties of gradualism even existed among those who advocated the gradual approach to emancipation. The movement suffered as a result of their lack of consensus.

Many sincere advocates of the gradualist approach rooted their ideology in the belief that society could not easily adapt to the sweeping social, political, and economic consequences that would result from the immediate emancipation of the slaves. Such a change, proponents argued, could be more effectively implemented and genuinely managed by societies if the mitigating factor of time was introduced to permit the kind of change that would be necessary to transition from a slave-based economic order to one based entirely on free labor. In addition, racist notions prevailed among some antislavery advocates who genuinely opposed the horrors of slavery, yet did not deem themselves to be the social and political equals of emancipated slaves. The gradualist ideology sought to soften the fears of "racial amalgamation" that prevailed among many in the United States.

The notion that society copes best with evolutionary change rather than with revolutionary change was one of the primary underpinnings of the gradualist philosophy. The lessons of history supported such an idea, for slavery had existed in ancient societies, but the notion disappeared when it became economically disadvantageous and socially untenable. Such historic precedent, rooted in the ideology of change over time, made the gradualist approach appealing to many within the antislavery movement.

The gradualists also believed that some type of education and training would be necessary to prepare the emancipated slave for life and labor beyond slavery. Advocates argued that some type of tutorship or apprenticeship would be necessary to complete the social and economic transformation from slavery to freedom, and believed that gaining this training would be much more manageable if it was spread out over time. Proponents believed that a corps of trained freedmen could become effective teachers and mentors to others, who would be freed in subsequent cohorts as gradual emancipation took shape. Such was the thinking that had animated efforts by the British government when it emancipated slaves throughout its colonial possessions in 1833 but instituted a five-year system of apprenticeship to shepherd the freedmen to their new lives as wage laborers.

The roots of gradualist thought can be found in the methods employed by several states to abolish slavery at the conclusion of the American Revolution. All states from Pennsylvania northward ended slavery, but each, with the noticeable exception of New York, incorporated elements of gradualism in its emancipation scheme. New Jersey, for example, announced the date at which emancipation was set to take effect and allowed slaveowners within that state to sell their slaves to owners in the southern states where slavery still existed.

Methods varied as to how slavery might be ended on a gradualist model. Some argued that passing a law declaring free all children born to slave mothers once the law was promulgated might be an effective means of ending slavery. Others believed that setting a target age at which one became free was another approach. In some slave societies, laws were passed that made free all slaves who had reached the age of sixty. Both of these methods belie the hypocrisy of gradualism because the purported emancipation of infants and the elderly did nothing immediately to free the many adults who labored as slaves in the prime of their life.

In the United States, some abolitionists who subscribed to the gradualist approach were also active supporters of the American Colonization Society. The combined effects of liberating slaves over the course of time and encouraging free blacks to emigrate to Liberia seemed to work well together for the gradualists, but such efforts were criticized vehemently by the more radical abolitionists who favored immediate emancipation. The opposition to colonization was so intense that by the 1830s many antislavery supporters distanced themselves from the American Colonization Society.

The battle between gradualism and immediatism became especially heated in the 1820s. During the 1824 and 1825 legislative sessions, eight of the twelve free states in the United States passed legislation urging the federal government to begin to take steps to bring an end to slavery. All eight of these proposals included gradualist approaches that combined various elements of compensated emancipation and colonization outside of the United States as additional components of a national emancipation scheme. Although the Congress took no action regarding any of these proposals, the measures had the unanticipated consequence of energizing the more radical abolitionists who favored immediate emancipation and believed gradualism to be anathema.

The opponents of the gradualists charged that if slavery was indeed evil, it was then rather inconceivable to understand how one could oppose slavery but work to prolong its effects. The divisive question of gradualism versus immediatism quickly became one that divided abolitionists, and passions on both sides of the issue were charged by polemic attacks. The English Quaker Elizabeth Heyrick wrote *Immediate, Not Gradual Emancipation* (1824) as Parliament began to consider the fate of slavery in the British colonies. In the United States, radical abolitionists like William Lloyd Garrison believed that gradualists were effectively in league with slaveholders since both groups sought to perpetuate an institution that was rooted in sin.

Although other questions also divided abolitionists, most notably the role of women and their rights both in the abolitionist movement and in society at large, the lingering debate between the proponents of gradualism and the advocates of immediatism created a chasm within the antislavery movement that made unified action impossible. Although abolitionists were a small but vocal minority in the early nineteenth century, the clarity of their message and the overall effectiveness of their efforts were diminished by factional infighting within the movement.

When emancipation did come in the United States, it was based on the immediate, noncompensated

model that Garrison and the other more radical abolitionists had long promoted.

— *Junius P. Rodriguez*

See also: Garrison, William Lloyd; Immediatism.

For Further Reading

Davis, David Brion. 1986. "The Emergence of Immediatism in British and American Antislavery Thought." In *From Homicide to Slavery: Studies in American Culture*. Ed. David Brion Davis. New York: Oxford University Press.

Gellman, David. 2001. "Pirates, Sugar, Debtors, and Slaves: Political Economy and the Case for Gradual Abolition in New York." *Slavery and Abolition* 22 (2): 51–68.

Macleod, Duncan. 1982."From Gradualism to Immediatism: Another Look." *Slavery & Abolition* 3 (September): 140–152.

Stirn, James R. 1979. "Urgent Gradualism: The Case of the American Union for Relief and Improvement of the Colored Race." *Civil War History* 25 (December): 309–328.

GREAT POSTAL CAMPAIGN

The Great Postal Campaign that the American Anti-Slavery Society initiated in May 1835 was a massive effort to disseminate antislavery literature throughout the nation by using the United States Postal Service as the means of distribution. Controversy associated with the plan polarized the views of both pro- and antislavery advocates, thus doing little to stimulate the informed discussion that abolitionists had unrealistically hoped to stimulate through their efforts. The campaign also evoked questions of states' rights as local authorities in the South sought to censor the mail to prohibit the distribution of any propaganda that supported the antislavery cause, literature they believed endangered the public peace and security of their region.

Designed, in the words of Lewis Tappan, "to sow the good seed of abolition thoroughly over the whole country," the Great Postal Campaign involved the expenditure of $30,000 by the American Anti-Slavery Society to distribute—free of charge—more than 1 million pieces of abolitionist literature (Stewart, 1996). The vast majority of the items that were distributed were sent to northern churchmen in the hope that they would join the antislavery cause and proselytize the merits of the movement to their congregations. Only about twenty thousand items were sent into the southern states, but these items were specifically addressed to persons of influence throughout the South including ministers, elected officials, and newspaper editors. It was not the intent of abolitionists, as was charged by their opponents, to place the materials into the hands of slaves and free blacks in the South.

Only in its second year of existence, the American Anti-Slavery Society was a still-fledgling organization that was seeking to expand its membership and attract financial backers to the cause of abolition. The Great Postal Campaign was in large part a public relations effort designed to attract converts to the cause and engender a national dialogue on the question of slavery.

The American Anti-Slavery Society developed a wide array of abolitionist literature designed to appeal to all types of readers in the South. These items included the small-folio newspaper *Human Rights,* a small magazine called *The Anti-Slavery Record,* copies of the *Emancipator,* an abolitionist newspaper, and a reader designed for children called *The Slave's Friend.* Yet despite the best plans and intentions of the northern abolitionists, few of these items were ever delivered to the persons to whom they had been addressed.

Abolitionists had an unreasonable expectation about the outcome of the Great Postal Campaign. Many antislavery advocates believed in the power of moral suasion to make individuals see the error of their ways and change their attitudes. Many early Quaker abolitionists had courageously traveled into the South where they conducted person-to-person conversations with slaveholders and used the powers of reasoned argument to convince these individuals to emancipate their slaves through manumission. It was believed, somewhat incredulously, that the arrival of unsolicited abolitionist literature in the mail would provide the same sanguine outcome in individuals whose views had become ever more strident.

Southern officials lambasted the abolitionists for sending "incendiary literature" through the mail and charged that the real purpose of this campaign was to foment slave insurrection throughout the South. In cities all across the South, local postmasters took it upon themselves to censor the mail of those items that had been sent by the northern abolitionists. A mob raided the post office in Charleston, South Carolina, on July 29, 1835, and removed the suspected abolitionist materials from the premises. The following evening a Charleston mob burned effigies of William Lloyd Garrison and Arthur Tappan using the stolen abolitionist newspapers as bonfire material.

During his 1836 Message to the Congress, President Andrew Jackson sided with the southern states' rights advocates who maintained that they were within their rights to censor the mails and remove abolitionist literature. Jackson urged passage of "such a law as will prohibit, under severe penalties, the circulation in the southern states, through the mail, of incendiary publications intended to instigate the slaves to insurrection" (Filler, 1960). Postmaster General Amos Kendall, a proslavery advocate, was questioned about the extralegal measures taken by southern postmasters, and he replied that "we owe an obligation to the laws, but we owe a higher one to the communities in which we live" (Filler).

Free blacks living in the South became some of the unintended victims of the Great Postal Campaign as southern legislatures enacted stricter codes regulating the liberties that were allowed to that group. Many in the South feared that the true purpose of flooding the mail with abolitionist literature was to place it in the hands of free blacks who could then place it—or the radical ideas contained therein—into the hands and hearts of slaves. There was a flurry of fear in many parts of the South in 1835–1836 that conspiracies between free blacks and slaves might be afoot. In several states authorities placed militias on alert to prevent the likelihood of slave insurrection.

The high-minded abolitionist plan that moral suasion through reading abolitionist literature would sway the minds of southern slaveholders had failed, but the abolitionists may nonetheless have gained ground in the national controversy that erupted in response to the Great Postal Campaign. The campaign was more successful in the northern states as many individuals who had not previously subscribed to Garrison's newspaper, the *Liberator,* began to do so and the membership rolls of the American Anti-Slavery Society experienced a growth spurt.

— *Junius P. Rodriguez*

See also: American Anti-Slavery Society; Garrison, William Lloyd.

For Further Reading

Filler, Louis. 1960. *The Crusade against Slavery, 1830–1860.* New York: Harper and Row.

Stewart, James Brewer. 1996. *Holy Warriors: The Abolitionists and American Slavery.* New York: Hill and Wang.

Wyatt-Brown, Bertram. 1965. "The Abolitionists' Postal Campaign of 1835." *Journal of Negro History* 50 (October): 227–238.

Wyly-Jones, Susan. 2001. "The 1835 Anti-Abolition Meetings in the South: A New Look at the Controversy over the Abolition Postal Campaign." *Civil War History* 47 (4): 289–309.

Angelina Grimké published the influential pamphlet "An Appeal to the Christian Women of the South" in 1836. (Library of Congress)

ANGELINA GRIMKÉ (1805–1879)

As a southern woman who became a leader of the abolitionist movement, Angelina Grimké attracted widespread notoriety by agitating publicly against slavery before mixed audiences of men and women, thus bringing into question traditional views of women's roles. Angelina was born into a prominent South Carolina slaveholding family. In 1829 she followed the lead of her elder sister Sarah, who wanted a more intellectually active life than that traditionally available to upper-class southern women, and moved to Philadelphia and converted to Quakerism.

Over the next six years, Angelina Grimké became interested in the abolitionist movement by reading William Lloyd Garrison's *Liberator* and attending meetings of the Philadelphia Female Anti-Slavery Society. In 1835 she wrote Garrison a letter praising his adherence to the principle of immediate emancipation and referring briefly to her own experience with slavery in the South. Garrison published the letter in the *Liberator,* and as a consequence, Grimké received and accepted invitations to speak before women's discussion groups. She also wrote the pamphlet *An Appeal to the Christian Women of the South* (1836), which implored southern women to use their influence upon men to end slavery immediately. Although well received among abolitionists, the work caused an uproar in the South where U.S. postmasters judged it seditious and destroyed copies of it.

A passionate and animated speaker, Grimké drew large crowds to her public lectures. In 1836 she and her sister began acting as unofficial agents for the American Anti-Slavery Society, traveling throughout New York and New England raising funds and boosting society membership. Grimké's nine-month speaking tour in 1837 broke attendance records, but she also attracted criticism from those within the society who did not like women challenging traditional gender roles by speaking before mixed audiences. In addition, she was criticized for her position that it was as important to end northern prejudice as it was to end southern slavery. Early in 1838, Grimké gained further notice when she gave evidence to a committee of the Massachusetts legislature about the horrors of slavery, as she was the first woman ever to testify before a legislative body in the United States.

On May 14, 1838, Grimké married fellow abolitionist Theodore Dwight Weld, and the marriage marked the end of her active involvement with the abolitionist cause. Her last significant contribution to the movement was a book, which she jointly authored with Weld and her sister, entitled *American Slavery as It Is* (1839). In this compilation of southern newspaper editorials and runaway notices, the authors hoped that the slaveholders' cruelty would speak for itself, and, indeed, the book became one of the antislavery movement's most influential works.

Although Grimké's involvement with the abolitionist movement was brief (1835–1839), she played a significant role in two ways. First, she had personal knowledge of slavery's cruelty, which made many New Englanders sympathetic to the antislavery cause. Second, her success as a public speaker heightened tensions within the abolitionist movement regarding women's proper roles and civil rights for blacks. Her stance on these two issues brought into question traditional notions of gender and race, sparked a series of controversies that contributed to a split in the abolitionist movement, and thus altered the course of the antislavery effort in the United States.

Near the end of their lives, the Grimké sisters once again sparked controversy by openly accepting as their nephews Francis and Archibald Grimké, the sons of their brother Henry and his slave Nancy Weston. The sisters provided the boys with support throughout their young adulthoods. Both men went on to become prominent figures in the African American community and outspoken advocates of civil rights as followers of W. E. B. DuBois.

— *Elizabeth Dubrulle*

See also: *An Appeal to the Christian Women of the South* (1836); Garrison, William Lloyd; Grimké, Sarah Moore; The *Liberator;* Philadelphia Female Anti-Slavery Society; Weld, Theodore Dwight.

For Further Reading

Barnes, Gilbert H., and Dwight L. Dumond, eds. 1934. *Letters of Theodore Dwight Weld, Angelina Grimké Weld, and Sarah Grimké, 1822–1844.* New York: D. Appleton.

Ceplair, Larry, ed. 1989. *The Public Years of Sarah and Angelina Grimké: Selected Writings, 1835–1839.* New York: Columbia University Press.

Lerner, Gerda. 1963. "The Grimké Sisters and the Struggle against Race Prejudice." *Journal of Negro History* 48 (October): 277–291.

Lerner, Gerda. 1967. *The Grimké Sisters from South Carolina: Rebels Against Slavery.* Boston: Houghton Mifflin.

Lumpkin, Katharine Du Pre. 1974. *The Emancipation of Angelina Grimké.* Chapel Hill: University of North Carolina Press.

Perry, Mark. 2001. *Lift Up Thy Voice: The Grimké Family's Journey from Slave Holders to Civil Rights Leaders.* New York: Penguin Books.

Sarah Moore Grimké and her sister, Angelina Grimké, occupied a special place in the abolitionist and women's rights movements. (Library of Congress)

SARAH MOORE GRIMKÉ (1792–1873)

Intelligent, pious, dedicated to justice, and withal a determined lecturer and essayist, Sarah Moore Grimké was a strong foe of southern slavery and a fearless proponent of women's rights. Born to a wealthy South Carolina slaveholding family, Sarah could have enjoyed an unusually leisured life. Yet like many other southern women, she abhorred the use of slaves and had trouble reconciling her principles with the culture of her home state. Formally educated in the scant manner thought appropriate for young ladies of good families, Sarah read widely in her father's library. She was denied her wish to study law, and for years, she tried to satisfy her restless mind in a giddy social whirl.

By 1817 she experienced a religious conversion and joined the Presbyterian Church; in 1820, after reading John Woolman's memoirs, she became a Quaker. A year later, Sarah moved to Philadelphia. She returned to Charleston in 1827 and persuaded her sister Angelina to join her in the Quaker faith. In 1829 the

Grimké sisters joined forces in Pennsylvania, and after 1831, Sarah never returned to the slaveholding states.

In Philadelphia, fellow religionists did not appreciate the Grimké sisters' participation in abolitionist activities. Relations grew more difficult when the pair moved to New York to be trained as activists and worse yet when Sarah and Angelina took to the lecture halls. As southerners familiar with, and disgusted by, slavery's daily realities, both women were valuable additions to the antislavery cause.

Because Angelina made more speeches and was judged the better orator, Sarah's contributions to abolition have been deemed less significant than her advocacy of women's rights. Sarah herself always held that her abolitionism and support for women's rights were inseparable, as both were predicated on a scriptural view of the moral responsibilities of women. She wrote an antislavery statement called *An Epistle to the Clergy of the Southern States* (1836), and a year later, she cowrote the "Letter to Clarkson," which answered a call for advice as to what nonslaveholders could do to bring an end to slavery. In 1839, Sarah edited the antislavery compendium, *American Slavery As It Is,* along with her sister Angelina and new brother-in-law, Theodore Weld.

After that project, Sarah Grimké's participation in antislavery activities waned despite importunings when abolitionists in the United States quarreled over the question of the role of women in the movement to free the slaves. In addition to teaching in progressive schools, she wrote on women's rights and translated a biography of Joan of Arc. In 1868 she and Angelina acknowledged and befriended two nephews who were mulattoes. An ardent supporter of woman suffrage, Sarah lived to vote in a local election.

— *Barbara Ryan*

See also: Grimké, Angelina; Weld, Theodore Dwight.

For Further Reading
Birney, Catherine H. 1885. *The Grimké Sisters.* Boston: Lee and Shepard.
Ceplair, Larry, ed. 1989. *The Public Years of Sarah and Angelina Grimké.* New York: Columbia University Press.
Lerner, Gerda. 1967. *The Grimké Sisters from South Carolina: Rebels against Slavery.* Boston: Houghton Mifflin.

JOSIAH B. GRINNELL (1821–1891)

An early Republican Party founder, Josiah B. Grinnell was also an abolitionist and western settler and developer. Born in New Haven, Vermont, he graduated from Oneida Institute (1843) and Auburn Theological Seminary (1846). Employed briefly at an integrated church in Union Village, New York, Grinnell left New York in 1851 to found the first congregational church in Washington, D.C. With his education and northern background, Grinnell made the mistake of preaching an abolition sermon, reportedly the first of its kind in the nation's capital. When he persisted, Grinnell was forced to leave Washington for the safety of New York. A chronic throat problem led Grinnell to refocus his career, and in 1854, he followed journalist Horace Greeley's advice to "go west." He and two business associates purchased 5,000 acres in central Iowa's Poweshiek County and founded the town of Grinnell. Two years later, Iowa College relocated from Davenport to Grinnell, and in 1909 the institution was renamed Grinnell College.

Grinnell was active in local affairs and was a prime mover in founding the state Republican Party at Iowa City in 1856. Elected to the Iowa Senate in 1856 (serving one term until 1860), he became a major voice in the free school movement. He likewise favored temperance and prohibition, but soon became Iowa's most

Josiah Bushnell Grinnell was an early Republican Party founder, abolitionist, and settler of the West. (Library of Congress)

recognized abolitionist. In February 1859 Grinnell hosted John Brown in his home as Brown escorted a group of fugitive slaves to Canada. According to legend, Brown penned part of his Virginia Proclamation while under Grinnell's roof.

In 1860 Grinnell represented Iowa at the Republican National Convention in Chicago, which nominated Abraham Lincoln for the presidency. His rise in national politics culminated with his election to two terms in Congress (1863–1867). An energetic supporter of Lincoln, Grinnell advocated using black troops in the Union army and a high protective tariff. He also supported the president's use of war powers, including the detention of wartime opponents.

Grinnell's visibility as an abolitionist held him in good standing among Iowa Republicans, but the state's Democrats distrusted him. He opposed Andrew Johnson's Reconstruction plan and voted against readmitting the southern states until they granted blacks the vote. Thus began Grinnell's decline as a public figure. He lost the Republican renomination for a third congressional term to William Loughride, a proponent of radical Reconstruction. His final stand was in favor of old friend Horace Greeley for president in 1872. Seemingly without the abolitionist cause, Grinnell's influence in the party disappeared.

— *Boyd Childress*

See also: Brown, John.

For Further Reading
Payne, Charles Edward. 1938. *Josiah B. Grinnell.* Iowa City: State Historical Society of Iowa.

Schuchmann, Mary. 2003. *Grinnell, Iowa, Jewel of the Prairie: Sesquicentennial, 1854–2004.* Grinnell, IA: Grinnell Sesquicentennial Committee.

GULLAH

There are various explanations for the meaning of the word "Gullah" as well as its origin within the United States of America. Gullah refers to the people who have populated the Sea Islands and low country of the southeastern United States since the Africans who were kidnapped and captured from the West African coast were enslaved in the region. These people of African descent and their kinspeople who are referred to as "Geechee" continue to have a unique African culture in America that is also called "Gullah."

Given the various ethnic groups of Africans that were brought to the Sea Islands and low country, there are two direct connections from which this name came into use in America. Since many Angolans were initially captured and brought in directly from the African continent to be enslaved in the Sea Islands, many Africans from that country were listed with the word "Gullah" as part of their names. The most well known of these is "Gullah Jack," who was involved in the Denmark Vesey Uprising (1822).

The word "Gullah" is also thought to be derived from an island in the Sierra Leone area of West Africa called Gola. The Gola were captured from the forest belt along Africa's windward coast (modern-day Sierra Leone and Liberia) and became heavily populated in the Sea Islands of the southeastern United States. This group was brought in because of their skills in rice cultivation, which proved to be one of massive financial benefit to the building of America. Rice as well as cotton and indigo became known as the cash crops.

Both Gullah and Geechee share many linguistic influences with the Fula, Mende, upper Guinea Coast, and Gambia River areas. Gullah has a linguistic equivalent in the "Krio" language, which is still in use in the Windward/Rice Coast region of West Africa today. For many years, Gullah was thought of as a dialect of English. However, scholarly research over the years has shown that Gullah is a unique Creole language with its own vocabulary, lexicon, and grammatical structure. The language was derived from the amalgamation of numerous African languages and dialects, with a sprinkling of Elizabethan English.

Being isolated from the mainland, the Gullah people were able to continue their African traditions and customs. Some of these people even joined forces with the Native or indigenous Americans of their area and became part of what is called the Seminole Nation" Many of them moved into Florida, and others even went west into what is now Oklahoma, Mexico, and Texas to escape the enslavement by Euro-Americans after fighting against them for over forty years during the "Gullah Wars" or the "Seminole Wars."

The people who remained in the Sea Islands and low country of the United States who share the African heritage that has come to be known as "Gullah" and "Geechee" came together under their international human right to self-determination to be recognized as the Gullah/Geechee Nation. On July 2, 2000, they had an official ceremony for this designation, at which they presented their governing principles and flag.

The Gullah/Geechee Nation Constitution states that "Gullah includes the people, history, language, and culture and Geechee is the 'descendant' of this. Gullah is the native tongue and pure language. Geechee is the creolization of the language in which loan words from other languages are used as the Gullah/Geechee people continue to interact with those that speak other languages."

— *Marquetta L. Goodwine*

See also: Geechee; Liberia; Rice Cultivation and Trade; Sea Islands; Seminole Indians; Vesey, Denmark.

For Further Reading
Goodwine, Marquetta L. 1998. *The Legacy of Ibo Landing: Gullah Roots of African American Culture.* Atlanta, GA: Clarity Press.

Montgomery, Michael. 1994. *The Crucible of Carolina: Essays in the Development of Gullah Language and Culture.* Athens: University of Georgia Press.

Pollitzer, William. 1999. *The Gullah People and Their African Heritage.* Athens: University of Georgia Press.

Turner, Lorenzo Dow. 1974. *Africanisms in the Gullah Dialect.* Ann Arbor: University of Michigan Press.

GULLAH JACK

Gullah Jack, who was also known as "Cooter Jack" and "Jack Pritchard," was born in Africa in the village of McChoolay Mooreema and spoke an Angolan language. One Zephaniah Kingsley purchased him as a prisoner of war at Zanguebar (later Zanzibar) on Africa's eastern shore and took him to the Florida Sea Islands early in the nineteenth century.

Gullah Jack was allowed to take a bag aboard ship, and he always retained it. As a priest, conjurer, root doctor, and medicine man, he carried his necessary implements in this bag. His knowledge and use of herbal medicine and supernatural traditions made some people respect him, but others feared and stood in awe of him.

Numerous accounts describe Gullah Jack as a small man, possessed "of tiny limbs, which look grotesque despite his small frame" with "enormous black whiskers" (Freehling, 1965). He had an animated manner and a changing countenance, and because of his demeanor, he was sometimes called diabolical, artful, cruel, and bloody.

Approximately forty people escaped or were taken in 1812 during a Seminole raid and attack on the Kingsley Plantation where Gullah Jack was enslaved. Gullah Jack was among the group and eventually ended up in Charleston, South Carolina. In 1821 one Paul Pritchard purchased him there.

While enslaved in Charleston, he became a member of the African Methodist Episcopal (AME) congregation that Denmark Vesey attended. Just after Christmas in 1821, Vesey recruited Gullah Jack to be a lieutenant in the uprising that he planned for the Charleston Township and the neighboring Sea Islands. Vesey chose Jack because he represented an Angolan company called the "Gullah Company" or the "Gullah Society." He also knew that people believed that Gullah Jack was "a man that could not be killed" and one who "had a charm to lead his people" (Freehling, 1965).

Gullah Jack fused African and European religious forms and summoned the spiritual powers that he knew would empower the Africans who were enslaved. He provided those who were participating in the Vesey conspiracy with charms to prevent injury in battle and to injure anyone who betrayed them. However, betrayal did come. Gullah Jack gave a specific warning to Vesey not to tell anyone who was "mulatto" of the plot, but this advice was not strictly followed. When the plan was exposed, Jack was captured on July 5, 1822. A total of 131 people, including Jack and Vesey, were put on trial as conspirators.

The people who testified against Gullah Jack stated that he had intended to implement the plans that Vesey, he, and others had developed despite Vesey's arrest. Testimony from Gullah Jack's trial mentions that he requested an extension of his life for one or two weeks. No one will ever know if he wanted this time in

order to complete what he and the others had planned, or if he asked for other reasons. Nonetheless, Gullah Jack was condemned to death and he was hung on July 9, 1822. He is still greatly remembered and admired within the Gullah/Geechee Nation.

— *Marquetta L. Goodwine*

See also: Geechee; Gullah; Sea Islands; Vesey, Denmark.

For Further Reading
Freehling, William W. 1965. *Prelude to Civil War: The Nullification Controversy in South Carolina, 1816–1836.* New York: Oxford University Press.

Goodwine, Marquetta L. 1998. *The Legacy of Ibo Landing: Gullah Roots of African American Culture.* Atlanta, GA: Clarity Press.

Lofton, John. 1964. *Insurrection in South Carolina: The Turbulent World of Denmark Vesey.* Yellow Springs, OH: Antioch Press.

Powers, Bernard E., Jr. 1994. *Black Charlestonians: A Social History, 1822–1885.* Fayetteville: University of Arkansas Press.

EDWARD EVERETT HALE (1822–1909)

Edward Everett Hale was a prominent nineteenth-century American minister and writer who was an active abolitionist and cofounder of the New England Freedmen's Aid Society. Hale was born in Boston on April 3, 1822, to a family with deep roots in Massachusetts society and history. His father was the owner and editor of the *Boston Daily Advertiser,* his maternal uncle was the prominent orator/statesman, Edward Everett, and his paternal great-uncle was revolutionary spy and martyr, Nathan Hale.

Hale graduated from Harvard in 1839 intending to become a teacher. After three years of teaching in several New England schools, however, he followed a new calling into the ministry. As a Unitarian minister, Hale served for a decade at the Church of the Unity in Worcester, Massachusetts. In 1856 he accepted a position as minister at the larger South Congregational Church in Boston where he served for forty-five years, from 1856 to 1901. Throughout his ministry Hale worked first for the abolition of slavery and after emancipation, for the social and economic improvement of freed slaves.

On February 7, 1862, Hale, along with fellow abolitionists and social activists Charles Bernard, William Cullen Bryant, Samuel Cabot, and William Lloyd Garrison, founded the New England Freedmen's Aid Society in Boston to promote education among free African Americans. The society raised funds to support schools throughout the region for native free blacks and for newly freed slaves, both children and adults, male and female.

Hale was a prolific writer, novelist, and biographer. His most successful literary work was the short story, "The Man Without a Country," which he published in 1863. That story's central character, a U.S. naval officer, curses his native land and announces his desire never to set foot again on U.S. soil. As punishment for betraying his country, he is condemned to spend the rest of his life aboard U.S. naval vessels, within sight of the United States but never being allowed to land. That story was widely reprinted and became a sentimental favorite during the years of post–Civil War patriotism that gripped late nineteenth-century readers.

In 1903 Hale was appointed chaplain of the U.S. Senate, a position he held until his death on June 10, 1909, in Roxbury, Massachusetts.

— *Frederick J. Simonelli*

For Further Reading

Adams, John R. 1977. *Edward Everett Hale.* Boston: Twayne Publishers.

JAMES H. HAMMOND (1807–1864)

James Henry Hammond, governor of South Carolina, U.S. senator, and states' rights advocate, was born at Stoney Point, in the Newberry District of South Carolina. He was the son of Elisha Hammond, a Massachusetts native, and Catherine Fox Spann of Edgefield District, South Carolina. Throughout his public career, slavery and the sectional politics that it engendered influenced his views on national policy.

Hammond attended South Carolina College and graduated in 1825. After a brief career as a teacher, he read law in Columbia, South Carolina, and was admitted to the bar in 1828. Hammond built a successful legal practice in Columbia and entered politics as a nullification supporter. In 1830 Hammond established a newspaper, the *Southern Times,* in which he upheld South Carolina's stand on nullification and states' rights. He also called for a convention to consider the state's course of action in the nullification crisis.

On June 23, 1831, Hammond married Catherine E. Fitzsimmons, daughter of Charles Fitzsimmons, a wealthy Charleston merchant. The couple moved to their cotton plantation at Silver Bluff on the Savannah River. Hammond's love of the land and his devotion to agricultural pursuits eclipsed his participation in politics for a time. In 1832 he ran unsuccessfully for a seat in South Carolina's nullification convention. When the danger of armed conflict became a possibility, Hammond urged his state to prepare for war. He became a colonel of a volunteer regiment and offered part of his cotton crop and the use of his slaves to defend South Carolina. After the immediate danger of conflict was over, Hammond still advocated military preparedness for his state.

Following the nullification crisis, Hammond gave his full support to the eventual secession of the southern states from the federal Union. Hammond became an ardent supporter of southern nationalism. He also supported the institution of slavery and proposed the death penalty for abolitionists.

In 1836, owing to ill health, Hammond left the country to travel in Europe. When he returned, he devoted his energies to his plantation. However, in 1840 he ran unsuccessfully for governor of South Carolina. Elected to the office in 1842, Hammond served two terms. As governor, he supported public education, had an agricultural survey made of the state, reformed the Bank of South Carolina, and established military academies in Columbia (the Arsenal) and Charleston (the Citadel).

By 1842 Hammond again advised the secession of the southern states from the Union. When the South did not secede, Hammond again turned his interests to politics by considering a run for the U.S. Senate. His ambition was thwarted by the threat of disclosure of a sexual liaison with a young girl. Nevertheless, Hammond maintained a high profile in South Carolina politics. In 1850 he supported the Nashville Convention and attended as a delegate. Disgusted by the South's lack of action on secession, Hammond returned to South Carolina and pursued his agricultural interests. In 1855 he established a plantation at Redcliffe where he lived the rest of his life.

In 1857 Hammond was elected to the U.S. Senate. He became convinced that the South could eventually control the destiny of the Union. On March 4, 1858, on the floor of the Senate, Hammond gave his famous "King Cotton" speech in which he stated that no power on earth dare make war on cotton, "Cotton is King." Although Hammond supported the secession of the South from the Union, he did not participate in politics after the formation of the Confederacy. Instead, he frequently criticized the leadership of Jefferson Davis and the Confederate Congress. By 1864 Hammond could see the end of southern independence and the defeat of the Confederacy. Exhausted and ill, he died at his beloved Redcliffe.

— *Ron D. Bryant*

See also: Nullification Doctrine.

For Further Reading
Bleser, Carol K. 1987. *The Hammonds of Redcliffe*. Oxford: Oxford University Press.

Faust, Drew Gilpin. 1986. *A Sacred Circle: The Dilemma of the Intellectual in the Old South, 1840–1860.* Philadelphia: University of Pennsylvania Press.

Hammond, James Henry. 1998. *Secret and Sacred: The Diaries of James Henry Hammond, a Southern Slaveholder.* Ed. Carol K. Rothrock Bleser. Columbia: University of South Carolina Press.

Merritt, Elizabeth. 1923. *James Henry Hammond, 1807–1864.* Baltimore: Johns Hopkins University Press.

HARPERS FERRY RAID (1859)

On visiting Harpers Ferry today, one is struck by its scenic beauty. Small houses perch atop hills overlooking the confluence of the Potomac and Shenandoah rivers in West Virginia. This tranquil scene, however, once witnessed a bold plan to incite slave insurrection and destroy the slave South. Harpers Ferry was established as the second federal armory of the new American republic in 1794. It was chosen for its strategic position, close proximity to Washington and Baltimore, and plentiful supplies of raw materials. By 1859 there were one hundred thousand arms stored at the arsenal. This ready supply of munitions, light defense by civilians rather than military troops, and easy access to the slave South down the Appalachian range, made Harpers Ferry an attractive target for an antislavery attack.

Conceived earlier, radical abolitionist John Brown planned an attack during the mid-1850s. In early 1858, while visiting with Frederick Douglass at Rochester, New York, Brown wrote his *Provisional Constitution and Ordinances for the People of the United States.* Consisting of forty-eight articles, the document condemned slavery, envisioned a mountain-based community, and outlined a political structure based on the U.S. Constitution. Later that year, Brown traveled to Chatham, Canada West, to drum up support for his planned raid, including raising companies of soldiers from local black communities. In December 1858, he led a raid in Missouri in which one slaveholder was killed and eleven slaves were liberated, eventually settling in Canada.

By summer 1859, Brown had secured financial backing from a secret six (Gerrit Smith, Samuel G. Howe, Franklin Sanborn, Theodore Parker, George L. Stearns, and Thomas W. Higginson). He moved to the vicinity of Harpers Ferry, renting a farm under the pseudonym Isaac Smith. Over the next few months, the farmhouse served as the base for his small army. Brown's wife Mary refused to come to the farmhouse, unlike sons Oliver, Watson, and Owen. Five men of African descent joined Brown. Shields Green was a fugitive from South Carolina, who had participated in a fugitive defense at Harrisburg, Pennsylvania. Dangerfield Newby, the oldest member at forty-four, was slave-born but since freed and working as a blacksmith. His enslaved wife wrote a letter to her husband in which she identified her "one bright hope to cheer me in all my troubles, that is to be with you, for if I thought I should never see you this earth would have no charms for me" (DeCaro, 2002). John Copeland, Jr., and Lewis Leary were both Oberlinites and antislavery activists drawn to Brown through his Missouri raid. Osborn Perry Anderson was born to free black parents in West Fallowfield, Pennsylvania, in 1830. After attending Oberlin, he became a printer and immigrated to Chatham in late 1850. He attended the May 8, 1858, convention in which Brown unveiled his plan for raiding Harpers Ferry and provoking a slave insurrection. The other liberators were Jeremiah G. Anderson, John E. Cook, Clay Coppoc, Edwin Coppoc, Albert Hazlett, John H. Kagi, William H. Leeman, Francis J. Merriam, Aaron D. Stevens, Stewart Taylor, Dauphin Thompson, William Thompson, and Charles P. Tidd. The youngest follower, twenty year-old Leeman, explained the nature of the plan in a letter to his mother: "We are now all privately gathered in a slave state, where we are determined to strike for freedom, incite the rebels to rebellion, and establish a free government" (Oates, 1970).

The raid on the federal armory began late Sunday evening, October 16, 1859. The twenty-two insurrectionists left the farmhouse and marched by stealth to Harpers Ferry, where they quickly occupied the lightly defended armory, arsenal, and bridge. Brown then ordered sorties into the surrounding countryside to capture hostages and liberate slaves. Between twenty and thirty slaves had joined the raiders by the early morning hours of October 17. Three hostages were seized, including Colonel Lewis W. Washington, the great-grandnephew of George Washington, and his sword. Brown believed both were important symbols of a past successful revolution against tyranny. This first phase of the raid was an unmitigated success.

Then problems began. Rather than seizing as many weapons as possible and taking to the hills

The capture of John Brown during the Harpers Ferry raid on October 16, 1859. Brown, an abolitionist, led the raid on the Virginia town in an attempt to seize the federal arsenal and initiate a full-scale rebellion against slavery by distributing its weapons to local slaves. (North Wind Picture Archives)

Spartacus-like, Brown and his raiders waited in the armory for an expected uprising by slaves and dissident whites. Some of Brown's men came across Heyward Shepherd, a free black baggage porter who panicked when confronted and was shot. Ironically, the first casualty of the war against slavery was black. Awakened by gunfire, Dr. John Starry treated Shepherd, after which he was released. He immediately made for Charlestown, capital of Jefferson County, Virginia, and alerted the garrison. The local militia was soon en route for Harpers Ferry and by late morning had seized the bridge and cut off the escape route. Realizing these problems, most of the slaves who had earlier joined Brown slipped back to their former plantations and farms. Brown's final error was his failure to stall an eastward-bound train traveling through Harpers Ferry. The conductor telegraphed news of the raid, and authorities in Washington, D.C., were alerted. Federal marines under the command of Virginians Lieutenant Colonel Robert E. Lee, seconded by Lieutenant J. E. B. Stuart, were soon on their way to Harpers Ferry.

During the early morning hours of Tuesday, October 18, federal troops surrounded the engine house of the armory and demanded the surrender of its occupants. The insurgents refused. The marines stormed the firehouse, using a ladder as a battering ram, with orders not to harm the valuable black chattel. One marine was killed, while the white raiders were quickly dispatched. Marine Lieutenant Israel Greene attempted to kill Brown, but his short sword bent and buckled so he smashed the head of the fifty-nine-year-old into unconsciousness.

Thirty-six hours later, and after fifteen deaths including Brown's sons Oliver and Watson, the raid was over. The group had failed to accomplish its stated objective of slave insurrection. The bodies of the black rebels were sliced and diced by students at Winchester Medical School. After a brief examination, short imprisonment, and show trial, Brown was convicted for treason against the state (although his was legally a federal offense). He used the forty days between his first newspaper interview on October 22 and his execution to proclaim his cause nationally. He spent his final night having supper in his cell with his wife Mary discussing his will, the education of their daughters, and Mary's future. He emerged from his cell the next morning to be met with heavy security provided by the militia in fear of an attempted rescue. Local blacks made their feelings known by burning the barns of all the jurors. On December 2, 1859, John Brown was hanged.

Many northerners praised Brown's principles, even if many of them disagreed with his methods. Southerners condemned the event, even as they used it to galvanize popular support for their cause. On October 25, 1859, the *Richmond Enquirer* wrote: "The Harpers Ferry Invasion advanced the cause of Disunion more than any other event." Most importantly, the raid served as the opening shot of the Civil War. As Brown scrawled on a small note the day of his execution: "I John Brown am now quite certain that the crimes of this guilty, land: will never be purged away; but with Blood" (Oates, 1970). At a eulogy held for Brown in New York City the same day, Black activist Henry Highland Garnet spoke of "the dreadful truth written as by the finger of Jehovah—For the sins of this nation there is no atonement without the shedding of blood." This was less a prophecy than a direct recognition that only warfare would abolish American slavery.

— *Jeffrey R. Kerr-Ritchie*

See also: Brown, John.

For Further Reading

Anderson, Osborne Perry. 1972. *A Voice from Harpers Ferry: A Narrative of Events at Harpers Ferry.* Freeport, NY.

Brown, John. 1969. *Provisional Constitution and Ordinances for the People of the United States.* Ed. Boyd Sutler. Weston, MA: M&S Press.

DeCaro, Louis A., Jr. 2002. *Fire from the Midst of You: A Religious Life of John Brown.* New York: New York University.

DuBois, W. E. B. 1909. *John Brown.* Philadelphia: G. W. Jacobs.

Finkelman, Paul, ed., 1995. *His Soul Goes Marching On: Responses to John Brown and the Harpers Ferry Raid.* Charlottesville: University of Virginia Press.

Oates, Stephen B. 1970. *To Purge This Land with Blood: A Biography of John Brown.* New York: Harper and Row.

Quarles, Benjamin. 1974. *Allies for Freedom: Blacks and John Brown.* New York: Oxford University Press.

JOEL CHANDLER HARRIS (1848–1908)

White southern journalist and author Joel Chandler Harris has been simultaneously praised and vilified by historians and scholars who have studied and reviewed his writings. Many critics view his Uncle Remus tales as a validation of plantation politics and as tacit approval of racism and slave mentality. However, some academic folklorists claim that his writing in the *Atlanta Constitution* during the 1870s helped to support the postslavery period in the New South by introducing black characters to literature in a recurring and nonthreatening scenario.

Harris was born on December 9, 1848, in Eatonton, Georgia. He was the illegitimate child of an Irish laborer and a village seamstress. As a youth and adolescent, Harris lived on a plantation. Living with poor white farmers had a profound influence on his ability to understand the social and economic structure of the antebellum South. Harris was a shy child but found that a keen sense of humor and a fondness for practical jokes helped him to fit in and gain acceptance.

Life on a plantation also contributed to Harris's literary style. In 1862 he took a job as an apprentice typesetter for plantation owner Joseph Addison Turner. It is likely that Turner's publication, *Countryman,* was the first weekly paper published at a plantation. Harris spent a lot of time, especially evenings, in the slave quarters where he learned the dialogue, tales, and folklore of the slave culture. It was during this period that he developed his major themes, which displayed paternalism and support of slavery, juxtaposed against a humanitarian concern for black people. Harris published some of the anecdotal lessons that he learned in *Countryman.*

Sherman's march into Georgia in 1864 all but ended plantation life and culture, resulting in the escape of slaves and the end of the publication of *Countryman* in 1866. Harris, now seventeen years of age, left the plantation, moving to Macon, Georgia, and another typesetting position at the *Telegraph.* Over the next decade he learned more about publishing through his work as a book reviewer, associate editor, and staff writer at various newspapers in Georgia and Louisiana.

In 1876 Harris became associate editor at the *Atlanta Constitution,* and he again wrote some sketches about the folklore of slavery. Harris's stories were critically acclaimed and were particularly noted for their entertainment value and verisimilitude. His recollections of life on a plantation became the genesis of the character of Uncle Remus, who was once a slave and narrates tales with a recurring storyline. He tells his stories to a young white child, and the tales are about a protagonist character named Brer Rabbit and his rival Brer Fox. Brer Fox is perpetually trying to capture Brer Rabbit but is never successful. Once the fox concedes defeat, the story reverts to a cabin setting. Harris

In the decades after the Civil War, Joel Chandler Harris, who was known for his Uncle Remus stories, used the African American folklore he had learned on a plantation in his youth to create literature for children. (National Archives)

pointedly emphasized that these stories were fictional and that animals were not subject to the same moral dilemmas as humans.

Harris's column in the *Atlanta Constitution* led to the publication of ten Uncle Remus books. While his tales were once very popular, they aroused a great deal of controversy, and in fact the controversy continues today. Some view his writings as contributing positively to the discussion of race relations after slavery, while others condemn him for perpetuating racial stereotypes.

Joel Chandler Harris died on July 3, 1908 in Atlanta, Georgia.

— *Anthony Todman*

See Also: Paternalism.

For Further Reading

Brasch, Walter M. 2000. *Brer Rabbit, Uncle Remus, and the "Cornfield Journalist": The Tale of Joel Chandler Harris.* Macon, GA: Mercer University Press.

Fluche, Michael. 1979. "Joel Chandler and the Folklore of Slavery." *Journal of American Studies* 9 (December): 347–363.

Jones, Alfred Haworth. 1983. "Joel Chandler Harris: Tales of Uncle Remus." *American History Illustrated* 18 (3): 34–39.

Mixon, Wayne. 1990. "The Ultimate Irrelevance of Race: Joel Chandler Harris and Uncle Remus in their Time." *Journal of Southern History* 56 (3): 457–480.

Price, Michael. 1997. "Back to the Briar Patch: Joel Chandler Harris and the Literary Defense of Paternalism." *Georgia Historical Quarterly* 81 (3): 686–712.

Trotsky, Susan M., and Donna Olendorf, eds. 1992. *Contemporary Authors.* Vol. 137. Detroit: Gale Research.

LEMUEL HAYNES (1753–1833)

A noted Revolutionary War veteran, abolitionist, and clergyman, Lemuel Haynes was one of the eighteenth century's most enigmatic African Americans. Born a mulatto of African and Scottish descent, Lemuel was the slave of John Haynes of Hartford, Connecticut, until the age of five months, when he was indentured to Deacon David Rose of Granville, Massachusetts, until age twenty-one.

In 1774, when his tenure ended, Haynes remained with the Rose family, only to leave twice. He joined General George Washington's army during the attack on Boston in 1775, and in fall 1776, he served in a garrison regiment during the battle at Fort Ticonderoga. These experiences made a deep impression on Haynes's political consciousness. Returning from the battle in Boston, in April 1775, he composed a ballad titled "The Battle of Lexington," in which he incorporated the revolutionary and patriotic sentiment that was sweeping many of the colonies. In his lyrical ballad, Haynes argued that the American colonies were no longer the land of freedom and equality, but had become a place where corruption and political savagery, stimulated by George III and Parliament, thrived.

In 1776, perhaps after returning from Fort Ticonderoga, Haynes wrote a pointed critique of slavery in an essay titled "Liberty Further Extended." His work contained three main arguments. First, based on his interpretation of the Declaration of Independence, Haynes urged his fellow revolutionaries to consider the broader implications of the independence struggle. Second, he proclaimed that the principles of freedom and liberty should be applied to all colonial citizens. Third, drawing closely on the arguments of early antislavery writers like Samuel Hopkins and Anthony Benezet, Haynes argued that slaveowners must liberate their African slaves to free themselves from the inherent corruption and sin of slavery.

After the American Revolution, Haynes devoted the rest of his life to spreading the gospel. In 1785 he was ordained by the Association of Ministers in Litchfield County, Connecticut, and moved to Torrington, Connecticut, to become the minister there. From 1788 to 1818 he served as pastor of West Parish Congregational Church of West Rutland, Vermont.

For six months, Haynes traveled throughout Vermont spreading Christianity, but in late 1818, he obtained a position as minister at a small church in Manchester, Vermont, for three years. In 1822 Haynes moved again when he became minister at the Granville Congregational Church in New York where he remained until his death on September 28, 1833.

— *Eric R. Jackson*

See also: Black Loyalists.

For Further Reading
Cooley, Timothy Mather. 1837. *Sketches of the Life and Character of the Reverend Lemuel Haynes, A. M., for Many Years Pastor of a Church in Rutland, Vermont and Late in Granville, New York.* New York: Negro University Press.

Newman, Richard, ed. 1990. *Black Preacher to White America: The Collected Writings of Lemuel Haynes, 1774–1833.* Brooklyn, NY: Carlson Publishing.

Roberts, Rita. 1994. "Patriotism and Political Criticism: The Evolution of Political Consciousness in the Mind of a Black Revolutionary Soldier." *Eighteenth Century Studies* 27 (Summer): 569–588.

Saillant, John. 1994. "Lemuel Haynes's Black Republicanism and the American Republican Tradition, 1775–1820." *Journal of the Early Republic* 14 (3): 293–324.

Saillant, John D. 2003. *Black Puritan, Black Republican: The Life and Thought of Lemuel Haynes, 1753–1833.* New York: Oxford University Press.

HAYNE–WEBSTER DEBATE (1830)

The 1830 Hayne–Webster Debate actually consisted of several speeches in the U.S. Senate between Robert Hayne of South Carolina and Daniel Webster of Massachusetts. Although the Senate discussion formally centered on a resolution concerning western lands, part of it, consisting of two speeches each by Hayne and Webster, has become known as the Hayne–Webster Debate. The debate focused on the issue of whether the United States was one nation united under the Constitution or merely a group of sovereign states united by a treaty called the Constitution. The second of Webster's replies guaranteed for all time his position as one of the Constitution's greatest defenders. The debate was widely covered in the period's newspapers, and 100,000 copies of Webster's second speech were reprinted in pamphlet form.

This debate was more than just a disagreement between Webster and Hayne. In a larger sense, it was between those in the South who promoted nullification (the argument that a state had the right to nullify federal law), including John C. Calhoun, vice president at the time of the debate, and those who opposed it. Nullification opponents, most prominently Webster and Henry Clay, believed in a strong union and a (relatively) strong role for the federal government, including the sponsorship of internal improvements and the use of tariffs to promote domestic industry, which was called the "American System."

In Hayne's first speech, on January 19, 1830, he addressed westerners who opposed the federal government's ownership of land in their states. He attacked such control of the land as transferring state funds to the federal government and suggested that the states should be able to control all land within their boundaries. He

Daniel Webster speaking in the U.S. Senate in 1830. Webster and fellow senator Robert Hayne of South Carolina conducted debates that discussed whether the United States was one nation united under the Constitution or merely a group of sovereign states united by a treaty called the Constitution. (Library of Congress)

cited the tariff (although not referring to it by name) and land sales as "taxation" and urged that it come to an end.

Webster replied to this argument on January 20, stating that the land policy had been successful in most areas. In support of his stand, he recalled that Ohio had moved from wilderness to a highly populated area (rising to a million people) in only thirty-five years. He also cited the need to pay off the national debt and the conditions under which the land was transferred to the federal government as reasons federal lands could not be given back to the states. Throughout the debate, he stressed the value of the Union. He mostly avoided the question of the tariff, but did praise New England as a great friend of the West. Webster also praised the Northwest Ordinance (1787), noting its ban against slavery.

Hayne's second speech, delivered the next day, mixed wit, Shakespeare, ridicule, and attack. He

cited Webster's participation in the supposed "corrupt bargain" that elected John Quincy Adams president in 1825, and he accused Webster of inconsistency regarding the public lands and the American System. Hayne also attacked the Federalists (Webster had once been a Federalist) for their role in the Hartford Convention, a meeting during the War of 1812 at which New England Federalists who were disenchanted with the war had met and discussed disunion. However, he also took Webster's bait, defending slavery and claiming that slaveholders defended freedom more than any other group in the country. Hayne finally defended nullification, contrasting it with what he saw as the evil of the Hartford Convention, and he closed with a claim that South Carolina's actions in resisting the tariff represented the only way to preserve the Union.

Webster responded on January 26–27 (in the interim, the Senate had been adjourned) with what has been called one of the greatest speeches in American history. He spoke for six hours over two days. Webster first answered some of Hayne's barbs with some of his own, even noting errors in Hayne's references to Shakespeare. Webster defended his own and New England's consistency on the public lands issue and the tariff, and also answered the charge regarding the "corrupt bargain" associated with the disputed presidential election of 1824. He accused the South of inconsistency on the tariff, implying that Calhoun had changed his opinion. Webster directly attacked the nullification doctrine, describing it as unconstitutional, and contrasted it with New England's earlier actions, which he described as constitutional.

Webster then suggested that South Carolina's actions in resisting the tariff would lead to civil war and a weak union. Throughout his speech, he noted how the government was one of constitutionally restricted powers, made by the people, responsible to it, and restricted by the Supreme Court rather than the states. Webster closed by arguing that the United States should not have "Liberty first and Union afterwards," but "Liberty and Union, now and forever, one and inseparable" (Baxter, 1984).

This debate was later echoed by a toast of President Jackson at the annual Thomas Jefferson banquet. Jackson rose and stated "Our Federal Union—It must be preserved," which clearly put him on Webster's side. Calhoun, also at the banquet, responded with this toast: "The Union—next to our liberty most dear. May we always remember that it can only be preserved by distributing evenly the benefits and burthens of the Union" (Baxter, 1984). Thus the Hayne–Webster Debate sharply defined, but did not resolve, the whole battle over nullification and states' rights.

— *Scott A. Merriman*

See also: Calhoun, John C.; Nullification Doctrine; Webster, Daniel.

For Further Reading

Baxter, Maurice. 1984. *One and Inseparable: Daniel Webster and the Union.* Cambridge, MA: Belknap Press of Harvard University Press.

Fuess, Claude. 1932. "Daniel Webster and the Abolitionists." *Proceedings of the Massachusetts Historical Society* 64: 29–42.

Jervey, Theodore D. 1970. *Robert Y. Hayne and His Times.* New York: Da Capo Press.

Remini, Robert V. 1997. *Daniel Webster: The Man and His Time.* New York: Norton.

Smith, Craig R. 1989. *Defender of the Union: The Oratory of Daniel Webster.* Westport, CT: Greenwood.

HINTON ROWAN HELPER (1829–1909)

Hinton Rowan Helper's most famous book, *The Impending Crisis of the South: How to Meet It,* published in 1857, was probably the harshest condemnation of slavery ever to be written by a southerner. Helper's argument, buttressed by statistical evidence and written in a combative prose style, ensured that the book could never be published in the South. In fact, a New York publisher, A. B. Burdock, published it only after Helper had guaranteed (with the help of financial backers) that the publisher would not suffer any financial loss.

Helper's main theme was that slavery retarded the economic growth of the South because slavery caused great suffering for both slaves and millions of poor white southerners. The poor whites were Helper's intended audience. Helper came from a yeoman family in North Carolina; however, he tended to lump yeoman farmers and poor whites together into one category he called "poor whites." He cast slaveholders as the enemies, not the friends, of the poor whites and disparagingly referred to slaveholders as "the lords of the lash."

To prove his point about economic underdevelopment, Helper contrasted the North and the South in both 1790 and 1850. Using statistical evidence culled from the census for each decade, Helper showed that after starting out equal to or even surpassing the northern states, by 1850 the southern states lagged woefully behind the North in commerce and industrial output. He used these statistics to reveal that the South's supposed superiority in agricultural production did not exist; rather, his numbers revealed that the North was superior in agricultural production and other key indices such as livestock holdings, the value of farm implements, and land valuations. Furthermore, southern backwardness extended into education and culture as well, with the North exceeding the South in rates of literacy, number of libraries, colleges, and writers. Helper placed the blame squarely on the South's devotion to slavery and the slaveholders' political, economic, and oratorical manipulation of poor whites.

The proper remedy for this situation, Helper maintained, was the abolition of slavery, which would encourage free white labor, which heretofore had been assigned a degraded status, raise land values, and destroy the slaveholding aristocracy's grip on economic power. To effect the abolition of slavery, Helper said, southern nonslaveholding whites had to unite in organized, independent political action. Slaveholders had to be rendered ineligible for political office. No political cooperation with slaveholders should occur, nor should there be religious fellowship or social affiliation with them. Poor whites should refuse to patronize slaveholding merchants. In fact, proslavery men should not be recognized, except as the criminals or ruffians they actually were. Poor whites should cancel their subscriptions to proslavery newspapers. To encourage free white labor, nonslaveholders had to refuse to hire slaves for work.

The last step was the immediate emancipation of the slaves. Helper apparently envisioned gradual emancipation because he recommended a tax of $60 per slave, with an additional $40 tax levied for each slave held after July 4, 1863. This tax money would be given to the slaves as recompense for their years of unpaid labor as well as to cover the cost of their colonization to Africa, Latin America, or elsewhere in the United States. Helper had genuine pity for the slaves, despite his thoroughgoing racism; he called the slaves "cowards" and "pitiable," yet he called slavery "the most horrific relic of the most barbarous age" (Helper, 1857). He saw both slaves and poor whites as victims of tyrannical slaveholders.

In effect, what Helper advocated, though not explicitly, was class conflict in the South. He hoped change would be peaceful and asserted that he sought "fair play, [to] secure to us the right of discussion, the freedom of speech, and we will settle the difficulty at the ballot box, not on the battle-ground by force of reason, not by force of arms" (Helper, 1857). The slaveholders, however, were not convinced of Helper's pacific intentions, especially when he noted that nine out of ten slaves "would be delighted with an opportunity to cut their masters throats" (Helper, 1857). Such violent rhetoric raised the ever-present specter of another Nat Turner rebellion. As Clement Eaton (1964) notes, ultimately, Helper's message had little impact in the Old South. Most poor whites rallied around slaveholders when war broke out in 1861, and racial antipathy toward blacks proved stronger than class interest. Yeoman farmers, whom Helper had lumped in with poor whites, also rallied around slaveholders when the war came. Many of these farmers supported slavery because they had ambitions to move into the planter class themselves.

— *James C. Foley*

For Further Reading
Bolton, Charles C. 1994. *Poor Whites of the Antebellum South: Tenants and Laborers in Central North Carolina and Northeast Mississippi.* Durham, NC: Duke University Press.
Degler, Carl. 1974. *The Other South: Southern Dissenters in the Nineteenth Century.* New York: Harper and Row.
Eaton, Clement. 1964. *The Freedom-of-Thought Struggle in the Old South.* Baton Rouge: Louisiana State University Press.
Fredrickson, George M. 1988. *The Arrogance of Race: Historical Perspectives on Slavery, Racism, and Social Inequality.* Middletown, CT: Wesleyan University Press.
Helper, Hinton Rowan. 1857. *The Impending Crisis of the South; How to Meet It.* New York: A. B. Burdock.
Owsley, Frank L. 1949. *Plain Folk of the Old South.* Baton Rouge: Louisiana State University Press.

SALLY HEMINGS (1773–1835)

One of Thomas Jefferson's slaves most of her life, Sally Hemings gained notoriety when a political opponent charged that she was also Jefferson's mistress. Sally was born to Betty Hemings, a slave woman alleged to have been a concubine of her owner, John Wayles. When that wealthy slave-trading Virginia planter died a year later, Sally became part of the estate of Thomas Jefferson, who had married Wayles's daughter Martha in 1772. Sally's first duties likely included caring for Jefferson's daughter Mary, often called Polly.

In 1787, five years after Martha Jefferson's death, Sally accompanied eight-year-old Polly to Paris where her father was serving as the U.S. minister to France. While there, Sally served as Polly's servant. Upon Jefferson's return to Virginia in 1789, Sally became a house slave at his home, Monticello. Over the next two decades, Sally had six children, four of whom survived to adulthood. After Jefferson's death in 1826, Sally lived with her sons Eston and Madison in Charlottesville, Virginia, until her death nine years later.

In 1802 Sally came into public notice as the subject of a story promoted by a frustrated office seeker, James T. Callender. Angry because he had failed to secure a government appointment during Jefferson's first term as president, Callender published a story in a Richmond, Virginia, newspaper charging that Jefferson was the father of Sally's children. Since he had never been to Jefferson's home, Callender based the story on little more than gossip gathered in the neighborhood around Monticello. The story spread quickly as other newspapers reprinted the allegations, sometimes in scurrilous verse. Jefferson's friends and political associates denied the story and condemned Callender. Although he issued no public statement on the charges, Jefferson denied them in private correspondence.

After a time, interest in the story flagged until Sally's son Madison granted an interview seventy years later to a reporter for the *Pike County Republican,* an Ohio newspaper. In this interview, the sixty-eight-year-old man, who had been freed in Jefferson's will and subsequently had moved to Ohio, contended that his mother became Jefferson's mistress while they were in Paris. Although Sally wished to remain in France, according to Madison, Jefferson promised her special privileges and to free any children she should have if she returned to the United States with him.

Most historians acknowledged the possibility of a relationship between Sally Hemings and Thomas Jefferson, but until the late 1990s, only three biographers—Fawn Brodie, Page Smith, and Annette Gordon-Reed—had found the circumstantial evidence persuasive. DNA test results published in 1998 in *Nature* magazine failed to resolve the questions surrounding a possible relationship. Scientists compared the DNA of descendants of Eston Hemings to the DNA of descendants of a paternal uncle of Jefferson's since the latter had no sons. The data demonstrated that Jefferson might have been the father of Sally's youngest son, Eston. However, Jefferson shared the same Y chromosome as over two dozen adult male Jeffersons living in Virginia at the time Eston was conceived. One distinguished panel of scholars examined all the available data in 2001 and concluded that the case has yet to be made that Jefferson likely was the father of any of the children of Sally Hemings.

Because the question cannot be resolved absolutely, Hemings's relationship with Jefferson will remain controversial, but the possibility that he had a liaison with one of his slaves adds another dimension to the intriguing study of a man who remained a slaveowner while being widely known as an opponent of slavery.

— *Larry Gragg*

See also: Jefferson, Thomas.

For Further Reading
Brodie, Fawn. 1974, *Thomas Jefferson: An Intimate History.* New York: Norton.

Foster, Eugene A., et al. 1998. "Jefferson Fathered Slave's Last Child." *Nature* 396: 27–28.

Gordon-Reed, Annette. 1997. *Thomas Jefferson and Sally Hemings: An American Controversy.* Charlottesville: University Press of Virginia.

Smith, Page. 1976. *Jefferson: A Revealing Biography.* New York: American Heritage.

Scholar's Commission on the Jefferson-Hemings Matter, "Final Report, 12 April 2001," www.geocities.com/tjshcommission/SCreport.htm (accessed August 24, 2003)

JOSIAH HENSON (1789–1883)

The Reverend Josiah Henson was born a slave in Charles County, Maryland. Henson's earliest recollections of slavery were of the selling of his father to a planter in Alabama, and the auctioning off of himself, five siblings, and his mother after the death of their master, one Dr. McPherson. Henson described himself in his youth as one who was full of energy and thrived on competition. Such characteristics were likely the reasons Henson's master, Isaac Riley, chose him to serve as the plantation overseer after a white overseer was fired for stealing. Henson's mother regularly gave her son lessons in Christian ethics.

Around the age of eighteen, Henson experienced a religious conversion, which he attributed to a sermon preached by John McKenny, a Christian man who lived in Georgetown in Washington, D.C. McKenny preached that all could receive spiritual salvation through Jesus Christ. Henson was moved by the sermon and began to think of his own salvation and that of other slaves. His belief in the possibility of personal salvation for all (even for slaves) likely influenced his decision to carry out a task for his master—one that he would later regret.

Mounting debt led Henson's master, Isaac Riley, to hide some of his slaves to prevent their seizure by debt collectors. Riley charged Henson with escorting eighteen of his bondspeople to his brother's home in Kentucky. Henson carried out this task. In April 1825, he arrived in Kentucky with the eighteen slaves. He later witnessed many of these same slaves sold on a Kentucky auction block, an event that had a transformative effect on Henson, making him obsessed with freedom.

In 1828 Henson met privately with a white preacher who was opposed to slavery. The two developed a plan for Henson to obtain his freedom by purchasing it from Riley. The plan was unsuccessful because Riley reneged on his part of the agreement. Henson eventually obtained his freedom by escaping to Canada with his wife and children in October 1830. He later assisted over one hundred slaves in escaping to freedom in Canada.

After arriving in Canada, Henson worked as a farm laborer, while continuing his efforts to spread the gospel. Financial support from northern philanthropists helped Henson establish the British American Manual Labor Institute, located near Chatham, Canada West (currently known as Ontario), in 1842. Henson envisioned the institution as a place where black boys could learn the mechanical arts and black

Josiah Henson escaped slavery by fleeing to Canada with his wife and children in 1830. Henson later helped more than one hundred slaves escape to Canada. Many believed that Harriet Beecher Stowe's *Uncle Tom's Cabin* was based on Henson's life. (Corbis)

girls, the domestic arts. Over the next several years, Henson toured England, raising funds to support the British American Manual Labor Institute, which eventually closed in 1868, amidst claims of mismanagement.

Henson was thrust into the limelight when Harriet Beecher Stowe's work, *Uncle Tom's Cabin,* was published in 1852. Many people believed the book was based on Henson's life, especially since Beecher had indeed interviewed Henson. In 1876 Henson took his last tour of England where he was received by Queen Victoria. After returning to the United States, Henson met with President Rutherford B. Hayes to discuss his travels abroad. He then returned to his home in Canada, where he died in 1883 at the age of ninety-two.

— *Beverly Bunch-Lyons*

See also: United States–Candian Relations on Fugitives; *Uncle Tom's Cabin.*

For Further Reading
Hartgrove, W. B. 1918. "The Story of Josiah Henson." *The Journal of Negro History* 3 (1): 1–21.

Johnston, Penelope. 1990. "Canada's Uncle Tom." *History Today* 40 (9): 3–4.
Lobb, John, ed. 1971. *"Uncle Tom's Story of His Life": An Autobiography of the Rev. Josiah Henson.* London: Frank Cass and Company.

HERMOSA CASE (1840)

Litigation involving the U.S. slaver *Hermosa* occupied admiralty courts for nearly fifteen years. On October 19, 1840, the American schooner *Hermosa,* commanded by a Captain Chattin, wrecked on one of the Abaco islands in the Bahamas. Bound for New Orleans from Richmond, Virignia, the *Hermosa* carried a cargo of thirty-eight slaves. Wreckers escorted the ship into Nassau, where Chattin refused to allow slaves to disembark the ship or to have contact with anyone on the wharf. Instead he met with the U.S. consul to arrange for another ship to deliver his cargo. While the two attempted to make arrangements, uniformed magistrates, armed and backed by British troops with muskets and bayonets, forcibly removed the *Hermosa's* slaves. After hurried proceedings before a Nassau magistrate, the slaves were freed, despite protests from the captain and U.S. consul.

The *Hermosa* case was one in a series of instances involving the removal of slaves from U.S. ships by the British. Despite different circumstances, there were similarities between the *Encomium, Comet, Enterprize,* and *Creole* cases. Each focused on a parliamentary act of August 28, 1833, which abolished slavery. In the *Comet* and *Encomium* cases, since the incidents occurred before abolition, the British paid indemnities, but the other three occurred after the parliamentary act became effective. Britain's position concerning the *Hermosa* was to deny liability, claiming instead that the slaves became free upon entering British jurisdiction. The Americans countered that the *Hermosa* had committed no illegality and had only sought aid. Like the other cases, that of the *Hermosa* became entangled in international arbitration for years.

The *Hermosa's* owner, H. N. Templeman, persisted in claims for compensation for the thirty-eight slaves, as did the U.S. government, but it took years before the case was resolved. The *Hermosa, Enterprize,* and *Creole* cases were considered together as a commission of claims was established to hear arguments. Meeting in London, the commission included Nathaniel L. Upham representing the United States and Edward Hornby of Great Britain. The commission operated under articles that established an umpire for cases where the two commissioners were at odds. The *Her-*

mosa claim was presented on March 14, 1854, and the commissioners heard arguments on May 23–25; further papers were filed on June 19.

The *Hermosa, Enterprize,* and *Creole* claims were submitted to the umpire on September 26, 1854. The umpire was Joshua Bates, a prominent London banker and partner in the Baring Brothers firm. Bates conducted hearings during October 19–21, 1854, with John A. Thomas representing the United States and James Hannen defending the British position. Bates announced his ruling in the *Hermosa* case on January 15, 1855, and decided in favor of the United States, awarding $8,000 to each of the two American firms to whom owner Templeman had transferred the claims.

— *Boyd Childress*

For Further Reading

U.S. Congress: Senate. 1856. Senate Executive Document 103, 34th Congress, 1st Session. *Report of the Decisions of the Commissioner of Claims under the Convention of February 8, 1833, between the United States and Great Britain, Transmitted to the Senate by the President of the United States, August 11, 1856.* Washington: Nicholson.

THOMAS WENTWORTH HIGGINSON (1823–1911)

A Unitarian minister, radical abolitionist and disunionist, social reformer, orator, and writer, Thomas Wentworth Higginson was the consummate nineteenth-century intellectual whose ideas and theories compelled him to a life of militant social activism. In the years following graduation from Harvard College in 1841, Higginson was intrigued by the possibility of study at Harvard's Divinity School, yet doubted his vocation for the ministry. Through his increasing involvement in several social reform movements, including temperance, antislavery, and women's rights, he discovered his immense attraction to the social activism of liberal Unitarian clergymen Theodore Parker and William Henry Channing. Thus inspired, he enrolled in the Divinity School to prepare for a ministry in which he would lead his congregants, or, as he once wrote, "take hold and shake them up a little" and exhort them to follow him in missions of committed social reform (Edelstein, 1968).

Higginson served as pastor of the First Religious Society in Newburyport, Massachusetts, from 1847 to 1849, and as minister of the Free Church in Worcester, Massachusetts, from 1851 to 1861. He used the pulpit to refine and promulgate his radical abolitionism and disunionism, which completely alienated his congrega-

Thomas Wentworth Higginson was a Unitarian clergyman and colonel of the first black regiment in the Union Army during the U.S. Civil War. He was also active in women's rights and antislavery movements. (Corbis)

tion in Newburyport. In 1850 he made an unsuccessful bid for Congress as a Free Soil Party candidate, eventually withdrawing from that party's politics for a deeper personal commitment to the principles of disunionism. He firmly believed that dissolution of the Union was the only way to extract slavery permanently from the lives and consciousness of northerners.

Higginson was actively involved in the effort to maintain the liberty of Boston's fugitive slaves. In 1851 he conceived a plan to free the fugitive slave Thomas Sims incarcerated in Boston. Although this plot failed and Sims was returned to slavery, the incident confirmed for Higginson the necessity of concerted militant action against a government responsible for upholding the evil institution of slaveholding. In 1854 Higginson and several other abolitionists devised a plan to free the fugitive Anthony Burns. This attempt also failed and resulted in Higginson's arrest and a facial wound. Higginson found that the more he engaged in "forcible resistance," the more convinced he became of its necessity and the more he sought its opportunities. As he noted in his journal, "I can only make life worth living for, by becoming a revolutionist" (Edelstein, 1968).

Higginson's personal writings from the 1850s display the beliefs and theories that led to his conviction that violence was essential to the eradication of slavery. Despite his obvious moral outrage against slaveholding, his militancy did not solely derive from his morality. Journals and letters reveal his obsession with a heroic, romantic ideal in which men proved their courage, their manliness, and the power of their moral fortitude through militant, armed action.

Following passage of the Kansas–Nebraska Act (1854), Higginson became the New England agent for the Massachusetts, State Kansas Committee, the militant branch of the New England Emigrant Aid Society, an organization that actively supported the settlement of free state emigrants in Kansas. As agent, Higginson made two trips to Kansas and also purchased arms and ammunition to help free state settlers defend their settlements against attacks by proslavery forces.

In 1857 Higginson became one of the group of six abolitionists, all members of the Massachusetts State Kansas Committee, who collaborated to provide John Brown with funds to stop proslavery forces in Kansas and who helped subsidize John Brown's raid on Harpers Ferry. Besides Higginson, the "Secret Six," including Samuel Gridley Howe, Theodore Parker, Frank Sanborn, Gerrit Smith, and George Luther Stearns, provided funding, arms, and other supplies Brown needed to execute his plan.

One scholar has argued that Higginson played a pivotal role in producing the "rationale for violence" that persuaded the group members who were most reluctant to accept militant action. Higginson possessed the fervent belief that participation in an insurrection would prepare enslaved African Americans to assume independent lives in a democratic society. Higginson also favored Brown's plan because he was convinced of the need to destroy the belief among northerners that all slaves were docile and submissive (Rossbach, 1982).

Unlike his five co-conspirators, once Higginson decided to support Brown's plan, he did not equivocate. He detested his collaborators' ambivalence, and from the earliest days of the group's collaboration, Higginson judged his colleagues' inability to support their moral imperatives with vigorous militancy as evidence of their moral and physical cowardice. After the raid's failure and Brown's capture, Higginson's colleagues panicked and frantically destroyed evidence of their involvement. Higginson neither destroyed his records nor denied his role, instead dedicating himself to raising money for Brown's defense and developing a plot to free Brown from captivity. Although these efforts were unsuccessful, Higginson was not as disturbed by them as he was by the failure of Brown's raid to trigger a massive slave insurrection that would break southern slaveowners. From this point on, Higginson realized that only unified action by northern whites could destroy slavery.

Higginson welcomed the outbreak of hostilities that began the Civil War. In November 1861 the governor of Massachusetts authorized him to raise a regiment, which he filled by August 1862. In November 1862 Higginson eagerly accepted an appointment as colonel of the first all-black regiment in the Union army, composed entirely of freed slaves, the First South Carolina Volunteers. He enthusiastically trained the recruits and then sought skirmishes with the enemy as a means of giving his men the opportunity to exercise, display, and prove their valor. In 1864 persistent ill health brought on by a leg wound and malaria forced Higginson to resign his post and return to civilian life.

Although Higginson became briefly involved in supporting radical Reconstruction after the war, including full citizenship and enfranchisement for freedmen, he soon recognized that his decades of radical militancy had passed. He wrote to Ralph Waldo Emerson of his new longing to be "an artist . . . lured by the joy of expression itself" (Edelstein, 1968). By 1867 African American concerns no longer captivated him. He devoted himself to writing, prolifically producing essays, literary criticism, fiction, and the memoir *Army Life in a Black Regiment* (1870). He remained an ardent supporter of women's rights and woman suffrage, and with fellow former abolitionists Lucy Stone and Henry Blackwell, he edited *The Woman's Journal* from 1870 to 1884.

— Judith E. Harper

See also: Brown, John; Burns, Anthony; Harpers Ferry Raid; Kansas–Nebraska Act.

For Further Reading

Edelstein, Tilden G. 1968. *Strange Enthusiasm: A Life of Thomas Wentworth Higginson*. New Haven, CT: Yale University Press.

Howe, Marc A. DeWolfe. 1932. "Thomas Wentworth Higginson." *Dictionary of American Biography*. Ed. Dumas Malone. New York: Charles Scribner's and Sons.

Poole, W. Scott. 2005. "Memory and the Abolitionist Heritage: Thomas Wentworth Higginson and the Uncertain Meaning of the Civil War." *Civil War History* 51 (2): 202–217.

Renehan, Edward J., Jr. 1995. *The Secret Six: The True Tale of the Men Who Conspired with John Brown*. New York: Crown.

Rossbach, Jeffrey. 1982. *Ambivalent Conspirators: John Brown, the Secret Six, and a Theory of Slave Violence*. Philadelphia: University of Pennsylvania Press.

HIRING OF SLAVES

Slave hiring was a practice whereby slaves were temporarily rented, or otherwise temporarily transferred, between persons for various reasons. Many hired slaves labored in cities or on internal improvements. Less noted by historians are hired fieldhands and slaves hired out for their upkeep, particularly those in poor health or of very young or advanced age. Hired slaves' terms of service ranged from one day to one year, sometimes longer. Although agreements varied, most stipulated that the hirer assumed the expenses of food, clothing, and taxes. However, owners of very young, very old, or infirm slaves often paid another person to feed and clothe them, or transferred the slaves in exchange for their food and clothing.

To varying degrees, slave hiring occurred nearly everywhere African slavery existed in the Western Hemisphere. It evolved as an institutional modification, reflecting slavery's flexibility in changing economic circumstances. It became most prevalent in areas characterized by diversified agriculture and urbanization. In the late eighteenth-century South, for instance, planters in parts of Virginia began shifting from labor-intensive tobacco to mixed agriculture, including wheat and other small-grain crops. Slave hiring became widespread in much of Virginia and remained so through the Civil War. The practice was even more ubiquitous in large cities, where diversified economies demanded flexible employment of slave labor. In Richmond and Petersburg, Virginia, for example, hired slaves worked as factory hands, house servants, and carriage drivers, among other occupations.

Similarly, in sixteenth-century Peru, slave hiring was widespread. Free persons rented slaves in Peru, as did the Spanish government, which rented slaves to work in shipyards and on fortifications. As in the United States, Peruvian slave hiring served the purpose of providing a more flexible employment of slave labor.

Although there has been little scholarly investigation of the practice, slave hiring is a subject of debate among historians. The main points of contention include the impact of the practice on hired slaves, on the institution of slavery, and on white society. Historians of urban slave hiring stress that in some cases, being hired out conferred special advantages on the affected slave. These historians show that urban tobacco-factory workers and carriage drivers, for instance, were often hired slaves and predominantly male, and they enjoyed relative freedom of movement between their homes and work sites. However, the many slave women hired as house servants in cities usually did not experience their male, urban counterparts' relative freedom of movement.

Recent research on rural slave hiring, however, shows that the experiences of these hired slaves—both women and men, agricultural and industrial—differed radically from those of their male, urban counterparts. With no need to find their own room and board away from the work site, rural hired slaves did not enjoy freedom of movement any more than slaves living and working on their owner's farm or plantation. Furthermore, much evidence shows that slaves rented out in rural areas were often unsuccessful in their attempts to manipulate the relationship among themselves, renters, and owners to their own advantage. Finally, slaves rented out in rural areas usually did not choose their own hirer but were rented to the highest bidder at public hirings.

Factors applicable to both urban and rural settings must also be considered. In both city and countryside, slave hiring frequently separated slave children from their mothers once children were considered old enough to work for a prospective renter. For this reason, slave hiring often entailed the rupture of a slave's ties with family and friends. In addition, the prospect of owners' lawsuits did not always deter hirers from beating or otherwise abusing hired slaves mercilessly. Since slave hirers lacked interest in the long-term welfare of the slaves they rented, many were probably even more likely to shoot or whip the hired slaves in their charge.

The effect of slave hiring on slavery's long-term economic viability is also a matter of debate. Some historians contend that freedom of movement and other aspects of city hiring were symptomatic of a fundamental incompatibility of slavery and an urban environment. Other scholars believe that slave hiring afforded slavery new vitality in regions characterized by mixed agriculture and urbanization because the practice permitted slaveowners to temporarily divert their surplus labor elsewhere. In 1850s Virginia, for instance, rapidly advancing hire rates and a growing demand for slave labor in other areas of the state combined to induce many slaveowners to hire out surplus slaves within Virginia rather than sell them to areas further south. Thus, these historians maintain, slave hiring afforded slavery the flexibility it required to survive in diversified economies.

Many of slave hiring's effects on white society occurred within the context of logistical tasks entailed in the hiring out of slaves. For example, slave hiring in antebellum Virginia was facilitated by whites being paid to transport, surveil, and auction off slaves for rent at slave-hiring sites. In this connection, what mattered most was not solely how many, or how few, whites *owned* slaves, but how many whites (including non-slaveowners and tenants) had opportunities to exercise some form of *authority* over slaves, either in the performance of logistical tasks connected to slave hiring or by hiring slaves owned by others. Ultimately, slave hiring in antebellum Virginia produced a white society whose otherwise seemingly disparate elements were linked by the authority all of them wielded over slaves.

— *John J. Zaborney*

For Further Reading

Dunaway, Wilma A. 2003. *The African-American Family in Slavery and Emancipation* and *Slavery in the American Mountain South*. Cambridge: Cambridge University Press.

Klein, Herbert S. 1986. *African Slavery in Latin America and the Caribbean*. Oxford: Oxford University Press.

Martin, Jonathan D. 2004. *Divided Mastery: Slave Hiring in the American South*. Cambridge, MA: Harvard University Press.

Takagi, Midori. 1999. *"Rearing Wolves to Our Own Destruction": Slavery in Richmond, Virginia, 1782–1865*. Charlottesville: University Press of Virginia.

Wade, Richard C. 1964. *Slavery in the Cities: The South, 1820–1860*. Oxford: Oxford University Press.

Zaborney, John J. 1999. "'They Are Out for Their Victuals and Clothes': Slave Hiring and Slave Family and Friendship Ties in Rural, Nineteenth-Century Virginia." In *Afro-Virginian History and Culture*. Edited by John Saillant. New York: Garland.

HISTORIOGRAPHY

The historiographical debate on U.S. slavery reflects most poignantly the changing paradigms, research agendas, and methodologies in the writing of history, particularly in the second half of the twentieth century. Historical research is concentrated on the antebellum South, that is, the period between 1830 and 1860, and mainly focused on large plantations; little attention has so far been paid to slaves in towns and to small slaveholdings.

Slavery has been studied by American historians since the foundation of the United States. Interest, however, and historiographical output were particularly strong in the decades after World War II and during the American civil rights movement. Black studies, and thus the history of slavery, gained recognition as a specific field of academic research in the late 1960s and early 1970s. Tensions arose about white contributions to a black experience, but black studies were gradually integrated into the mainstream of the historical profession.

Historiography in the postrevolutionary era initially focused on state histories. Although slavery was seen as a product of British rule, historians of slave states such as Hugh McCall in his *History of Georgia* (1811) described the slaves as "naturally fitted" for the plantation economy, thus offering an explanation for the continuation of the "peculiar institution." George Bancroft in his *History of the United States* (1834–1874) picked up these arguments. In accordance with his political ideas of Jacksonian Democracy, he criticized U.S. slavery as a remnant of British rule that was alien to the true American nature. However, he also emphasized the "naturally inferior" character of the African race, whose members could profit from the civilizing contact with their white masters. Arguments on the perceived racial inferiority of Africans dominated the historiographical discourse on slavery over the following decades in both the abolitionist and proslavery camps. Africans were portrayed as children who needed guidance and moral support. They could essentially be moulded into saints or sinners depending on the attitudes of their masters. Ulrich B. Phillips's major study *American Negro Slavery* (1918) further developed the paradigm of the paternalistic South and presented the plantation household as an essentially unprofitable, but beneficiary institution, which underlined white supremacy and reduced the slaves to objects of their masters' policy. Phillips's research was based on plantation records, which did not leave much room for black voices. He dismissed slave narratives as a source that could shed light on the slave experience. His interpretation of the slave system remained largely unchallenged for more than thirty years. Only in 1956 did the northern historian Kenneth Stampp challenge Phillips's interpretation of slavery as a mild but inefficient system. In his *The Peculiar Institution,* which was also based on plantation records, Stampp characterized slavery as a harsh but profitable economic system that left the slaves as maltreated victims of calculating planters. For Stampp, slavery was an exploitative mode of production, not an institution to regulate race relations, since there were no inherent racial differences between blacks and whites other than the color of their skin.

These conflicting views of the slave economy set the agenda for a debate on the character of the plantation South, which dominated the historiography in the following twenty years. Two major studies, which coincidentally appeared in the same year—1974—epitomized the debate, which centered on a group of historians at the University of Rochester. In his *Roll,*

Jordan, Roll Marxist historian Eugene D. Genovese supported the idea of southern paternalism, which used both kindness and cruelty to ensure a system of exploitation. In his interpretation of the master–slave relationship Genovese applied Antonio Gramsci's theories of hegemony, which were based not on force but on consent. Although the power structures were obviously in favor of the white masters, the slave system also depended on the collaboration of the slaves, who, within very restricted limits, could manipulate the working relationship. Genovese became increasingly fascinated with "the world the slaves made" (the subtitle of his book) and the aspects of slaves' culture that oscillated between white values and norms and black traditions. Robert W. Fogel and Stanley L. Engerman's *Time on the Cross* also addressed the question of the slave economy. They argued that slavery was an economically viable and successful system with future potential, which was based on incentives rather than fear. Slave life was initially based on stable families, who had internalized the Protestant work ethic of their masters and profited from the success of the plantation economy. Their book, which appeared in two parts and was based on a close reading of plantation records, caused considerable reaction because it applied new quantitative methods to the writing of history. They presented graphs, tables, and diagrams in Volume 2, which did not always stand the test of cross-examination.

Both books not only discussed the economic viability of slavery, but also shed light on the identity of the slaves. They also reacted to earlier studies, such as Stanley Elkins's *Slavery: A Problem in American Institutional and Intellectual Life* (1959) and the devastating government report issued by Daniel P. Moynihan in 1965, which had argued that slavery had greatly contributed to the contemporary "pathology" and "instability" of black families. Elkins had applied behavioral theories taken from the social sciences to present slaves as essentially traumatized and corrupted by a system that he compared to Nazi concentration camps. In his interpretation, blacks were racially equal to whites but severely crippled by a depersonalizing system. Elkins's book and Moynihan's verdict provoked a wave of research that attempted both to challenge the image of the slave as a mere victim and object of the white masters and to reconstruct the black personality and culture. This took the form of studies on slave revolts and, more importantly, on *Black Culture and Black Consciousness*—the title of Lawrence W. Levine's groundbreaking book on the slave world as seen through black folklore and reports of ex-slaves collected in the 1930s through interviews of the Works

Progress Administration (WPA). These approaches reflected not only the historians' interest in hitherto unexplored sources, but they also paid tribute to the growing self-confidence in the American black community in search of their own past. Black culture was no longer seen as a corrupted adaptation of white society. African roots and their development in the slave society became a new field of research that attracted anthropologists like Charles Joyner and Norman Yetman and radical black historians like Sterling Stuckey.

In the 1980s gender historians became interested in the role of gender in slave societies. Deborah Gray White's *Ain't I a Woman?* (1985) and Elisabeth Fox-Genovese's *Within a Plantation Household* (1988) discussed issues of race, gender, and class in the antebellum South. Drawing on women's diaries, letters and memoirs, and the WPA interviews, they reconstructed the world of plantation women that was based on race and class distinctions rather than female solidarity. These and more recent studies such as Walter Johnson's *Soul by Soul* (1999) try to reconstruct the experience of slaves as men and women who had to adapt to a cruel, degrading system. Hitherto neglected sources such as slave narratives and court records are used to give the slaves their own voices and to capture the daily life of those in bondage.

— *Raingard Eßer*

See also: DuBois, W. E. B.; Elkins, Stanley M.; Engerman, Stanley L.; Fox-Genovese, Elizabeth; Genovese, Eugene; Phillips, Ulrich Bonnell; Women and the Antislavery Movement; Works Progress Administration Interviews.

For Further Reading

Foner, Philip S. 1983. *History of Black Americans.* 2 vols. Westport, CT: Greenwood.

Meier, August, and Elliot Rudwick. 1986. *Black History and the Historical Profession 1915–1980.* Chicago: University of Illinois Press.

Miller, Randall M., and John David Smith, eds. 1997. *Dictionary of Afro-American Slavery.* Westport, CT: Praeger.

Parish, Peter J. 1989. *Slavery, History and Historians.* New York: Harper & Row.

JULIA WARD HOWE (1819–1910)

A poet, author, and abolitionist, Julia Ward Howe is best known for writing "Battle Hymn of the Republic," the rallying song for the North during the Civil War. Born and raised in New York City, she moved to Boston in 1843 upon marrying Dr. Samuel Gridley Howe, head of the Perkins Institute for the Blind and an ardent abolitionist. Unhappy in her new surroundings and prohibited by her husband from participating in public reform work, she attended lectures; privately studied foreign languages, religion, and philosophy; and wrote poetry and drama while maintaining a household with children.

In the 1850s, while embarking upon a literary career, Howe became a convert to abolitionism. Having been raised in a family that feared abolitionism as a threat to society, she became thoroughly convinced in her thirties that it was a just and necessary cause. Although she supported ending slavery, she did not believe in racial equality. She thought that freed slaves would have to be trained, educated, and "refined by white culture" in order to be more than "the laziest of brutes." Her derogatory comments about blacks, published in her book *A Trip to Cuba* (1860), drew public criticism from fellow abolitionist William Lloyd Garrison.

Howe wrote the "Battle Hymn of the Republic" on November 19, 1861, while in Washington, D.C., with her husband to distribute supplies to Massachusetts regiments. Seeing Union troops return from the battlefield and personally witnessing President Lincoln's sadness over the war deeply affected her. She wrote the "Battle Hymn" as her personal contribution to the Union cause, and upon returning to Boston, she submitted it to the *Atlantic Monthly* for publication. The magazine's editor, James T. Fields, gave the poem its title and published it on the cover page of the February 1862 issue. In April 1862 Oliver Ditson and Company published sheet music setting the poem to the tune of "John Brown's Body," a song already popular among Union troops. Not long after its publication, regiments throughout the North were singing the new "Battle Hymn of the Republic."

In the work, Howe used biblical imagery from both the Old and the New Testaments to depict a powerful, wrathful God marching alongside Union troops to the battlefield. She depicted a God who "sounded forth the trumpet that shall never call retreat" and "loosed the fateful lightning of His terrible swift sword." God marched with the Union to preserve truth and justice, and "crush the serpent [symbol of the South] with his heel." In the last of the song's five verses, Howe gave the Union the emotional boost it needed to legitimize and continue the war by proclaiming it a crusade to end slavery. Referring to Christ, she wrote, "As he died to make men holy, let us die to make men free, While God is marching on." The "Battle Hymn of the Republic" remained popular even after the Civil War and was a serious contender for the national anthem until 1931 when "The Star-Spangled Banner" was chosen instead.

— *Mary Jo Miles*

See also: Abolitionism in the United States; Garrison, William Lloyd.

For Further Reading

Clifford, Deborah Pickman. 1979. *Mine Eyes Have Seen the Glory.* Boston: Little, Brown and Company.

Grant, Mary H. 1994. *Private Woman, Public Person: An Account of the Life of Julia Ward Howe from 1819 to 1868.* Brooklyn, NY: Carlson.

Ream, Debbie Williams. 1993. "Mine Eyes Have Seen the Glory." *American History Illustrated* 27 (1): 60–64.

ILLEGAL SLAVE TRADE

The illegal slave trade in the modern era involved two aspects: the smuggling of slaves to avoid paying tax and customs duties, and the smuggling of slaves in violation of international laws prohibiting the slave trade. Because of the nature of the illegal slave trade, little data exists on the number of slaves traded illegally.

Smuggling slaves to avoid paying customs and tax duties on them was an integral part of the slave trade, and throughout the period of that trade, Dutch, English, French, Danish, Swedish, and Genoese smugglers supplied, at varying times, French, English, Portuguese, and Spanish colonies with illegal slaves. Obviously, those slaves were unrecorded in customshouse ledgers. For example, in the eighteenth century, the Spanish *asiento* (which licensed foreigners to trade slaves in the American viceroyalties) contributed to slave smuggling, as quality standards and duty payments required by the Spanish government were often too high to allow for substantial profits on the sale of slaves. Indeed, the *asiento* was used more for the illicit sale of other goods other than slaves, but the illicit cargoes often contained untaxed slaves. In addition, the failure of official *asiento* holders to meet the demand for slaves often led to a market for smuggled slaves. Thus the illegal slave trade was profitable in most periods, albeit difficult to estimate.

The second aspect of the illegal slave trade, the smuggling of slaves in violation of the international laws that prohibited the international slave trade, meant, of course, that the illegal trade's practitioners strove to keep their dealings secret. Legal abolition began with the

Slaves disembark at Key West from the U.S. steamer *Wyandotte* in 1860. The slaves were rescued when they were discovered on the American bark *Williams*, whose captain was illegally trading in slaves. (Corbis)

Dutch in 1805, and Great Britain and the United States prohibited engagement in the international slave trade in 1807. Following the Vienna Treaty (1815), all European maritime powers, often under British diplomatic pressure, passed piecemeal abolition acts.

In 1817 the British established a naval squadron off Africa's western coast to suppress the slave trade, and the United States followed suit. Great Britain and the United States also established a court to enforce their agreement, but formal abolition rarely meant an end to the trade. Neither Spain, Portugal, nor France took effective measures to enforce legislation, so much of the history of the illegal slave trade centers on efforts of the British and U.S. naval squadrons to suppress the trade. In 1845 a British House of Commons report suggested that although most nations had agreed to abolish the trade, an illegal trade remained active; the report also listed 2,313 known slavers.

Exact figures for the number of slaves illegally smuggled into the New World after 1808 are unavailable. Indeed, only estimates and educated guesses are possible. For example, W. E. B. DuBois argued that nonenforcement by the United States of its international agreement with Britain implied high levels of imports to the United States after 1808, and he estimated the number of those illegal imports to be two hundred fifty thousand. Recent scholarship has suggested that DuBois's figures were too high and that the correct figure (still only an educated guess) was

more like one thousand illegal imports per year until 1860.

Because it is nearly impossible to determine the total number of slaves illegally smuggled into the New World, students of the illegal slave trade have concentrated on specific cases in which illegal slave traders were caught (for example, the *Wanderer* case of 1859) and on records of both the antislavery squadron and the courts. As those data suggest, the illegal slave trade constituted a significant part of the overall slave trade.

— *John Grenier*

See also: Atlantic Slave Trade, Closing of.

For Further Reading

Curtin, Philip D. 1969. *The Atlantic Slave Trade: A Census.* Madison: University of Wisconsin Press.

Daget, Serge. 1979. "British Repression of the Illegal French Slave Trade: Some Considerations." In *The Uncommon Market: Essays in the Economic History of the Atlantic Slave Trade.* Ed. Henry A. Gemery and Jan S. Hogendorn. New York: Academic Press.

Drake, Frederick C. 1970. "Secret History of the Slave Trade to Cuba Written by an American Naval Officer, 1861." *Journal of Negro History* 55: 218–235.

Emmer, Pieter. 1981. "Abolition of the Abolished: The Illegal Dutch Slave Trade and the Mixed Courts." In *Abolition of the Atlantic Slave Trade.* Ed. James Walvin and David Eltis. Madison: University of Wisconsin Press.

ILLNESS. *See* Diseases and African Slavery in the New World.

IMMEDIATISM

Immediatism was a term used among abolitionists in Britain and America beginning in the late 1820s to define their stance toward emancipation and to distinguish themselves from a gradualist approach to abolition. Immediatists advocated the immediate and unconditional abolition of slavery; they fervently believed that sin must never be compromised, and therefore they refused to resort to such intermediate agencies as the closing of the slave trade, colonization, or apprenticeship as gradual remedies for the evil. The shift from gradual to immediate emancipation signaled a fundamental transformation in reformers' worldviews and a major turning point in intellectual history.

The doctrine of immediatism had its roots in the natural rights philosophy of the Enlightenment and in Quaker theology. Abolitionists in the eighteenth century theoretically believed that slaves had a right to their immediate freedom; and many Quakers, viewing slavery as an embodiment of worldly sin that corrupted masters and slaves alike, concluded that the evil must be immediately cast off to escape moral contamination. But while immediatism was latent in the origins of antislavery thought, the overwhelming majority of eighteenth-century abolitionists advocated gradual abolition. Despite their understanding of slavery as a horrible sin that needed to be rooted out, their stance toward emancipation was detached and indirect. They sought gradual and cautious measures that retained Enlightenment attitudes toward linear progress and history; natural law and property rights; and a stable, orderly, and hierarchical universe. Consequently, British and American reformers focused on the abolition of the slave trade as an indirect means that they felt would lead to emancipation. Gradualists in America also embraced the American Colonization Society, which was organized in 1816 as a way to rid the country of both the stain of slavery and blacks without upsetting the social order or natural rights doctrines.

But slaveholders continually sought to block the path to gradual emancipation; and when reformers concluded that indirect means did not accomplish their morally urgent objectives, a crisis emerged that led to immediatist views. In 1824 the British Quaker Elizabeth Heyrick provided one of the most eloquent early pleas for immediate emancipation. Slavery, she said, was a "*holy war*" against "the very powers of darkness" that precluded any compromise with the sin. By 1830 many prominent British abolitionists had converted to immediatism, and the following year the British Anti-Slavery Society officially embraced immediate emancipation. Similarly, by the 1820s many American abolitionists concluded that the American Colonization Society was founded on racist principles and not interested in ending slavery, and reformers increasingly viewed gradualism as ineffectual. William Lloyd Garrison, the most persistent American immediatist, rejected colonization in 1829 and two years later began publishing the *Liberator*. And in 1833 the American Anti-Slavery Society was organized on the basis of the doctrine of immediate abolition.

In one sense the turn to immediatism reflected a shift in strategy; but in a much more fundamental sense it represented a conversion experience in the reformer and a shift from Enlightenment to romantic worldviews. Immediatists became "born again," free from the fetters of original sin and ready to make the world sacred. They defined themselves as outsiders and stood apart from what they considered to be the vague and insincere policies of gradualists. Immediatism was at once their religion and their "sacred vocation"; it defined who they were, and it shaped everything they

did. And in contrast to Enlightenment thought, immediatists affirmed a sharp break with the past, an eschatological leap that transcended the previous limits of history and progress. They understood that emancipation was a root and branch operation that would severely disrupt prevailing conventions, order, and stability. Their worldview "was essentially romantic," in the words of David Davis, "for instead of cautiously manipulating the external forces of nature, [they] sought to create a new epoch of history by liberating the inner moral forces of human nature."

— *John Stauffer*

See also: American Anti-Slavery Society; American Colonization Society; Atlantic Slave Trade, Closing of; Garrison, William Lloyd; Gradualism.

For Further Reading
Davis, David Brion. 1962. "The Emergence of Immediatism in British and American Antislavery Thought." In *From Homicide to Slavery: Studies in American Culture*. New York: Oxford University Press.
Loveland, Anne C. 1966. "Evangelicalism and 'Immediate Emancipation' in American Antislavery Thought." *Journal of Southern History* 32 (2, May): 172–188.
Scott, Donald M. 1979. "Abolition as a Sacred Vocation." In *Antislavery Reconsidered: New Perspectives on the Abolitionists*. Ed. Lewis Perry and Michael Fellman. Baton Rouge: Louisiana State University Press.

INDENTURED SERVANTS

Indentured servitude was a widespread system of bound labor in British colonial America that foreshadowed many later aspects of slavery. Servants generally signed articles of indenture in Britain that bound them to serve a master without pay for a period ranging typically from about three to seven years. In return the masters would pay their passage to America and at the end of their time give them "freedom dues of goods" and sometimes land. Indentured servitude had become fully established in Virginia by the 1620s, allowing tobacco planters cheap labor and creating a profitable sideline for merchants in importing servants, encouraged by the headright of 50 acres for each person they paid to be brought into the colony. Essentially the same system was adopted with great success and profit in the English West Indies and wherever the British settled in North America. It has been estimated that 50 to 75 percent of British emigrants to colonial America crossed as servants, most of them going to plantation colonies.

The system developed in order to supply labor to

grow American cash crops by adapting existing elements of the English labor system, such as the hiring of unmarried agricultural laborers for "service in husbandry" and craft apprenticeship. There were a number of significant changes in the system used in America. First, the servant contracts or indentures were far longer and more formal than was usual in the case of English agricultural labor, where such agreements were often verbal and lasted only a year, the laborer frequently shifting master. This was a result of the planters' need for a long-term workforce and the considerable investment they made in paying for a servant's migration. Second, masters were allowed to sell their servants' contract, as in medieval apprenticeship, a practice that had become illegal in England. Transferable contracts evolved because servants were bound in England by an agent, who sometimes engaged them under false pretenses or even kidnapped them and then sold them to masters on arrival in America. Families also sold relatives as servants because of debt, and English parishes used the system to provide cheaply for orphans.

Servants in early Virginia seem to have faced far harder work regimens and harsher treatment than was normal in Britain; they also suffered heavy mortality from disease. Court records reveal that in response servants frequently ran away, or disobeyed. As a result, a complex code of laws evolved to handle servant problems, including restricting their movement by a pass system and imposing severe punishment, including extensions of time in service. Servants also could not marry without their master's consent, nor had they much control over their terms of work and living conditions. Whereas in the early period the difference between bound English servants and African slaves was not always clear, particularly in the Chesapeake, the development of this sort of legislation clearly defined the two groups by guaranteeing the servants legal protection from abuse and rights (e.g., testifying in court and property) denied to slaves. For any servants, generally younger ones, who arrived without a written contract the "Custom of the Country," varying from each colony, regulated the freedom dues and length of service, which was generally longer than for those who arrived with indentures.

In many early colonies, when their time was over servants who survived gained land and might do well for themselves, but as time went on, in established colonies it became uncommon to give land to ex-servants, and freed servants had to find waged work or move to frontier areas. This resulted in a discontented class of poor white ex-servants that backed Bacon's Rebellion in Virginia in 1676, but ironically as the number of slaves grew, these poor whites became vital allies for planters against the danger of slave rebellion.

Throughout the colonial period, the type and number of servants recruited and their destinations and length of service varied considerably. At first, in northern colonies of New England no crops were profitable enough to warrant serious agricultural investment in servants, so servants were usually domestic and well treated. In the southern colonies indentured servants were at first cheaper than slaves, but as demand grew prices for servants could rise because the number of migrating servants was limited, especially if wages rose in Britain, whereas slave prices remained constant once the slave trade became well established. Following a pattern established in the West Indies, a move from servant to cheaper slave agricultural labor occurred in the Chesapeake over a longer period of time, and it was not till the turn of the eighteenth century that a major shift had occurred because of shortages in the supply of servants. At first, slaves merely were fieldhands and there was still a demand for indentured servants as domestics, skilled artisans, and overseers, but by the eighteenth century these positions were filled either by American whites or increasingly by native-born slaves trained to fill skilled positions.

During the seventeenth century most servants used as fieldhands on plantations were young, unskilled, single, male, and British, but by the eighteenth century there was a shift to more varied skilled labor for service trades and various industries such as construction, iron-works, and shipbuilding in the urbanized Mid-Atlantic region, especially New York and Philadelphia. Many of these servants came from Germany, traveling in family groups. They were transported under the redemption system in which migrants promised to pay for passage within about two weeks of arrival; if the fare was not paid, they were sold into servitude, with families sometimes being split. The "redemptioner" trade acquired an evil and dishonest reputation as the risk now lay with the migrants rather than the merchants. Thus traders could overcrowd the ships and give insufficient rations, commonly resulting in a death rate of 25 percent, frequently making it more deadly than the Middle Passage. This trade disappeared as an increasing urban underclass made cheap wage labor possible. Also in the eighteenth century, penal servitude became a significant source of labor in the colonies with the arrival of a total of fifty thousand British convicts.

By 1800 indentured servitude had grown uncommon, having been replaced by slavery or wage labor, but clearly it had played a paramount role in making British America an economic success and populating it. Revolutionary ideas about liberty had made the idea of keeping bound white servants distinctly unfashionable, and cheaper transatlantic fares now made it uneconomic. Nonetheless, the social and economic patterns that surrounded indentured servitude remained ingrained in plantation colonies and in increasingly stratified northern cities, it was merely transferred to a new system of labor. The growth of racism may have ensured that the main comparable institution in the nineteenth century was the frequently exploitative debt contract schemes that funded migration from Japan and China to California. Its modern, carefully regulated descendant is the migrant labor system, which employs hundreds of thousands of workers in the United States, mainly in agriculture.

— *Gwilym Games*

See also: Atlantic Slave Trade, Closing of.

For Further Reading
Galenson, David W. 1981. *White Servitude in Colonial America: An Economic Analysis*. Cambridge: Cambridge University Press.

Menard, Russell R. 2001. *Migrants, Servants and Slaves: Unfree Labour in Colonial British America*. London: Variorum.

Sallinger, Sharon. 1987. "*To Serve Well and Faithfully*": Labor and Indentured Servants in Pennsylvania. Cambridge: Cambridge University Press.

Smith, Abbot Emerson. 1947. *Colonists in Bondage: White Servitude and Convict Labor in America 1607–1776*. Gloucester, MA: Peter Smith.

INFANTICIDE

Cultural definitions of infanticide are highly variable. The *Oxford English Dictionary* offers the following definitions: (1) One who kills an infant. (2) The crime of murdering an infant after its birth perpetrated by or with the consent of its parents, especially the mother. (3) The killing of infants, especially the custom of killing newborn infants, which prevails among savages, and was common in the ancient world. Infanticide is usually carried out immediately after birth.

Infanticide has been practiced on every continent and by many ethnic groups at every level of cultural complexity. Archaeological evidence for child sacrifice dates back to Jericho, 7000 BCE. Infanticide is not currently legally sanctioned by any society, although it is still practiced. Infanticide is an action that bears moral weight relative to its embedded cultural belief systems. Cultural practices that are as widely distributed as infanticide, both temporally and geographically, tend to

have practical functions that perpetuate their existence. No single factor can account for infanticide; it serves many different societal functions. Some of these functions include: eliminating defective children, motherless infants, multiple births, and illegitimate children; interbirth spacing; regulating future adult sex ratios; and controlling population. The most common methods used to commit infanticide are suffocation, abandonment, drowning, and exposure. Infanticide in general is rarely practiced to express violence or cruelty, but rather it is usually carried out for economic or demographic reasons. The practice of infanticide among slave populations had additional dimensions.

The life of a female slave consisted of many harsh realities. For the female slave, it was race rather than gender that determined her status. A woman born into slavery could expect to be subjected to austere labor conditions, violence, and exploitation throughout her lifetime. Southern laws did not recognize the rape of an enslaved woman as a crime, and sexual abuse of female slaves was common. Any child borne by a slave became the property of her master and could be sold away from the mother at any time. According to Works Progress Administration slave narratives and contemporary court documents, infanticide was practiced among slave populations and had many motives.

Some women told of committing infanticide to free their children from a life of bondage. These acts can be viewed as a form of resistance in which the women actively exercised a form of control over the bodies of their children. Margaret Garner murdered her two-year-old infant daughter in 1856 and attempted to kill her two young sons after she ran away and realized that she was going to be recaptured. She did not want her children to live as slaves. She was tried for this crime unsuccessfully under the Fugitive Slave Law. Another woman allegedly killed her newborn to prevent her master from selling him, as he had sold her three previous children. Another woman said she killed her child to end its suffering from the continual abuse of her mistress. She claimed that the master was the father of her child and cited paternity as the cause of the abuse.

Infanticide was one method used to deal with unwanted pregnancies resulting from sexual abuse by the master. Because slave marriages were not legally recognized, technically all slave children were illegitimate. Illegitimacy and infanticide have had a strong association throughout history. Cross-culturally, biracial children are the illegitimate class that most often suffers infanticide. An enslaved woman in Virginia was convicted of killing her mulatto child, but she was released when whites petitioned on her behalf. She claimed that "she would not have killed a child of her own color" (King, 1996).

In general, infant mortality was high among slave populations in the Americas and fertility rates were low, though there was temporal and regional variation. In 1850 slave infant mortality was twice that of whites in the United States (Jones, 1986). Owing to unhygienic living conditions, the absence of medical care for slaves, and the lack of a mother's attention to her child necessitated by her commitments as a slave, many children died of enforced neglect (Fox-Genovese, 1988; White, 1985). In addition, some slave mothers served as wet nurses and were nursing the children of their masters at the same time as their own. These slave mothers were sometimes forced to wean their own children, and some may have consequently died from lack of nutrition. Conditions created by the slaveholder contributed to high infant mortality considerably more than acts of infanticide.

Because of scarce space and/or cultural practices, small children often slept with the mother. The mother might accidentally, or intentionally, roll over onto her child and smother it in her sleep. Recent historical and medical research suggests that many children who were supposedly suffocated by a mother were actually victims of what today is known as Sudden Infant Death Syndrome (SIDS) (White, 1991). According to Michael P. Johnson, the 1850 census showed that 82 percent of the victims of suffocation were slaves. African cultural practices, such as tying up the umbilical cord with a rag for nine days, may also have contributed to high infant mortality rates (Bush, 1996).

Because infanticide is difficult to detect and prove, the act often went undetected and unpunished. But if a slaveholder suspected infanticide, even if the infant died of natural causes, the slave could be punished harshly and sometimes fatally. It was an issue of economics for the slaveholder; infanticide meant a loss of property. But for slave women it meant much more. Infanticide among slave populations was not a common act committed by women with no maternal feelings for their children, but rather an atypical, compassionate act of freedom or resistance, or a means of self-survival.

— *Lori Lee*

See also: Works Progress Administration Interviews.

For Further Reading

Bush, Barbara 1996. "Hard Labor: Women, Childbirth, and Resistance in British Caribbean Slave Societies." In *More than Chattel: Black Women and Slavery in the Americas.* Ed. David Barry Gaspar and Darlene Clark Hine. Bloomington: Indiana University Press.

Fox-Genovese, Elizabeth 1988. *Within the Plantation Household: Black and White Women of the South.* Chapel Hill: University of North Carolina Press.

Jones, Jacqueline 1986. *Labor of Love, Labor of Sorrow: Black Women, Work and the Family, from Slavery to the Present.* New York: Vintage Books.

King, Wilma. 1996. "Suffer with Them till Death." In *More than Chattel: Black Women and Slavery in the Americas.* Ed. David Barry Gaspar and Darlene Clark Hine. Bloomington: Indiana University Press.

White, Deborah. 1985. *Ar'n't I a Woman? Female Slaves in the Plantation South.* New York: Norton.

Williamson, Laila. 1978. "Infanticide: An Anthropological Analysis." In *Infanticide and the Value of Life.* Ed. Marvin Kohl. New York: Prometheus Books.

ISLAM

Recent studies suggest that perhaps as much as 20 percent of the Africans brought to the Americas as slaves during the era of the transatlantic slave trade may have been adherents to the Islamic faith. The presence of Muslim cultural influence was strong in portions of Brazil, especially in the so-called Hausa States, but it seemed less apparent within the slave society that emerged in the United States. One of the ultimate goals of the "seasoning" or conditioning of slaves to the Americas was the attempt to break the slave of all cultural ties with Africa. Thus efforts to eliminate any connection with religious practices of the Motherland culture would have been part of this effort. Still, in spite of these efforts, evidence persists that large numbers of slaves within the United States surreptitiously maintained the practices of their Muslim faith during the days of slavery.

Presumed evidence of Muslim association is sometimes determined by examining the manifests of slave ships and early auction records to identify the names associated with recent African arrivals. It appears that Muslim names such as Muhammad and Fatima do appear in these records, as do individuals named for the day of the week on which they were born. Common West African day names included, for male slaves, Cuffee, Cudjo, and Quashee, while female names included Phibba, Cubba, and Quasheba. These African names—whether or not of religious origin—were stripped away from recent arrivals who received new "slave names" as a means of symbolizing their cultural break with their former selves.

Some slave narratives and autobiographies published during the antebellum era acknowledge the presence of "old Muslim slaves" who continued to maintain their religious practices, like daily prayer, despite the deterrent efforts of owners and overseers. It appears that some African slaves were punished repeatedly in an effort to break them of their religious and cultural ties to Africa. Occasionally, records indicate a limited tolerance of non-Christian religious practices among some slaves. An eighty-nine-year-old North Carolina slave named Uncle Moreau (Omar Ibn Said) was permitted to maintain the fast of Ramadan when he first arrived in North Carolina, but later in his life he abandoned Islam and was baptized as a Presbyterian (Blassingame, 1977).

Muslim slaves were preferred by some slaveowners and were distrusted by others, so when it was possible to determine an African slave's religious background planters generally sought such knowledge. There did not always exist physical evidence or scars to indicate what Africans might be Muslim. The practice of male circumcision at the age of thirteen was common throughout the Islamic world, but its adaptation and use in West Africa seemed to be sporadic. Often the geographic region from which the slave originated or the tribal ethnicity was used to determine the likelihood of a slave's association with Islam. Some slaveowners found Muslim slaves to be more civilized than their non-Muslim brethren, and for this reason the Muslim slaves were sometimes given positions of trust such as slave driver on a plantation. In Brazil, many owners came to fear the influence of Muslim slaves because they were perceived as being prone to insurrection and to use their faith to fan anti-Western defiance among their fellow slaves.

One of the most celebrated examples of an African Muslim who was enslaved in the United States was the case of Abdual-Rahahman Ibrahima (1762–1829) who labored for forty years as a slave on a Natchez, Mississippi, plantation. The son of a Timbo king from present-day Guinea, Ibrahima was an African prince who struggled over four decades to effect his manumission so that he and his family could return to their African homeland. The emancipation of the African prince and his return to Guinea was finally accomplished through the intervention of Secretary of State Henry Clay and President John Quincy Adams, who supported pleas on behalf of "the Moor" to obtain his freedom.

Muslim slaves tended to be well educated, and most came from affluent families in Africa. In many West African societies, the politically well-connected and the merchant class tended to convert first when Islam arrived in the region. The social dislocation caused by prolonged centuries of tribal conflict resulting from the slave trade and the expansion of some Muslim states in the African Sudan like Futa Jalon created conditions in the eighteenth century that made anyone in West Africa liable to be captured by raiding parties. Some scholars estimate that in this era alone as many as thirty thousand Muslim slaves may have been transported to the Americas.

In the new scholarship, like that produced by Michael A. Gomez, efforts are being made to make the place of Muslim slaves more central in the discussion of slavery in the United States.

— Junius P. Rodriguez

See also: Names and Naming.

For Further Reading

Austin, Allen D., ed. 1996. *African Muslims in Antebellum America: Proud Exiles.* New York: Routledge.

Blassingame, John W. 1977. *Slave Testimony: Two Centuries of Letters, Speeches, Interviews, and Autobiographies.* Baton Rouge: Louisiana State University Press.

Curtin, Philip D. 1968. *Africa Remembered: Narratives by West Africans from the Era of the Slave Trade.* Madison: University of Wisconsin Press.

Gomez, Michael A. 1994. "Muslims in Early America." *Journal of Southern History* 60: 671–710.

Gomez, Michael A. 2005. *Black Crescent: The Experience and Legacy of African Muslims in the Americas.* Cambridge: Cambridge University Press.

Judy, Ronald A. T. 1993. *(Dis)forming the American Canon: African-Arabic Slave Narratives and the Vernacular.* Minneapolis: University of Minnesota Press.

HARRIET ANN JACOBS (1813–1897)

Born a slave in Edenton, North Carolina, Harriet Jacobs underwent severe trials before escaping to the North and publishing her narrative about the sexual vulnerability of slave women. Though attacks on southern masters' concubinage and even rape had been standard abolitionist fodder for years, Jacobs's *Incidents in the Life of a Slave Girl* (1861) revealed horrors that strengthened the antislavery cause. The book was also remarkable for its portrait of free and enslaved blacks working together and for its indication that southern white women also suffered from slavery.

Born to comparative comfort, since her grandmother had a small business and was free, Jacobs was
taught to read and write by a mistress whom she recalled with a sense of love betrayed. This woman's decision to will Harriet to a three-year-old niece put the
young slave girl into the hands of the toddler's father.
James Norcom harassed Jacobs to the extent that the
slave girl felt trapped by impossible ideals of virtue and
chastity. Although Jacobs foiled Norcom's designs by
taking a white lover, with whom she had two children,
this desperate expedient did not free her from her mistress's father's power.

Forced to hide in her grandmother's garret to elude
Norcom, Jacobs finally escaped to Philadelphia in 1842
with the help of her grandmother and uncle. Aided by
abolitionists, she joined her daughter in Brooklyn but
was forced to flee to Boston when Norcom put slave
catchers on her trail. After supporting herself and her
children as a seamstress, Jacobs returned to the job of
nursemaid in a New York family. Later, she moved to
Rochester, New York, where her brother was an active
abolitionist, but she remained unsettled because of
Norcom's relentless pursuit. In 1852 Jacobs was purchased and freed by Cornelia Willis, whom she served
in New York.

Jacobs asked Harriet Beecher Stowe to write the
story of her life, but Stowe refused. Determined to
make her experiences known, Jacobs decided to write
her own book and practiced with shorter antislavery
pieces, signed "Linda," which appeared in New York's
reformist *Tribune*. In 1859 Jacobs arranged for the publication of her manuscript with a Boston firm. Their
request for a preface from Maria Child led to one final
editing and the decision that characters' identities
should be disguised. Thus Jacobs's autobiography is
told as the story of Linda Brent. Favorably received,
Incidents in the Life of a Slave Girl was republished in
England as *The Deeper Wrong* (1862), and portions of
the book appeared in Child's *Freedmen's Book* (1865).

During the Civil War, Jacobs did relief work among
former slaves in Washington, D.C., and then taught
and nursed in Alexandria, Virginia. After the war, Jacobs and her daughter traveled to southern cities carrying relief supplies. In 1868 the two women sailed to
England to try to raise funds for a Savannah orphan-
age and home for the aged, but Jacobs later advised
against building because of southern racist agitation.
She died in 1897 and was buried in Massachusetts,
near her brother John.

— *Barbara Ryan*

See also: Child, Lydia M.; Narratives; Stowe, Harriet
Beecher.

For Further Reading
Yellin, Jean Fagan, ed. 1987. *Incidents in the Life of a
Slave Girl*. Cambridge, MA: Harvard University Press.

JOHN JASPER (1812–1901)

John Jasper was a prominent Baptist preacher in Richmond, Virginia, whose sermon "De Sun Do Move"
made him nationally renowned. He was slave-born on
a plantation in Fluvanna County, Virginia, to Nina, a
domestic slave, and Philip, a field slave and preacher.
His father's death two months after Jasper's birth left
Nina to raise the family. Years later, Jasper recalled the
harshness of these years "when the July sun cooked de
skin on my back many er day when I wuz hoein in de
corn fiel, and he knowed nuthin wuth talkin bout con-
sarnin books, but thusted fer de bread uv learnin."
Jasper was eventually sold to Samuel Hargrove, who
put him to work as a stemmer in his Richmond tobacco factory. While there, Jasper married fellow slave
Elvy Weadon.

In July 1837, Jasper converted to Christianity. He
subsequently joined Richmond's First Baptist Church
and began preaching regularly. Like many fellow
slaves, he taught himself to read through the Bible.
"Since then, I aint keerd bout nuthin cept ter study an
preach de Word uv God." Soon after his conversion,
Jasper left Elvy and married Candus Jordan. They had
nine children. Beginning in 1839, he gained recognition for his funeral orations in and around Richmond.

During the Civil War, Jasper preached in hospitals
to the wounded. After emancipation, he moved with
his congregation to the northern part of Richmond
and helped found the Sixth Mount Zion Church. He
preached there for some four decades until his death,
gaining national reputation.

Jasper was historically significant for several reasons.
First, he was an old-style preacher thundering fire and
brimstone from the pulpit. This style stood in marked
contrast to the more measured tones of his theologi-
cally trained contemporaries. Second, he preached in
the honest dialect of poor rural black folk and new migrants to Richmond, who made up most of his congregation. "An lemme say dat it I doant giv it ter you
straight," he was fond of preaching, "if I gits one word
crooked or wrong, you jes holler out Hol on dar, Jasper,
yer aint got dat straight an Ill beg pardon." In such
ways, he linked the pulpit with the congregation, life
and religion, the countryside and the town. Jasper's first
biographer recalled one inspirational sermon he had
witnessed: "He painted scene after scene. He lifted the
people to the sun and sank them down to despair. He

plucked them out of hard places and filled them with shouting" (Hatcher, 1908). Third, he was a consummate performer. Hatcher recalled his first sighting of Jasper: "He circled around the pulpit with his ankle in his hand; and laughed and sang and shouted and acted about a dozen characters within the space of three minutes. He was a theatre within himself, with the stage crowded with actors" (Hatcher, 1908). Finally, the Bible in his hands became a liberation text through which human oppression was both understood and overcome. "I preach dis sermon, he pronounced, jest fer ter settle de mins uv my few brutherin."

The sermon "De Sun Do Move" was the most famous feature of Jasper's performance. Drawing upon the biblical stories of Hezekier, Joshwer, and Malerki, Jasper asserted that the earth was flat and the sun revolved around it. He delivered this sermon over 250 times, including to the Virginia General Assembly, much to the chagrin of his fellow preachers who thought the content, style and popularity outlandish. Their dislike was fueled by class tensions among Richmond's black elite; while the organic nature of the sermon is suggested by its failure to rouse much excitement when Jasper toured northern states.

Jasper is an important figure in African American, Virginia, and religious history. He belongs to a long line of inspirational black religious leaders and he was long remembered: former slave Allen Wilson fondly recalled Jasper's old sermons decades later during the 1930s.

— *Jeff R. Kerr-Ritchie*

See also: Slave Preachers.

For Further Reading
Brawley, Benjamin. 1937. *Negro Builders and Heroes.* Chapel Hill: University of North Carolina Press.
Hatcher, William E. 1908. *John Jasper: The Unmatched Negro Philosopher and Preacher.* New York: F.H. Revell.
James, Isaac. 1954. *"The Sun Do Move": The Story of the Life of John Jasper.* Richmond, VA: Whittet and Shepperson.
Perdue, Charles L., et al. 1976. *Weevils in the Wheat: Interviews with Virginia Ex-Slaves.* Charlottesville: University of Virginia Press.

JAYHAWKERS

In the 1850s the jayhawkers of Kansas became a major obstacle to the expansion of slavery in the United States. In the contest to determine the status of slavery in the territory, partisan bands engaged in frequent violent episodes that foretold the future Civil War. The antislavery forces were called "jayhawkers." The origins of the term are obscure, and numerous conflicting explanations have been given. The jayhawkers' resistance to the proslavery forces, or border ruffians, eventually helped make Kansas a free state.

The Kansas–Nebraska Act, signed in 1854, opened two new territories with no reference as to the status of slavery in either of them. The residents of the territories were to vote on slavery prior to the formation of state constitutions—a practice called popular sovereignty. Kansas's close proximity to Missouri, a slave state, virtually ensured conflict since most of the early settlers of Kansas Territory were antislavery farmers from free states in the Midwest.

After slavery advocates from Missouri flooded across the border to cast fraudulent votes in the 1855 territorial elections, the region exploded in violence. In the polarized political climate of the 1850s, Bleeding Kansas became a national issue, since many people perceived the territory to be a crucial test over the future of slavery.

The jayhawkers were the frontier vanguard of the American antislavery movement, but they differed from their high-minded eastern abolitionist counterparts in important ways. Most jayhawkers wanted to exclude not only slaves but all blacks from settlement in Kansas, although most of them were content to allow the institution to remain in Missouri. By and large they had little love or sympathy for blacks—free or slave—as they saw them as competitors for land and jobs.

The key political leaders of the jayhawkers were James Lane, James Montgomery, and Charles R. Jennison. During the American Civil War, the jayhawkers formed Union bands that roamed the Kansas–Missouri area and engaged proslavery forces in fierce guerrilla fighting. The jayhawkers and their proslavery counterparts often matched each other in violence.

— *Richard D. Loosbrock*

See also: Border War (1854–1859); Popular Sovereignty.

For Further Reading
Castel, Albert. 1958. *A Frontier State at War: Kansas, 1861–1865.* Ithaca, NY: Cornell University Press.
Monaghan, Jay. 1955. *Civil War on the Western Border, 1854–65.* Boston: Little, Brown.

THOMAS JEFFERSON (1743–1826)

Thomas Jefferson, one of the most recognized figures in early U.S. history, advocated the emancipation of slaves, an end of the slave trade, and prohibition of the

Thomas Jefferson advocated the emancipation of slaves, an end to the slave trade, and a prohibition of slavery's spread in the United States' new territories. (National Archives)

spread of slavery in acquired territories of the United States. Nonetheless, no figure was more enigmatic in his views on slavery than Jefferson, who was truly trapped by the institution in both public and private life. Influenced by Enlightenment ideas, Jefferson clearly recognized slavery's moral wrong, yet when he was governor of Virginia and president for two terms, he did nothing to encourage an end to the institution. Writing in 1820, Jefferson lamented, "We have the wolf by the ears," concluding that slavery was evil but the South could not live without it. On one side he saw the concept of justice, and, on the other, self-preservation.

Born on April 13, 1743, in Shadwell, Virginia, Jefferson was educated at the College of William and Mary and studied law under George Wythe, Virginia's leading legal mind of the era. He was a significant figure in the nation's history after 1775: he wrote the Declaration of Independence, served as a minister to France, was secretary of state, was vice president (1797–1801), and served as president (1801–1809). All aspects of Jefferson's public career suggest an opposition to slavery.

His authorship of the Declaration of Independence included the concept that all men are equal; his Virginia Statute of Religious Freedom (1786) implied a sense of freedom of, at least, religion; and in *Notes on the State of Virginia* (1781–1782), the only book he ever wrote, Jefferson stated his opposition to slavery. Historically, he believed all slaves should be freed. Yet he found emancipation incompatible with his practical actions.

Despite his political stance on slavery, Jefferson's personal actions have been questioned for nearly two centuries. Jefferson was a slaveholder—at one time, he owned more than one hundred slaves. He often considered freeing his slaves and allowing them to become tenants on his property, but financial problems kept him from doing so, as he apparently put personal economics above his social philosophy. Jefferson also believed that blacks were intellectually inferior and that the negative impact of slavery on whites was far more significant than the consequences of society supporting an enslaved race. Jefferson, a complex man, was puzzling in his attitudes on race and social relations.

During Jefferson's first term as president, *Richmond Recorder* newspaperman James Callender published a rumor that Jefferson had fathered a mulatto child by one of his slaves, Sally Hemings. Callender's attack was clearly politically motivated and lacked an accurate basis, but the charges, ironically, were made possible by Jefferson's own insistence on freedom of the press. In *Thomas Jefferson: An Intimate History* (1974), Fawn Brodie explored Jefferson's involvement with Hemings, the historical importance of that association, and his interest in other women. Brodie's evidence is circumstantial, however, leaving history and historians to make a final decision. Scientific studies conducted in the late 1990s compared DNA evidence from Hemings's son's descendants with that of the Jefferson family to try to determine the likelihood of the paternity of Heming's children by Thomas Jefferson. Although it is likely that someone from the Jefferson family fathered at least one of Hemings's children, the DNA evidence could not determine exclusively that Thomas Jefferson was the father of the child.

Jefferson's stance on slavery was confused by a draft he prepared in 1784 proposing the abolition of slavery in the West, in the new region of the nation gained during the American Revolution. The Articles of Confederation Congress met in Annapolis in 1784 to decide the future of that territory, and as chair of a committee assigned to establish a governmental system and land policy, Jefferson wrote a draft that became the Ordinance of 1784 (which never went into effect).

In his proposal, slavery (and involuntary servitude) was prohibited in all territories of the United States—

North and South. His plans included the areas that became Alabama, Mississippi, and Tennessee, but only one southern representative supported Jefferson. Ironically, the antislavery provision lost by one vote, that of an absent New Jersey delegate. The Northwest Ordinance (1787) did ban slavery in a portion of the expanding nation, but in areas south of the Ohio River, slavery could exist. Although Jefferson had no connection with the Northwest Ordinance, his ideas from the Ordinance of 1784 did influence this later legislation. From the perspective of southern interests, the decision to allow slavery to spread was clearly economic.

As president, Jefferson's dichotomy on slavery persisted. Most historians agree that Jefferson's two major accomplishments as president were the Louisiana Purchase (1803) and the abolition of the slave trade (1808). The contradiction lies in Jefferson's fight to abolish trade in human beings, yet allowing human bondage to expand into land purchased from France. From Jefferson's perspective, he envisioned the northern half of the Louisiana territory as a huge Indian reservation. Yet critics, citing Jefferson's earlier view of the nation as an "empire of liberty," now saw an "empire of slavery" when the administration took no action on slavery in the vast region. In the 1780s Jefferson favored limits on the spread of slavery, but he had become resigned to the fact that slavery was an economic necessity for southerners.

Jefferson's second term featured an end to the foreign slave trade, which had been the object of national scorn for years. In 1787 antislavery forces pushed for a constitutional ban on importing slaves, but an odd alliance of southern slave interests and New England shippers, who profited from the slave trade, had combined to recognize a moratorium on federal interference with the slave trade for twenty years.

In 1794 a federal law was enacted to prohibit ships access to any U.S. port when the cargo was slaves. By 1799 all states had banned importing slaves, but the cumulative impact of the legislation was ineffective. Smuggling was widespread, and in 1803 South Carolina bent to the planters' economic necessity and rescinded earlier acts. Over the next five years, an estimated forty thousand slaves were imported through South Carolina's various ports. But in March 1807 Congress passed an act that totally abolished the slave trade after January 1, 1808. Jefferson supported the legislation, but it reflected national sentiment and preference more than his presidential leadership. Ironically, the foreign slave trade continued after 1808, but in total numbers such illegal smuggling was not excessive (estimates vary, but the total was fewer than sixty thousand). Instead, slaveowners turned to natural reproduction to increase their slave numbers.

Jefferson's views on slavery survived his death in 1826. From 1829 to 1832, the Virginia legislature wrestled with the issue, but emancipation was not forthcoming, even though Jefferson had advocated freeing the slaves. Nat Turner's Rebellion (1831) was a defining reason for the outcome of the debate, but even a captured Nat Turner wondered: if all men were created equal, why then was he not free? Critics have continued to address the crucial question: Why did the father of democracy, the author of his nation's independence document, not free his slaves?

— *Boyd Childress*

See also: Hemings, Sally; *Notes on Virginia* (Jefferson).

For Further Reading
Brodic, Fawn. 1974. *Thomas Jefferson: An Intimate History.* New York: Norton.

Jefferson, Thomas. 1950–. *The Papers of Thomas Jefferson.* Princeton, NJ: Princeton University Press.

Miller, John C. 1977. *The Wolf by the Ears: Thomas Jefferson and Slavery.* New York: Norton.

ANTHONY JOHNSON (D. 1670)

Anthony Johnson, a black indentured servant, gained his freedom in early seventeenth-century Virginia. Through hard work, Johnson and his family built a successful tobacco enterprise. But changing racial attitudes by the middle of the century eroded the socioeconomic livelihood enjoyed by Johnson and his heirs.

Sometime during 1621, Anthony Johnson, then called Antonio a Negro, arrived in Virginia aboard the *James* as an indentured servant. Sold to a white planter named Bennett at Jamestown, Johnson was listed as a servant in early census and tax records. Perhaps impressed by Johnson's work ethic, Bennett gave him a small piece of land to farm. By the middle of the decade, Johnson married Mary, an African who had also arrived as an indentured servant.

The next records for Anthony Johnson are more revealing. By 1641 he had gained his freedom and owned both a tobacco plantation and a black indentured servant named John Casor. Johnson and his wife also raised livestock on their modest estate along the banks of the Pungoteague Creek. Since he owned an indentured servant, Johnson claimed 250 acres of land based on the headright system.

By the early 1650s, Johnson's sons John and Richard owned land adjacent to him. As shown in the tax records, the Johnson clan, despite their African ancestry, had become quite successful tobacco farmers. To this point, their race had not been a barrier to upward mobility.

Beginning in 1653, however, the fortunes of the Johnson family changed significantly. In February, a fire swept through Anthony Johnson's buildings. Johnson made every effort to recover from this setback. He petitioned Northampton County justices for tax relief based on the disaster. The justices granted relief to Mary and their two daughters. The exemption allowed the Johnsons to save money and rebuild their plantation. A year later, Anthony Johnson lost his indentured servant Casor to a nearby white planter, who claimed that the servant was held illegally. Johnson did not challenge the claim. In 1655, perhaps learning that Johnson indeed had legal custody of Casor, county officials returned him to Johnson. In 1657 another white planter contested 100 acres of land adjacent to Anthony Johnson. Again, Johnson did not defend his right of ownership. Virginia's racial climate was less hospitable than it had been even a decade earlier.

During 1665 the Johnsons relocated to Somerset County, Maryland, where they named their tobacco farm Tonies Vineyard. Despite the move, Anthony Johnson's troubles continued. Another white planter forged a letter contending that Johnson owed him for tobacco. Although Johnson was illiterate, the court upheld an attachment of his land. Anthony Johnson died in 1670, leaving his estate to his wife. Mary Johnson negotiated a forty-year lease on the land and with her sons tried to make it profitable. But her sons died during the 1670s, and Mary Johnson died in 1680.

The land was inherited by a grandson named John Johnson, Jr. It was now reduced to 40 acres, which he named Angola, in honor of his grandfather's birthplace. Perhaps because he was unable to pay taxes on the property, it was seized by a white planter. John Johnson, the last heir, died in 1721, and the Johnson name along with the hard work of Anthony Johnson perished too.

The increasing racial hostility faced by Anthony Johnson was likely exacerbated during the lifetime of his sons and grandson. Barriers to success for Virginia's blacks, as reflected in Anthony Johnson's experiences were hard to overcome. The establishment of slavery in late seventeenth-century Virginia clearly marked blacks like Anthony Johnson as inferior. Now more than before, skin color defined the changing nature of colonial America.

— *Jackie R. Booker*

See also: Indentured Servants; Virginia's Slavery Debate.

For Further Reading

Berlin, Ira. 1998. *Many Thousand Gone: The First Two Centuries of Slavery in North America*. Cambridge, MA: Harvard University Press.

Berlin, Ira. 2003. *Generations of Captivity: A History of African American Slaves*. Cambridge, MA: Harvard University Press.

Breen, Timothy, and Stephen Innes. 1982. "Seventeenth-Century Virginia's Forgotten Yeomen: The First Blacks." *Virginia Cavalcade* 32 (1): 10–19.

Johnson, Charles, and Patricia Smith. 1998. *Africans in America: America's Journey Through Slavery*. New York: Harcourt, Brace, and Company.

JONES V. VAN ZANDT (1847)

The *Jones v. Van Zandt* case tested the constitutionality of the federal Fugitive Slave Act of 1793. John Van Zandt of Ohio, known for his support of abolition and actively involved in the Underground Railroad, was accused of assisting a runaway slave in escaping his master, Wharton Jones. The Supreme Court upheld the constitutionality of the 1793 act and ordered Van Zandt to pay the slaveowner for his lost slave, plus the costs of his recapture, and a $500 penalty.

Van Zandt had been driving his wagon in Ohio when he encountered several black men walking along the road. He offered them a ride, which they accepted. A few hours later two slave catchers confronted the party claiming the men were runaways. All the men were recaptured, except for one, who made his escape. Van Zandt claimed that he did not know they were runaways: he had encountered them walking along the road, in daylight, in the free state of Ohio. They had not urged him to make his wagon go faster once they were riding in it, but proceeded rather slowly, as if they were unhurried about reaching their destination. Nothing about them suggested that they were fugitives. Van Zandt claimed that he could not have known that the men were runaways, and so he should not be charged for aiding their escape.

Van Zandt made various other legal arguments to oppose the Fugitive Slave Law and to challenge the federal government's role of assisting in the recapture of runaways. Van Zandt's lawyer, Salmon P. Chase, argued that slavery was unlawful because it conflicted with the Declaration of Independence and violated aspects of the Bill of Rights, especially the Fifth Amendment. Most importantly, Chase contended that the federal government had no power to support slavery or to assist in the recapture of fugitive slaves (attacking the fugitive slave clause of the Constitution, found in Article IV). The Supreme Court rejected all of these arguments in the opinion written by Levi Woodbury. Perhaps seeking political prestige and elective office in 1852 with the support of southern slaveholders, Woodbury called the fugitive slave clause one of the Constitution's "sacred compromises," which could not be subverted or undone. Only three years later, Congress revised the 1793 act and replaced it with even harsher provisions in the Fugitive Slave Act of 1850.

Jones v. Van Zandt [46 U.S. 215 (1847)] was one of a series of slavery cases decided by the Supreme Court in the decades before the Civil War in which the justices supported slavery and rejected any argument attacking it. As in *Prigg v. Pennsylvania* (1842), *Dred Scott v. Sandford* (1857), and *Ableman v. Booth* (1859), the Supreme Court solidly defended slaveowners' rights to recapture runaways and made many northerners uneasy about how far the Supreme Court would go to defend slavery from legal challenges.

— *Sally E. Hadden*

See also: *Ableman v. Booth;* Abolitionism in the United States; *Dred Scott v. Sandford; Prigg v. Pennsylvania;* Underground Railroad; United States Constitution.

For Further Reading

Cover, Robert. 1975. *Justice Accused: Antislavery and the Judicial Process.* New Haven, CT: Yale University Press.

Finkelman, Paul. 1985. *Slavery in the Courtroom. An Annotated Bibliography of American Cases.* Washington, D.C.: Library of Congress.

Swisher, Carl. 1974. *History of the Supreme Court of the United States: The Taney Period, 1836–1864.* New York: Macmillan.

Wiecek, William E. 1978. "Slavery and Abolition before the United States Supreme Court, 1820–1860." *Journal of American History* 65 (1978): 34–59.

A Quaker from Indiana, George Washington Julian was a devout abolitionist throughout his forty-year career in public life. (Library of Congress)

GEORGE WASHINGTON JULIAN
(1817–1899)

Throughout his forty-year public career, George W. Julian consistently stood at the forefront of antislavery politics and battles for black civil rights in the United States. Perhaps owing to his Quaker upbringing in Indiana, Julian demonstrated a moral disgust for human bondage at an early age. A devoted abolitionist, Julian began practicing law in 1840 and quickly joined such lawyers as Salmon P. Chase of Ohio at the head of the western antislavery movement. In 1845 Julian entered the Indiana legislature as a Whig, but when the Whig Party chose slaveholder Zachary Taylor as its 1848 presidential candidate, Julian bolted the organization and allied himself with the nascent Free Soil Party—an organization explicitly devoted to arresting the progress and expansion of slavery. In 1849 Indiana voters elected Julian to the U.S. House of Representatives, where the Free Soilers opposed the Compromise of 1850 because of its fugitive slave provisions and its noninterventionist posture regarding slavery in the territories acquired as a result of the Mexican War (1846–1848).

Julian lost his congressional seat in 1851 and did not hold another public office for a decade, though he remained politically active throughout the 1850s. He ran for the vice presidency on the Free Soil ticket in 1852, and he consistently strove to build free soil coalitions at the state and regional levels, hoping to unite disparate antislavery elements into a single party of liberty. To this end, Julian joined and promoted the Republican Party when it emerged from the fallout over the Kansas–Nebraska Act in 1854, and he helped the fledgling antislavery party gain a firm foothold in the Midwest. Julian's tireless activism commanded attention from ally and adversary alike. His antiabolitionist opponents, for example, assigned him the deprecatory moniker "orator of free dirt," while the black abolitionist Frederick Douglass once praised Julian as "one of the truest and most disinterested friends of freedom whom [antislavery activists] have ever met" (Sewell, 1976).

In 1861 Julian began the first of five consecutive terms in Congress, where he emerged as a leading Radical Republican spokesman. From the outset of the Civil War, Julian pressed President Abraham Lincoln to proclaim a general emancipation, to enlist black troops, and to guarantee equal citizenship rights for blacks. After the war Julian joined other Radicals in denouncing President Andrew Johnson's pro-southern plan of restoration, which contained no safeguards for the legal and civil rights of freedmen. A leading figure in the implementation of congressional Reconstruction in 1866–1867, Julian supported the Thirteenth and Fourteenth Amendments to the Constitution, backed the Reconstruction Acts of 1867, and even tried to introduce legislation granting suffrage to women.

After 1868 Julian turned his attention to matters of civil service reform. A vocal critic of President Ulysses S. Grant's graft-ridden administration, Julian soon fell out of favor with the Republican Party hierarchy. He failed to win reelection to Congress in 1871 and quickly faded from the political limelight.

— *Eric Tscheschlok*

See also: Free Soil Party.

For Further Reading
Blue, Frederick J. 1973. *The Free Soilers: Third Party Politics, 1848–54.* Urbana: University of Illinois Press.
Foner, Eric. 1970. *Free Soil, Free Labor, Free Men: The Ideology of the Republican Party before the Civil War.* New York: Oxford University Press.
Riddleberger, Patrick W. 1966. *George Washington Julian, Radical Republican.* Indianapolis: Indiana Historical Bureau.
Sewell, Richard H. 1976. *Ballots for Freedom: Antislavery Politics in the United States, 1837–1860.* New York: Oxford University Press.
Trefousse, Hans L. 1969. *The Radical Republicans: Lincoln's Vanguard for Racial Justice.* New York: Knopf.

JUNETEENTH

Juneteenth is a hybrid of the words June and nineteenth. It was first recognized on June 19, 1865. In the weeks following General Robert E. Lee's surrender at Appomattox, General Gordon Granger and a regiment of Union army soldiers sailed into Galveston, Texas, and issued a freedom proclamation for nearly two hundred thousand slaves. This was the catalyst for a number of celebrations in the state and throughout the southwestern United States. Currently a Texas state holiday, Juneteenth is commemorated all over the country with parades, concerts, and cultural festivities.

President Abraham Lincoln signed the first Emancipation Proclamation on September 22, 1862. It was a preliminary document, announcing that emancipation would become effective on January 1, 1863. Enforcement, however, was stalled until the end of the Civil War in April 1865 and the passage of the Thirteenth Amendment to the U.S. Constitution on December 18, 1865. Texans were not notified of these developments and did not learn of their freedom until June 19 of that year.

The reasons surrounding the lapse in delivering the news are legendary. One account details the sojourn of a soldier traveling by mule at the request of President Lincoln who stopped in Arkansas and Oklahoma before finally arriving in Texas. However, this does not coincide with the landing of General Granger in Galveston Bay. It is generally accepted that plantation owners purposely delayed the news announcing the end of slavery in order to orchestrate one final harvest and planting of the cotton crops.

Despite its Texas origins, Juneteenth parallels the segregation and migration of former slaves to the western and northern territories of the United States. People who believed they would never live to see freedom were eager to observe and celebrate their culture and traditions.

The initial gatherings were held in rural locations that were not subject to the laws of segregation. Later, as the freedom celebrations became more popular Houston waived its segregation rules for the event. This led to the purchase of 10 acres of land near Houston in 1872. In 1878 a community group was chartered, and they purchased the land that became Booker T. Washington Park in Mexia, near Waco. It soon became the home of the earliest Juneteenth celebrations. The traditions established at this time included a reprieve from work, the donning of elaborate costumes to symbolize freedom from the rags of slavery, barbecuing, and enjoying an elaborate picnic. Contemporary celebrations include prayer services, African art sales, and a variety of musical concerts.

Integration, the Great Depression, and World War II contributed to the decline of Juneteenth emancipation gatherings. In 1979 Houston Representative Al Edwards proposed legislation to make June 19 an official Texas state holiday. The bill became law on January 1, 1980. The renaissance of African American cultural pride and ethnic identification prevalent in the country over the last twenty-five years has helped to resurrect Juneteenth. It is now visible in a variety of places in the United States.

— *Anthony Todman*

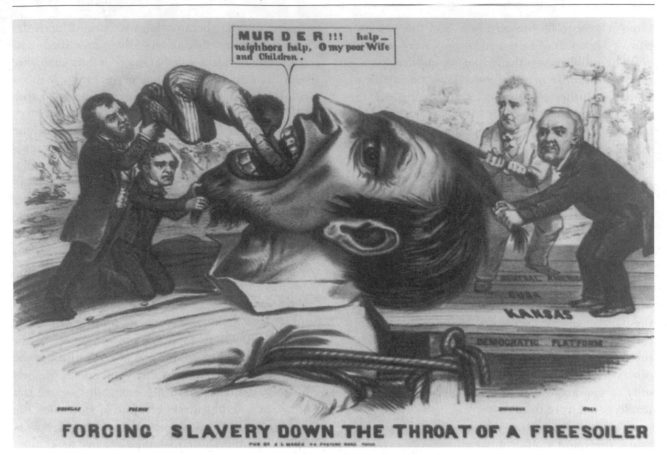

President Franklin Pierce, presidential nominee James Buchanan, Senator Lewis Cass, and Senator Stephen A. Douglas force a man down the throat of a giant in an 1856 political cartoon that satirized the Kansas–Nebraska Act of 1854, which allowed popular sovereignty to decide slavery-related issues in the two territories. The act nullified the Missouri Compromise of 1820. (Library of Congress)

See also: Emancipation Proclamation.

For Further Reading

Chase, Henry. 1997. "Juneteenth in Texas." *American Visions* 12 (June–July): 44–49.

Galloway, Lula Briggs, and Audrey Beatty. 1999. *Juneteenth, Ring the Bell of Freedom.* Saginaw, MI: National Association of Juneteenth Lineage.

Pemberton, Doris Hollis. 1983. *Juneteenth at Comanche Crossing.* Austin, TX: Eakin Publications.

Thomas, Karen M. 1992. "Juneteenth Remembers Slavery, Celebrates Freedom." *Chicago Tribune* June 18, final edition: 1.

Wiggins, William H. 1993. "Juneteenth: Tracking the Progress of an Emancipation Celebration." *American Visions* 8:3 (June–July): 28–31.

∾ K ∾

KANSAS–NEBRASKA ACT (1854)

The Kansas–Nebraska Act, passed by the U.S. Congress on May 30, 1854, repealed the Missouri Compromise (1820), which had specifically excluded slavery from the region north of latitude 36°30'. Illinois Senator Stephen A. Douglas introduced the bill organizing Kansas and Nebraska into territories that would be in a position to determine the status for slaves via popular sovereignty. This meant that whether or not slavery was instituted in the state would be decided by popular vote.

In addition to repealing the Missouri Compromise (1820), the act abrogated certain portions of the Compromise of 1850 since northern Texas, California, and

Oregon were to be free territories and the remaining part of Texas was to be settled by proslavery southerners. The problem was that if the act nullified parts of the Compromise of 1850, then slavery could be extended to other territories. Later, during the Lincoln–Douglas debates (1858), Abraham Lincoln criticized Douglas, stating that popular sovereignty did nothing to address the moral and ethical concerns of slavery. Whig congressman Samuel P. Benson of Maine noted during the congressional debate that the Northwest Ordinance (1787) indicated that for no reason was slavery to be extended. In other words, the prohibition of slavery in the territory was a compact against the extension of slavery.

Not surprisingly, the Kansas–Nebraska Act was unacceptable to those traditionalists who believed in and supported slavery vehemently. It upset many people in the North who considered the Missouri Compromise to be a long-standing binding agreement. In the proslavery South, it was also strongly opposed. Still others felt that the agitation caused by Douglas was only to guarantee that the transcontinental railroad would be built westward from Chicago. The problem was that any such plan would need the support of southerners and would thus encompass the issue of slavery. Although Douglas had no personal stance on the issue of slavery, congressional "nonintervention" may have led to the conflict between rival factions called Bleeding Kansas. After the act was passed, pro- and antislavery supporters hurried to Kansas in an attempt to influence the outcome of the first election held after the law went into effect. When the final results indicated that proslavery settlers won the election, the charge of fraud was made by antislavery proponents who argued that the results were unjustified. When the second election was held, proslavery settlers refused to vote. This refusal resulted in the establishment of two opposing factions of the Kansas legislature. It also led some historians to contend that the Civil War began when proslavery and antislavery forces began to debate over whether land north of latitude 36°30' should be slave or free territory.

The disagreement escalated until 1861. People's opinions about the Kansas–Nebraska Act were so vehement that it was not uncommon for premeditated attacks, which often led to death, to be waged against opposing factions. Georgia native Charles A. Hamelton was the leader of the proslavery forces in the region. He originally went to Kansas to garner support for making it a slave state, but he was forced to leave. He then gathered a group of men, who, on their way to Missouri, captured eleven free state supporters, lined them on the side of a road, and fired their weapons in what became known as the Marais des Cygnes massacre. Five of the eleven men died. The irony of this incident was that many of these men were his former neighbors. Only one of this group, William Griffith, was caught for the crime and punished with death by hanging.

Public sentiment over the incident was intense and horrific. This event was so troubling that John Greenleaf Whittier wrote a poem on the act, and it was published in the September 1858 *Atlantic Monthly.* President Franklin Pierce, in support of the proslavery settlers, sent in federal troops to stop the violence and disperse the antislavery legislature. Another election was called. However, Congress did not recognize the constitution adopted by the proslavery settlers and subsequently did not allow Kansas into the Union.

Feelings over the situation in Missouri and Kansas even prompted violence on the floor of the Senate. In the end, antislavery supporters, who comprised the majority, won the election and a new constitution was penned. President Franklin Pierce supported the new antislavery constitution, which eventually became law. Both Kansas and Nebraska chose to be free states. On January 29, 1861, prior to the start of the Civil War, Kansas was admitted to the union as a free state.

— *Torrance T. Stephens*

See also: Border War (1854–1859); Douglas, Stephen A.; Lecompton Constitution; Missouri Compromise; 36°30' North Latitude.

For Further Reading

Drake, Ross. 2004. "The Law That Ripped America in Two." *Smithsonian* 35 (2): 60–66.

Johannsen, Robert. 1989. *The Frontier, the Union, and Stephen A. Douglas.* Urbana: University of Illinois Press.

Morrison, Michael A. 1997. *Slavery and the American West: The Eclipse of Manifest Destiny and the Coming of the Civil War.* Chapel Hill: University of North Carolina Press.

Stampp, Kenneth M. 1990. *America in 1857: A Nation on the Brink.* New York: Oxford University Press.

ELIZABETH KECKLEY (C. 1818–1907)

Born a slave in Virginia, Elizabeth Keckley earned the money to buy her freedom and eventually became a successful dressmaker in Washington, D.C. Her skills were so much admired that the fashionable Mary Todd Lincoln hired Keckley frequently, and soon the former slave was a Lincoln family friend and confidante. After Abraham Lincoln was killed and his widow had returned to Illinois, Keckley published an autobiographical narrative that recounted scenes from the Lincolns' private life. Keckley blamed the resultant scandal on her editor's unauthorized decision to print Mrs. Lincoln's personal letters, yet it was the dressmaker who took the brunt of Robert Lincoln's anger when he had *Behind the Scenes; or, Thirty Years a Slave and Four Years in the White House* (1868) suppressed.

No one could have foreseen this scandal when as a young slave Keckley labored as a bondwoman or when she was forced to be a white man's concubine. Yet this woman's talents appeared early enough that one master set her to earning, with her needle, the money to support his entire family. After she was taken to St. Louis, the enterprising seamstress negotiated an agreement to work herself out of slavery, and equipped with a ready needle and loans from appreciative clients, Keckley was able to purchase her own and her son's freedom in 1855. Five years later, the loans repaid, Keckley moved to the nation's capital, and became the modiste of dress-conscious ladies' choice. It was in this setting that Keckley met Mary Lincoln and became a White House intimate.

No one questioned Keckley's right to compose a narrative of slavery or even to describe her life as a freewoman during the Civil War. It was because *Behind the Scenes* revealed inside knowledge of Mary Lincoln's staggering debts and provided details on the "old clothes" sale, which titillated gossipmongers that Keckley's memoirs caused a scandal, one its author apparently did not foresee. Soon, Mary Lincoln's "dearest Lizzie" was persona non grata amid former friends, and though Keckley spent the rest of her life working as a dressmaker and teaching sewing, she did not write again.

Acquaintances from Keckley's final days recalled her as dignified and ladylike. Often, she would recall the days in which she was Mary Lincoln's friend. She contended that her editor was to blame for the narrative's infelicities, and indeed, James Redpath may have had a grudge against Lincoln's widow. But it is also possible that Keckley overestimated the friendship that Mary Lincoln felt for her. *In Behind the Scenes,* Keckley claimed that bonds of affection could exist between slaveholders and their slaves; she did not note that such sentiments rested on unequal relations to social power.

— *Barbara Ryan*

See also: Narratives.

For Further Reading
Keckley, Elizabeth. 1868. *Behind the Scenes; or, Thirty Years a Slave and Four Years in the White House.* New York: G.W. Carleton.

Washington, John E. 1942. *They Knew Lincoln.* New York: E. P. Dutton.

FRANCES ANNE KEMBLE (1809–1893)

Frances Anne Kemble was a famous English actress who was also well known for the publication of her antislavery *Journal of a Residence on a Georgian Plantation in 1838–1839* (1863). Frances Anne (Fanny) and her father, Charles Kemble, both accomplished Shakespearean actors, toured the United States from 1832 through 1834. During the tour she met and eventually married Pierce Mease Butler, a wealthy Philadelphia resident. At the time of their wedding Fanny was unaware of the source of Butler's wealth—plantation lands and slaves located in coastal Georgia.

Headstrong and opinionated, Fanny Butler strongly opposed slavery. Believing she could persuade her husband of slavery's evils, she openly condemned his "living in idleness from the unpaid labor of others," and sought "to bring him to a realization of the sins of slaveholding" (Kemble, 1863). Pierce Butler reluctantly assented to his wife's suggestion that they both visit the Georgia plantations as Christian "missionaries," and in late December 1838 the Butler family arrived in Darien, Georgia. Nearby was Butler's Island, the family's rice plantation of nearly 2,000 acres, and there was another property in the vicinity, a 1,700-acre tract on St. Simons Island called Hampton Point where Sea Island cotton was cultivated. The two plantations combined had a slave population of several hundred.

Already convinced of the degrading nature of slavery when she arrived in Georgia, Fanny Butler not only confirmed but strengthened her antipathy to slavery. During this sojourn in the South she kept a diary, subsequently expanded, and eventually published as the *Journal of a Residence on a Georgian Plantation in 1838–1839* (1863). Her chronicle reveals a particular concern for slave women as she recounts in great detail how pregnant slaves were overworked and even whipped. Laboring in the fields until delivery, female slaves were allowed only a short period to recover from childbirth. Fanny Butler condemned medical care on the plantations as barbaric. Not surprisingly, miscarriages, stillbirths, and infant mortality were shockingly high.

Slave dwellings were regarded as "filthy and wretched in the extreme," and the children were depicted as having "incrustations of dirt on their hands, feet, and faces." During her months in Georgia, Fanny

Frances Ann Kemble was an accomplished Shakespearean actress who was also well known for publishing the antislavery *Journal of a Residence on a Georgian Plantation* in 1838 and 1839. (Library of Congress)

Butler did what she could to improve sanitary conditions in the slave infirmary and slave dwellings. Her journal also gives details regarding slave music, funerals, food and its preparation, and other customs.

Considered to be quite an indictment of slavery, the *Journal* was published in England in 1863. The Butlers were divorced by this time, and Frances Kemble had been persuaded by friends that publication would help the antislavery cause of Union forces during the Civil War. The *Journal* was actually published too late to have any substantial effect on Britain's foreign policy regarding the Confederacy—government opinion had already shifted from its previous pro-southern views. Nevertheless, the *Journal* gives a firsthand and very thorough account of slavery.

—*Mary Ellen Wilson*

See also: Georgia; Sea Islands.

For Further Reading

Bell, Malcolm. 1987. *Major Butler's Legacy: Five Generations of a Slaveholding Family.* Athens: University of Georgia Press.

Blainey, Ann. 2001. *Fanny & Adelaide: The Lives of the Remarkable Kemble Sisters.* Chicago: I.R. Dee.

Jenkins, Rebecca. 2005. *Fanny Kemble: A Reluctant Celebrity.* New York: Simon & Schuster.

Driver, Leota S. 1969. *Fanny Kemble.* New York: Negro Universities Press.

Kemble, Frances Anne. 1863. *Journal of a Residence on a Georgian Plantation in 1838–1839.* New York: Harper and Brothers.

Scott, John Anthony. 1961. "On the Authenticity of Fanny Kemble's Journal of a Residence on a Georgian Plantation in 1838–1839." *Journal of Negro History* 46: 233–242.

KNIGHTS OF THE GOLDEN CIRCLE

A colorful example of antebellum southern expansionism, the Knights of the Golden Circle was a secret filibustering society that sought to extend U.S. control—and slavery—throughout the lands bordering the Gulf of Mexico. Founded, according to some sources, on July 4, 1854, in Lexington, Kentucky, the organization was the brainchild of Virginia-born George W. L. Bickley (1819–1867), a physician, scholar, and journalist from Cincinnati, Ohio. A self-proclaimed crusader for "southern rights," Bickley planned to achieve sectional equality with the North by carving new slave states from territory seized in Mexico, Central America, and the Caribbean.

Little is known of the organization's activities im-

mediately after its formation, but the outbreak of civil war in Mexico spurred Bickley to action in spring 1859. During a convention held in White Sulphur Springs, Virginia, on August 8, Bickley announced that Mexico would be the first field of operations. In early 1860, he ordered his followers to rendezvous in Texas and prepare for active operations.

Bickley was probably encouraged because both President James Buchanan and Governor Sam Houston of Texas openly advocated U.S. intervention for the purpose of restoring order in Mexico. However, Houston, a staunch unionist, was unwilling to support Bickley's efforts to extend slavery south of the Rio Grande. He refused to sanction Bickley's invasion and on March 21, 1860, issued a proclamation against the Knights' activities.

Houston's proclamation, coupled with Bickley's failure to arrive with promised reinforcements, led his Texas followers to abandon the enterprise. Charging their leader with betrayal, the Texas Knights met in New Orleans in early April and expelled Bickley from the organization. The latter retaliated by summoning a grand convention at Raleigh, North Carolina, on May 7, where he was reinstated as president of the national organization.

Bickley immediately resumed efforts to lead his followers into Mexico, and on July 18, in an open letter published in the Richmond, Virginia, *Daily Whig,* he urged fellow Knights to rendezvous at Fort Ewen, Texas, on September 15. Claiming that Mexico's liberal faction would welcome the Knights as allies and colonizers, Bickley predicted that the Conservatives' defeat would pave the way for the "Americanization" of the strife-torn nation. Published in newspapers throughout the South, Bickley's address assured southerners that the acquisition of Mexico would prevent the North from reducing the slave states to "vassalage." He further promised that the abolitionists would be silenced, the South's free black population would vanish, and cotton production would soar.

Arriving in Texas on October 10, "General" Bickley established his headquarters in San Antonio and began recruiting activities throughout the state. However, the secession movement that swept the South after Abraham Lincoln's presidential victory led Bickley to abandon the Mexican venture. He announced to his followers that, henceforth, promoting secession, not filibustering, would be the society's mission.

Leaving Texas in late 1860, Bickley spent spring and summer 1861 in a futile effort to promote secession in the crucial border state of Kentucky. He eventually established a recruiting camp across the state line in

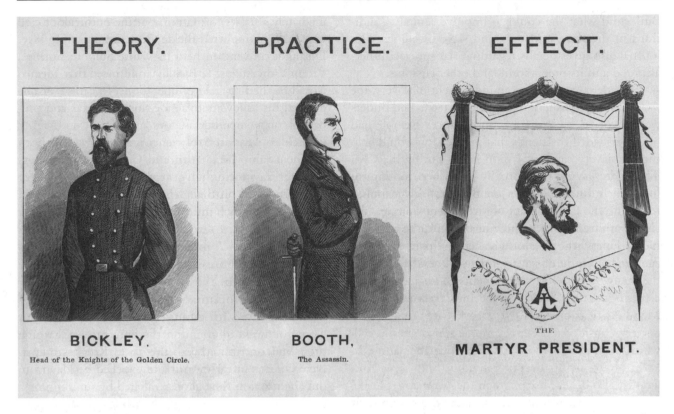

THEORY.   PRACTICE.   EFFECT.

BICKLEY.
Head of the Knights of the Golden Circle.

BOOTH,
The Assassin.

THE
MARTYR PRESIDENT.

Founded by George W. L. Bickley, the Knights of the Golden Circle was a secret filibustering society that sought to extend U.S. influence—and the practice of slavery—throughout the lands bordering the Gulf of Mexico. (Library of Congress)

Clarksville, Tennessee, but disbanded his volunteers in late summer 1861 after a dispute with Confederate leaders in the state. Bickley later attempted to organize a mounted command in Virginia before securing a place as a rebel surgeon.

Deserting the Confederate cause in 1863, Bickley was arrested by Union military authorities in July as he attempted to return to his former home in Cincinnati, Ohio. The ex-filibuster chief was charged with spying and kept under close confinement until his release on October 14, 1865. He reportedly died a "broken man" in Baltimore on August 3, 1867.

Often confused with a similarly named secret antiwar society that existed in the North during the war, Bickley's "Knights of the Golden Circle" was a separate organization that arose from the sectional discord and expansionism that characterized the 1850s. Far from being a man of action, like William Walker, Bickley, whom many regarded as a fraud, never saw the fulfillment of his grandiose scheme. Nevertheless, many northerners regarded Bickley's organization as symbolic of the South's determination to preserve and extend slavery. In this respect, the organization contributed significantly to the sectional misunderstanding that led to war.

— *James M. Prichard*

See also: Filibusters; Lopez, Narciso; Walker, William.

For Further Reading

Bridges, C. A. 1941. "The Knights of the Golden Circle: A Filibustering Fantasy." *Southwestern Historical Quarterly* 44 (January): 287–302.

Crenshaw, Ollinger. 1941. "The Knights of the Golden Circle: The Career of George Bickley." *American Historical Review* 47 (October): 23–50.

Emerson, Mason. 2002. *Missouri's Secret Confederate Agents: The Knights of the Golden Circle.* Independence, MO: Blue & Grey Book Shoppe.

May, Robert E. 1973. *The Southern Dream of a Caribbean Empire 1854–1861.* Baton Rouge: Louisiana State University Press.

∼ L ∼

LADIES' NEW YORK CITY ANTI-SLAVERY SOCIETY (1835–1840)

The Ladies' New York City Anti-Slavery Society was founded at the time of the Second Great Awakening, a religious revival movement of the early nineteenth century that encouraged women in particular to use their moral superiority to reform society. With the encouragement of their ministers, women founded and joined the many moral reform movements and benevolent societies of the time, including the antislavery movement. Members of the Ladies' New York City Anti-Slavery Society considered slavery a moral and domestic evil, which motivated their efforts toward emancipation. In addition to being deeply religious, the New York women also believed strongly in the "woman's sphere," an ideology that placed women's activities within their homes and left public actions to men. The society's documents bear witness to the fact that, aside from its more radical cause, the Ladies' New York City Anti-Slavery Society looked and operated similarly to other benevolent and moral reform societies.

The Ladies' New York City Anti-Slavery Society circulated petitions to Congress and the Presbyterian Church's General Assembly, distributed antislavery tracts, and collected funds for the national society. In addition, a special auxiliary sewed antislavery articles for sale. In 1836 the group sponsored a series of parlor lectures featuring the Grimké sisters in an effort to widen the society's audience. Besides organizing this lecture series, the members hosted a four-day national convention of antislavery women in May 1837 and sent eighteen delegates and eighty corresponding members to the meeting.

The society represented the most homogeneous of the autonomous female antislavery societies in the United States. All of the women belonged to evangelical denominations, and unlike either the Boston Female Antislavery Society or the Philadelphia Female Antislavery Society, the New York women did not attempt to integrate black women into their society.

In 1840, during a debate within the American Anti-Slavery Society over the role of women in the abolitionist movement, the members of the male New York City Anti-Slavery Society, led by Lewis Tappan, walked out of the American Anti-Slavery Society's convention and formed the American and Foreign Anti-Slavery Society.

The Ladies' New York City Anti-Slavery Society members walked out with the men, many of whom were husbands and fathers. Shortly thereafter, these ladies declared themselves an auxiliary of the newly formed men's organization. After 1840 no record exists of further organizational activity by this women's group, although many members' names later appear on the rolls of more conventional reform societies.

The Ladies' New York City Anti-Slavery Society thus operated for only five years. Its members took up abolition based on their religious beliefs and with the encouragement of their ministers, and they left the movement for the same reasons they entered it. Although the New York City women were mostly conservative abolitionists in their beliefs and actions, they surpassed most of the city's women in their understanding and commitment to action outside the domestic sphere. In addition, most contemporary women shared their conservative ideology, which probably contributed to a favorable climate to antislavery and made New York one of the first states to put abolition on the ballot.

— *Sydney J. Caddel-Liles*

See also: Grimké, Angelina; Grimké, Sarah Moore; Women and the Antislavery Movement.

For Further Reading

Jeffrey, Julie Roy. 2001. "Permeable Boundaries: Abolitionist Women and Separate Spheres." *Journal of the Early Republic* 21 (1): 79–93.

Swerdlow, Amy. 1994. "Abolition's Conservative Sisters: The Ladies' New York City Anti-Slavery Societies, 1834–1840." In *The Abolitionist Sisterhood: Women's Political Culture in Antebellum America*. Ed. Jean Fagan Yellin and John C. Van Horne. Ithaca, NY: Cornell University Press.

JOHN LAURENS (1754–1782)

Born into a well-respected South Carolina family, John Laurens earned distinction as a Revolutionary War soldier and diplomat. His father, Henry Laurens, was a planter, Continental Congress delegate, and diplomat. Young John enrolled in school in London in 1771, but after a year he and his two brothers traveled to Geneva, Switzerland, to attend a liberal-minded institution following classical studies. In September 1774 Laurens returned to London to study law. Though married, Laurens returned to America in April 1777, without his wife and daughter. Using family influence, he joined George Washington's staff as aide-de-camp. Young, ambitious, and brave to the point of rashness, Laurens fought at Brandywine, Monmouth, and Germantown, where he was wounded. His continental education served him well as his French fluency made him a valuable liaison. Laurens returned to South Carolina in May 1779, where he was both an elected official in the state assembly and a soldier. Though captured when Charleston fell in May 1780, he was paroled in a prisoner exchange.

Laurens shifted his career when Congress appointed him special minister to the Court of Versailles in late 1780. Though unconventional, Laurens successfully negotiated French aid and returned to America in August 1781, with ships, supplies, and money for the cause of independence. Laurens immediately joined Washington's force at the Yorktown siege, and he negotiated the surrender terms for Cornwallis's British army.

Returning to South Carolina, Laurens was again elected to the state assembly. He maintained his military commission and commanded American forces near Charleston. In a meaningless and insignificant skirmish with a superior British unit at Chehaw Neck on the Combahee River (August 17, 1782), Laurens was killed, a result of his rash behavior as a military commander.

Laurens was a product of his age and his education. He was essentially a republican and a progressive, a believer in the rights of man. As early as 1776, he advocated emancipating blacks for their participation in military service. Washington's Continental Army utilized whatever troops the states provided, and reluctance to use blacks as troops disappeared owing to impending shortages. Congress acted on March 29, 1779, recommending that Georgia and South Carolina form separate black battalions, 3,000 troops in all. Slaveowners would be compensated up to $1,000 per able-bodied male up to age thirty-five. The troops would be outfitted at government expense, freed at the war's end, and paid fifty dollars each. Congress selected Laurens to elicit South Carolina's support for the idea; he was the ideal choice. When his father had earlier mentioned freeing his slaves, John wrote to him in 1778 suggesting raising a troop of blacks to fight as a unit. But young Laurens found South Carolina's planters horrified by the thought of black troops. A key shortage of available soldiers in South Carolina led General Benjamin Lincoln to support using blacks in his ranks. General Nathanael Greene shared this view.

In early 1782, with Laurens back from his French mission and serving in the state legislature, the state assembly took two votes on enrolling black troops. Despite the presence of the popular and gregarious Laurens, the measures failed. Georgia also refused the request, even when facing superior British forces. Slaveowners and planters had spoken, proving that fear of the British paled in comparison to images of blacks earning their freedom through military service.

— *Boyd Childress*

See also: Compensated Emancipation.

For Further Reading
Bailey, N. Louis, and Elizabeth Ivey Cooper, eds. 1981. "John Laurens." In *Biographical Directory of the South Carolina House of Representatives*. Columbia: South Carolina University Press.
Massey, Gregory D. 2000. *John Laurens and the American Revolution*. Columbia: University of South Carolina Press.
Quarles, Benjamin. 1961. *The Negro in the American Revolution*. Chapel Hill: North Carolina University Press.

JOSHUA LEAVITT (1794–1873)

Joshua Leavitt was a prominent American antislavery newspaper editor and political activist. A Yale graduate, he took up the practice of law in Vermont in 1821 but abandoned it two years later to become a Congregational clergyman. Like many Congregationalists, he was opposed to slavery, and he supported the American Colonization Society's efforts to purchase slaves, free them, and transport them to Africa. In 1825 he wrote his first antislavery articles for the *Christian Spectator*, an evangelical magazine with close ties to Yale Theological Seminary, his alma mater. In 1831 he became editor of the New York *Evangelist*, a weekly newspaper devoted to reforming American society.

By 1833 Leavitt had changed his views about abolition. Realizing that colonization was unfair to blacks who had been born and raised in the United States, he decided that slavery could best be ended by convincing slaveholders to free their slaves voluntarily. That same year he cofounded the New York City Anti-Slavery Society and became the recording secretary of the American Anti-Slavery Society. He also bought the *Evangelist*, which he used as a pulpit from which to preach voluntary emancipation. His constant harping about abolition alienated most of his southern subscribers and many northern ones, especially those who were more interested in other reform movements such as temperance. On one occasion, he had to hide from an angry proslavery mob to avoid being done bodily harm. By 1837 the *Evangelist*'s circulation had dropped to the point that the threat of bankruptcy forced him to sell the paper.

Shortly thereafter, Leavitt was named editor of the *Emancipator,* the official weekly newspaper of the American Anti-Slavery Society that was struggling to survive. Here he found an audience eager to hear his fire-and-brimstone pronouncements concerning the need to abolish slavery, and he soon turned the paper around. At about the same time, he realized that slaveholders would never free their slaves voluntarily, and he began to insist that direct political action was required to coerce the slave states into giving up slavery. This position brought him into direct opposition to the prominent abolitionist William Lloyd Garrison, who declared that the very act of voting in a federal election supported slavery because federal law and the U.S. Constitution supported slavery. Leavitt cared little for this argument, and in 1839 he called for the nomination of antislavery candidates independent of both major political parties. This stance cost him many subscribers from the ranks of Garrison supporters and from supporters of the Whig Party, many of whom were already working to end slavery through the political system.

In 1840 Leavitt heeded his own call by joining the abolitionist Liberty Party. He enthusiastically supported James G. Birney, its candidate for president, and he traveled extensively to build a party organization at the grassroots level. Shortly after the election of 1840, in which Birney polled fewer than one hundred thousand votes, Leavitt opened an office in Washington, D.C. For the next five years he reported back to the nation what Congress was doing about matters pertaining to slavery, and his reports did much to increase antislavery sentiment in the North. Meanwhile, his editorials helped to bring the slavery question to the floor of the House of Representatives, despite that body's rules against debate on that topic.

Leavitt became sole owner of the *Emancipator* in 1840, and the next year he moved its offices to Boston, where he merged it with the *Free American* and began publishing under the auspices of the Massachusetts Abolition Society. From 1844 to 1847 he served as chairman of the Liberty Party's national committee. In 1848 he sold the *Emancipator,* but he continued to work privately for abolition.

— *Charles W. Carey*

See also: American Colonization Society; Birney, James G.; Gag Resolution; Garrison, William Lloyd.

For Further Reading
Davis, Hugh. 1990. *Joshua Leavitt, Evangelical Abolitionist.* Baton Rouge: Louisiana State University Press.
McPherson, James M. 1963. "The Fight against the Gag Rule: Joshua Leavitt and Antislavery Insurgency in the Whig Party, 1839–1842." *Journal of Negro History* 48 (July): 177–195.

LECOMPTON CONSTITUTION

The Lecompton Constitution was drawn up in 1857 by proslavery Kansans to admit the territory into the United States as a slave state. The Kansas–Nebraska Act (1854) had established that slavery in the area would be decided by popular sovereignty, which led to anti- and proslavery forces battling in Kansas over the slavery question. Kansas's proslavery party met from September 7 to November 7, 1857, at Constitution Hall in Lecompton, territorial capital of Kansas, to frame the Lecompton Constitution.

The constitution stated the functions of the state government and included provisions for slavery. It maintained that the legislature could not deny owners property rights to their slaves, nor could it emancipate slaves without compensation to owners or prevent immigrants from bringing slaves into the area. It also protected the legal and civil rights of slaves with provisions for trial by jury and protection against brutal punishment.

The vote on the Lecompton Constitution was not a choice between accepting or rejecting the constitution. The choice was between adopting the Lecompton Constitution "with slavery" or "with no slavery." "With no slavery" meant that "slavery shall no longer exist in the territory of Kansas, except that the right of property in slaves now in this Territory shall in no manner be interfered with." In short, whatever the outcome of the vote, slavery would still exist in Kansas.

Angered by this deception, Kansans who opposed the extension of slavery into the territory boycotted the polls, and on December 21, 1857, the constitution "with slavery" was ratified by a vote of 6,226 (2,720 of which were fraudulent, mostly from Missouri border ruffians) to 569. Another vote on January 4, 1858, this one involving both the free state contingent and the proslavery faction—but largely boycotted by the proslavery people—denounced the Lecompton Constitution 10,226 to 162.

Despite Kansans clear mandate to repudiate the Lecompton Constitution, Democratic president James Buchanan recommended to Congress on February 2, 1858, the admission of Kansas under the corrupt Lecompton document. Coming on the heels of the Supreme Court's *Dred Scott v. Sandford* (1857) decision, which stated that Congress could not pass a law depriving persons of their slave property, Buchanan urged Congress to accept Kansas as a slave state under

Masthead of William Lloyd Garrison's abolitionist newspaper, *Liberator,* ca. 1850. (North Wind Picture Archives)

the Lecompton Constitution. The U.S. Senate passed Buchanan's legislative recommendation, but Illinois Democrat Stephen A. Douglas denounced the illegal constitution and prevented it from passing in the House of Representatives.

Partly to avert further division in the Democratic Party, the English Bill (named after its author, William H. English of Indiana) was proposed as a compromise to offer Kansans a third vote on the slavery issue. Although it did not directly confront the slavery issue and sought to spare Buchanan the embarrassment of his political blunder, the English Bill attached land grants to the voting. Kansans would vote to either accept or reject the standard 4 million acres of land for new states (considerably less than originally requested).

On August 2, 1858, in a strictly supervised election, Kansans voted 11,300 to 1,788 to reject overwhelmingly the land grant offer and indirectly repudiated the Lecompton Constitution. The renunciation of the illegal Lecompton Constitution demonstrated Kansas' preference for remaining a territory rather than becoming a slave state. Kansas was admitted into the Union as a free state in 1861.

The Lecompton Constitution split the country on several levels. Kansans first battled each other over the legality of slavery in their territory. The Topeka (antislavery) and Lecompton (proslavery) factions clashed in a civil war that alerted the rest of the country to the divisiveness of the slavery question. The national Democratic Party and the U.S. executive and legislative branches also passionately debated the validity of the Lecompton Constitution, further demonstrating the frenzied state of the nation over the slavery issue. The conflict that the Lecompton Constitution provoked foreshadowed the American Civil War.

— *Julieanne Phillips*

See also: Democratic Party; Free Soil Party; Kansas–Nebraska Act; Popular Sovereignty.

For Further Reading

Connelley, William E. 1918. *A Standard History of Kansas and Kansans.* Chicago: Lewis.

Meerse, David E. 1995. "Buchanan, the Patronage, and the Lecompton Constitution: A Case Study." *Civil War History* 41 (4): 291–313.

Stampp, Kenneth M. 1990. *America in 1857: A Nation on the Brink.* New York: Oxford University Press.

Wilder, Daniel W. 1875. *The Annals of Kansas.* Topeka, KS: G.W. Martin.

THE *LIBERATOR*

The *Liberator* (Boston, 1831–1865) was a radical abolitionist weekly newspaper owned and edited by William Lloyd Garrison. It provides an excellent record of Garrison's views on slavery, antislavery, national politics, contemporary events, women's rights, nonresistance, institutional religion, and racism over the antebellum period and prints many of his speeches, most of which have not been published elsewhere. Its accounts of antislavery meetings animate the passion and range of ideas within the antislavery movement.

The paper describes the activities of the Garrisonian antislavery societies, in particular the American Anti-Slavery Society, the Massachusetts Anti-Slavery Society, and smaller affiliated groups. It reports the speeches and experience of both prominent and lesser known abolitionists, and it is a useful source of proslavery, antiabolitionist, and non-Garrisonian antislavery texts and Garrison's responses to them. Equally as significant, the *Liberator*—or Garrison speaking through it—helped set the terms of the antislavery debate; the paper's astute deployment of the American Revolution's patriotic language and the religious language of apocalypse and its oppositional stance forced others to respond in kind. Although neither the first antislavery newspaper nor the one with the largest subscription list, it was the best known, longest lived, and most influential.

Garrison began the paper to advocate abolition to both North and South, for he believed the entire nation was implicated in the sin of slavery. Most of the paper's subscribers lived in the North and West and in the first ten to fifteen years were predominantly free blacks, but the subscription lists do not accurately depict the *Liberator's* influence. In 1831, for instance, the paper was exchanged with some one hundred southern newspapers. For southerners and many northerners as well, the *Liberator* embodied abolitionist propaganda, reliably printing the very worst ideas (according to southern readers) in consistently extreme language. Southern newspaper editors printed excerpts from the *Liberator* along with attacks on both it and Garrison, and they and their readers wrote letters to him. Garrison published these letters in the front-page feature, "The Refuge of Oppression," and the more scurrilous the better.

The *Liberator's* reputation was made in 1831 when a southern newspaper editor, trying to explain Nat Turner's violent uprising, claimed Turner had been incited by abolitionist propaganda and specifically by the *Liberator*. Clearly, Turner did not need abolitionists to identify the cruelty and injustice of slavery, and the *Liberator* was a new, struggling, and obscure paper, one of which few Americans were aware. Even so, the claim stuck. Since even moderate or nominal abolitionists received similar accusations, Garrison functioned as a representative abolitionist for the South as his newspaper was an easily identified target. The language of the *Liberator* was not moderate; Garrison believed he needed strong language to win the war against slavery.

Garrison made the *Liberator* a powerful propaganda tool by exploiting the newspaper's form and meaning. The outstanding character of a newspaper, particularly the tremendously popular penny papers, which first appeared in the 1830s, is variety. The *Liberator* offered speeches, proslavery gibes, clippings from southern papers, editorials, descriptions of abused slaves, reports about Congress's doings, poems, and, for a time, small illustrations in addition to its large and impressively illustrated masthead. Although Garrison wanted to "diversify the contents of the *Liberator* so as to give an edge to curiosity" (January 1, 1831), he also kept the reader focused on a small body of abolitionist truths. Hence the paper fell between the new kind of popular newspaper and the older sort of political paper, which made no pretensions to express anything other than a partisan opinion.

In fact, Garrison turned his newspaper into a pulpit, imbuing it with the language and moral force of the sermon, following a long tradition of joining the sacred and the secular in the press and pulpit. A vigorous religious press had begun in the 1820s, and the pulpit had always been a place to comment on vital secular topics and to urge congregations to carry sacred lessons into the world. The substitution of page for pulpit was essential for Garrison, who was mild mannered and, unlike some other abolitionists or the charismatic revivalist preachers, an ineffective orator. The *Liberator's* sermon-speeches and editorials have all the fire and force his oral delivery lacked. Through his newspapers, Garrison's words gave him a moral and social stature, even heroism: just because he published the *Liberator,* he was hailed as a modern Martin Luther or John the Baptist, and he became a catalyst for inciting mobs and riots. In a sense, Garrison became the *Liberator;* as a poem on the first page of the first issue (January 1, 1831) put it:

> My name is LIBERATOR! I propose
> To hurl my shafts at freedom's deadliest foes!
> My task is hard—for I am charged to save
> Man from his brother!—to redeem the slave!

Although most of Garrison's early subscribers were free blacks, he directed much of the *Liberator* at a white audience or else at "Americans," who were implicitly white. Perhaps he did not feel a need to appeal to free blacks because he believed they already sympathized with his cause. But this force on a white audience also assumed that black Americans lacked the power to end slavery, that they needed white "liberators."

Garrison published the *Liberator* every week for over thirty years, an astonishing record for any antebellum newspaper, and more so for one that constantly rested on the edge of financial collapse. In the early years Garrison did much of the work himself—writing, setting type, printing, and even delivering the papers to Boston-area subscribers. In later years other prominent abolitionists assumed editorial duties, among them Oliver Johnson and Maria Weston Chapman. The *Liberator* finally suspended publication on December 29, 1865; with the Civil War over, Garrison believed the *Liberator* had accomplished its task.

— *Andrea M. Atkin*

See also: American Anti-Slavery Society; Garrison, William Lloyd.

For Further Reading

Atkin, Andrea M. 1995. "Converting America: The Rhetoric of Abolitionist Literature." Ph.D. dissertation, Department of English, University of Chicago, Chicago, Illinois.

Merrill, Walter M. 1963. *Against Wind and Tide: A Biography of William Lloyd Garrison.* Cambridge, MA: Harvard University Press.

LIBERIA

Liberia was settled in 1822 by freed slaves from the United States; its organizers intended to fight the slave trade being conducted along the western coast of Africa as colonists spread the Christian religion and "civilization" among the indigenous population. Under white governors appointed by the American Colonization Society, the colonists had little success in persuading Africans to abandon either domestic slavery or the coastal sale of slaves.

After gaining independence in 1847, the Americo-Liberians continued dressing in European clothes, speaking English, and modeling their government and society after their "mother" country. Their stated policy toward the African population was assimilation, but they maintained almost complete separation despite a system of apprenticeship that brought children into their homes as servants. They did mix somewhat more with the five thousand "Congoes," Africans freed by the U.S. Navy from slave ships captured before reaching the Americas. The native African population considered the Congoes Americo-Liberian slaves, but the Congoes adopted Christianity and English and became a buffer between the fifteen thousand Americo-Liberians and the 2 million natives.

Using trade goods supplied by U.S. and European donors, the Americo-Liberians purchased control of 600 miles of coastline, but they made little impact on the hinterland before 1900. Pressured by British and French expansion during the late 1800s, the Americo-Liberians claimed as much of the interior as possible,

but they had no way of imposing their will until the founding of the Liberian Frontier Force (LFF) in 1908. Relying on U.S. assistance, they established the LFF but never adequately paid or disciplined its members. The LFF pillaged, raped, and enslaved hinterland peoples who did their best to escape its depredations. The national government imposed a "hut tax" in 1916 and used the LFF and taxes to saddle the interior with district commissioners, who used their official positions to establish plantations manned by forced labor and to extort rice from the local people. Complaints by the chiefs and missionaries led to the hiring of white commissioners from the United States in an effort to reform local government. When a U.S. commissioner arrested a slave-owning district commissioner and had him marched in chains to Monrovia, the Americo-Liberians reacted with indignation at the Americans' racism, and by 1921, they had forced all foreign commissioners out of the country.

Market farming in the interior proved unprofitable because there were no roads to transport products to the coast, so the Americo-Liberians turned to exporting labor. The government sold licenses to Germans and later to the Spanish to allow them to recruit workers. A scandal ensued when the Spanish employed Americo-Liberians as agents to produce labor for the unhealthy cocoa plantations on Fernando Po, a Spanish island in the Bight of Biafra. The League of Nations investigated and found that both fraud and later the LFF had been used to capture Liberians for export. The vice president of Liberia had been the principal organizer—both he and the president resigned.

Domestic slavery was outlawed in the 1930s, but there was little basic change following the scandal. Firestone Tire Company established a massive rubber plantation and, bowing to the pressure of Americo-Liberian planters, accepted the forced-labor system, paying chiefs to "recruit" labor. As late as 1965, one-quarter of all wage laborers in the country were forced workers.

After World War II, the Liberian government dropped assimilation in favor of a unification policy and established a Bureau of Folkways to generate respect for indigenous cultures, but that policy made little difference in ethnic relationships. The International Labor Organization (ILO) found that Liberian laws did not meet the standards set by the 1930 international labor convention and that forced labor remained legal. In response to international condemnation, in 1961 the government made it illegal for chiefs to use force or threats to recruit labor but still retained that right for the state. In 1962 Liberia repealed the forced-labor and cultivation laws, and Firestone stopped paying chiefs for labor recruitment. Nevertheless, in the mid-1960s, a U.S. group, Growth Without Development, reported that "recruitment" continued.

The Americo-Liberians remained in control of the government, exploiting most of the population, until 1980 when Sergeant Samuel Doe, an African, overthrew and murdered the Americo-Liberian president in a coup. Rebellion and ethnic warfare followed. Despite U.S. support, Doe was overthrown and murdered and the country descended into anarchy and civil war. In 1997 Charles Taylor, a warlord of indigenous and Americo-Liberian ancestry, won the presidency. He made his followers "security forces" in his government. A United Nations-sanctioned court in Sierra Leone convicted Taylor of crimes against humanity, and rebel organizations backed by neighboring countries took over the country. Both Taylor's government and the rebels enslaved Liberians as soldiers and as sex slaves.

The U.S. State Department, the ILO, and nongovernmental organizations reported forced labor to be an enduring feature of Liberian society. Local leaders forced farmers to work on "community projects" for private benefit. The Liberian government lagged behind in ratifying international agreements such as ILO Convention 182 to end the worst forms of child labor. Taylor encouraged foreign logging operations that practiced forced labor and some NGOs reported that President Taylor used forced labor on his private farm. Without a functioning national government, international slavery resumed in a fashion as Liberia exported sex slaves to Belgium and the Netherlands in 2003.

— *Dennis J. Mitchell*

See also: American Colonization Society.

For Further Reading

Akpan, M. B. 1973. "Black Imperialism: Americo-Liberian Rule over the African Peoples of Liberia, 1841–1964." *Canadian Journal of African Studies* 7 (2): 217–236.

Fleishman, Janet. 1994. *Easy Prey: Child Soldiers in Liberia.* New York: Human Rights Watch.

Gershoni, Yekutiel. 1985. *Black Colonialism: The Americo-Liberian Scramble for the Hinterland.* Boulder, CO: Westview Press.

Shick, Tom W. 1977. *Behold the Promised Land: A History of Afro-American Settler Society in Nineteenth-Century Liberia.* Baltimore: Johns Hopkins University Press.

Sundiata, I. K. 1980. *Black Scandal: America and the Liberian Labor Crisis, 1929–1936.* Philadelphia: Institute for the Study of Human Issues.

Williams, Gabriel I. H. 2000. *The Heart of Darkness.* New Bern, NC: Trafford.

ABRAHAM LINCOLN (1809–1865)

As president of the United States during the Civil War, Abraham Lincoln issued the Emancipation Proclamation (1863), which freed African American slaves in parts of the Confederacy unoccupied by Union forces, and he laid the legal groundwork for the eventual eradication of slavery in the United States. Lincoln is often associated with giving freedom to an enslaved people and restoring the values of equality contained in the Declaration of Independence to the forefront of the American experience.

Economic issues rather than slavery dominated Lincoln's thinking during his early career as an attorney and a leading Illinois politician, particularly the problems of ensuring equal opportunities for white Americans in an increasingly complex national economy. He absorbed his father's antislavery attitudes, and he never publicly defended slavery. Yet he said little about the institution while serving in the Illinois state legislature (1834–1840) and the U.S. Congress (1846–1848). As a lawyer, he defended the rights of slaveholders and runaway slaves alike with no apparent moral qualms.

By the early 1850s, Lincoln concluded that slavery's degradation of free labor and entrepreneurship was anathema to his ideals of equal economic opportunity for all citizens. The period's national political crises also propelled the problems associated with slavery to the forefront of Lincoln's political consciousness. The repeal of the Missouri Compromise line by the Kansas–Nebraska Act (1854), which opened newly acquired western territories to slavery, and the extreme proslavery language of the Supreme Court's *Dred Scott* decision (1857), led Lincoln to believe that some white southerners and northern white Democrats were engaged in a secret plan to make slavery a national institution. Searching for a constitutional and political basis to combat this plan, he concluded that the Declaration of Independence contained an antislavery ideal that the Constitution's language and provisions should fulfill. By setting the Declaration's high ideals of equality as the moral goal toward which the republic must always strive, Lincoln believed the Founders had placed slavery "in the course of ultimate extinction."

Lincoln carried his ideas with him upon joining the fledgling Republican Party in 1856. He avoided the radical plans of some Republicans and abolitionists for an immediate and possibly violent end to slavery, calling instead for preventing slavery's spread into western lands while leaving it untouched to die of its own accord in the South. He also supported colonization schemes to ship ex-slaves to Africa, and he expressed

Sculpture of Abraham Lincoln, the "Great Emancipator," standing over a crouched slave who wears shackles on his arms. (Library of Congress)

doubts as to whether the two races could ever live together in peace. Lincoln was also keenly aware of the virulent prejudice exhibited by many of his white neighbors toward African Americans, and he was sometimes compelled to cater to those prejudices to win votes. During an unsuccessful campaign for the U.S. Senate in 1858, for example, he stated, "I have no purpose to introduce political and social equality between the white and the black races" (Donald, 1995).

Once elected president in 1860 and facing the country's subsequent dissolution, Lincoln declared that he had no intention of making war on slavery. "My paramount object in this struggle is to save the Union," he wrote, "and is not to either save or destroy slavery" (Donald, 1995). He quashed early emancipation schemes by Union generals John Frémont and David Hunter, and was ambivalent toward congressional legislation such as the Confiscation Acts that appeared to be legal precursors of emancipation.

Lincoln began a gradual movement toward emancipation in 1862 for several reasons. Abolitionist leaders

like Frederick Douglass and Charles Sumner constantly pressured Lincoln to end slavery; the war itself created tremendous pressures on the institution as thousands of African Americans escaped into Union-held territory, and their presence demanded clarification of their legal status; and a manpower shortage compelled Lincoln to contemplate the unprecedented employment of African American soldiers, which would necessarily be accompanied by the promise of freedom. Primarily, Lincoln himself achieved a deeper and more profound understanding of the war's ultimate meaning. He began understanding that Americans required a loftier goal than restoration of the Union to justify the war's dreadful cost. He believed that what was at stake was nothing less than the future of all humankind's free institutions.

On January 1, 1863, Lincoln issued the Emancipation Proclamation. Ever mindful of public opinion, he crafted the document carefully to avoid antagonizing northerners on such a sensitive subject. It freed only those slaves in areas of the Confederacy that were not yet occupied by Union forces and was devoid of the inspirational eloquence that characterized the Gettysburg Address and other speeches. But Lincoln's proclamation ended national legal protection that had been afforded human bondage in America for over two centuries, and paved the way for the Thirteenth Amendment's final eradication of slavery. Lincoln believed the Emancipation Proclamation was his greatest achievement as president.

With emancipation came a variety of related policies and measures from Lincoln's administration designed to hasten slavery's demise. Chief among these was the recruitment of African American soldiers, which Lincoln encouraged to help freedmen erase slavery's stigma. He also tried quietly to persuade leaders of the conquered South to allow African Americans limited legal and political rights. Lincoln's assassination in 1865 cut short whatever further efforts he may have made in behalf of freedmen; we will never know what his policies might have been concerning slavery's legacy.

Lincoln's actions concerning slavery have been debated ever since his death. Generations of Americans, white and black, revered him as the "Great Emancipator." Beginning in the 1960s, however, some Americans began questioning this reputation, arguing that he freed the slaves because of wartime necessity, rather than any internal antislavery or egalitarian values. Perhaps Frederick Douglass provided the best assessment of Lincoln's legacy in this regard. "Viewed from the genuine abolition ground, Mr. Lincoln seemed tardy, cold, dull, and indifferent," Douglass declared, "but measuring him by the sentiment of his country, a sentiment he was bound as a statesman to consult, he was swift, zealous, radical, and determined" (Cox, 1981).

— *Brian Dirck*

See also: Abolitionism in the United States; American Colonization Society; Border War (1854–1859); Civil War; Confiscation Acts; Douglas, Stephen A.; Douglass, Frederick; *Dred Scott v. Sanford;* Emancipation Proclamation; Lincoln–Douglas Debates; United States Constitution.

For Further Reading
    Cox, LaWanda. 1981. *Lincoln and Black Freedom: A Study in Presidential Leadership.* Urbana: University of Illinois Press.
    Donald, David. 1995. *Lincoln.* New York: Simon & Schuster.
    Johannsen, Robert. 1991. *Lincoln, the South and Slavery: The Political Dimension.* Baton Rouge: Louisiana State University Press.
    Paludan, Phillip Shaw. 1994. *The Presidency of Abraham Lincoln.* Lawrence: University Press of Kansas.

LINCOLN–DOUGLAS DEBATES (1858)

In the summer and fall of 1858, two candidates for the U.S. Senate from Illinois, Republican Abraham Lincoln and Democrat Stephen A. Douglas, faced each other in a series of seven debates. This in itself was unusual because since the state legislature would decide who would fill the Senate seat, such a campaign for this office was unprecedented. The tense political climate of the period made these debates even more significant, as they represented an articulate statement of conflicting views on slavery and its expansion, a capstone of a generation of controversy during which these issues dominated the American political scene.

The participants were polar opposites, both physically and politically. Senator Stephen A. Douglas was one of the most powerful politicians in the United States. Nicknamed "the little giant" because of his small stature and oratorical prowess, Douglas had extensive political experience. After serving several terms in the House of Representatives, he had been elected to the U.S. Senate in 1846. As a member of that body, he rose to chair the important Committee on Territories, and as such, he sponsored the Kansas–Nebraska Act (1854), which brought the debate over slavery in the territories and the idea of popular sovereignty to the political forefront.

Douglas believed that the settlers of each territory should be allowed to decide the slavery question for themselves; popular sovereignty was the solution to a

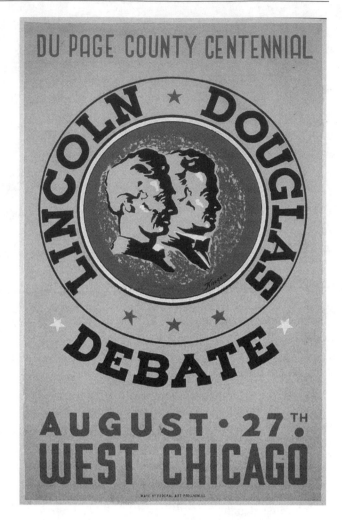

Poster for the centennial celebration of the Lincoln–Douglas debate, 1858. (Library of Congress)

persistent political problem. First, he believed that under the U.S. Constitution, states, not the federal government, had the authority to enact legislation dealing with slavery. Second, he believed the institution would die out without any federal intervention. Third, he understood that his political future, and that of his party, rested on a fragile coalition of northern and southern Democrats, which a strong stand on either side of the issue would dissolve. So Douglas, the consummate politician, chose what he believed to be a safe, moderate position. When Kansas erupted in civil war over the issue of slavery, Douglas's critics argued that popular sovereignty was merely another way to protect slavery's westward expansion. One of his most vocal opponents was a tall, rough-hewn former Whig, Abraham Lincoln.

In 1858 Lincoln was not a politician of national stature. He had served several terms in the Illinois legislature and a single term in Congress. A successful

Springfield lawyer, he had left the Whigs over the issue of slavery in 1856 and joined the fledgling Republican Party. Lincoln believed slavery was a moral wrong and opposed its expansion. He argued that the institution was a corrosive force in American society, and he felt it should be eliminated as quickly as possible. Therefore Lincoln and Douglas represented the two opposing views on the expansion of slavery that dominated American politics before the Civil War.

The debates themselves were a departure from political tradition because Senate candidates normally did not campaign, as the state legislatures elected senators and the party that controlled the state assembly usually elected powerful party leaders to such a post. In 1858 the controversy over the expansion of slavery and the resulting political turmoil meant that for the first time, the Senate election was an important issue in the Illinois legislative races. It was, in fact, a referendum on the future of slavery in the United States.

The voters had an unprecedented opportunity to evaluate the Senate candidates after the Chicago *Times* suggested that Lincoln and Douglas debate across Illinois. Lincoln quickly agreed and was followed, somewhat more reluctantly, by Douglas. As the incumbent, Douglas realized that he had much more to lose than his relatively unknown Republican challenger. Seven debates were scheduled, all similar in content and form to modern political forums.

The first debate, in Ottawa, Illinois, on August 21, set the tone for those that followed as the issue of slavery expansion came to the forefront. Douglas declared that it was "the sovereign right of each State to decide the slavery question . . . for themselves, without interference from any other states or power whatsoever" (Jaffa, 1959). According to Douglas, this right also extended to territories, which should be allowed to decide the question through the democratic process. He went on to accuse Lincoln and the Republican Party of being "in favor of the citizenship of the negro" (Jaffa, 1959). Lincoln denied that he favored black equality, but he admitted that he believed the institution was a moral blight on the nation. He argued that "we shall not have peace upon the question until the opponents of slavery arrest the further spread of it" (Donald, 1995). During the second debate in Freeport, Illinois, Lincoln questioned Douglas's support of the *Dred Scott* decision (1857), as it seemed to contradict the continued endorsement of a popular sovereignty position. Douglas's response, which thereafter became known as the Freeport doctrine, was to assert that slavery could effectively be prohibited from any region if local police regulations were not in place to enforce it.

The debates had far-reaching effects, the least of

which was the outcome of the 1858 Illinois legislative races. Voters, to some degree, cast their ballots for legislators based on the senatorial candidates. Although Democrats carried both houses of the state legislature and reelected Douglas to the Senate, the Republicans showed impressive strength. Also, Douglas, who had been reluctant to enter the debates, lost much of his national prestige. Southern Democrats questioned his view of the use of the federal government to protect slave property, and northerners accused him of pandering to slave interests. In attempting to take a moderate position, Douglas became something of a pariah in an increasingly polarized political climate. Lincoln, the heretofore unknown, emerged from the debates with a national political reputation.

Most importantly, the debates brought increased attention to the issue of slavery and its expansion. Two years later, in the presidential campaign of 1860 in which Lincoln and Douglas were both candidates, the debates took on increased political importance. Douglas, whose earlier positions had angered southerners, could not unite the Democratic Party. Lincoln, however, was able to use his speeches to attract Free Soil Democrats and former Whigs to win the election. So this series of debates, which began as a forum for senatorial candidates in Illinois, contributed in no small way to the course of American history during its most trying time.

— *Richard D. Starnes*

See also: Douglas, Stephen A.; *Dred Scott v. Sandford;* Freeport Doctrine; Lincoln, Abraham; Popular Sovereignty.

For Further Reading
Donald, David. 1995. *Lincoln.* New York: Simon & Schuster.

Jaffa, Harry. 1959. *Crisis of the House Divided: An Interpretation of the Lincoln–Douglas Debates.* Garden City, NJ: Doubleday.

Johannsen, Robert. 1973. *Stephen A. Douglas.* New York: Oxford University Press.

Johannsen, Robert. 1989. *The Frontier, the Union, and Stephen A. Douglas.* Urbana: University of Illinois Press.

LITERATURE

Slavery was legally abolished in Great Britain by the emancipation of slaves in the British colonies (1834–1838) and in the United States by the Emancipation Proclamation (1863) and the Thirteenth Amendment (1865). Nevertheless, slavery, as a topic, pervaded all aspects of Western literature and remains central to a large body of works, especially in the United States, even today.

Historically, the discourse of slavery is detectable in literature as diverse as Aphra Behn's *Oroonoko; or, The History of a Royal Slave* (1678), Jane Austen's *Mansfield Park* (1814), and Richard Wright's *Native Son* (1940). On entering London's Tate Gallery, built on the proceeds from British sugar plantations, or when singing "Amazing Grace," written by John Newton, a slave-ship captain who underwent a conversion to abolitionism, or when listening to a Billie Holiday rendition of "Strange Fruit," the all-pervasive nature of slavery and oppression in Western art can be recognized.

Slavery often appears in literature, not as subject, but as a sensational backdrop to a story that is essentially about other things, as in Margaret Mitchell's *Gone With the Wind* (1936). Literary texts also use the subject to articulate other concerns about the power structures of the day. Thus Behn's *Oroonoko* comments specifically on female oppression and the struggle for political power in seventeenth-century England, and in Austen's *Mansfield Park,* Sir Thomas Bertram's departure for interests in the West Indies precipitates a moral collapse in the comfortable and respectable nineteenth-century English country home, leaving only the modest and withdrawn Fanny to raise the issue of slavery and its relationship to the beautiful Mansfield Park. She does this, however, through an underlying theme in the text: that of the nature of the patriarchy under which all of the weak and the powerless live. In Charlotte Brontë's *Jane Eyre* slavery is also used as a metaphor for male tyranny. Jane's cousin is called a "slave driver" when he forces her to stand still as he hurls books at her head and, later, the Creole blood of Bertha, Rochester's wife, is used as a signifier of that dark other that was to be both feared and oppressed.

In the nineteenth century slavery was an obvious presence in British novels. A perceived analogy between British workers and the slaves of the Americas was exploited in factory novels, such as Francis Trollop's *Michael Armstrong, the Factory Boy* (1839) or Elizabeth Gaskell's *Mary Barton* (1848). Harriet Beecher Stowe's *Uncle Tom's Cabin* (1852) and her second novel, *Dred* (1865), were used by British workers and philanthropists to build support for the Reform Act of 1867, which began the emancipation of British labor. It was felt that the lives of factory workers were little better than those of slaves. This analogy was strenuously refuted by African Americans, most famously by James Baldwin in *Notes of a Native Son* (1955), in which he argued that Uncle Tom wore his badge upon his face and

could not, therefore, better his lot through education and social mobility.

More directly, pro- and antislavery literature abounded during the eighteenth and nineteenth centuries. Proslavery literature, given the traditional association of darkness with evil in Western culture, commonly used the myth of barbarism to assert its arguments. Thus Thomas Jefferson, in *Notes on the State of Virginia* (written in 1781–1782), compares the American slave to the Roman slave and, after commenting on the artistic and intellectual capacities of the latter, concludes that it is nature, not slavery, that creates distinctions between black and white. Some writers used biblical and providential arguments to justify slavery, while others, such as Edward Long in *The History of Jamaica* (1774), searched for a scientific and anthropological rationale, prefiguring the nineteenth-century pseudoscientific justifications perpetrated by Josiah Nott and others.

Any relationship between blackness, nature, and slavery was systematically refuted in the antislavery literature, perhaps indicating the degree to which these ideas were associated in the common mind. Writers insisted that it was slavery, not skin pigmentation, that was responsible for the African's condition. The colonial argument, prior to the American Revolution, that all men were created equal was extended to include slaves in writings such as James Otis's *The Rights of the British Colonies Asserted and Proved* (1764) and David Cooper's *A Serious Address to the Rulers of America* (1773), while a mischievous footnote to John Trumbull's *M'Fingal* (1775), pondering the nature of liberty, insists that the thirteen stripes on the new American flag are to be associated with neither prison bars nor the stripes on the backs of slaves. Trumbull, like other American satirists such as Artemus Ward and David Ross Locke, wrote against slavery, but the author of the most famous antislavery novel, *Uncle Tom's Cabin,* was able to draw her "facts" of the book from a vast quantity of slave literature circulating at the time in narratives, histories, tracts, and pamphlets.

Many slave narratives used their sensationalist appeal, with gruesome tales of cruelty, beatings, and lynchings, to turn public opinion against slavery. Because it was illegal to teach a slave to read or write, many of the narratives had to be transcribed or even written by white abolitionist editors, as was Harriet Ann Jacobs's *Incidents in the Life of a Slave Girl* (1861). Others were written by African Americans themselves, most famously the narratives, essays, and works of Frederick Douglass, an escaped slave. Douglass was an activist and established the antislavery newspaper, the *North Star.* His *Narrative of the Life of Frederick Dou-*

glass (1845), besides relating the story of his escape to freedom, finds common ground with other literature of the period through its questioning, like Emerson and Thoreau, of what it is that separates the human from the animal and in what forms, therefore, did human freedom exist. For Ralph Waldo Emerson, the question was largely esoteric but not for Henry David Thoreau. He was involved with the antislavery movement, and he took a political and moral stand against it. He delivered speeches, such as his "Slavery in Massachusetts" speech in 1854, and profoundly stirred by his meeting with John Brown at Emerson's home in 1857, he wrote three lectures: "A Plea for Captain John Brown," "The Last Days of John Brown," and "After the Death of John Brown." For Douglass, questions of human freedom were not abstract but vital. His capacity to "think himself free" empowered his emancipation.

The African American voice on slavery in literature, however, was at best marginalized and at worst silent. It was an oppressive silence, broken only sporadically during the centuries of slavery and then by slaves like the poet Phillis Wheatley (c. 1755–1784), who had been taught by her "owners" to read and write and did not, in any direct sense, question her servitude, regarding it as the price paid for bringing her to God. In the period following emancipation, recuperation began. Charles Waddell Chesnutt wrote *The Conjure Woman* (1899), a series of dialect stories about slavery told by an African American gardener to his northern employers that denied the plantation's romanticism and slavery's glorification and emphasized the divisions between black and white. The poet Paul Lawrence Dunbar blended the use of African American dialect and refrains with a rich mixture of pathos and humor in his collected poems, *Lyrics of Lowly Life* (1896). There were others, but it was with the age of the Harlem Renaissance and writers such as Jean Toomer (who published *Cane* in 1924), the poets Langston Hughes and Countee Cullen, and the novelist Zora Neale Hurston that writers began to write a literature that allowed those who had suffered under the oppression of slavery to speak with their own voice.

The Harlem Renaissance, fueled by the interest in jazz, was not a school and the aims of its writers differed, but a popular term at the time described these self-assertive and racially conscious African Americans as the "new Negro." The term marked the shift of the black intellectuals from the agrarian South to the urban North, and a movement from the world of Booker T. Washington to that of W. E. B. DuBois. These writers created characters and perspectives that considered African Americans as people; as subjects in their own literature rather than as the objects of other peoples' literature. They countered the invisibility of their people, as passive Uncle Toms or as the singing and dancing caricatures of the minstrel shows, with strong literary characters who spoke to their own people.

The writers of the Harlem Renaissance did not, on the whole, deal directly with stories of slavery. It exists in their texts as a brooding and inevitable presence— in the laconic question in Countee Cullen's poem of the same name, "What is Africa to me?" or in the attitudes and actions of Janie, whose grandmother was born into slavery, in Hurston's *Their Eyes Were Watching God* (1937). Janie is bullied into marrying a staid and much older man because that will keep her "safe" from the atrocities common to her grandmother's experience. After World War II, works such as Richard Wright's *Native Son* (1940), Ralph Waldo Ellison's *Invisible Man* (1952), and the poetry of Gwendolyn Brooks confront the social and psychological problems inflicted by the racism, bigotry, and stereotyping that was the legacy of slavery.

The Black Arts movement of the 1960s was a call to action. Amiri Baraka's "Black Art" (1969) declares: "We want 'poems that kill'/Assassin poems, Poems that shoot/guns." The movement, essentially a cry for civil liberties, gave impetus to an explosion of new African American writers, among them those who worked to reclaim their peoples' past. The theme emerges in Alice Walker's "Everyday Use" (1973) when Dee, named for her Aunt, decides to break with her past and call herself Wangero, but in so doing loses her own identity. Other writers confronted the silences of slavery by remembering those whose existence as slaves meant that their stories remained untold. On a popular level, Alex Palmer Haley wrote *Roots: The Saga of an American Family* (1975), which traced his own slavery background back to Africa. The television series that followed demonstrated to people worldwide what the loss of country, home, language, freedom, even one's name, meant and what it could mean for generations to come. Toni Morrison's *Beloved* (1987) similarly explores the ongoing legacy of slavery in terms of the nature of possession and freedom. Beloved, the child Sethe killed rather than allowed to live in slavery, returns. The return brings little joy. Beloved takes possession, holding Sethe from life just as her would-be lover, Paul D., is held from life by the memory of slavery's atrocities. As Sethe loosens her hold on life, it is the black community itself that frees her, and ultimately, it is from among this community that depictions of slavery in literature have found their finest form.

— *Jan Pilditch*

See also: Autobiographies; Chesnutt, Charles W.; Douglass, Frederick; Locke, David Ross; Narratives; Stowe, Harriet Beecher; *Uncle Tom's Cabin.*

For Further Reading

Bruce, Dickson D. 2001. *The Origins of African American Literature.* Charlottesville: University Press of Virginia.

Crane, Gregg. 2002. *Race, Citizenship, and Law in American Literature.* Cambridge: Cambridge University Press.

Fisher, Philip. 1985. *Hard Facts: Setting and Form in the American Novel.* New York: Oxford University Press.

Gates, Henry Louis, Jr. 1987. *Figures in Black: Words, Signs, and the "Racial" Self.* New York: Oxford University Press.

Karcher, Carolyn L. 1980. *Shadow over the Promised Land: Slavery, Race, and Violence in Melville's America.* Baton Rouge: Louisiana State University Press.

Sekora, John, and Darwin T. Turner, eds. 1982. *The Art of Slave Narrative: Original Essays in Criticism and Theory.* Macomb: Western Illinois University

DAVID ROSS LOCKE (1833–1888)

David Ross Locke was born in New York State and spent his working life as a freelance printer and journalist, mainly in Ohio. He was the author of a number of political pamphlets and a popular lecturer. During the American Civil War, he invented his famous pseudonym Petrolium V. Nasby, late pastor uv the Church uv the New Dispensation, Chaplain to his excellency the President, and P.M. at Confederate x roads, kentucky. The character, a dissolute and illiterate country preacher, satirized the southern cause during the Civil War through his own fervent support of it. This support took the form of a long series of misspelt letters and ludicrous arguments, after the manner of Artemus Ward, Seba Smith's Major Jack Downing letters, and others. Although it must be admitted that Locke's Petrolium V. Nasby is the most conniving, rationalizing, and generally appalling of all the writers of misspelt letters. If it is the satirist's duty to lash the vice and folly of humanity, it is no accident that this epitome of all cracker-box philosophers should emerge in the course of the Civil War. His very presence, his disruption of logic and grammar, signify the deep disharmony felt among the general population. The Petrolium V. Nasby letters appeared for the first time in the Findlay *Jeffersonian* on March 21, 1861.

The misspelt letters made their point through a series of puns, ludicrous spelling, deformed grammar, incongruous juxtaposition, and anticlimax. Petro-lium V. Nasby, an office seeker who unfailingly points to the superiority of his lineage remarks: "My politiks hez ever bin Dimocratic, and I may say, without egotism, I hey bin a yooseful member uv that party. I voted for Jackson seven times, and for every succeedin' Dimocratic candidate ez many times as possible." Nasby is the most corrupt of men and despite his enthusiasm for the southern cause is unable to fight. On reading in the newspaper that the government had instituted a draft, Nasby writes on August 6, 1862: "I know not wat uthers may do, but ez for me, I cant go. . . . My teeth is all unsound, my palit aint eggsackly rite, and I hev hed bronkeetis 31 yeres last Joon. At pesent I hev a koff, the paroxisms uv wich is friteful to behold."

This appalling human frame embodies a collection of equally appalling values that are supported by spurious appeals to God and nature. When the Civil War ends, he reacts to an election taking place, after passage of the Fourteenth Amendment to the U.S. Constitution, by rigging it. Nasby drags voters from jails and poorhouses and sobriety was not a requirement: "One enthoosiastic Dimekrat, who cost us $5, hed to be carried to the polls. He hed commenced early at one uv the groseries, and hed succumbed afore voting." The way in which misspelling can reinforce satire is evident in the spelling of Dimekrat. Elsewhere in Nasby's letters the word is spelt "dimocrat," but here the issue of bribing voters is paramount, and this so that the Fourteenth Amendment, which gave black Americans voting rights, could be voted down by the "liberty-lovin freemen uv Ohio."

If Harriet Beecher Stowe was told by President Lincoln that she was the "little woman who started a war," then David Ross Locke was the writer who was credited with helping him win it. Lincoln is said to have read the latest Nasby letters to his cabinet for a little comic relief before outlining the Emancipation Proclamation. *The Nasby Papers* by David Ross Locke were published in 1864, the first of many collections, and a political novel, *The Demagogue* was published in 1891.

— *Jan Pilditch*

See also: Civil War; Literature.

For Further Reading

Barucky, Jerry M. 1969. "David Ross Locke: A Muckrake Man." M.A. Thesis, Bowling Green State University, Bowling Green, Ohio.

Clemens, Cyril. 1936. *Petroleum Vesuvius Nasby.* Webster Groves, MO: International Mark Twain Society.

Harrison, John M. 1969. *The Man Who Made Nasby: David Ross Locke.* Chapel Hill: University of North Carolina Press.

LONG-STAPLE COTTON

Long-staple cotton (G. *barbadense*) was one of the most valuable commodities produced in the antebellum South. Variously known as Sea Island cotton and black seed cotton, this type of cotton had a long growing season and therefore flourished in the Caribbean basin and in the Sea Island region just off the South Carolina and Georgia coastline. Long-staple cotton was the first variety of cotton to be commercially cultivated in the United States, but its regional distribution as a "cash crop" was limited by climatic considerations.

Long-staple cotton was valued as an exportable commodity for many reasons. The smooth black seeds of the cotton boll did not stick to the cotton lint and were therefore relatively easy to remove by hand. It was possible for slave laborers to remove the cotton lint from the cotton seed by hand without the necessity of using any type of blade-based gin (though roller-gins were used on some plantations). In addition, the long-staple cotton was so named because the cotton fiber that was produced within each boll tended to be long and relatively silky. Textile manufacturers in Great Britain and in the northern United States valued the product greatly.

Sea Island cotton was not cultivated in South Carolina and Georgia during the colonial era but was only introduced into the region in the 1780s. At this point, long-staple cotton still vied with rice and indigo as regional exports—the southern cotton boom had not yet occurred. That transformation would take place as new technologies encouraged the cultivation of short-staple cotton (G. *hirsutum*), which could grow practically anywhere in the upland South almost like a weed. Alexander Bissett of Sapelo Island, Georgia, sold the first bale of long-staple, Sea Island cotton in 1788, and by the early 1790s the product was selling for 10.5 cents per pound. The value placed on this product was clearly noted, and by 1805, Sea Island cotton reached an all-time high of $2.00 per pound. It was said that the finest French mills imported only Sea Island cotton because of its high quality, and during the nineteenth century, Britain's Queen Victoria reputedly only used handkerchiefs made out of Sea Island cotton.

In 1792 Eli Whitney arrived in Savannah to study law and to tutor the children of General Nathanael Greene, a hero of the American Revolution. While he was living in Mulberry Grove, Georgia, the Massachusetts native recognized the problems inherent in cultivating cotton in the area—particularly the difficulty of removing cotton seeds from cotton fiber by hand. Whitney's ingenious solution to this problem—the development of the cotton gin—would do much to transform the agricultural economy not only of coastal Georgia and South Carolina but also of the entire antebellum South. In addition, the expansion of cotton cultivation would trigger an insatiable demand for slave laborers throughout the region.

It would be false to argue that slavery was a more benign institution in the days when long-staple cotton was cultivated exclusively, but slavery was certainly more localized and a smaller part of the local economy during this earlier era. The expansion associated with the cotton boom that brought the cultivation of short-staple upland cotton would extend the region of cultivation westward to the Mississippi and beyond to East Texas. This rapid expansion of territory to be cultivated carried with it the demand for tens of thousands of additional slave laborers to make the cotton economy viable.

— *Junius P. Rodriguez*

See also: Georgia; Sea Islands; South Carolina.

For Further Reading

Chaplin, Joyce E. 1991. "Creating a Cotton South in Georgia and South Carolina, 1760–1815." *Journal of Southern History* 57: 171–200.

Cohn, David L. 1956. *The Life and Times of King Cotton.* New York: Oxford University Press.

Gray, Lewis C. 1933. *History of Agriculture in the Southern United States to 1860.* 2 vols. Washington, DC: Carnegie Institution.

Keber, Martha L. 2002. *Seas of Gold, Seas of Cotton: Christophe Poulain DuBignon of Jekyll Island.* Athens: University of Georgia Press.

Mirsky, Jeannette, and Allan Nevins. 1952. *The World of Eli Whitney.* New York: Macmillan.

Woodman, Harold D. 2000. *King Cotton and His Retainers; Financing and Marketing the Cotton Crop of the South, 1800–1925.* Washington, DC: Beard Books.

Works Progress Administration. 1941. *The Story of Sea Island Cotton.* Tallahassee: State of Florida Department of Agriculture.

NARCISO LOPEZ (1798–1851)

The pivotal year 1848, which saw the acquisition of the vast Southwest from Mexico, also witnessed great enthusiasm throughout the United States for the annexation of Cuba—one of Spain's last colonial possessions in the Western Hemisphere. The same year saw Cuban revolutionaries issue a proclamation stating that the island's future lay with the rising American nation. Foremost in promoting trade with the United States, and determined to thwart Spanish efforts to abolish slavery,

Cuban annexationists contended that admission to the Union would see the island's "farms and slaves . . . double their value" (Brown, 1980).

Led by General Narciso Lopez, a native of Venezuela, who married into a Cuban planter family, these patriots planned a revolt for June 29. Once a loyal Spanish soldier, Lopez fought against Latin American revolutionary, Simon Bolívar, and served in the Carlist War, a Spanish civil war in the 1830s fought over problems of succession. Although he subsequently held several administrative posts in Spain and Cuba, he was apparently driven to support the island's anti-Spanish faction by serious financial reverses.

Ironically, Lopez and his followers were betrayed by the American government who, in the process of negotiating the purchase of the island, exposed the plot to Spanish authorities. Lopez barely escaped capture, fled to New York, and with the support of Cuban exiles and American expansionists, raised a private army to liberate Cuba in 1849. However, President Zachary Taylor's strong stand against filibustering, coupled with legal and military precautions taken by federal officials, effectively thwarted Lopez's invasion plans.

When federal authorities foiled efforts to organize a second expedition, Lopez transformed his base of operations from New York to New Orleans. Strongly proslavery, Lopez was well known in Cuba for harsh sentences against free blacks while serving as president of the military commission in the early 1840s. Although he failed to persuade prominent southerners like Robert E. Lee and Jefferson Davis to lead a new expedition, he received substantial support from Governor John A. Quitman of Mississippi who believed that the annexation of Cuba as a slave state would balance the recent admission of California to the Union as a free state.

"Cuba fever" spread rapidly through the South, and by spring 1850, Lopez had assembled an invasion force of nearly 600 men. Sailing from New Orleans, he landed on Cuba's northern coast on May 19 and captured the Spanish garrison at Cardenas. The local populace failed to rise, and Spanish reinforcements forced Lopez's "liberators" to reembark hastily and sail for Key West. Closely pursued by a Spanish warship, the filibusters scattered upon reaching Key West, narrowly avoiding arrest by local federal officials.

Lopez and sixteen followers, including Quitman, were subsequently indicted by a federal grand jury for violating the Neutrality Law (1818), which banned private military expeditions from American soil against foreign nations. Released after three hung juries compromised the government's case, Lopez promptly organized a fourth expedition. Ignoring a proclamation by President Fillmore, Lopez sailed from New Orleans on August 3, 1851.

Lopez's 400 filibusters landed at Bahia Honda on August 11 and marched inland only to discover, as before, that Cuban support failed to materialize. Discipline soon fell apart, and Lopez's force was overwhelmed by Spanish troops. Colonel William L. Crittenden of Kentucky and over fifty others were shot in Havana on August 16, while over 162 filibusters were sent to Spain in chains. Hunted down by Spanish troops, Lopez himself was captured and publicly garroted in Havana on September 1.

The news of Crittenden's fate, which reached New Orleans prior to Lopez's capture, sparked anti-Spanish riots that wrecked the Spanish consulate there. However, the American government was unwilling to protest Spain's harsh measures against what was regarded as an illegal expedition. Spain subsequently released all surviving prisoners after the U.S. Congress voted a $25,000 indemnity for the damage in New Orleans.

For many Cubans and Americans, Narciso Lopez died a martyr for liberty. However, as one historian contends, he was in reality "an agent of annexation." Many of Lopez's followers subsequently participated in Quitman's abortive filibuster expedition against Cuba and fought under William Walker in Central America.

— *James M. Prichard*

See also: Filibusters; Quitman, John A.; Walker, William.

For Further Reading

Brown, Charles H. 1980. *Agents of Manifest Destiny: The Lives and Times of the Filibusters.* Chapel Hill: University of North Carolina Press.

Chaffin, Tom. 1995. "'Sons of Washington': Narciso Lopez, Filibustering, and U.S. Nationalism, 1848–1851." *Journal of the Early American Republic* 15 (1): 79–108.

Chaffin, Tom. 2003. *Fatal Glory: Narciso Lopez and the First Clandestine U.S. War against Cuba.* Baton Rouge: Louisiana State University Press.

May, Robert E. 1973. *The Southern Dream of a Caribbean Empire 1854–1861.* Baton Rouge: Louisiana State University Press.

Thomas, Hugh. 1971. *Cuba: The Pursuit of Freedom.* New York: Harper and Row.

LOUISIANA

Slavery in Louisiana falls into two periods: the colonial, alternating between French and Spanish rule from 1699 until 1803; and the American, from 1803 until emancipation at the end of the Civil War. Unlike developments in the Caribbean and along the Atlantic coast of North America, colonial Louisiana was not initially a plantation society. Large-scale slave ownership did not become crucial until after the mid-1700s when varieties of sugarcane and a method of sugar processing suitable to Louisiana's climate were introduced. During the American period, cotton became Louisiana's most widely cultivated crop north of the latitude of Baton Rouge. As the size of plantations grew and commodity production became more profitable, Louisiana slavery became harsher and legendary.

After the French claimed Louisiana in 1682, colonizers established permanent settlements in 1699 at Biloxi, Mississippi and in 1702 at Fort Louis on Mobile Bay, Alabama. The colony's first slaves were Indians, who numbered eleven in the 1704 census and eighty in the count four years later. Colonists quickly became dissatisfied with Indian slaves, however, and in 1706 petitioned for Africans. Although the date the first Africans arrived in the colony is unknown, the first black child was born in 1712 and the black population at that time totaled approximately twenty. In 1719, a year after the founding of New Orleans, French ships brought in five hundred slaves. This number increased modestly at first and then dramatically. At the end of the French rule in the 1760s, slaves in the colony numbered approximately ten thousand; by the end of the Spanish colonial era, there were about twenty-eight thousand; and in 1860, under the Americans, the number reached a peak of 331,726. Despite the introduction of African slaves, Indian slavery continued on a small scale. Individuals from the two groups sometimes ran off together, held each other in bondage, mated to produce offspring referred to in the colonial records as *grifes,* and on occasion joined in conspiracies against the colonial governments, including the 1729 massacre of the French at Natchez. Following this revolt the French clamped down on the slave trade to Louisiana, allowing only one ship to enter the colony between 1731 and 1769. The trade resumed afterward, however, under the Spanish. Another major conspiracy against slavery occurred in Pointe Coupée Parish in 1795, bringing together Africans, Indians, Europeans, Americans, and free people of color motivated by ideas of egalitarianism and the revolutions in France, the United States, and St. Domingue. Again, in 1811, five hundred slaves began a march on New Orleans, killing whites, burning plantations and crops, and taking weapons and ammunition. Planters organized a militia, reinforced by the U.S. Army, and massacred sixty-six slaves during the revolt. Others were captured, tried, and executed—their heads raised on poles along the Mississippi River Road to intimidate others who might be tempted to rebel.

Although slaves destined for Louisiana were taken from several regions of Africa, two-thirds of the direct arrivals during the French colonial rule came from the Senegambia, with the Bambara being the largest group, and thereby, the most significant contributors to the formation of the colony's Afro-Creole culture. The Spanish continued to bring slaves from the Senegambia, taking others from Central Africa, the Bight of Benin, and the Bight of Biafra. The 1791 Revolution in St. Domingue strengthened French and Afro-Creole culture in Louisiana as many slaveowners along with their slaves fled Hispaniola and settled in the colony. This occurred again in 1808 as another migration of St. Domingue exiles came to Louisiana from Cuba, where they had originally sought refuge. Although slaves from elsewhere in the United States had been brought into Louisiana during the colonial period, this number increased dramatically after 1803. This was due in large part to the exhaustion of the soil in the Upper South, creating a surplus of slaves in that region, and the cotton boom in the Lower South and Southwest, leading to a demand for labor. Consequently, Louisiana's Afro-Creole culture became partially Anglicized, and in this form following Reconstruction spread throughout much of the rest of the United States.

Slaves arriving in Louisiana from Africa were often technically skilled and had considerable knowledge of tropical crop production. Their experiences in Louisiana varied considerably, however. Although cotton planters in the northern part of the state attempted to maintain a sexually balanced labor force and increased their slaves through sexual reproduction, sugarcane planters in the South needed more males than females and consequently depended on a continuation of the slave trade with Africa. In urban areas, such as New Orleans, slaves worked as domestic servants or skilled laborers, such as blacksmiths, masons, metalworkers, and carpenters, some of whom leased themselves out for hire and returned a portion of these earnings to their owners. Government authorities responsible for maintaining levees and constructing roads, wharves, and public buildings also purchased the labor of slaves. On such jobs, slaves sometimes worked alongside free people of color. This segment of the population grew slowly under the French but increased dramatically under the Spanish, who allowed masters to manumit their salves with little interference from the government and slaves to more easily purchase their own freedom, a practice known as *coartación.* Free people of color, many of whom were of mixed European and African ancestry, were often educated, held property including plantations, and in some cases owned slaves. Although the number of free people of color in Louisiana increased from seventy-five hundred to over twenty-five thousand between 1810 and 1840, their proportion of the state's population of African descent declined from 18 to 13 percent during this period.

In several of its features, slavery in colonial Louisiana developed along lines similar to those in French and Spanish societies in the Caribbean and gave rise to cultural patterns that endured, in part, into the American period. These included: (1) tolerance of widespread interracial matings so that large numbers of mulattoes existed alongside pure Africans; (2) creation of a syncretic religious tradition, Voodoo, that drew on Catholicism and traditional African beliefs; (3) continuation of African language or ethnic communities that facilitated marronage; (4) production of language patterns that evolved into a form of widely spoken Creole French; and (5) continuation of African traditions of drumming, dancing, and cooking to produce the most Africanized slave culture on the North American continent.

— *Claude F. Jacobs*

See also: Derham, James; Durnford, Andrew; German Coast Uprising (1811); Pointe Coupée Conspiracy (1795); Rillieux, Norbert.

For Further Reading

Hall, Gwendolyn Midlo. 1992. *Africans in Colonial Louisiana: The Development of Afro-Creole Culture in the Eighteenth Century.* Baton Rouge: Louisiana State University Press.

Haas, Edward F., ed. 1983. *Louisiana's Legal Heritage.* New Orleans: Louisiana State Museum.

Macdonald, Robert R., John R. Kemp, and Edward F. Haas, eds. 1979. *Louisiana's Black Heritage.* New Orleans: Louisiana State Museum.

Mills, Gary B., 1977. *The Forgotten People: Cane River's Creoles of Color.* Baton Rouge: Louisiana State University Press.

Northup, Solomon. 1968. *Twelve Years a Slave.* Eds. Sue Eakin and Joseph Logsdon. Baton Rouge: Louisiana State University Press.

Taylor, Joe Gray. 1963. *Negro Slavery in Louisiana.* Baton Rouge: Louisiana Historical Association.

ELIJAH PARISH LOVEJOY (1802–1837)

Elijah Parish Lovejoy was an abolitionist, antislavery activist and advocate, newspaper editor, and publisher, who earned a reputation as an uncompromising opponent of slavery. He was born in Albion, Maine, on November 9, 1802. His parents, the Reverend Daniel Lovejoy and Elizabeth (Pattie) Lovejoy, were both of New England origin. A brilliant young man, Lovejoy attended Waterville (now Colby) College and graduated with honors in 1826. He taught school for about a year and then moved to St. Louis, Missouri, where he continued teaching. Perhaps influenced by his father, young Lovejoy entered the ministry. He attended the Theological Seminary at Princeton and was licensed to preach in 1833 by the Philadelphia Presbyterian Church. He returned to St. Louis that same year, this time driven by a deep sense of mission and determined to contribute to the antislavery cause.

In November 1833 he began publishing and editing the *St Louis Observer,* a Presbyterian weekly. He was driven by an inner revulsion against slavery, and an inner determination to destroy the institution. He transformed the paper into a vocal antislavery organ. Early in his antislavery crusade, Lovejoy came under the influence of Garrisonian moral-suasionist ideology. Followers of the New England abolitionist William Lloyd Garrison embraced moral suasion, and nonviolence, and believed strongly that the most viable and effective weapon against slavery was the force of moral condemnation and exposition. Lovejoy accepted the creed and became a radical pacifist who rejected violence, while persistently criticizing and exposing slavery's evils. Such persistence, Lovejoy and other nonviolent abolitionists felt, would eventually influence public opinion against slavery, bringing down the institution in the process. Consequently, although his editorials were harsh and often fiery, Lovejoy remained a pacifist at heart.

But St. Louis proved intolerant of his antislavery activities, and opposition to Lovejoy developed, becoming increasingly militant and life-threatening. He was confronted with the choice of either moderating his criticism or leaving the city completely. He chose to leave. He strongly believed in his constitutionally given right to protest and criticize slavery and vowed not to "give ground a single inch." His unpopularity deepened with his coverage of the public roasting of a St. Louis mulatto sailor in May 5, 1836, for killing a white deputy. The perpetrators were never punished. Lovejoy reported the incident in his paper, bitterly denouncing the perpetrators and the judge who was lenient on them. Enraged by Lovejoy's coverage, public sentiment against him turned violent, and fearing for his life and his family, his antislavery friends advised Lovejoy to leave the city. He relocated across the Mississippi River in Alton, Illinois, home to many antislavery New Englanders. But even there Lovejoy was not completely safe. An antiabolitionist mob from St. Louis followed him to Alton and destroyed his press as it stood on the dock.

An anti-abolition mob attacks the warehouse of the Alton *Observer,* a newspaper in favor of abolition, in Alton, Illinois, on November 7, 1837. Editor Elijah P. Lovejoy, a leader in the movement, was shot dead defending his press. (Library of Congress)

Altonians initially welcomed Lovejoy and expressed regret over the destruction of his press, pledging to assist him in replacing it. They also made clear their discomfort with abolitionism, and Lovejoy allegedly promised to restrict the content of his newspaper to religious matters. Illinois was not quite an ideal haven for abolitionists. The state legislature recognized the constitutional right of southerners to maintain slavery and had condemned abolition. Nevertheless, abolitionist sentiments were rising in the state, and Lovejoy felt at ease, believing that he had finally found a safe place to propagate antislavery ideas. He replaced his press, thanks to the generosity of antislavery friends in Ohio.

The Alton *Observer,* like its predecessor, assumed the character of a staunch opponent of slavery, and soon the tone of his writings and his activities became worrisome to Altonians. Lovejoy criticized and condemned slavery and gave wide publicity to antislavery activities, both local and distant. He supported abolitionists and began to advocate forming an abolitionist society in Alton. On July 4, 1837, the paper called for an antislavery meeting in Alton to consider establishing a state branch of the American Anti-Slavery Society. Opposition to

his activities mounted. However, after several deliberations, the society was finally formed on October 26.

The formation of an antislavery society brought the wrath of Altonians down on Lovejoy, and people began publicly discussing the possibility of violence to stop him. His press was destroyed by mobs three times, and each time a replacement arrived from Ohio. When the third press was destroyed, Lovejoy, with the concurrence of Alton's mayor, decided to arm himself in order to protect his family and press against further attacks. He thus abandoned pacifism, believing that self-defense was justified in such a situation of helplessness and vulnerability. Unfortunately, the townspeople were just as determined to end his editorial career permanently. Lovejoy sought protection for his property and his right to free speech, but to no avail. The mayor claimed that he lacked the necessary force with which to protect Lovejoy, and advised him to consider leaving town. Angry mobs invaded his home several times, threatening the safety of his family. Finally, Lovejoy was compelled to abandon nonviolence. Determined not to be bullied any longer, Lovejoy procured guns with which to protect his family and business. Explaining his resolve, he wrote in the *Liberator,* "But dear-bought experience has taught me that there is at present no safety for me, and no defense in this place, either in the laws or the protective aegis of public sentiment. I feel that I do not walk the streets in safety, and every night when I lie down, it is with the deep settled conviction, that there are those near me and around me, who seek my life. I have resisted this conviction as long as I could but it has been forced upon me." For Lovejoy, the die seemed cast. He was abandoning Garrisonian nonresistance and pacifism. He would fight back.

His fourth press arrived from Ohio, and just as in the past, a mob gathered to destroy it. Lovejoy stood his ground, beside a group of armed supporters, in defense of his new press. Tension mounted, and in the ensuing confrontation, shots were fired. Lovejoy was hit and fatally injured. He died on the spot, thus becoming a martyr of the antislavery cause—in fact, the American Anti-Slavery Society proclaimed him the "first martyr of American liberty." Fellow pacifists bemoaned Lovejoy's decision to defend himself and seemed to blame him for his death.

Lovejoy's death strengthened the abolitionist movement. Angry meetings were held throughout the country to denounce his killing, and thousands of men and women were drawn to the antislavery cause. His death also reduced northern antagonism to abolition, giving abolitionists a freer and more permissive atmosphere in which to meet, speak, publish, and agitate. Lovejoy's devotion to antislavery and the sacrifice of his life for the cause inspired generations of abolitionists, black and white. Perhaps the most outstanding was John Brown, who at a memorial meeting in Ohio, vowed to dedicate his own life to the destruction of slavery.

— *Tunde Adeleke*

See also: Alton (Illinois) *Observer;* Antiabolition Riots; Beecher, Edward; Brown, John; Garrison, William Lloyd.

For Further Reading

Blight, David W. 1972. "The Martyrdom of Elijah P. Lovejoy." *Pennsylvania History* 39: 239–249.

Curtis, Michael Kent. 1997. "The 1837 Killing of Elijah Lovejoy by an Anti-abolition Mob: Free Speech, Republican Government, and the Privileges of American Citizens." *UCLA Law Review* 44 (April): 1109–1184.

Mabee, Carlton. 1970. *Black Freedom: The Nonviolent Abolitionists from 1830 through the Civil War.* London: Macmillan.

Richards, Leonard L. 1975. *Gentlemen of Property and Standing: Anti-Abolition Mobs in Jacksonian America.* New York: Oxford University Press.

Sorin, Gerald. 1972. *Abolitionism: A New Perspective.* New York: Praeger Publishers.

MADISON COUNTY SLAVE WAR

The 1859 Madison County, Kentucky, "slave war" resulted from a series of misunderstandings and prejudices that occurred in and around the small settlement of Berea, Kentucky. Encouraged by the abolitionist Cassius M. Clay's emancipation of his slaves in Kentucky, followers of Reverend John G. Fee, a noted abolitionist, settled in the Berea area in 1855 and established a school and church where the principles of racial equality were taught. Clay became disenchanted with the teachings of those at Berea and gave them little support after 1856, but Fee continued his efforts to attract recruits and to raise money for the colony.

In October 1859, Fee traveled throughout New England to garner support for a proposed college at Berea, and while in the North, he was invited to speak to Henry Ward Beecher's congregation at the Plymouth Congregational Church in Brooklyn. During his speech, Fee invoked the name of the abolitionist, John Brown. The Kentucky papers reported the incident in a sensational manner, and calls for Fee and his followers to be driven out of Kentucky, or to be arrested, were numerous.

Madison County citizens were outraged at Fee's words. On December 5, 1859, a group of influential residents met in the courthouse at Richmond, Kentucky, to discuss the situation regarding the Berea community. Among their resolutions was a pledge to stop Fee and his followers by "fair and proper means and measures." On December 23, 1859, sixty men rode to Berea to warn the inhabitants to leave the state within ten days, or be forced out. Kentucky governor Beriah Magoffin refused to send the militia to protect them.

Fear of mob violence prompted a group of ten families consisting of thirty-six people to leave their homes, and twenty went to Cincinnati and free territory. Although feelings among many slaveowners ran high against Fee and the Berea community, some Madison County residents did not feel completely negative about the Bereans, as at least one-third of the students at the Berea school were from slaveholding families.

The threat of violence did not end with the exodus of some of the Berea residents. In March 1860, a group of twenty-five armed men rode into the community to find that John C. Hanson, one of the former residents, had returned to settle some business and to sell his sawmill. This time the proslavery people met resistance, and shots were exchanged. The infuriated mob returned to Richmond to get reinforcements, and the following day a larger force of over two hundred returned to Berea and destroyed Hanson's mill. Cannons were ordered from Lexington to aid in the attack. Hanson escaped capture and fled the state, and because of continued threats and violence, in April 1860, some sixty additional members of the Berea community left Kentucky for the free states.

Madison County experienced some of the same difficulties that occurred in Kansas and Nebraska just a few years earlier, though on a smaller scale. The clash of antislavery forces with proslavery forces gave Madison County a foretaste of what Kentucky and the nation would endure with the coming of the Civil War.

— *Ron D. Bryant*

See also: Brown, John.

For Further Reading
Dorris, Jonathan T. 1936. *Old Cane Springs.* Louisville, KY: Standard Printing.
Ellis, William. 1985. *Madison County: 200 Years in Retrospect.* Richmond, KY: Madison County Historical Society.
Harrold, Stanley C., Jr. 1988. "Cassius M. Clay on Slavery and Race: A Reinterpretation." *Slavery & Abolition* 9 (May): 42–56.

MARGARET MERCER (1791–1846)

As an antislavery advocate, teacher, and author, Margaret Mercer is considered to have been Virginia's preeminent female supporter of Negro colonization. Driven by religious motives, Mercer entered into altruistic activities as a young woman, beginning by supporting church activities as well as giving money and time during the Greek War of Independence from Turkey (1821–1832). Her main focus, however, was her interest in antislavery causes, specifically those embodied by the American Colonization Society (ACS). The goal of the ACS was to provide funds for free blacks to emigrate to Africa and to encourage the emancipation of slaves by asking slaveowners to send their slaves to the newly created colony of Liberia. The ACS believed that this manner of dealing with slavery would ultimately rid the United States of the practice. ACS supporters also clearly stated that removal of free slaves to Africa would open up job opportunities for white citizens and would eventually accomplish the creation of a white (and therefore more acceptable) populace.

Mercer, the daughter of a Maryland governor (John F. Mercer, served 1801–1802), emancipated the fifteen slaves she inherited from her father, diligently worked on fund-raising for the colonization project, sponsored education projects in the Liberian colony, and was a forthright voice in the argument for Liberian colonization. Eventually, enthusiasm for the ACS began to wane among some of its leading members, who felt the ACS was ineffective and divisive among abolitionists. The American Union for the Relief and Improvement of the Colored Race was organized in its stead, and Mercer, deeply offended, turned her efforts to teaching. She was the author of two books published in 1837: *Studies for Bible Classes* and *Popular Lectures on Ethics or Moral Obligation for the Use of Schools.* Mercer died of tuberculosis in Virginia.

— *Maria Elena Raymond*

See also: American Colonization Society.

For Further Reading
Jeffery, Julie. 1961. *The Great Silent Army of Abolitionism: Women in the Antislavery Movement.* Chapel Hill: University of North Carolina Press.
Malone, Dumas, ed. 1933. *Dictionary of American Biography.* New York: Charles Scribner's Sons.
Staudenraus, P. J. 1961. *The African Colonization Movement 1816–1865.* New York: Columbia University Press.

MASON–DIXON LINE. *See* Free Persons of Color.

MIDDLE PASSAGE

The label Middle Passage has long been used to describe the voyage of slaving vessels from African to American ports. Beginning in the sixteenth century, this involuntary voyage was taken by over 11 million people before slave trading ended in the nineteenth century. Voyage lengths could vary considerably. Gambia River slavers made the passage to Barbados in as little as three weeks, while those from Angola to Virginia or Cartagena might take several months. Abolitionists and then historians have used descriptions of the treatment of slaves aboard ship, the terror experienced by the captives, and the high mortality rates on some of the voyages to demonstrate some of slavery's worst aspects.

Before embarking on the transatlantic voyage, slaves had already endured significant trauma. Most had been enslaved by fellow Africans, as Europeans rarely ventured into the interior to capture slaves and purchased them from African merchants instead. Some slaves had been sentenced to their status for criminal activity, indebtedness, or religious infractions while others were victims of political disorders or wars of aggression by imperialist African nations. Prior to 1700, over half of all slaves were prisoners of war, but in the eighteenth century, banditry and large-scale kidnapping expeditions were responsible for about two-thirds of the slaves delivered for coastal sale. Exhausted from long treks from the interior and crowded conditions of detention in pens awaiting the arrival of European traders, slaves were often ill because of inadequate diets and fouled water supplies. In all, most slaves spent at least six months from capture until being placed aboard ships for transport across the Atlantic. Adding to their misery was the terror of seeing the ocean and hearing the pounding of the surf for the first time and their fear that the mysterious white men with long hair and strange languages might be cannibals.

After boarding the sailing ships, the slaves faced almost indescribable conditions. Although women and children had some freedom of movement, men were usually shackled in pairs. Slave traders bought primarily men because planters in the tropics preferred them for plantation laborers. Throughout the slave-trading era, men outnumbered women by nearly two to one, and children under ten seldom constituted more than 10 percent of the cargo. Whenever possible, captains permitted slaves on deck during the day, but at night and during stormy weather, they faced the horrors of the conditions below deck.

Olaudah Equiano, an eighteenth-century slave from the Niger Delta, published an account of his travail. He related that slaves first noticed an overwhelming smell when forced below deck. There was little breeze through portholes or ventilators, and sanitation facilities rarely were adequate. The resulting foul odor overcame Equiano, as it did countless others, who not only became ill but also found it difficult to eat amid the horrid stench. It became common knowledge that one could smell a slaving vessel five miles downwind.

Some captains preferred packing their slave cargoes more tightly than others. Below deck on most ships there was seldom more than 5 feet of headroom. The "tight packers" installed shelves to halve the headroom and increase the number of slaves transported. Eighteenth-century abolitionists circulated widely a diagram of a Liverpool slave ship named the *Brookes,* which showed a cargo of slaves barely having enough room to move. The captain had allotted an area of only 6 feet by 16 inches for each man to lie in.

Although it is doubtful that the *Brookes* was typical of most of the slave ships, even under ideal circumstances on the "loosely packed" vessels, the space allotted to slaves for the passage was seldom half that provided on ships for indentured servants, soldiers, and convicts. By the eighteenth century, the typical slaving vessel carried nearly two slaves for every ton of displacement. With slaving vessels averaging 200 tons by 1750s, the average slaving voyage carried over 350 slaves, and several far exceeded that figure, with a few carrying up to seven hundred slaves. During the years of peace in the eighteenth-century Atlantic, nearly 170 vessels carried slaves in these cramped conditions.

The meals furnished by ship captains usually depended on the African region where they procured their cargoes. They supplied plantains and manioc for Angolans, yams for slaves from the Bight of Biafra, and rice and cornmeal for those from the windward coast of Africa. Most captains supplemented these meals with boiled horsebeans and, on rare occasions, a small ration of meat. Two meals a day were common, served with water.

The cramped vessels were horrible disease environments in which Europeans and Africans with little immunity to each other's diseases spent much time in close contact. Yellow fever, measles, malaria, leprosy, scurvy, and syphilis were all threats, but smallpox and gastrointestinal disorders, particularly dysentery, often were the biggest killers. Smallpox outbreaks could claim half or more of the slaves during a voyage, as could dysentery. Dr. Alexander Falconbridge, testifying to the British Parliament when that body was investigating the slave trade in the late eighteenth century, explained that a combination of having to keep slaves below deck in bad weather and an outbreak of dysentery created a hell of blood, mucus, and fever that could kill dozens. Even when it did not kill large numbers, the "bloody flux," as contemporaries called dysentery, often so weakened the slaves that they were unable to handle the harsh work environment of the plantations in the Americas. Crew members also faced great risks, as a higher proportion of the crew members than the slaves died during the Middle Passage. Overall, about 17 percent died in the eighteenth-century voyages, but on English slave ships late in the century nearly 22 percent perished, mostly while they obtained cargoes along the African coast.

Most slave ships had at least one doctor on board. Even the most successful ones could do little more than urge captains to keep the holds as clean as possible, to provide the slaves with ample opportunities for exercise and fresh air, and to supply adequate rations of food. Some doctors used traditional herbal treatments they encountered along the African coast. Yet, given their limited knowledge of hygiene and medicine, the doctors could do little when there was an outbreak of disease on board.

The psychological trauma endured by many slaves often was more devastating than the physical ailments. Slaving crews often noticed that a few slaves became so unresponsive that they even refused to eat. To combat this "fixed melancholy"—a depression caused by shock, fear, or the memory of lost home and family—some crews made the slaves dance on deck each day. If the slaves remained unresponsive, crews used threats, violence, and even forced feeding to keep them alive. Occasionally, nothing could be done, and despondent slaves committed suicide by leaping overboard.

The treatment of slaves on the voyages was invariably harsh. Lashings were routine for minor infractions, and sexual assaults on female slaves were commonplace. Captains hired about twice as many crew members for a slaving voyage as for a normal Atlantic crossing, taking about one crewman for every ten slaves to feed and control the cargo. The crewmen were well armed because of a constant fear of slave mutinies, and there certainly was good reason to be concerned. There were nearly four hundred revolts on slave ships crossing from Africa to the Americas. In addition, there were almost one hundred attacks from the African shore on ships or the longboats transporting slaves to slaving vessels.

As ships neared the American markets, the captains began preparing their cargoes for sale. They gave the slaves extra food rations and plenty of water to drink. Crews bathed and shaved the slaves, coated their skin with palm oil to give it a healthier looking sheen, and dyed the gray hair of older slaves. Some captains even provided tobacco and pipes to raise spirits, but it was too late for some. So weakened after surviving the horrors of the passage, perhaps as many as 5 percent of slaves died while awaiting sale or shortly after being sold.

There long has been an effort to determine the mortality rate on the Middle Passage. A few voyages experienced very high death tolls. In 1716, the *Windsor* lost 216 of its 380 slaves before arriving in Brazil. Sixty-five years later, the captain of the *Zong,* a ship from Liverpool, started a voyage with 440 slaves; 60 of them died en route to the West Indies, and 132 others were so sick that the captain ordered them thrown overboard to collect insurance for losses at sea. Such catastrophes were rare. The overall mortality rate was 12 percent, although through the early seventeenth century, the rate hovered around 20 percent. By the late eighteenth century, losses on British slave ships remained under 10 percent of their cargoes.

Historians have offered a number of explanations for the improvement. Some have suggested that captains, with an ever-closer eye on profit margins, slowly moved away from the tight packing of ships. Others have argued that captains decided to sell slaves in the closest ports, thus shortening voyages and improving the chances of reaching markets with a higher percentage of their cargoes. Drawing upon information on over twenty-seven thousand voyages identified in the Trans-Atlantic Slave Trade Project, historians have found that those two factors played only a small role, although they did find that very lengthy voyages led to much higher mortality rates. Beyond the small gains achieved by sailing shorter distances, perhaps the doctors' increasing use of citrus juices to combat the ravages of scurvy and their efforts to improve sanitation aboard ship also contributed. Whatever the explanation, mortality on the Middle Passage declined, as it did on voyages carrying troops, contract laborers, convicts, and free immigrants in the eighteenth and nineteenth centuries.

Despite the ever-greater likelihood that slaves would survive the journey, there is no way to minimize its horror. The ridicule, whippings, sexual exploitation of women, poor rations, disease, disorientation, and terror combined to create a living hell for those forced to sail the Middle Passage.

— *Larry Gragg*

See also: Diseases and African Slavery in the New World.

For Further Reading

Allison, Robert, ed. 1995. *The Interesting Narrative of the Life of Olaudah Equinao Written by Himself.* Boston: Bedford Books.

Eltis, David, Stephen D. Behrendt, David Richardson, and Herbert S. Klein, eds. 1999. *The Trans-Atlantic Slave Trade: A Database on CD-ROM.* Cambridge: Cambridge University Press.

Klein, Herbert S. 1978. *The Middle Passage: Comparative Studies in the Atlantic Slave Trade.* Princeton, NJ: Princeton University Press.

Klein, Herbert S., Stanley L. Engerman, Robin Haines, and Ralph Shlomowitz. 2001. "Transoceanic Mortality: The Slave Trade in Comparative Perspective." *William and Mary Quarterly* 58 (1): 93–117.

Mannix, Daniel, and Malcolm Cowley. 1962. *Black Cargoes: A History of the Atlantic Slave Trade, 1518–1865.* New York: Viking Press.

MISSOURI

When the Missouri Territory applied for statehood in 1819 with a proposed constitution that recognized the existence of slavery within the state, the action touched off a national debate on the expansion of slavery into the western lands recently acquired through the Louisiana Purchase (1803). Although this debate was settled by compromise, the argument prefigured later sectional animosity of the late 1840s and 1850s that would ignite as the same question resurfaced after the United States acquired additional western territories as a result of the Mexican War (1846–1848). Compromise would be less successful in healing the national rift over slavery, and the United States would find itself inextricably drawn toward civil war over the question of slavery's expansion into the western territories.

Slavery first came to Missouri when the area was colonized as part of French Louisiana in the early eighteenth century. The French colonizers made an effort to establish a series of frontier outposts connecting the poles of New France (i.e., Quebec) with Louisiana (i.e., New Orleans) and extending throughout the heartland of the North American continent. As such, French colonial settlements were established at Ste. Genevieve, Kaskaskia Island, and St. Louis to extend French hegemony into the interior of North America. According to the standard labor regimen of the day, the French introduced African slaves into these settlements to labor as artisans, household servants, and eventually, once the settlements were firmly established, within the area's saltworks and as agricultural laborers. This practice continued during the era when the Louisiana Territory came under Spanish colonial control (1763–1803), as the Spanish, too, used slave labor within their colonial establishment.

The United States acquired the Louisiana Purchase territory from France in 1803 after the area had been retroceded by the Spanish. When the United States took formal possession of Upper Louisiana (i.e., Missouri) in the spring of 1804, the colonial population of the region, albeit small, included a number of slaves who had labored for either French or Spanish colonial masters in the region. Although the white Creole colonials became citizens of the United States by treaty arrangement, their slaves were also transferred as chattel property and were not granted the benefit of citizenship by the transfer of national sovereignty in the region.

In many respects the Missouri Territory, like much of the entire Louisiana Purchase lands, was an unknown quantity at the time of American acquisition. It was not until after the Lewis and Clark Expedition (1804–1806) successfully explored the Missouri River Valley and traversed the continent to the Pacific Coast and back, that many came to understand and appreciate the bountiful lands of the Missouri Territory and the possibilities that they presented for settlement and agricultural development. William Clark, a leader of the famed expedition, eventually served as territorial governor of Missouri and did much to conclude treaties with Native American tribes in the region that would clear the way for the establishment of farms, plantations, and towns throughout the Missouri Valley. According to the historic custom of the community, slave labor extended into these new settlements.

Pioneer settlers from Kentucky, Tennessee, and Virginia were attracted to Missouri, especially after the War of 1812, by the legendary fertility of the Missouri valley's alluvial bottomlands, and the population of the territory swelled as did its slave population. Large plantations tended to be rare in Missouri, but the ownership of small numbers of slaves by landed farmers tended to be the dominant pattern that emerged in the state. By the time that Missouri sought statehood in 1819, roughly ten thousand slaves, or 15 percent of the territorial population consisted of slaves. By the time of the Civil War, there would be nearly one hundred fifteen thousand slaves in Missouri.

The area of Missouri that sustained the largest population of slaves in the antebellum era was the Missouri River Valley region of the northern part of the state. Physical geography and cultural demographics limited the practical use of or desired ownership of slaves in other Missouri regions. The Ozark Plateau in south-central Missouri produced a region of hills and mountains where large-scale agriculture involving the use of slave labor was marginal. In urban St. Louis some slaves were used as house servants and as workers on the wharves, but the ever-expanding German immigrant population that swelled in the city during the late 1840s and 1850s had decidedly antislavery sentiments. Even though the population of slaves in Missouri increased substantially in the decades leading up to the Civil War, slaves as a percentage of the state's population declined to the point where less than 10 percent of the state's population in 1860 consisted of slaves.

As a state of the Upper South, Missouri was not ideally situated for cotton cultivation by either climate or geography, and the state's primary agricultural pursuits were focused on cultivation of tobacco and hemp and the raising of livestock. Missouri slaves were engaged in all of these pursuits throughout the Missouri Valley settlements. In some parts of the state, slaves continued to be used in an industrial setting in both the saltworks and the lead mines of the state. Slaves working in Missouri may have had some of the most diversified experiences of all the slaves in antebellum America.

Missouri slaveowners played a significant role in neighboring Kansas as that state sought to employ popular sovereignty to determine whether the region would join the union as a slave or as a free state. So-called border ruffians from Missouri crossed the boundary into Kansas to settle in proslavery towns and to influence both with their ballots and with force if necessary the justice of their position. Similarly, free soil advocates from Iowa and elsewhere—the Jayhawkers—also entered Kansas to counter the effects of the "border ruffians" on the territory. By the mid-1850s, as "Bleeding Kansas" erupted into factional violence, the wisdom of popular sovereignty was called into question by a divided nation that saw no easy solution to the question of slavery and its potential expansion into the western territories.

Missouri was the scene of some of the more spectacular legal battles involving slaves in the antebellum era. Missouri was the point of origin for the famed *Dred Scott v. Sandford* (1857) decision, which originated as a case in the historic courthouse in St. Louis in 1846. Similarly, a slave woman named Celia was involved in a historic case in Callaway County in 1855 when she was charged with murdering her master, a man who had repeatedly raped her over the course of several years.

Since most of Missouri's slaves were located in the northern part of the state, a region adjacent to the free states of Iowa and Illinois, it was common for many Missouri slaves to run away and seek freedom either in the adjacent states or in Canada. Both Iowa and Illinois had many active supporters of the Underground Railroad who assisted Missouri fugitives to make their way to freedom.

Though it remained a slaveholding state, Missouri did not leave the Union during the Civil War, but it remained a border state. As such, the state was the scene of much of the fratricidal violence that a war of brother against brother might bring when families often divided their allegiance to the North or to the South. Keeping Missouri within the Union was one of the key war aims of Abraham Lincoln, and he resisted all efforts that might drive the state into the hands of the Confederacy. Lincoln prevented General John C. Frémont from implementing an announced plan that would have emancipated all Missouri slaves who sought refuge with the Union lines. In Lincoln's view, such a policy would have torn Missouri from the Union.

— *Junius P. Rodriguez*

See also: *Dred Scott v. Sandford;* Missouri Compromise; Tallmadge Amendment; 36°30' North Latitude.

For Further Reading

Fehrenbacher, Don E. 1981. *Slavery, Law, and Politics: The Dred Scott Case in Historical Perspective.* New York: Oxford University Press.

Frazier, Harriet C. 2001. *Slavery and Crime in Missouri, 1773–1865.* Jefferson, NC: McFarland.

Hunter, Lloyd A. 1974. "Slavery in St. Louis 1804–1860." *Missouri Historical Society Bulletin* 30 (July): 233–265.

Hurt, R. Douglas. 1992. *Agriculture and Slavery in Missouri's Little Dixie.* Columbia: University of Missouri Press.

McLaurin, Melton A. 1991. *Celia, a Slave.* Athens: University of Georgia Press.

Trexler, Harrison Anthony. 1914. *Slavery in Missouri, 1804–1865.* Baltimore, MD: Johns Hopkins University Press.

MISSOURI COMPROMISE (1820)

The Missouri Compromise (1820) raised the important question of whether or not slavery would be allowed to expand into the Louisiana Territory that the United States had purchased from France in 1803. Although the territory in question was west of the Mississippi River, the most important debate over the issue occurred in the nation's capital. Representatives and senators from North and South clashed over the sensitive issue of slavery in heated debate, the likes of which would not be seen again until the 1850s.

The long-term cause of the Missouri crisis was the gradual evolution of slavery in the United States. Following the American Revolution, the northern states began to abolish slavery, and many northerners began to question the place of slavery in a country that had fought a war for liberty and that professed in its Declaration of Independence that all men were created equal and possessed inalienable rights to life, liberty, and the pursuit of happiness. Many southerners, however, retained slavery despite the inconsistency between slavery and a war fought for independence. Southerners defended slavery by asserting that the Revolution had preserved liberty, including the protection of private property, which included slaves. Although they clung to slavery, many southerners often professed the wish to be rid of slavery. Those statements kept hopes alive in the North that the institution of slavery could be abolished, but such hopes grew dimmer after the invention of the cotton gin in 1793. After 1793, the cultivation of short-staple cotton, which had been difficult to grow because of the lengthy cleaning by hand of the cottonseeds, became the staple crop of choice in the lower South states. As cotton planters exhausted eastern lands and searched for new lands, they moved west into new territories such as Alabama, Mississippi, and Louisiana. Slavery came with the planters and soon covered the lower South from the Atlantic to the Gulf of Mexico. This rapid expansion of slavery, and slave states, worried many northerners who saw the prospect for abolition fading.

In the summer of 1818 the residents of Missouri Territory applied to Congress for the right to form a state government and draft a constitution. Henry Clay presented this petition on December 18, 1818. Little happened until February 13, 1819, when James Tallmadge, a Republican congressman from New York, introduced an amendment that sought "the further introduction of slavery or involuntary servitude be prohibited, except for the punishment of crimes" (*Annals of Congress*, 15th Cong., 2d sess.). His amendment also provided that all children born into slavery in Missouri were to be freed when they reached the age of twenty-five. After furious debate on February 15, 1819, the House passed the Tallmadge Amendment, but the Senate rejected it. Northern representatives and senators overwhelmingly supported the measure, while southerners overwhelmingly opposed it.

During the months between the close of the Fifteenth Congress and the opening of the Sixteenth Congress, antislavery sentiment blossomed in several northern states. Newspaper articles, private and public letters, and mass meetings condemned the spread of slavery to Missouri and urged northern congressional delegations to vote against statehood for Missouri. This outpouring of antislavery sentiment contributed to bitter sectional feelings between northerners and southerners as well as a siege mentality among supporters of slavery in Missouri. In many ways these editorial exchanges in rival newspapers offered a preview of what was to come when Congress resumed its deliberations on the Missouri Question.

When Congress returned to the issue of slavery in Missouri in December 1819, one of the main questions was whether the national legislature had the authority to regulate slavery. Northerners tended to argue that the federal government had previously regulated slavery by alluding to the Northwest Ordinance of 1787 as precedent. Several northern congressmen also argued that the general welfare clause, the commerce clause, the migration and importation clauses, and the territorial authority clause of the Constitution vested power with Congress to regulate slavery in the territories. Southerners replied that slavery was a state institution and Congress could not regulate it. The debates in the winter of 1820 also featured northern attacks on slavery and southern defenses of it. Northerners criticized slavery as an unrepublican institution and asserted that slavery blighted the southern landscape and made a

mockery of national values such as liberty for all men. Southern defenders of slavery counterattacked, offering readings of the Constitution and the Declaration of Independence and defending the right of slaveholders to move their human property to Missouri. In addition, southerners stated that efforts to exclude slavery from Missouri would make the residents of that state second-class citizens, unable to share in the common rights enjoyed by Americans living in other states.

After months of heated debate, Congress, led by Henry Clay, speaker of the House, decided to affect a compromise. Maine, then a province of Massachusetts, sought admission to the Union as a state. Southern members of Congress decided to hold up the admission of Maine, in effect using Maine as a bargaining chip to get Missouri admitted into the Union. The ploy worked. The resulting compromise admitted Maine to the Union as a free state and allowed the Missouri legislature to decide the future of slavery in that state, although most observers expected Missouri to enter the Union as a slave state. Through this arrangement the balance of power in the Senate remained equally divided between North and South. Another crucial part of the compromise called for a line to be drawn in the Louisiana Purchase at 36°30' north latitude, a line that represented the southern border of Missouri. Land north of this line in the remaining territory of the Louisiana Purchase, except for Missouri, would be free territory. Land to the south of the line would be open for settlement by slaveholders.

In the second session of the Sixteenth Congress, which met in the autumn of 1820, there was an episode that nearly scuttled the agreement reached only months earlier. Missouri's constitutional convention included a provision in the new state constitution that called for the legislature to prohibit the immigration of free blacks and mulattoes into the state, an action that raised the thorny question of black citizenship. Northern opponents of this proposed measure asserted that the Constitution made no mention of color as a prerequisite for citizenship, while southern supporters of the proposed law pointed to custom for evidence to buttress their position. Southerners noted that states in both the North and the South denied suffrage to most free blacks, prohibited interracial marriage, and forbade free blacks from serving in the militia. These arguments proved quite powerful because they expressed a common belief that blacks were inferior to whites, and no northern opponent of Missouri's constitutional stipulation expressed unqualified sentiments that contradicted such beliefs.

As a result of this provision in Missouri's constitution, Congress delayed the admission of Missouri into the Union. Competing resolutions for and against the offending clause lacked majorities in Congress, and once again, Henry Clay managed to affect a compromise. This second compromise required the Missouri legislature, in a solemn public act, to ignore the principles of their state's constitution and not pass laws that contradicted the federal Constitution. The Missouri legislature responded by passing a law stating that Congress lacked the right to order such a bill and that the order of Congress lacked binding authority on the state. President James Monroe accepted this law, and Missouri became a state on August 10, 1821.

The Missouri Compromise revealed an important lesson to the political generation of that day. Slavery had to be kept from becoming a topic of debate in Congress. The heated passions expressed during the debates exposed a growing antislavery sentiment in the North and a growing commitment to slavery in the South. Slavery in the territories provoked a crisis that shook the nation to its foundation in 1819. In the heated politics of the 1850s, slavery in the territories provoked a crisis that resulted in civil war.

— *James C. Foley*

See also: Missouri; Tallmadge Amendment.

For Further Reading

Ashworth, John. 1995. *Slavery, Capitalism, and Politics in the Antebellum Republic. Volume 1: Commerce and Compromise, 1820–1860.* New York: Cambridge University Press.

Dangerfield, George. 1952. *The Era of Good Feelings.* New York: Harcourt, Brace and Company.

Forbes, Robert Pierce. 1994. "Slavery and the Meaning of America, 1819–1837." Ph.D. diss., Yale University. New Haven, CT.

Freehling, William W. 1990. *The Road to Disunion: Volume 1: Secessionists at Bay, 1776–1854.* New York: Oxford University Press.

Moore, Glover. 1953. *The Missouri Controversy, 1819–1821.* Lexington: University Press of Kentucky.

Robinson, Donald. 1979. *Slavery in the Structure of American Politics.* New York: Norton.

MIXED-RACE AMERICANS. *See* Miscegenation; Mulattoes; Octoroons; Passing; Quadroons.

LUCRETIA COFFIN MOTT (1793–1880)

Quaker minister, abolitionist, and early feminist, Lucretia Mott has long been acknowledged as the most universally respected antebellum feminist-abolitionist. Unusu-

Depiction of Lucretia Mott during a confrontational meeting. Mott and several other women reacted to discriminatory treatment from the American Anti-Slavery Society by forming the Philadelphia Female Anti-Slavery Society in 1833. Their initiative sparked the creation of similar female abolition groups across the nation. (Bettmann/Corbis)

ally well educated for a woman of her time, Mott had a Quaker education that supported the development of her intellectual prowess and scholarly reputation. Following a long-standing Quaker tradition of opposition to slavery, Lucretia and her husband James Mott became involved in antislavery activities in the 1820s and supported the antislavery teachings of Elias Hicks. Lucretia was chosen to be a Quaker minister in 1821.

Both Lucretia and James were devout supporters of the free-produce movement, a Quaker-instigated reform devoted to promoting goods produced without slave labor. Through her ministering, Mott persuaded women to purchase wool and linen instead of cotton, maple sugar instead of cane sugar, and to make other appropriate substitutions.

In August 1830, William Lloyd Garrison visited the Mott home in Philadelphia. He convinced them that immediate emancipation, not colonization in Africa, was the only viable solution to the slavery problem and urged them to increase their activism. The Mott residence soon emerged as the hub of Garrisonian abolitionism in Philadelphia. In 1833 Lucretia and several other women were invited to attend the first national antislavery convention in Philadelphia at which the American Anti-Slavery Society was formed.

Spurred by the national convention's call for the creation of more female antislavery societies, Lucretia founded the Philadelphia Female Anti-Slavery Society. Besides serving as corresponding clerk for the organization, she was its principal leader and activist throughout her years in the movement. Most of the women members were Quakers, though some were Unitarians and Presbyterians. The society also included several middle-class black women. It was unique among women's antislavery organizations in its efforts to provide for the needs of Philadelphia's African American community. The women also petitioned Congress to abolish the domestic slave trade and to eradicate slavery in Washington, D.C., and the territories. They raised funds for the American Anti-Slavery Society and the Pennsylvania Anti-Slavery Society, collected a vast library of abolitionist literature, and popularized free-produce purchasing practices.

Although Lucretia acknowledged the importance of raising money for the abolitionist cause, she resisted the efforts of male abolitionists to define money-making as the sole function of the female societies. Nor did Lucretia confine her abolitionist efforts to all-female organizations. She was an outspoken, prolific activist in both the American Anti-Slavery Society and the Pennsylvania Anti-Slavery Society, serving on the latter's executive committee.

Lucretia was a major organizer of the First Anti-Slavery Convention of American Women held in New York City in 1837. In 1838, when the Second Annual Convention convened in Philadelphia, a mob of seventeen thousand, incensed by the role of women in the city's much-despised abolitionist activities, disrupted the proceedings. The attendants were forced to flee when the mob destroyed Pennsylvania Hall by fire. Lucretia and her fellow organizers refused to dissolve the convention, instead moving the site and proceeding with the convention.

In 1840 Lucretia and James attended the World's Anti-Slavery Convention in London. Although other American women were sent as delegates from various antislavery organizations, Lucretia was the only woman among the five delegates sent by the American Anti-Slavery Society. Despite her considerable stature in American abolitionism, Lucretia (and all other women delegates) were not permitted to participate and were forced to sit in the adjoining gallery.

Although this event is often credited, erroneously, as the impetus that impelled Lucretia and Elizabeth Cady Stanton to organize the Seneca Falls Convention of 1848, the actual motivating force behind Mott's feminist activism was her need to redress the years of obstacles that men placed in the path of women abolitionists. Lucretia believed that such impediments unjustly restricted women's ability to eradicate the evils of slavery and seriously limited the potential of the abolitionist movement.

Throughout the 1840s and 1850s Lucretia lectured widely throughout the eastern United States, speaking against slavery. An eloquent orator, she also addressed the legislatures of Delaware, Pennsylvania, and New Jersey. During the Civil War, she was a member of the Women's National Loyal League, which petitioned Congress in support of a thirteenth amendment. Long distressed by the pervasiveness and intractability of racial prejudice in Philadelphia, she led a committee of the Friends Association for the Aid and Elevation of Freedmen in investigating the practice of barring African Americans from the passenger cars in that city. In 1866 she was selected president of the divisive American Equal Rights Association, which was formed to push for universal suffrage. From the late 1860s until the time of her death in 1880, Lucretia continued her interest and involvement in the women's rights and suffrage movements, peace organizations, and the free religion movement.

— *Judith E. Harper*

See also: American Anti-Slavery Society; Immediatism; Philadelphia Female Anti-Slavery Society; Women and the Antislavery Movement.

For Further Reading

Bacon, Margaret Hope. 1999. *Valiant Friend: The Life of Lucretia Mott.* Philadelphia, PA: Friends General Conference.

Cromwell, Otelia. 1958. *Lucretia Mott.* Cambridge, MA: Harvard University Press.

Hersh, Blanche Glassman. 1978. *The Slavery of Sex: Feminist-Abolitionists in America.* Urbana: University of Illinois Press.

Lutz, Alma. 1968. *Crusade for Freedom: Women in the Antislavery Movement.* Boston: Beacon Press.

Palmer, Beverly Wilson, ed. 2001. *Selected Letters of Lucretia Coffin Mott.* Urbana: University of Illinois Press.

MULATTOES

In the United States, mulatto, a term of Spanish and Portuguese origin, technically identified a progeny of one black and one white parent. Popularly, however, it signified an individual with any mixture of black and white ancestry. Debates over the categorization and status of mulattoes within the American racial order began during the colonial era and continued well into the twentieth century.

Interracial bonding began soon after the first Africans landed in the English colony of Virginia in 1619. The first mulattoes were the offspring of European indentured servants and Africans and were of uncertain legal status. Although colonial authorities did not prohibit miscegenation, they discouraged it by enacting a series of legislation. The first of such laws was instituted in 1662 and stipulated that children of mixed parentage inherited the status of their mothers and therefore, those born of slave women would likewise be enslaved. This same act also imposed double punishment for any "Christian who shall commit fornication" with an African person. Growing disdain for free mulattoes born of white women led to a 1691 decision specifying that persons of such "abominable mixture" would be "bound out" as servants for thirty years and their mothers suffer five years of servitude or a heavy fine. Furthermore, the Virginia assembly banished European Americans in intermarriages from the colony. In 1705 a six-month jail sentence was imposed on whites in such unions.

Although estimations of mulatto populations varied throughout American history, owing partly to differing and unreliable census-taking practices, it is generally agreed that in spite of such obstructive antimiscegenation laws, the number of people of mixed heritage grew steadily. In 1755 the colony of Maryland counted 108,000 European Americans and 45,000 African Americans. Among the black population were 3,600 mulattoes, 1,500 of whom were free. After the American Revolution (1775–1783), the number of free people of color increased dramatically. In the 1790s, 60,000 lived in the United States, and by the turn of the nineteenth century, their numbers would grow to 108,000, approximately 11 percent of the entire African American population. In spite of the fact that some mulattoes were manumitted, the great majority remained in bondage as slaves.

During the antebellum era, most mixed-race individuals lived in the South. At this juncture, there were two Souths, differentiated by the treatment of mulattoes within each region. The Upper South included North Carolina and areas northward and westward, and was characterized by the presence of a large mulatto population early in the colonial period. Many were free but relatively poor and rural, similar to their Euro-American forebears. Anxiety over emancipated mulattoes passing for whites was prevalent and hence the "one-drop rule," which categorized an individual with any African American blood as "black," dominated in all avenues of life but was not made into law. In such a situation, a biracial society was reinforced.

In contrast, mulattoes appeared later in the Lower South and grew slowly in numbers in the eighteenth and nineteenth centuries. Most were born of well-to-do Euro-American fathers and those few who were unfettered dominated the free black communities and lived in prosperity. Beginning in the 1790s, their numbers were augmented by a huge influx of West Indian mulattoes who emigrated to Louisiana and South Carolina. Before the 1850s, successful free mulattoes were valued by Euro-Americans as "a barrier between our own color and that of the black—and in case of insurrection, are more likely to enlist themselves under the banner of the whites" (Berlin, 1974). Influenced by racial policies practiced under French and Spanish rule, European Americans valued people of mixed heritage above the slave. The manumitted African American masses were thus deemed to be a third intermediary caste, especially in South Carolina and lower Louisiana where free mulattoes were most affluent. A review of local and state records reveals that they rose highest in position in these regions with 242 property-holding planters by the mid-nineteenth century.

According to the Census of 1850, mulattoes comprised 1.8 percent of the national total population and numbered 406,000 out of an African American population of 3,639,000. By 1860 they grew to a little over five hundred thousand. In the Old Slave South, those areas settled prior to 1750, approximately half were free. In contrast, only 10.4 percent were not enslaved in the New Slave South. During the antebellum era, miscegenation occurred most frequently between upper-class Euro-American planters and mulatto slave women who were often perceived as breeders and objects of sexual pleasure. As a result, they suffered from their owners' aggression and produced numerous "white children of slavery." Although some of these mixed offspring were liberated, most were used for bonded labor.

As the sectional conflict between the North and the South grew in the 1850s, so did hostility and animosity against free mulattoes. Motivated by fresh fears of abolitionism from abroad and internal insurrections, the Lower South, traditionally a haven that esteemed individuals of mixed lineage, grew increasingly intolerant and joined the Upper South in clamoring for "two classes, the Master and the slave [since] no intermediate class can be other than immensely mischievous to our peculiar institution" (Williamson, 1980). In 1856 the New Orleans newspaper the *Picayune* urged the removal of all free people of color, who were considered to be a "plague and a pest in our community." Order and stability through rigid dichotomies of slave or free, black or white, were desired and implemented; there was no longer any room for a triracial society. Increasingly, the one-drop rule predominated. Stripped of their privileged position, free mulattoes who had previously identified with white southerners before and at the beginning of the Civil War (1861–1865) turned to African Americans for alliance. During the Reconstruction era (1863–1877), they assumed leadership roles in helping to better freedmen's lives. Miscegenation with Euro-Americans was minimal throughout this time period. For the most part, whites, blacks, and people of mixed parentage all came to accept the one-drop rule. At the same time, however, literary portrayals of the "tragic mulatto" began to appear, thereby continuing the discussion of the ambiguous status of these individuals. By 1910, the number of mixed offspring, mostly of mulatto and African American parents, would grow to over 2 million.

— *Constance J. S. Chen*

See also: Octoroons; Quadroons.

For Further Reading

Berlin, Ira. 1974. *Slaves Without Masters: The Free Negro in the Antebellum South.* New York: Pantheon Books.

Johnson, Michael P., and James L. Roark. 1984. *Black Masters: A Free Family of Color in the Old South.* New York: W.W. Norton.

Mencke, John G. 1979. *Mulattoes and Race Mixture: American Attitudes and Images, 1865–1918.* Ann Arbor, MI: UMI Research Press.

Williamson, Joel. 1980. *New People: Miscegenation and Mulattoes in the United States.* New York: Free Press.

MUTILATION

The institution of slavery has seldom been humane. Although some historians like Robert Fogel and Stanley Engerman in *Time on the Cross: The Economics of American Negro Slavery* (1974) argue that white slave masters treated their slaves with respect and kindness, the documentary evidence suggests that slavery was a horrible practice. Thus it was not unusual for slaves to be subjected to cruel and unusual punishment—including mutilation.

The mutilation of slaves was often implemented under the guise of punishment, or for the purposes of doing things for the slaves' personal well-being. Punishment through mutilation is well recorded, and it was more often an act of brutality rather than one of rehabilitation. The record shows, for example (in the case of Captain Philippe Loit), that a common practice was to break the teeth of female slaves considered to be recalcitrant. Other accounts show that mutilation was no different than death. For many ship captains on the Middle Passage, one means of trying to prevent slaves from jumping ship was to recapture those who had jumped and to behead them in front of other slaves.

Documents also show that on the Middle Passage, ship captains would make use of a tool called the speculum oris, an instrument shaped like a pair of scissors with serrated blades that was forced in the mouths of captives who refused to eat. On sugar plantations in the West Indies, slaves who fell asleep in the mill because of the long work hours might have a limb cut off as an example to the other slaves of the dangers of falling asleep on the job. Slaves were also placed in metal cast-iron weights or boots in which it was not unusual for them to lose an appendage. Such practices were not nearly as horrendous as other acts practiced by slave and plantation owners. In Grenada, slaves were taken to open forums for punishment in which mutilation was not out of the ordinary. One female slave taken to St. George's, Grenada, in 1789 was supposed to have her finger removed as punishment. However, she was suspended from a crane and her thighs, breast, and back were split open. In Jamaica, it was not extraordinary for female slaves to have their skin peeled off from heel to back and breast to waist. One 1692 account tells of a freed slave whose master and mistress had cut off her ears.

Moses Roper, who had lived as a slave in the Carolinas and Georgia recalls in her narrative of her master pouring tar on her head and face and setting her on fire, and following up this action by placing the fingers of her hand in a vise and removing her fingernails and having another man smash her toes with a sledge hammer. Other tools of mutilation included the thumbscrew and pickets, the latter being used so extensively in Jamaica that the weight of standing on them more than likely resulted in the mortification of feet. Accounts also indicate the use of nails being inserted or hammered into body parts such as appendages and ears and hammers being used to knock out teeth. Some slaves who accidentally touched whites had their hands or the body part used in the touching cut off. Breaking legs in piecemeal fashion, removing sensory organs, and castration were just additional means for masters to get their point of control across to captives.

A broad range of activities were used to justify acts of maiming and mutilation. Frederick Douglass in his *Narrative* stated that looking at a person in the wrong way, saying certain words, making a simple mistake, and running away, could result in permanent injury or death for slaves. Mutilation of slaves was so bad that in French colonies, Louis XIV published the *Code Noir* to curtail cruelty.

Since slaves in most parts of the New World were under the complete control of their masters, it was difficult to gauge the true extent of mutilation practices. Moreover, slave codes in the United States were developed and implemented in all slave states to maintain and enhance this absolute control and justify the power of whites to treat Africans as they willed. Consequently, the slave patrols created to enforce the codes often employed mutilation to discipline slaves who were considered to be breaking the law.

The system of slavery was an inhuman institution in which descendants of European ancestry maintained control over slaves through beliefs and brutish actions against slaves. Although practiced by Africans, the Chinese, and Arabs, slavery as used by Europeans was replete with atrocities that often resulted in the mutilation of slaves. This may be why many have noted that slavery practiced in the Americas was quite unlike slavery instituted by prior civilizations.

— *Torrance T. Stephens*

See also: Punishment; Slave Patrols.

For Further Reading

Blake, W. O. 1860. *The History of Slavery and the Slave Trade, Ancient and Modern.* Columbus, OH: H. Miller.

Douglass, Frederick. 1846. *Narrative of the Life of Frederick Douglass, An American Slave.* London: Leeds.

Farmer, Paul. 2004. "An Anthropology of Structural Violence." *Current Anthropology* 45 (3): 305–325.

Jordan, Winthrop. 1974. *The White Man's Burden: Historical Origins of Racism in the United States.* London: Oxford University Press.

Stein, Robert L. 1979. *The French Slave Trade in the Eighteenth Century: An Old Regime Business.* Madison: University of Wisconsin Press.

Index

—m—

Note: Page numbers in **bold** type indicate primary encyclopedia articles on the subject. Page numbers followed by (photo) indicate a photograph or illustration and (doc) indicates a primary source document.

AASS. *See* American Anti-Slavery Society (AASS)
Abda (mulatto), 10
Ableman v. Booth (U.S.), 56, 62, **151**, 303, 354, 415, 474
The Abolition Intelligencer (Crowe), 37
abolitionist movements, **152–153**
    among Quakers, 8, 18, 19, 21, 93, 558–559 (doc), 577–578 (doc)
    Atlantic Abolitionist Movement, 178–180
    convention in Philadelphia, 28
    death of Lovejoy and, 380
    divisions within, 105, 152, 318–319, 620 (doc)
    in England, 101–102
    First Continental Congress and, 21
    Germantown Protest, 8, 93, 432, 532–533 (doc)
    Great Postal Campaign of, 42, 43, 44, 51, 120–121, 132, 173, 174, 252–253, 277, 313, 319–320, 502, 597–599 (doc)
    Kansas-Nebraska Act and, 135
    in Kentucky, 31, 37
    in Maryland, 23, 54
    in Massachusetts, 9, 12, 20, 21, 32, 36, 39, 42, 44, 45, 47, 49, 56, 58, 93–94, 183, 199, 208, 212 (photo), 212–213, 364, 401, 436
    in Missouri, 42, 50
    in New Jersey, 16, 27
    in New York, 41, 42, 45, 46, 48, 50, 51, 53, 54, 363, 488–489, 522
    in North Carolina, 33
    number of societies, 44
    at Oberlin College, 41–42
    in Ohio, 33, 36, 44, 45, 48, 58, 161, 185
    in Pennsylvania, 9, 11, 14, 18, 21, 23, 25–26, 27, 38, 42, 93, 94, 103, 129, 204, 280, 388, 456, 464
    petitions to Congress, 43, 45, 103
    purchase of fugitive slaves, 488
    removal from southern states, 120
    in Rhode Island, 22, 26, 39
    rise of societies, 130, 131–132
    romanticism and, 152, 279, **439–440**
    spread to the West, 131
    in Tennessee, 33, 35, 36, 42
    thought processes energizing, 92–93, 99, 110, 152, 308
    transatlantic cooperation, 42, 99
    transcendentalism and, 477–479
    use of slave autobiographies/narratives, 9–10, 183
    in Vermont, 39
    in Virginia, 27, 28
    women in, 199
    See also anti-slavery movements; gradualism; immediatism; *specific abolitionist society or abolitionist by name*
Abolitionist Party. *See* Liberty Party
abolitionists
    division over slavery, 619–620 (doc)
    early plans of, 18
    establishment of American Anti-Slavery Society, 42
    first elected to U.S. House of Representatives, 45
    founding of New England Anti-Slavery Society, 41
    fundamental reasoning of, 92–93, 110, 115
    Garnett's chastisement of, 674–675 (doc)
    rescue of fugitive slaves from courts, 53, 54, 151, 212, 447–448, 488–489
    view of colonization plans, 20, 34, 41, 105
    See also specific man or woman by name
An Account of the European Settlements in America (Burke), 18
"An Act for the Better Ordering and Governing of Negroes and Slaves," 11
"An Act to Regulate the Negroes on the British Plantations" (England), 5–6, 89
Adams, Abigail, 21
Adams, Charles Frances, 51, 298
Adams, James H., 59
Adams, John, 21, 97, 182, 404, 483
Adams, John Quincy, 153 (photo)
    antislavery activities of, **153–154**